HARDPRESS.NET
HOME OF HARD-TO-FIND BOOKS

An Abridgement of the Book of Martyrs
by John Foxe

Address:
HardPress
8345 NW 66TH ST #2561
MIAMI FL 33166-2626
USA
Email: info@hardpress.net

James Harrison
Born Jan 28 1809

Elnor Harrison
Born August 19 1810
at to past twelve at

John Harrison
Born July 30th 1812
to past 5 in morning

See Page 107

AN

ABRIDGMENT

OF

THE BOOK OF MARTYRS:

TO WHICH ARE PREFIXED,

THE LIVING TESTIMONIES OF THE CHURCH OF GOD, AND
FAITHFUL MARTYRS, IN DIFFERENT AGES OF THE
WORLD; AND THE CORRUPT FRUITS OF
THE FALSE CHURCH,

IN THE TIME OF THE APOSTACY.

TO THIS WORK IS ANNEXED,

AN ACCOUNT

OF

THE JUST JUDGMENTS OF GOD

ON

PERSECUTORS, &c.

ALSO,

A CHRISTIAN PLEA AGAINST PERSECUTION

FOR

THE CAUSE OF CONSCIENCE.

New-York:

PRINTED AND SOLD BY SAMUEL WOOD,

NO. 357, PEARL-STREET.

....
1810.

DISTRICT OF NEW-YORK, ss :

BE IT REMEMBERED, that on the 15th day of May, in the thirty-fourth year of the independence of the United States of America, Samuel Wood, of the said district, hath deposited in this office, the title of a Book, the right whereof he claims as proprietor, in the words following, to wit :

"¶ An Abridgment of the Book of Martyrs : to which are prefixed, The living testimonies of the church of God, and faithful Martyrs, in different ages of the world ; and the corrupt fruits of the false church, in the times of the Apostacy. To this work is annexed, an account of the just judgments of God on Persecutors, &c. Also, A Christian Plea against Persecution for the cause of Conscience."

In conformity to the act of the Congress of the United States, entitled, " An act for the encouragement of learning, by securing the copies of maps, charts and books, to the authors and proprietors of such copies, during the times therein mentioned :" And also, to the act, entitled, " An act supplementary to an act, entitled, ' An act for the encouragement of learning, by securing the copies of maps, charts and books, to the authors and proprietors of such copies, during the times therein mentioned,' and extending the benefits thereof, to the arts of designing, engraving, and etching historical and other prints."

CHAR. CLINTON,
Clerk of the District of New-York.

PREFACE.

THE PUBLISHER of this First American Edition of 'An Abridgment of The Book of Martyrs,' thinks proper to observe, that it has not been with a view to revive, or to expose the malice, or misguided zeal of the persecutors, so much as to show the excellency and sufficiency of that power and confidence, which supported the sufferers under their keenest torments: nor is it intended to reflect on the liberal and enlightened of the present day. It is hoped, that light and knowledge have now so spread, in various parts of the world, that it is not considered as doing God service, to destroy men's lives, especially for their religious opinions; and experience abundantly shows, the good effects of religious toleration; and that no man ought to be accountable to man, for his religious sentiments; but that all should have free liberty to worship God, in the way that is most agreeable to their own convictions of duty; and that, while their practice is peaceable, none should be molested. God is the only sovereign of the conscience, and whenever man takes it upon him to control or direct, in these matters, he assumes the right and prerogative of God himself.

All oppression and cruelty, are hateful both to God and man; and it is strange, that men should conceive an opinion, that by persecuting and destroying the lives of their fellow creatures, they would render themselves acceptable to that God, who delighteth not in the death of a sinner, but rather that all should return, repent, and live.

It is, indeed, true, that under the former dispensations, the Children of Israel had positive orders from the Almighty, to cut off nations whose cup of iniquity was full. But Christ has given a new and special command, to love our enemies, &c. and not even to resist evil.

Most precious in the sight of the Lord, is the death of his saints; and, surely, if a sparrow does not fall without his notice, he will not be inattentive to the sufferings of his noble creature, man, whose cries and prayers ascend both day and night, like sweet incense, before his throne, desiring to be preserved in the way that is most pleasing in his holy sight. His commands are, " touch not mine anointed, and do my prophets no harm:" and whosoever oppresses these, may expect to receive their just reward, both in time and eternity, they that injure them, will be found fighting against God, who regardeth them as the apple of his eye." Christ commanded to "let the tares grow with the wheat, lest, in destroying the former, the latter should also be rooted up;" his special command also, is, "whatsoever ye would that men do to you, do ye even so to them." And when his officious disciples would have commanded fire from heaven, to consume those who would not receive him, he rebuked them, and said, "ye know not what manner of spirit ye are of. For the Son of Man is not come to destroy men's lives, but to save them." The whole tenor and spirit of the gospel is love. It breathes "peace on earth, and good will to men."

It may be proper to remark, that as this History of the Martyrs, &c. is brought down to a later period than any work of the kind, heretofore published, it embraces transactions and events which have occurred in America, and particularly in New-England; exhibiting the operation of a sanguine and persecuting spirit, which prevailed in the early settlement of that country, and by which, the religious people, called Quakers, greatly suffered. It is however but justice due to the present inhabitants of the state of Massachusetts, to observe, that so far from approving the conduct of their predecessors, they are now as much distinguished for the mildness and liberality of their laws, and kind treatment of this people, as their predecessors were for their cruelty towards them : hence, we cannot forbear to add, that such are the religious toleration of that government, and its regard to conscientious scruples, as not only to excuse the society of Friends, from personal military service, but also from any commutation; an indulgence, which, we apprehend, is not so fully granted to that people, by any other state in the Union. In delineating the character of the first settlers of New-England, and comparing it with that of the present day, we are struck with a contrast, which, at one view, evinces the progress of light and knowledge; and in proportion as it pervades the understanding, men are inclined to cherish that disposition towards each other, which is calculated to promote the religion of Jesus Christ, who 'came not to *destroy*, but to *save* men's lives.'

In commencing this work, it was intended to give a revised edition of the Book of Martyrs, as abridged by Ellis Hookes, which was first published in England, in 1719; but, in the prosecution, recourse being had to a variety of books, of esteemed authenticity, it was thought proper to select from them, as appeared most suitable; particularly from Southwell's 'New Book of Martyrs,' and others mentioned in the course of the work.

CONTENTS.

A

INDEX

Of the names of sufferers contained in this work.

The letter m. signifies martyred.

A

BRIEF COLLECTION

OF

THE MOST REMARKABLE PASSAGES AND LIVING TESTIMONIES

OF

THE CHURCH OF GOD,

AND FAITHFUL MARTYRS, IN ALL AGES;

AND OF THE CORRUPT FRUITS OF THE FALSE CHURCH,

IN

THE TIME OF THE APOSTACY.

B

A LIVING TESTIMONY

OF

THE TRUE CHURCH.

PART I.

Shows how God, under the several dispensations of him-self to mankind always led and guided his Church and seed by his Spirit and power to worship and serve him, and to bring forth the fruits of righteousness and holi-ness, which were acceptable to him: and how the serpent or evil one hath from the beginning, made it his work to deceive, and lead man from God to sin, and to work wickedness, which always brought the wrath and judg-ments of God upon man.

AFTER God had created heaven and earth, and all things in them, he created man in his own im-age; that is to say, pure, holy and innocent, giving him power to govern and rule the creation to God's glory; and God said, " it is not good for man to be alone, I will make him an helpmeet for him;" and he caused a deep sleep to fall upon Adam, and he took one of his ribs, and closed up the flesh thereof, and of the rib he made woman, and brought her unto the man; and Adam said, " this is now bone of my bone, and flesh of my flesh, she shall be called woman :" and the Lord plac-ed them in the garden of Eden, there to live in a blessed state, giving unto them a commandment of obedience,

which was, that they were not to eat of the tree of knowledge of good and evil; for, in the day they did eat thereof, they should die ; but, of all the rest of the trees of the
garden, they might eat, and receiving comfort therefrom,
might give the praise and glory thereof to their Maker,
to whom it did belong : and whilst man and woman stood
in this condition they were happy and blessed.   And
now God beheld all that he had made, and behold all
was good : for sin had not as yet entered upon man.

But the devil, envying God's honor and man's felicity,
tempted the woman to sin by the serpent ; the woman
being beguiled by the serpent, the man was also beguiled by her, and broke the ordinance of God by eating
the forbidden fruit : and thus, man and woman lost the
dignity and excellency of their first creation, and were
enslaved by the serpent, who, by his wiles and subtilty,
had entangled and ensnared them, and persuaded them
to believe him more than God ; for God said, that, in
the day they did eat thereof, they should die ; but the
serpent said, they should not surely die ; " for God doth
know," said he, " that ye shall be as Gods, knowing good
and evil ;" and thus was man, by a lie, drawn from the
pure command of his maker.

Now, after they had sinned, in the cool of the day, the
Lord called unto Adam, saying, " Where art thou ?" and
Adam, who hid himself, said, " I heard thy voice in the
garden, and I was afraid, because I was naked :" and God
said, " who told thee that thou wast naked ? Hast thou
eaten of the tree whereof I commanded thee that thou
shouldest not eat ?" and having brought guilt and shame
upon themselves by transgression, they began to make
coverings by sewing fig leaves to make themselves aprons,
of which, it seems, they had no need before they had
transgressed.

And, by this, all men may see, that it was the serpent's work from the beginning (and indeed, it has been
in all ages his work) to beguile men and women with
his lies and subtilties, and to darken their eyes and pol-
lute their understandings that he may keep them in subjection to himself ; and from hence spring the wicked

thoughts and actions, which all mankind are apt to lean and incline to, and have been, and are readier to give ear to the voice of the serpent and wicked one, than to the voice of God their maker : and this has been the fountain and source from whence have come all the disorders, miseries, and woes, that have happened unto mankind throughout the world, in all ages ; they have been feeding and delighting themselves in eating the forbidden fruit, which their forefathers also delighted in : and all nations upon the earth are in this state and condition at this day, led away by the voice of the serpent from the purity and righteousness in which man was first created, except a little remnant, which God hath gathered by his light and power, to be witnesses to his name.

And, the Lord having convicted Adam of his evil, and pronounced several punishments upon him, and on Eve his wife ; yet, with this promise, added, that the seed of the woman should bruise the serpent's head : and man being put out of the garden of Eden, and a fiery flaming sword being set to keep the way, leading to the tree of life ; man was in an undone condition, had not the Lord condescended in his tender love and mercy to restore him, and make that promise to him ; and this was the Lord's great love, to open a door of hope to lost man, that he might not be destroyed by Satan's power ; and now the power of God, by which man was first created, appeared again to restore him.

After the fall of Adam, Cain was the first man that was born of a woman ; and after Cain, his brother Abel was born ; and in process of time, these two offered offerings unto the Lord, being, doubtless, instructed in righteousness by their father Adam after his restoration ; but Cain's sacrifice, being only outward in show, and nothing inward in the spirit, wherein doth consist the true worship of God, the Lord accepted not his offering ; but unto Abel and his offering, which was from the uprightness and sincerity of his heart, the Lord had respect. At this, Cain was wrath, and being inflamed with anger, rose up against his brother Abel, and, in his envy, slew him ; here was the beginning of persecution, and that upon a righteous person for serving God in a pure mind ; and here the envy of the wicked one appeared again, to extinguish, if he could, the righteous seed : but the Lord shewed regard again to mankind, and in his tender love repaired this loss ; for Abel being slain, Adam's wife bore another son, whose name was Seth ; for God, said she, hath appointed me another seed, instead of Abel, whom Cain slew ; and this Seth proved a godly man, and had a son called Enos, who kept up the holy seed and true religion, as it is recorded of him ; and in his days, men did begin to call on the name of the Lord. Now Enos signifies the lamentable condition of all mankind ; for even then, as some men write, was the worship of God wretchedly corrupted, by the race of Cain : whence it came that men were even so distinguished, that they who persisted in the true worship of God, were known by the name of the children of God, and they who forsook him were termed the children of men.

The next of the righteous stock was Jared, to whom was born Enoch, another of the righteous seed, whose life and conversation were so innocent, that it is recorded of him, he walked with God.

And thus, the reader may see how the righteous plants were such, as took the Lord to be their guide in their actions and undertakings, and were as patterns of righteousness in the midst of a perverse generation, and it is the same with all the faithful and upright at this day : and now Enoch having this testimony, that he pleased God, the Lord, as a requital of his faithfulness, translated him, so that he saw no death and took him to himself.

And it came to pass, when men began to multiply on the face of the earth, and daughters were born unto them, these sons of God saw the daughters of men, that they were fair, and they took them wives of all that they chose ; this displeased the Lord, so that he said, my spirit shall not always strive with man, for that he also is flesh ; and his days were shortened to one hundred and twenty years, who before lived many hundred years.

And God saw that the wickedness of man was great in the earth, and that every imagination of the thoughts of his heart was only evil continually : and it repented the Lord that he had made man, and it grieved him at his heart ; and the earth was corrupt, and filled with violence, and God looked upon the earth, and behold it was corrupt, for all flesh had corrupted his way upon the earth.

And God said unto Noah, "the end of all flesh is come before me ; for the earth is filled with violence through them; and behold I will destroy them with the earth;" and he commanded Noah to make an ark, and behold, I bring a flood upon the earth to destroy all flesh, wherein is the breath of life, and every thing that is in the earth shall die ; but with thee will I establish my covenant, and thou shalt come into the Ark, thou and thy sons, and thy wife, and thy sons' wives ; for thee have I seen righteous before me in this generation.

But before the Lord brought the deluge of waters upon the world of the wicked, he sent this just man Noah, a preacher of righteousness unto them, giving them one hundred and twenty years' space to repent them of their evil ways ; and Noah having provided an ark at the commandment of God, was directed when he should enter into the ark, whilst the world in the mean time void of all fear, sat eating and drinking, and marrying and giving in marriage.   In the six hundredth year of the life of Noah, upon the seventh day of the second month, when he and his children were entered into the ark, God sent a rain upon the earth forty days and forty nights, and the waters continued upon the earth a hundred and fifty days; the waters abating upon the seventeenth day of the seventh month, the ark rested upon one of the mountains of Ararat ; the waters still abating, upon the first day of the tenth month, the tops of the mountains appeared above the waters ; and after forty days, Noah opened the window of the ark, and sent forth a Raven ; and seven days after, sent forth a dove ; and she returning, after seven days more, he sent her forth again, and about the evening, she returned, bringing the leaf of an olive tree in her mouth ; and then staying yet seven days more he sent the same dove out again, which returned no more unto him.

In the six hundredth and first year of the life of Noah, when the surface of the earth was all dry, Noah took off the covering of the ark ; and, all that were with him in the ark being gone forth, he offered unto God for his preservation an offering ; " and the Lord smelled a sweet savour; and the Lord said in his heart, I will not again curse the ground any more for man's sake ; for the imagination of man's heart is evil from his youth :" and God spake unto Noah and to his sons, saying, " I establish my covenant with you, and with your seed after you, neither shall all flesh be cut off any more, by the waters of a flood to destroy the earth ;" and gave the rain bow for a sign of the covenant which he then made with man.

And Noah made a division of land among his grandchildren, and they went from those eastern parts, whither they first repaired from the Mountains of Ararat, unto the valley of Shinar, where they took in hand to build the city and tower of Babylon, whose top might reach to Heaven ; lest they should be scattered abroad upon the face of the earth ; which purpose of theirs being frustrated by the confusion of languages sent among them, from whence they took the name of Babel, the dispersion of nations followed, and one language was lost, which the whole earth was of until this attempt.

The next of the righteous stock that succeeded was Abram, the second son of Terah: he was born in the year 2008. And ten years after was Sarai, who was afterwards Abraham's wife, born, daughter of Haran, Abram's brother. Some writers relate, that Abram was educated in the idolatry of his father's house, who, they say, was a maker of statues and images : and the Jews relate of Abram's going into the shop in the absence of his father, of his breaking the images, and jeering those that came to buy, or worship them ; of his father's carrying him to Nimrod to be punished ; his witty answers and miraculous escapes : thus, the Jews write of him : but however these things may be credited, we have a sure record in the scriptures, that the Lord had a great regard to the sincerity of Abram, and had a purpose to make use of him to be an instrument in his work and service ; and that appears by his calling him from his kindred, and from his father's house, and promising a blessing to him and his seed ; and now Abram, who had chosen the Lord for his delight above all earthly things, consulted not, but departed as the Lord had commanded him ; and he took Sarai his wife, and Lot his brother's son, and travelled to the land of Canaan, where God promised to Abram, that to his seed he would give that land ; but afterwards Abram, compelled by a famine, went from thence down into Egypt, where Sarai his wife, to escape a danger, went for his sister, and was taken into Pharaoh's house, being fair and beautiful, but was not long after sent back unto him untouched. Then Abram, accompanied by just Lot, returned into Canaan, where, when the country which they pitched upon was not sufficient, to feed both their herds of cattle, strife arose between the herdsmen ; and Abram loving peace, said to Lot, "let there be no strife, I pray thee, between me and thee and between my herdsmen and thine, for we be brethren;" and they parted ; and Lot went into the country of Sodom ; and after they were parted, the promise both of the possession of that land of Canaan, and also of his numberless posterity, was again renewed unto him.

Abram being now ninety nine years old, God made a covenant with him, touching the seed of Isaac, (who was to be born of Sarai that time twelve month) and gave him the seal of circumcision, changing both their names; Abram into Abraham, and Sarai into Sarah, for a sure pledge and testimony of his promise.

When Abraham was an hundred, and Sarah ninety years of age, Isaac was born unto them, and Abraham instructed his family in righteousness ; for God said, I know Abraham, that he will command his children, and his household after him, and they shall keep the way of the Lord to do justice and judgment.

By faith, Abraham offered up his son Isaac ; considering with himself, that God was able to raise him again from the dead. Josephus reports, that at this time Isaac was twenty five years old, and that he was at that time well grown may be gathered from this, that he was able

c

to carry so much wood as was to go to the burning and consuming of such a whole burnt-offering as himself was, then intended by Abraham to have been made. Sarah being now one hundred and twenty seven years of age, died in Hebron ; and as Abraham, for his integrity and uprightness to the Lord, is recorded to posterity for the father of the faithful; so is Sarah for the mother of the faithful ; and she is the only woman whose full and entire age is mentioned in scripture.

Abraham being also advanced in age was careful to get a wife for his son Isaac ; and he was likewise careful that he might not marry with any of the idolatrous and corrupt nations, it being looked upon as a great evil by this righteous stock, that their sons should marry with the daughters of men that were corrupted, and despisers of the true religion, as it appears by Abraham's care for his son, that he should not take a wife of the daughters of the Canaanites among whom he dwelt ; and also by the strict charge he gave to his servant to look out a wife for him, who going by the guidance of God into Mesopotamia, where praying to the Lord to shew kindness unto his master Abraham, he there obtained for him Rebekah, the daughter of Bethuel, sister to Laban the Syrian, whom Isaac receiving for his wife, brought into the tent of his mother Sarah ; and he loved her, and had comfort in her after his mother's death ; and he was forty years old when he married with Rebekah.

Abraham, when he was an hundred and seventy-five years old, and an hundred years after his coming into Canaan, departed this life, and was buried by his two sons in his cave at Machpelah, with Sarah his wife. He lived fifteen years after the birth of Jacob, with whom he is said also to have lived in tents.

And Abraham being dead, Isaac was raised up, as the next of the righteous line and seed of God, to whom the Lord often appeared in his divine power, confirming the covenant he had made with Abraham his father ; for he walked in the steps of his father in faithfulness to the Lord, and when his father's servant brought Rebekah to him, they found him meditating in the field at eveningtide, by which it appears, his mind was delighted in that which was good. When his wife had continued barren nineteen years after her marriage, Isaac entreated the Lord for her, because she was barren, and the Lord was entreated of him, and his wife conceived, and when the twins strove in her womb, Rebekah asked counsel of God ; and the Lord said unto her, " two nations are in thy womb, and two manner of people shall be separated from thy bowels ; and the one people shall be stronger than the other, and the elder shall serve the younger." Being born, the children grew, and one of them, named Esau, was a cunning hunter, a man of the field ; and Jacob was a plain man, dwelling in tents : and Isaac loved Esau, because he did eat of his venison, but Rebekah loved Jacob.

Isaac being grown old and blind, in the forty fourth year before his death, sent Esau his eldest son to take some venison for him, purposing to bless him at his return ; but Jacob, the younger son, by the counsel of his mother, coming disguised in his cloaths, and with savoury meat in his hand, stole away the blessing unwittingly to his father ; and the blessing though so got, God confirmed ever after ; but Jacob seeing that for so doing, his brother followed him with a deadly hatred, and being desirous to avoid his snares, and willing to take a wife of his own kindred, his father blessing him, he took his journey into Mesopotamia, to his uncle Laban ; for his father had charged him not to take a wife of the daughters of Canaan ; and in his journey the Lord appeared unto him by his presence, and renewed the covenant to him, which he had made before to his father and grandfather ; and the Lord manifesting his presence unto him, he covenanted with the Lord, saying, " if God will be with me, and keep me in this way that I go, and will give me bread to eat, and raiment to put on, so that I come again to my fathers house in peace, then shall the Lord be my God ;" and coming at length to Haran, and continuing a time with Laban, he fell in love with Rachel his daughter, for whom he served seven years, and they seemed to him but a few days, for the love he had to her.

Esau had now been married thirty seven years, and was seventy seven years old, whereas Jacob had all this while lived unmarried: but being now mindful of his father's command, he demanded Rachel his wife to be given to him, using this for a reason, that his days were now full ; but by the fraud of Laban, instead of Rachel, Leah the elder daughter was put in bed unto him, nevertheless Rachel also was afterwards espoused to him, upon covenant of serving seven years more for her.

At first, Rachel was barren but afterwards, by the blessing of God, proving fruitful, bore Joseph unto Jacob. At the end of the fourteen years service, Jacob asking leave of Laban to return into his own country, was held there six years more, upon another bargain made between him and his father-in-law Laban, for a certain part of his flock.

Jacob perceiving the heart-burning of Laban, and his son's malice towards him, was warned of God to return into his own country, which having communicated to his wives, whilst Laban was shearing his sheep at the latter end of spring, after his twenty years service, went away unknown to Laban, with all his substance, wives and family, and passed over the river Euphrates. Laban, three days after, hearing that his son-in-law was gone, took some of his friends and kindred along with him, and pursued after him seven days journey and at last overtook him at Mount Gilead, which took its name from their meeting there; for, after many and diverse expostulations which passed between them, making all fair at last, for a testimony and monument of their covenant there made, Jacob erected a pillar with a heap of stones, which Laban the Syrian called, Jegar-Sahadutha, but Jacob the Hebrew called, Gilead, that is, the heap of testimony or witness between them. Jacob being sent away in peace by Laban, but affrighted with the news of his brother Esau's approach with four hundred men, divided his company into two, saying, " if he smite one, then the other company which is left shall escape ;" and called upon God, saying, " O God of my father Abraham, Isaac, &c. which saidst unto me return into thy country, and to thy kindred, and I will deal well with thee, deliver me, I pray thee, from the hand of my brother Esau" Esau having entertained his brother courteously, after much entreaty, accepted of his presents. Jacob then went on to Succoth, and there he built him an house, and afterwards passing over Jordan, he came into Canaan, and pitched his tent in Salem, and there he built an altar, which he called by the name of El-Elohe-Israel, or, the Mighty God, the God of Israel, to wit; in the same place where Abraham had heretofore built his first Altar, and where Jacob's well was.

I am now come to write of Joseph, who being seventeen years of age, when his brethren saw that their father loved him more than them, they hated him, and could not speak peaccably to him ; and Joseph declaring his dream to them, the Lord having shewed him that he should be set above his brethern, and be the chief of his father's family, they hated him yet the more ; and first they conspired his death, and at length agreed, to sell him away for a bond-slave into a far country ; so drawing him out of the pit, whereinto they had cast him, they sold him to the merchants for twenty pieces of silver, and he was by them carried into Egypt, and there sold for a slave to Potiphar, a captain of the guard to Pharaoh, where he was tempted by Potiphar's wife to uncleanness ; and, because he refused to do such evil, she by her lies, instigated Potiphar her husband against him, who put him in prison ; but the Lord was with Joseph, and shewed him mercy, and gave him favour in the sight of the keeper of the prison, and that which he did the Lord made to prosper.

Two of the officers of Pharaoh's court, being imprisoned in the same prison with Joseph, having both of them dreamed, Joseph interpreted their dreams unto them, which came to pass according to his interpretation ; and Joseph said to one of them, " When thou art restored into thy place, after thy former manner, think on me when it shall be well with thee, and shew kindness, I pray thee, unto me, and make mention of me unto Pharaoh, and bring me out of this house ; for indeed I was stolen away out of the Land of the Hebrews, and here also have I done nothing, that they should put me into the dungeon :" but when this officer was restored again into Pharaoh's court he remembered not Joseph.

Two years after, Pharaoh dreamed two dreams, who seeing he could not get them expounded by his own wise men, but hearing of Joseph's expertness to interpret dreams, sent for him, being then thirty years old, who opened to the king his dreams : first, that of the seven years of plenty ; then the seven years of famine : he added moreover, as his counsel and advice, how to provide out of the store of the first years of plenty, against the famine of the other seven years of scarcity, which were to follow ; whereupon, by the general consent of his nobles, he made him governor of the kingdom.

From the harvest of this year, were counted seven years of plenty, wherein Joseph laid up an infinite treasure of corn.

The seven years of the famine began from the harvest of this year, wherein the forecast and wisdom of Joseph did not only sustain Egypt, but were a help and relief to other countries.

Jacob dispatched ten of his sons into Egypt to buy corn, whom Joseph seeming not to know, caused to be taken for spies ; and being laid hold on, he spake roughly unto them, and said, whence came ye ? and they said, from the land of Canaan to buy food : and Joseph knew his brethren, but they knew not him ; and he said they were come as spies to see the nakedness of the land : they said, they were true men, and thy servants are twelve brethren, the sons of one man in the land of Canaan ; and behold, the youngest is this day with our father, and one is not ; and Joseph said, "ye are spies : hereby it shall be proved ; if ye be true men, let one of your brethren be bound in prison : go ye, carry corn for the famine of your houses ; but bring your youngest brother unto me, so shall your words be verified, and you shall not die," and they did so : and they said one to the other, " we are verily guilty concerning our brother, in that we saw the anguish of his soul, when he besought us, and we would not hear, therefore is this distress come upon us :" and Reuben answered them, saying, " spake not I unto you, saying, do not sin against the child, and ye would not hear, therefore, behold his blood is required ;" and they knew not that Joseph understood them, for he spake unto them by an interpreter ; and he turned himself about from them, and wept, and returned to them again, and communed with them, and took from them Simeon the chiefest of them, who consented to sell him, and cast him into prison ; and being dismissed, they carried away their corn, and with it the money that they had paid for it, being conveyed into their sacks by the secret appointment of Joseph. They told their father Jacob all that happened unto them, and withal declared unto him the necessity that laid upon them of carrying their younger brother Benjamin into Egypt, persuading him by all means to let him go ; but Jacob their father said unto them, " me have ye bereaved of my children ; Joseph is not, and Simeon is not, and you will take away Benjamin : all these things are against me ;" but Jacob, pressed with famine sent again his sons, and with them his son Benjamin, furnished with double money, and other presents to Joseph, to buy more corn ; and they, at their return, were courteously entertained ; for when Joseph saw Benjamin with them, he said to the ruler of his house, " bring these men home, and slay and make ready, for these men shall dine with me at noon." And the man did as Joseph bade, and brought the men into Joseph's house, and the men were afraid, because they were brought into Joseph's house : and they said, " because of the money that was returned in our sacks the first time, are we brought in, that he may seek occasion against us :" but the steward comforted them, saying, " peace be unto you, fear not ; your God and the God of your fathers hath given you treasure in your sacks, I had your money ;" and he brought Simeon out unto them.

And Joseph asked them of their welfare, saying," Is your father well, the old man of whom you spake, is he yet alive ? And they answered, " Thy servant our father is in good health ; he is yet alive," when he saw his brother Benjamin, his mother's son, he made haste, for his bowels did yearn upon his brother, and he sought where to weep, and he entered into his chamber, and wept there : and after they had eaten, he commanded the steward of his house to fill their sacks with food, and to put a silver cup in the sack's mouth of the youngest ; and when they were gone, Joseph sent after them, and caused them to be stopt for taking away his cup, which crime they endeavoured to put of, by shewing how truly they meant, by bringing again the money which they found in their sacks when they came home ; offering themselves to die, or to be his bond-slaves, if any such thing could be proved against them ; but in the end, the cup being found with Benjamin, and they brought back to Joseph, they all yielded themselves to him, for his bond-slaves, which he refused, saying, he would have none but him with whom the cup was found. Judah then humbly offered himself to serve him in Benjamin's stead, saying, " when I come to thy servant my father, and the lad be not with us, seeing that his life is bound up in the lad's life it shall come to pass, that when he seeth that the lad is not with us, that he will die, and thy servants shall bring down the grey hairs of thy servant our father with sorrow to the grave : " Then Joseph could not refrain himself before all them that stood by him : and cried, cause every man to go out from me, and there stood no man with them, while Joseph made himself known unto his brethren ; and wept aloud, and the Egyptians and the house of Pharaoh heard ; and Joseph said unto his brethren, I am Joseph, doth my father yet live ? And his brethren could not answer him, for they were troubled at his presence ; and Joseph said unto his brethren, " come near to me, I pray you," and they came near, and he said, " I am Joseph your brother, whom ye sold into E-gypt ;" and seeing them troubled, he comforted them, by shewing how that act of theirs was by the providence of God.

And he said unto them, haste ye and go up to my fa-ther, and say unto him, " thus saith thy son Joseph ; God hath made me Lord of all Egypt : come down unto me ;

tarry not, and thou shalt dwell in the land of Goshen, and thou shalt be near unto me, thou and thy children, and thy children's children, and thy flocks and thy herds, and all that thou hast, and there will I nourish thee ; for there are yet five years of famine :" and he fell upon his brother Benjamin's neck, and wept, and Benjamin wept upon his neck ; moreover he kissed all his brethren, and wept upon them ; so he sent his brethren away, and they told Jacob all the words of Joseph, and when he saw the waggons which Joseph had sent to carry him, the spirit of Jacob their father revived ; and Israel said, " It is enough, Joseph my son is yet alive ; I will go and see him before I die ;" and God spake unto Israel saying, " I am God, the God of thy father : fear not to go down into Egypt, for I will there make of thee a great nation ; I will go down with thee into Egypt, and I will surely bring thee up again ;" and Jacob was an hundred and thirty years old when he went down into Egypt.

Joseph letting Pharaoh know of the arrival of his kindred in Egypt, brought his father and five of his brethren into his presence, and having communed with him, assigned them a place in the land of Goshen, where they were provided with all necessaries by Joseph.

The book of Genesis ends with the death of Joseph, containing the history of two thousand three hundred and sixty nine years space ; which book was written by Moses himself, in the opinion of the Talmudists, in their Baba-Bathra, Lib. 1.

At this time, lived Job, a man of whom it is recorded, that he was a man of a perfect and upright heart, and one that feared God and shunned evil, and embraced the knowledge of the true God, and all righteousness ; rich in substance, and the more noted, as neither the enjoyment of riches corrupted, nor the loss of them depraved him in his way ; for, being first spoiled of his goods by satan ; also bereft of his children ; and at last tormented with sore biles, from the sole of his foot to his crown, nevertheless he could yet never be drawn through impatience to sin in any sort ; whereof, having first received a testimony from God's own mouth, he was afterwards re-

D

stored to his former health, and had cast into his bosom double of whatever he possessed before.

And when Joseph and all his brethren, and that generation were dead, and the children of Israel were fruitful, and increased abundantly, and multiplied, and waxed exceedingly mighty, and the land was filled with them, there arose up a new king over Egypt, who knew not Joseph, and he began to afflict them, but the more they were afflicted, the more they multiplied and grew : and the Egyptians made the children of Israel to serve with rigor, and they made their lives bitter with hard bondage, and kept them under with great severity.

Aaron was born three years before his brother Moses, and eighty three years before the departure of the children of Israel out of Egypt.

The ungodly king of Egypt, when he could not prevail with the midwives of the Hebrew women privily to destroy the male children of them, made a barbarous edict to destroy them all, by drowning them in the river.

About this time, Moses the son of Amram, of the house of Levi, was born, and when his mother saw that he was a goodly child, being willing to preserve him, she hid him three months, and when she could no longer hide him, she took for him an ark of bulrushes, and daubed it with slime, and with pitch, and put the child therein, and she laid it in the flags by the river's brink, his sister standing afar off from the place, to see what would become of him ; and Pharaoh's daughter finding it there, caused her maids to fetch it ; and when she had opened it, she saw the child, and, behold, it wept, and she had compassion on him, and said " this is one of the Hebrew children :" then said his sister to Pharaoh's daughter, " shall I go and call a nurse to thee of the Hebrew women, that she may nurse the child for thee ?" and Pharaoh's daughter said, " go ;" and the maid went and called the child's mother, and she nursed him ; and Pharaoh's daughter called him Moses, because she drew him out of the water ; and she caused him to be brought up as her son, and caused him to be instructed in the science and learning of the Egyptians : and thus did the Lord wonderfully preserve him, which noted no less than that he intended to make him an instrument in some great work, as indeed it so came to pass ; for as he grew in years, the Lord put it in his heart to slight the honors of Pharaoh's court ; for he refused to be called the son of Pharaoh's daughter, choosing rather to suffer affliction with the people of God, than to enjoy the pleasures of sin for a season ; esteeming the reproach of Christ greater riches than the treasures in Egypt, for he had respect to the recompense of reward. And now the Lord having chosen him into his work and service, indued him with such a spirit of meekness, that none was like him upon the earth ; and being thus fitted he often had trials and exercises of his patience by the people he was to govern, who were often murmuring and repining against him. And the Lord appeared unto him, whilst he was keeping his father-in-law Jerthro's sheep in the mountain of Horeb, and the angel of the Lord appeared unto him in a flame of fire, out of the midst of a bush ; and behold the bush burned with fire, and the bush was not consumed ; and the Lord said unto him, " I am the God of thy father, the God of Abraham, the God of Isaac, and the God of Jacob ;" and Moses hid his face, for he was afraid to look upon God ; and the Lord said, " I have surely seen the affliction of my people which are in Egypt, and have heard their cry, by reason of their task-masters ; for I know their sorrow, and am come down to deliver them out of the hands of the Egyptians." And he chose Moses as an instrument to go unto Pharaoh, and to bring the children of Israel out of Egypt, to whom as an assistant in his work, Aaron was added.

Moses and Aaron having declared unto Pharaoh the message, with which they were sent unto him from God, were sent away with many harsh words ; and many more greivous oppressions were inflicted upon the Israelites than before.

Moses being now eighty, and Aaron eighty three years of age being moved by the Lord, returned again to Pharaoh, where the magicians, imitating the miracles of Aaron's rod made Pharaoh harden his heart, so that he would not let the children of Israel go ; werefore, the Lord sent diverse plagues upon Pharaoh before he would let the children of Israel go ; and when the last plague was brought upon them, Pharaoh and his servants made haste to send away the Israelites, with all their substance, being six hundred thousand men, besides children ; and they being departed, Pharaoh with his host pursued and overtook them. Here Moses divided the waters with his rod, and with the children of Israel, passed through the sea ; but Pharaoh and his army following were all overwhelmed by the waters coming together again. When the Israelites were thus freed from the bondage of the Egyptians, they forthwith sang a song of praise and thanksgiving unto God, for their deliverance, which is called the song of Moses.

After their encamping in the desert of Sinai, Moses went up into the mount, and the Lord said unto him, " thus shalt thou say to the house of Jacob, and tell the children of Israel ; ye have seen what I did unto the Egyptians, and how I bore you on eagles' wings, and brought you unto myself; now, therefore, if you will obey my voice indeed, and keep my covenant, then ye shall be a peculiar treasure unto me above all people ; for all the earth is mine, and ye shall be unto me a kingdom of priests, and an holy nation." And Moses told the people what the Lord had commanded him ; all the people answered together, and said, " all that the Lord hath spoken we will do." But the reader may see how ready and apt these people were to forget the tender dealings of the Lord towards them ; for Moses and Aaron, and several of the elders of Israel went up into the mount, and there beheld the glory of God ; and the rest returning, Moses with his servant Joshua, abode there still, and waited there six days, and upon the seventh day, God spake unto him, and there he continued forty nights, eating no meat all that while, nor drinking water : and there he received God's command, and the law written in tables of stone, with God's own finger ; God bidding him withal to get him down ; for that the people had already made themselves a molten calf to worship.

Moses, seeing this, brake the tables at the foot of the mount, and having burnt and defaced the idol, many of the people were put to death by the hands of the Levites.

The next day, Moses returned into the mount, and there again entreated the Lord for the people ; and having drawn them into a deep sense of the wrath of God, to repent of their sin, he by his prayer, obtained, that God himself should be their leader in their way.

God commanded Moses to frame new tables of stone ; and the next day, to bring them with him into the mount ; Moses staying again forty days and forty nights in the mount, without meat or drink, prayed there for the people ; when God was pleased to renew his covenant with the people ; and he gave his law anew, and bade Moses commit it to writing ; who, after forty days, returned from the mount with the tables in his hands ; and covering his face with a vail, because it shone, he published the laws of God to the people, enjoining the observation of them, and commanded a free-will-offering to be made, toward the building of the tabernacle, according to God's order. · Nadab and Abihu, the two eldest sons of Aaron, going with their father up into the mount Sinai, had there seen the glory of God, and having gone into the sanctuary with strange or common fire, were struck dead in the place by· fire sent from heaven, and for them the priests were forbidden to make lamentation : moreover, for some particular men's neglect of duty, all the priests were charged to forbear wine and strong drink, before they were to go into the tabernacle.

Moses, finding the government of the Israelites to be weighty, complained to the Lord of the burden thereof ; saying, " I am not able to bear all this people alone, because it is too heavy for me ;" and to ease him, the Lord said, " gather seventy of the elders of Israel, whom thou knowest to be the elders of the people, and officers over them, and bring them to the tabernacle of the congregation, that they may stand there with thee ;" and Moses gathered the seventy elders, and the Lord gave of the same spirit that was on Moses unto them, and it rested upon them, and they prophesied ; and Eldad and Medad remained in the camp, and prophesied, and when it was told Moses, that they prophesied, Moses, being pleased therewith, said, " would to God that all the Lord's people were prophets, and that the Lord would put his spirit upon them."

The Israelites lusting after flesh, and loathing the food that God gave them, the Lord was wrath with them, and brought quails from the sea, and let them fall by the camp, and the people gathered them ; but whilst the flesh was yet between their teeth, ere it was chewed, the wrath of the Lord was kindled against the people, and the Lord smote the people with a very great plague ; and thus God punished them again for their murmuring.

Twelve spies were now sent, one for every tribe, to discover and spy out the land of Canaan. After forty days spent in searching out the land, the spies returned to Kadesh, in the wilderness of Paran, bringing with them one branch of a vine, with a cluster of grapes upon it, gathered in the valley of Eshcol. Ten of the twelve spies, by speaking ill of the country, and the barrenness thereof, and withal magnifying the cities for their strength, and the gigantic stature of the men therein, disheartened the people from marching any further toward it, whilst Caleb did all he could to persuade the people to go on ; and now the people began again to murmur against Moses and Aaron, and would go back again into Egypt, and were ready to stone Caleb and Joshua, for saying, " The land was an exceeding good land, and, that it flowed with milk and honey ;" and because of the people's complaining. the Lord threatened them with sudden destruction ; but, through Moses's intercession and prayer, the Lord spared them yet, so, that withal he denounced to them, that all of them which were then twenty years old and upwards should die in the wilderness, and should never see the land which was promised unto them ; and that they should wander in that wilderness forty years ; " but my servant Caleb, because he had another spirit, and hath followed me fully, him will I bring into the land, whereinto he went, and his seed shall possess it."

Upon this calamity, and the continual dropping away of the Israelites in the wilderness, Moses prayed unto the Lord, and thereupon it is supposed he wrote the nine-tieth psalm, in which he sheweth, that the ordinary age of men was reduced to seventy or eighty years at the most, so that now the age of man was again contracted, and cut shorter.

And at length the people for lack of water, murmured against Moses and Aaron, whom God commanded to call water out of the rock, only by speaking to it. Moses being moved in his mind, said, " hear now, ye rebels, must we fetch you water out of the rock ?" And with the rod, he smote the rock twice, and the water came forth abundantly ; Moses and Aaron for their unbelief, here shewn in executing the command of God, were de-barred from entering into the land of Canaan : and the waters were called Meribah, or, waters of strife.

In the fortieth year after the coming of the children of Israel out of Egypt, Aaron died ; and shortly after, God signified to Moses, that he should die ; and Moses de-sired the Lord to set a man over the people, which might go in and out before them : and that they might not be as sheep without a shepherd ; and the Lord chose Josh-ua, a man in whom was the spirit of God ; and Moses laid his hands on him, and gave him a charge, as the Lord had commanded him. And here ends the matter of the five books of Moses, containing the history of the two thousand five hundred and fifty-two years and a half ; and the children of Israel mourned for Moses, as they had done for Aaron, thirty days in the land of Moab.

Joshua succeeding Moses, the Lord promised Joshua to be with him, and to assist him ; and the Lord was with him until he had conquered all the enemies of the Israel-ites ; and when God was about to give the Israelites rest round about them, so that they might dwell there secure-ly, it was requisite also, that a place should be appointed, which himself should choose, to place his name there ; wherefore, coming together at Shiloh, they there fixed the tabernacle of the congregation, after the whole land was subdued unto them. Shiloh, both by the signification of the name, and also by the situation of the place, seemeth to be the same with Salem, both which words signify peace or rest.

Joshua built the city of Timnah-Sera, in Mount Ephraim, in which he dwelt many years, after God had given rest to Israel, and having lived an hundred and ten years, he there died and was buried.

After the decease of Joshua, and of the elders, who out lived him, the wonders which God had wrought for the children of Israel, from the time of their being brought out of Egypt, began to be forgotten by the young men, every man now doing what seemed good in his own eyes. All those disorders were committed, which are reported in the five last chapters of the book of Judges, to wit, the idolatry of Micah, and the children of Dan, and the war of the Benjamites, and the cause thereof; and there succeeded a generation of men who forgot God, and mingled themselves with the Canaanites by marriage, and worshipped their Idols; and God thereby was provoked to wrath, and gave them up to Cushan, king of Mesopotamia, which first calamity of theirs held them eighty years, until Othniel, son-in-law to Caleb, being stirred up by God as a judge and avenger of his people, defeated Cushan, and delivered the Israelites out of their bondage, and the land had rest forty years, after the rest which Joshua procured them.

After the decease of Othniel, the Israelites falling again to sin against God, were again given over into the hands of Eglon, king of Moab, who joining with the Ammonites and Amalekites, overthrew the Israelites, and possessed the city of Palm-Trees; and this second oppression of theirs continued for the space of eighteen years.

Then the Lord raised up Ehud to be an avenger of his people, who slew Eglon and ten thousand of the valiant men of Moab, and the land of Israel had rest forty years. But when Ehud was dead, they returned to their old sin; wherefore they were brought again into servitude for twenty years, until Jabin's army was routed, and Sisera, captain of his army was killed by Jael, the wife of Heber, in her own tent, with a nail struck into the temple of his head ; whereupon, Deborah a prophetess, who at that time judged Israel, made a song thereof, for a memorial of that victory, and the land rested forty years.

The Israelites sinning again, and doing evil in the sight of the Lord, he delivered them into the hand of of Midian seven years. The Israelites, falling into this fourth servitude, cried unto the Lord for help, and he sent a prophet unto them, who reproved them, and shewed them what great things the Lord had done for them, and encouraged them, that they should not fear the Gods of the Amorites ; and the Lord raised up Gideon, being stirred up by an Angel sent from God to deliver them ; and first, by command from God, he overturned the altar of Baal, and burnt his grove ; and the Midianites and Amorites pitching their camp against him, the spirit of the Lord came upon Gideon, and out of thirty-two thousand men, he chose only three hundred, according to God's commandment, to fight against them, that so the victory of salvation might appear to be of the arm of the Lord, that Israel might not vaunt themselves against him. After he had obtained the victory, when the Israelites offered to settle the kingdom on his posterity, he refused it, saying, the Lord shall rule over you ; but receiving their golden earrings, he made thereof an Ephod, whereof they afterward took an occasion to fall into idolatry ; but the Midianites being vanquished, the land had rest forty years. As soon as Gideon was dead, the Israelites falling back to idolatry, worshipped Baal-Berith for their God ; and Abimelech the son of Gideon, purposing to get unto himself the kingdom, which his father had refused, slew seventy of his brethren, all upon one stone. When Abimelech had gotten the kingdom, and had reigned three years, Gaal, a man of Shechem, conspired against him, which being discovered to Abimelech, the city of Shechem was utterly destroyed, and the inhabitants put to the sword : and from thence, Abimelech, going to besiege Thehez, was knocked on the head with a piece of a millstone cast at him by a woman, and then killed out right by his own armour-bearer.

E

Now the Israelites forsaking again the true God, and falling to worship the Gods of several nations, were given up into the hands of the Philistines.

Samson the Nazarite was born at Zorah, who avenged the Israelites twenty years in the time of the Philistines, and who slew a thousand of them at one time, with the jaw-bone of an ass: in which place, called Lehi, from that jaw-bone, God, at the prayer of Samson, clave an hollow place that was in the jaw, and there came water thereout, and when he had drunk, he was revived, wherefore, he called the name thereof En-bekkore, that is, the fountain of him which called upon God.

Samson being betrayed by Delilah, and spoiled of the hair of his Nazariteship, was delivered to the Philistines, who, plucking out his eyes, carried him away prisoner to Gaza, and put him there in prison, fast bound in chains, where his strength renewing again, he pulled down the house, to which they brought him to make sport, killing the princes of the Philistines, with a very great multitude of people which were therein ; more men being killed at the fall thereof, including himself, than he had slain in all his life before ; and he was buried with his fathers, after he had been the avenger of the Israelites twenty years.

The Israelites being grievously oppressed by the philistines, and Samson being dead, Samuel was raised up of the Lord to be a prophet unto them; who, by his faithfulness, was found a true prophet, and by his word, he was known to be faithful in vision. He exhorted them to turn to the Lord with all their hearts, and to put away their strange Gods, and to prepare their hearts unto the Lord, and to serve him only ; and he would deliver them out of the hands of the Philistines. Then the children of Israel put away their Gods, and served the Lord only; and the Philistines came no-more to invade the borders of the Israelites, because they saw the hand of the Lord was against them all the days of Samuel, till Saul came to be king, under whom they returned again, and grievously oppressed Israel. And Samuel being now grown old, took to him his two sons to be his assistants, to judge the people, and his sons walked not in his ways, but turned aside after lucre, and took bribes, and perverted judgment; wherefore, the Israelites were offended, and desired Samuel that they might have a king to rule them, as other nations had ; this displeased Samuel, and he prayed unto the Lord, and the Lord said, " hearken unto the people, for they have not rejected thee, but they have rejected me, that I should not reign over them:" whereupon the Lord gave them a king in his wrath, to wit, Saul : and now began the Israelites' trouble again, for the Amorites besieged them; and Saul reigned but a short time until he was put from the kingdom by the philistines, and the Israelites were again grievously enslaved by them.

Jesse the Ephrathite, in his old age, had his youngest son David born at Bethlehem, which, therefore, was afterwards called the city of David, thirty years before he succeeded Saul, in the kingdom.

God having now rejected Saul, and debarred his race and family from succeeding in the kingdom, sent Samuel, after his long mourning for Saul, to Bethlehem, there to anoint David to be king, forty years before the rebellion of Absalom, who, was called from keeping his father's sheep, and preferred before his elder brethren ; and being anointed in their presence, he incurred their envy, no less than Joseph did of his brethren; and at last, was set over the tribe of Judah, at the same age that Joseph was made ruler over all Egypt. From the very day of his anointing, the spirit of God came upon him; to wit, the spirit of courage and wisdom, in both which respects, even whilst Saul lived, he was made captain over Israel, and withal grew a great warrior to fight the Lord's battle, and besides was a prophet, and was made the sweet singer of Israel, as one who by his divine psalms should teach and instruct the people of God.

The armies of the Israelites and Philistines being ready for battle, Goliah of Gath the Philistine, their great champion, defied the armies of Israel ; wherefore David being stirred in his zeal, said, " who is this uncircumcised Philistine, that he should defy the armies of the living God ?" but Eliab, David's eldest brother, hearing him, was offended, and asked, with whom he had left the sheep in the wilderness; and told him, he knew the pride and haughtiness of his heart; and said he, thou art come down t. at thou mayst see the battle. David said; "what I have now done, is there not a cause?" Saul being acquainted with David's words, sent for him; and David told Saul, he would fight the Philistine; Saul replied, " Thou art not able to fight him, he is a man of war, and thou art but a youth;" David told him, whilst he was keeping his father's sheep, he had killed a lion and a bear, and that this uncircumcised Philistine, who had defied the armies of the living God, should be as one of them; then Saul bade him go, and said, the Lord be with thee, and armed him with his armour, which David put off again, and took only his staff, and five smooth stones out of the brook, and put them in his Shepherd's bag; and with his sling in his hand, he drew near to the Philistine. The Philistine despised his coming so meanly armed : David said, " thou comest with sword, spear, and shield; I come in the name of the Lord of hosts; and all the assembly shall know, that the Lord saveth not with sword and spear, for the battle is the Lord's." And David slew the Philistine with a stone and a sling; and Saul taking notice of David's valour, inquired whose son the stripling David was; and David brought the Philistine's head to Saul, which he had cut off with the Philistine's own sword, having first slain him with a stone which he slung at him : and David told Saul whose son he was; and after this, David went out whithersoever Saul sent him, and behaved himself wisely.

And David returning from the slaughter of the Philistines, because it was said, Saul hath slain his thousands, and David his ten thousands, Saul was very wroth with David from that day forwards, and an evil spirit entered Saul, and the Lord departed from him, and he was afraid of David, because he saw the Lord was with him; and David behaved himself wisely, and all Israel and Judah loved him, but especially Jonathan the son of Saul, who made a covenant with David, because he loved him as his own soul; and David fearing he might at last fall into

Saul's hands, fled ; for Saul became David's enemy continually.

And David being fled, and the armies of the Philistines invading the land, Saul fell into a fear, and sought counsel from the Lord, but receiving no answer from him neither by dream, nor by Urim, nor by prophets, he went to Endor by night to consult with a witch : where, in a vision, he saw Samuel, who said to Saul, "God shall deliver Israel, together with thyself, into the hands of the Philistines ; for the Lord hath rent the kingdom out of thine hand, and given it to thy neighbour, even to David, because thou didst not obey the voice of the Lord, and didst not execute his fierce wrath upon Amalek."

The host of Israel being routed, the sons of Saul were all slain, and Saul killed himself. When David heard it, he much lamented the death of Saul and Jonathan, saying, " tell it not in Gath, publish it not in the streets of Askelon, lest the daughters of the Philistines rejoice, lest the daughters of the uncircumcised triumph ;" and further, he said, " I am distressed for thee my brother Jonathan ; very pleasant hast thou been unto me ; thy love to me was wonderful, passing the love of women."

David, having now built him an house of cedar, and living in a full and perfect peace, imparted unto Nathan the prophet, the purpose he had of building a house for God ; but was answered from God, that this was a work which should not be done by him, because he was a man of blood, but by his son Solomon, a man of peace, which should be born unto him.

Now David subdued the Philistines, the Edomites, the Amalekites, the Moabites, the Ammonites, and the Syrians ; and the bounds of Israel were stretched out to the outmost part of all that land, which had been formerly promised to the seed of Abraham, but never before possessed so fully by any of them, as by David and Solomon his son.

At the end of this year, whilst David took his ease at Jerusalem, he there defiled by adultery Bathsheba, the wife of Uriah, the hittite, who was then in the army, and in consequence thereof, he caused the husband to be slain by the hands of the Ammonites. When the child so gotten in adultery was born, David, being convinced by Nathan the prophet of his evil, acknowledged his transgression, saying, " my sin is ever before me ;" and he repented of his sin, as may be seen at large in Psalm 51 ; yet the new-born babe was taken away by death. Bathsheba being now his wife, bare David a son, unto whom, as to one who should prove a man of peace, God gave the name of Solomon.

David for numbering the people, kindled the wrath of God against the Israelites : wherefore, Gad the Prophet said to David, " thus saith the Lord ; choose one of them, that I may do unto thee, viz. whether famine, sword, or pestilence ;" and David said, " I am in a great strait ;" and his heart smote him ; for he saw the evil he had done in numbering the people, and said, " let us now fall into the hands of the Lord, for his mercies are great ; and and let me not fall into the hands of men." So the Lord sent the pestilence upon Israel, and there died seventy thousand men in one day.

David being now seventy years of age, and being broken with continual cares and wars, grew weak and feeble ; and Adonijah his son seeing his father thus declining, by the counsel and advice of Joab and Abiathar the high priest, made himself king ; whereof, when David was advertised by Bathsheba and Nathan, he presently caused his son Solomon to be anointed king, by Zadock the priest, and Nathan the prophet, and Benaiah the son of Jehoiada in Gihon ; upon which, as soon as Adonijah heard it, he fled ; and afterwards, laying hold on the horns of the altar, was pardoned by the favour of Solomon, and set at liberty ; and David assembling all the governors and chiefs of Israel, together with his sons and servants, exhorted them all to fear and worship God.

David departed this life, having reigned in Hebron seven years and six months ; and thirty three years in Jerusalem over all Israel.

Solomon loved the Lord, and walked in the statutes of David his father ; and in Gibeon the Lord appeared to

him in a dream, and bade him ask and choose what he
would, and it should be given him ; and Solomon said,
" thou hast shewed unto thy servant David my father,
great mercy, according as he walked before thee in truth
and righteousness ; and now, O my Lord God ! Thou
hast made thy servant king, instead of David my father ;
and I am but a little child, I know not how to go out or
come in :"¹ and he asked wisdom, and an understanding
heart to be given him of God ; and the speech pleased
the Lord, that Solomon had asked this thing ; God,
therefore, gave wisdom from above, exceeding any that
was before him, or should come after him, and of his
wisdom, the first experiment was made, in deciding the
controversy between the two women, about the child,
which first gave him an esteem among the people, when
they saw the wisdom of God, was in him to do judgment.

Solomon having, according to his father's direction, in
whose heart it was to build an house for the name of the
Lord God of Israel, built the temple, which was seven
years and a half in building ; in the building of which
there was neither hammer nor axe, nor any tool of iron,
heard in the house, and Solomon, having built the temple, placed there the ark, wherein was the covenant of
the Lord, which he made with the children of Israel,
when he brought them out of the land of Egypt ; and
Solomon stood before the altar of the Lord ; and, in the
presence of the people, said, " Lord God of Israel, there
is no God like thee in heaven above, or in earth beneath !
who keepest covenant and mercy with thy servants, that
walk before thee with all their heart." And he made
a long prayer for the preservation of the people ; and
desired the Lord would be with them, as he was with
their fathers, and not leave them, nor forsake them ; and
that he would incline their hearts unto him, to walk in all
his ways, to keep his statutes and judgments, which he
commanded their fathers : thus, was Solomon's beginning ; but it was not long until he was drawn away by
many strange women, who, towards his latter days, drew
away his heart unto idolatry, and his heart was not per-

fect with the Lord his God, as was the heart of David his father; for he went after the abominations of the Ammonites; and he did evil in the sight of the Lord, and went not fully after the Lord, as did David his father; and he built an high place for Chemosh, the abomination of Moab; and for these things, the Lord was angry with Solomon, and said, "because thou hast not kept my covenant, I will surely rend the kingdom from thee; yet in thy days I will not do it for David thy father's sake;" but after this, Solomon repented deeply, and made his peace with the Lord, as may be seen at large in the book called the Preacher; and at last he died when he had reigned forty years.

Rehoboam the son of Solomon, when all Israel met at Sechem to make him king, by a harsh answer made unto them, alienated the hearts of the ten tribes from him, who presently sending into Egypt for Jeroboam the son of Nebat, made him king over them; and fell off both from the house of David, and also from the true worship of God; in memory of which sad disaster, the Jews afterward kept a solemn fast yearly, upon the twenty-third of the third month, called Sivan, from this dismal rent made in that kingdom. Rehoboam reigned over Judah and Benjamin, seventeen years; and Jeroboam over Israel, that is, over the ten tribes, the space of twenty years.

Jeroboam fearing est his new-gotten subjects should revolt from him again, in order to divert their thoughts from looking any more after Jerusalem, introduced a new devised form of religion, setting up two golden calves; the one at Bethel, the other at Dan; and there he offered sacrifices to his calves, and the people ran after his idolatry.

At which time, a prophet, and man of God out of Judea, went to Bethel, and cried out against the altar, in the word of the Lord, and bore his testimony against the king's idolatry; and when the king stretched forth his hand to lay hold on him, his hand was dried up, and the prophet foretold, that the altar should be rent. After this prophet had done his message, he was charged by the

Lord not to eat bread, nor to drink water, nor return by the way that he came ; but being deceived by another, who said he was a prophet, and abused the word of God unto him, was unfaithful unto God's command : wherefore as he was returning homeward, he was slain by a lion whereof, when tidings came to the prophet who deceived him, he took up his body and buried it, mourning over him, saying, alas ! my brother, and assured his sons, that what had been foretold by the man of God should come to pass.

The Israelites who feared God, falling off from Jeroboam to Rehoboam, maintained the kingdom of Judah three years, which time they walked in the ways of David and Solomon.

Rehoboam being once settled in his kingdom, forsook the law of the Lord, and all Israel and Judah with him ; for the Jews who, by their good example, should have stirred up their brethren the Israelites to repentance, provoked the Lord with their own sins, wherein they offended more than any of their fore-fathers had done ; they made also to themselves high places, images, and groves upon every high hill, and under every green tree, doing according to all the abominations of the Gentiles, which the Lord had therefore cast out before them.

After Rehoboam, succeeded Abijah, who putting his trust and confidence in God, obtained a great victory against Jeroboam, and slew five hundred thousand men, and took Bethel, where one of the idolatrous calves was set up.

After the death of Abijah, Asa his son succeeded, and God gave ten years peace, without interruption in the land ; and this godly king Asa put away all idolatry, and reformed the kingdom ; but when Asa died, though he was good, yet a better succeeded in his stead his son Jehoshaphat, who being settled in his kingdom, began with taking away the high places, and the groves : but when Jehoshaphat died, Jehoram, his wicked son, slew all his brethren, and many of the princes of Israel ; and following the counsel of his wicked wife Athaliah, he set up in Judah, and even in Jerusalem itself, the idolatrous worship of

Baal, after the manner of his father-in-law Ahab and his house; for which he was reproved in a letter by the prophet Elijah, who foretold him what calamities should fall upon him, because he had not walked in the ways of his father, but had made Judah, and the inhabitants of Jerusalem, go a whoring, like the whoredoms of the house of Ahab, and also had slain his brethren of his father's house, who were better than himself; and according to what the prophet had foretold, the Lord struck Jehoram with an incurable disease in the bowels, and he died a miserable death.   And his son Ahaziah succeeded him, who also walked in the ways of the wicked house of Ahab for his mother was his counsellor to do wickedly, and the evil that he did in the sight of the Lord, was his destruction: being sick, he asked counsel of Baalzebub, the God of the Ekronites, concerning his recovery.   The prophet Elijah told the king plainly that he should die, and accordingly he died.

Athaliah the daughter of Ahab, seeing her own son Ahaziah dead, destroyed all the race of the house of Judah, and possessed herself of the kingdom; but Jehosheba, the Daughter of king Joram, and wife to Jehoiada the high priest, took Joash, being then an infant, and son to her brother Ahaziah, and hid him, with his nurse, six months in the temple, whilst Athaliah ruled; and at seven years end, brought him forth, and anointed him king, and caused Athaliah to be slain, and restored the worship of the true God, destroying the worship of Baal.

This Joash did that which was right in the sight of the Lord, all the days of Jehoida the priest. After the death of Jehoida, the king hearkening to the princes of Judah, they left the house of the Lord God of their Fathers, and served Groves and idols, for which sin the Lord sent his wrath upon them; yet he sent his prophets to testify against them, and to bring them back again; but they would not hear, and Zachariah, the son of Jehoida, was moved by the spirit of God to tell them that they had forsaken God, and that he had forsaken them; for which message, they stoned him to death, at the commandment of the king.   Thus Joash the king remembered not the kindness which Jehoida, Zachariah's father, had done to him ; and when the prophet died, he said, " the Lord look upon it and requite it." And, now mark, what was the end of this king ; his own servants conspired against him, and slew him in his bed, as may be seen more at large in the account given of God's judgments against persecutors.

Amaziah succeeded Joash, and he did that which was right in the sight of the Lord, but not with a perfect heart, for at last he set up the gods of the children of Seir, and bowed himself before them, and burnt incense unto them ; wherefore the anger of the Lord was kindled a gainst him, and he sent a prophet unto him to reprove him, to whom the king said, " art thou made of the king's council, forbear, wherefore shouldst thou be smitten ?" " Nevertheless, the prophet said, " I know God hath determined to destroy thee ;" and after the time that this king turned away his heart from the Lord, he was slain.

After him succeeded Uzziah, under whom did the kingdom of Judah flourish no less than that other of Israel did under Jeroboam the second, and he did that which was right in the sight of the Lord, and he sought God in the days of Zechariah and as long as he sought the Lord and applied his mind to matters of piety, God made him to prosper, and he subdued the Philistines, and other bordering enemies : And thus, whilst he was weak and low, he was marvellously helped against his enemies ; but when he was strong, and looked at his own strength, his heart was lifted up to his destruction ; for he transgressed against the Lord, and burnt incense ; wherefore, the Lord smote him with the leprosy, and he remained a leper to the day of his death, and dwelt in a house separately, for he was cut off from the house of the Lord ; and he being dead, Jotham his son reigned, and he did that which was right in the sight of the Lord, howbeit the people did yet do corruptly ; but he became mighty, because he prepared his ways before the Lord his God. After him reigned Ahaz his son, who did not that which was right in the sight of the Lord ; for he walked in the ways of the kings of Israel, who made also molten images for Balaam, and burnt incense on the high places.

and under every green tree, wherefore, the Lord delivered him into the hands of his enemies.   And thus the
reader may see how these people and the children of Judah
and Israel, to whom God had given a commandment
that they should fear him, and not forget him, and that
then he would deliver them from their enemies, did not
hearken, but were ready often to backslide, and to serve
their graven images, both their children and their children's children unto this day.

Ahaz being dead. Hezekiah his son began to reign,
and he did that which was right in the sight of the Lord,
according to all that his father David did, he removed
the high places, and broke the images, and cut down the
groves, and brake in pieces the brazen serpent that Moses had made ; for, in those days, the children of Israel
did burn incense to it ; and he called it Nehushtan, that
is to say, a little piece of brass.   And thus, this good reformer trusted in the Lord God of Israel, and he left not
off throwing down the altars and high places, until he
had destroyed them all, causing a thorough reformation.
And his zeal was so great for the Lord, that after him,
as it is recorded, was none like him among all the kings
of Judah, nor any that was before him ; for he clave to
the Lord, and departed not from following him, and the
Lord was with him, and he prospered him whithersoever he went forth.

Hezekiah falling sick unto death, the prophet Isaiah
being commanded of the Lord, said unto him, "set thine
house in order, for thou shalt die, and not live."   This
moved Hezekiah's heart, that he wept sore, and turning to
the wall, prayed unto the Lord, saying, " I beseech thee,
O Lord, remember now how I have walked before thee
in truth, and with a perfect heart, and have done that
which is good in thy sight ;" wherefore, the Lord had
compassion on him, and added fifteen years more to his
days.   And Hezekiah dying, Manasseh his son, reigned, and did that which was evil in the sight of the Lord,
after the abomination of the heathen, building the high
places which his father had destroyed, and again reared up
altars for Baal, and worshipped all the host of heaven,

and served them, and used enchantments ; and dealing with familiar spirits and wizards, he wrought much wickedness in the sight of the Lord, to provoke him to anger ; which abominations the Lord sent his servants and prophets to foretel, that he would bring such evil upon Jerusalem and Judah, that whosoever should hear it, their ears should tingle : and the Lord brought upon Manasseh, the host of the Assyrians, who took Manasseh, and bound him with fetters, and carried him captive to Babylon. And now being in affliction, he besought the Lord, and humbled himself greatly before the God of his fathers ; wherefore, the Lord restored him his kingdom, and then he knew that the Lord was God, and he cast out the altars that he had built, and took away the strange Gods and idols, and commanded the people to serve the Lord God of Israel ; but still the people retained the high places to worship in. And after his death, his son Amon was punished by the Lord, being slain by his servants in his own house. And now these two bad kings being taken away, the Lord raised up another good king, which was Josiah the son of Amon, who reigned thirty-four years in Jerusalem ; and caused again a blessed and thorough reformation amongst the people of Judah and Jerusalem, making a covenant before the Lord to walk after the Lord, and to keep his testimonies with all his heart, and with all his soul ; and he likewise cleansed away the abominations from the people, and again stirred them up to serve the Lord their God ; and all his days, they departed not from following the Lord God of their fathers.

Neco, king of Egypt, by God's command, went against the king of Assyria, who at that time made war upon him, 2 Kings, xxiii. 29, 2 Chron. xxxv. 20, 21. Josiah unadvisedly engaging in this war, was slain ; and this good king being taken out of the world, there were such lamentations, that it grew almost a common proverb, The lamentation of Hadadrimon, in the valley of Megiddo ; for not only the whole people living, wonderfully bewailed the death of Josiah, but the ages following were sensible of the loss of him : and the prophet

Jeremiah, in remembrance thereof, wrote his mournful book of Lamentations, wherein bewailing the calamities which were shortly to befal the people, as if he had then presently beheld them, using these words, " the breath of our nostrils, the anointed of the Lord, is taken in their pits ; of whom, we said, under the shadow of his wings, we shall live among the heathen."

After the death of Josiah, his youngest son was anointed king, who presently fell to doing that which was evil in the sight of God ; but Neco, king of Egypt, removed him after he had reigned three months, and made Eliakim, his elder brother, king in his room, changing his name into Jehoiakim, that thereby he might testify to the world, that he ascribed the victory by him gotten against the Assyrians, to the Lord only, by whom he professed he was formerly sent against them.

In the beginning of this king's reign, Jeremiah, commanded by God, went and stood in the court of the temple, and there exhorted the people to repentance ; and when they would not, he denounced the judgment of God against them, saying, that that house should become as Shilo, and that city should be cursed among all the nations of the earth ; whereupon, he was apprehended by the priests and prophets, and all the people then in the court, and was accused as a man worthy of death ; but was acquitted and set at liberty by the public judgment of the princes and elders.

At this time also, Uriah prophesied against Jerusalem, and the land of Judah, agreeable to the sayings of the prophet Jeremiah ; for which, the king put him to death by the sword, and threw his carcass among the sepulchres of the basest common people ; but Ahikam, who had formerly been a man of great authority with king Josiah, appeared so much in behalf of the prophet Jeremiah, that he was not delivered over into the hands of the people to be put to death at that time.

To these, might be added the prophet Habbakkuk, to whom, when he complained of the stubbornness of the Jews, God made this answer, That he would shortly send the Chaldeans into Judah ; and further declared his purpose concerning this matter, in these words, I will do a work in your days which you will not believe when it shall be told unto you ; for, behold, I will stir up the Chaldeans, a fierce nation, and a swift, which shall walk through the breadth of the land which is none of theirs, as their own inheritance.

In the fourth year of this king Jehoiakim, the prophet Jeremiah reproved the Jews for not hearkening to the word of the Lord, which he had spoken unto them from time to time, and for not regarding the exhortations of the prophets which the Lord had sent unto them ; and then again told them of the coming of Nebuchadnezzar upon them, and of their being carried away captives to Babylon, and that captivity to last seventy years ; and during the seventy years captivity, Daniel prophesied of the coming of the Messiah, who should bring in the law of everlasting righteousness, and put an end to the Levitical sacrifices.

Jehoiakim being taken prisoner by the Chaldeans, was thrown out without burial ; that is, was buried like an ass, his carcass being drawn without the gates of Jerusalem, as was foretold by the prophet Jeremiah ; though, in reference to the common course of nature, he also may be said to have slept with his fathers, as he is 2 Kings, 24. 6.

After him, came his son Jehoiachin, who was also called Jeconiah, and reigned three months and ten days in Jerusalem, who also did evil in the sight of the Lord, as his father had done before him, against whom, the Lord, by his prophet Jeremiah, declared a most dreadful decree, saying, " O earth, earth, earth, hear the word of the Lord ;" thus saith the Lord, " Write ye this man childless, a man that shall not prosper in his days, for no man of his seed shall prosper, sitting upon the throne of David, and ruling any more in Judah ;" and pronounced a woe to the pastors that scattered the sheep, and that had not fed nor visited the people ; and therefore, the Lord would visit them for the evil of their doing, and he would gather the remnant of his flock, and would set up shepherds over them that should feed them ;

and that would raise unto David a righteous branch, that should execute judgment and justice in the earth ; and that in his day, Judah shall be saved, and Israel shall dwell safely ; and this is his name wherewith he shall be called, "The Lord our Righteousness." And in the sense of this, the prophet cried out, "Mine heart within me is broken, because of the prophets ; all my bones shake : I am like a drunken man, and like a man whom wine hath overcome, because of the Lord, and because of the words of his holiness."

And Isaiah the prophet had a true sight of the coming of the blessed Messiah ; for he said, "The spirit of the Lord God is upon me, because the Lord has anointed me to preach good tidings unto the meek ; he hath sent me to bind up the broken-hearted ; to proclaim liberty to the captives, and the opening the prison to them that are bound ; to proclaim the acceptable year of the Lord, and the day of vengeance of our God ; to comfort all that mourn ; to appoint unto them that mourn in Sion ; to give unto them beauty for ashes, the oil of joy for mourning, the garment of praise for the spirit of heaviness, that they might be called trees of righteousness, the planting of the Lord, that he might be glorified ; and they shall build the old wastes ; they shall raise up the former desolations, and they shall repair the waste cities, the desolations of many generations."

And thus, the reader may see the many glorious dispensations and manifestations of God's love unto mankind, to the holy patriarchs and prophets in all generations ; and now we are come, according to what the prophets foretold, to the day of the appearance of that great Saviour of the world, whose dispensation far exceedeth all others in glory, being that eternal substance, which ended all types, shadows, and figures.

And thus, these Jews, who had been the true worshippers, apostatized and degenerated from their primitive glory and institutions ; and their worship became merely outside ; for, it is said, "they drew near to God with their mouths, and honoured him with their lips, but their hearts were far from him." The prophets were raised up, and sent from the Lord to cry against them, and to foretel the desolation and destruction that were to come upon them, which accordingly came to pass, as will be seen anon. And, in this condition, did Christ at his coming, find these ancient people the Jews, to whom God had formerly committed his laws and commands, and given his oracles ; but they were wholly apostatized from them, as will appear by their fruits in the following discourse.

After the Jews had apostatized, as the prophets had foretold, and that the Messiah and Deliverer should come ; in the fulness of time, Christ Jesus the son of God was born of the Virgin Mary, whom she wrapped in swaddling clothes, and laid in a manger, because there was no room for him in the inn. The birth of Christ was revealed, by an angel of the Lord, to shepherds, keeping their flock by night in the field ; and " suddenly there was with the angel a multitude of the heavenly host praising God, and saying, Glory to God in the highest, and on earth peace, good will towards men." The shepherds making haste to Bethlehem, found Mary and Joseph, and the child lying in a manger, and they published that which was told them concerning the child, and they returned praising and glorifying God ; but Mary kept all these things, and pondered them in her heart.

The child was called Jesus (signifying Saviour,) which was so declared by the angel, before he was conceived in the womb. The wise men from the east, the star being their guide, coming to Herod at Jerusalem, and there being taught, that the birth-place of Christ was at Bethlehem of Judea, went thither ; and entering into the house which was shewn them by the star, which stood over it, they found the little child, and Mary his mother, and falling down worshipped him ; and having opened their treasures, they offered unto him gold, frankincense and myrrh. Afterwards, being warned of God in a dream, that they should not return unto Herod, they departed into their own country another way.

G

And when the child was brought by his parents to Jerusalem, to be presented to the Lord, there came into the temple one Simeon, a just and devout man, who had waited for the consolation of Israel; and the Holy Ghost was upon him; and it was revealed unto him by the Holy Ghost, that he should not see death before he had seen the Lord's Christ; and he came by the spirit into the temple; and when the parents brought the child, to do for him after the custom of the law, he took him up in his arms, and blessed God, and said, "Lord, now lettest thou thy servant depart in peace, according to thy word; for mine eyes have seen thy salvation, which thou hast prepared before the face of all people, a light to lighten the Gentiles, and the glory of thy people Israel." And Joseph and his mother marvelled at those things which were spoken of him; and Simeon blessed them, and said unto Mary his mother, "Behold, this child is set for the fall and rising again of many in Israel, and for a sign which shall be spoken against."

In the same moment, came Anna, a prophetess, the daughter of Phanuel. She also openly acknowledged the Lord, and spake of him to all that looked for redemption in Jerusalem.

When Joseph and Mary had performed all things, according to the law of the Lord, they returned into Galilee, unto their own city Nazareth.

The angel of the Lord appearing unto Joseph in a dream, shewed him, that he should flee into Egypt, that he might provide for the life of the child, and escape the devices of Herod. Joseph being awakened, took the young child and his mother by night, and departed into Egypt; where he remained until the death of Herod; who thinking the young child had been still at Bethlehem, that he might destroy him amongst the rest, killed all the children that were in Bethlehem, and in all the coasts thereof, from two years old and under, according to the time which he had inquired of the wise men.

Herod being dead, the angel of the Lord appeared unto Joseph in a dream in Egypt, and commanded, that he should return, with the young child and his mother, into the land of Israel; but when he heard that Archelaus did reign in Judea, in the room of his father Herod, he feared to go thither; and being warned of God in a dream, he departed into the parts of Galilee, and there dwelt in the city Nazareth, from whence Jesus took the name of Nazarene, and the Christians of Nazarenes.

In the year of the world 4010, it being the passover, Christ, in the twelfth year of his age, was brought by Joseph and Mary to Jerusalem. His parents returning home, he staid behind; they, not knowing where he was, sought him three days, and found him in the temple, sitting in the midst of the doctors, hearing them, and asking them questions; and all that heard him were astonished at his understanding and answers; and he went down with his parents to Nazareth, and was obedient unto them, and followed his father's trade of a carpenter.

In the year of the world 4030, and in the thirtieth year of Christ, John came forth in his ministry, crying with a loud voice in the wilderness, "prepare ye the way of the Lord, make his paths straight;" and opening the acceptable year of the Lord, or the time of his divine pleasure, preaching repentance and remission of sins, being clothed with a garment of camel's hair, and a girdle of skin about his loins; and his food was locusts and wild honey.

And Jesus being filled with the Holy Ghost, was led by the spirit into the desert, where he fasted forty days and forty nights, and was tempted, but the tempter could find no place in him. When John was asked by the sect of the Pharisees, who he was? he told them, he was not the Christ, denying that he was Elias, or that prophet; but said, he was the voice of one crying in the wilderness, "make straight the way of the Lord;" and told them, " I baptize with water, but there standeth one amongst you, whom ye know not; he it is who cometh after me, who is preferred before me, whose shoe-latchet I am not worthy to unloose." The next day, John seeing Jesus coming to him, saith, "behold the Lamb of God, that taketh away the sin of the world; this is he of whom I spake, there cometh one after me, that is preferred before me, and I saw him, and testify, that this is the son of God."

Jesus going into Galilee, commanded Philip to follow him; he finding Nathaniel under a fig-tree, brought him to Jesus, who pronounced him to be truly an Israelite, in whom was no guile.

Jesus working miracles, many believed on him; but he did not commit himself unto them. Leaving Jerusalem, where he had been at the passover, he went into the land of Judea, with his disciples; where, after he had staid eight months, he went into Galilee again; but he must needs go through Samaria, where he brought the Samaritan woman off from their worship, to the worship of the Father, in the spirit and truth; and in Galilee, he worked many miracles, healing the sick, casting out devils, going through all Galilee, preaching in their synagogues, and healing every disease; and his fame went into all Syria; and a great multitude followed him: and in a certain city, he healed a leper, which, though he was forbid, he published; and they came to him from every place to hear him, and to be healed, insomuch, that he could no more enter openly into the city, but was in desert places and prayed.

After these things, was the feast of the Jews; and Jesus went up to Jerusalem; where, for healing a man on the Sabbath-day, that had had an infirmity thirty-eight years, lying at the pool of Bethesda, the Jews persecuted Jesus, and sought to slay him, because he had done these things on the Sabbath-day. Jesus told them, " my Father worketh hitherto, and I work:" wherefore, the Jews sought the more to kill him, because he said, that God was his father: Jesus said, the Son can do nothing of himself, but what he seeth his Father do; for whatsoever he doeth, these also doth the Son; for the Father loveth the son, and sheweth him all things that himself doth, and he will shew him greater things than these, that ye may marvel; for the Father judgeth no man; but hath committed all judgment unto the son, that all men should honour the Son, even as they honour the Father: he that honoureth not the Son, honoureth not the Father that hath sent him.

'And it came to pass in those days, that he went into a mountain to pray, and continued in prayer all night ; and when it was day, he chose twelve, whom he called Apostles, and he came down with them, and stood in the plain ; and a great multitude coming unto him, he went up into a mountain again, and there spake, first, to his a-postles, and afterwards, to the people, exhorting his disciples to lowliness, pronouncing a blessing to the poor, and to them that weep now, but a wo unto them that were rich and full, and unto them that laughed now, for they should mourn and weep ; and that they should love their enemies, and do good to them that hated them : And when he ended all his sayings, in the audience of the people, he entered into Capernaum, and healed the Centurion's servant, that lay sick ready to die ; and af-terwards he went from city to city preaching ; and his disciples were with him, and certain women ministered unto him : And whilst he spake to the people, it was told him, that his mother and brethren stood with-out, desiring to see him, and to speak with him ; he an-swered, and said, my mother and brethren are these which hear the word of God and do it.

And as Jesus was going to the house of Jairus (who fell down at Jesus's feet, and besought him, that he would come to his house ; for he had only one daughter, of a-bout twelve years of age, and she lay a dying) the peo-ple thronged him as he went ; and a woman, having an issue of blood twelve years, who had spent all her living upon physicians, and could not be healed of any, came be-hind him, and touched the border of his garment ; and she was healed ; and the daughter of Jairus, already dead, was restored to life by his word only ; and he strait-ly charged that no man should know it.

When he departed thence, two blind men followed him, whose eyes he opened, straitly charging, that no man should know it. As they went out, behold, they brought unto him a dumb man, possessed with a devil ; and when the devil was cast out, the dumb spake, and a mul itude marvelled, but the Pharisees blasphemed ; and he went round about their cities and villages, teaching and healing all their diseases; and he was moved with compassion towards the great multitude. When he saw the great harvest and the few labourers, he said unto his disciples, that they should pray the Lord that he would send forth labourers; and he sent forth the twelve apostles to preach the gospel.

He said to his disciples, wo unto them by whom offences come; and he taught them, that if thy brother sin against thee, he is to be forgiven.

Lazarus of Bethany being sick, his sisters sent to Jesus, to tell him of it. When he heard that he was sick, he tarried two days in the place where he was; but afterwards he said to his disciples, let us go again into Judea: they said unto him, the Jews of late sought to stone thee, and goest thou thither again? Jesus answering, said unto them, Lazarus sleepeth (speaking of his death, not of his sleep) let us go to him, said Thomas, that we may die with him; Jesus came nigh unto Bethany, and found that Lazarus had been buried four days in the grave; Martha came to meet him; they discoursed concerning the resurrection. Mary hearing of it, came quickly to him without the town, where Martha met him, who seeing her weep, Jesus wept and came to the grave, bidding them remove the stone, and giving thanks to his father, called Lazarus out of his grave; whereupon many believed on him, and some going to the Pharisees, telling what things Jesus had done, they called a council, where Caiphas prophesied concerning Jesus, and from that day consulted together, that they might put him to death, commanding that if any knew where he was, they should give notice, that they might take him; and, at another time, the Pharisees said, behold, the whole world has gone after him.

Jesus travelled towards Jerusalem, and when he came nigh, seeing the city, he wept over it, foretelling the utter destruction thereof; and being come to Jerusalem, and having spoken of the desolation and ruin of it, as he sat on the mount of olives, over against the temple, his disciples asked him, when these things shall be, and what shall be the signs of the coming? To whom he answered at large, and warned them to watch, and to be ready ; for they knew not the hour when the Lord will come, and taught the same thing by the parable of the ten virgins ; as also by the parable of the talents, delivered to the servants to trade with.

When Jesus had finished these sayings, he said to his disciples, ye know that after two days is the passover, and the son of man shall be betrayed to be crucified.—Then they consulted together, in the palace of the high-priest that they might kill Jesus, but they said, not on the feast-day, lest there be an uproar among the people ; then entered satan into Judas, who offered himself, and covenanted to betray him.

In the first day of the unleavened bread, when the passover was slain, and in the evening, he came with the twelve ; and when they had sat down and eaten, Jesus said, I have greatly desired to eat this passover before I suffer ; and he further said, one of you shall betray me ; and they began to be sorrowful, and to say unto him, one by one, is it I ? He answered, it is he that dippeth his hand with me in the dish ; and to Judas, asking, is it I ? He said, thou hast said.

Jesus knew that the hour was come, that he should depart out of this world unto the father ; having loved his own which were in the world, he loved them unto the end ; knowing that the father had given all things into his hands, and that he was come from God, and went to God. There being a strife among his disciples who should be the greatest, he rose after supper, and laid aside his garments, took a towel and girded himself ; after that, he poured water into a bason and began to wash his disciples' feet. Peter said, thou shalt never wash my feet. Jesus answered him, " if I wash thee not, thou hast no part with me." Peter said, " not my feet only, but also my hands, and my head." After he had washed their feet, and had taken his garments, and had set down again, he said unto them, know ye what I have done to you. You call me master and Lord, and ye say well ; for so I am : if then your Lord and master hath washed your feet, you ought also to wash one another's feet ; for I have given you an example, that you should do as I have done to you. And speaking further to his disciples, he was troubled in spirit, and said, one of you shall betray me. They looked one upon another, doubting of whom he spake : one of the disciples whom Jesus loved, lying on Jesus's breast, said, Lord, who is it? Jesus said, he it is to whom I shall give a sop, after I have dipped it ; and he gave it to Judas, and said to him, what thou doest do quickly. After Judas had received the sop, he went immediately out ; when Jesus said, " now is the son of man glorified, and God is glorified in him." " Little children, yet a little while I am with you ; ye shall seek me; and as I said unto the Jews, whither I go, you can-cannot come, so now I say unto you, a new commandment I give unto you, that you love one another, as I have loved you ; by this shall all men know that ye are my disciples, if ye have love one to another" : Peter said, Lord, whither goest thou?" Jesus answered, "whither I go thou canst not follow me now, but thou shalt follow me afterwards ;" Peter said, "why cannot I follow thee now?" I will lay down my life for thy sake. " Jesus answered, the cock shall not crow till thou hast denied me thrice."

Against their sorrow, conceived by them for his death, he comforted them, saying, let not your hearts be troubled ; and, that in his father's house, were many man-sions ; and that the comforter, the holy ghost, should come and be their teacher : And he exhorted them to a-bide patiently the hatred of the world, which hated him, and that they should not be offended, though persecutions attended them.

Again, entering into a garden with his disciples, unto whom he said, "pray ye that ye enter not into temptation; sit here till I go and pray yonder"; and he took Peter and the two sons of Zebedee, with him, and said unto them, tarry here and watch: " and having withdrawn from them about a stone's cast, he kneeled down and prayed, saying, father, if thou be willing, remove this cup from me, nev-ertheless, not my will but thine be done" ; and there ap-peared an angel from heaven strengthening him: Then returning and finding his disciples sleeping, he reprehended and admonished them ; and being in an agony, he prayed more earnestly ; and his sweat was as it were great drops of blood ; and while he was yet speaking to his disciples, Judas came and betrayed him to the chief priests, who took him ; and he said unto them, this is your hour and power of darkness ; and the disciples left him, and fled ; and they bound Jesus, and brought him first to Annas, who sent him to Caiphas the high priest, where all the chief priests, elders, and scribes of the people were gathered together ; then Caiphas asked him concerning his disciples, and his doctrine ; Jesus answered him, I spake openly to the world ; ask them that heard me ; therefore, one of the officers struck him with a staff, to whom he answered ; if I have well spoken, why smitest thou me ? Then all the council sought false witness against him, and found none ; at last, two witnesses came ; but their testimony agreed not. Caiphas then said, answerest thou not to what they witness against thee ; but Jesus held his peace; then he adjured him that he should tell whether he were the Christ, and he answered, I am ; wherefore, they judged him guilty of death, for this blasphemy (as they accounted it.) Then they mocked him, and spat on him, and cruelly beat him with buffets and staves ; and covering his face, they said prophesy who smote thee ; and many other things they reproachfully spoke against him.

They led him bound unto Pontius Pilate the governor, from Caiphas to the hall of judgment ; and they began to accuse him, saying, we found this man perverting the nation, and forbidding to give tribute to Cæsar, saying that himself is Christ, a king. And when he was accused of the chief priests and elders, he answered nothing. Then said Pilate unto him, hearest thou not how many things they witness against thee ; but he answered not a word, so that Pilate marvelled. Then said Pilate, take ye him, and judge him according to your law ; but they urged, it is not lawful for us to put any man to death. Pilate then entered into the judgment-hall again and called Jesus, and said unto him, art thou the king of the jews ? Jesus answered, sayest thou this of thyself, or did others

H

tell it thee of me? Pilate answered, am I a Jew? Thine
own nation and t e chief priests have delivered thee unto
me; what hast thou done? Jesus answered, my kingdom
is not of this world.   Pilate therefore said unto him, art
thou a king then? Jesus answered, for this cause came I
into the world that I might bear witness unto the truth.
Pilate said unto him, what is truth? And when he had
said this, he went out again unto the Jews, and said unto
them, I find in him no fault at all; and they were the
more fierce, saying, he stirreth up the people, teaching
throughout all Galilee to this place.   Pilate therefore
hearing of Galilee, asked if he were a Galilean ? And
when he knew that he belonged to Herod's jurisdictions,
he sent him to Herod, who was at Jerusalem in those
days ; and when he saw Jesus, he was exceedingly glad ;
but being deceived in his hopes of seeing a miracle, and
not vouchsafed any answer either to him or the   chief
priests and scribes,   vehemently accusing him ; after
Herod had set Jesus at nought and mocked him, he sent
him back to Pilate arrayed in a gorgeous robe ; and both
the governors were made friends that same day.   And
Pilate, when he had called the chief priests, the rulers, and
the people, said unto them, neither I, nor Herod, finds
any fault in him, or any thing worthy of death : I will
therefore chastise him, and release him ; for the governor was of necessity every feast, as the custom was,
to deliver to the people one prisoner whom they would ;
and the multitude crying out aloud, began to desire that
he would do unto them as he had ever done.   Pilate
therefore calling them, said unto them, ye have a custom that I should release unto you one at the passover ;
will ye therefore that I release unto you the king of the
Jews ? which will ye, either this man or Barrabas ? For
he knew that the chief priests had delivered him for envy ; but they stirred up the people that he should rather
deliver Barrabas unto them.   Now he was a notable
thief, who lay bound with them that made insurrection ;
and for insurrection and murder in the city, was cast into prison ; and when Pilate had sat down in the judgment seat, his wife sent unto him, saying, have nothing

to do with the just man ; for I have suffered many things in my dream by reason of him this day. Pilate therefore spake unto them again, being willing to release Jesus. Which of the twain will you that I release unto you ? But they all cried out, not him, but Barrabas. Pilate therefore answering, said unto them, what will you that I should do unto him that ye call king of the Jews ? And they all cried out again, crucify him. Pilate said, but what evil hath he done ? I find no cause of death in him. I will therefore chastise him, and let him go ; but they cried more earnestly, crucify him, and were very instant with loud voices desiring the same : then Pilate took Jesus and scourged him ; and the soldiers platted a crown of thorns, and put it on his head, and clothed him with purple, saying, hail ! king of the Jews ; and beat him with staves. Pilate therefore went forth again, and said unto them, behold, I bring him forth unto you, that you may know I find no fault in him. Then Jesus came forth wearing the crown of thorns, and the robe : and Pilate said unto them, behold the man. When the chief priests and officers saw him, they cried out, saying, crucify him, crucify him : Pilate said, take ye him and crucify him, for I find no fault in him ; the Jews said, he ought to die, because he made himself the son of God. When Pilate therefore heard that saying, he was the more afraid, and went again into the judgment-hall, and said to Jesus, whence art thou ? but Jesus gave him no answer. Then said Pilate, speakest thou not unto me? knowest thou not that I have power to crucify thee ? Jesus answered, thou couldst have no power, unless it were given thee from above ; and from thenceforth Pilate sought to release him, but the Jews cried out, then thou art not Cæsar's friend. When Pilate heard this, he brought forth Jesus, and sat in the judgment seat in the place called the pavement, and it was the preparation of the passover, and about the sixth hour. Then said he unto the Jews, behold your king ; but they cried out, away with him ; away with him ; crucify him. Pilate said unto them, shall I crucify your king ? Then answered the chief priests, we have no king but Cæsar. When

Pilate therefore saw that he prevailed nothing but that rather a tumult was made, he took water and washed his hands before the multitude, saying, I am innocent of the blood of this just person, see you to it ; and all the people answered and said, his blood be upon us and our children.   Then willing to content the multitude, he released unto them Barrabas ; and when he had scourged Jesus, he delivered him over to their will, that he might be crucified.

And the soldiers of the governor, when they had led Jesus into the hall, called Prætorium, called together the whole band ; and when they had stripped him, they put upon him a scarlet robe, and platted a crown of thorns, and put it on his head, and a reed in his right hand ; and bowing the knee, mocked him, saying, hail, king of the Jews ; and when they had spit on him, they took that reed, and smote him on the head ; and when they had mocked him, they took off the purple from him and put his own clothes on him, and led him out to crucify him.

Then Judas, who had betrayed him, when he saw that he was condemned, repented himself, and brought the thirty pieces of silver to the chief priests, confessing his sin unto them ; and casting the silver pieces into the temple, went and hanged himself ; and they bought with them the potters-field, that the prophecy might be fulfilled.

And Jesus came forth carrying his cross ; but as they were leading him, they found one Simon of Cyrene, who came out of the country, whom they took and compelled to carry the cross after Jesus ; and there were two thieves that were led with him, that they might be crucified, and there followed a great multitude of people, and of women that lamented him, to whom he turned and foretold the lamentable destruction of Jerusalem : and when they were come into the place called Calvary, but in the Hebrew Golgotha, they gave unto him wine mingled with myrrh, and vinegar mingled with gall ; and when he had tasted it, he would not drink it ; and they crucified him there, (at the third hour) and the two thieves with him, one on the right hand, and the the other on the left; and Jesus said, Father, forgive them; for they know not what they do. And Pilate wrote a superscription in Hebrew, Greek and Latin, and put in on the cross, which, at the request of the high priest, Pilate would not alter; and after they crucified him, they parted his garments into four parts, to every soldier that was employed in the execution a part, casting lots; and likewise upon his seamless coat, whose it should be, that the scripture might be fulfilled, and they sitting down, watched him there : and the people stood beholding him, but they that passed by reviled him, wagging their heads, and saying, thou that destroyest the temple, and buildest it in three days, save thyself, if thou be the son of God, come down from the cross : likewise, also the chief priests and rulers, with the people, mocking and scoffing, with the scribes and elders, said among themselves, he saved others, himself he cannot save. If he be the king of Israel, if that Christ the chosen of God, let him come down from the cross, and we will believe him: he trusted in God : let him deliver him; for he said, I am the son of God. The soldiers also mocked him, and coming unto him, offered him vinegar, saying, if thou be the king of the Jews, save thyself. One of the thieves also which were crucified with him, continued railing against him; the other being converted, rebuked him that railed, and said unto Jesus, Lord, remember me when thou comest into thy kingdom; to whom, Christ answered, " to day shalt thou be with me in paradise." And there stood by his cross, the mother of Jesus, and his mother's sister Mary, the wife of Cleophas, and Mary Magdalene. When therefore Jesus saw his mother, and the disciple whom he loved, standing; he said unto his mother, behold thy son, and to the disciple, behold thy mother : And when the sixth hour was come, there was darkness in all the land until the ninth hour; and about the ninth hour Jesus cried with a loud voice, Eli, Eli, lama-sabachthani; and some that sood by said, that he called Elias. After this, when Jesus knew that all things were accomplished, that the scrip-

ture might be fulfilled, said, I thirst. Now there was set
there a vessel full of vinegar, and they filled a spunge
with vinegar, and put it upon a reed, and gave him to
drink, the rest saying, let be, let us see whether Elias
will come to save him, and take him down : but Jesus
said, it is finished ; and again he cried with a loud voice,
Father, into thy hands I commend my spirit, and bowing
his head, he gave up the ghost. And when the centurion saw that he so cried out, and gave up the ghost, he
said, truly, this man was the son of God.

And behold ! the veil of the temple was rent in twain
from the top to the bottom, and the earth did quake, and
the rocks rent, and the graves were opened, and many
bodies of the saints which slept arose, and came out of
the graves after his resurrection, and went into the holy
city, and appeared unto many ; and the centurion, and
they that stood over against, and those that watched Jesus, when they saw the earthquake, and the things that
were done, feared greatly, saying, truly, this was the son
of God. And all the people that came together to that
sight, beholding the things that were done, smote their
breasts and returned ; and his acquaintance, and the women which followed him from Galilee, stood afar off, beholding these things ; among whom were Mary Magdalene, and Mary the mother of James the less, and the
mother of Joses and Salome, who also, when he was in
Galilee, followed him, and ministered unto him ; there
were also many other women that came up to Jerusalem
with him.

The Jews, therefore, that the bodies should not remain
on the cross on the Sabbath, because it was the preparation, (for that Sabbath was an high day) besought Pilate,
that their legs might be broken, and that they might be
taken away. The soldiers therefore came and broke the
legs of the two thieves, but not of Jesus, because he was
already dead ; but one of the soldiers with a spear pierced his side, and there came out straightway blood and
water ; and these things were suffered to be done, that
the scripture might be fulfilled.

And when evening was come, because it was the preparation, that is, the day before the Sabbath came Joseph of Arimathea, a rich man, and an honourable counsellor, who also looked for the kingdom of God, and had not consented to the council and deed of them, being a disciple, but secretly, for fear of the Jews, came boldly unto Pilate, and begged the body of Jesus. Pilate marvelled if he were already dead, and calling the centurion, asked him, and when he knew it, he gave the body to Joseph. There came also Nicodemus (who at the first came to Jesus by night) and brought a mixture of myrrh and aloes, about an hundred pounds weight : then took they the body of Jesus, and wound it in linen clothes with the spices, as the manner of the Jews is to bury ; and Joseph, when he had wrapped him in a clean linen cloth, laid it in his own sepulchre, which he had hewn out of a rock, wherein never man was laid, and which was in a garden, in the place where Jesus was crucified : and Joseph rolled a great stone to the door of the sepulchre ; and Mary Magdalene, and Mary the mother of Joses, which came with him from Galilee, beheld where they had laid him, and sat over against the Sepulchre ; and they returned, and prepared spices and ointments, and rested the Sabbath day, according to the commandments. The Pharisees besought Pilate, that he would command the sepulchre to be made sure until the the third day, shewing him a reason, which, when he had yielded unto, they went and made the sepulchre sure, sealing the stone, and setting a watch.

In the end of the Sabbath, when it dawned towards the first day of the week, came Mary Magdalene and Mary the mother of James, and Salome. bringing spices which they had bought, that they might see the sepulchre, and anoint Jesus ; and they said among themselves, who shall roll away the stone from the door for us? coming to the sepulchre, they saw the stone was rolled away ; for behold there was a great earthquake, and the angel of the Lord came down from heaven, and rolled away the stone, and sat upon it; and they went in and found not the body of the Lord Jesus ; and it came to

pass, as they were much perplexed thereat, that behold
two men came to them in shining riament, their countenances were as lightning, and their garments white as
snow (Matthew and Mark speak but of one angel) and
the keepers for fear did shake, and became as dead men;
and when the women were afraid, and bowed their faces
to the earth, the angel said unto them, fear not ye, I
know ye seek Jesus who was crucified; why seek ye
the living among the dead? he is not here, he is risen,
as he said; come and see the place where the Lord was
laid, and remember what he said while he was in Galilee
with you, saying, the son of man must be delivered into
the hands of sinful men, and be crucified, and the third
day rise again; but go ye quickly and tell his disciples,
and Peter, that he has risen again from the dead, and behold he goeth before you into Galilee, there shall ye see
him; behold I have told you: then the women remembered the words of Jesus, and they departed quickly out
of the sepulchre, with fear, and wonder, and great joy,
and ran that they might tell his disciples; but they said
nothing to any man (as they went) for they were afraid;
and when the women told these things to the eleven, and
to all the rest, their words seemed unto them as idle tales;
but Mary Magdalene telling Peter, and the other disciple
whom Jesus loved, they have taken away the Lord, and
we know not where they have laid him; Peter, therefore,
and that other disciple, went out and came to the sepulchre; but that other disciple outran Peter, and came
first to the sepulchre, and when he stooped down, he saw
the linen clothes lying, but went not in; then came Peter
following him, and went into the sepulchre; and he saw
the linen clothes lying, and the napkin that was about his
head, not lying with the linen clothes, but wrapped together in a place by itself; then went in that other disciple, and saw, and believed; and Peter went unto his
own home, wondering at what was done, for as yet, they
knew not the scriptures, that he must rise again from the
dead; and the disciples went unto their own home:
but Mary Magdalene stood without at the sepulchre
weeping, and whilst she yet wept, she stooped down into

the sepulchre, and saw two angels in white sitting, the one at the head, and the other at the feet, where the body of Jesus had lain, who said unto her, " woman, why weepest thou ?" She said unto them, " they have taken away my Lord, and I know not where they have laid him ;" and when she had said thus, she turned herself back, and saw Jesus standing, but knew not that it was he ; and Jesus said unto her, " why weepest thou ? whom seekest thou ?" She supposing him to be the gardener, answered and said, " if thou hast borne him hence, tell me where thou hast laid him, and I will take him away." Jesus said unto her, " touch me not, for I am not yet ascended to my Father ; but go to my brethren, and say unto them, I ascend unto my Father, and your Father ; and to my God and your God." And she came and told his disciples, and those that had been with him, as they were weeping and mourning, that she had seen the Lord, and that he had said these things unto her ; but they, when they heard that he was alive, and had been seen of her, believed not : and as the women went from the sepulchre, that they might tell his disciples, behold, Jesus met them, and spake unto them, saying, be not afraid ; go ye and tell my brethren, that I go into Galilee, there shall they see me.

Now, when they were going, behold, some of the watch came into the city, and shewed unto the high priests all things that were done ; and when they were assembled with the elders, they took counsel that they should give large sums of money to the soldiers, that they should say, that his disciples came by night, and stole him away whilst they slept ; and if this comes to the governor's ears, we will persuade him, and secure you ; so they took their money, and did as they were taught ; and this saying is commonly reported among the Jews to this day.

And behold, two of them went into the country, that same day, to a village sixty furlongs from Jerusalem, called Emmaus ; and as they journeyed, Jesus went along with them, they telling what things were done in those days, concerning Jesus of Nazareth, how he was crucified, and that he rose again ; and Jesus shewing

I

them out of the scriptures, that it behoved Christ to suffer, and to enter into his glory. And in the village, when he had taken bread, and given thanks, and broken it, and given it unto them, he was known unto them, their eyes being opened. Although he appeared in another form, he vanished out of their sight. And they rose up that same hour, and returned to Jerusalem to the eleven, and those that were with them, who told them, the Lord is risen indeed, and hath appeared unto Simon : then they told them what things were done in the way, and how he was known of them in the breaking of bread ; but neither believed they them. But whilst they yet spake, whilst it was evening, in the first day of the week, the door being shut, where the disciples were gathered together, for fear of the Jews, came Jesus himself, and stood in the midst of them, and said unto them, peace be unto you; but they were terrified and affrighted, supposing they had seen a spirit ; but he upbraided them with their unbelief and hardness of heart, because they believed not them that had seen him since he was risen. And he said unto them, " why are ye troubled ? see my hands and my feet ; a spirit hath not flesh and bones;" and he shewed them his hands, and his feet, and his side; and when they believed not for joy, and wondered, he said unto them, have ye here any meat ? and he ate a piece of broiled fish, and an honey-comb ; and the disciples rejoiced that they had seen the Lord : and he said unto them, " these are the words that I spake unto you, that all things must be fulfilled that were written in the law of Moses, and in the Prophets, and in the Psalms of me." Then opened he their understandings, that they might understand the scriptures, and said unto them, " thus it is written, and thus it behoveth Christ to suffer, and to rise from the dead the third day, and that repentance and remission of sins should be preached in his name among all nations, and ye are witnesses of these things ; and behold I send the promise of my Father among you, but tarry ye at Jerusalem till ye be endued with power from on high. He said unto them again, peace be unto you, as my Father sent me, so send I you;

go ye into the world, and preach the gospel to every creature : He that believeth and is baptized, shall be saved, but he that believeth not shall be damned ; and these signs shall follow them that believe : In my name they shall cast out devils, and they shall speak with new tongues ; they shall take up serpents, and if they drink any deadly thing, it shall not hurt them ; they shall lay their hands on the sick, and they shall recover." And when he had said these things, he breathed on them, and said unto them, " receive the Holy Ghost ; whose sins ye remit, they are remitted unto them, and whose sins ye retain, they are retained." (And thus Jesus appeared five times in the very first day of his resurrection ;) but Thomas, who is called Dydimus, one of the twelve, was not with them when Jesus came ; and the rest of the disciples telling him, "we have seen the Lord;" he very confidently professed he would not believe it. About eight days after, Thomas being then together with the rest, Jesus came, the doors being shut, and stood in the midst, and said unto them, " peace be unto you," and abundantly satisfied Thomas's unbelief.

Then the eleven disciples went into Galilee, unto the mountain that he had appointed them ; and when they saw him, they worshipped him, but some doubted : And when Jesus came unto them, he said, " all power is given unto me, both in heaven and earth ; go, therefore, and teach all nations, baptizing them, &c. And I am with you to the end of the world." After that, Jesus was seen of above five hundred brethren at once ; after that, by James. 1 Cor. xv. 6, 7.

Afterwards, Jesus shewed himself to his disciples again at the sea of Tiberius, or at least to seven of them, as they were fishing, after they had fished all night, and caught nothing ; in the morning, Jesus, unknown to them, stood upon the shore, and bade them cast their net on the right side of the ship, where they took a great number of fish.

Last of all, he appeared to his disciples in Jerusalem, and led them out as far as Bethany, and he lifted up his

hands and blessed them ; and it came to pass, as he blessed them, he was parted from them, and carried up into
heaven.

Hitherto reacheth the history of the four evangelists,
declaring the sufferings of Christ ; and now I shall give
the reader a short account of what Josephus, the Jewish
historian, in his eighteenth book of Antiquity, writeth of
John the Baptist and Christ. Concerning the Baptist,
Cap. v. he saith, Herod the tetrarch killed John, sur-
named the Baptist, a most excellent man, who stir-
ed up the Jews to the study of virtues, especially of
piety and justice, and also to the washing of baptism,
which he said then would not be acceptable to God, if
abstaining from some sins only ; but having their
minds first purged through righteousness, they also
added cleanness of body. And whereas there was great
resort unto him, the common people being greedy of
such doctrine, Herod fearing lest the great authority of
the man should raise some rebellion, because they
seemed as though they would decline nothing to which
he advised them, thought it safer to take him out of the
way, before there was any alteration in the state, than to
repent too late, when the state was once embroiled :
wherefore, he commanded him to be sent prisoner to Ma-
charas; and then to be put to death.

Concerning Christ, he saith thus, Cap. xlv. In the
same time, there was a wise man, (named Jesus) if we
may call him a man ; he was a worker of miracles, and a
teacher of them that willingly receive the truth ; he had
many, both Jews and Gentiles, that were his followers,
and was believed to be the Christ : and when Pilate had
crucified him, through the envy of our rulers, nevertheless those that loved him, continued constant in their affections ; for he appeared to them alive the third day ;
the prophets in their prophecies foretelling both these,
and many other wonderful things concerning him, and
the christians (from him so called) continue to this very
day.

After the Apostles had seen Christ, and had worshipped him, after his resurrection, they returned to Jerusa-

lem with great joy from the mount of Olives, which is from thence a Sabbath day's journey ; and in Jerusalem they abode in an upper room, and continued with one accord in prayer, with the women, and Mary his mother, and his brethren ; and they were filled with the holy ghost, and began to speak with tongues, as the spirit gave them utterance ; and many received the truth, and continued stedfastly in the Apostles' doctrine and fellowship; and breaking bread from house to house, did eat their meat with gladness and singleness of heart, praising God, and having favour with all the people ; and the Lord daily added to the church such as should be saved ; and the multitude of them that believed were of one heart, and one soul; and there was none among them that lacked ; for as many as had possessions of lands or houses, sold them, and brought the prices, and laid them down at the apostles' feet, to be distributed for the use of the poor ; in which business, Barnabas, that is, the son of Consolation, shewed the first example.

By the hands of the apostles, were many miracles done among the people, and many believed, and were added to the Lord.

But the high priest and sadducees that were with him, moved with envy, cast the apostles into prison ; from whence, the night following, being freed by an angel, they were commanded to teach the people boldly, and without fear ; and being brought to the council by the advice of Gamaliel a Pharisee, a doctor of law, in much esteem among the people, they were delivered from death, (after they had been scourged) and let go ; and they went from the council rejoicing that they were counted worthy to suffer for the name of Jesus ; and they taught daily in the temple ; and the word of the Lord increased ; and the number of disciples multiplied.

Stephen did many wonders and miracles among the people, and stoutly defended the cause of Christ against the Jews, of the synagogue of the Libertines, Cyrenians, and Alexandrians, and of them of Cilicia, and of Asia, disputing with them ; but when they could not resist the wisdom and spirit by which he spake, they turned to

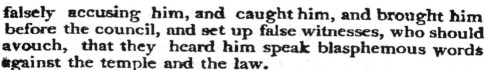

falsely accusing him, and caught him, and brought him before the council, and set up false witnesses, who should avouch, that they heard him speak blasphemous words against the temple and the law.

Stephen, before Annas the high priest and council, shewed that the true worship of God was observed by Abraham and his posterity, before the temple was built by Solomon; yea, before Moses was born, and that Moses gives testimony of Christ, and that the outward ceremonies that were given to their fathers, were to endure but for a time: then he sharply reprehended the Jews, because they always resisted the holy ghost, and had wickedly put Christ to death, who, the prophets had foretold, should come into the world. See the death of Stephen, at large, in the testimony of the Martyrs.

Afrer the death of Stephen, there arose a great persecution against the whole church that was at Jerusalem; in which, Saul, exceedingly raging, made havock of the church; for having received authority from the chief priests, he not only, when the saints were put to death, gave his voice against them, but also he himself, entering into every house, and taking from thence both men and women, bound them, and put them in prison, and some were compelled, by denying Christ, to blaspheme.

This persecution dispersed the church into divers countries, but with great advantage to the church; for some that were dispersed into the regions of Judea and Samaria, preached the gospel wheresoever they came; others went to-Damascus, amongst whom was Ananias, a devout man according to the law, and one who had a good report among all the Jews who dwelt there; others travelled as far as Phenice, Cyprus, and Antioch, preaching the word of God to those that were dispersed among the Gentiles. Amongst them that went to Samaria, was Philip, who preached Christ there. When the aopstles, at Jerusalem had heard that Samaria had received the word of the Lord, they sent unto them Peter and John, upon whose praying for them, and laying their hands on them, they received the holy ghost, and, Simon Magus (who had a long time bewitched the people of Samaria with his sorceries, they giving heed to him, from the least to the greatest, saying, he was the great power of God) seeing the great signs and wonders that were done by the apostles, offered them money, that he also might receive the gift of conferring the Holy Ghost; whose mad impiety, Peter sharply rebuking, warned him to repent of his wickedness, and to ask pardon of God ; and desired the apostles that they would pray for him to the Lord. The apostles having cleared themselves in these parts, they returned to Jerusalem, preaching the gospel in the villages of Samaria as they went.

Saul, yet breathing out threatenings and slaughter against the disciples of the Lord, obtained of the high priest Annas, and the council, letters to the synagogues of Damascus, that if he found any that were christians, he should bring them bound to Jerusalem, that they might be punished ; and as he came nigh to Damascus about noon, suddenly there shone from Heaven a great light, above the brightness of the sun, round about him, and them that journeyed with him : and when they were fallen to the earth, he heard a voice speaking to him in the Hebrew tongue, " Saul, Saul, why persecutest thou me ? 'Tis hard for thee to kick against the pricks." And when he had said, " who art thou, Lord" ? It was answered him, " I am Jesus, whom thou persecutest ;" but rise, and stand upon thy feet, I have appeared unto thee for this purpose, to make thee a minister and a witness, both of these things that thou hast seen, and those things in which I will appear unto thee, delivering thee from the people, and from the Gentiles, unto whom now I send thee, that thou mayst open their eyes, and turn them from darkness to light, and from the power of satan unto God, that they may receive remission of sins, and an inheritance among them that are sanctified, by faith that is in me. And when Saul, full of fear and trembling, asked further, " Lord, what wilt thou have me to do" ? the Lord said unto him, " arise, and go into the city, and it shall be told thee what thou must do: But the men that journeyed with Saul were so amazed, that they were speechless, seeing indeed a light, and hearing the sound of words, but neither seeing Christ which spake, nor understanding any thing which he spake : Saul arose from the earth, and being blinded with the glory of the light, being led by the hand, he came to Damascus, and he was three days without sight, and did neither eat nor drink. Now there was a certain disciple, named Ananias, to whom the Lord spake in a vision, " arise and go into the street which is called straight, and inquire in the house of Judas, for one called Saul of Tarsus ; for, behold, he prayeth ;" and Saul then saw in a vision, Ananias entering, and laying his hand on him, that he might receive his sight, but Ananias answered, " Lord, I have heard by many of this man, how much evil he hath done to thy saints at Jerusalem ;" yea, in this place, he hath authority, from the chief priests, to bind all that call upon thy name : and the Lord said unto him, " go thy way, for he is a chosen vessel unto me, to bear my name, before the Gentiles, and kings, and the children of Israel ; for I will shew him how great things he must suffer for my name's sake."

And Ananias went, and entered into the house ; and laying his hands on him, said, " brother Saul, the Lord even Jesus, that appeared unto thee in the way as thou camest, hath sent me, that thou might receive thy sight, and be filled with the Holy Ghost ; and immediately there fell from his eyes as it had been scales, and he received sight forthwith." And Ananias said, the God of our fathers hath chosen thee, that thou shouldst know his will, and see that just one, and shouldst hear the voice from his mouth ; for thou shalt be a witness before all men of those things that thou hast heard and seen : and now, why tarriest thou here ? arise, and be baptized, and wash away thy sins, calling on the name of the Lord : and Saul arose and was baptized, and when he had received meat, he was strengthened.

What was revealed to Saul at Damascus that he should do, Luke shews not in the Acts , but out of those things which in the Epistle to the Galatians, he saith happened unto him, immediately after his conversion ; it

appears among other things, it was commanded him, that
he should not confer with flesh and blood, nor return to
Jerusalem to them that were Apostles before him, but
that he should go for some time into Arabia, or places
near Damascus, where he should receive the knowledge
of the gospel, not being taught of men, but by the revelation of Jesus Christ.

: Saul then returned to Damascus, and tarried there with
the disciples a few days, and straightway, in the synagogue, he preached, that Christ is the son of God ; and
they were all amazed who heard these things, and said,
" is not this he, that destroyed at Jerusalem those that
called on his name ? And came hither for that intent,
that he might bring them bound unto the chief priests ;"
and Saul increased the more in strength, and confounded
the Jews that dwelt at Damascus, teaching that Jesus is
the Christ ; for to the Jews that dwelt at Damascus, was
the gospel first preached by him.

: Tiberius being certified, by Pilate out of Palestine,
concerning the affairs of Christ, he proposed to the senate, that Christ might be reckoned among the Gods,
which the senate opposing, and he remaining in his opinion, threatened, that it should be dangerous for any to
accuse a christian, as Tertullian relates, [in Apologetic.
[Chap. 5, and 21.] and others that follow him, as Eusebius
in Chronic. and Histor. Eccles. Lib. 2. 2.] and Gildas,
in an epistle of the destruction of Britain, which being
granted, we may lawfully say, that the first persecution,
after the murder of Stephen, that arose in Judea, ceased
partly by the conversion of Saul, who greatly promoted
it, and partly through the fear of Tiberius.

: When Saul had preached the gospel a long time at
Damascus, the Jews took counsel to kill him, and watch-
ing the gates of the city day and night, that they might
take him : but, being let down by a rope by night in a
basket, he escaped from them.

: The first three years after his conversion being finish-
, Saul returned to Jerusalem to see Peter ; and abode
with him fifteen days: and he then assaying to join himself to the disciples, they all were afraid of him, not

K

believing him to be a disciple ; but Barnabas took him, and brought him to the apostles Peter and James the brother of the Lord. He declared unto them, how he had seen the Lord in the way, and that he had spoken to him, and how he had preached boldly at Damascus in the name of Jesus.

Saul also spake boldly in the name of Jesus at Jerusalem, but the Jews went about to kill him. Saul, being in the temple praying, was in a trance, and saw the Lord speaking unto him, saying, "make haste, and get thee quickly out of Jerusalem, for they will not receive testimony of me ;" to whom he answered, "Lord they know that I imprisoned, and beat in every synagogue, those that believed on thee, and when the blood of thy martyr Stephen was shed, I also was standing by, and kept the garments of them that killed him :" and the Lord said unto him, "go, and I will send thee to the Gentiles."

The brethren at Jerusalem brought him to Caesarea, and sent him into his own country of Tarsus, and he came into the countries of Syria and Cilicia, being as yet unknown by face to the churches of Judea ; but they heard that he preached the faith which once he destroyed, and they glorified God in him ; and the churches had rest through all Judea, Galilee, and Samaria, and were edified ; and walking in the fear of the Lord, and comfort of the holy ghost, they multiplied.

About this time, king Herod troubled the church, laying hands upon some, for contradicting the institutions and rites of the country, of which he was a most religious observer, as Josephus, Lib. xix. Chap. ult. relates.

He slew James, the brother of John, with the sword ; and seeing that the death of James pleased the people, he cast Peter into prison in the days of Azincus, delivering him to four quarternions, that is, sixteen soldiers to guard him, intending after the passover to bring him out to the people, but there were prayers made daily in the church for him ; and an angel of the Lord delivered him miraculously in the night ; and he went to the house of Mary, the mother of John Marcus, where many were congregated, at prayer, and telling them that they might certify James the son of Alpheus, and brother of our Lord, and the rest, of the manner of his deliverance; from whence he went into another place.

Herod, being frustrated of his hope, in his rage commanded the innocent keepers to be dragged to execution; and he going down to Cæsarea, staid there; and was prejudiced in his mind against the Syrians and Sidonians, whose land being not sufficient to maintain them (especially in that year of scarcity) they were forced to seek for themselves sustenance from Galilee, and other places under Herod's jurisdiction : they came therefore unanimously to him by the mediation of Blastus, the king's chamberlain, whom they had made their friend, desiring peace of him ; a day being appointed, Herod in his royal apparel, and sitting before the tribunal, made a speech to them ; the people with acclamations shouting out, " 'tis the voice of a God, and not a man ;" but presently, the angel of the Lord smote him, because he did not give the glory to God; and being eaten of worms, he gave up the ghost.

The very same history Josephus exemplifies, saying, " he had now finished the third year of his reign when he came to Cæsarea, which was formerly called Straton's tower, where he solemnized some yearly plays for Cæsar's health ; to which festivity, a great multitude of noblemen and youngsters came together out of the province. On the second day of this celebrity, he went all attired with his princely robes, richly and curiously wrought with silver, which, by the reflection of the rising sun, yielded an angelical or extraordinary lustre, and struck reverence into the spectators ; and presently some wicked parasites, with acclamations from a far off, saluted him God, desiring him to be propitious to them ; for that hitherto they had only honoured him as a man, but now they saw there was something more in him than human : this impious adulation he neither refused nor repelled, and was suddenly struck to the very heart ; afterwards, his belly began to torment him more and more grievously, wherefore, turning to his friends, he said, " behold, I, who, by your appellation, am a God, am commanded out of this life, my certain fate, giving the lie to your flattery ; and I, whom you saluted immortal, am forced to death ; but I must endure the pleasures of the heavens." Having spoken these things, his pain grew worse and worse, and presently these things being divulged about the country, the rumour went, that he was dying, and in the end his pain lasted in great extremity, and without intermission for five days space ;" he then ended his life, Joseph. Lib. xix. Chap. ult.

About this time, Saul is always found named by his new name Paul. Paul and Barnabas coming to Antioch, and entering into the synagogues, almost the whole city came to hear the word of God ; but the Jews, seeing the multitude were filled with envy, and contradicted what Paul spoke, with whose blasphemies Paul and Barnabas being grievously offended, they left the Jews, and preached only to the Gentiles, who with joy embraced the gospel; and the word of God was divulged over that whole nation ; they staid at Antioch a great while, and suffered those things which, in his latter Epistle to the Corinthians, he writes of, to wit, that as at Philippi afterwards, so twice elswhere by the Gentiles, he had been whipped with rods, and received five times forty stripes of the Jews, save one.

Certain professors of the name of Christ, of the sect of the Pharisees, came down from Judea to Antioch, and said, that the christians of the Gentiles ought to be circumcised, and to keep the law of Moses, if they would be saved, disturbing the souls of many of the brethren in Syria and Cilicia with their perverse doctrine ; against whom, Paul and Barnabas stiffly opposed themselves, Paul calling them brethren brought in unawares : Philastrius de Heres. cap. 87. and Epiphanius, Heres. 28. say, that Cerinthus, that arch-heretic, was the first broacher of this opinion.

Paul, fourteen years after his conversion, went again to Jerusalem with Barnabas, being both sent from the church at Antioch with some others, that they might ask the judgment of the apostles and elders at Jerusalem (whose names those disturbers had abused to favour their opinion) concerning the crontroversy newly risen; but Paul would not compel Titus to be circumcised, lest he should seem to give place to the false brethren for a moment.

Peter and Paul had foretold at Rome, that it should come to pass, after a little time, God would send a king that should overcome the Jews, and that should lay their city even with the ground, and should besiege them, being pined with hunger and thirst; and then it should come to pass, that they should eat each other, and one consume the other; and, at last, that they should come into their enemies' hands, and should see their wives most grievously tormented in their sight; and their virgins violated and prostituted; their sons torn asunder; and their little ones dashed in pieces; and, in short, that all things should be wasted by fire and sword, and themselves forever banished out of their own land; and all this because they exalted themselves against the son of God. Lactan. lib. iv. cap. xxi.

On the 29th day of the month called June, (which last day of that month falls to be within the reign of Nero) Paul was beheaded at Rome, as the records, both of the eastern and western churches confirm; whereupon Chrysostom affirms, that undoubtedly the day of his death was more certainly known than that of Alexander himself, [in 2 Cor. Homil. xxvi.] Dionysius, the bishop of the Corinthians, affirms, in an Epistle to the Romans, that Peter also suffered Martyrdom at the same time with him; [in Eusebius, lib. ii. Histor. Ecclesiast. cap. xxiv.] whom also Origen relates, in the third tome of his commentaries upon Genesis, that at Rome, he was crucified with his head downwards, as he had desired. [Ibid. lib. iii. Hist. cap. i.]

Four years before the Jewish war (that was managed by Vespasian) when the city of Jerusalem enjoyed both peace and plenty, one Jesus, the son of Ananus a countryman, and one of the common people, coming to the feast of tabernacles, began suddenly to cry out, " a voice from the east, a voice from the west, a voice from the four winds, a voice against Jerusalem and the temple, a voice against new married men and women, a voice against all this people ;" and crying thus night and day through all the streets of the city, some of the nobility disdaining any token of adversity, took the fellow and scourged him with many stripes ; but he spake nothing secretly for himself, nor unto them that scourged him, but continued still in the same cry. But the magistrates, thinking it rather to be some motion in him from God, brought him to the Roman captain, where being beaten till his bones appeared, he made no entreaty, but with a weeping voice, at every stroke, he said, " woe, woe, to Jerusalem". Albinus then asked them, who he was, and where he was born, and why he still cried after this manner ; but he answered nothing : yet he ceased not to bewail the city, till Albinus, thinking he was mad, suffered him to depart : he crying thus most on the feast days, and that for seven years space, (or rather six, as it is in Phot. Biblioth. Cod. xlvii.) and five months, and yet was neither hoarse nor weary. At last, he was killed by a stone shot out of an engine in the time of the siege. [Joseph. lib. vii. bel. cap. xii.]

And according to these, and many other prophecies concerning the destruction that was to come upon the Jews, for the hardness of their hearts, it came to pass ; for Cornelius and Suetonius relate, that there were six hundred thousand of the Jews killed in this war between Vespasian the emperor, and the Jews ; but Josephus, a Jew, and a commander in that war, writes, that ten hundred thousand perished by sword and famine : and of the rest of the Jews that were dispersed all the world over, and put to death divers ways, the number is said to be ninety thousand ; (so Orolius, Lib. vii. cap. ix.) but I find not in Suetonius the num- of six hundred thousand of them that were killed. In Josephus, (Lib. vi. bel. cap. xvii.) the number of captives is ninety seven thousand, but the other number, eleven hundred thousand, is only the number that perished in the six months' siege in Jerusalem. And thus did the Lord afflict with wars and destruction the apostatized and stiff-necked people the Jews, until they were a scattered and dispersed people, as at this day they are throughout the world.

PART II.

Shews the corrupt fruits of the false church, and the seed of the serpent in the time of apostacy, darkness, and persecution, amongst them called Christians.

ALTHOUGH the sufferings of the christians were very great, after the death of the apostles, for some time; and it cannot be denied but there was a sincerity in some of the christian churches ; yet as John testified in his day, he saw the true church flee into the wilderness ; and the apostle foretold, that there would be a departing from the faith; and Paul saw the apostacy coming in in his day, and said, perilous times should come, and that men should be lovers of themselves, covetous, &c. and repro-bate concerning the truth. And it was not long after the apostles' time, before these prophecies were fulfilled; for if the reader peruse the following discourse, he will find a great decay, and apostacy from that life and power that the apostles were in, and the corrupt fruits of many of these called christians brought forth, which manifested the great degeneracy that was come upon the christian church : for, as Eusebius writes, when persecution at any time ceased, then began heresy to spring apace a-mong the christians, until at last there were continual discord and contention, and they broke out into sects and opinions, and persecuted one another about their sev-eral forms of faith, and became so far degenerated from the doctrine of Christ, which taught to love enemies, that they became haters of one another, and manifested to the world, that they had lost the blessed love and unity, that were amongst the apostles and brethren of the christian church in the beginning. But before a particular ac-count be given of that, it is necessary that the reader understand, that the purest state of the christians, in the first times after the apostles, was their most suffering times, when as yet the christian religion was accounted by the heathen but an upstart thing ; and therefore they persecuted them greatly, as may be seen at large in the testimony of the martyrs hereunto annexed.

But, through the tenderness of Adrian the emperor, the christians had some intermission from their sufferings, and they began to be in some request ; for, after Adrian's death, Antonius Pius succeeding, he continued that peace with the christians which he found begun in Adrian's last days, for which he had the name of Pius ; yet by the people's tumult, without the emperor's consent, some were martyred ; to this emperor, Justin made an apology on the behalf of the christians ; divers other supplications were also made unto him on their behalf ; which supplications produced an edict from the emperor, remitting the persecutions against the christians.

The copy of the edict is as follows : " The emperor Cæsar Marcus Aurelius Antonius Augustus Amenicus Pontifex Maximus, fifteen times tribune, thrice consul, unto the commonalty of Asia, sendeth greeting. I know the Gods are careful to disclose hurtful persons, for they punish such as will not worship them, more grievously than you do them you bring into trouble concerning that opinion which they conceive of you, to be wicked and ungodly men ; it is their desire in God's quarrel to die rather than to live, so that they become conquerors, yielding their lives unto the death, rather than to obey your edicts : it shall seem very necessary to admonish you of the earthquakes which have and do happen among us, that being therewith moved, you may compare our estate with theirs ; they have more confidence towards God than you have ; you, during the time of your ignorance, despise other Gods, condemn the religion of the immortal God, banish the christians which worship him, and persecute them unto death. In behalf of these men many of the provincial presidents have written heretofore unto our father of famous memory, whom he answered in writing again, that they were no longer to be molested,

L

unless they had practised treason against the Roman empire, and many have given notice unto us of the same matter, whom we answered as our father did before ; if any therefore hereafter be found thus busied in other men's affairs, we command, that the accused be absolute and free, though he be found such a one, I mean faulty, and that the accuser be grievously punished."

In the hearing of the great assembly of Asia, this edict was proclaimed at Ephesus. Thus far of Antonius Pius, who was so called for his gentle and good disposition ; of whom it is recorded, that this quiet emperor in life, of all other emperors of those times, died the quietest death.

But Vesus, one of his successors, was a wicked and cruel man, under whom multitudes of christians suffered, as may be seen in my testimony of the martyrs, which may give the reader a taste of what they endured, who were faithful to give a testimony concerning their faith.

About this time, the christians began to have a little respite and peace again, from the heathens' persecution of them ; and having a little peace, they now began to jangle about the celebration of Easter ; but though they differed in the ceremony, they were not yet grown so bad as to be out of charity one with another, but left it as an indifferent thing in the church until the time of Victor.

This Victor was so violent set upon, upholding the Roman determination of his former predecessor as unnecessary, that he would excommunicate all the bishops and churches of Asia, unless they would be of his opinion, had not Ireneus restrained him, who though he was of Victor's opinion concerning the celebration of Easter, yet seeing Policratus bishop of Ephesus, and divers other bishops of Asia, of another opinion, alleging for their practice scripture, and the example of other fathers; therefore Ireneus still took off the edge of sharp contentions, and so the controversy remained free till the time of the Nicene council ; and other doctrines of the christian religion were free till Victor's time, which was about two hundred years after Christ.

About this time, was one Philippius made president of Alexandria, who had a daughter Eugenia, of rare beauty, who, to avoid marriage with a Pagan, and heathen persecutor, fled from her father, going in man's apparel, calling herself Eugenius; and for her parts was made head of a society of christians, where a lustful matron being enamoured with her beauty, supposing her to be a man, laboured to draw her into uncleanness with her, but Eugenia not consenting, this matron accused Eugenia of having laboured to deflower her; whereupon, the matter was brought before Philippius the president, who according to allegations, being about to condemn her to death, Eugenia seeing no other evidence would serve, discovered herself to Philippius to be an innocent woman, and his daughter, who not long after converted her father to christianity, who afterwards died also a martyr ; and after his death, Eugenia returning to Rome was also martyred.

Maximinus persecuted the christians sorely, though at times he would seem to be otherwise minded ; but the hand of God pursued him, so that he was afflicted with sore distempers, when he pondered with himself the rash enterprises he had practised against the worshippers of God ; wherefore, returning unto himself, he confessed his sins to God, and gave forth a command, that with all speed they should cease from persecuting the christians.

The christians having a little ease and liberty, they began to grow in favour of the emperor's courts, and to be employed in the emperor's palaces, and to be eminent in the management of public affairs, whereby they degenerated from the natural rule of piety, and after that, one pursued another with open contumely and hatred, bishops against bishops, and people against people, raised seditions, which caused persecution against them again ; for the shepherds (saith the historian) practised contention and schism among themselves : but these persecutions ended, when Constantine came to be emperor, who being a christian, and a wise and mighty prince, struck all these cruelties and death under foot, and gave peace unto all ; but as peace and rest came, divisions still arose up among them, and when they had power, they began to impose their faiths and forms of worship one upon another, as the heathen did to them.

No sooner were the heathen persecutions laid aside, than these that had jointly withstood the force of heathenish persecution, came to be at variance, and at length to do the same things one to another as the heathen had done unto them together.

And now being at rest, and differing among themselves in some things, they knew not how to bear one another, but being insensible of the hand that had wrought their deliverance, they began to impose one upon another, and to enforce their several faiths with torments and the sword, which wrought sore destruction and trouble among them, and shamed the christian religion.

In the days of Constantine, free liberty was given to all men, to use what religion they pleased, as by the particular constitutions and edicts may be seen at large ; so that there was liberty now of complaints, and synods were called to refute, at least, take off the opposition of the contrary ; but when the sueceeding emperors, leaned to this or that party, or confession of faith, or opinion, then force of arms, or carnal extremities, were exercised towards those who were of the contrary dispositions. And thus, as religion became national, and was required by the laws of men, and imposed, such were the consequences of it; for a difference fell out between Cicilianus bishop of Carthage, and the bishops with him, the one siding against the other in Africa, which occasioned Constantine to summon a synod of bishops to meet at Rome, for the hearing and reconciling thereof ; at which, something being attempted, and the judgment given by the other party not being acquiesced in, but after the rising of the synod, the difference increasing instead, of being ended amongst them, he called a second synod at Orleans in France, to the end it might be determined ; as a scourge and rebuke, unto which dissentions, or the differences that then arose among the christians, Lucinius, (who being emperor, and, together with Constantine, had

written, enjoining the liberty of the christians) came forth
and fell upon the christians under his dominion, who
never did him evil, practising the same things upon them
as those had done, whom, for so doing, he had cut off.
First, he banished them from his court, and such as would
not sacrifice, he spoiled of their honour and dignities,
commanded no charity to be given to them that were in
prison and in fetters, no not by their kindred, overthrowing the meeting-places of the christians to the ground ;
some of the bishops, his presidents, he caused to be tormented, cutting their bodies into small pieces, as butchers
do their meat, casting pieces into the sea for food for fish-
es. He revoked sundry good laws of the Romans, brought
in barbarous and cruel laws, unjust and unlawful, making away noble and honest personages, whose youthful
and tender wives he delivered to his servants to be shamefully abused ; for these things, Constantine made war
against him ; by which means, the persecutions against
the christians again ceased, and they had rest.

The christians came now to have rest and peace again;
see what Socrates, in the continuation of the history,
saith, concerning the differences that were among the
christians, and the consequences thereof.

Arius was the first he takes notice of, who, hearing
Alexander, bishop of Alexandria, treating somewhat
more curiously of what is called the Trinity in unity,
among the priests that were under him, said, " If the
Father begot the Son, then had the Son, which was begotten, a beginning of essence ; hereby it is manifest
that there was a time when the Son was not, and the
consequence to follow necessarily, that he had his essence of nothing." This began a great deal of reasoning amongst them. Arius had his favourers, both of
bishops and others, of this his blasphemous opinion,
which beginning at Alexandria, spread itself throughout
all Egypt, Lybia, and the upper Thebais, and at length,
passed through the rest of the cities and provinces ; the
spreading of this moved Alexander, who calling a council of many bishops, deprived Arius, and such as favoured his opinion, of the priestly order, and after-

wards writing to the bishops throughout the cities against him, spread the thing farther than it was before, because those unto whom the letters were directed, began to burn among themselves with the sparks of contention and discord.

So the nicety of the bishop on the one hand, and his sharp proceeding and writing on the other, gave occasion for this little spark to burn out into a great flame, which made sore distraction and divisions, and which in no wise could be quenched, but ran over all as a loathsome leprosy, bishop against bishop, people against people, and synod against synod, doing the things which the heathen had done to them, which rended them asunder, and caused the religion which the Christians professed, to be openly derided by the heathens in the public theatres.

Constantine was sorely troubled at these things, and by a principal person whom he entirely loved, he wrote both to Alexander and Arius, blaming Alexander for demanding a question of the elders touching a certain place of scripture ; yea, rather (saith his letter) touching a certain vain piece of a question what every one's opinion was : and Arius, for unadvisedly blazing abroad, and setting a broach that which thou shouldst (saith the emperor) not at the first have conceived, and having conceived it, thou shouldst have passed over with silence. He wrote smartly to them both, and very reasonably, concerning an accommodation, and that union might be again, exhorting them to pardon each other, but neither of them would hear ; he summoned a council at Nice about that, and near the time of celebrating the feast of Easter, about which there was no small controversy at this time also ; at which council, three hundred and eighteen bishops met, the emperor being present, and endeavoured to persuade them to unity, where making a creed, they generally subscribed it, except five bishops, who admitted not of the clause of ' one substance with the Father,' and who thus affirmed, that to be of one substance, which had its original of something, either by divison, or derivation, or production ; by production, as a bud out of a root; by derivation, as children of the parents; by division, as two or three pieces out of one piece of gold. The Son of God by relation was after none of these manners, and therefore, they said, they would not agree to the form of faith confirmed in the council of Nice; and, by the emperor's edict, some of the dissenting bishops were exiled.

The decree of this synod, by a solemn epistle, was sent unto the churches throughout Egypt, Lybia, &c. and Constantine wrote to the church at Alexandria, and other places, concerning the matter, wherein he calls the censure of this assembly, or the decree of this synod, the sentence of God himself; neither doubted he, that so great a company of bishops was so united and linked together in one opinion and mind, but by the motion and instinct of the Holy Ghost; notwithstanding Sabinus (who was termed the ring-leader of the Macedonian heresy) impugned those things, terming those that met at Nice, unlearned and doltish idiots.

Thus things grew on to a height, for the emperor, favouring the strongest side, made decrees and laws, so that there came to be an injunction; and the emperor commanded, that if any book or work of Arius could be found, it should be burnt to ashes, and that it should be death to keep it; and, as soon as he was taken, his head should be stricken off from his shoulders; and thus the contest grew high, and woful wreck came upon Christian assemblies, although the emperor, in his letters to Arius and Alexander, reasoned contrary to his actions; for writing concerning the unity, he said to them, " wherefore let every one of you pardon each other, like that which your fellowminister, not without cause, exhorteth you unto, (as aforesaid) and what is that? That you neither object at all, nor answer any objection that concerneth such matters; for such questions as no law or ecclesiastical canon necessarily defineth, but the fruitless contention of idle brains setteth abroad, though the exercise thereof avail for the sharpening of the wit, yet ought we to retain them in the inward closet of our minds, and not rashly to broach them in the public assembly of the

eople; neither unadvisedly to grant the common
hearing thereof; for how many be there that can
worthily explicate, and sufficiently ponder, the weight
of so grave, so intricate, so obscure a matter; but if
there be any such, that persuadeth himself easily to
compass and attain unto it; how many parts are there, I
beseech you, of the multitude whom he can sufficiently instruct therein? And who is there, who in sifting
out so curious a question, that can well pass the peril of
plunging into error? Wherefore, in such cases, we must
refrain from verbal disputations, lest that either we, by
reason of the imbecility of our wit, cannot explicate our
mind, when we teach, or our auditors by reason of their
dull capacity, cannot comprehend the curious drift of
our doctrine, whereby the people, of necessity, incur
the danger, either of blasphemy, or the poisoning infection of discord; wherefore, both the rash objection,
and the unadvised answer, being the cause of the heretical sect of the Arians, Eunomians, and as many as favour the like folly, ought each one of each other to
crave pardon.

The difference between the heathen and the christians
was, whether Christ was the Son of God? The difference betwixt the Christians was, whether the Son of
God was eternal? And in at this door entered the enemy to make shipwreck of the flock.

Arius being sent for to Constantinople, and coming
there, he framed a recantation at the emperor's demand,
whereupon the emperor sent him to Alexandria again.
Athanasius, bishop of Alexandria, (for Alexander was
dead) refused to receive him. Eusebius, bishop of Ni-
comedia, wrote to Athanasius, and also procured the
emperor's letters to command Athanasius to admit
Arius. Athanasius wrote back again to the emperor,
that it was not lawful for such as had made shipwreck of
their faith, and had been censured, after this their turn
and conversion, to receive their former dignities. This
vexed the emperor, so that he was much displeased with
Athanasius, and wrote sharply to him; but he refused,
notwithstanding, to receive him; whereupon, six bish-

ops took their opportunity to lift him out of his bishopric; afterwards, by the consent of all the bishops, assembled at Jerusalem to consecrate the temple, built by the emperor, Athanasius was exiled.

The thirteenth year of Constantine expired, while these things were doing, yet he saw no peace among the christians. Arius, with his company, returning to Alexandria, they set the whole city in an uproar, for they were not only disturbed with the return of Arius, but the banishment of Athanasius. The emperor understanding the perverse mind, and corrupt purpose of Arius, sent for him again to Constantinople, to render an account of the tumult and sedition he had raised afresh; the city being divided into two parts, one for the Nicene creed, the other for Arius. Arius being come to Constantinople, the emperor demanded of him to sign the Nicene creed, and he subscribed it cheerfully. He put him to his oath, and he swore it also. His juggle is said to be this: he wrote his opinion in a piece of paper, which he carried under his arm in his bosom, and coming to the book, he took his oath, that he verily believed as he had written: the emperor, believing he had dealt plainly, commanded the bishop of Constantinople to receive him to communion. This was on Saturday, the day after he looked to be received by the church: but see what happened upon his lewd and bold enterprise, being departed out of the emperor's hall, passing through the city in great pomp, coming nigh Constantine's market, he was suddenly taken with a great lax and faintness, and he voided his bowels, and immediately died like a dog; and the place was then to be seen; and passengers were wont, as they went by, to point their fingers thereat, in remembrance of the miserable end of Arius. Shortly after, the emperor died; but, neither with the death of Arius, nor of Constantine, was there an end of the troublesome discord, that was among the christians; for a council being called by both the emperors at Sardis, the bishops of the east would not come to the bishops of the west,

M

unless they would bear Paulus and Athanasius their
company ; which the bishops of the west not brooking,
the eastern bishops departed ; and at Pilippi, a city in
Thracia, there assembled a private council, and thenceforth openly began to curse the creed, condemning the
clause of one substance, and writing to sow abroad their
opinion, that the Son of God was not of one substance
with the Father.

The western bishops that continued at Sardis, first
condemned them which fled from the hearing of their
cause ; next, deposed, from their dignities, the accusers of Athanasius ; afterwards, ratified the creed of the
Nicene council, and abrogated the heretical opinion,
which said, that the Son was of a different substance
from the Father ; lastly, they set forth more plainly the
clause of one substance, and wrote letters thereof, and
sent them throughout the whole world.

And thus things often changed and altered, men having lost that which should give a weighty understanding
in these matters, and going about to make faiths, and
to force and compel one another thereto; as also to determine and give judgment in things beyond their reach,
being in their fallen wisdom, they turned the world up-
side down, in reference to conformity to their faith, and
broke asunder the bond of unity and concord, which
once flourished among the true christians.

But these cruel divisions, because of faith and doctrines, in relation unto God, were not let pass without
rebukes from the Lord ; for the Persians proclaimed
wars against the Romans ; and now Constantine, the emperor, died, and Julianus succeeded him, who, though
brought up a christian, yet had a secret inclination unto Paganism ; who set open the idolatrous temples and
groves, and sacrificed to pictures, and entitled himself
an high priest.

In the reign of this Julian, called the apostate, by reason of his inclining to Heathenism, the christians suffered very deeply, and some were run through with
swords; some killed with clubs ; some stoned to
death ; some strangled with halters ; some nailed

to trees, casting in their teeth the death of the cross ; one friend fell upon another; one brother sought anothers's life ; parents put their chidren to death ; and, to be short, one cut the other's throat. This blood and murder the emperor Julian seemed to be troubled at, thinking it might give a sudden start to his settlement in the empire ; therefore, he wrote a cruel angry letter to those of Alexandria, shewing his dislike of their enterprise.

Shortly after, Julian put forth a proclamation, that such as would not renounce the christian faith, should warfare no longer in the emperor's palace, but all should prepare to do sacrifice ; that no christian should bear office in the commonwealth ; for their law, said he, forbiddeth the use of the sword, unto such as deserve death, and therefore they are not fit to be magistrates.

As a scourge for Julian, who undertook these enterprises against the christians, wars broke out against him; and considering that many inconveniences and evils attended war, and great sums of money were requisite, he set a great fine on the heads of those that would not sacrifice : so that the christians were assessed, and he greatly enriched himself with large sums of money unjustly exacted ; then did the Gentiles insult over the christians, the philosophers solemnizing their detestable rites and ceremonies, making slaughter of infants, sparing neither sex, using their entrails for sooth-saying, they tasted of their tender flesh. These detestable practices were both at Athens and Alexandria, and elsewhere.

At Marais in Phrygia, Amachius the governor commanded the temple to be set wide open, and to be cleansed, and set himself to worship the idols, which pricked not a little in conscience the zealous christians ; wherefore Masidonius, Theodulus and Tattanus broke, in the night season, into the temple, threw down their idols ; and stamped them to powder ; at which, when the governor was exceeding wroth, and threatened to execute divers of the citizens, the men aforesaid presented themselves, who were the authors thereof, that the guiltless of that act might not suffer, and chose to die themselves for the truth, the governor commanded them to clear themselves by sacrifice, threatening severely to punish them, if they did not : they set nought by his threats, and made themselves ready to suffer. The governor, when he had assayed them with every kind of torments, last of all, set them on the gridiron, and caused fire to be made under, and broiled them to death ; who nobly said, " if thou dost long, O Amachius, after broiled meat, turn up the other side of us, lest in the eating, we seem raw unto thee, and the blood run about thy teeth."

Julian being dead, Jovianus succeeded, who, being proclaimed emperor, refused the crown, and being compelled thereto by loud speeches, expressed himself, that he was a christian, and he would not be emperor where Ethnics should be his subjects ; but, when they cried with one voice, and confessed themselves christians, he yielded, and was crowned emperor; and now peace came again to the church, but it was no sooner come, than the sedition began again among the christians ; and now the emperor sticking fast to the faith of one substance, the bishops, who had been exiled for the same faith, he also restored ; the Pagans' temple he shut up, and stopped their worshipping devils, which Julian gave way to, and which they had their fill in, in his reign.

Now went on the old work, of tearing and rending one another, among the christians. The Macedonians made a supplication to the emperor, that such as avouched the unlikeness and dissimilitude between the son and father, should be banished the church, and themselves substituted in their rooms. The emperor gave them no answer at all, but with these words sent them away ; " I tell you truly, I cannot away with contention, but such as embrace unity and concord, I do both honour and reverence;" which cooled the fiery contention of others.

The Acacians also signed a supplication to the emperor, acknowledging the faith of one substance. The emperor told them, he would not molest any, what faith and religion soever they professed ; but above all others, that he would honour and reverence such as shewed themselves peace-makers, and went about to maintain the bond of unity and concord.

And Athanasius being dead, after he had been bishop forty six years, Peter was left behind to succeed him. The emperor Jovianus being also dead, and the Arians coming in favour, Lucius the Arian was settled in Alexandria, whereupon great persecution followed in Egypt, wherein some were imprisoned, some tormented, and others exiled; Peter, the bishop of Alexandria, was imprisoned, and not long after an edict was proclaimed, by virtue of which, the religious houses in the desert were spoiled, the people thrown down, and cruelly beaten to the ground; for the armed soldiers setting upon those accounted silly and unarmed souls, who would not stretch out the hand in their own defence, were miserably slain: the manner of which slaughter was so lamentable (saith the record) that it cannot sufficiently be manifest to the world; and throughout Alexandria and Egypt, there were great persecutions to them that maintained the faith of one substance; they were brought before the bar; they were put in prison; they were diversly tormented and vexed with sundry punishments; set at nought; scourged; spoiled of their raiment; fettered in prison; crushed with stones; beheaded with bloody swords; shut up in the desert; covered with sheep and goat skins; destitute of aid and succour; grievously afflicted; whom the world was not worthy to enjoy, nor the earth to bear so holy a burden (saith the historian Rufinus) who is said to have been an eye-witness and partaker with them in the same calamity; many wandered in many and dangerous ways, and hid themselves in mountains, caves, dens, and hollow rocks; all which, when Lucius had accomplished, he persuaded the captain to banish the fathers and ring-leaders of them.

In those days, these sufferings brought the christians into a lowly frame and state, leading a self-denying life in deserts and other retired places; the historian mentions one of them, by which may be seen what principles were amongst the rest.

There was, said he, one Moses, who led in the desert, a solitary or retired kind of life, and is said, for his
zeal to religion and constant faith, to be famous among
them: this Moses was taken from the wilderness and sent
to Alexandria, with intent to be made bishop; and being
come to be made bishop, he refused to receive orders from
Lucius; and after this sort, reasoned with him, " I
think myself unworthy of the priestly order, yet if it
be for the profit of the commonwealth, that I be called
unto the function, truly, thou, Lucius, shalt never lay
hand upon my head; for thy right hand is imbrued in
slaughter and bloodshed." Then Lucius said again, that
it became not him so contumeliously to revile him, but
rather to learn of him the precepts of the christian religion.   Moses answered, " I am not come to reason of
matters of religion; but sure I am of this, that thy horrible practice against the brethren, proves thee to be utterly void of the true principles of the christian religion;
for the true christian striketh no man, revileth no man,
fighteth with no man; for the servant of God should be
no fighter; but thy deeds in exiling some, throwing
others to wild beasts, burning some others, do cry
out against thee; yet are we surer of the things we see
with our eyes, than of those we hear with our ears. So
Moses was brought to a mountain, and made priest by
such as were exiled; for now the wars ceased, and the
persecuted found some comfort.

But now the affairs of the church being quiet from
persecution, they began to jangle about their creeds,
and to differ again, and falling together by the ears,
when a little outward peace from the emperor sprang in
among them, which was occasioned by forcing their
faith one upon another: this was the division among
themselves, when there was no division made of them
by the Roman governments; and this was the trade a-
mong the christians, striving and contending for each
other's bishoprics, worse than some of the emperors,
who were willing, many times, to leave things free as to
matters of religion; the manner of the bishops at the general councils and synods being to cleave hairs (as they

used to say) at arguments, and they that were most curious and subtle therein, were accounted the best masters of faith, and so carried the matter, not according to the revelation of truth, but according to the subtlety of man, through which came all this ado and trouble in the world; and that side which the emperor took part with, prevailed, keeping the other under. Thus matters of religion began to be guided by policy, and to be enforced to be believed, by the emperor's sword, or else great persecution followed. Now the Christians were divided into a diversity of opinions, viz. Arians, Novatians, Macedonians, and Eunomians, one severing himself from the other; and these schisms and rents were many, as is usual where the unity of the spirit is not known in the bond of peace, and where logic and wit, and the wisdom which is from beneath, take upon them the determination of truth.

The other chief matters in which they differed, were, the time of observing Easter, their Lent, Communion, days of fasting, setting of their altar, priests marrying, &c. Concerning Easter, the greater part throughout the lesser Asia, held no discord with them that held the contrary opinion, until Victor, bishop of Rome, through broiling heat and choler, had excommunicated all Asia, for not believing his opinion in the same; for which, Ireneus inveighed bitterly, by letter, against him, and rebuked him for his harsh dealing, and furious rage.

Though many councils were called, thinking thereby to make reconcilement in the matter of difference, yet the breach rather grew wider, deposing and banishing one another for refusing to be subject to the decrees and canons of councils; for they were so strict, that they would not admit of the change of one syllable, avoiding the company, and refusing to communicate with them that were otherwise minded; on the other hand, others condemned the council, and their decrees, and accursed them, contending, among themselves, whether Christ had one or two natures; insomuch, that all the churches were divided into sundry factions, the bishops refusing to communicate one with another.

Thus the reader may see how far the Christians were degenerated from the life that the Apostles, and first Christians were in, contending with, and destroying one another, about their forms and outward observations, as if they had wholly forgotten the doctrine of the Apostle, who wrote after this manner, " how turn you again to these weak and beggarly elements, whereinto ye desire again to be in bondage ? Ye observe days, months, times, and years ; I am afraid of you, lest I have bestowed on you labour in vain."

Yet at this time, there were some sincere persons raised up to testify against the looseness and evils the pretended christians were run into ; for Chrisostome (saith the history) was bold and free in rebuking sin, especially in his public preaching ; and for that cause, was he hated by the clergy. He withstood Gainas, who requested of the emperor that he might obtain a temple at Constantinople for his people.

About this time, was John, patriarch of Alexandria, who of a hard sparing man, became bountiful in hospitality to to the poor ; he would twice a week, sit all the day at his door, to take up matters, and make unity where there was any variance. He lamented much one day, because none came that day to him, as having done no good ; but his deacon persuaded him rather to rejoice, that he had brought the city into that good order, that it needed no reconcilement.

Near this time, died Gregory, bishop of Rome, in whose time, it is recorded, that the purity of the ecclesiastical doctrine was almost lost ; for it was imbrued and darkened with human traditions, and many and sundry sorts of superstitions were daily brought in, and there grew horrible and bitter darkness ; yet, saith my author, the Lord raised up some good men betimes. In this bishop's time, there happened a great controversy about the primacy of the church ; for John, bishop of Constantinople, was declared, in the whole synod of the Greeks, universal patriarch ; and Maritius, the emperor, commanded Gregory to obey the said patriarch of Constantinople ; but Gregory would not abide that any bishop should be universal above all the rest. It is further said of Gregory, that he was the basest of all his predecessors, and the best of all his successors.

Boniface the third, being bishop of Rome, it is said, he did more hurt in one year than Gregory could do good in many. He obtained of Phocas (the wicked emperor, who had murdered Mauritius, his master) that he and his successors in that see, should have an universal dominion over all the churches in Christendom.

And it was observable, that as in the time of Constantine, the christians had more liberty, so they grew more ambitious; for then the bishops began first to think on mitres, who before time thought nothing else but to be martyrs; and now no less would satisfy the ambition of the bishop of Rome, but to be head of all other bishops.

In the year of Christ one thousand, religion was wholly decayed, to what it was in former times; and from the year three hundred to that time, many dark institutions and ceremonies were set up in the church of the pretended christians; insomuch, that it became midnight for darkness, and the popes began to draw their swords to war in defence of Peter's keys.

And now Henry the fourth, emperor, attended upon Hidlebrand, with his wife and children, bare-foot, at his palace-gate, and then he was made to swear unreasonable subjection to the pope in all things; and when all was done, the pope gave away his crown to Redolph, duke of Swevia.

The emperor this while sitting quietly at home, and considering how the people had wrested his power, in elections of popes, investing of prelates, &c. how he had robbed all nations by his legates, and had spread discord in his empire; he required homage and oaths of allegiance of all his bishops, and forbade all appeals to Rome, and the pope's legates to enter into his empire, without being sent for. Finally, in his letters, he prefixed his name before the pope's. Hereupon the pope wrote a rebuking letter to the emperor; the emperor wrote back, in defence of his doings, an apologetical epistle: the pope replied with a bull of excommunication: the empe-

N

ror made answer to that, with accusatory letters against
the vileness, pride, &c. of the see of Rome; then the
pope wrote to the German bishops to work against the
emperor; but they wrote excusing the emperor.

This pope, towards the end of his life, (who died a-
midst these broils, being choked with a fly as he was
walking abroad) used to say, that there was not a more
miserable kind of life than to be a pope.

About this time, William the first, king of England,
took down the prelates in temporalities in England; for
he ordained, that they should exercise no temporal authority at all, but rather in spirtualities; and he raised
them, as may be seen by a passage between Aldred,
archbishop of York, and the king; for at a time, upon
the repulse of a certain suit, the archbishop, in great dis-
contentment, offered to depart; when the king, in awe
of his displeasure, fell down at his feet, desired pardon,
and promised to grant his suit; the king all this while
being down at the archbishop's feet, the noblemen that
were present, put him in mind, that he should cause the
king to rise; nay, said the archbishop, let him alone, let
him find what it is to anger Saint Peter.

About this time, William the second, king of England, claimed the making of bishops to be his right, and
forbade appeals and intercourse to Rome; for appeals
had been seldom used, till Anselm, in this king's reign,
appealed to the pope, upon whose complaint, the pope
was about to excommunicate the king; but having a little before excommunicated the emperor, Henry the
fourth, he forbore at that time to do it, lest by making excommunication common, he should make it to be slighted:
at this time, great contention arose between the king and
archbishop Anselm; and Anselm not yielding to the king
in any point prejudicial to the pope's authority, nor the
king yielding to Anselm in any point prejudicial to his
own prerogative, the contention continued long and hot;
Anselm often threatening his going to Rome, the king
told him plainly, he would not trust him out of the realm,
but if he would go without his leave, he would then keep

him out during his pleasure; and besides, he should carry nothing out of the realm with him. Yet Anselm ventured it, and the king performed it; for William Warlswast was sent to rifle him in his passage at sea of all he had; neither was he suffered to return as long as the king lived, during all which time, the king took all the profits of his archbishopric to his own use.

At this time, Henry the first, being king of England, at his first coming to the crown, he forbore his claim to the investitures of bishops; but after he had been king some time, he claimed that both to invest bishops, and to allow or hinder appeals to Rome, belonged to him. In these, Anselm, archbishop of Canterbury, who was now returned into England, opposed him, affirming, that both of them belonged to the pope. The contention at last was brought to the pope, to whom king Henry sent William Warlswast, elect bishop of Exeter; who saying to the pope, that his master would not, for the crown of his realm, lose the authority of investing his prelates; the pope started up, and answered, neither will I lose the disposing of spiritual promotions in England, for the king's head that wears the crown; before God I avow it. So the contention grew long and hot, and many messengers were sent to and fro about it. The conclusion was, that the king should receive homage of the bishop elect, but should not invest them by staff and ring; to which the king said nothing, for the present, but forbore not to do it nevertheless; for five years after the death of Anselm, Ralph, bishop of Rochester, was by the king made archbishop of Canterbury, notwithstanding all the pope's threatenings.

At this time, there being two popes chosen at a time, made a great schism and tumult. The emperor, to quiet them, sent for them to appear before him. Alexander being one that was chosen, scorned the motion; Victor appeared; him, therefore, the emperor aided to the city, and settled to be pope. Alexander fled to France and Venice, and required aid against the emperor; at last, the emperor was fain to submit to the pope, who putting his foot upon the emperor's neck spoke these words, "thou shalt walk upon the adders and basilisks, and shalt tread down the lion and dragon." Mean while, the emperor speaking to the pope from under his foot, "not to thee, but to Peter" the pope answered, "both to me, and to Peter." Thus the emperor, having subjected himself, promising to take Alexander for the true pope, and to restore all that he had taken from Rome, departed.

Henry, the emperor, was crowned (on condition of restoring many things to Saint Peter, pretended by the pope to have been taken away,) the pope holding the crown between his feet, and so the emperor stooping with his head to take it on, the pope immediately, with his foot, struck it off again, intimating his power to depose him, as well as to crown him ; the cardinals taking up the crown, thus kicked off, put it on again.

About the year 1216, after the death of Hubert, archbishop of Canterbury, the monks at that convent, secretly in the night, elected one Reginald, their subprior, to succeed him, and caused him to go to Rome for confirmation ; but afterwards doubting how the king would take it, being done without his knowledge, they craved leave of king John to choose a fit man ; the king was content to allow them the election, but required himself to have the nomination, and thereupon commended unto them John Gray, bishop of Norwich, whom he had especially favoured, and accordingly the monks elected him ; but the matter being afterward referred to the pope; which of these elections should stand good, after many allegations on both sides, the pope, to shew himself indifferent to both, disallowed them both, and nominated a third man, one Stephen Langton, an Englishman, and a cardinal. The monks admitted him, but the king opposed it. The contest grew hot, and as the pope threatened the king to excommunicate him, and to interdict the kingdom; and the king threatened the pope to nullify his authority, and to banish the clergymen out of the realm; and the pope acted as much as he threatened; for he interdicted the kingdom ; so the king performed as much as he had spoken; for he drove the monks out of the cloisters ; yet at last, when the pope's legate came into England, he told the king in what great danger he stood ; first, of the king of France by invasion, and then of his own subjects by rebellion, for both which, there was no other help, but reconcilement with the pope : this so touched him to the quick, that he made him leave his great words, and fall to ask him forgiveness ; and taking off his crown from his head, he laid it down at the legate's feet, to be disposed of as the pope should please, and the legate stuck not to take up his crown, and to keep it three or four days in his hands before he restored it ; and did not then, neither, but upon condition, that he and his successors should hold the kingdom of the see of Rome, at the annual tribute of a thousand marks.

This king John was shortly after poisoned by one Simon a monk, who was absolved of his abbot before hand, for doing this act. To accomplish his design, he found a toad in the garden, and pricked him with a penknife until he made him vomit up all his poison, which he having conveyed into a cup of wine, began to the king with a smiling countenance, speaking these words : " if it shall please your princely majesty, here is such a cup of wine, as you never drank a better ; I trust this wassail shall make all England glad :" the king having drunk, and anon being ill, inquired for Simon the monk; to whom some answered, that he was departed this life, the king replied, then God have mercy on my soul ; and so he died, much repenting of his former life.

About this time, several persons were stirred up by the Lord, to declare against the pope as an Heretic, and were by him condemned for their pains, viz. Arnoldus, Johannes, Semeca, Gulielmus de Santo amore, Gallus, and Grosthead, great writers against the pope's decrees, giving many signs of false teachers ; of whom see more in the testimonies of the martyrs.

The pope being at variance with the emperor, Frederick the second, would not on any terms be reconciled, though the king of France strongly interceded, and the emperor cleared himself of all imputation, and offered full satisfaction for all pretended wrongs, and to go out of his empire (if the pope would not endure him there) to the holy land, never to return into Europe again, so as his son Henry, nephew to king Henry, of England, might succeed him; with offers of other most reasonable conditions.

And thus, having given a brief relation of the most material passages in the affairs of the pretended christian church till this time; I shall now proceed to give a discovery of the beginning and proceedings of the monks, friars, and jesuits, who now began to swarm in the apostatized church of the papists.

We read, that many religious men heretofore, contemning the world, and all the pomp, pride, and vanity thereof, withdrew themselves, into the wilderness and desert places, in Syria, Egypt, and other countries, it being in the time of great persecution, to the end they might the better, (being not troubled with worldly cares and encumbrances,) bestow their time in reading the scriptures, fasting, praying, meditating, and such divine exercises, whereof Paul, sirnamed the first hermit, Anthony, Hilarion, Basil, and Jerome, were the first and chiefest among the christians, who, for their sanctity in life, were in those days had in great honor; for then this kind of life was simple and free, and not bound or tied to unlawful vows and ridiculous ceremonies, as afterwards came to be observed by such as were called monks and friars; their habit was then homely, and yet decent, as every man was best pleased to wear; neither were they bound to abide or remain in any one particular place, nor tied to one kind of life by vow, but free to stay where they liked best, or to go into any city or country where they would, at their own pleasure: they sought out the most desert place that they could find, that is, in the wilderness, working with their hands, and getting their living by the sweat of their brow, and gave a singular good example to all men to live virtuously and godly, instructing their families, and others that resorted unto them, to lead a godly and christian life; and were admired and honoured of all good men for their doctrine, integrity of life, and godly zeal ; for as yet, the christians had but one law and one religion, which afterwards fell out otherwise, to the grief and sorrow of the upright among them, to see what rents and divisions, sects and factions, superstitions and ceremonies, were brought in amongst them, although good stirrings there might be amongst these that lived this private life.

Their successors and imitators were far from being like them, for the words of Philo, cried by Euschius, are these; "now let our monks," saith he, " who live like kings, who swim in all manner of delights and pleasures, who affect nothing more than promotion and honour, and whose chiefest care and study are to gather wealth and to hoard up gold, silver, &c."

About this time several sects of monks began to spread forth out of the order of Benedictus : their habit was, to wear a black loose coat of stuff, reaching down to their heels, with a cowle or hood to cover their bald heads, hanging down to their shoulders ; and under that coat, another white habit as large as the former : they shave the hairs off their heads, except one little round circle, which they call corona ; they are bound to abstain from flesh, unless it be when they are sick : these Benedictine monks would have the world believe, that they are godly and religious men, and would not be ranked with the jesuits, who were statesmen, for they (poor monks) meddle not with matters of state, or with kings' affairs. But notwithstanding their counterfeit holiness, an English Benedictine monk of Swinsted abbey, poisoned king John, as is before related; for which fact, he was, and still is highly honoured by all papists in general ; and one said of him thus: "regem perimere meritorium ratus est:" he thought it a meritorious deed to kill the king.

About this time, began to peep out another sect of monks, called Montelinetences, at the time when there were three several popes living who troubled all christendom for their Papacy. The institutor of this family of monks, was one Bernardus Ptolomeus. They lived, at the first, at Sienna in Italy, but afterwards (having gathered their crumbs together) they built an abbey on the top of an hill not far from thence ; and they wore a white habit.   This family was approved by pope Gregory the twelfth.

The Bethlemite friars began in 1257. Their first dwelling was at Cambridge ; and their habit was like the Dominican friars, saving these wore a star on their breast, wrought upon their habit, in memorial of the star which appeared at the time that Christ was born at Bethlehem. There started up so many sects of monks, friars, and nuns, at this time, in England, that the Commonwealth was so oppressed and exhausted by them, that it was not able to satisfy their exhorbitant and greedy desires.

The monks, called Præmonstratensis descended, down from heaven (as they themselves brag) in the bishopric of Lodan, at a place, which they call Præmonstratum. The author of this order was Northbertus, a priest, born in Lorain, who patched up an order, or rule, for his new-begotten monks, out of Augustin's rule, which was afterwards approved and confirmed by pope Calixtus the second ; they wore a long white cloth coat, open before, and a linen surplice over, and over that a long white cloak, a corner cap or hat (when they go abroad) of the same colour, and underneath all doublets, breeches, linen shirts, shoes, and white stockings. These monks have lands and revenues to maintain themselves, and are rich wheresoever they live. This sect began about the year 1170, and had abbeys in England.

About this time appeared first in England, the order of crutched friars ; this order is more ancient than all the former orders, if the reader will believe them, for they say, that Clitus, Peter's disciple, the third bishop of Rome after him, was warned by an angel, to build for him an house, to entertain all those that fled thither for the christian religion's sake, which he with all speed performed; so that, in a short time many godly men repaired thither, and were entertained, who, for many years after bore a cross in their hands, in memorial of the death of Christ.   A thing unlike to be true, that Clitus should be warned by an angel, to build an house for a company of lazy friers, to entertain all those that fled to Rome for the

christian religion's sake, whereas the very names of monks
and friars were not then, or many hundred years after,
either known or heard of in the church of God, and with
all, the persecution was then so great in Rome, that the
saints themselves were constrained to forsake the city,
and therefore it is not creditable, that christians should
fly thither for relief. Pope Pius commanded these friars to wear a sky-coloured habit, but now this order
wear black, and a cross of red cloth or scarlet, fixed to
their habit on their breast; they likewise live by their
lands and revenues. They had a monastery heretofore at
Tower-hill, which is now put to a better use, being built
up into tenements.

In the time of pope Innocent the third, the Trinitarian
friars began to shew themselves to the world. One Johannes Matta, and one Felix Anchorita, who lived a solitary life in France, were warned in their sleep, (as they report) to repair to Rome to the pope, and to seek for a
place for him to build a cloister; and this pope (as they
say) was warned in a vision to entertain them, which he
did, and ordained, that they should wear a white habit,
with a red and sky-coloured cross wrought on their
breast. Their charge was to go and gather money
to redeem christians, that were captives under the
Turks, and were called monks of the redemption of captives, but instead of redeeming captives, they purchased
lands with the money they gathered; so that the captives,
if they had no reward from Christ for suffering for his
sake, were like to have no redemption from these
friars.

Bridget, of Sweethland, being a widow, did institute an
order of friars and nuns, and coming herself to Rome,
obtained of pope Urban the fifth, a confirmation of the
same order or institution, that both sexes should live together in one cloister, having a wall between them, and
that the nuns should lie in the uppermost chambers, and
the friars underneath them.

The next is the Minorite friars. They wear a morish-
coloured habit, and never eat flesh, butter or cheese, but
feed on the best fish, and oil, the finest bread and purest

wine, the best spices, fruit, herbs, and roots, that they can buy for their money. They had a cloister built for them, at Barkhempsted in England, in the year 1257.

The Mendicant, or begging friars wear a long white coat of cloth down to their heels, all loose, with a cowle or hood of the same, when they are in their cloisters; when they go abroad, they wear another black coat over the other, with another cowle; both their coats are then bound close to their bodies, with a broad leather girdle or belt, which girdle is a very holy thing (if they may be believed) for they call it St. Austin's girdle, and many lame people wear it for pure devotion's sake, looking upon it to have some singular virtue in it; this leather belt is given to none but those that are special benefactors, and such as pay dearly for it, which brings them in no small benefit.

The next is the Carmelite friars : that is, friars of the order of the blessed Virgin Mary, of mount Carmel.—Their first appearance in the world was in the year 1270; at first they were ordained to wear a party-coloured habit, white and red, made in the form of a man, the which they then dreamed to be like unto that which Elias used to wear; but afterwards pope Honorius forbid them to wear that habit, as being not well befitting their profession, and therefore a black long habit and a cowle was given them, and over that a long white robe or cloak, as best agreeing with virginity.

Another sort is the Franciscan, or gray friars, of whom it is said, they would not touch any money, and made a show, as if they abstained from all flesh, and did eat nothing but raw herbs and roots, and wore wooden clogs instead of shoes, railing against other friars, who possessed money, and eat meat, wore shoes and stockings, &c. But these did not long persevere in this austere life, their delight being to fare deliciously.

There is a sort of these Franciscans, called Penitentiarians : they wear no linen, as they say, neither doublet, breeches nor hose, except a little pair of linen drawers to save their skin from their coarse habit; instead of shoes, they wear wooden clogs, which are under their feet.

bound over with leather straps, their habit is made of a very coarse cloth, and close before, reaching down to their heels, with a cowle close to their head made of the same, and also a gray rope made of hair, full of knots, instead of a girdle about their loins ; they never ride, but go a foot, when they travel ; they have a pair of great wooden beads, with a wooden cross tied to their girdle before them : if these Franciscan friars may be believed, they say, all that they wear about them is holy ; yea, all that they eat, drink or touch is sanctified ; their cowle, habit, sandals, and especially their knotty girdles, they say, have many virtues, and therefore they have no small profit from the lay-people, that they may wear them.

The origin of the society of jesuits is but of a new institution, whereof the founder was one Ignatius Loyala, born in Spain, who had been a soldier, and was hurt on both of his knees, and halted ever after : his order was confirmed by Paul the third, in the year 1504, and himself sanctified by pope Paul the fifth in the year 1622, not for his holiness and sanctity of life, but for an infinite sum of money given unto the pope by the jesuits ; and withal, because the duke of Bavaria (by the wicked practice, and policy of his children the jesuits, and the help of the king of Spain) had taken the Palatinate from the prince elector, the true and lawful owner thereof : this Ignatius, ordained that all those of this society, should call themselves jesuits, or patres societatis Jesu ; fathers of the society of Jesus.

Valderama preached, that when this St. Ignatius resolved to quit the soldier's life, the very walls of the house wherein he then was, shook, the beams and posts trembled ; all that were in it betook themselves to flight, and ran out of doors as fast as they could : even as when a strange eruption of fire suddenly breaks out in some high mountain ; so when interior fire began to be discovered in him, who before was cold and frozen, as to religion, it lightened forth in such sort, that it caused a thousand amazements, a thousand firing of houses, &c. there was never any Ætna, or flaming mountain, that did the like ; thus far are the words of Valderama.

And further the reader may see what ignorance was among the papists at this time, for the heathen people heretofore had many Gods, and every one of them had his distinct office, as Apollo was the God of wisdom ; Mars of wars ; Æolus of the winds ; Neptune of the seas, &c. the papists have many saints which they honour, and every one hath his several charge assigned unto him ; as St. Anthony for swine and for fire ; St. Roch to cure the plague, and sheep ; St. Lucy for the tooth-ach ; St. Petronal for the fever ; St. Martin for the itch ; St. Valentine for lovers ; St. Crispine for shoe-makers ; St. Clement for bakers, brewers and victuallers ; St. Sebastine for archers ; St. Nicholas for butchers ; and many more.

AN

ABRIDGMENT

OF

THE BOOK OF MARTYRS.

AN

ABRIDGMENT

OF

THE BOOK OF MARTYRS.

The history of the persecutions, and great sufferings sustained by the faithful servants of the Lord, both before and after the Jews' apostacy, and before the coming of Christ.

THE great enemy to all mankind is that wicked spirit of persecution, which moved Cain against his righteous brother Abel: the Lord had respect unto Abel, and to his offering; but unto Cain, and to his offering he had not respect: and Cain rose up against Abel his brother, and slew him: and the Lord said unto Cain, where is Abel thy brother? And he said, I know not: and the Lord said, a fugitive and a vagabond shalt thou be in the earth. And Cain said unto the Lord, my punishment is greater than I can bear.

And Pharaoh afflicted the people of God a long time, which grieved the good spirit of God in his people; but they cried out to the Lord in their oppressions; for the Egyptians made the childen of Israel to serve with rigour; and they made their lives bitter with hard bondage; the king commanding the midwives to slay all the male children, yet the Lord delivered his people out of all these afflictions with a mighty hand; and he poured out his judgments upon Pharaoh, and upon the Egyptians that oppressed his people; and he set his people free; for while the people of God had a sense of their bondage and sufferings, and cried unto the Lord, through the multitude of their oppressions, the Lord heard and answered them, and delivered them by the hand of his servant Moses, by whom he gave them laws, which they were to obey and which they submitted to.   Then God was with them as a mighty defence, and in this time of sufferings, they kept nigh to the Lord, and he was with them, and was a rock of defence unto them.

And because Mordecai, the servant of the Lord, could not bow, nor do reverence to proud Haman, Haman was full of wrath, and he thought scorn to lay hands on Mordecai alone ; wherefore he sought to destroy all the Jews that were throughout the whole kingdom of Ahasuerus, even the people of Mordecai.   And Haman said unto king Ahasuerus, there is a certain people scattered abroad, and dispersed among the people in all the provinces of thy kingdom, and their laws are diverse from all people, neither keep they the king's laws ; therefore it is not for the king's profit to suffer them : if it please the king, let it be written that they may be destroyed, and I will pay ten thousand talents of silver.   And the king said, the silver is given to thee, and the people also, to do with them as seemeth good to thee.   And letters were sent to the rulers of all the provinces to destroy all, both young and old, little children, and women, and to take the spoil of them for a prey.   Thus this proud persecutor endeavoured to destroy this people, had not queen Esther made supplication to the king on their behalf, and by that means, a stop was put to the wicked design ; and he was hanged on the gallows that he prepared for Mordecai.

Jezebel cut off the prophets of the Lord ; but Obadiah (who was governor of Ahab's house) being one that feared the Lord greatly, took an hundred of the prophets, and hid them by fifty in a cave, and fed them with bread and water.

Ahab persecuted Elijah, and said to him, art thou he that troubleth Israel ? He answered I have not troubled Israel, but thou and thy father's house, in that you have forsaken the commandments of the Lord, and thou hast followed Baalam.

Jezebel persecuted Elijah, so that he fled into the wilderness.

Manasses persecuted the prophet Isaiah for reproving him, and caused him to be sawn asunder with a wooden saw.

Jeremiah was persecuted for declaring the word of the Lord to all the cities of Judah, and for saying, " thus saith the Lord, if ye will not hearken to me, to walk in my law, which I have set before you, &c. then will I make this house like Shiloh, and will make this city a curse to all the nations of the earth," and all the people were gather-red against him in the house of the Lord, and the priests and prophets said unto the princes and people, " this man is worthy to die, for he hath prophesied against this city." Jeremiah said, " the Lord sent me to prophesy against this house, and against this city."

" As for me," (saith he) " behold, I am in your hand, do with me as seemeth good and meet unto you : but know for certain, that if ye put me to death, ye shall sure-ly bring innocent blood upon yourselves, and upon this city."

And Jeremiah was shut up in the court of the prison, which was in the king of Judah's house.

And the princes were wroth with Jeremiah, and smote him, and put him into a dungeon.

Nebuchadnezzar persecuted Shadrach, Meshach, and Abednego, because they would not bow to the golden image he had set up. The king told them, that if they would not worship the image which he had made, they should be cast into the burning fiery furnace. They an-swered, " O Nebuchadnezzar, we are not careful to an-swer thee in this matter ; if it be so, our God whom we serve is able to deliver us from the burning fiery furnace ; and he will deliver us out of thy hand, O king ; but if not, be it known unto thee, O king, we will not serve thy gods, &c." Then was he full of fury, and commanded the furnace to be heated seven times more than it was wont to be, and commanded that they should be bound with their hats and coats on, and cast into it ; but the Lord pre-served them in the flames, so that the fire had no power over them.

P

The princes under Darius also persecuted the prophet Daniel, against whom they confessed they could find no occasion, except it were concerning the law of his God ; wherefore, they persuaded the king to make a decree, that whosoever should ask a petition of God or man for thirty days, save of the king, should be cast into the den of lions : but Daniel, as he did afore-time, opened his windows towards Jerusalem, and kneeled down, and prayed, and gave thanks before his God ; of which these persecutors acquainted the king ; then the king commanded, and they cast Daniel into the den of lions, but the Lord preserved him that the lions hurt him not, because he believed in his God ; which the king hearing of, caused Daniel to be taken up out of the den, and commanded them that were his persecutors to be cast into it, which was done, and they were soon destroyed.

———— ❖ ————

The constancy and faithful suffering of some of the ancient people of the Jews, rather than they would be forced to depart from the laws of their fathers, and to live contrary to the laws of God.

ELEAZER, one of the principal scribes, an aged man, and of a well-favoured countenance, was constrained to open his mouth, and to eat swines' flesh ; but he choosing rather to die gloriously, than to live stained with such an abomination, spit it forth, and came of his own accord to the torment, as it behoved them to come, that are resolved to stand out against such things as are not lawful, for love of life, to be tasted : but they that had the charge of that wicked feast, for the old acquaintance they had with the man, taking him aside, besought him to bring flesh of his own provision, such as was lawful for him to use, and make as if he did eat of the flesh taken from the sacrifice commanded by the king ; that in so doing, he might be delivered from death, and from the old friendship with them, find favour. But he began to consider discreetly, and as became his age, and the excellency of his ancient years, and the honor of his grey head, whereunto he was come, and his most honest education from a child, or rather the holy law made and given by God; therefore, he answered accordingly, and willed them straightway to send him to the grave: "for it becometh not our age (said he) in any wise to dissemble, whereby many young persons might think that Eleazer, being fourscore years old and ten, was now gone to a strange religion, and so they, through my hypocrisy, and desire to live a little time longer, should be deceived by me, and I get a stain to my old age, and make it abominable; for though, for the present time, I should be delivered from the punishment of men, yet should I not escape the hand of the Almighty, either alive, or dead; wherefore, now manfully changing this life, I will shew myself such an one as mine age requireth, and leave a notable example to such as be young, to die willingly and courageously for the honourable and holy laws." And when he had said those words, immediately he went to the torment; they that led him changing the good-will they bore him a little before into hatred, because the aforesaid speeches proceeded, as they thought, from a desperate mind. But when he was ready to die with stripes, he groaned, and said, "it is manifest unto the Lord, that hath the holy knowledge, that whereas I might have been delivered from death, I now endure sore pains in body, by being beaten, but in soul am well content to suffer these things, because I fear him." And thus this man died, leaving his death for an example of a noble courage, and a memorial of virtue, not only unto young men, but unto all his nation.

————

The constancy and cruel death of seven brethren and their mother in one day, because they would not eat swines' flesh at the king's commandment.

SEVEN brethren, with their mother, were taken, and compelled by the king, against the law, to taste swines' flesh; and were tormented with scourges and whips; but one of them that spake first, said thus, "what wouldst thou ask or learn of us ? We are ready to die, rather than to transgress the laws of our fathers ; then the king, being in a rage, commanded pans and caldrons to be made hot, which forthwith being heated, he commanded to cut out the tongue of him that spake first, and to cut off the utmost parts of his body, the rest of his brethren, and his mother looking on. When he was thus maimed in all his members, he commanded him, being yet alive, to be brought to the fire, and to be fried in the pan ; and as the vapour of the pan was for a good space dispersed, they exhorted one another, with the mother, to die manfully, saying thus ; " the Lord God looketh upon us, and in truth hath comfort in us ; as Moses, in his song, which witnessed to their faces, declared, saying, " and he shall be comforted in his servants." So when the first was dead, after this manner, they brought the second to make a mocking stock ; and when they had pulled off the skin of his head with the hair, they asked him, " wilt thou eat, before thou be punished throughout every member of thy body ? But he answered in his own language, and said, no ; wherefore, he also received the next torment, in order as the former did ; and when he was at the last gasp, he said ; " thou, like a fury, takest us out of this present life, but the king of the world shall raise us up, who have died for his laws, unto everlasting life." After him, was the third made a mocking stock ; and when he was required, he put out his tongue, and that soon, holding forth his hands manfully, and said courageously ; " these I had from Heaven, and for his laws, I despise them ; and from him I hope to receive them again; insomuch, that the king, and they that were with him, marvelled at the young man's courage ; for he did not regard the pains. Now, when this man was dead also, they tormented and mangled the fourth in like manner ; so when he was ready to die, he said thus : " it is good being put to death by men, to look for hope from God, to be raised up again by him ; as for thee, thou shalt have no resurrection to life." Afterwards, they brought the fifth also, and mangled him ;

then looked he unto the king, and said, "thou hast power over men; thou art corruptible; thou dost what thou wilt; yet, think not, that our nation is forsaken of God; but abide a while. and behold his great power, how he will torment thee, and thy seed." After him, also they brought the sixth, who being ready to die, said, "be not deceived without cause, for we suffer these things for ourselves, having sinned against our God, therefore, marvellous things are done unto us; but think not, thou that takest in hand to strive against God, that thou shalt escape unpunished." But the mother was marvellous above all, and worthy of honorable memory; for when she saw her seven sons slain within the space of one day, she bore it with good courage, because of the hope she had in the Lord; yea, she exhorted every one of them in her own language, filled with courageous spirit, and stirring up her womanish thoughts with a manly stomach, she said unto them; "I cannot tell how you came into my womb, for I neither gave you breath nor life; neither was it I that formed the members of every one of you; but doubtless the Creator of the world, who formed the generation of man, and found out the beginning of all things, will also, of his own mercy, give you breath and life again, as you now regard not your own selves for his law's sake." Now, Antiochus thinking himself despised, and suspecting it to be a reproachful speech, whilst the youngest was yet alive, did not only exhort him by words, but also assured him with oaths, that he would make him both a rich and happy man, if he would turn from the laws of his fathers; and that also he would take him for his friend, and trust him with affairs; but when the young man would in no case hearken unto him, the king called his mother, and exhorted her, that she would counsel the young man to save his life; and when he had exhorted her with many words, she promised him that she would counsel her son; but she bowing herself towards him, laughing the cruel tyrant to scorn, spake on this manner. "O my son, have pity upon me that bore thee nine months in my womb, and gave thee suck three years, and nourished thee, and brought thee up unto this age, and endured the troubles of education. I beseech thee, my son, look upon the heaven and the earth, and all that is therein, and consider that God made them of things that were not, and so was mankind made likewise ; fear not this tormentor, but being worthy of thy brethren, take thy death, that I may receive thee again in mercy with thy brethren." While she was yet speaking these words, the young man said, " whom wait ye for ? I will not obey the king's commandment, but I will obey the commandment of the law that was given unto our fathers by Moses ; and thou that hast been the author of all mischief against the Hebrews, shalt not escape the hand of God ; for we suffer because of our sins ; and though the living Lord be angry with us a little while, for our chastening and correction, yet shall he be at one again with his servants. But thou, O Godless man, and of all other most wicked, be not lifted up without a cause, nor puffed up with uncertain hopes, lifting up thy hands against the servants of God ; for thou hast not yet escaped the judgment of Almighty God who seeth all things ; for our brethren, who now have suffered a short pain, are dead under God's covenant of everlasting life ; but thou, through the judgment of God, shalt receive just punishment for thy pride ; but I, as my brethren, offer up my body and life, for the laws of our fathers, beseeching God that he would speedily be merciful unto our nation, and that thou, by torments and plagues may confess that he alone is God ; and that in me, and my brethren, the wrath of the Almighty, which is justly brought upon all our nation, may cease." Then the king, being in a rage, handled him worse than all the rest, and took it grievously that he was mocked ; so this man died undefiled, and put his whole trust in the Lord : last of all, after the sons, the mother died. When her sons were apprehended, she exhorted them in the Hebrew tongue, saying, " O my most dear and loving children, let us hasten to that agony which may credit our profession, and be rewarded by God with eternal life ; let us fearlessly present our bodies to those torments which aged Eleazer endured ; let us call to mind our father Abraham, who having but one only son, willingly sac-

sacrificed him at God's command, and feared not to bring him to the altar, whom, with many prayers, he had obtained in his old age. Remember Daniel, the three children, &c." Antiochus being enraged against her, caused her to be stripped naked, hanged up by the hands, and cruelly whipped; then was she herself put into the red hot frying-pan, where, lifting up her hands and eyes to heaven, in the midst of her prayers, she yielded up her chaste soul unto God. But God suffered not the cruel tyrant to escape unpunished; for, in his wars against the Persians, the Lord struck him with madness; his entrails were devoured with worms; and stinking like carrion, in the extremity of his torments, he gave up the ghost.

An account of the great persecutions and martyrdoms of the christians, after the coming of Christ.

AFTER the Jews, who were once the people of God, and had the laws, statutes, ordinances, and commands, of God made known to them, as is before related, had apostatized from the holy spirit, or life, they provoked God, and soon forgot him, and shamefully entreated and killed the servants and messengers of God; yet the Lord had compassion on mankind, and remembered his promise; and in love to the world, he sent forth his Son, who said when he was come, he was the "true light which lighteth every man that cometh into the world," yet the world knew him not, but God sent his messenger to prepare his way, and the voice of one cried in the wilderness, "prepare ye the way of the Lord, and make straight paths for our God;" and when this messenger, whose name was John, was come, the hand of the Lord was with him, and he preached repentance for the remission of sins; and for reproving Herod of his evils, he was shut up in prison; and Christ testified of him, "that among those that were born of women, there was not a greater prophet than John."

To this Herod, who had married Herodias, his brother's wife, John said, "it is not lawful for thee to have thy brother's wife;" therefore, the persecuting spirit arose in Herodias, and she would have killed him, but could not; yet afterwards she was the cause of John the Baptist's being beheaded in prison.

And when Christ Jesus appeared, who is the light of the world, whom John called the lamb of God, who testified against the apostatized Jews, and their false worship in their dead forms, saying, " God is a spirit, and they that worship him, must worship him in spirit and in truth;" yet him these Jews rejected, and would not receive, that they might have life ; and when he said, " I am the bread of life," and, " I am the living bread which came down from heaven ; if any man eat of this bread, he shall live for ever ; and the bread that I will give is my flesh, which I will give for the life of the world ;" the Jews, in their ignorance, reasoned, saying, " how can this man give us his flesh to eat ? And they would not believe in him, though he did such great works and miracles amongst them, that never man did the like, yet they sought to kill him ; nevertheless, they would be accounted of Abraham's seed, and called him their father ; but, said Christ, " if ye were Abraham's children, ye would do the work of Abraham ; but now ye seek to kill me, a man that hath told you the truth ; ye are of your father the devil, and the lusts of your father ye will do ; he was a murderer from the beginning, and abode not in the truth, because there is no truth in him." And this blessed lamb of God, Christ Jesus, did these persecuting Jews crucify and put to death, as may be read at large in the scriptures. After they had crucified the Lord of life, then they persecuted his disciples and apostles as followeth.

When the Jews heard what Stephen had declared, they were cut to the heart, and they gnashed on him with their teeth ; but he being full of the Holy Ghost, looked up steadfastly into heaven, and saw the glory of God, and Jesus standing on the right hand of God, and said, behold, I see the heavens opened, and the Son of man standing on the right hand of God ; then they cried out with a loud voice, and stopped their ears, and ran upon him with one accord, and cast him out of the city, and stoned him ; and Stephen called upon God, saying, Lord Jesus, receive my spirit ; and he kneeled down, and cried with a loud voice, Lord, lay not this sin to their charge ; and when he had said this, he fell asleep.''

After the martyrdom of this blessed Stephen, the apostle James suffered next ; mention of which is in the acts of the apostles ; how, that not long after the stoning of Stephen, king Herod stretched forth his hand to vex certain of the church, and slew James, the brother of John, with the sword. Of this James, Eusebius also makes mention, quoting Clement, who writes this memorable story of him : " when he who brought James to the tribunal seat, and was the cause of his trouble, saw him condemned, and that he should suffer death, as he went to the execution, being moved therewith in heart and conscience, confessed himself also, of his own accord, to be a christian : and so were they led forth together, where, in the way, he desired of James to forgive him what he had done ; after James had a little paused upon the matter, turning to him, he said, peace be unto thee, brother, and kissed him, and they both were beheaded together, in the year 36.''

James, the brother of Christ, was termed a just and perfect man. It is said, that he took in hand the government of the church, after the apostles ; and when many of the princes were persuaded to believe, there arose a tumult of the Jews, Scribes, and Pharisees, saying, " it is very dangerous lest the whole people look after this Jesus, as though he were Christ ;" and being gathered together, they said to James, " we pray thee stay this people, for they err in Jesus, as though he were the true Christ : we pray thee persuade this people concerning Jesus, for we all obey thee ; yea, we and all the people testify of thee, that thou art just, and respectest not the person of any man ; stand, therefore, upon the pinnacle of the temple, that thou mayst be seen aloft, and

Q

that thy word may be heard plainly of all the people." The aforesaid Scribes and Pharisees placed James upon the pinnacle of the temple, and shouted to him, and said, "thou just man, at whose commandment we are all here, insomuch as this people are seduced after Jesus, who was crucified, declare unto us which is the door, or way of Jesus crucified;" and he answered with a loud voice, " why ask ye me of Jesus the Son of man, when as he sitteth at the right hand of great power in heaven?" When as he had persuaded many, so that they glorified God at the testimony of James, and said, " Hosanna in the highest to the Son of David." Then the Scribes and Pharisees said among themselves, " we have done very ill in causing such a testimony of Jesus to be brought forth; but let us climb up and take him, to the end that the people may be stricken with fear, and so may be brought to renounce his faith;" and they shouted, saying, " Oh! Oh! and the just also is seduced;" so they climbed up, and threw Justus down headlong, saying, " let us stone James Justus;" and they began to throw stones at him; for, after his fall, he was not fully dead: and he fell upon his knees, saying, " I beseech thee, Lord God and Father, forgive them, for they wot not what they do." And as they were stoning him, one of the priests, the son of Rachab, spake to them the testimony which is in Jeremiah, the prophet, and cried out, " cease, what do you? this just man prayeth for you." And one of them that were present, taking a fuller's club, struck Justus on the head, and killed him. This James was so notable a man, that for his justness, he was honoured by all men; insomuch, that the wise men of the Jews, shortly after his martyrdom, imputed the cause of the besieging of Jerusalem, and other calamities which happened unto them, to the violence and injury done to this man. Also, Josephus hath not left this out of his history; for he speaketh of him after this manner: " these things so happened unto the Jews for a vengeance, because of that just man James, who was the brother of Jesus; for shortly after his suffering, Vespatian, the emperor, destroyed the land of Jury, and brought them into captivity."

A relation of the persecutions raised by the Romans against the Christians, in the primitive age of the church, during the space of three hundred years.

EUSEBIUS, and most writers, number the first persecutions to be ten; wherein great numbers of the christians were slain and tormented; some were slain with the sword; some were burnt with fire; some were scourged with whips; some were stabbed with forks of iron; some were fastened to the cross, or gibbet; some were drowned in the sea; some had their skins plucked off; some had their tongues cut out; some were stoned to death; some were killed with cold; some were starved with hunger; some had their arms cut of, or were otherwise dismembered; and others were left naked to the open shame of the world; in which kinds of punishment, though they were diverse, yet the constancy of all these martyrs was the same.

The first of these ten persecutions was stirred up by Nero Domitias, about the year 67, after the birth of Christ. Orosius writeth of Nero, that he was the first within Rome who raised up persecution against the christians, and not only in Rome, but in all the provinces thereof, thinking thereby to abolish the name of christians in all places.

In this persecution, the apostle Peter suffered death, with many more christians, as Hierome said. Simon Peter, the son of Jona, of the province of Galilee, and of the town of Bethsaida, the brother of Andrew, about the year 44, after Christ's birth, came to Rome to withstand Simon Magus, in the time of Nero, and was crucified with his head downwards, and his feet upwards, himself so requesting; "because," said he, "I am unworthy to be crucified after the same manner as the Lord was."

Paul the apostle, after his great travel and labours in preaching the gospel in divers countries, at last suffered martyrdom in this first persecution under Nero. He was beheaded, some writers say, on the same day of the year on which Peter was crucified, although not in the same year, but in the year following, which was the thirty-seventh year after the passion of Christ.

He was delivered by Nero, bound, unto Longimus and Magistus, the chief officers, and Acestus, the Centurion, that they should lead him without the city, and cause him to be beheaded. And Paul being full of the Holy Ghost, spake the words of eternal life, that Nero, and all the people, should believe in Jesus Christ, who was king of heaven and earth, and who would destroy the glory of the world with fire. When they had led him away, Longimus, Magistus, and Acestus, began to say unto him, "tell us, Oh, Paul, where is that king? and where will he appear unto you? and how will you know him? and what will he give unto you, or what good will he bestow upon you, that you christians so mightily love him, that by no means you will consent unto our religion, that you may live and enjoy the good of this life; but rather, than all the pleasures of delight, to be led to die for him with divers torments? For this seems to us to be a great error, to hate this joyful life, and to embrace, with all your desire, punishment and death." Paul, therefore, said, "O ye wise men, and flourishing in knowledge, depart out of the darkness and error wherein the nobility of your understanding is clouded with darkness, lest you should see the truth, which lieth hid in you: turn the eyes of your minds to the eternal true light, that ye may be able first to know yourselves; and so come to the knowledge of that king with gladness, and to be saved from the fire which is to come upon the world, and to remain unhurt; for we do not war, as you think, for some earthly king, but for the living God, and the kingdom without end, who, by reason of the iniquities that are done in this world, will come a judge, and will judge it by fire. Happy will that man be who will believe in him; he shall have eternal life, and shall live world without end; and most unhappy is he, who, despising the riches of his bounties and long suffering, will not return unto him, for he shall perish eternally."

The first persecution, beginning under Nero, as afore-said, ceased under Vespatian, who gave some rest to the poor christians. Not long after whose reign, the second persecution was begun by the emperor Domi-tian, brother of Titus. His tyranny was unmeasurable; for he put to death all the nephews of Jude, called the Lord's brothers, and caused to be sought out, and to be slain, all that could be found of the stock of David. In the time of this persecution, Simon, bishop of Je-rusalem, after other torments, was crucified to death. In this persecution, John the evangelist, was banished into Patmos, for the testimony of the word ; and, after the death of Domitian, in the reign of Pertinax the em-peror, he came to Ephesus, and was released in the year 100. He lived to a great age ; some write, till he was 120. And this was his practice to his dying day, when age and weakness grew upon him at Ephesus, that he was no longer able to preach to them, he used, at every public meeting, to be led to the meeting, and say no more to them, than, little children, love one another.

He expressed great care for the good of souls, un-weariedly spending himself in the service of the gospel, in order to beget people to the truth. Witness one in-stance : in his visitation to the churches, near Ephesus, he made choice of a young man, of a goodly appear-ance, and a fervent mind, whom, with a special charge for his instruction and education, he committed to the bishop of that place : afterwards, John returned to Ephe-sus. But in process of time, the young man became very dissolute, and accompanied himself with idle, dis-solute persons, of ill behaviour, who put him in a way to steal and rob ; so after he forsook the right way, he brought himself unto a bottomless pit of all disorder and outrage ; and a rout of thieves being gathered to-gether, he became their captain, which John, at his re-turn, understanding, was sorely troubled, and said, I have left a wise keeper of our brother's soul : prepare me a horse, and let me have a guide ; he hastened and rode post : being come to the place appointed, he was straightway taken by the thievish watch; he neither fled nor resisted, but said, " bring me to your captain;" who, in the mean time, as he was armed, beheld him coming; but as soon as he saw his face, and knew it was John, he was stricken with shame, and fled away; the old man pursued, and cried, " my son, why fleest thou? O son, tender my case, be not afraid, as yet there remaineth hope of salvation : I will undertake for thee with Christ : I will die for thee, if need be, as Christ did for us." Which words seized so on the young man, that his countenance changed, and he shook off his armour, and trembled, and wept bitterly, and embraced the old man, and answered as well as he could for weeping; so afterwards, the apostle brought him into the church again. Yet nowithstanding all these continual persecutions and horrible punishments, the christians daily increased, being deeply rooted in the doctrine of the apostles, and watered plenteously with the blood of saints, as saith Nicephorus.

Everastus, bishop of Rome, was martyred under Trajan, in the year 102, after Christ; and Ignatius, bishop of Antioch, was martyred in his reign; with many more christians. This Trajan was very impious towards the christian religion, and cruel towards the christians, and caused the third persecution; in which persecution, Pliny the second, a heathen philosopher, a man learned and famous, seeing the lamentable slaughter of the christians, and moved therewith to pity, wrote to Trajan, of the pitiful persecution, informing him, that there were very many thousands of them daily put to death; of which none did any thing contrary to the Roman laws, worthy of persecution, saving that they used to gather together, in the morning before day, and sing hymns to a certain God, whom they worshipped, called Christ. In all their other ordinances, they were godly and honest; and for proof hereof, said he, I caused two maidens to be laid on the rack; and with torments to be examined about the same; but finding nothing in them, but immoderate superstition, I resolved to cease farther inquiry, till I received further instructions from you in this matter. Trajan having read this epestle, returned for answer, that it was his mind, that the christians should not be sought after; but if they were brought and convicted, that they should suffer execution. Whereof, Tertullian speaking, said, "oh! confused sentence, he would not have them sought for, as men innocent, and yet would have them punished as men guilty." This Trajan sent a command to Jerusalem, that whosoever could be found of the stock of David, should be inquired for, and put to death. In this persecution, suffered Phocas, bishop of Pontus, whom Trajan, because he would not worship Neptune, caused to be cast into a hot lime-kiln; and afterwards to be put into a scalding bath, where he ended his life in the cause of Christ. Then, also, Ignatius, bishop of Antioch, was apprehended and sent to Rome, where he was devoured by wild beasts; and besides these, many thousands more were martyred.

In the reign of Antolius Verus, a great number of the christians suffered most cruel punishments and torments, especially in Asia and France; among whom was Policarp, bishop of Smyrna, who was burnt at a stake at Smyrna. About this time also, suffered Blandina and Ponticus, a youth of fifteen years old, who, defying their idols, and constantly cleaving to Christ, were put to all the torments their enraged enemies could devise, till at last, the youth gave up the ghost. Blandina was first pitifully whipped, and then thrown to the wild beasts; then tormented on the gridiron; and at last slain. Comolus the emperor, upon his birth-day, calling the people of Rome together in great royalty, clothed in his lion's skin, sacrificed to Hercules, causing it to be proclaimed, that Hercules was the patron of the city; whereupon Vinsencicus Eusebius, Perigrenous, Potentionous, learned men, being stirred up with zeal, went about from place to place, converting the heathen to the faith of Christ; and hearing of the madness of the emperor and people, they reproved that idolatrous blindness, exhorting them to believe in the living and true God; and that forsaking the worshipping of devils, they should honour God alone. The emperor, hearing thereof, caused them to be apprehended, and required them to sacrifice to Hercules, which they refusing to do, he caused them to be grievously tormented, and pressed to death with weights of lead.

Severus, another emperor, put forth proclamations, that no christians should be suffered to live; hereby a great persecution was stirred up on every side, and an infinite number of martyrs were slain. Potamtena was tormented with boiling pitch poured upon her, and afterwards, with her mother Mersila, and Rhais, was burnt in the fire; and when Basilides, the captain, having the maid to execution, as he led her to the place, he repressed the raging of the multitude, who followed with raging and reviling, which she seeing, prayed to the Lord for his conversion, to the true faith; and so with admirable patience suffered martyrdom.

Shortly after, Basilides being required to give an oath in the behalf of his fellow soldiers, he denied the same plainly, affirming, that he was a christian, and therefore he could not swear; they who heard him, thought he jested at first; but when he constantly affirmed it, they had him before the judge, who committed him to custody. The christians wondering at it, went to him and inquired the cause of his conversion; he told them, that Potamtena prayed for him, and so he saw a crown put upon his head, adding, that it should not be long before he received it; and accordingly, the next day, he was beheaded.

A certain christian, being examined before the judge, and through fear, being ready to shrink back, there were certain persons standing by, who were ready to burst for grief, making signs to him, by their hands and gestures, to be constant; which being observed, they were ready to be laid hold on; but they of their own accord pressed up to the judge, professed themselves to be christians, which much imboldened the weak christian and terrified the judge: this being done, they departed away, rejoicing for the testimony they had given of their faith.

The crimes and accusations that were laid to the charge of the christians, by the persecutors, were, that they refused to worship idols, and the emperors, and that they professed the name of Christ; and besides, all the calamities and evils, that happened in the world, as wars, famine, pestilence, &c. were imputed only to the christians. But Cyprian and Tertullian confuting these slanders, proved, that the special cause of all those miseries, which befel the empire, proceeded from shedding the innocent blood of the christians; Cyprian was at last condemed to have his head cut off, and he patiently and willingly submitted his neck to the stroke of the sword.

Sixtus, bishop of Rome, and his six deacons, for the christian faith, were all beheaded.

Laurence, also, another of his deacons, following Sixtus, as he went to his execution, complained that he might not suffer with him, but that he was secluded, as the son from the father; to whom the bishop answered, that within three days, he should follow him, bidding him in the mean time to go home, and if he had any treasures, to distribute them amongst the poor; the judge hearing mention of treasures, supposing that Laurence had great store in his custody, commanded him to bring the same to him. Laurence craved three days respite, promising then to declare where the treasure might be had. In the mean time, he caused a great number of christians to be gathered together; and when the day of his answer was come, the persecutors strictly charged him to make good his promise; but valiant Laurence, stretching his arms over the poor said, "these are the precious treasures of the church; these are the treasures in whom Christ hath his mansion, &c." But the tyrant, in a great fury and madness, cried "kindle the fire, make no spare of wood; hath this villain deluded the emperor? Away with him; whip him with scourges; jerk him with rods; buffet him with fists; brain him with clubs; Jesteth the traitor with the emperor? Pinch him with fiery tongs; gird him with burning plates; bring out the strongest chains and fire-forks; bind the rebel hand and foot, and when the grate is red hot, on with him; roast him; broil him; toss him; turn him; upon pain of our high displeasure, do every man his office, oh! ye tormentors." Immediately his commands were obeyed; and

R

after many cruel handlings, this meek lamb was laid on the gridiron ; but what he endured was with such patience, that the emperor seemed tormented more than he : though his flesh broiled, the other's heart burned.

Dionysius writeth, that, "the number of those that suffered martyrdom, about that time, was great, men, women, young men, maidens, old wives, and men of all sorts and ages, of whom, some with scourgings and fire, and some with sword, obtained the victory, and got the crown ; neither, saith he, to this day, doth the president cease, cruelly murdering such as are brought before him, tearing some with torments ; imprisoning others ; and commanding that no man should come to them ; yet God with the daily resort of the brethren, did comfort the afflicted."

Not long after this time, the church had peace for about the space of forty four years, during which time, it did mightily increase and flourish ; and divers of the christians were preferred, both to court and elsewhere ; but, through this great prosperity, the christians began to degenerate, and to grow idle, striving and contending among themselves upon every occasion, with railing words bespattering one another in a despiteful manner, bishops against bishops, and people against people, moving hatred and sedition against each other, besides great hypocrisy and dissimulation more and more, by reason whereof, God's judgments broke forth against them, the pastors being inflamed in mutual contempt against each other. Then did the Lord raise up adversaries against his people ; then did Dioclesian, the emperor, raise a great and grievous persecution against the church ; commanding all the meeting places of the christians to be spoiled and cast down, and the scriptures to be burnt, which was executed with all rigour and contempt that might be, giving out edicts for the displacing of all christian magistrates ; and for imprisoning the elders and bishops ; and a great persecution ensued : but the christians manfully passed through exceeding bitter torments, by scourging, whipping, racking, and being put to death ; so that it cannot be expressed what number of martyrs suffered ; what blood was shed through cities and regions, for the name of Christ, in this emperor's time by divers torments ; some being hanged up by the feet, and by the smoke of a small fire strangled:

One Peter was hoisted up naked, and so beaten and torn with whips, that his bones might be seen : then they poured on salt and vinegar; and afterwards roasted him with a slow fire.

Many christians being met together, Maximinian, the emperor, sent some to burn the meeting-place and all the people in it ; but first they commanded a crier to proclaim, that whosoever would have life, should come out, and sacrifice to Jupiter, otherwise they should be all burnt ; then one stepping up boldly, in the name of all the rest, said, " we are all christians, and believe that Christ is our only God and king; and we will sacrifice to none but him :" hereupon the fire was kindled and many men, women, and children, were burnt in that place.

The punishments that these christians endured were so great and horrible, that no tongue is able to express ; as whippings, scourgings, rackings, horrible scrapings, sword, fireship-boats, whereinto many were put, and sunk in the sea ; also, hanging upon crosses, binding some to the bodies of trees, with their heads hanging downwards ; hanging others by the middle upon gallowses, till they died of hunger ; throwing divers alive to bears, leopards, wild bulls, pricking others with bodkins, and talons of beasts, till they were almost dead.

The christians being assembled at Antioch, one Romanus ran to them, declaring to them that the wolves were at hand, which would devour them ; yet he exhorted them not to fear : a band of armed men was sent against them, but they kept their faith ; whereupon the soldiers sent word to their captain, that they could not force the christians to deny their faith, by reason of Romanus, who did so mightily encourage them. The captain commanded that he should be brought before him, which was done accordingly. "What," said the captain, " art thou the author of this sedition ? Art thou the cause that so many loose their lives ? By the gods, I swear, thou shalt answer for them all, and shalt suffer those torments that thou encouragest them to undergo." Romanus answered, " thy sentence O em-

peror, I willingly embrace. I refuse not to be sacrificed.
for my brethren, and that by as cruel torments as thou canst
invent." The captain being much enraged with this stout
answer, commanded him to be suspended, and his bowels
drawn out ; whereupon, the executioner said, " not so, sir ;
this man is of noble parentage ; and therefore, he may not
be put to so ignoble a death : " scourge him then," said
the captain, "with whips, having knobs of lead at the end ;"
"but Romanus sung all the time of his whipping, requiring
not to favour him for nobility's sake ; "not the blood of
progenitors," said he " but the christian profession makes
me noble." Then he derided their idol gods, which enraged the tyrant, so that he commanded his sides to be lan-
ced with knives, till the bones were laid bare ; yet, still did
the holy martyr preach the living God, and the Lord Jesus
Christ to him ; for which, the tyrant commanded them to
strike out his teeth ; also, his face was buffetted ; his eye-
lids torn, his cheeks gashed with knives ; the skin of his
beard pulled off; yet the meek martyr said, " I thank thee,
O captain ! that thou hast opened to me so many mouths
as wounds, whereby I may preach my Lord and Saviour
Jesus Christ. Look how many wounds I have, so many
mouths I have lauding and praising God." The captain,
astonished at his constancy, bade them give over tormenting him, yet he threatened to burn him, reviled him, and
blasphemed God, saying, " thy crucified Christ is but a
yesterday's God, the gods of the Gentiles are of the greatest
antiquity." But Romanus, taking occasion from thence declared to him the eternity of Christ, withal, saying, " give
me a christian child of seven years old, and thou shalt hear
what he will say ;" hereupon a boy was called out of the
multitude, to whom Romanus said, " tell me, my pretty
babe, whether thou thinkest it reason that we worship
Christ, and in Christ one father, or else that we worship infinite gods ?" The child answered, " that certainly what
we affirm to be God, must needs be one, which with one is
one and the same ; and inasmuch as this one is Christ, of
necessity, Christ must be the true God ; for that there be
many gods, we children cannot believe." The captain,
amazed at this, said, " thou young villain and traitor,

where, and of whom learnedst thou this lesson ?" Of my
mother, said he, with whose milk, I sucked in this lesson,
that I must believe in Christ. The mother was called, and
she gladly appeared. The tyrant commanded the child to
be tied up and scourged. The bystanders beholding this
merciless act, could not refrain from tears. The joyful
mother alone stood by, with dry cheeks: she even rebuked
her sweet babe for desiring a cup of cold water, charging
him to thirst after the cup that the babes of Bethlehem once
drank of: she advised him to remember little Isaac, who
willingly offered his neck, to the dint of his father's sword,
&c. Then the cruel tormentor pulled off the skin and
hair from the crown of the child's head ; the mother crying,
" suffer, my child, anon thou shalt pass to him that will a-
dorn thy head with a crown of eternal glory." Thus the
mother counselled and encouraged the child ; and he received the stripes with a smiling countenance. The captain,
seeing the child invincible, and himself vanquished, commanded him to be cast into the stinking prison, whilst the
torments of Romanus were renewed and increased. Then
was Romanus brought forth again to receive new stripes
upon his old sores, the flesh being torn, and the bare bones
appearing; yet the cruel tyrant raging like a madman, quar-
relled with the tormentors for dealing so mildly with him,
commanding them to cut, prick, and punch him ; and then
he passed sentence upon him, together with the child, to
be burned to death ; to whom, Romanus said, " I appeal
from this unjust sentence of thine to the righteous throne
of Christ, that upright judge ; not because I fear thy cruel torments, and merciless handling, but that thy judgments
may be known to be cruel and bloody." When they came
to the place of execution, the tormentors required the
child of his mother ; for she had carried it in her arms from
the prison. She kissed it, delivered it to them ; and as
the executioner was striking off his head, she said, farewell,
my sweet child.

> All laud and praise, with heart and voice,
>   O Lord, we yield to thee ;
> To whom the death of all thy saints
>   We know most dear to be.

The child's head being cut off, the mother wrapped it in her garment, laid it to her breast, and so departed. Then was Romanus cast into a mighty fire, which being quenched by a great storm of rain, the tyrant commanded his tongue to be cut out, and afterwards caused him to be strangled in the prison.

Gordius, a centurion in Cæsarea, in the heat of this persecution, left his charge, living a solitary life in a wilderness, for a long time; at last, when a solemn feast was celebrated to Mars in that city, and multitudes of people were assembled in the theatre to see the games, he came, and got up into a conspicuous place, and, with a loud voice, said, " behold, I am found of those that sought me not." The multitude hereupon looked about to see who it was that spoke this; and Gordius being known, he was immediately brought before the sheriff; and being asked, who, and what he was, and why he came thither? He told him the whole truth, professing that he believed in Christ; valued not their threatenings; and chose this as a fit time to manifest his profession: the sheriff called for scourges, gibbets, and all manner of torments; to whom, Gordius answered, " that it would be a loss and damage to him, if he did not suffer divers torments and punishments for Christ, and his cause." The sheriff, more incensed thereby, comanded all those torments to be inflicted on him; with which Gordius could not be overcome, but sang, " the Lord is my helper, I will not fear what man can do unto me; and I will fear no evil, because thou, Lord, art with me, &c." Then he blamed the tormentors for favouring him, provoking them to do their uttermost. The sheriff not prevailing that way, sought by flattery to seduce him, promising him preferment, riches, treasures, honour, &c. if he would deny Christ; but Gordius deriding his foolish madness, saying, " that he looked for greater perferment in Heaven, than he could give him here upon earth." Then was he condemned, and taken out of the city, and burnt, multitudes following him, and some kissing him, with tears, entreated him to pity himself; to whom, he answered, " weep not, I pray you, for me, but for the enemies of God, which fight against the christians. Weep, I say, for them, which prepare a fire for us; purchasing hell-fire thereby for themselves in the day of vengeance: and cease, I pray you, thus to molest my quiet and settled mind; for truly, for the name of Christ, I am ready to suffer a thousand deaths, &c." Others persuaded him to deny Christ with his mouth, and to keep his conscience to himself: " my tongue, said he, which, by God's goodness I have, cannot be brought to deny the author and giver of the same : for, with the heart, we believe unto righteousness ; and, with the tongue, we confess unto salvation." And thus persuading and encouraging the people to be willing to die in the like cause, with an unparalleled countenance, he willingly gave himself to be burnt.

Basil, in one of his orations, relates a story of one Julitta, from whom, one of the emperor's officers took all her goods, lands, and servants, contrary to equity; whereupon she complained to the judges, and a day of hearing was appointed, when the spoiled woman immediately declared her case ; but the wicked villain that had robbed her, said, that her action was of no force, for she was an outlaw for not observing the emperors's gods, and that she was a christian. His allegation was allowed : incense was prepared for her to offer to the gods, which, if she refused, she should neither have protection nor benefit of the emperor's laws, nor continue her life ; she hearing this, in the mighty strength of God, said, " farewell, riches, welcome, poverty ; farewell, life, welcome, death ; all that I have, were it a thousand times more, would I loose, rather than speak one wicked word against God my Creator: I yield thee most hearty thanks, O my God, for this gift of grace, that I can contemn and despise this frail and transitory world, esteeming the profession of Christ above all treasures."— And thenceforth, when any question was proposed to her, her answer was, " I am the servant of Jesus Christ." Her kindred and friends earnestly solicited her to change her mind, but she constantly refused, with detestation of their idolatry. Then the cruel judge condemned her to be burnt ; which sentence she embraced joyfully, as a thing most sweet and delectable ; and so she addressed herself to the flames, in countenance, gesture, and words, declaring the joy of her heart, coupled with singular constancy, and embracing the fire, she sweetly slept in the Lord.

Thus, near the space of three hundred years, was the church of Christ assaulted on every side, and had but little rest, and no joy, nor outward safety, in this present world, but in much bitterness of heart, in continual tears and mourning, under the cross, passed their days; being spoiled, imprisoned, contemned, reviled, famished, tormented, and martyred every where; they by night assembling to sing praises to God; in all which, their dreadful dangers, and sorrowful afflictions: notwihtstanding, the goodness of the Lord left them not desolate, but the more their outward tribulations increased, the more their inward consolations abounded; and the farther off they seemed from the joys of this life, the more present was the Lord with them with grace and fortitude to confirm and rejoice their souls; and though their possessions and riches in this world were lost and spoiled, yet were they enriched with heavenly gifts and treasures from above, an hundred fold; then was true religion felt in the heart; then was christianity not in outward appearance shewn only, but in inward affection received: then were the name and fear of God true in heart, not dwelling in lips alone. Faith then was fervent, zeal ardent, prayer not swimming in the lips, but groaning out to God from the bottom of the spirit: then was no pride in the church, no leisure to seek riches, nor time to keep them: contention for trifles was then so far from christians, that well were they when they could meet to pray together.

But after this, the christians coming to be in favour with the emperors, riches and worldly wealth crept into the clergy, and the devil poured his venom into the church, so that true humility began to decay, and pride to set in its foot; and afterwards the church, through favour of the emperors, was indued with lands, donations, possessions, and patrimonies; and the bishops feeling the smack of wealth, ease, and prosperity, began to swell in pomp and pride; and the more they flourished in this world, the more God's holy spirit forsook them; till at last, the bishops, who were for a long time kept low, and persecuted, as before is related, now of persecuted people, began to be persecutors of others; and, through their pride and riches, were wholly degenerated from the true religion, and became adversaries to God; and persecuted and destroyed his living witnesses and members, as they were raised up from time to time, to bear a testimony against their apostacy, as, in the following history, will appear.

----------◆----------

The grievous sufferings, persecutions, and martyrdom of the servants of the Lord, by the priests.

JOHN saw there would be an apostacy from the blessed faith in his days: for he " saw a beast rise up out of the sea, and the dragon gave him his power, and his seat, and great authority; and all the world wondered after the beast; and they worshipped the dragon, which gave power unto the beast; and they worshipped the beast, saying, who is like unto the beast? Who is able to make war with him? And he opened his mouth in blasphemy against God, to blaspheme his name and his tabernacle, and them that dwell in heaven; and it was given unto him to make war with the saints, and to overcome them; and power was given him over all kindreds, and tongues, and nations. And all that dwell upon the earth shall worship him, whose names are not written in the book of life of the lamb, slain from the foundation of the world."

After this great darkness had spread over nations and people for some years, the Lord raised up some, from time to time, to bear testimony, according to the measures of light and knowledge they had received, against the blindness and ignorance that the world was under, as in the following instances, the reader may observe.

Robert Grosthead, living in the year 1240, wrote sharply to the pope, (particularly for the evils he committed in England) that he was opposite to Christ, a murderer of souls, and an heretic; and complained on his death of the corruption which had sprung up in the church, and inveighed bitterly against the manifold abominations of the church and court of Rome.

For his thundering against the Romish church, and for his publicly reproving the covetousness, pride, and manifold tyrannies of the pope, he was excommunicated to the pit of hell, by Innocent the fourth, and was cited to come to his bloody court; but he appealed from the pope's tyranny to the eternal tribunal of Jesus Christ; and shortly after died. Even before this, there were some found in England, who testified against the corruptions of the church of Rome, and suffered for the same; for, in the year 884, John Patrick Erigena wrote a book about the Lord's supper, which was afterwards condemned by the pope, and he was martyred for it.

In the year 960, some were branded in the face at Oxford, and banished, for saying, that the church of Rome was the whore of Babylon; monkery, a stinking carrion; their vows, nurses of sodomy; and purgatory and masses, &c. inventions of the devil.

In the year 1126, there was one Arnold, an English preacher, cruelly butchered, for preaching against the prelates' pride, and priests' wicked lives.

About the year 1160, about thirty Waldenses came into England, one Gerrard being their minister. These people labouring to win disciples to Christ, were quickly noticed by the popish clergy; and great complaints were made against them to king Henry the second, who caused them to be brought before an assembly of bishops, at Oxford, where Gerrard speaking for them, said to this effect; "we are christians, holding the doctrine of the apostles." In their examinations, they would not admit of salt, spittle, and exorcisms in baptism, and the eucharist; nor of binding with the stool, in marriage. And being admonished to repent, and to return to the unity of the church, they despised that counsel, and scorned threats, saying, "blessed are they which are persecuted for righteousness' sake; for theirs is the kingdom of heaven." Then the bishops excommunicated them, and delivered them over to be corporeally punished by the king, who caused them to be burnt as heretics in the forehead, and to be whipt through Oxford, they singing all the while, "Blessed are ye when men hate you." And the king further commanded, that none should presume to receive them into their houses, nor to cherish them with any comfort; whereby they miserably perished with hunger and cold, none affording any comfort to them.

These Waldenses are reputed the first reformers, after the darkness of popery had overspread the christian world, as before is related. And pope Alexander the third, being informed, that divers persons in Lyons questioned his sovereign authority over the whole church, cursed Waldow and his adherents, commanding the archbishop to proceed against them by ecclesiastical censures to their utter extirpation: whereupon, they were wholly chased out of Lyons. Waldow and his followers were called Waldenses, who afterwards spread themselves into divers countries and companies; and for their religion, many of them were burnt to death; and fleeing into Germany and other countries, many of them were put to death. Pope Alexander made a decree, that these gospellers, and all their favourers, should be excommunicated, and that none should sell them any thing, or buy any thing of them.

But the Waldenses, notwithstanding all the pope's curses, continued publishing, "that the pope was antichrist, the mass an abomination, the host an idol, and purgatory a fable;" whereupon, pope Innocent the third, A. D. 1198, seeing that the other remedies were not sufficient to suppress these heretics, as he called them, authorized certain monks, inquisitors, who by process should apprehend and deliver them to the secular power, by a far shorter, but much more cruel way than was used formerly; for, by this means, they were by thousands delivered into the magistrates' hands, and by them to the executioners, whereby, in a few years, all Christendom was moved with compassion to see so many burnt and hanged, that trusted only in Christ for Salvation.

From the year 1170, to the year 1470, many noble witnesses were raised up in England, and elsewhere, to write against the pope's pride, calling him antichrist,

&c. and to bear à public testimony in these dark times against the corruption and abominable idolatry which had crept into the church, with the hazard of their lives and liberties. Amongst which, were the Lollards, of the increase of whom, the pope had often complained in Richard the second's time, but could not prevail. And king Henry the fourth, coming to the throne by usurpation, to ingratiate himself with the clergy, made a law, that the Lollards should be burnt, at the discretion of the bishops; whereupon, divers suffered martyrdom, as followeth.

William Sawtry, of London, in the year 1400, was imprisoned by Thomas Arondell, archbishop of Canterbury. William Sawtry desired his cause might be heard by the parliament then sitting, for the whole realm; but the bishops would not allow it, and caused him to be brought before them, who examined him upon eight articles, the last whereof was about transubstantiation; to which, he answered, that after the words of consecration, there remained the very same bread, which it was before the words were spoken; whereupon, he was condemned by Robert Hall, the bishop's chancellor; after which, they got a warrant from the king, directed to the mayor and sheriff of London, for his burning.

William Thorp, for the same cause, was examined and imprisoned; and, after a long examination, before the archbishop, was committed to another foul, bad prison, where he never was before; of which place, he wrote as followeth: "After I was brought to prison, when all men were gone forth from me, and the prison-doors fast, being by myself, I began to think on God, and to thank him for his goodness; and I was then greatly comforted, not only for that I was then delivered for a time from the presence of the scorning, and from the menacing of my enemies, but much more I rejoiced in the Lord, because that through his grace, he kept me so, both among the flattering especially, and among the menacing of my adversaries, that without heaviness and anguish of my conscience, I passed away from them.

In this examination, the bishop told him, that it was certified against him, that he preached openly and boldly in Shrewsbury, that priests have no title to tithes ; the substance of his answer was,

"One came to prison to me, and asked, what I said of tithes ? To whom, I said, ask the priests and clerks of the town : the man replied, " our prelates say, they are cursed that withdraw their tithes." I said, I wonder that any priests say, men are cursed, without the ground of God's word ; and I put the man to inquire of the priest of that town, where the sentence of cursing them that tithed not, was written in God's law? And I said further, In the old law, which ended not fully till Christ rose up from death to life, God commanded tithes to be given to the Levites, but the priests were to have but the tenth part of those tithes given to the Levites. Now, said I, in the new law, neither Christ, nor any of his apostles took tithes of the people, nor commanded the people to pay tithes ; but Christ taught the people to shew works of mercy. And I said, not of tithes, but of pure alms of the people, Christ and the apostles lived, when they were so busy in preaching the word to the people, that they could not otherwise work to get their livelihood."

Then the bishop said, " thou preachest openly at Shrewsbury, that it is not lawful to swear in any case."

Thorp said, "by the authority of the epistle of James, and by the witness of divers others, I have preached openly in one place or other, that it is not lawful for any to swear in any case by any creature."

Then the clerk asked him, whether it were not lawful for a subject, at the command of his prelate, to kneel down, and touch the holy gospel-book, and kiss it, saying, so help me God, and this holy dome.

Thorp said, " ye speak full largely ; what, if a prelate command his subject to do an unlawful thing, should he obey ?"

Archbishop. A subject ought not to suppose that his prelate will bid him do an unlawful thing.

Thorp related the opinion of a master in divinity in the matter of swearing ; who said, It was not lawful either to give or take any such charge upon a book, for every book is nothing else but divers creatures, of which it is made : therefore, to swear upon a book, is to swear by creatures, and this swearing is ever unlawful.   This sentence (said Thorp) witnesseth Chrysostom plainly, blaming them greatly that bring forth a book to swear upon, charging clerks, that in no wise, they constrain any body to swear, whether they think a man to swear true or false.   Then the archbishop scorned me, and threatened me with sharp and great punishment, except I left this opinion of swearing.

Thorp said, it is not only my opinion, but the opinion of Christ, James, and Chrysostom, and of divers others.

The clerk said, wilt thou tarry, my lord, longer ? Submit thee here meekly to the ordinance of the holy church and lay thy hand upon a book, touching the holy gospel of God, promising, not only with thy mouth, but also with thine heart, to stand to my Lord's ordinance.

Thorp said, have I not told you here, how that I heard a master of divinity say ; that, in such a case, it is all one to touch a book, as to swear by a book ?

Bishop.   There is no master of divinity in England, but if he hold this opinion before me, I shall punish him, as I shall do thee, except thou swear as I shall charge thee.

Thorp.   Is not Chrysostom a doctor ?

Bishop.   Yea.

Thorp.   If Chrysostom proveth him worthy of great blame that bringeth forth a book to swear upon, it must needs follow, that he is more to blame that sweareth on that book.

The clerk said, lay thine hand upon the book, touching the holy gospel of God, and take thy charge.

Thorp.   I understand that the holy gospel of God may not be touched with man's hand.

It was mentioned before, that he was imprisoned by Thomas Arondell, archbishop of Canterbury ; and it is recorded that he was, by the said bishop, at last secretly put to death in the year 1407.

In the year 1413, Roger Acton, John Brown, and John Beverly were persecuted, and put to death for their testimony to the truth, at Giles, in the fields, together with divers others, to the number of thirty six, all which were hanged, with fire made under them. These godly persons, in these dangerous times, used too meet in the night, at Giles, in the fields, to pray and preach, which the bishops had notice of, and they informed the king as if they intended to rebel; whereupon, the king going with many armed men, at midnight, took these thirty six, and caused them to be executed; the number that were assembled was greater, but they fled; amongst whom, was William Murle of Dunstable, Malster, who being afterwards apprehended, was drawn, hanged, and burnt. But within a few days after their execution, Thomas Arondell, archbishop, was so striken by God in his tongue, that he could neither swallow any food, nor speak for divers days before his death, whereby he died in much misery. And this was thought to come upon him, for that he so bound the word of the Lord, that it should not be preached in his days.

John Purvey was imprisoned by Henry Chichley, archbishop of Canterbury, in the year 1421. He wrote a book against the pope, wherein he called him antichrist, and that his censures were like the blast of Lucifer. He complained, that many before him, who had impugned the Romish errors, had been imprisoned, killed, and their books burnt, and that none were suffered to preach, but such as would swear obedience to the pope: for which, he was imprisoned, and secretly made away, by the aforesaid bishop.

About this time, there began to spring forth some light in Bohemia. The Bohemians having received some of Wickliff's books, began first to taste and favour Christ's gospel, till at length by the preaching of John Hus, they increased more and more in knowledge, insomuch that pope Alexander the fifth hearing thereof, began to stir coals, and directed his bull to the archbishop of Swinco, requiring him to look to the matter, that no persons should maintain that doctrine; and not long after this, John Hus and Jerome of Prague were both condemned, and burnt, at Constance, by the council held there ; and yet their blood did not satisfy their adversaries, but they took further counsel for the destruction of these people in the whole nation ; for when fifty eight of the chief nobles of Bohemia, in the name of all the commons, A. D. 1416, had sent letters from Prague to the council, complaining, that John Hus their pastor, an innocent and holy man, and faithful teacher of the truth, was unjustly condemned, the council, instead of answering them, wrote letters to some violent papists who were in authority, to assist their legate in oppressing the heretics ; and thereupon they persecuted them all manner of ways, using great violence towards them ; insomuch that they raised tumults, and one Zisca, a nobleman of that country, being sorely grieved for the death of John Hus, and Jerome of Prague, and minding to revenge the injuries which the council had done, greatly to the dishonour of the kingdom of Bohemia, upon their accomplices and adherents he gathered together a number of men of war, subverted the monasteries, and idolatrous temples, pulling down and breaking in pieces the images and idols, driving away the monks and priests, which he said were kept up in their clositers like swine in their styes to be fatted.— When this Zisca died, in remembrance of him, the Bohemians engraved over his tomb, in the Greek language, this epitaph : " John Zisca, a Bohemian, enemy to all wicked and covetous priests, but with a godly zeal."

Yet still as the popish party prevailed, they exercised all manner of cruelty upon the poor servants of Christ, till they were utterly suppressed by force, many of whom fled into the hilly country, near Silesia, to inhabit ; where throwing off all superstitious practices, they applied themselves to the best form that they, according to the best of their understandings, judged to be nearest to the primitive christians, calling themselves brethren and sisters : they were branded with the name of Picards, a a name by which the Waldenses in Picardy were called. The purity that was amongst them much displeased the devil ; for he raised a sudden and violent tempest against them, and an edict was proclaimed, threatening death to all that should administer to the picards ; whereupon they were brought to great extremity. A second edict came forth, that none of them should be suffered either to live in Bohemia, or Moravia; hereupon they were dispersed amongst the woods and mountains, dwelling in caves, where yet they were scarce safe, so that they were forced to make no fire, nor dress any meat, but in the night time, lest the smoke should betray them. In the cold winter nights, sitting by the fire, they applied themselves to the reading of the bible, and holy discourse.—— When in the snow, they went abroad to provide them necessaries, they went close together ; and, lest their footsteps should betray them, the hindermost of them drew after him a great bough, to cover the prints which their feet had made.

But, to return again to give a farther account of sufferers in England. John Claydon, of London, currier, in the year 1415, being examined before Henry Chichley, archbishop of Canterbury, upon suspicion of heresy, he confessed that for the same cause, he had been formerly imprisoned by R. Braybrock, bishop of London, in Conway prison two years, and at another time, three years in the fleet ; and also, that he had several English books that he took delight to hear read to him. One of the books was entitled, "the lantern of light," in which books was contained, speaking or treating on the text, how the enemy did sow the tares ; "that wicked antichrist, the pope, hath sowed his popish and corrupt decrees, which are of no authority, strength, nor value ; and that the bishop's licence for a man to preach, is the true character of the beast and antichrist : and that the court of Rome is the chief head of antichrist : and that no reprobate is a member of the church." His books being examined, were condemned as heretical, to be burnt in the fire ; and sentence of condemnation was passed upon him, by the archbishop ; and he was delivered to the secular power, by whom he was carried into Smithfield, and there burnt, with Richard Turning, a baker.

T

The next year after the burning of these men, the prelates of England, seeing the daily increase of the gospel, and fearing the ruin of their papal kingdom, took counsel together, with what diligence they could to maintain the same. Wherefore, to make their state and kingdom sure, by statutes, laws, constitutions, and terrors of punishment, Henry Chichley. archbishop, in his convocation holden at London, made another decree against the poor Lollards, which was sent abroad. A.D. 1416 to be straightly executed ; in which, their officials (or commissaries) were required twice every year at least, to make diligent inquiry after such persons as were suspected of heresy ; and parishoners were to be sworn upon the evangelists, to discover whether they knew any frequenting privy conventicles, or differing in their life and manners from other common catholic men, or that should have any books in the English tongue.

After the setting out of the decree aforesaid, great inquisition hereupon followed in England ; and many good men, who began to have a love for the gospel, were much troubled, and great sufferers.

John Gale, of London, was summoned before the archbishop, for having a book in English, entitled, "a book of the new law."

Ralph Maungin, for the same doctrine, was condemned to perpetual imprisonment.

William White, a follower of John Wickliffe, was of a devout holy life, and is recorded as a morning star in the midst of a cloud, a man well learned, an upright man, and well spoken. For the love of the truth, he gave over his priesthood. but not his preaching ; for he continually laboured to advance the glory of God, by reading, writing, and preaching. The chief matters charged against him were, that he held,

That men should seek for the forgiveness of their sins only at the hand of God.

That the pope was an enemy unto Christ's truth.

That men ought not to worship images.

That the Romish church was the fig-tree which Christ cursed, because it brought forth no fruit of the true belief.

That such as wear cowls, or are anointed, or shorn, are the soldiers of lucifer: and that all such, because their lamps are not burning, should be shut out when the Lord shall come.

He was apprehended (for preaching and teaching such like doctrine) in Norfolk; and being had before the bishop of Norwich, he was convicted, condemned, and burnt in the seventh month, 1424.

When he was at the stake, beginning to open his mouth to speak to the people, to exhort them and confirm them in the truth, one of the bishop' servants struck him in the mouth, thereby to force him to keep silence: and thus this good man received the crown of martyrdom, and ended this mortal life, to the great grief of all good men in Norfolk. His wife Joan following her husband's steps, according to her power, teaching and sowing abroad the same doctrine, confirmed many in God's truth; wherefore, she suffered much trouble and punishment the same year at the hands of the said bishop.

John Goose, 1473, being called before the bishops and accused of heresy was, condemned and delivered to Robert Bellisdon, one of the sheriffs of London, to see him burnt, in the afternoon. The sheriff, like a charitable man, had him home to his house, and there exhorted him to deny his errors. He desired the sheriff to be content, for he was satisfied in his conscience. The sheriff giving him some meat, he being very hungry, did eat so freely as if the hour of his death had not been known to be so nigh, saying to the bystanders, " I eat now a good and competent dinner, for I shall pass a little sharp shower ere I go to supper;" and having dined, he required that he might be led to the place where he should yield up his spirit unto God.

About this time, there being a war begun by the Turks against the christians, so called, there were great invasions, and victories were obtained by the Turks over them, insomuch that the Turks, in the space of thirty years, subdued Arabia, got Palæstina, Phœnica, Syria, Egypt, and Persia, raging with their armies throughout all Asia and Europe, conquering as they passed. The causes of which invasions and victories, as is recorded, were the dissension, discord, falsehood, idleness, inconsistency, greedy avarice, lack of truth and fidelity amongst christian men of all states and degrees, both high and low; for, by the wilful defection and backsliding of the christians, the Turkish power did exceedingly increase, and they, called christians, were by multitudes destroyed; and as it is written, there was hardly a town, city, or village, in all Asia and Greece, or in a great part of Europe and Africa, whose streets did not flow with the blood of the christians, whom these cruel Turks murdered after an inhuman manner; men and women being by them cut in pieces, children stuck upon poles and stakes, till they gored them to death in the sight of their parents, dragging some at their horses' tails, till they worried them to death, tearing some in pieces, tying their arms and legs to four horses, treading the aged and feeble under their horses' feet. The princes of Rasia had both their eyes put out, with basons red hot, set before them, cutting some asunder in the midst, and with other torments, putting many to death, insomuch that the streets and ways of Chalrides did flow with the blood of them that were slain. The Pretor's daughter, of said city, being the only daughter of her father, and noted to be a singular beauty, was saved out of the slaughter, and brought to Mahomet the Turk, to be his concubine; but she denying to consent to his Turkish filthiness, was commanded therefore to be slain. It would be long to recite, and incredible to believe, the cruel and horrible slaughters, and miserable tortures inflicted upon the christians by these Turks, in most parts of Asia and Africa, and especially in Europe.

And during all these wars and slaughters, the pope ceased not, continually calling upon christian kings, princes, and subjects to take the cross, and to war against the Turks, lest he should loose all; whereupon, in that time of darkness and popery, many took voyages to the holy land, and many battles were fought for winning the holy cross; and yet without success, neither ever came prosperously forward, whatsoever the pope attempted against him. What the cause was may be easily judged, if the reader considers the gross idolatry, profaneness, and degeneration those called christians were fallen into, having lost the true faith once delivered to the saints : and instead of being sufferers, which was once the portion of the true christians, they now became the persecutors and destroyers of such as would not stoop to their idolatry, and to every foolish invention, that the popes from time to time set up, and commanded to be observed. It is recorded, that in the time of pope Julius, partly with his wars, and partly with his cursings, in the space of seven years, about two hundred thousand christians were destroyed. So addicted to bloodshed was this pope; and it is written, he so far surpassed many other popes in iniquity, that Wicelius wrote thus of him, Marti illum quam Christo deditiorem fuisse, that is, that he was more given to war and battle, than to Christ.

In the year 1512, there was a fight, between Lewis, the French king, and this pope Julius, at Ravenna, upon Easter-day, where the pope was vanquished, and had of his army slain, to the number of sixteen thousand ; and the next year, this apostolic warrior, who had resigned his keys to the river Tybris before, made an end both of his fighting and living.

About this time, began the reign of Henry, the eighth, king of England, in whose reign, great alterations and turns of religion, were wrought by the mighty operation of God's hand, not only in England, but in Germany, and other parts of Europe, such as had not been seen (although much groaned for) many hundred years before ; nevertheless, many suffered great persecutions and martyrdom in this king's reign, both in England and elsewhere ; and many good men were raised up to bear witness to the truth; yet some were of opinion, that it was not wholly the king's fault, that so much blood was spilt in his time : for the bishops were the dragon to make the bloody laws, and it was the bishops that were earnest to see the laws put in execution, the king oftentimes scarce knowing what was done, and hearing of a woman that was the second time put upon the rack, he exceedingly condemned the party that was the cause of it, for using such extreme cruelty.

J. Brown passing from London, in a Gravesend-barge, in which there was a priest; sat close by him; whereupon, the priest said, "dost thou know who I am? Thou sittest too near me." Brown said; No, sir, I know not who you are: I tell thee, said he, I am a priest. What, sir, said Brown, are you a parson, or a vicar, or a lady's chaplain? I am, said he, a soul priest, and sing for a soul. I pray you, sir, said Brown, where find you the soul, when you go to mass? I know not, said the priest: and where do you leave it when you have done mass? I cannot tell, said the priest. Brown replied, if you neither know where the soul is when you begin, nor where you leave it when you have done; how then do you save a soul? Go thy ways, said the priest, thou art an heretic, and I will be even with thee. And accordingly, when they came to land, the priest, taking two others with him that were present in the barge, went and complained to archbishop Warham, who sent a warrant presently to apprehend Brown; and being apprehended, the messenger bound his feet under his horses' belly, and carried him away to the archbishop, neither his wife nor friends knowing whither he went, nor what they would do with him. The bishop cast him into prison, where he lay about six weeks: then he was carried to Ashford, where he dwelt, and was there set in the stocks all night. His wife hearing of it, came and sat by him all night, to whom he shewed how cruelly he had been handled by the archbishop, telling her she could not set his feet to the ground, for they had burnt them to the bones, to make him deny Christ, which, said he, "I durst not do, lest my Lord, Christ, should deny me hereafter; therefore, good wife, continue as thou hast begun, and bring up my children virtuously, and in the fear of God." And so, the next day, this godly martyr was burnt, calling upon God, and saying, "into thy hands, I commend my spirit, thou hast redeemed me, O Lord God of truth!" At the fire, the bailiff bade, cast in his children also; for, said he, "they will spring out of his ashes." And in queen Mary's time, his son Richard Brown was sentenced to be burnt, being a prisoner a Canterbury; but the queen dying, he escaped suffering.

About this time, many suffered very greatly, for speaking against the worshipping of saints, and against Pilgrimage, for having scripture-books in English, and a book called Wickliffe's Wicket.

One of which sufferers, by name, Elizabeth Stamford, being brought and examined before Fitz James, bishop of London, A. D. 1517 confessed, that she was taught by one Thomas Beale, of Henly, these words, eleven years before, viz. That Christ feedeth and nourisheth his church with his own precious body, that is, the bread of life coming down from Heaven : this is, said she, the worthy word that is worthily received and joined unto man, to be in one body with him ; so it is, that they be both one, they may not be parted ; this is not received by chewing of teeth, but by hearing with ears, and understanding with the soul, and wisely working thereafter, and as Paul saith, I fear amongst us brethren, that many of us be feeble and sick, therefore my counsel is, brethren, to rise and watch, that the great day of doom come not suddenly upon us, as the thief doth upon the merchant : and she said further, that the said Thomas Beale taught her, that she should confess her sins to God, and that the pope's pardons and indulgences were nothing worth.

John Stillman, in the year 1518, was apprehended and brought before the bishop of London, and examined for speaking against worshipping, praying, and offering unto images, and for saying, Wickliffe's Wicket was a good book ; and that when he was apprehended, he hid the same in an old oak, and did not bring it out to the bishop. He was sent to the Lollards' tower ; and being afterwards brought openly to the consistory at Paul's, it was further objected against him, that he should say, " the pope was antichrist, and not the true successor of Peter, or Christ's vicar on earth ; and that his pardons and indulgences, which he granted in the sacrament of Penance, were nought, and that he would have none of them ; and likewise, that the college of cardinals were limbs of antichrist, and the priests the synagogues of satan ; and that the doctors of the church had subverted the truth of holy scripture, and expounded it after their own minds ; and that he should say, he would abide by these doctrines, and die for it; and wished there were twenty thousand of his opinion, to witness against the scribes and pharisees : but for his constant persevering in these principles, Doctor Head, vicar general, passed sentence against him as an heretic ; and so delivered him to the sheriffs of London, to be openly burnt in Smithfield.

The next that suffered was Thomas Man, who, for saying, " the popish church was not the church of God, but a synagogue ;" and for holding several other articles contrary to the popish church, was a long time imprisoned ; but through frailty and fear, having an opportunity, he fled the diocess of Lincoln ; but not long after, was again apprehended, and brought before the bishop of London, and was shortly after delivered, by Dr. Head, to the sheriff of London, to be presently burnt, with this protestation, that he might not consent to the death of any.

This popish chancellor would not seem to consent to his death, but yet sent him to the shambles to be killed ; for these were the words he sent to the sheriff : " receive this person, and we desire, in the bowels of our Lord, Jesus Christ, that the punishment and execution of due severity of him, and against him in this part, may be so moderate, that there be no rigorous rigor, and yet no dissolute mansuetude, but to the health and wealth of his soul," &c.

Thomas Man was burnt by the sheriff, without any warrant, for Head delivered him to the sheriff in paternoster-row, protesting he had no power to put him to death, and therefore desired the sheriff to see him punished, et tamen citra mortem, that is, without death ; but the sheriff had him to Smithfield, and there caused him to be burnt.

This Thomas Man, after he had escaped out of the diocess of Lincoln, travelled about in divers places and counties in England, and instructed many in the truth, as at Amerham, London, Billericy, Chelmsford, Stratford, Uxbridge, Henly, Newberry, Suffolk, and Norfolk, and divers other places ; and he testified himself, as he went westward, he found a great company of well-disposed persons of the same judgment with him, especially at Newbury, where, he said, was a glorious and sweet society of faithful followers, three or four of which were burnt for religion.

And he travelled into divers other places, where he found many faithful brethren.

This Thomas Man confessed, as is registered in the bishop's book, that he had turned seven hundred people to his religion, for which, he thanked God; which people were afterwards called by the name of Protestants.

William Sweeting and James Brewster had the like Catholic charity shewed them by the bishop, they being imprisoned for their zeal to the truth and religion; and being surprised with fear, said, they submitted themselves to the mercy of Almighty God, and to the favourable goodness of the judge; upon which submission, the popish fathers were contented to give out a solemn commission, to release and pardon them from the sentence of excommunication; but immediately, the bishop pronounced upon them the sentence of death and condemnation; whereupon, they were both delivered to the secular power, and both burnt together at one fire, in Smithfield.

I find further upon record, that as the light of the gospel began more and more to appear, and the number of the professors thereof to grow, so persecution increased, and the bishops stirred themselves to keep the truth from increasing and growing. Whereupon ensued great persecutions, and grievous afflictions upon divers in several counties, epecially in Buckinghamshire, Norfolk, Suffolk, and Essex; but although they were thus afflicted outwardly, yet their inward fervency and zeal for the truth were very great, as appeared by their sitting up all night in reading and hearing; and by their expense in giving great prices for a few chapters of James and Paul, in English. And further, their great travels, their earnest seeking, their burning zeal, their reading, their watchings, their sweet assemblies, their love and concord, their godly living, their faithful marrying only with the faithful; all which, it is written, they were faithfully practising and observing, being noted or known among themselves by the name of known men, or just fast men. The bishop of Lincoln, in his inquisitions and examinations of these known men, was so strict and cruel, that he caused the wife to detect the husband, and the husband the wife, the father the daughter, and the daughter the father; brother against brother, and neighbour against neighbour, to witness one against another, and that to death; causing them to swear upon the evangelists, whether they knew the persons to be known men.

Agnis Ashford, being one of the said people, for preaching these words following, was articled against, viz. " we be the salt of the earth, if it be putrefied and vanished away, it is nothing worth; a city set upon a hill may not be hid; ye light not a candle and put it under a bushel, but set it on a candlestick, that it may give a light to all in the house; so shine your light before men, that they may see your works, and glorify your father which is in heaven." And further she did teach, saying, " Jesus seeing his people, as he went up a hill, was set, and his disciples coming to him, he opened his mouth, and taught them, saying, blessed be the poor men in spirit, for the kingdom of heaven is theirs; blessed be mild men, for they shall inherit the earth." For teaching this doctrine, the bishop strictly enjoined and commanded her to teach no more such lessons to any man, especially to her children.

There were three persons accused for sitting up all night, reading in a book of scriptures, in the house of one Durdant, in Iven court, near Stains; and for having certain English books, as Wickliffe's Wicket, in which it was asserted, that man could not make the body of Christ, who made us; another crime was, having some part of the New Testament, and a book called The Prick of Conscience; for these, and such like allegations, did these men greatly suffer; but the Lord's hand worked marvellously amongst them, so that, in a short space, they did exceedingly increase, in such sort, that the bishop was driven to make his complaint to the king, to require his aid to suppress them. The king being then young, and easily incensed with the bishop's suggestions and cruel complaints, sent letters to the sheriffs to aid the bishops a-against these known men, whom he termed heretics. Upon the king's letter, he renewed his former fierceness, and began to shew further violence upon the poor flock of Christ, calling them before his tribunal seat, passing judgment upon some, and committing them to the secular arm to be burnt, namely, Thomas Bernard, James Morden, Robert Rave, John Scrivener, and others; compelling children to set fire to their own fathers: an example of such cruelty as is contrary both to God and nature.

The judicious reader, whose eyes are enlightened, may see what darkness the world was drowned in at this time, the purity of the christian religion being wholly lost, and turned into outward observations, ceremonies, and idolatry, worshipping saints, and making pilgrimages to see the relics, which were as so many lying miracles. Instead of worshipping the living God, they worshipped dead stocks and stones; the pope's laws and canons being more set by, than Christ's testament or the scriptures; laying another foundation than Christ and the apostles laid; upon which, the papists planted their infinite number of masses, dirges, obsequies, matins, hours of singing-service, midnight-rising, barefoot-going, fish-tasting, lent-fast, ember-fast, stations, rogations, jubilees, invocation of saints, praying to images, pilgrimage-walking, vows of chastity, wilful poverty, pardons, indulgences, penance, auricular confessions, shaving, powling, anointing, saying prayers by their beads, making laws that none should wear sumptuous garments, or ouches, or rings on their fingers, but bishops only when they were saying mass. These, with other such like doings, have been set up by the pope's power in the night of apostacy, and people have been forced to swallow it down, though some did it against their consciences; and if the least light appeared in any to testify against their conduct, the beast and false prophet made war with them; and rather than they would fail in extinguishing the truth, they would destroy the persons in whom the least appearance thereof manifested itself, as in the relation before, and hereafter will appear. About this time, there were many eminent men raised up, who were accounted fathers of the protestant church, as Zuinglius,

Oecolempadius, Melancton, and Martin Luther. Luther was a German born; and, being oppressed with the popish idolatry, began to preach against the authority of the pope, and to bring in a reformation of religion; for repressing whom, the council of Trent was called by pope Paul the third, in the year 1542; which council continued about forty years to no purpose; for they made many decrees which caused a great confusion amongst the papists themselves. It is recorded of Luther, that he shined in the church as a bright star, after a long, cloudy, and obscure sky. He preached expressly, that sins are freely remitted for the love of the Son of God, and that we ought faithfully to embrace this bountiful gift. These good beginnings got him great authority, especially seeing his life was also correspondent to his profession, the consideration whereof took place in the hearts of his hearers, some of whom were persons of note. These things, and his preaching against indulgences and pardons, incensing the pope, he put forth a new edict, wherein he declared this to be the Catholic doctrine of the mother church of Rome, prince of all other churches; that bishops of Rome, which are successors of Peter, and vicars of Christ, have this power and authority given to release and dispense; also to grant indulgences available, both for the living, and for the dead, lying in the pains of purgatory. And this doctrine he charged to be received by all faithful christian men, under pain of the great curse and utter separation from all the holy church; whereupon, Luther's books were condemned as heretical, and the pope's legate caused them to be burnt, which Martin Luther hearing of, got a company together at Wittemberg, and making a fire, burnt the pope's decrees and bull then lately sent out against him; for which, the pope accursed him at Rome. Afterwards, he was sent for by the emperor to Wormes, and, though he was much persuaded not to go, he said, " as touching me, since I am sent for, I am resolved, and certainly intend to enter Wormes in the name of our Lord Jesus Christ," and did appear; and according to a promise made by the emperor, he was safely conducted thither, and home again. Before the emperor, he said, " I can affirm no other thing but only this, that I have taught hitherto in simplicity of mind, that which I have thought to tend to God's glory." Being asked, whether he owned these books published in his name; he said, they were his books; but he could not submit his books to the judgment of men, which he had fortified by the authority of scripture, unless they could prove by the scripture the contrary; professing, that except they could convince him by testimonies of the scriptures, (for he did not believe the pope, nor their general councils, which have erred many times, and have contradicted themselves) he could not submit to their judgment.

This opposition, made by Luther, much troubled the pope, especially seeing the followers of Luther to increase; and therefore, he earnestly desired some speedy remedy against the same; and to that end, sent to the German princes to move them thereunto; but the German princes, instead of putting the pope's sentence in execution against Luther and his followers, exhibited at the council of Nuremberg an hundred grievances and oppressions against the court of Rome: as, forbidding marriage to some, forbidding meats, times of marriages restrained, and after released again for money, selling remissions of sins for money, the licentious life of the priests, and their great number of holy-days; and such like other things, as would be too much to mention.

Luther continued, notwithstanding all the opposition against him; twenty nine years a preacher, and at last died in peace in his own country.

But there continued great disputations and reformations in divers parts of Europe, abolising the mass, and all images and foolish ceremonies, making decrees against them, that they should be utterly abandoned. After the preaching of Luther, great troubles and persecutions followed in many parts of the world; and many laws and decrees were made against such as bore testimony against the ignorance and error of those times; whereby many good christians were cruelly handled; and lamentable it is to read, how many poor men were troubled in Germany, France, and England; some being racked, some exiled, some driven to caves in woods, and others burnt to death ; with many other cruel torments. It will be too much to mention every person that suffered in those days for religion ; but some of the chief are as followeth.

In the year 1523, John Esch, and Henry Voes, two young men, for owning the doctrine of Luther, were proceeded against as hereties, being examined by the pope's inquisitors at Lovaine. The greatest thing that they were accused of as error, was, believing that men ought to trust only in God, inasmuch as men are liars, and deceitful in all their words and deeds.   Being condemned, they were led to the place of execution in Bruxels, and went joyfully, saying, they died for the glory of God, and the doctrine of the gospel, as true christians, believing and following the holy church of the son of God, saying also, that it was a day which they had long desired.   Being come to the place of execution, and stripped to their shirts, they stood so a great space, patiently and joyfully enduring whatsoever was done unto them ; praising God, and singing for joy. A doctor standing by, exhorted Henry to take heed so foolishly to glory himself ; to whom he answered, "God forbid that I should glory in any thing, but only in the cross of our Lord Jesus Christ :" another counselled him to have God before his eyes, to whom he said, "I trust, I carry him truly in my heart."

The next that suffered was Henry Stutven, burned in the borders of Germany.   When he was apprehended, they fell upon him in a very great rage and fury, drawing him naked out of his bed, and bound his hands behind him.   When he was brought to Hemmingstead, they asked of him, what his intent was in coming to Diethmar ; unto whom, he gently declared the cause of his coming, which was to preach the gospel.   They all, in a rage, cried out, away with him, away with him, for we will hear him talk no longer.   Then he being very weary and faint, required to be set on horseback, for his feet were all cut and hurt with the ice, because he was led all night bare foot ; but they mocked him, and said he was an heretic, and he should go on foot.   That night, they had him to a man's house, called Calden, and there they bound him in chains in the stocks; but the master of the house being compassionate, would not suffer the cruel deed long; wherefore, he was carried away to a priest's house, and there shut up in a cupboard, and by the rude people mocked and scorned all night: in the morning, about eight of the clock, they gathered together in the market place, to consult what they should do; where the rustic people, boiling in drink, cried out, burn him, burn him, to the fire with the heretic. Then they bound him, hands, feet, and neck; and being brought to the fire, one of the presidents appeared to pass a sentence upon him, to be burnt and consumed with fire. Henry lifting up his hands, said, " Lord, forgive them, for they know not what they do: thy name, O Almighty God, is holy." The fire, as often as it was kindled, would not burn; notwithstanding they satisfied their minds upon him, striking and pricking him with their several kinds of weapons, he standing in his shirt; and when he began to pray, one struck him on the face, saying, " thou shalt first be burnt, and afterwards pray and prate as much as thou wilt:" and thus, this godly preacher finished his martyrdom, which was in the year 1529.

John Clark, of Melden in France, for setting up a paper upon the door of the house of worship, against the pope's pardons, and calling the pope antichrist, was whipped three several days, and marked in the forehead. His mother seeing their cruelty towards her son, constantly and boldly encouraged him, blessing the Lord with a loud voice that he was worthy to suffer. After the execution of the foresaid punishment, the said John Clark removed to Mentz, and there followed his trade, being a wool-comber, where understanding that the people of the city, after the old accustomed manner, worshipped certain blind idols; he being inflamed with th zeal of God against them, went to the place where the images were, and broke them all down in pieces; the next morning, the canons, priests, and monks, accompanied with the people, according to their accustomed manner, went to their idolatrous place of worship, where they found all their blocks and stocks broken to pieces upon the ground, which sight sorely offended them: and searching out for the author of the fact, and John Clark being suspected, was apprehended; and, upon examination, confessed he did it, and shewed them the cause wherefore; and being brought to trial, he defended the pure doctrine of the Son of God, against their images and their false worships, for which, he was condemned. Being led to the place of execution, he there sustained extreme torments; for, first, his right hand was cut off; then, his nose, with sharp pincers, was violently plucked from his face; all which, and much more, he quietly and constantly endured, testifying at the fire against his persecutors, saying, their images were silver and gold, the work only of man's hand.

George Carpenter, of Emering in Bavaria, was burnt to death. When he was led out of the tower, where he was prisoner, before the council, divers friars and monks followed him, to instruct and teach him, whom he willed to tarry at home, and not to follow him. When he came before the council, they read his offences, viz. that he did not believe that a priest could forgive a man his sins; and that he did not believe that God was in the bread which the priests hang over the altar; and that the element of water in baptism doth not give grace. Being urged to revoke these his opinions, and that then he should be set at liberty, and go home to his wife and children; to which, he answered, " my wife and children are so dearly beloved unto me, that they cannot be bought from me for all the riches and possessions of the duke of Bavaria; but, for the love of my Lord God, I can willingly forsake them;" At his execution, a schoolmaster repeating the Lord's prayer, George Carpenter said as followeth; " truly, thou art our father, and no other, this day I trust to be with thee; Oh! my God, how little is thy name hallowed in this world! for this cause, O Father, am I now here, that thy will might be fulfilled, and not mine: the only living bread, Jesus Christ, shall be my food; with a willing mind, do I forgive all men, both my friends and adversaries. Oh! my Lord, without doubt, shalt thou deliver me, for upon thee only have I laid all my hope; in thee alone do I trust, in thee only is all my confidence: I knew that I must suffer persecution, if I did cleave unto Christ, who said, where the heart is, there is the treasure also ; and whatsoever thing a man doth fix in his heart to love above God, that he maketh his idol. And then being cast into the fire by the hangman, he joyfully yielded up his spirit unto God.

Weendel Muta, a widow of Holland, receiving the truth of the gospel into her heart, was apprehended and committed to the castle of Werden ; and from thence shortly after was brought to the Hague to trial, where certain monks were appointed to talk with her, to win her to recant but she constantly persisted in the truth in which she was planted. A woman of her acquaintance coming to prison to visit her, said to her, " why dost not thou keep silence, and think secretly in thine heart these things which thou believest, that thou mayst prolong thy life here ?" " O ! (said the widow) you know not what you say, it is written, with the heart we believe to righteousness ; with the tongue, we confess to salvation." At her execution, she commended herself into the hands of God ; and, after a fervent prayer, was burnt to death.

About this time, there suffered many more in Germany for the witness of the gospel, viz. John Pistorius, coming from Wittemberg, for speaking against the mass and pardons, and against the subtil abuses of the priests. He was committed to prison, with ten malefactors, whom he comforted : to one of whom being half naked, and in danger of cold, he gave his gown. His father visiting him in prison, did not dissuade him, but bade him be constant. Being condemned, and coming to the stake, he gave his neck willingly to the band wherewith he was first strangled ; and was then burned, saying at his death, " O death ! where is thy victory ?"

There using to be a great meeting near Antwerp, where one used to preach to a great number of people ; of which, Charles the emperor hearing, gave leave to any that would to take the uppermost garment of all them that came to hear, and offered thirty guilders to him that would take the preacher ; afterwards, when the people

x

were gathered, and their usual minister being not there, one Nicholas, of Antwerp, stood up, and preached to the people ; wherefore, being apprehended by a butcher's servant, he was put in a sack, and drowned at the crane at Antwerp, 1524.

Some of the city of Lovaine, were suspected of Lutheranism, and the emperor's procurator came from Brussels thither to make inquisition ; after which inquisition, certain bands of armed men came and beset their houses in the night, where many were taken in their beds, plucked from their wives and children, and sent to divers prisons, through the terror whereof, many citizens revolted from the gospel, and returned again to idolatry ; but twenty eight remained constant in that persecution, unto whom the doctors and inquisitor of Lovaine resorted, disputing with them, and thinking either to confound, or convert them ; but so strongly the spirit of the Lord wrought with the saints, that the doctors went rather confounded away themselves. When they saw disputing would not do, they used cruel torments to enforce them. One of them was condemned to perpetual prison, which was a dark and stinking dungeon, where he was neither suffered to write nor read, nor any man to come at him, and commanded only to be fed with bread and water. Two of the said prisoners were also burnt; receiving with constantcy their martyrdom.

There were an old man, and two aged women, brought forth, of whom the one was called Antonia, born of an ancient stock in that city. These were condemned, the man to be beheaded, and the two women to be buried alive ; which death they received very cheerfully ; and the rest of the prisoners, that would not abjure the doctrine of Luther, were put to the fire.

One Percival, of Lovaine, for owning the truth, was adjudged to perpetual imprisonment : there to be fed only with bread and water ; which punishment he took patiently for Christ's sake. He was secretly made away with, either famished or drowned, no man could learn how.

Justus Jusberge, a skinner in Lovaine, in the year 1544, for having a new testament in his house, was persecuted by one Darsardus, and committed to prison ; and the gaoler was commanded that none should speak with him; shortly after, the doctors examined him, touching the pope's supremacy, sacrifice of the mass, purgatory, &c. ; wereunto he answered plainly and boldly, confirming his answers by the scriptures. When they saw he would not be moved from his faith, then they condemned him to be burnt; but as a pretended favour to him, he was only beheaded.

Giles Tilman, of Brussels, cutler, born of honest parents, at about the age of thirty years, began to receive the light of the gospel, for which he was very zealous and fervent. He was in his nature very mild and pitiful, passing all others in those parts, giving whatsoever he had to spare to the poor, and living only upon his trade. He was persecuted by the priest of Brussels, being taken at Lovaine spreading that religion which the pope called heresy. His adversaries used great care to make him abjure, but being a man of a singular wit, and constant in his religion, they went away many times with shame. After he had been kept eight months in prison, he was sent to Brussels to be judged, where finding Franciscus Ensenes, and others of the same religion, in prison, he exhorted them to be constant to the truth, that they might receive the crown that was prepared for them. When the gray friars, being sent unto him, would miscal and abuse him, he ever held his peace at such private injuries ; wherefore, they reported he had a dumb devil in him. He might have several times escaped out of prison, the doors being set open, but he would not. Being removed to another prison, and on the twenty-second of the month called January, 1544, he was condemned to be burnt privately ; for openly they durst not do it, for fear of the people, he being so well beloved. When tidings were brought him of his sentence, " he thanked God, that the hour was come wherein he might glorify the Lord ;" and being had to the fire, he willingly resigned up his life into the hands of the Lord.

Great persecution in Gaunt, and other parts of Flanders,
Annis 1543, *and* 1544.

CHARLES the emperor lying in Gaunt, the friars and
doctors obtained, that the edict made against the Lutherans might be read openly twice a year, which caused a
great persecution to follow ; so that there was no city or
town in all Flanders, wherein some were not either expulsed, beheaded, condemned to perpetual imprisonment,
or their goods confiscated, without respect either to age
or sex, especially at Gaunt, where some of the chief
men in the town were burnt for their religion.

Afterwards, the emperor coming to Brussels, there
also were terrible slaughters and persecutions of God's
people, namely in Brabant, Honeygrow, and Artois, the
horror and cruelty whereof are almost incredible ; insomuch that two hundred men and women were brought
out of the country into the city, some of whom were
drowned, some buried quickly, some privately destroyed
and others sent to perpetual imprisonment, whereby the
prisons were filled, to the great sorrow of them which
knew the gospel, the professors whereof being now compelled either to deny the same, or confirm it with their
blood; the history whereof was at large set forth by Francis Ensenes, in Latin, who himself was a prisoner at the
same time in Brussels for the truth's sake.

Martin Hœurblock, fishmonger in Gaunt, 1545, being
converted to the truth from the superstitious idolatry of
the Papists, and a great change wrought in him, having
all his time till then lived a wicked and fleshly life, was a
wonder to his neighbours to see such a sudden change.
The Franciscan friars, who before knew him, remembering how beneficial he had been to them, now seeing him
so altered, and taking notice of his visiting the prisoners,
and comforting them in persecution, and confirming them
that went to the fire, they soon caused him to be detected and imprisoned ; and, with grievous and sharp torments, would have constrained him to discover more of
the same religion ; to whom he answered ; " that if they
could prove by the scripture, that his detecting and ac-

cusing his brethren, whom they would afflict with the like torments, were not against the law of God, then he would not refuse to prefer the honour of God before the safeguard of his brethren." But he was soon after had to the council in Flanders, where the causes laid against him were, the sacrament, purgatory, &c. for which, he was condemned and burnt at Gaunt, all his goods being confiscated.

Nicholas and Francis Thiesten, Anno 1545, for standing firm in the truth, and bearing witness against the church of Rome, and their auricular confession, purgatory, &c. were condemned to be burnt; and coming to the place of execution, for exhorting the people, they put wooden gags in their mouths. When they were fastened to the stake, they patiently endured the fire. The mother of these two men was for her steadfastness to the truth condemned to perpetual imprisonment.

Adrian Taylor, and Marion his wife, of Dornick, Anno 1545, by reason of the emperor's decree at Wormes against the Lutherans, were apprehended and persecuted. Adrian, not so strong as a man, for fear gave back, and was only beheaded: the wife, stronger than a woman, withstood their threats; and abode the uttermost; and being enclosed in an iron grate, formed in the shape of a pasty, was laid in the earth, and buried quickly. When the adversaries first told her, that her husband had relented, she believed them not, but as she was going to the place where she was to die, passing by the tower where he was, she called to him to take her leave, but he was gone before.

Peter Bruly, of Stratsburg, at the earnest request of faithful brethren, went down to visit the lower counties about Artois, which the magistrates of Dornick hearing, shut the gates of the town, and made search for him three days. He was privately let down the wall in the night by a basket; and as he was let down into the ditch, ready to take his way, one of them which let him down, leaning over the wall, to bid him farewell, caused, unawares, a stone to slip out of the wall, which falling upon him, broke his leg; by reason whereof, he was heard by the

watchmen, complaining of his wound, and so was taken.
As long as he remained in prison, he ceased not to preach
the truth to all that came unto him ; and he wrote his
own confession, and examination, and sent it to the brethren.   He wrote also another epistle to them that were in
persecution ; another to all the faithful ; and another letter he wrote to his wife, the same day he was burned.
He remained four months in prison, before he was sentenced to be burnt.   Letters were sent from duke Frederick, of the Landsgrave, to entreat for him ; but he was
burnt before the letters came.

Peter Moice being converted to the truth, by Peter
Bruly, was apprehended and let down into a deep dungeon, under the castle-ditch, which was full of filthy vermine.   The friars coming to examine him, he told them,
" whilst he lived an ungodly life, they never concerned
themselves with him, but, now for favouring the word of
God, they sought his blood."   Being brought before the
senate, he would have boldly answered to what they objected against him, but they interrupted him ; to whom,
he said, " if you will not suffer me to answer for myself,
send me back to prison among the toads and frogs, which
will not interrupt me, while I talk with my God."   And
continuing constant in the truth, he was at last burnt to
death.

Nicholas Frenchman, having been at Geneva, intended to go into England ; but in his way, was apprehended by the lieutenant of Dornick ; and, being bound
hands and feet, was brought to Burgis, and there laid in
a dungeon.   The friars, when they came to examine
him, went away in a shameful rage, saying, " he had a
devil ;" and crying, " to the fire with him."   Soon after, the judges condemned him to be burnt to ashes ; at
which sentence, he blessed the Lord, which had counted
him to be a witness in the cause of his beloved son. Going to the place of execution, he was threatened, that if
he spake, they would put a wooden-ball in his mouth ;
nevertheless, being at the stake, he minded not their
threats, but cried out with a loud voice, saying, " Oh
Charles ! Charles ! how long shall thy heart be harden-

ed ?" with that, one of the soldiers gave him a blow; then he said, " O! miserable people, who are not worthy, to whom the word of God should be preached." Then the friars cried out, " he hath a devil." To whom he said, " depart from me all you wicked, for the Lord hath heard the voice of my weeping." So, in the midst of the fire he commended his spirit unto God, and ended this life.

Bertrand le Blais, at Dornick, in the year 1555, suffered lamentably; his torments being almost incredible, and his constancy admirable. He being a silk-weaver, and having something upon his spirit, set his house in order; and desired his wife and brother to pray, that God would establish him in his enterprise, that he was going about; which was upon Christmas-day (so called). He went to the high place, at Dornick, where he took the cake out of the priest's hands, as if he would have lifted it over his head, at mass, and stamped it under his feet, saying, " that he did it to shew the glory of that God, and what power he hath." At the sight hereof, the people were amazed; and he hardly escaped with his life. It was not long, before the governor of the castle heard of this passage, who, like a mad-man, threatened he should be an example to all posterity. Bertrand being brought before him, he asked him, if he repented of his fact? He answered, " no: and if he had a hundred lives he would give them in the quarrel." Then was he thrice put to the torture, and tormented most miserably. Then they passed sentence against him, and this was executed: first, he was drawn from the castle of Dornick to the market-place, having a ball of iron put in his mouth: then he was set upon a stage, where his right-hand was crushed and pressed between two hot irons, with sharp edges; in the like manner, they served his right foot; which torments he endured with marvellous constancy; that being done, they took the ball of iron out of his mouth, and cut out his tongue. Notwithstanding his tongue was cut out, he still called upon God, as well as he could, whereby the hearts of the people were greatly moved; whereupon the tormentors thrust the iron ball into his mouth again : from thence, they brought him down to a lower stage ; where his legs and hands were bound behind him, with an iron chain going about his body ; and so he was let down flat upon the fire. The governor standing by, caused him to be plucked up again, and so down, and up again, till at last this whole body was consumed to ashes.

James Faber, and three others, suffered at Valens. Faber being an old man, said, "that though he could not answer, nor satisfy them in reasoning, yet he would constantly abide in the truth of the gospel."

Godfrey Hamell, a tailor, was taken and condemned at Dornick, by the name of an heretic : "nay, said he, not an heretic, but a servant of Jesus Christ." When the hangman went about to strangle him, to diminish his punishment, he refused, saying, "that he would abide the sentence that the judges had given."

Besides those that suffered in Germany before mentioned, there were great numbers, both in the higher and lower countries of Germany, who were put to death for religion. Many of them were burnt ; some buried alive ; and others secretly drowned ; whose names are mentioned in the "Acts and Monuments," and which I have omitted for brevity's sake.

Sufferers in France, for bearing the like witness to the gospel.

DENNIS RENNIX, at Melde, in the year 1558, was burnt for testifying against the mass. He was always used to have in his mouth the words of Christ, "he that denieth me before men, him will I also deny before my Father." He was burnt in a slow fire, and suffered cruel torments.

Upon a complaint made to the council, called Le Chamber Ardante, that the judges suffered heretics to have their tongues ; a decree was immediately made, that all who were to be burned, unless they recanted at the fire, should have their tongues cut off, which law afterwards was strictly observed.

Stephen Polliard coming out of Normandy, (where he was born) in the year 1546, to Meux, tarried there not long; but he was compelled to flee; and went to a town called Frea, where he was apprehended and brought to Paris; and there cast into a foul and dark prison; in which prison, he was kept in bonds and fetters a long time; and saw almost no light. At length, being called for before the senate; and his sentence given to have his tongue cut out, and to be burnt alive, his satchel of books hanging about his neck; "O Lord," said he, " is the world in blindness and darkness still ?" For he thought, being in prison so long, that the world had been altered from its old darkness to better knowledge. At last, with his books about his neck, he was burnt to death.

Florent Venote remained a prisoner in Paris four years; during which time, he was put to divers torments. One kind of torment was, he was put into a narrow place, so strait that he could neither stand, nor lie, which they called the hose, or boots, because it was strait below, and wide above. In this, he remained seven weeks, where the tormentors affirmed, that no thief or murderer could endure fifteen days, but was in danger of life or madness; and at last, on the ninth of the month, called July, he was burnt to death, with divers other martyrs, who were burnt as a spectacle at the king's coming into Paris.

The next that suffered, was a poor tailor in Paris, who, for working upon holy-days (so called,) and for denying to observe them, was clapped in prison. The king hearing of it, sent for him before him, and some of his peers. Being before the king, he answered with great boldness, wit, and memory, defending the cause of Christ; neither flattering their persons, nor fearing their threats, which struck the king in a great damp, in musing in his mind; which the bishop seeing, committed the poor tailor again to the hands of the officer, saying, " he was a stubborn fellow, and fitter to be punished, than to be marvelled at." A few days after, he was condemned to be burnt alive.

The next year, two men, for friendly admonishing a certain priest, who, in his sermon, abused the name of God,

Y

were both burned. Another young man, of the age of eight en years, for rebuking a man in Paris for swearing, being suspected to be a Lutheran, was apprehended, and brought before the council at Paris, who committed him to prison; where he was so cruelly racked and tormented, that one of the persecutors seeing it, could not but turn his back and weep. When he was brought, and put in the fire, he was plucked up again upon the gibbet; and was asked, whether he would turn? to which, he said, " that he was in his way towards God; and therefore, desired them to let him go."

John Joyer, and his servant, being a young man, in the year 1552, coming from Geneva to their country with certain books, were apprehended by the way; and had to Tholouse, where the master was condemned. The servant being young, was not so prompt to answer, but directed them to his master to answer them. When they were brought to the stake, the young man first going up, began to weep; the master fearing lest he should recant, ran to him, and he was comforted. As they were in the fire, the master standing upright to the stake, shifted the fire from him to his servant, being more careful for him than for himself; and when he saw him dead, he bowed down himself in the flame, and so expired.

Matthias Dimonetus, merchant, at Lyons, in the year 1553, having been a man of a vicious and detestable life, was, notwithstanding, through the grace of God, brought to the knowledge and savour of his truth; for a testimony of which, he was soon after imprisoned. Being in prison, he had great conflicts with the infirmity of his own flesh, but especially with the temptation of his parents, brethren, and kinsfolk, and the great sorrow of his mother; nevertheless the Lord so assisted him, that he endured to the end, and was burnt to death.

In the year 1558, the fourth day of the month, called September, there was a company of the faithful, to the number of three or four hundred, met together, at Paris, in a certain house. In the beginning of the night, they were discovered by some priests; and the house was soon beset; and the city was in an uproar, many being in an extreme rage, furiously seeking to have their blood. At the suddenness of this thing, the people were struck in great fear, and fell to prayer. About six or seven score of them having weapons, escaped through the multitude, save only one, who was knocked down with stones, and destroyed. The women remaining in the house, were taken by the magistrates, and had to prison. In their passing to the prison, they were plucked and haled by the rude multitude, who tore their garments, pulled off their hoods, and disfigured their faces with dirt. They were accused to the king, by a priest, that they put out the candles in their meetings, and that they maintained, that there was no God; and denied the divinity and humanity of Christ, the immortality of the soul, and the resurrection of the body. &c. These things a lying doctor charged on them, without any proof, moving the king and people to destroy them; and shortly after, a commission was directed out by the king to certain counsellors to try and give judgment upon the aforesaid sufferers; a particular relation of whose execution, is at large inserted by my author; but there being little material, either in their trial, or execution, I thought not meet to insert.

About this time, many suffered martyrdom, under the cruel and bloody inquisition in Spain, first begun by king Ferdinandus, and Elizabeth his wife. The Spanish priests maintain, that the holy and sacred inquisition, as they call it, cannot err, and that the holy fathers, the inquisitors, cannot be deceived. If one be apprehended as a favourer of heretics, he is carried and put into a horrible prison, and none permitted to come to him, but there he is kept alone in a place, where he cannot see so much as the ground, and often whipped, scourged, put in irons, tortured, and racked, sometimes brought out and shewed in some higher place to the people, as a spectacle of rebuking infamy; and thus some are detained there many years, and murdered by long torments, by which they are more cruelly executed, than if they were at once slain by the hangman; during all their time of imprisonment, whatsoever process is done against them, no person knows it, but only the holy fathers and tormentors, which are sworn to execute the torments; all the proceedings of the court of that execrable inquisition, are done in secret; by the rigor of which inquisition, many good men have been destroyed, both in Spain and Italy.

In the kingdom of Naples, in the year 1560, in the time of Pope Pius the fourth, was begun a hot persecution against the protestants, many men and their wives being slain.

Likewise, in the same year, in Calabria, the number of eighty-eight persons, both old and young, suffered, for the protestant religion, by the papists : all of whom were put together in one house, and taken out one after another, and laid upon the butcher's stall, like sheep in the shambles; and with one bloody knife, they were all killed ; a spectacle most tragical for all posterity to remember, and almost incredible to believe ; but it is confirmed by two epistles of sufficient credit, which are at large inserted in the Book of Martyrs.

The next matter to be treated of, is the great persecution and destruction of the people of Merindol and Cabries, in the county of Provence; where not a few persons, but whole villages and townships, with the most of the men, women, and children, were put to all kinds of cruelty ; and suffered martyrdom for the profession of the gospel.

From the year 1200, they had refused the bishop of Rome's authority ; for which, they were often accused and complained of, to the king, as contemners and despisers of the magistrates, and as rebels ; wherefore, they were called by divers names, according to the countries and places where they dwelt ; for, in the country about Lyons, they were called the poor people of Lyons: in the borders of Sarmaria and Livonia, and in other countries towards the north, they were called Lollards; in Flanders and Artois, Turrelupines, from a desert where wolves haunt ; in Dauphin with great despite, they were called Chagnars, because they lived in places open to the sun, without house or harbour ; but most commonly, they were called Waldows, from Waldow, who first instructed them in the word of God, as before is related ;

which name continued till the name of Lutherans came up, which, above all others, was most hated and abhorred.

Notwithstanding these most spiteful reproaches and slanders, the people dwelling at the foot of the Alps, and in Merindol and Cabries, always lived so Godly, uprightly, and justly, that in all their lives and conversation, there appeared to be in them a great fear of God; and that little light of true knowledge, which God had given them, they laboured by all means to kindle and increase daily more and more, sparing no charges, whether it were to purchase the scriptures in their own language, to encourage one another in godliness, or travelling into other countries, even to the farthest parts of the earth, where they had heard that any light of the gospel began to shine.

But the more zealous these people were for a reformation in their religion, the more did the fury and rage of persecution stir in the bishops, priests, and monks, in all Provence, against them. Amongst the rest, one Jo. de Roma, a monk, obtaining a commission to examine those that were suspected to be of the Waldow or Lutheran profession, forthwith ceased not to afflict the faithful with all kinds of cruelty that he could devise or imagine: amongst other horrible torments, this was one, which he most delighted in, and most commonly practised: he filled boots with boiling grease, and put them upon their legs, tying them backward, to a form with their legs hanging down over a small fire, and so he examined them. Thus he tormented very many; and in the end, most cruelly put them to death. This cruelty coming to the French king's ears, he was much digusted; wherefore, he wrote to the parliament at Provence, that the monk might be apprehended and punished; but he conveyed himself away. The Lord, not long after, smote him with a most horrible and strange sickness, his body being tormented with pain, and he could get no help. Being had to an hospital, his flesh rotted away, and stunk so that none cared to come near him: and in this rage and torment, he often cried out, " who will deliver me ?

Who will kill me, and deliver me out of these torments and pains, which I know I suffer for the evils and oppressions that I have done to the poor men?" And, in this anguish, he most miserably ended his unhappy days.

After the death of this persecuting monk, the bishop of Aix, by his official, continued the persecution, and put a great multitude of them in prison, of whom, some by force of torments revolted from the truth; and the others, who proved constant, after he had condemned them of heresy, were put into the hands of the ordinary judge, who at that time was one Merianus, a cruel persecutor, and who, without any form of process, or order of law, put such as the official had pronounced to be heretics, to death with most cruel torments.

After this persecutor was dead, one Bartholomew Casenes, president of the parliament of Provence, became a a pestilent persecutor, whom God at length struck with a fearful and sudden death. In the time of this tyrant, those of Merindol were cited personally to appear before the king's attorney; but they hearing that the court had determined to burn them, without any process or order of law, durst not appear at the day appointed; for which cause, the court awarded a cruel sentence against Merindol, and condemned all the inhabitants to be burned, men, women, and children, and their town and houses to be razed to the ground, and their country to be made a desert and wilderness, never more to be inhabited. This bloody arrest or decree seemed strange and wonderful, some openly saying, " they marvelled that the parliament should be so mad as to give out an arrest so manifestly injurious and unjust, and contrary to all reason and humanity;" others said, " the judges are not bound to observe either right or reason in extirpating such as are suspected to be Lutherans :" but whatever was said in opposition to this decree, the bishops, from time to time, used all the opportunities to endeavour to put the same in execution, as appears in the following relation.

Amongst these poor men that suffered in Merindol, there was a bookseller, who, for setting publicly to sale certain bibles in French and Latin, in the sight of the bishop of Aix, and other prelates, was apprehended, and and committed to prison ; and afterwards, was sentenced and burnt. The prelates seeing great dissension among the people of Avinion ; and that many murmured at the death of this bookseller, for selling the bible, to scare the people, the next day, they put out a proclamation against all French bibles, that none should keep them in their hands, upon pain of death.

After this proclamation, the bishop of Aix endeavoured his utmost to persecute the people of Merindol, being very earnest with the president to that effect, and to put the parliament's arrest and decree in execution. The president, shewing himself unwilling to the bishop to shed innocent blood, pleaded, " the king would be displeased to have such destruction made of his subjects." Then said the bishop, '· though the king, at the first, do think it ill done, we will so bring it to pass, that in a short space, he should think it well done ; for we have the cardinals on our side, especially the cardinal of Tournon."

By these arguments of the bishop, the president and council of the parliament were persuaded to raise a force, and destroy the people of Merindol, according to the decree. The inhabitants of Merindol hearing thereof, and seeing nothing but present death to be at hand, with great lamentation commended themselves and their cause unto God, by prayer, and made themselves ready to be murdered, as sheep for the slaughter. Whilst they were in this grievous distress, there was one raised up, called the Lord of Alner, to plead with the president on their behalf, giving the president several reasons, why he ought not to destroy these poor chirstian men of Merindol ; by which reasons, the president was persuaded, and immediately called back his commission which he had given out ; and caused the army to retire, which was within a mile and a half of Merindol ; the people of Merindol understanding, that the army was retired, gave thanks unto God, comforting one another with admonition and exhortation, always to have the fear of God before their eyes, and to seek after the everlasting riches.

The noise of these proceedings, and of this arrest and decree, coming to the king of France's ears, he appointed persons to make inquiry into the whole matter, and to make a report to him thereof, and what manner of people these Merindolians were.

These deputies brought a copy of the arrest, decree, and proceedings, to the king's lieutenant, declaring unto him the great injuries, polling, extortions, exactions, tyrannies, and cruelties, which the judges, as well secular as ecclesiastical, had used against them of Merindol and others. They reported, touching the behaviour and disposition of those who were persecuted, " that the most part of the men of Provence affirmed them to be men given to great labour and travel ; and that about two hundred years past, (as is reported) they came out of the country of Piedmont, to dwell in Provence, and took to tillage, and to inhabit many villages destroyed by the wars, which they had so well husbanded, that there was now great store of wine, oil, honey. and cattle, so that strangers were greatly relieved ; and that they were a peaceable, quiet people, beloved of all their neighbours, men of good behaviour, constant in keeping their promise, and paying their debts, without suing men at law ; that they were also charitable men, giving alms, relieving the poor, suffering none amongst them to lack, or to be in necessity, harbouring and nourishing poor strangers and passengers, in their necessities." Moreover, " that they were known by this throughout all the country, that they would not swear ; and that, if they heard any swear, blaspheme, or dishonour God, they straightways departed out of their company." This was the tenor of the report made by the king's lieutenant, touching the life and behaviour of these inhabitants of Merindol, who were persecuted by the popish bishops and cardinals ; of which, the lieutenant advertised the king, who was a good prince; and moved with mercy and pity, sent letters to the parliament, expressly charging and commanding them, that they should not, hereafter, proceed to prosecute the said arrest and decree so rigorously, as they had done before, against this people, and not to molest or trouble them in person or goods ; and to command them to set at liberty all prisoners, who either were accused or suspected of Lutheranism ; and withal included in his letter, that if any of them should be convicted of heresy, by the scriptures of the Old and New Testament, they should be caused to abjure.

Notwithstanding this letter was written in favour to the people of Merindol, yet the bishop of Cavaillon took advantage of one part of it, to prosecute his malice against them ; for, upon the king's letter, the parliament ordained, that John Durand, counsellor of the parliament, the secretary, and the bishop of Cavaillon, with a doctor of divinity, should go to Merindol, and there declare to the inhabitants the errors and heresies, which they knew to be contained in their confession of their faith, and make them apparent by good and sufficient information ; and having so convicted them, by the word of God, they should make them renounce and abjure the said heresies ; and, if they refused to abjure, then to make report thereof, that the court might appoint how to proceed against them. The bishop of Cavaillon would not tarry till the time appointed by the court, for the execution of this matter ; but he himself, with a doctor, went to Merindol, to make them abjure ; and they refusing, he grew very angry with them.

Shortly after, John Durand , counsellor of the parliament, went to execute the commission, according to order, to whom the bailiff of Merindol said, " it seemeth unto me, that there is no due form of process in this judgment ; for there is no party here, that doth accuse us ; if we had any accuser present, who, according to the rule of the scripture, either should prove by good demonstration, out of the New and Old Testaments, that of which we are accused ; or, if he were not able, should suffer punishment due unto such as are heretics ; I think he will be as greatly troubled to maintain his accusation, as we to answer unto the same."

Thus, things debated for some time; but the bishop and doctor were much confounded ; and the inhabitants of Merindol enjoyed rest and quiet for a space, until John

z

Miniers, an exceeding bloody tyrant, began a new persecution. He put five or six of his own tenants into a cistern under the ground, and closing it up, he kept them there, till they died with hunger, pretending that they were Lutherans ; but it was to get their goods and possessions. By these practices, this wretch grew great and wealthy, and became president of the parliament, and lieutenant-general in the country of Provence. He employed all his powers to obtain letters patent from the king, to prosecute the decree against the people of Merindol, which, by the help of the cardinal of Tournon, he did obtain. After this, he gathered all the king's army, and employed them to the destruction of Merindol, Cabries, and other towns, to the number of twenty-two, giving commission, to spoil, ransack, burn, and destroy all together, and to kill man, woman, and child without mercy. The people of Merindol, seeing all in a flame round about them, left their houses, and fled into the woods, carrying their children upon their shoulders a day's journey ; but the way through which they were to pass, being rough and cumbersome, they thought it expedient to leave the women and children behind, hoping that the enemy would shew mercy to them, being destitute of all succour. No tongue can express, what sorrow, what tears, what sighings, and what lamentations there were at that woful parting, when they were compelled to be thus separated ; the husband from his wife, the father from his tender children, and never like to see each other again. They had not gone far, when the enemy suddenly came upon them, and, finding them assembling together at prayer, spoiled them of all that they had : some they ravished ; and others they scourged, practising what cruelty and villainy they could devise against them ; the women being in number about five hundred. Miniers caused thirty men to be carried into a meadow, and there to be miserably cut and hewed to pieces by soldiers; and he had forty women put in a barn full of straw, and the barn was set on fire, which destroyed them. Of those that were so unmercifully murdered by this bloody tyrant, there were about one thousand persons, men, women, and

children.   It is inexpressible, how lamentably and cruelly these poor people were persecuted, insomuch that no
kind of cruelty and tyranny was left unpractised ; for
they that escaped into the woods and mountains, being
taken, were either slain out-right, or put in the galleys and
made slaves.   Some were famished in rocks and caves
with hunger ;   and thus it continued, till God, by his
just judgments, cut off the bloody tyrant Miniers, by
death.

*The persecution of the Waldenses in Angrogna, Lu-
cerne, Perouse, Piedmont, and other places, from the
year 1555, to 1561.*

THOUGH these people, by long persecution, were
driven from place to place ; and in all places, were afflicted ; yet they were not utterly destroyed, and would never yield to the superstitions of the popish religion, but
abstained from their idolatry.   They had many books of
the New Testament translated into their own language ;
they lived, in great simplicity, by the sweat of their
brows ; and they were quiet and peaceable among their
neighbours, abstaining from oaths, games, dancing, and
filthy songs.   The said people, at Angrogna, having
drawn up a confession of their faith, it was by learned
men, at the king's court, condemned as heretical ; wherefore, the king required them to give obedience to the
church of Rome, on pain of loss of goods and life : and
to give their answer in three days ; but, upon some of
the German princes interceding with the French king,
on their behalf, and desiring him to show some pity to
these churches, they were not molested for three years ;
only one of their ministers, viz. Jeffery Varnigle, who
travelled from place to place, was apprehended, and suffered martyrdom.   But the pope envying this liberty, obtained through the moderation of the German princes,
who entreated on their behalf, he stirred up the duke of
Savoy against them (who in his own nature was rather in-

clined to let them live in quietness,) telling him, " that he ought to banish the Waldenses, for they were a rebellious people against the holy mother, the church." These instigations caused great persecutions on these poor people : for, soon after, several of them were burnt ; many fled, and their houses were ransacked ; some were taken and sent to the galleys ; and proclamations were put out, that none should go to their assemblies, on pain of death. In the midst of this suffering, they thought the best way to put a stop, was to send to the duke a declaration of their religion, and wherefore they suffered, which they did, withal declaring, " that, if by the word of God, it could be proved, that they were in error, they should not be obstinate, but be reformed, &c." After this, the persecution seemed somewhat to abate for a time ; but in the month called June, following, it was first proposed to them, to put away their ministers that were strangers; which they refusing to do, it was then commanded, in the duke's name, that they should banish from them all their ministers that were strangers. A new proclamation was put out, persecution began afresh, and many of the said people were slain, and many imprisoned, and cruelly handled ; the monks being very active in this persecution ; in one place, causing two women to carry faggots to the fire, where their minister was burnt, and to speak these words to him : " Take this, thou wicked heretic, in recompense of the naughty doctrine thou hast taught us." To whom, he said, "ah! good women, I have taught you well, but you have learned ill." Great were the havoc and ruin they made upon these poor people's estates and bodies, in this persecution. And not long after, an army was raised to destroy the Waldows ; which they hearing, their ministers met with the chief rulers, to advise what, in such an extremity, it was best to do. Upon due consideration, they concluded not to defend themselves by force of arms, but to flee to the mountains, and carry their goods with them. Others of the ministers, hearing of the resolution, that they at Angrogna and Lucerne had made, thought it strange, that they might not defend themselves, against their enemies' violence, in so just a cause, knowing that it was the pope and his ministers who were the cause of their troubles. And some stood in their own defence, and made great slaughter upon their enemies at times; and when they pursued their enemies, they often retired to avoid shedding blood, meaning only to defend themselves : and they held their adversaries so tightly to it, that they were at last brought to make a peace, upon articles and conditions, so that the persecution was stopped; and the pride, malice, and rage of their adversaries were abated.

Thus, having given a brief account, of the troubles and persecutions, sustained by the faithful martyrs, in foreign parts, it remains to give a farther relation, of such as suffered in England, in this king's reign.

After the light of the gospel began to shine and increase, beyond sea, the beams of it began to spread and grow more in England; and a great stir and alteration followed in the hearts of many, so that coloured hypocrisy and painted holiness began to be spied more and more, by such as in any measure tasted of the truth : and some there were that could distinguish Christ from antichrist : amongst whom, was one Simon Fish, of Gray's Inn, who wrote a sharp book, entitled, "The Supplication of beggars, against the corruption of the clergy ;" which book was written beyond sea, he having fled thither for fear of cardinal Woolsey, who had taken a distaste against him; in this book, was shewn what a great oppression the priests and clergy were to the nation; and that they had got into their hands more than a third part of the realm, besides their tithes of all the increase of corn, hay, &c. The book being read to the king, after a pause, he said, " If a man should pull down an old stone wall, and begin at the lower part, the upper part thereof might chance to fall on his head ;" and he took the book, and put it in his desk, and seemed to be pleased with it ; for he encouraged Simon Fish's wife, to send for her husband to come before him ; but notwithstanding he liked it, he would make no show of it openly ; for that book, and others, being spread about London, the cardinal acquainted the king therewith, and bade him beware of them; and the cardinal and bishop of London consulted, how they might stop the mischief that might accrue by that and other books, being spread about. Whereupon they agreed, that the bishop of London should send forth a proclamation to call in the New Testament, translated into English; the Supplication of Beggars; the Revelation of Antichrist, by Martin Luther; and other books in English. This was one way they took, by which they thought to have suppressed the growth of those they accounted heretics; but not thinking that sufficient, they obtained a proclamation from the king to suppress the sectaries, heretics, and Lollards, and for abolishing divers of their books, in English. The bishops having now what they would have, there was no diligence wanting on their part, for putting the same in execution; whereupon ensued a grievous persecution and slaughter of the faithful.

The first that went to wreck was Thomas Bilney, who, after his examination and condemnation, by Dr. Pell's chancellor, was committed to the sheriffs of the city of Norwich. A day before his execution, some friends being with him, comforted him, that though he was to go through the fire, the Lord would refresh him in it. At this, he put his finger in the candle, (as he used to do divers times) saying, " I know the fire is hot; and my body shall be wasted by it; and it is a pain for the time;" but he would often rehearse this scripture for his comfort; " fear not, for I have redeemed thee, I have called thee by thy name: thou art mine; when thou passet through the waters, I will be with thee: when thou walkest through the fire, thou shalt not be burnt; neither shall the flame kindle upon thee; for I am the Lord thy God, the holy one of Israel, thy Saviour." Going to execution, he said, "the mariner, for a while, meets with a troubled sea; and is tossed with the waves; but he is in hopes, when he comes to the haven, he shall be at quiet; I doubt not (though I feel storms) but by God's grace, I shall attain to the haven." And being brought to the stake, he very patiently endured the fire till death.

The next that suffered was Richard Bayfield, who received the truth, in a measure, and for reading the Testament in English, and a book called " The Wicked Mammon," &c. he was cast into prison, and there severely whipped, with a gag in his mouth, and then stocked, and continued in prison three quarters of a year ; and then was set at liberty ; but was soon after taken again, and put in the coal-house, where he was tied by the neck, middle, and legs, standing upright by the wall. This punishment was inflicted on him, to make him confess who bought his books ; but he accused none, stood to his religion, and told them he would dispute for his faith. At his trial, he was accused of divers things ; but the chief were, for bringing books over from beyond sea, and spreading them in England. On the twentieth day of November, 1532, he was had into the choir of Paul's cathedral ; where the bishop of London, with other prelates, passed sentence on him, and he was delivered to the sheriffs of London, to be carried to Newgate; and from thence, to the place of execution ; but first, the sheriffs were commanded to have him into the vestry, and to bring him forth again in antichrist's apparel, to be degraded, having been a monk. Then the bishop took his crosier and smote him on the breast, by which he threw him down backwards, and broke his head, and he swooned ; but coming to himself again, he thanked God, that he was delivered from this malignant church of antichrist ; and being led to Newgate, after one hour's respite, he was had to the fire and burnt.

John Tewksberry, leather-seller, of London, was converted by the reading of the Testament in English, and the book called " The Wicked Mammon." In the month, called April, in the year 1529, he was brought before the bishop of London, in the open consistory ; where he disputed with the bishops and the prelates, concerning his faith ; and was very expert and prompt in his answers to them ; being so indued with heavenly wisdom, that they were not able to resist him, insomuch that the bishops were ashamed, that a leather-seller should so confound them. · He affirmed in his doctrine, that there was no purgatory after this life, but that the souls of the faithful, departing this life, rest with Christ ; that prayers ought not to be made to saints, there being no other advocate but Christ alone. For which, and other principles, he was condemned to die by the bishop of London : and by him delivered to the sheriffs thereof ; and by them burnt in Smithfield.

Edward Freese, painter, for painting upon clothes in an inn, certain sentences of scripture, was noted to be a heretic ; and was apprehended, and brought to London ; and from thence, had to the bishop's house at Fulham, where he was imprisoned, with several other men and their wives ; and fed with bread, part of which was made of saw-dust; and they were kept so close in prison, that their relations were not suffered to come at them. The painter's wife being pregnant, was very desirous to see her husband; and pressing to go into the prison, the bishop's porter kicked her on the belly, so that her child died immediately, and she died soon after.

The prisoners were all put in the stocks for a long time; and after they were let loose, some had horse-locks put on their legs, and some other irons. The painter would often be writing on the walls with chalk or coal ; which so provoked his adversaries, that they manacled his wrists so long, that the flesh of his arms grew higher than the iron. From that prison, he was brought to the Lollard's tower, and there kept three days, without meat, and used so hard, that he lost his understanding and sense.

Valentine Freese, (brother of the said Edward Freese,) and his wife, were both burned, at one stake in York, for the testimony of Jesus Christ.

James Bainham, son of a knight in Gloucestershire, was a man of virtuous disposition, and a godly conversation; much given to prayer and reading the scriptures, a great maintainer of the godly, a visiter of the prisoners, liberal and merciful, delighting in doing equity and justice to the poor, very diligent in giving counsel to all widows, fatherless, and afflicted, without money or reward, being a man bred in the knowledge of the law. He, for his religion, was apprehended by the instigation of Thomas Moore, chancellor of England, who kept him prisoner in his own house, and whipped him at a tree in his garden, which he called, the tree of troth. From thence, he sent him to the tower, to be racked, being himself present to see it effectually done, till in a manner he had lamed him, to make him confess where his books were ; and because his wife denied that they were at his house, she was sent to the fleet, and their goods were confiscated. These tortures making him confess nothing, the chancellor sent him to the bishop of London, in the year 1531, who examined him, upon certain points, concerning his religion ; and asked, " whether he believed there was any purgatory of souls hence departed ?" to which he, answered, " if we walk in the light, as he is in the light, we have fellowship one with another and the blood of Jesus Christ his Son cleanseth us from all sin. If we say that we have no sin, we deceive ourselves, and the truth is not in us. If we confess our sins, he is faithful and just, to forgive us our sins, and to cleanse us from all unrighteousness. Several other things they objected against him, and often had him again before them, threatening him with the danger that would ensue, if he did not abjure his religion; whereupon, being overtaken with fear, he consented unto them. After he had abjured, the chancellor fined him twenty pounds to the king, and enjoined him penance, which was, to go before the cross in procession at Paul's, and to stand before the preacher, during the sermon at Paul's cross, with a faggot upon his shoulder, and to return with the sumner to prison again ; but soon after, he was discharged of his imprisonment; and before he had been at liberty a month, he bewailed his fact and abjuration, and never was quiet in his mind and conscience, until, before a congregation of the people of God, who in those days met in a warehouse in Bow-lane, he uttered his condemnation of the fact, asking of God and that assembly forgiveness. And the next Sunday (so called) afterwards, he went to a place called St. Austins, and stood up in a pew, with a Testament in English in his hand ; and with tears declared to the people, " that he had denied God, and desired the people to forgive him, and to beware of his weakness, and rather to choose to die, than to do as he did; for he would not, for all the world, feel again such a hell as he had done:" to this purpose, he also wrote to the bishop, whereupon he was shortly after apprehended, and committed to the tower of London ; from thence, he was removed to the bishop's coal-house, where he lay two weeks in the stocks, with irons upon his legs : then he was carried to the chancellor's, and there chained to a post two nights : from thence, he was had to Fulham, where he was cruelly handled, for the space of a week : from thence, he was committed to the tower, where he lay a fortnight, and was scourged with whips, to make him revoke his opinions : from thence, he was carried to Barking : and from thence, to Chelsea, and was there condemned : and from thence, conveyed to Newgate ; and by the sheriffs of London, was had into Smithfield ; and there burnt to death, the last day of the month called April, about three o'clock in the afternoon.

In the year 1532, Robert King, Nicholas March, Robert Gardner, all of Dedham; and Robert Debnam, of Esthergholt, being burdened in their consciences to see the honour and power of the Almighty living God blasphemed, by people's adoring an idol, called, the Rood of Dovercourt, to which many people greatly resorted, ignorantly believing a common rumour spread abroad, that no man had power to shut the door of the house of worship, where that idol stood ; whereupon, the aforesaid four men were moved, by the spirit of God, to travel out of Dedham, in a frosty moonshiny night, ten miles, to the place where the idol stood; and they took it from its shrine, and carried it a quarter of a mile, and there struck fire, and set it on fire; for which fact, three of them were indicted as felons, and were hanged in chains about half a year after. And it is recorded, that at their death, through the working of the spirit of God, they bore such a living testimony, that the people were more edified in the truth, than they had been by all the sermons they had heard preached before.

The fourth man, viz. Robert Gardner, would have suffered the same death, had he not fled away, and thereby escaped their hands.

The same year, there were many more images cast down, and destroyed in many places.

John Frith, a godly young man, and one of great parts and wit, of a ready capacity, and a great scholar, becoming acquainted with William Tindal, he first, through his instructions, received into his heart the seed of the gospel, and sincere godliness.

The said John Frith, and divers young men of grave judgment and sharp wit, conferring together upon the abuses of religion, which at that time had crept into the church, were therefore accused of heresy, to cardinal Woolsey; and cast into a prison within a deep cave, under a college in Oxford, where they used to lay their salt fish, the stink of which so infected their bodies, that three of them died in a little space. The fourth was John Frith, who was shortly after discharged out of prison, and travelled beyond sea; and, after two years, returning into England, and being at Reading, it happened that he was taken as a vagabond, and was put in the stocks; and there kept so long that he was almost starved with hunger; yet would not discover who he was; but desired to speak with the school-master of the town, with whom he discoursed in Latin: the school-master perceiving that he was a scholar, and a young man of excellent parts, obtained of the magistrates his liberty, which he enjoyed not long, being pursued by sir Thomas Moore, chancellor, who persecuted him both by sea and land, promising a great reward to any that could bring tidings of him. Soon after, he was apprehended, and committed to the tower of London, where he had many conflicts with the bishops; but especially, in writing, with the chancellor; and afterwards was carried to Lambeth, before the bishop of Canterbury, and from thence to Croyden, before the bishop of Winchester; and, last of all, he was brought before the bishop, in a common assembly at London. The whole matter of his examination before them, was comprehended in two special articles; purgatory, and the substance of the sacraments; to which, he answered very fully and wisely, and in great moderation and uprightness; but no reason would prevail against the force and cruelty of his adversaries. On the twentieth day of the month, called June, 1533, he was brought before several bishops at Paul's, who seeing, that by no means, they could persuade him to recant, the bishop of London condemned him to be burnt, and passed sentence against him to that effect.

. About this time, John Chapman, Andrew Hewet, and John Tibauld, being men zealous for religion and piety, were informed against; and, by the bishop of London's chancellor, and others, were apprehended and carried to the bishop's house. Hewet was sent to the Lollard's tower; and Chapman and Tibauld were kept asunder in the bishop's house, till the next day when he came from Fulham, and examined them; and not liking their confession, he committed Chapman to the stocks, with this threat, that he should tell another tale, or else he should sit there till his heels dropped off. He shut Tibauld up in a close chamber; but afterwards delivered him out of prison, with this injunction; that he should not come within seven miles of his own house. Chapman, after many threatenings and five weeks imprisonment, three weeks whereof he sat in the stocks, by suit made to the chancellor on his behalf, was discharged out of prison. Hewet being brought before the bishops, and asked, what he thought concerning the sacrament? he answered, "even as Frith doth." At which the bishop smiled; and one of them said, "why Frith is an heretic, and is condemned to be burnt; and except thou revoke thy opinion, thou shalt be burnt with him." "Truly," said he, "I am contented therewith." Whereupon, he was sent to the prison to Frith; and on the fourth day of the month, called July, he was carried to Smithfield with Frith, and there burnt.

Thomas Bennet, a school-master, in Exeter, a man of a godly conversation, and a favourer of such as suffered for their zeal to the true religion, after he had lived in a retired condition six years, he could no longer refrain from bearing a testimony against the idolatry of those times, though his blood were shed for the same. He wrote on a paper which he set upon the doors of a house of worship in the city, "the pope is antichrist, and we ought to worship God only, and not saints." This paper being seen, great search and inquiry were made, what heretic had set it up ; but seeing they could not find the author out at that time, they agreed, that the sentence of a curse should be pronounced against him that did it ; the manner of which curse was as followeth.

The priest being in the pulpit, clothed in white; and the monks and friars standing about him, the cross was held up with candles fixed to the same. Then said the priest, " by the authority of God, the Father Almighty, and of the blessed Virgin Mary, of St. Peter and Paul, and of the holy saints, we excommunicate, we utterly curse and bann, commit and deliver to the devil of hell, him, or her, whatsoever he, or she be, that has in spite of God, and of St. Peter, whose church this is, in spite of all holy saints, and in spite of our most holy father the pope, God's Vicar here in earth ; and in spite of the reverend Father in God, John our Diocesian, and the worshipful canons, masters, priests, and clerks, which serve God daily in this cathedral church, fixed up with wax such cursed and heretical bills, full of blasphemy, upon the doors of this, and other holy churches within this city ; excommunicated be he, she, or they plenarily, and delivered over to the devil, as perpetual malefactors and schismatics ; accursed they be, and given body and soul to the devil : cursed be they, he, or she, in cities and towns, in fields and ways, in houses and out of houses, and all other places, standing, lying, or rising, walking, running, waking, sleeping, eating, drinking, and whatsoever thing they do besides. We separate them, him, or her, from the threshold, and from all the good prayers of the church, from the participation of the holy mass, and from all sacraments, chapels, and altars ; from holy bread, and holy water ; from all the merits of God's priests and religious men ; and from all their cloisters ; from all their pardons, privileges, grants, and immunities, which all the holy fathers, popes of Rome, have granted to them ; and we give them over utterly to the power of the devil ; and let us quench their souls, if they be dead, this night, in the pains of hell-fire, as this candle is now quenched, and put out ; (and with that he put out one of the candles) and let us pray to God, if they be alive, that their eyes may be put out, as this candle light is ; (so he puts out another candle) let us pray to God and our lady, and to St. Peter and Paul, and all holy saints, that all the senses of their body may fail them ; and that they may have no feeling, as now the light of this candle is gone, (and so he put out the third candle) except they, he, or she come openly now, and confess their blasphemy; and by repentence (as in them shall lie) make satisfaction unto God, our lady, St. Peter, and the worshipful company of this Cathedral church.''

Bennet, being not able to digest these fooleries, wrote other bills, and caused them to be set upon the gates of the grave-yard ; but the person that set them up, being taken in the action, Thomas Bennet was thereby discovered; and being apprehended, confessed they were his bills, and that he would do it again, to discover the abominable blasphemy of their antichrist, the pope, and to let people see, that he is the boar come out of the wood, which destroyeth and throweth down the hedges of God's church. Whereupon, he was committed to prison ; and the next day, was had to the bishop, who committed him to prison again, where he was kept in the stocks with strong irons, without much favour. Then his house was searched for books, and his wife shamefully abused, which she bore with patience, being contented to bear the cross with her husband, to fare hardly with him, and to subsist on coarse meat and drink. A gray friar reminding Bennet of the many dangers that he was liable to fall into, in that condition, Thomas replied, '' my life is not dear to me ; I had rather by death, which I know is not far off, depart this life, than to partake of your detestable idolatries and superstitions, or be subject to antichrist, your pope.''

During the time of his imprisonment, the hate of the people, through ignorance, was great against him, notwithstanding they could never move his patience. In his imprisonment, his wife provided sustenance for him : when she lamented, he comforted her, and gave her many good and godly exhortations ; and desired her not to move him to comply with his adversaries. After the clergy saw, they could by no means cause him to recant, they condemned him to be burnt, and delivered him to the sheriff of Devonshire to see him executed. The mild man rejoicing to see his end approach so near, as the sheep before the shearer, yielded himself, with all humility, to abide and suffer the cross of persecution. Being brought to his execution, in a place called Livery Dole, without Exeter, he gravely and soberly advised the people, "to seek the honour of God, and the knowledge of him, and to leave the devices and imaginations of men's inventions;" and saying, "Oh Lord, receive my spirit!" he patiently endured the cruelty of the fire until his life was ended.

. Thus, the reader hath an account of such as sustained death for Christ's cause, through the rigorous proclamation aforesaid, published in the name of the king, but indeed procured by the bishops; and by them so strictly executed, that a good man could scarcely appear abroad without being apprehended, and either brought to the fire, or forced to abjure his religion. A great number of instances are particularly mentioned in Fox's Acts and Monuments, which, for brevity sake, are here omitted.

Thomas Philip was one of them that was prosecuted; and being asked by the bishop, whether he would abjure or not, he said, "except ye shew me cause wherefore I should abjure, I will not say, yea, or nay to it; but will stand to my appeal." Then the bishop read openly the bill of excommunication against him, charging all men to have no company, or any thing to do with him. After this excommunication, what became of him, whether he was burnt, or died in the tower, no mention is made in the register. I mention him, because a letter that was found in his pocket, is worth taking notice of. It is as followeth:

A letter directed to Thomas Philip, in the name of the brethren, and given him by the way going to the tower.

"THE favour of him that is able to keep you, that you fall not, and to confess your name in the kingdom of glory, and to give you strength by his spirit to confess him, before all his adversaries, be with you, ever, Amen.

The brethren think, that there be divers false brethren craftily crept in among them, to seek out their freedom in the Lord, that they may accuse them to the Lord's adversaries, as they suppose they have done you ; wherefore, if it be so that the spirit of God move you thereunto, they, as counsellors, desire you above all things, to be steadfast in the Lord's truth, without fear ; for he shall and will be your help, according to his promise, so that they shall not diminish the least hair of your head without his will, unto which submit yourself, and rejoice ; for the Lord knoweth how to deliver the godly out of temptation, and how to reserve the unjust, unto the day of judgment to be punished; and therefore cast all your care on him, for he careth for you ; and in that you suffer as a christian man, be not ashamed, but rather glorify God on that behalf, looking upon Christ the author and finisher of our faith, who, for the joy that was set before him, abode the cross and despised the shame ; nevertheless, though we suffer wrong, after the example of our master Christ, yet we are not bound to suffer the wrong cause ; for Christ himself suffered it not, but reproved him that smote him wrongfully, ; therefore, according both to God and man's law, you are not bound to make answer to any cause, till your accusers come before you, which, if you require, and thereon do stick, the false brethren shall be known, to the great comfort of those who now stand in doubt whom they must trust : and also, it shall be a means, that they shall not craftily by questions take you in snares ; and, Acts xxv. 16, it is written, " it is not the manner of the Romans, to deliver any man to die, before he which is accused have the accusers face to face, and have license to answer for himself, concerning the crime laid againgst him." And also Christ said, " that in the mouth of two or three witnesses, all things shall stand ;" wherefore, seeing that in accusations such witnesses should be, you may with a good conscience require it ; and thus, the God of grace, settle, strengthen, and establish you, that to him may be glory and praise for ever."

William Tracy, of Taddington, in the county of Gloucester, in his will, amongst other things, touching the burying of his body, asserted that it availed him not what was done thereto when he was dead " for," said he, " funeral pomps are rather for the solace of them that live, than for the wealth and comfort of them that are dead."

This will being brought by his son, his executor, to the bishop of Canterbury to be proved, the bishop shewed it to the convocation, which ordered, that a commission should be sent to doctor Parker, chancellor of the Diocess of Worcester, to take up Tracy's dead body, and to burn him as a heretic, for making such a will; which, accordingly was executed, notwithstanding he had been buried almost two years.

About this time, the house of commons, assembled in parliament, put up a supplication, by way of complaint to the king, against the clergy. This complaint, the king, at first, took but little notice of; but afterwards coming to have a clear understanding of the abuses and enormities of the clergy, especially of the corrupt authority of the See of Rome, he provided certain acts against the same, and wholly excluded the pope's authority out of his realm; but thinking the work not sufficiently done, as long as abbeys and priories kept their stations, which were, as it were, his fortresses and pillars, there were not long after means found to have them suppressed; for aspersions being laid upon them of adulteries and murders, they, by act of parliament, or at least near four hundred of them, were supprest, and all their lands and goods conferred upon the king, and afterwards all the rest; the colleges, chanteries, and hospitals. The same parliament also enacted, that bishops should pay no more annals' or money for their bulls to the pope; and that no person should appeal for any cause out of the realm, to the court of Rome: and an act was made, that the king should be the supreme head of the church of England, &c.

Although the pope's power and authority in England were abrogated by act of parliament, as before mentioned, yet the bishops went on persecuting such as they accounted seetaries and heretics. But, before I give an account of such as further suffered in England for religion, it falls in order to give an account of the sufferings of William Tindal, beyond sea.

This William Tindal was born near Wales, being a man zealous for reformation and religion, and consid-

2 a

ering, that if the scripture were translated into common language, it might conduce much to the propagation thereof; and finding his purpose could not be well effected in England, by reason of the strictness of the bishops and chancellor, he travelled into Germany; and there he first translated the New Testament, and then the Old; and wrote several other books against the irreligious practices of the prelates, which books being published and sent over into England, opened a door of light to the whole English nation, which before was many years shut up in darkness.

But though the spreading of these books wrought much good to the upright, and such as had in any measure a desire to advance the truth, yet the envious and persecuting spirit of the bishops was also much stirred up thereby, seeking by all means how to stop them from being spread, lest their hypocrisy and works of darkness should be discerned. Wherefore, they made a great stir and search, as Herod did at the birth of Christ, and sought by what means they might hinder this Tindal from travelling, and from printing and publishing the said books. And they set persons to search and examine how he was situated at Antwerp. And when the bishops and chancellor in England, understood how things were, they sent over one Henry Philips to betray him into the hands of the emperor's procurator-general, at Brussels. The said procurator through the treachery of Philips, seized upon all Tindal's books, and apprehended him, and sent him prisoner to Filford castle, eighteen English miles from Antwerp. Being brought to his trial, they offered him counsel to plead for him, but he refused, saying, " he would answer for himself." After much reasoning and dispute, he was condemned by virtue of the emperor's decree, made in the assembly at Ausbrough; and upon the same, was brought to the place of execution at Filford, Anno 1536; where, being tied to the stake, he cried with a fervent zeal, and a loud voice, " Lord, open the king of England's eyes;" and so was burnt to death.

When the king had taken the title of supremacy from the bishop of Rome, and stated the same to himself, he perceived by the wisdom and advice of Thomas Cromwell, one of his privy council, that the corrupt state of the church had need of reformation in many things.

This Cromwell was, through the goodness of God, raised up to be a friend and favourer to those that professed the gospel.   Though but a smith's son, born at Putney, for the pregnancy of his wit, he was first entertained by cardinal Woolsey, and by him employed in many great affairs.   The cardinal falling, the king took him into his service, and finding his great abilities, advanced him for his worth to places of great honour and trust: and through his persuasions, several injunctions were put out by the king for reformation in religion ; and he was the great instrument in overthrowing abbeys, monasteries, and friaries, which were a little before, by act of parliament given into the king's hands. 'Whereupon, not only their houses were razed, but their possessions were divided amongst the nobility, insomuch that all friars, monks, canons, nuns, and other such sects, were so rooted out of the land, that there seemed to be no room left for them to grow any more.

As this Cromwell was raised up for good, and being so greatly in favour with the king, he used all means he could to persuade him to reform the errors in the church; but satan raised up his instrument, Stephen Gardner, bishop of Winchester, who used all the wiles and, subtil means he could, to persuade the king against the same, casting upon the professors of truth, the names of heretics, sectaries, anabaptists, and sacramentaries ; and so far prevailed with the king, that by his authority, certain injunctions were published, prohibiting the publishing of any books in English, written by the sectaries and sacramentaries, under pain of the forfeiture of all their goods and chattels, and their bodies to be imprisoned during the king's pleasure.   And further, Gardner instigated the king, not only against the queen (who was a favourer of religion and reformation) but also against Cromwell, who, no doubt, had brought true religion, according to his understanding, to greater perfection, had not this Gardner and other malignant opposers thereof, set themselves against it, to hinder the prosperity thereof. But now, through the said Gardner's evil advice, the king, who before had raised Cromwell for his worth and integrity, for his pleasure forsook him, and suffered him to be beheaded. After his death, religion and the reformation more and more decayed; whereby, the reader may see how variable the state of things stood in reference to religion at this time; and with what difficulty any thing of light and truth came forth, and how often things changed, as the king was ruled and inclined; sometimes it went a little forward, and then backward again, according as the persons prevailed that were about the king.

The king, influenced by Gardner's suggestions, began to decline shewing any favour to the reformation in religion, concluding that it was most for his safety, both at home and abroad; having so much displeased the pope, and other popish princes, in what he had already done. And, though he had rejected the pope's authority, he would declare himself nevertheless to be a good catholic, son of the mother church, and a withstander of new heresies; and then calling a new parliament, and a convention of prelates, they agreed to six articles concerning religion, which were afterwards commonly called, a whip with six strings. It was pretended to be done for the unity of the church, but what unity followed, the groaning hearts of many that suffered by the same, both in this king's time and in queen Mary's, declare.

The six articles, condemning all to be burnt as heretics that should hold them, were these:

First, That the body of Christ was not really present, in the sacrament after the consecration.

Secondly, That the sacrament might not truly be administered under one kind.

Thirdly, That priests who entered into holy orders, might marry.

Fourthly, That vows of chastity entered into, upon mature deliberation, were not to be kept.

Fifthly, That private masses were not to be used.

Sixthly, That Auricalar confession was not to be used in the church.

Before these articles were published, bishop Gardner, having obtained his desire with the king, he and the rest of the prelates began again to persecute the protestants ; and the first they stretched forth their hands against, was John Lambert of Norfolk, one zealous for the spreading of the truth, according to the manifestation of it then broken forth ; and to that end, he was conversant with Tindal and Frith at Antwerp, until, by the instigation of Sir Thomas Moore, he was apprehended and brought to London, where he was first brought to examination at Lambeth, and then at the bishop's house at Oxford, before Warham archbishop of Canterbury, and others. Forty-five articles were objected against him, to all which he answered in writing very fully and wisely, both according to the scriptures and reason. The articles, and his answers may be read at large in Fox's Acts and Monuments.

The bishop of Canterbury shortly after died, whereby Lambert for that time, was delivered out of prison ; but coming to London, it was not long before he fell into trouble again ; for having a private conference with one doctor Tayler, what passed between them in their dispute in private, grew at last to be a public and common talk, which coming to the archbishop's ears, he sent for Lambert, and forced him to defend his cause openly. In in that disputation, Lambert appealed to the king from the bishops.

Upon this appeal, bishop Gardner went to the king, and privately insinuated to him, that now he had an opportunity, to quiet the minds of the people, who were offended with him, for abolishing the bishop of Rome's authority, and for subverting the monasteries and abbeys, &c. and that he might now remedy these troubles, if he would manifestly appear in this matter against Lambert, and shew himself stoutly to resist the heretics. The king immediately received this wicked counsel of the bishop, and forthwith sent out a general commission, commanding all the bishops and nobles of the land, to come with speed to London, to assist him against the heretics. These preparations being made, a day was set, upon which Lambert should appear before the king, and the rest assembled with him, to be tried and judged.

The day being come, the king ascended his throne, clothed in white. He looked upon the prisoner with a stern countenance, as if his mind were full of indignation; and then he called forth the bishop of Chichester, and commanded him to declare to the people the causes of their being assembled. He informed them, "that the king would have none to conceive, that whereas the authority and name of the bishop of Rome being utterly abolished, he would also extinguish all religion, or give liberty to heretics, to trouble the churches of England without punishment." The chief thing that the king pressed Lambert to declare, was, what opinion he held touching the sacrament of the altar. To which, he answered fully; and the dispute held, chiefly concerning that point, for some hours, until the king and bishops, enraged against him, forced him to silence at last.

The king, being minded to end the dispute, said to Lambert, "what sayest thou, after all these labours and reasons of these learned men? Art thou yet satisfied? Wilt thou live or die? Thou hast yet free choice." Lambert answered, "I yield and submit myself wholly unto the will of your majesty." Then said the king, "commit thyself unto the hands of God; and not unto mine." Lambert said, "I commend my soul into the hands of God, but my body I wholly yield and submit unto your clemency." Then said the king, "if you do commit yourself unto my judgment, you must die; for I will not be a patron to heretics." So he caused the sentence of death to be read against him. Shortly after, he was had to Smithfield, and there burnt. In the midst of the flames, he cried unto the people in these words, "none but Christ, none but Christ;" and so ended his life.

The aforesaid six articles being consented unto, and concluded by the king and parliament, the bishops caused further to be enacted, "that whosoever denied transubstantiation, or whosoever should be aiders, comforters, counsellors, consentors, and abbettors therein, should be adjudged heretics ; that every such offender should have and suffer judgment, execution, and pain of death, by way of burning, without any abjuration, benefit of the clergy, or sanctuary ; and should forfeit to the king all their land and tenements, goods and chattels, as in cases of high treason. And all such as did preach, teach, uphold, maintain, or defend any thing contrary to the five last articles, should be adjudged as felons, and lose both life and goods, as in the case of felony.

When these articles were in debate in the parliament-house, doctor Cranmer, in favour of the professors of the truth, earnestly disputed in defence of the truth against them ; but notwithstanding all his opposition, the act was passed.

By reason of these six articles, a great number were apprehended in London and other places, so that all the prisons in London were insufficient to hold them ; and many were imprisoned in halls.

Amongst them, was one John Porter, of London, who, for reading to the people in a bible, was sent for by Bonner, and sharply reproved. Porter answered, " he trusted he had no way offended contrary to the law thereby." Bonner charged him with making expositions upon the text, and with gathering multitudes about him. This Porter denied. Yet Bonner sent him to Newgate, where he was miserably loaded with irons, both hands and legs, with a great collar of iron about his neck, whereby he was fastened to the wall in the dungeon. After a while, he sent for a kinsman of his, through whose influence, by bribing the keeper, he was put amongst thieves and murderers ; but Porter hearing and seeing their wickedness, exhorted them to amendment of life, giving them good instructions ; for this, he was complained of, and carried down into the lowest dungeon ; where he was so cruelly pressed with bolts and irons, that within a few days after, he was found dead.

In the year 1544, one Robert Testwood, living at Windsor, being a favourer of the Lutherans, and seeing people licking and kissing a white alabaster image, that stood behind the high altar; his zeal was so stirred, that with a key, that he had in his hand, he struck off the image's nose, saying, " see, good people, what it is : it cannot help itself; how then would you have it help you ?" The noise thereof being spread abroad, one Symonds, a lawyer, took up the nose and said, that one day, it should be a dear nose to Testwood.

This act so offended the clergy, that they said, " he is an heretic, and will roast a faggot one day for this geer." But, notwithstanding their threats, he lived in quiet till the death of the lord Cromwell, and till Winchester had insinuated into the affections of the king, and wholly ruled ; at which time, Testwood, being sick in bed, was fetched out, and cast into prison, together with one Anthony Person, John Marbeck, and Henry Filmer. After a while, they were all brought forth to judgment, before Dr. Capon, bishop of Salisbury, and others. The substance of Testwood's indictment was, that, when the priest lifted up the sacrament, he said, " what, wilt thou lift it up so high ? what, yet higher ? take heed that thou let it not fall." As also, that, at such times, when the sacrament was lifted up, he used to look down on his book, or another way, that he might not see the sacrament ; whereupon, he said, " whereon did he look, that marked me so well ?" Quoth the king's attorney, " he could not be better occupied, than to mark such heretics." The prisoners being condemned, they spent the greatest part of the night preceding their execution, in praying that the Lord would strengthen them, and enable them, with steadfast faith and power, to go through their exercise.

About this time, there rose a great persecution in Calais, in France, which was then under England's power. There were, at one time, twelve persons imprisoned for their religion ; but lord Cromwell hearing of it, wrote immediately to the commissioners in Calais, in the king's name, requiring, that the heretics, with their accusers, should be sent over into England. Forthwith the commissioners, loading them with chains, sent them over. As soon as Cromwell heard that they had arrived, he sent for them to his house; and smiling upon them, said, " go your ways to the fleet, and submit yourselves prisoners there; and be of good cheer; for if God give me life, you shall shortly go home with as much honesty, as you came with shame." But shortly after this, Cromwell was beheaded; so that the poor men had no hopes, but in the providence of their heavenly Father, who comforted them in their deep troubles, that as their afflictions abounded, their joys and consolations abounded much more; for when all hope was past, lord Audley, chancellor of England, sent for them, and without any further examination, discharged them from their imprisonment.

In the year 1541, the king sent out a commission, for apprehending such as offended against the six articles, and when the commissioners sat, at Mercer's Chapel, being such as were chosen for the purpose, they inquired not only for such as offended against the six articles, but for such as came seldom to church, and received not the holy bread and water; so that they indicted above five hundred persons, most of whom would either have died in prison, or been burnt in Smithfield, but the king, being informed, by lord Audley, that they were indicted for malice, granted them his pardon.

About the same time, one Richard Meekins, a boy of fifteen years old, was accused for speaking some words against the sacrament of the altar; and when the first jury would not find the indictment against him, they were severely censured by the bishop of London; and another jury was empannelled that found it, and the poor boy was burnt in Smithfield.

On account of the diligent preaching of Adam Damplip, and one William Smith, at Calais, the devil raised up his instruments to persecute them, and others, their hearers; and letters were written over to the council in England, suggesting, that by the means of Damplip, they were infected with horrible heresies and errors. The persons accused were Thomas Brooke, Ralph

2 c

Hare, James Cock, and James Barber, who were sent for over, and committed to prison at Westminster. Afterwards, they were brought before the bishops. Grievous letters were written against them from Calais by their adversaries, so that if God had not preserved them, they had all certainly perished.

One of these, viz. Ralph Hare, though so unlearned, that he could scarcely read, yet was very zealous; and so holy and inoffensive in his life, that none of his adversaries could accuse him of evil. He was charged with speaking against auricular confession, holy bread, and holy water; as also, that he would not swear, nor use any pastime, but used to be in a corner by himself, looking on his book, when others were at liberty. Thus being charged, he said to the commissioners, " I take God to witness, I would not willingly maintain any error or heresy; wherefore, I beseech you, let my accusers come before me face to face; for if they charge me with what I have spoken, I will not deny it; and, if it be truth, I will stand to it, if an error, I will with all my heart forsake it; I mean, if it be against God's holy word; for the Lord is my witness, I daily pray to God that I may know the truth, and shun errors; and I hope God will preserve me from them."

The bishop of Winchester said, " I perceive now thou art a naughty fellow." " Alas!" said Hare, " what evil have I spoken?" the bishop replied, " sir, you said, the Lord, the Lord; and that is symbolum hereticorum." What is that, said Hare," " thou art naught, thou art naught," said the bishop; and further said, " I pity thee, for I think thou art a good simple man, and meanest well enough, if thou hadst not had bad school-masters." And then Thomas Brooke was called for, who was charged with sedition; and that he had contributed towards maintaining Adam Damplip, and that he had said, that what the priest held up at mass was not the body of Christ. Brooke denied the charge; and after some debate, he was for that time dismissed.

The suffering and martyrdom of Anne Askew.

ANNE ASKEW was apprehended for her religion, and examined before one Christopher Dare an Inquisitor, who asked her, if she did not believe the sacrament of the altar to be the real body of Christ? to this question, she refused to answer. Then he told her, that she was accused for reading, that God dwelt not in temples made with hands; thereupon she shewed him the 7th and 17th chapters of the Acts for it. Then he asked her, how she undersood those texts? she answered, " that she would not cast pearls before swine :" then he charged her with saying, that she had rather read five lines in her bible, than hear a mass. She said, the reason was, because one did greatly edify her, and the other did not. And after other questions asked her, he had her before the mayor of London; the mayor, after some discourse with her, ordered her to be had to prison. She asked, if sureties would not serve? he said, he would take none : after some time, she was released from that imprisonment, but not long after, she was apprehended again, and carried before the king's council, where the chancellor asked her her opinion about the sacrament. She said, that she believed, that so oft as she received the bread in remembrance of Christ's death, she received therewith the fruits of his most glorious passion. The bishop of Winchester bid her answer directly. She answered, she would not sing the Lord's song in a strange land. The bishop told her, she was a pariat : to which she replied, that she was willing not only to receive rebukes from him, but whatsoever should follow besides, and that gladly. After much other debate, she was imprisoned until the next day ; at which time, they asked her again, what she said to the sacrament? she answered, that she had said what she could say.

Then the bishop of Winchester said, she would speak with her familiarly. She said, so did Judas when he unfriendlily betrayed Christ. Then the bishop desired to speak with her alone : but she refused. He asked her, why? she said, that in the mouth of two or three witnesses every matter should stand, after Christ and Paul's doctrine.

Then the chancellor began to examine her again of the sacrament. She asked him, how long he would halt on both sides? He would know, where she found that? she said, in the scripture. Then he went his way. And the bishop told her, she would be burnt; she answered, that she had searched all the scriptures, and could never find that either Christ, or his apostles, put any creature to death; and told them, God would laugh their threatenings to scorn.

After much other arguing, wherein she answered them wisely and holily, they dismissed her. A few days after, she was taken very sick, and was likely to die; and in that extremity of her sickness, they sent her to Newgate.

After a time, she was brought to her trial at Guildhall, where she was required to recant, or else she should be condemned by the law for an heretic. She answered, she was no heretic, neither deserved death by the law of God. Then they asked, if she would deny the sacrament to be Christ's body and blood? she said, "yea." They wished her, to confess herself to a priest: at which, she smiled, and said, she would confess her faults to God, for she was sure he would hear her with favour.

Then they would know of her, whether the bread in the box were God or not: she said, God is a spirit, and will be worshipped in spirit and truth." After she was condemned, she wrote a few lines to the king to this effect.

" I Anne Askew, of good memory, although God hath given me the bread of adversity, and the water of trouble; yet be it known, that forasmuch as I am by the law condemned as an evil-doer, (here I take heaven and earth to record,) that I shall die in my innocency; and as I said at first, I say at last, I utterly abhor and detest all heresies. And concerning the supper of the Lord, I believe so much as Christ hath said therein, which he confirmed with his most blessed blood. I believe so much as he willed me to follow, for I will not forsake the commandment of his holy lips, but look what God hath charged me with his mouth, that have I shut up in my heart ; and thus briefly I end.

ANNE ASKEW.

Shortly after, she was sent from Newgate, to the sign of the crown, where, she said, one Rich, and the bishop of London, used all their power, by flattering words, to persuade her from God ; but they prevailed not with her. One Nicholas Shaxton counselled her to recant, as he had done. She told him, it had been good for him, he had never been born. Then Rich sent her to the tower to be racked, where, first, he and one of the council examined her, telling her, that the king was informed, that if she would, she could name a great number of her sect. She answered, that the king was as well deceived in that, as he was in other matters.

"The manner of her racking was thus : she was let down into a dungeon, where the lieutenant of the tower commanded the gaoler to pinch her with the rack, which being done, as much as he thought sufficient, he went about to take her down; but Wrisley, the chancellor, not contented that she was loosed so soon, confessing nothing, but lying still, and not crying, commanded the lieutenant to strain her on the rack again; and because he refused to do it, pleading the weakness of the woman, the chancellor threatened him that he would signify his disobedience to the king. Then Rich and the chancellor took pains to rack her themselves, till she was nearly dead, first asking her, whether she was with child ? to whom she answered, " you shall not need to spare for that, but do your wills upon me;" and so quietly and patiently, praying unto the Lord, she abode their cruelty till her bones and joints were almost plucked asunder. After she was loosed from the rack, she swooned ; but they recovered her again ; and she was carried away in a chair to a house, and laid in a bed, with weary and painful bones. The chancellor sent her word, that if she would leave her opinion, she should want for nothing ; if she would not, she should forthwith be sent to Newgate, and so be burnt. She sent him word again, that she would rather die than break her faith. Before her death, she composed the following prayer.

"O, Lord! I have more enemies now, than there be hairs on my head; yet, Lord, let them never overcome me with vain words; but fight thou, Lord, in my stead; for on thee cast I my care. With all the spite they can imagine, they fall upon me, which am thy poor creature; yet, Lord, let me not set by them which are against me; for in thee is my whole delight. And, Lord, I heartily desire of thee, that thou wilt, of thy most merciful goodness, forgive them that violence which they do, and have done unto me. Open also thou their blind hearts, that they may hereafter do that thing in thy sight, which is only acceptable before thee, and to set forth thy truth aright, without all vain fantasy of sinful men. So be it, O Lord, so be it."

The day of her execution being appointed, she was brought into Smithfield in a chair, for she could not on her feet, by reason of her great torments. When she was brought to the stake, she was tied by the middle, with a chain that held up her body; and so was encompassed with the flames of fire. As a blessed sacrifice unto God, she resigned up her life, in the year 1546, leaving behind her a singular example of christian constancy, for all men to follow. There were, at the same time, three others burnt with her in Smithfield.

After the death of this woman, the popish clergy consulted together, how they might further proceed to keep the truth under, and the people in ignorance; and for that end, they obtained another proclamation, in the king's name, for abolishing the scriptures in English, and all other English books, that might give any light to the people, which made sore work, and caused persecution for a time; but it was not long it continued, by reason of the king's death, which took place shortly after.

But, before there be a full conclusion of the transactions, in this king's reign, it is necessary, that a short account be given of the rise and fall of Thomas Crom-

well, of whom mention is made before, he being a
man zealous for reformation of both church and commonwealth.

*A short relation of the life and death of Thomas, lord
Cromwell.*

He was born at Putney, his father being a Smith, as
is before related. In his youthful days, it is said, he
had little regard to God and religion, but travelled beyond sea; and for a time, was there a soldier. At
length, getting the New Testament in English, and oft-
ten reading it, he began to be touched, and awakened:
and coming into England again, cardinal Woolsey entertained him in his service; where, after remaining
some years, he was preferred to be solicitor to the cardinal. After the fall of cardinal Woolsey, he was, by the
master of the rolls, preferred to the king, who was then
opposing the pope, as a fit person to be employed by
him; and being brought to the king, at his garden in
Westminster, he informed him, that his authority was
abused by the clergy; who, by being sworn to the pope,
had run themselves into a premunire; and that now the
king had an opportunity to enrich himself. To this, the
king gave ear, and liking his advice, admitted him into
his service, and sent him to the convocation-house, a-
mongst the bishops, where he made a speech to this
effect: "that inasmuch as they had sworn to the pope,
contrary to their fealty due to the king, they had forfeited all their goods, chattels, lands, and possessions, to the
king, &c." This amazed the bishops at first, but after
a little a pause, they began to shrink; and before they
could be quit of the premunire, by act of parliament, it
cost them, to the king, no less than one hundred and
eighteen thousand eight hundred and forty pounds.

Afterwards, Cromwell grew greatly in favour with
the king, and was made one of his privy council, and
master of the rolls; and afterwards knight of the garter,
and earl of Essex; and now being come into such authority, and seeing the superstition, blindness, hypocri-

sy, and idolatry of the monks, friars, and papists, he, like a champion, was raised up to root them out; which, while the king favoured him, he prosecuted with effect, as is before related; but when the popish bishops saw the pope's power abolished in England, they never gave over using their utmost endeavours, and politic contrivances, till they had accomplished his destruction.

It would be tedious to recite, what benefit, this Cromwell, by his prudence and zeal, wrought in a little time for the public good; what good orders he established; what wickedness and vices he suppressed; what corruptions he reformed; what abuses he brought to light; and the popish idolatry and images he suppressed; one of which was called the rood of Grace, wherein a man stood with an hundred wires, to make the image goggle its eyes, nod its head, move its lip, and shake its jaws, according to the value of the gift offered. If it were a small piece of silver, then it would hang a frowning lip; if it were a piece of gold, then would its jaws go merrily. Thus, were poor people's souls seduced, and and their pockets picked, by these idolatrous forgers, until Cromwell caused the said image to be carried publicly to Paul's, where the people tore it to pieces.

He was a man, not only zealous for the public reformation, but also always ready to help private persons, that were in distress; and though it is common amongst men, that are raised from low estate to great place, and outward preferment, to forget themselves, and what they formerly were, and the persons from whom they received benefits, it was not so with him.

His care and zeal, for settling the protestant religion, brought him to his end; for, for the better establishing thereof he effected a marriage between the king, and the lady Anne of Cleve, whose sister was married to the duke of Saxony, a protestant prince; by which marriage, it was supposed, there would be established a perpetual peace and amity, between that kingdom and the protestant princes of Germany, which would much strengthen the protestant party, against the tyranny and oppression of the pope and his adherents. But presently after the marriage, Stephen Gardner, who had crept into favour with the king, (as is before related) suggested to him some occasions of distaste against the duke of Saxony, and some apprehensions of fear, by reason of that odium which he had drawn upon himself, by rejecting the pope, and demolishing abbeys and monasteries, whereby (as he told him) he had made the pope, the emperor, the king of France, and the king of Scotland, his enemies ; and especially his own subjects, who much disliked the innovations in religion ; and that the only way to heal all, was to shew himself sharp and severe against the new sectaries. This occasioned the king to withdraw his favour from Cromwell ; for, being one day in the council-chamber, he was suddenly apprehended and committed to the tower of London; at the hearing whereof, many good men were much troubled. The charge laid against him was, that he was a supporter of heretics, and a spreader of their books ; and, that he had caused to be translated into English, books written against the sacrament of the altar ; and, that he had spoken words against the king. But whatever he was accused of, he was soon after condemned in the tower, without any opportunity to answer, and was beheaded. His death the king shortly after bewailed, wishing he had his Cromwell alive again. So that it appears, it was more the malice of his adversary, that stirred up the king against him, than any real cause given or acted by him, that might justly occasion his death.

Persecutions in Scotland.

In the year 1634, the archbishop of St. Andrews called before him, David Stratton, and Norman Gourley. The first of these having a fishing-boat that went to sea, the bishop of Murray demanded tithe-fish of him ; to whom, he answered, " that if they would have tithe of that which his servants caught in the sea, they should take it in the place where it was caught." And so he caused his servants to throw the tenth fish into the sea again. All this while, he had nothing in him of religion. But when he was summoned to answer for heresy, it troubled him exceedingly, and then he began to frequent the company of such as were godly, and there appeared a wonderful change in him ; so that, whereas, before, he despised the scriptures, now all his delight was in hearing them read to him ; and he became an earnest exhorter of all men to peace and concord, and to a contempt of the world. He much frequented the company of the laird of Dun Arisken, whom God in those days had marvellously illuminated. And hearing that text read (for he could not read himself,) " he that denieth me before men shall be denied before the angels of God," he fell upon his knees, and steadfastly lifting up his eyes and hands, he at length burst out into these words, " O Lord ! I have been wicked, and justly mayst thou withdraw thy grace from me ; but, Lord ! for thy mercy's sake, let me never deny thee nor thy truth for fear of death, nor any corporal pains." Soon after, Norman and he were brought to judgment, to holy-rood-house, the king himself being present, and many means were used to draw Stratton to make a recantation ; but he persevered in his constancy, still denying that he had offended ; and so they were both condemned to the fire ; and after dinner, they were both first hanged, and then burnt.

Not long after the burning of these two, there was one Thomas Forret, a Dean, who used to preach every first day to his parishioners the epistles and gospels. This was counted a great novelty in those times ; for none used to preach but the friars; and, therefore, they envying him, accused him to the bishop of Dunkelden, for a heretic, and one that read the mysteries of the scripture to the vulgar people. The bishop, instigated by the complaints of the friars, called the said Thomas Forret before him ; to whom he said, " my joy, dean Thomas, I love you well, and therefore I must give you counsel how to govern yourself." The dean thanked him ; and then he proceeded : " my joy, dean Thomas, I am informed that you preach the epistles and gospels every Sunday to your people ; and that you take not your dues from them, which is very prejudicial to the church men ; and therefore, my joy, dean Thomas, I would have you to take your dues, or else it is too much to preach every Sunday ; for, by so doing, you make the people think, that we should do so also."

Thomas answered, " my lord, I presume none of my parishioners complain for my not taking my dues ; and whereas you say, it is too much to preach every sunday, I think it is too little ; and wish that your lordship would do the like."

" Nay, nay, dean Thomas," said the bishop, " let that be, for we are not ordained to preach ; and, dean Thomas, go your ways, and let all these fancies be ; for if you persist therein, you will repent, when it is too late."

" I trust," said the dean, " my cause is good and just in the presence of God ; and therefore, I care not what follows thereupon ;" and so he went away, but shortly after, he was summoned to appear before the cardinal, by whom he was condemned and burned for a chief heretic, and teacher of heresy.

But notwithstanding their bloody cruelty, the knowledge of God wonderfully increased in this country, partly by reading, and partly by brotherly conference, which, in those dangerous days, were much used, to the comfort of many, which so enraged the popish party, that in the year 1538, there were four persons burned in one fire.

The year after, Jeremy Russel, and Alexander Kenedy were apprehended, and brought before the bishop. Jeremy, was a man of a meek and quiet nature. Alexander was a young man, about eighteen years old, who at first was faint, and would fain have recanted; but when all place of repentance was denied him, the spirit of God began to refresh him, yea, the inward comfort began to break forth, as well in his visage, as in his words; and he cried in prayer to God, " oh eternal God! how wonderful are thy love and mercy, who hast made me to feel heavenly comfort, who takest from me that ungodly fear, which before I was oppressed with. Now I defy death. Do with me what you please, I praise God I am ready." Then they railed upon him and Jeremy, who also said unto them, " this is your hour and power of darkness. Now sit ye as judges; and we stand wrongfully accused, and more wrongfully to be condemned; but the day will come when our innocency will appear, and ye shall see your own blindness to your everlasting confusion: go forward, and fulfil the measure of your iniquity." Shortly after, they were condemned to die; and as they went to execution, Jeremy comforted Alexander, saying to him: " brother, fear not, greater is he that is in us, than he that is in the world. The pain that we are to suffer, is short, and shall be light; but our joy and consolation shall never have end: let us therefore strive to enter into our master and saviour's joy, by the same straight way, which he hath taken before us. Death cannot hurt us; for it is already destroyed by him, for whose sake we now suffer." And thus, they constantly continued steadfast in the flaming fire, till they finished their course by death.

In the year 1543, George Wiseheart, a man of a courteous, modest, and temperate behaviour, fearing God and hating covetousness, very charitable and moderate in his apparel and diet; and, for his innocence, well beloved, was accused of several articles by the bishops; and afterwards was condemned by them as a heretic to be burnt. When he came to the fire, he said, " Father of heaven, I commend my spirit into thy holy hands;" and then turned himself to the people, and said these words: " I beseech you, christian brethren and sisters, that you be not offended in the word of God for the afflictions and torments which you see already prepared for me; but I exhort you, that you love the word of God, and suffer patiently, and with a comfortable heart, for the word's sake, which is your undoubted salvation, and everlasting comfort. Moreover, I pray you, shew my brethren and sisters, which have heard me oft before, that they cease not, nor leave off the word of God, which I taught unto them, after the grace given unto me, for any persecutions or troubles in this world, which last not; and shew unto them, that my doctrine was no old wives' fable, after the constitution made by men; and if I had taught men's doctrine, I had gotten great thanks of men, but for the word, and the true gospel's sake, I suffer this day by men, not sorrowfully, but with a glad heart and mind; for this cause, I was sent, that I should suffer this fire for Christ's sake; this grim fire I fear not, and so I pray you to do, if that any persecution come unto you, for the word's sake; and fear not them that kill the body, and afterwards have no power to kill the soul."

Then he prayed for them which accused him, saying, "I beseech thee, Father of heaven, forgive them, that have, through ignorance, or an evil mind, forged lies against me. I forgive them with all my heart; and I beseech Christ to forgive them, who have condemned me to death this day ignorantly." So being first hanged, he was then burnt, many people bewailing his death.

We must not pass over, in silence, the constancy of Walter Mille, one of the martyrs of Scotland, out of whose ashes sprung thousands of his religion in Scotland. Many articles were drawn up against him, for which, he had sentence pronounced against him, that he should be delivered to the temporal judge, and punished as a heretic, which was to be burnt.

When all things were ready for his death, and he was conveyed, with armed men, to the fire, Andrew Olifant, the judge that passed sentence upon him, bade him "go to the stake," he said, "nay; except thou pull me up with thy hand; for I am forbidden by the law of God, to lay hands on myself." Then Olifant put him up with his hand; and he went gladly, saying, "I will go the altar of

God ;" and desired that he might have time to speak to the people, which his executioner denied, saying, " that he had spoken over-much ; and that the bishops were offended that the matter was so long continued." But some young men, that stood by, desired him to speak what he pleased ; so, after he had prayed, he rose up, and standing upon the coals, said :

" Dear friends, the cause why I suffer this day, is not for any crime laid to my charge, but only for the defence of the faith of Christ Jesus ; for which, as the faithful martyrs have heretofore gladly offered themselves, being assured, after the death of their bodies, of eternal felicity ; so this day I praise God, that he hath called me of his mercy, among the rest of his servants, to seal his truth with my life ; which, as I have received it of him, so willingly I offer it to his glory. Therefore, as you will escape the eternal death, be no more seduced by the lies of priests, monks, and bishops, and the rest of the sect of antichrist ; but depend only upon Jesus Christ, and his mercy, that you may be delivered from condemnation."

All that while, there were great mourning and lamentation of the multitude ; for they perceiving his patience, stoutness, boldness, and constancy, were not only moved and stirred up, but their hearts also were so inflamed, that he was the last martyr that died in Scotland. After his prayer, he was hoisted up on the stake ; and being in the fire, he said, " Lord, have mercy on me ! pray, people, while there is time." And so he departed.

Persecutions in the reign of Edward the sixth.

———— ❊ ————

HENRY the eighth being dead, Edward the sixth succeeded him, at the age of nine years. He was a youth of a meek nature and disposition, much inclined to clemency and mercy; so much so, that when one Joan Butcher, was condemned to be burnt for heresy, all the council could scarcely move him to set his hand, saying to Cranmer; " what, will you send her quick to the devil in her error ?" Doctor Cranmer persuaded him, with much reluctance, to put his hand ; to whom, he said, he would lay all the charge as before the Lord.

King Edward being of so mild a nature, and a person inclining to love religion from a child, he was very zealous for a further reformation in the church, abolishing the mass, &c. and his uncle, the duke of Somerset, a man also very zealous for reformation, and an encourager of such as professed the gospel, being appointed protector during his nonage, the sword was taken out of the hands of the popish party, which used all means and endeavours to stir up persecution, and to hinder that good they found the king and his uncle inclinable to ; yet there were some that suffered for religion, viz. Joan of Kent, an English woman ; one George, a Dutchman ; and one Thomas Dobb.

Dobb was a man fervent and zealous for religion ; and so innocent, that he was more apt to receive injuries than to do wrong to any one. It happened, that as he was passing St. Paul's, in London, seeing the priest at mass, being at the elevation, the young man, filled with godly zeal, pitying the ignorance and idolatry of the people, in so devoutly honouring that which the priest lifted up, was not able to forbear, but turning to the people, exhorted them, testifying against their idolatry, for which cause, he was apprehended by the mayor ; and being accused by the bishop of Canterbury, he was committed to the compter in Bread-street, where falling sick, he soon after died.

In this king's time, there was also John Home, a servant to one Lewnax, for denying the sacrament of the altar to be the real flesh and blood of Christ; and for saying, that he would never vail his bonnet to it, if he were burnt therefor; and that if he heard mass, he should be damned; for these things, he was accused by his master and mistress, and sent up by them to the bishop of Canterbury, with letters, desiring that he might be severely punished for the same; but no mention is made of his execution. I return to give a short account of the reformation in this king's time, and how far it extended.

Injunctions were made in his time, that bibles in English should be placed in some convenient place in the meeting-house, that the people might read in them when they pleased, and rather be encouraged to read them, than hindered by the priests or curates. That the priests or curates should not at any time haunt taverns or ale-houses, neither spend their time idly in unlawful games, but should give themselves to read and hear the scriptures read; and that every beneficed preacher should preach twice a year; and that all monuments of idolatry in meeting-houses and windows, should be taken away; and that homilies should be read every Sunday.

He repealed and abrogated all acts, made by former kings, for the reformation of heretics and Lollards, and the act of the six articles, and all acts published, prohibiting the spreading of the scriptures in English.

He also sent a letter to the archbishop, signed by the council, to abolish images, and that the altar should be taken down, and a table set up instead thereof.

Though this may be accounted but a little reformation, yet it so troubled the popish party, that they sought all the ways and means they could, to hinder its further progress; and would not be satisfied until they had found out a way to answer their wicked purposes. They charged the protector with being the occason of all the sedition that had happened in the realm, &c. And though he was in a high state, yet that did not preserve him; and, indeed, it is a vain thing for man to put confidence in worldly prosperity, how high soever he seemeth, considering that where virtue is most perfect, it is there most envied by wicked men, as in the example of this duke appears.

Whilst the protector and his brother, who was admiral of England, were knit and joined together in love and concord, they preserved themselves, the king, and the whole commonwealth, from the violence of all their adversaries, who, after a while, succeeded, through slanderous tongues, in sowing matter, first of discord between them, then of suspicion, and last of all extreme hatred, insomuch, that the protector suffered his brother to be condemned, and to lose his head; whereby it came to pass, that not long after, he himself was overmatched by his adversaries, and overthrown by them; and being cast into the tower, at last he lost his head also, to the great grief of many good men; and so the fall of one brother was the ruin of the other; for it was not long after the admiral was beheaded, that insurrections began in several parts of the kingdom; and after they were subdued, several of the lords assembled at Baynard's Castle, and at the mayor of London's house, and had great consultations against the protector, who was then with the king at Hampton Court; which the king hearing of, sent the secretary to them with a message, to which they made no answer; and not long after published a proclamation, in the city, against the protector, charging him with divers crimes; as, that he was the chief occasion of all the sedition that had of late happened in the kingdom; and, that he did what was in his power to cause variance between the king and the nobles; and desired the city to aid them. The king also sent the mayor and city a letter, requiring aid likewise. This put the mayor and citizens in a strait, some being for helping the king, and others for helping the lords, and against the protector. The recorder pressed the citizens to assist the lords against the protector, who, he said, had abused the king and the whole realm. He also pressed the common council for an answer, and that they would declare what they would do; but they were silent in the matter, until one George Stadlow stood up, and said to them, "It is good to consider of things past, to avoid dangers in things to come;" and then related to them, what inconveniences and damage befel the citizens, in assisting the barons in their wars against king Henry the third. In conclusion,

2 E

the lords hearing what passed in the city, assembled in the star chamber next day, and sent to the king, at Windsor, a messenger, who so ordered his matter with the king, that the protector was apprehended, and shortly after, was had to the Tower in London, and there was charged with several articles ; and a terrible proclamation was issued against him ; but through the king's love and labouring in his behalf, he was shortly after let out of the Tower, and the proclamation repealed ; after which trouble, he continued two years at liberty, though not restored to his former office.

But after this respite, he was again apprehended and committed to the tower, from whence he was, in a short time, conveyed through the city, (with the tower axe carried before him,) to Westminster, and there tried by the peers ; where in a quiet, patient, and suffering spirit, he modestly behaved himself, shewing himself an example of meekness ; wisely replying to the articles objected against him, and was at last cleared of the treason laid to his charge, which the people understanding, were greatly rejoiced at ; but his adversaries quickly found out another snare ; for they charged him with felony, for intending and purposing the death of the earl of Northumberland, according to a law, wherein it was enacted, that it should be felony for any subject to seek or procure the death of any privy counsellor. And, being condemned, he was again conveyed to the tower, and shortly after, from thence was had to the place of execution, where neither his voice nor countenance changed, but after his usual manner, he spake to the people, to this effect : " Dearly beloved friends, I am brought hither to suffer death, though I never offended the king, either in word or deed, and have been always as faithful and true to this realm, as any man hath been." And after other words, he said, " moreover, dearly beloved friends, there is yet somewhat that I must put you in mind of, as touching the christian religion, which, as long as I was in authority, I always diligently furthered to my power ; neither do I repent me of my doings, but rejoice therein, seeing the state of the christian religion cometh nearer to the order of the primitive church; which thing I esteem as a great benefit, given of God, both unto you and me; most heartily exhorting you all, that this which is most purely setforth unto you, you will with the like thankfulness embrace and accept of, and shew forth the same in your living, which thing, if you do not, without doubt, greater mischief and calamity will follow.'' And, after other good exhortations to the people, he kneeled down, without shewing any token of trouble or fear, and like a meek lamb, received the stroke of death.

As touching his disposition and conversation, whilst alive, they could not be sufficiently commended, according to his worth, being a man of so meek and gentle a nature, as is rarely found in so high a state. He was always ready to give ear to the complaints of the poor, and was very attentive to the affairs of the commonwealth. He was destitute of all craft and deceit, and as void of pride and ambition, as he was of doing injury. He was, from his disposition, more apt to be deceived, than to deceive. And last of all, he was a man zealous for religion and truth, so far as it appeared, and had broken forth in that day; and, in all likelihood, he would have been a good instrument in the work of reformation, had not this difference between the lords and him happened, which put a period to his days; for as long as they agreed, and there was concord between them, the two great persecuting bishops, Winchester and Bonner, were kept under, and their power was but small; but afterwards, upon seeing the great division amongst the nobles, they began again to have hopes, that they should have another day and time further to execute their persecuting power, which soon after they had; for the next year, after the death of the duke of Somerset, the king died; and queen Mary ascended the throne; of the bloody work in whose reign, a relation will be given in its place.

Sufferings of William Gardner, an English merchant, in Portugal, for his testimony to the truth, against Popish idolatry.

WILLIAM Gardner was born at Bristol, of honest parents. He was naturally given to gravity, of a mean stature of body, but of a comely and pleasant countenance, possessing excellent inward qualities of the mind, which, from a child, he had kept without spot of reprehension. While an apprentice with a merchant in Bristol, his master sent him a voyage to Spain; but, by accident, the ship arrived at Lisbon, in Portugal; where, after he came ashore, he was very strict in keeping himself, lest he should be defiled with the Portugal superstition. Whilst he remained there, a great marriage was solemnized, between the king of Portugal's son and the king of Spain's daughter; which the young man, amongst other people, going to the public place to see, and there beholding the people's great idolatry, he was sorely pricked and moved in his conscience against it; but had not an opportunity to bear his testimony against it at that time; and left the place, and went away with a great burden upon him; and so it continued upon him, insomuch that he sought out secret and solitary places, where he might call upon God with tears, and ease his mind, bewailing himself for neglecting his duty, in testifying against the impiety and superstition of that people; concluding in his mind to take another opportunity to clear himself; and to that end, he made up his accounts with all men; and then gave himself continually to prayer and meditation on the Lord, taking little meat by day, or sleep by night.

Shortly after, he went, on the first day of the week, to the public place of worship, where the king was present, and a great assembly of people. Getting as near to the high altar as he could, and having a Testament in English in his hand, in which he read while the mass was celebrated by the cardinal, until the cardinal took the host in his hand: then William, being moved with zeal, and not longer able to forbear, he stepped speedily, and snatched the cake out of the priest's hand, and trod it under his feet, and overthrew the chalice. This made the people all amazed, and rise in a great tumult; and one pierced him in the shoulder with his dagger, and immediately they would have killed him, had not the king commanded he should be saved.

After the tumult ceased, he was brought before the king, who asked him, what countryman he was? and how he durst be so bold as to do such an action, in contempt of him and the sacrament of the church?

William Gardner told him, he was an Englishman, and came thither a merchant; and seeing so great idolatry, in so famous an assembly, he was not satisfied in his conscience, until he had acted what he had done. Further telling the king, there was not any thought in him of acting any thing in contempt to his presence.

When he was urged to discover the persons that instigated him to the action, he desired there might be no such suspicion conceived of him, saying, he was not moved thereunto by any man, but by his own conscience, and that he did it as required of God, and for the people's salvation.

While he was thus examined, he was ready to faint with the wound he received; whereupon, surgeons were sent for to cure him, if possible, to the end he might be further examined, and receive greater punishment; for they were fully persuaded some others had stirred him to do the action; and thereupon the English merchants were apprehended, and his bed-fellow was examined, and cruelly tormented, and kept in prison two years after. And having searched William Gardner's chamber, thinking there to find out some of the authors of the enterprise, but finding none, they repaired to him again, urging him to discover who was the author or instigator of him to do the fact, using an unheard of piece of cruelty, to make him confess, which was thus: They made fast a thread to a cloth ball, and thrust it down his throat, and then pulled it up again, and so pulled it to and fro for some time, till they were wearied; and seeing they could work nothing that way, they asked him, whether he did repent of his wicked deed? He answered, that he thought, that if it were to do again, he should do it.

After they had used divers torments to make him confess, and saw it was to no purpose, they had him to execution; but first, they carried him into the vestry, and cut off his right hand: then he was had into the market place, and there they cut off his left hand: then his arms were bound behind him, and his feet under the horse's belly, and so he was carried to the place of execution, where he was let down by a pulley into the fire; and then pulled up and let down again; all which cruelty he endured with a constant spirit, saying, "O Eternal God! Father of all mercies, look down upon thy servant." And with patience he suffered, till at last, the rope burning, he fell down into the fire, and was consumed. This was in the year 1552.

Persecutions in the reign of queen Mary, beginning anno 1553.

After the death of Edward the sixth, queen Mary succeeded; and after she was settled on her throne, a synod was assembled, for consulting about matters of religion; and especially the point of the real presence in the sacrament. After a long disputation, in which, reason and the scripture were not so much weighed as voices numbered, the papal side, having most voices, carried it; and thereupon was that religion again restored, and the mass commanded again in all meeting houses, to be celebrated after the ancient manner.

Shortly after, cardinal Poole, an Englishman, who had fled to Rome for succour, in a former time, was sent for over again to England, by the queen. He had no sooner come, than the attainder upon record against him was, by act of parliament, taken off, and he restored; and a few days after, coming to the parliament, before the queen and both houses assembled, after the bishop of Winchester, who was chancellor, had made a short speech to them, signifying the presence of the cardinal, and that he was sent from the pope, as his legate, for their good and benefit; the cardinal stood up, and made a long oration to them, thanking them for restoring him, whereby he was made a member of their society. Then he exhorted them to return into the bosom of the church; for which end, he was come, not to condemn, but to reconcile; not to compel, but to call and require. And for their first work of reconcilement, he required them to repeal and abrogate all such laws as had formerly been made in derogation of the catholic religion.

After which speech, the parliament drew up a supplication, which, within two days after, they presented to the king and queen; wherein they shewed themselves to be very penitent for their former errors, and humbly desired them to intercede for them, to the cardinal and the see apostolic, that they might be pardoned of all they had done amiss, and be received into the bosom of the church, being themselves most ready to abrogate all laws prejudicial to the see of Rome.

This supplication being delivered to the cardinal, he then gave them absolution in these words: " We (by the apostolic authority given unto us, by the most holy lord pope Julius the third, Christ's vicegerent on earth) do absolve and deliver you, and every of you, with the whole realm and dominions thereof, from all heresy and schism, and from all judgments, censures, and pains, for that cause incurred; and also, we do restore you again, to the unity of our mother the holy church." The report hereof coming to Rome, was cause that a solemn procession was made, for joy of the conversion of England to the church of Rome.

And now all bishops, who had been deprived of their bishoprics in the time of Edward the sixth, were restored to them, and the new bishops removed; and all that would not turn and forsake their religion, were turned out of their livings. Stephen Gardner and Bonner became again to be had in favour, and were restored to their former places; and several old laws were again revived, by act of parliament, for the trial of heresy: and commissions and inquisitors were sent abroad into all parts of the realm; whereby many were apprehended and brought to London, and there imprisoned; and afterwards most of them were burnt to death; or they, through his cruel usage, died in prison, and were buried in dunghills in the fields, to the number of near three hundred persons, men and women, in the short reign of this queen.

Bonner, being reinstated into his bishopric, sent forth injunctions, that six in every parish, upon their oath, should present before him such as would not conform; and soon after, about three score inhabitants of the city of London, were apprehended and imprisoned, for dispersing and selling certain books, sent over into England out of Germany and other countries.

About this time, the people going in procession in Smithfield; and the priest being under the canopy with the box, according to the usual custom, one John Street, a joiner in Coleman street, going by in haste about his business, by chance went under the canopy by the priest, at which the priest was so surprised, and overcome with fear, that he let the pix fall down. The people being amazed, presently apprehended the poor man, and committed him to the compter; and the priest accused him to the council, as if he came to slay him. From the compter, he was removed to Newgate, where he was cast into the dungeon, and there chained to a post, and so miserably used that he lost his senses; and then they sent him to Bedlam.

These were but the beginnings of Bonner's cruelty, in this queen's time. The next thing he did was, he put out a mandate to the curates within his diocess, requiring them to abrogate and blot out all scripture texts written upon the walls in houses of worship, in Edward the sixth's time; which, he said, was opening a window to all vice; and he further commanded, that comely roods should be again set up in all churches.

The same injunction for setting up roods, was published in other diocesses at this time; for at Cockram, in Lancashire, the parishioners and wardens had agreed with a carver to make them a rood, and to set it up in their house of worship, at a certain price, which the

carver did ; but the rood being made of an ugly grim
countenance, they disliked it, and refused to pay the
workman that made it ; whereupon, by warrant, he
brought them before the mayor of Lancaster, who was
a favourer of the protestants, and a man against images.
When they came before the mayor, he asked them,
" why they did not pay the man according to their agreement ?" They replied, " they did not like the grim-
ness of its visage ; saying, they had a man formerly
with a handsome face, and they would have had such another now." " Well, said the mayor, though you like
not the rood, the poor man's labour has been nevertheless, and its pity he should lose ; but I tell you what
you shall do, pay him the money you promised him,
and if it will not serve you for a God, you may make
a devil of it." At which, they laughed, and so departed.

Near this time, about thirty men and women were
taken at a religious assembly, in Bow-yard, in Cheapside ; and were committed to prison. Their preacher,
one Rose, was had before the bishop of Winchester,
Stephen Gardner, and by him committed to the tower.

Shortly after, Cranmer, Ridley, and Latimer, three
bishops, were sent to the tower ; and from thence conveyed to Oxford ; there to dispute with Oxford and
Cambridge men on points of religion, but especially of
the eucharist. The Oxford men were Cole, Chadsey,
Pye, Harpsfield, Smith, and Weston, prolocutor ; the
Cambridge men were Young, Seaton, Watson, Fecknam, Atkinson, and Sedgwick. The matter was so carried by these twelve men, that it went against the prisoners ; and after the disputation was ended, the prisoners were brought again upon the stage, and demanded,
whether they would persist in their opinion, or recant ?
They affirming that they would persist, were all three
adjudged heretics, and condemned to the fire ; but their
execution was not till a year or two after.

In the mean time, we have an account of John Rogers, an aged minister, who was the proto-martyr offered up in this reign to popery ; and led the way for

2 r

those sufferers, whose blood has been the seed of the church.

Rogers had been some time chaplain to the English factory at Antwerp. There he became acquainted with Tindal, and assisted him in his translation of the New Testament. Rogers, knowing that marriage was lawful, and even enjoined in scripture, entered into that state with a virtuous woman; and soon after set out for Saxony, in consequence of an invitation for that purpose.

When young king Edward ascended the throne of England, Rogers returned to his native country; and was promoted by bishop Ridley to a prebendary of St. Paul's. He was also appointed reader of the divinity lecture in that cathedral, and vicar of St. Sepulchre's.

As the queen was returning from the tower, where she had been attending Gardiner's councils, Rogers was preaching at St. Paul's Cross. He inveighed much against popery, expatiated on the many virtues of the late king Edward, and exhorted the people to abide in the protestant religion.

For this sermon, he was summoned before the council; but he vindicated himself so well, that he was dismissed.

This lenity shewn by the council was rather displeasing to the queen; and Rogers's zeal against popery being equal to his knowledge and integrity, he was considered as a person who would prevent the re-establishment of popery.

For this reason it was, that he was summoned a second time before the council; and although there were many papists among them, yet such was the respect that most people had for Rogers, that he was again dismissed, only that he was commanded not to go out of his own house. This order he complied with, although he might have made his escape, if he would. He knew he could have had a living in Germany, and he had a wife and ten children: but all these things did not move him. He did not court death, but met it with fortitude when it came.

He remained in prison, as it were, in his own house

several weeks, till Bonner, bishop of London, procured an order to have him committed to Newgate, where he was lodged among thieves and murderers.

He was brought a third time before the council, where Gardner, the bishop of Winchester, presided. The questions asked him were of a very frivolous nature; but still they were such, that answers to them served to criminate him.

He made a most elaborate defence, which, however, did not avail him in the minds of his persecutors. He shewed them; that the statute upon which he was prosecuted, had never legally passed; and. even if it had, it was, in all respects, contrary to the word of God. For whatever emoluments might have been bestowed upon the clergy from time to time, they had no right to prosecute those who differed from them in sentiment.

After he had been examined several times before the council, which was only a mere farce, he was turned over to Bonner, bishop of London, who caused him to go through a second mock examination; and, at last, declared him to be an obstinate heretic. A certificate of this was, in the ordinary course, sent into chancery, and a writ was issued for the burning of him in Smithfield.

When he was taken out of Newgate, to be led to the place of execution, the sheriff asked him, if he would recant his opinions? To this, he answered, " that what he had preached he would seal with his blood." " Then (said the sheriff) thou art an heretic." To which, Rogers answered, " that will be known when we meet at the judgment seat of Christ."

As they were taking him to Smithfield, his wife and children went to take their last farewell of a tender husband. and an indulgent parent. The sheriffs, however, would not permit them to speak to him. So unfeeling is bigotry, so merciless is superstition! When he was chained to the stake, he took notice, that God would, in his own good time, vindicate the truth of what he had taught, and appear in favour of the protestant religion. Fire was then set to the pile; and he was, in about two hours, consumed to ashes.

The next person who suffered in this reign, was Laurence Saunders; of whom, we have the following particulars: his father had a considerable estate somewhere in Oxfordshire; but dying young, he left a large family of children. This Laurence was sent to Eton college, as one of the king's scholars.

From Eton, he was, according to the rules of the foundation, sent to king's college in Cambridge, where he studied three years, and made great progress in the different sorts of learning then taught in the schools. At the end of three years, he left the university; and returning to his mother, he prevailed upon her to article him to William Chester, a rich merchant in London, who was afterwards sheriff of that city. He had not been long in this employment, when he became sick, as it were, of a life of trade. He sunk into a deep melancholy, and afterwards went into a chamber, where no person saw him, to mourn for his imprudence, and to beg of God that he would, in some manner or other, deliver him from a life so disgustful.

His master, who was a worthy man, took notice of this, and asked him his reason for being in that desponding condition. The young man prudently told him; upon which, he immediately gave him up his indentures, and sent him home to his relations.

This the young man considered as a happy event; and that no time might be lost, he returned to his studies at Cambridge; and, what was very uncommon in that age, he learned the Greek and Hebrew languages. After this, he devoted himself wholly to the study of the sacred scriptures, in order to qualify himself for preaching the gospel.

In the beginning of king Edward's reign, when the true religion began to be countenanced, he entered into orders, and began to preach with great success. His first appointment was at Fotheringham, where he read a divinity lecture; but that college having been dissolved, he was appointed a preacher in Litchfield. In that new station, his conduct entitled him to great respect; for such was his sweetness of temper, his knowledge in his profession, his eloquent manner of addressing his hearers, the purity of his manners, and his affectionate addresses to the heart, that all conspired to make him an amiable object, and his ministry useful.

After being some months in Litchfield, he removed to the living of Church Langton, in Leicestershire. There he resided with his people, and instructed many who before were ignorant of the true principles of the christian religion. He was the same to men's bodies, as to their souls. All that he received, besides the small pittance that supported his person, was given away to feed the hungry, and clothe the naked.

His next removal was to Alhallows, in Bread street, London; and when he had taken possession of it, he went down into the country, to part, in an affectionate manner, with his friends.

It was while he was in the country, that the pious king Edward died; and Mary succeeding, published a proclamation, commanding all her subjects to attend mass. Many pious ministers refused to obey the royal proclamation; and none were more forward in doing so than Saunders. He continued to preach, whenever he had an opportunity, and to read the prayer book, with the scriptures, to the people, till he was apprehended, in the following manner.

He was advised to leave the nation, as pious Dr. Jewel, and many others did; but he would not, declaring to his friends, that he was willing to die for the name of the Lord Jesus. Accordingly, he left his people in Leicestershire, and travelled towards London. On his arrival near which, he was met by John Mordant, a privy counsellor to queen Mary, who asked him where he was going? Saunders said, to his living in Bread-street, to instruct his people. Mordant desired him not to go; to which Saunders answered: "how shall I then be accountable to God? If any be sick and die before consolation, then what a load of guilt will be upon my conscience, as an unfaithful shepherd, and an unjust steward!"

Mordant asked him, whether he did not frequently preach in Bread-street? and being answered in the affirmative, he endeavoured to dissuade him from doing so any more. Saunders, however, was resolute, and told him, he would continue to preach as long as he lived; and invited the other to come and hear him the next day; adding that he would certainly confirm him in the truth of those sentiments which he taught. Upon this, they parted; and Mordant went and informed bishop Bonner, that Saunders would preach in his own church the next Sunday.

In the mean time, Saunders went to his lodging, with a mind resolved to do his duty. When a person came to visit him, and took notice to him that he seemed to be in trouble, he said he was; adding, " I am, as it were, in prison, till I speak to my people." So earnest was his desire to discharge his duty, and so little did he regard the malice of his enemies!

Soon after he preached to his hearers, and made a most elaborate discourse against the errors of popery. He exhorted the people to remain steadfast in the truth; not to fear those who can only kill the body, but to fear him who can throw both soul and body into hell. He was attended by a great concourse of people, which gave much offence to the clergy, particularly to bishop Bonner.

No notice, however, was taken of him in the forenoon; but, in the afternoon, when he intended to have preached again, Bonner sent an officer to apprehend him; accordingly, he went with the officer; and John Mordant appeared to give evidence against him.

Saunders was charged with treason and sedition, for having disobeyed the queen's proclamation; but Bonner had other objects in view than that of bringing this man to trial at common law. Heresy was the main thing he had in view, and nothing else would go down. And here it is necessary to observe, that the bishop was too hasty, for the queen's proclamation could not be law, unless sanctioned by an act of parliament, which it was not.

After much conversation on the different points in religion, the bishop desired him to write what his sentiments were concerning transubstantiation. To this request, Saunders replied, " my Lord, I know you want to insnare me ; you seek for my blood, and you shall have it. Perhaps the reflection of taking my life, without cause, may bring you to a sense of guilt, and make you a better man."

The next thing the bishop did, was, to send Saunders, under the care of Mordant, to the house of the chancellor, who happened not to be at home ; so that he was obliged to tarry for him four hours in the servants' hall. During the whole of this space of time, Saunders did not so much as receive the least refreshment, but stood bareheaded, while Mordant kept walking backwards and forwards across the room.

At length, Gardner, the chancellor, arrived ; and, sending for Saunders into his chamber, asked him, how he could be so bold as to disobey the queen's proclamation ? Saunders acknowledged, that he had preached contrary to the proclamation ; and that he thought it his duty to do so, even although it should cost him his life. He added, that what he did, arose from the dictates of his heart, which commanded him to preach the gospel in season, and out of season : that he should be accountable at the judgment seat of Christ, if he neglected any part of his duty in teaching and comforting his people in their most holy faith, so as to meet them on the right hand of the judge.

The chancellor poured out much abuse on Saunders, telling him he was a hypocrite and a heretic, notwithstanding all his pretensions to a tender conscience. He accused him farther, of having called the queen a bastard, or rather worse, namely, that she had been born in a state of incest.

It is well known, that Henry's first marriage with Catharine had been declared inconsistent with the canons of the church ; and, therefore, had Saunders called her by such names, he might, according to law, have sheltered himself under an act of parliament. But the truth is,

Saunders never traduced the queen's character; but, in speaking to Gardner, he made use of a most severe sarcasm, by telling him, that there need not be much dispute concerning this matter with his lordship, who had actually signed the declaration concerning the illegitimacy of Mary's birth. This was bringing the argument home to him ; but the severity of the satire filled Gardner with strong motives of revenge.

Saunders told the chancellor, he had no objection against suffering for that God who had given him courage to declare his sentiments without fear, and would support him under all sorts of afflictions ; and although he would never give intentional offence, yet he was not, by any means, to injure his conscience, by giving up the truth as it was revealed in the word of God.

Gardner, upon this, remanded Saunders to prison, where he continued no less than one year and three months ; during which time, he wrote several letters to those great and worthy persons, who afterwards fuffered for the truth.

As this pious minister saw no hopes of getting released from prison, he drew up a paper which he sent to the chancellor, containing sentiments to the following purport : namely, that he did not believe he had transgressed against the proclamation, for it did not command ministers to preach against the dictates of their consciences.

As for his religion, he said it was the same as that taught in the New Testament. He worshipped the God of his fathers, after the manner they called heresy : that it was an easy matter to call people heretics, and to proceed against them by the assistance of the civil power : but the best way was to attempt, and, if possible, to confute their notions by solid argument.

The next observations made use of by Saunders were of a striking nature indeed. He declared, that no man could be a faithful servant of Christ, who acknowledged the papal supremacy. He said, it was the noblest of his glory ; and this is no more than what has been certified by most of the martyrs who suffered under the papal power. He observed, that traditions were not commanded

by the word of God, nor did they make any any part of religion.

In some other of his letters, he speaks of his entire confidence in God; and, in every one of them, there is something inviting the faithful to abide by the truth.

Saunders was a married man; and, in a letter to his
wife, he declared his firm attachment to the truth of the
gospel, according to the reformed religion, as it had
been set forth in the reign of king Edward VI. The
sentiments in this letter are truly evangelical; and such
as would have done honour to one of the primitive martyrs.

He told her, there could be no confidence in the divine
being, where a fixed truth was not placed in the righteousness of a redeemer. He added further, that she must not
consider him any longer as a husband for her in this world,
but that he hoped to spend an eternity with her. He told
her, that, if she should be molested for the truth, it was
her duty to examine her own mind, and attend to every
thing that could lead her to happiness; that the blessings
of the everlasting covenant could only be insured to believers in consequence of the death of Christ; and that the firm
persuasion of the resurrection of our Redeemer, was the only means the infinite wisdom could contrive, in order to
bring us to a state of happiness.

In one of his letters to Cranmer, who was then a prisoner, as well as himself, he expressed a firm belief of the immortality of the soul, and the resurrection of the dead, according to the gospel dispensation. At the same time, he
lamented that darkness which the corruption of human nature has thrown over our understandings: that as we see
here but through a glass darkly, so our faith should increase
in strength, in consequence of a longing desire for immortality. He added a great deal concerning the vast importance of the ministerial office, and the necessity for ministers to keep themselves from giving offence, lest the gospel
should be blamed.

In another letter to his wife, he said much concerning
that long friendship and happiness which he had enjoyed
with her. He expressed his earnest desire still to have en-

2 G

joyed her company, had it been consistent with the will of God. But as he knew his death was resolved on, he begged she would pray, that God would enable her to bear such an event, and that he might likewise be enabled to go through it as became a good soldier of Christ Jesus. He gave her the utmost encouragement to trust in the merits and mercies of Christ Jesus; to make him her only friend; and then he would never leave nor forsake her. He said much concerning the strength he had in Christ Jesus, who had gone the road of suffering before him; and cautioned her against denying the truth, whatever punishments the papists, and other enemies of Christ, might threaten her with.

In another letter to his wife, he said much concerning those consolations which God gives to those who suffer for his name's sake. He takes notice, that the whole of human life is one continual torment; and therefore, when we are just going to take possession of a glorious and eternal inheritance, we should not repine at going through a few hardships. And what are these hardships, when compared with the dreadful punishments which God will inflict on apostates hereafter!

He was confined in the Marshalsea prison; and strict orders were given to the keepers, not to suffer any person to converse with him. His poor wife, however, came to the prison with her young child in her arms; and the keeper had so much compassion, that he took the child and carried it to its father.

Saunders seeing the child, rejoiced greatly, saying it was a peculiar happiness for him to have such a boy. And to the standers by, who admired the beauty of the child, he said, what man, fearing God, would not lose his life, sooner than have it said, that the mother of this child was a harlot?

He said these words, in order to point out the woful effects of popish celibacy; for the priests being denied the privilege of marriage, seduced the wives and daughters of many of the inhabitants, thereby producing illegitimate children, who were left exposed to all sorts of hardships.

After all these afflictions and sufferings, Saunders was brought before the council, where the chancellor sat as president; and there he was asked a great number of questions concerning his opinions. These questions were proposed in so artful and insnaring a manner, that the prisoner, by telling the truth, must criminate himself; and to have stood mute, would have subjected him to the torture.

Under such circumstances, God gave him fortitude to assert the truth, by declaring his abhorrence of all the doctrines of popery.

The examination being ended, the officers led him out of the place, and then waited till some other prisoners were examined. While Saunders was standing among the officers, seeing a great number of people assembled, as is common on such occasions, he exhorted them to beware of falling off from Christ to antichrist, as many were then returning to popery, because they had not fortitude to suffer.

The chancellor ordered him to be excommunicated, and committed him to the compter, which was in his own parish of Bread-street. This was a great comfort to him, because he was visited by many of his people, whom he exhorted to constancy; and, when they were denied admittance, he spoke to them through the grate.

On the 4th of the month called February, the sheriff of London delivered him to the bishop, who degraded him; and Saunders said, " thank God, I am now out of your church."

The day following, he was given up to some of the queen's officers, who were appointed to convey him down to Coventry, there to be burned. The first night, they lay at St. Albin's, where Saunders took an opportunity of rebuking a person who had ridiculed the christian faith.

After they arrived at Coventry, a poor shoe-maker, who had formerly worked for Saunders, came to him, and said, " O, my good master, may God strengthen you!" " Good shoe-maker, (answered Saunders) I beg you will pray for me, for I am at present in a very weak condition; but I hope my gracious God, who hath appointed me to it, will give me strength."

The same night, he spent in the common prison, praying for, and exhorting all those who went to hear him.

The next day, he was led to the place of execution, in the Park, without the gate of that city, going in an old gown and shirt, barefooted ; and, he often fell flat on the ground and prayed. When he approached the place of execution, the under-sheriff told him, he was an heretic, and that he led the people away from the true religion ; but yet, if he would recant, the queen would pardon him. To this, Saunders answered, "that he had not filled the realm with heresy ; for he had taught the people the pure truths of the gospel ; and, in all his sermons, while he exhorted the people, he firmly desired his hearers to be obedient to the queen."

When brought to the stake, he embraced it ; and, after being fastened to it, and the fagots lighted, he said, " welcome, the cross of Christ ! welcome, everlasting life!" soon after which, he resigned his soul into the hands of him who gave it.

The sufferings and Martyrdom of bishop Hooper.

John Hooper was a student and graduate of the university of Oxford, where he applied himself to a diligent search of the holy scriptures, joined with earnest prayers, that God would enlighten his understanding, and guide him in the right way.

When the six articles were published, Dr. Hooper did all he could to oppose them, as maintaining every thing in the popish system, except the supremacy. He preached frequently against them, which created him many enemies in Oxford ; but Henry VIII. had such an opinion of him, that he would not suffer him to be molested.

Soon after this, he was compelled by persecution to leave the university, and afterwards the kingdom ; and as he was flying from city to city, he came at length to Basil, where he married a pious woman ; and afterwards settled at Zurick, in Switzerland. There he applied so close to his studies, that he made himself master of the Hebrew language.

At length, when the true religion was set up, after the death of king Henry VIII. amongst other English exiles that returned, was Hooper. In the most grateful manner, he returned thanks to all his friends abroad, who had shewn him so much compassion; particularly to the learned Bullinger, who was a great friend to all those who were persecuted for the gospel. When he took an affectionate leave of Bullinger, he told him, that he would write to him as often as he could find an opportunity; but added, probably I shall be burned to ashes, and then some friend will give you information.

When Dr. Hooper arrived in London, he was so much filled with zeal to promote the gospel, that he preached every day to crowded congregations. In his sermons, he reproved sinners in general, but particularly directed his discourse against the erroneous vices of the times.

After he had preached some time, with great success in the city, he was sent for by king Edward VI, who appointed him one of his chaplains, and soon after made him bishop of Gloucester, by letters patent under the great seal; having at the same time the care of the bishopric of Worcester committed to him.

As Dr. Hooper had been some time abroad, he contracted an aversion to the popish ceremonies; and, before he went to his bishopric, he requested of the king that he might not be obliged to give countenance to them, which was complied with, though much against the inclinations of the other bishops. He and his brethren had many disputes about the Romish tenets, which may serve to shew that there are some remains of corruption in the best of men. Some men seek honours with unwearied zeal, and seem to take more pleasure in titles, than in considering that an elevated rank only increases the necessity of being more enlarged in duty.

Dr. Hooper differed from this set of men; for, instead of seeking after any preferments, he would never have accepted of any, had they not been offered him. Having the care of two diocesses, he held and guided them both together, as if they had been but one. His leisure time, which was but little, he spent in hearing causes, private prayer, and reading the scriptures. He likewise visited the schools, and encouraged the youth in their learning. He had children of his own, whom he likewise instructed, and treated them with all the tenderness of an indulgent parent.

Fox tells us, he kept great tables, with provisions for the poor, which was a very pious action in those times, because the people who had been driven out of the convents, roved up and down the country starving. He relieved a certain number of these every day ; and, when they had done eating, he delivered a discourse to them on the principles of the christian religion.

After this manner, he continued to discharge his duty as a faithful pastor, during the whole of king Edward's reign. But no sooner was the pious young king laid in the grave, and Mary proclaimed, than a serjeant at arms was sent to arrest bishop Hooper, in order to answer to two charges.

First, to answer to Dr. Heath, who had been deprived of the diocess of Gloucester, for his adherence to popery, but was now restored by the queen. Secondly, to answer to Dr. Bonner, bishop of London, who was restored by the queen, for having given evidence to king Edward against that persecuting prelate.

Bishop Hooper was desired by some of his friends, to get away ; but his answer was, " I once fled for my life, but I am determined, through the strength and grace of God, to witness the truth to the last."

Being brought before the queen and council, Gardner was sitting as president, who accused bishop Hooper of heresy, calling him by the most opprobrious names. This was in the month of Septemper, 1553 ; and he lay in prison, on a charge of being indebted to the queen in several sums of money. The Spring following, 1554, when he was called again to appear before Gardner, the chancellor, and several of the bishops would not suffer him to plead his cause, but deprived him of his bishopric.

Being asked, whether he was a married man, he answered in the affirmative, and declared that he would not be unmarried until death occasioned a separation ; hence he looked upon the marriage of the clergy necessary.

The more they attempted to brow-beat him, the more resolute he became, and the more pertinent in his answers. He produced the decrees of the council of Nice, which first ascertained the canon of scripture, where it was ordained to be lawful, as well as expedient for the clergy to marry. This was to very little purpose with men who had their instructions from the queen ; and therefore, the bishop was committed to the tower, but afterwards removed to the fleet.

As the determination for burning him was not agreed on, he was only considered as a debtor to the queen, for the rents of his bishopric, which was the reason of his being sent to the fleet. This, however, was a most unjust charge ; for the protestant religion had been established in the first year of the reign of her brother Edward, by act of parliament ; so that Dr. Hooper's accepting of a bishopric was in all respects legal and constitutional.

As a debtor, he was to have the rules of the fleet, which the warden granted him for five pounds sterling ; but went immediately and informed Gardner, who, notwithstanding he had paid the money, ordered him to be close confined.

He was now in a dreadful situation ; and the warden, whose name was Babington, informed against him for not going to mass ; upon which, he was locked up in a small room, where he had nothing but straw to lie upon, with a rotten covering, and such other things, till at last, some pious people sent him a bed.

During this time, he was taken ill, and the doors being all fast locked, he mourned and called for help ; but the warden would neither give him any assistance, nor suffer the prisoners, who were willing, to do so, telling them, it would be well if he should die.

Notwithstanding all this cruelty, Dr. Hooper always paid the warden every fee that he demanded, besides an additional allowance for his board. His servant, who had been many years with him, came to see him, and the warden caused him to be stripped and searched for letters, but could find none, besides the names of a few of his friends who wished him well. The warden was so base as to carry the names of these persons to the chancellor, who ordered several of them to be taken into custody, and all Hooper's goods were seized.

After he had been eighteen months in prison, the warden of the fleet was ordered to bring him before the chancellor Gardner, who, with other bishops, was appointed to examine him a second time, at Gardner's house in Southwark.

When brought before these merciless persecutors, the chancellor made a long speech to him, desiring him to forsake the opinions he had embraced, and return to the bosom of the church ; adding that as the pope was the church, so it was breaking through her unity to separate from her. He promised to procure him the pope's absolution, if he would recant his opinions ; but this was nothing more or less than a farce ; for Gardner knew well that Hooper was too well grounded in his religious opinions, to comply with any such request.

To this, Dr. Hooper answered, that as the popes's doctrine was contrary to the sacred scriptures : and as he could not be the head of the church, because there was no head of it but Christ, so he would live and die asserting the doctrines he had taught.

Gardner replied, that the queen would never shew any mercy to the enemies of the pope ; whereupon, Babington, the warden, was commanded to take him back to the fleet. It was likewise ordered, that he should be shifted from his former chamber, which was done ; and he was searched to find, if possible, whether he had any books concealed about him ; but none were found.

Three days after, he was again brought before the chancellor to be examined, whether or not he would recant, but nothing could shake his constancy.

He continued in prison about ten days longer, when the bishop went to degrade him, which was done in the usual form, by putting the different robes upon him worn by priests, and then taking them off. The reason why they did not put on him the bishop's robes was, that they did not admit of the validity of his ordination. While they were taking these robes off from him, he told them he was glad to part with them, because his mind had always been against them, and considered them as no better than heathenish relics. In fact, they were such; for the same robes were worn by the priests before the time of the emperor Constantine the great.

A few hours after he was degraded, the keeper came to him, and told him, he was to be sent down to Gloucester to suffer death. Upon this, he lifted up his eyes and hands to heaven, praising God that he was to die among his own people, as it would be the means of confirming them in the truth of what he had taught them. He immediately sent to his servant for his boots and cloak, that he might be in readiness to attend them, whenever they should come for him.

About four in the morning, he was taken out of prison by the sheriff, and conducted to the sign of the angel, Fleet street. There he was received by the queen's officers, who had the warrant for his execution; after which, they permitted him to take some refreshment.

About the break of day, he cheerfully mounted on horseback, without help, having a hood on his head under his hat, that he should not be known; and thus equipped, with a serene and cheerful countenance, he proceeded on the road for Gloucester, attended by his keepers. The guards asked him, what houses he was accustomed to use on the road; and, when they were informed, in order to perplex him, they took him to others.

After three days, they arrived at Cirencester, a town in his own diocese, and about eleven miles from Gloucester. It being about eleven o'clock in the forenoon, they dined at a woman's house who had always hated the protestants, and traduced bishop Hooper's character as much as possible. This woman, seeing his constancy, was so affected, that she lamented his case with tears,

2 H

and begged his pardon for the manner in which she had treated him.

Dinner being over, they proceeded to Gloucester, where they arrived about five in the afternoon. A great crowd of people were assembled about a mile without the town; so that one of the guard, fearing a rescue, rode up to the mayor's house, to demand aid and assistance. This being granted, the officers desired the people to disperse, with which they very readily complied.

Hooper was that night lodged in the house of one Ingram, where he ate his supper with a good appetite, and slept very quietly, as the guard declared, for they continued in the chamber with him all the night. In the morning he got up, and having prayed most fervently, was visited by sir Anthony Kingston, who was one of the persons appointed to see him executed. When sir Anthony came into the chamber, he found him at his prayers, and waiting till he had done, asked him if he did not know him? To this, bishop Hooper answered, that he did know him, and was glad to see him in good health. He added, that he was come there to end his life, and blessed God that it was to be in the midst of his diocess. He said, he loved life as well as it ought to be loved, but he was not to enjoy it at the expense of his future welfare. He was not to blaspheme his Saviour by denying his name, through which alone he looked for salvation; but trusted, that he should be endowed with fortitude sufficient to bear all the torments his enemies could inflict upon him.

Sir Anthony Kingston had profited much from the preaching of bishop Hooper; and taking his leave, told him, with tears, that he was extemely sorry to lose such a worthy person. Dr. Hooper answered, that it was his duty to persevere in the truth, and not to be ashamed of the gospel, lest Christ should refuse to acknowledge him before his father in heaven.

The same day, in the afternoon, a poor blind boy came to visit bishop Hooper; and falling on his knees before him, said, " ah, my lord, I am blind in my eyes, but your pious instructions have removed a spiritual blindness from my heart. May God support you under all your sufferings, and bring you, even through flames, to heaven!"

Several other persons visited bishop Hooper, amongst whom was a very wicked man. a bigotted papist, who had known him formerly. This man upbraided him with what the papists call heresy, but he bore all his insults with patience and meekness.

The time appointed for the execution of this pious bishop drawing nigh, he was delivered to the sheriffs of Gloucester, one of whose names was Bind, and the other Jenkins, who, with the mayor and aldermen, repaired to bishop Hooper's lodgings, and at the first meeting, having saluted him, took him by the hand. The resigned martyr thanked the mayor, with the rest of the officers, for taking a condemned man by the hand, and for all the friendship that had formerly subsisted between them, for he had been long acquainted with them. He begged of the sheriffs that they would make the fire as violent as possible, that his pains might be of the shorter duration; adding, that he might have had his life, if he chose it, but could not, consistent with the duty he owed to God, and his own conscience. He said, he knew the bishop of Rome was antichrist, and therefore he could not be obedient to him.

A consultation was held by the sheriffs, whether or not they should lodge him, the evening preceding his execution, in the common gaol, over the north gate of the city; but the guards, who brought him from London, interceded so earnestly in his behalf, that he was permitted to remain in his former lodgings.

When bishop Hooper arose in the morning, he desired that no person whatever should disturb him in his devotions, till the officers came to lead him to execution.

About eight o'clock, the lord Chandois, attended by several other noblemen and gentlemen, came to conduct him to the place of execution; and at nine, Dr. Hooper was ready. Being brought down from his chamber, when he saw the guards, he told the sheriffs that he was no traitor, but one who was willing to die for the truth; and that, if they would have permitted him, he would have willingly gone unguarded to the stake, without troubling any officers. Afterwards, looking upon the multitude of people that were assembled, who were above seven thousand in number, it being the market day, he said, "alas! why are so many people assembled? I dare not speak to them as formerly."

He was led forward between the two sheriffs, as a lamb to the slaughter, having on a gown which the man of the house, where he was confined, had given him; and being much afflicted with an illness he had contracted in prison, he was obliged to walk with a stick in his hand. The sheriff having commanded him not to speak one word, he was not seen to open his mouth, but beholding the people, who mourned bitterly, he sometimes lifted up his eyes towards heaven, and looked cheerfully on such as he knew; and, indeed, his countenance was more cheerful than it had been for a long time before.

When he was brought to the stake, he embraced it, and looked with cheerfulness at a place where he used formerly to preach. He then kneeled down to pray, and beckoned several times to one whom he knew, to come near him, that he might give an account of what he said, after his death, as he was not permitted to speak aloud. When he had been some time at prayer, a pardon was brought, and laid down before him, on condition he would recant his opinions; but neither promises of pardon, nor the threatenings of punishment, could have any effect on him; so immovable was he in the faith, and so well established in the principles of the gospel.

Prayers being ended, he prepared himself for the stake, by taking off his landlord's gown, which he delivered to the sheriffs, requesting them to see it restored to the owner. He then took off the rest of his clothes, except his doublet and hose, in which he designed to be burned; but the sheriffs not permitting that, he patiently submitted. After this, a pound of gunpowder was placed between his legs, and the same quantity under each arm. Three chains were then fixed round him, one to his neck, another to his middle, and a third to his legs ; and with these, he was fastened to the stake.

This being done, fire was put to the fagots; but they being green, he suffered inexpressible torment. Soon after this, another load of dry fagots was brought, but still the wind blew away the flames ; so that he begged for more, that he might be put out of his misery.

At length, the fire took effect, and the martyr expired triumphantly, after such a fiery trial as almost exceeds any thing we meet with in the primitive ages.   His last words were, " Lord Jesus, have mercy upon me ; enable me to bear my suffering for thy name sake, and receive my spirit."

Such was the end of the temporal life ; and such was the passage into glory, of the pious John Hooper, some time bishop of Gloucester, and a most illustrious reformer !

The martyrdom of Dr. Rowland Taylor.

DR. ROWLAND TAYLOR was born in the town of Hadley, which was one of the first places in England that received the gospel.   Here it was, that Dr. Taylor, who was, in many respects, a very learned man, preached constantly to the people during the reign of king Edward. Archbishop Cranmer, who was a good judge of merit, and loved to reward it in learned men , took him into his family, and presented him to this living.   Here he behaved as a most excellent preacher, and a faithful pastor. He made himself acquainted with every individual in his parish ; and he taught them like the apostles and primitive christians, who went from house to house.

His preaching was not all : his life was one continued comment on his doctrine : it was a life of holiness.   He studied nothing so much as doing good : he was a stranger to pride ; and it might justly be said of him, that he was clothed with humility. While he rebuked sinners for their enormities, he was ready to relieve all their wants. This was a godlike disposition, and a mark of the true character of a real christian.

In the course of his ministerial labours, he often met with opposition, and even with abuse; but he attended to the old maxim laid down by the apostle, that we must go through evil, as well as through good report. He was a married man, but never sat down to dinner with his family, without first inquiring whether the poor wanted any thing. To those who were distressed, he gave relief before he eat any thing himself. He familiarized himself with all ranks of men, in order that he might, at least, gain them to the knowledge and practice of the truth. To his wife, he was an indulgent, tender, affectionate husband; and he brought up his children in the fear of God, well knowing, that the laying of a good foundation, is the only way to have a beautiful superstructure.

In this heavenly manner, Dr. Taylor continued to discharge his duty at Hadley, as long as king Edward lived; but no sooner was this pious monarch dead, than things took a different turn.

And here it is necessary to observe, that let a man be ever so pious; let him be ever so saithful in the discharge of his duty, yet he will find many enemies in this world. This was the case with Dr. Taylor. In his parish, notwithstanding all his endeavours to suppress popery, yet some papists remained; and it is well known, that popery and the protestant religion can no more agree together than light and darkness.

Two persons in his parish, one named Clarke, and the other Foster, hired a Romish priest to come to Hadley to say mass. For this purpose, they ordered an altar to be built up with all convenient speed, and appointed that mass should be said on the day called Palm Sunday. But the people met together in the evening, and beat the altar in pieces: however, it was built up again, and a watch was appointed, lest it should be demolished a second time.

The day following, Clarke and Foster came, bringing along with them their popish priest, who was to perform the service of the mass. The priest was dressed in all his robes for that purpose, and had a guard with him, lest he should be interrupted by the populace.

When Dr. Taylor heard the bells ring, he went into the house of worship to know the reason, according to the duty of his station, but found the doors of the chancel barred against him. However, getting within the chancel, he saw the popish priest at the altar, attended by a great number of people, with their swords drawn. The doctor accused the priest of idolatry, but the priest retorted upon him, and called him traitor, for disobeying the queen's proclamation. Dr. Taylor said he was no traitor, but a minister of the gospel, commanded to teach the people; and then ordered the popish priest to retire, as one who came in there to poison the flock of Christ with his most abominable doctrines. Foster, who had a share in this business, called Dr. Taylor a traitor, and violently dragged him out of the church ; while his wife, on her knees, begged that God would vindicate his innocence, and avenge the injuries he had so wrongfully received, which was what he had not deserved, because he had not done more than his duty.

The next thing done by Foster and Clarke, was to exhibit a charge of heresy against Dr. Taylor, to Gardner the chancellor. The chancellor sent a messenger, commanding Dr. Taylor to appear before him, in order to answer to the charge that had been exhibited.

When Dr. Taylor's friends heard of this, they were much grieved ; and suspecting what was likely to happen, as law and justice were both trodden under foot, desired him to go abroad to save his life. But this he would by no means comply with ; for he said, that it was more honourable to suffer for the cause of God, than to flee from the wrath of wicked men. " God (said he) will protect me from sufferings, or he will enable me to bear them." He added, " that he knew his dying for truth would be of more service to Christ, than his flying away from the malice of his persecutors."

When his friends saw that nothing could prevail upon him, they took farewell of him with tears; after which, he set out for London accompanied by a servant, named John Hull, who had been a considerable time in his family. This faithful servant advised him to make his escape, but all to no purpose; for he said, that the good shepherd should never leave his sheep, till he was torn from them by force. In the same heavenly manner, he exhorted John to be constant, in the profession of christianity, and not to return again to popery. He said, that worldly wisdom was apt to take too deep a root in our hearts, and that it was, therefore, our duty to do all we could to triumph over the world, the flesh, and the devil; to be constant in our attachment to the truth; to keep in view the great glories of eternity; to consider the vast difference between temporal and spiritual things; to trample, as it were, on the earth, while we keep heaven in our eye; to fear God more than men; to prefer sufferings, in this world to all temporary enjoyments; to believe that God will sweeten all our sufferings, by the influences of his holy spirit; to think nothing too hard to endure, so that we can but obtain a blessed immortality; and, with a christian courage, to trample on death, and triumph over the grave.

When Dr. Taylor was brought before the chancellor Gardner, that prelate reviled him in the most shocking manner, calling him a traitor and a heretic; all which, the pious martyr patiently submitted to. In the opinion of Gardner, he might have been an heretic; but, according to law, he could not have been a traitor; for the statute of high treason, and the statute of heresy, enforced different punishments: for the one, the offending party was to be hanged and quartered; for the other, he was to be burned alive. Had queen Mary proceeded against this man, and many others, on the statute of high treason, they must have been acquitted, as the trial would have been conducted according to the principles of common law. But this was what she had no intention to do: her design was to gratify the clergy, and have all those who opposed their sentiments, executed upon their infamous statute.

Dr. Taylor answered the chancellor's questions with a becoming firmness : he accused him of being the persecutor of God's people, and asserted that he himself had adhered to our Saviour and his words. He put bishop Gardner in mind of the oath he had taken in the beginning of king Edward's reign, to maintain the protestant religion, and oppose the papal supremacy ; but Gardner answered, that the oath had been extorted, so that he was not obliged to abide by it.

Dr. Taylor explained to the Bishop the nature of an oath, and told him, that as he had not been forced to take one contrary to the dictates of conscience, so he was either prejudiced in what he did, or what was still worse, he trifled with a sacred obligation ; that no man whatever could dispense with an oath, unless he knew it was his duty to do so, in consequence of its having been imposed on him by violence.

Gardner who was self-convicted, turned the subject to the disputed points concerning the real presence, and some other things in popery.

With respect to the real presence in the sacrament, Dr. Taylor told him, that it had no foundation in scripture, but had been first taught about the tenth century. He quoted the book of Bertram, which was written about that time, wherein the real presence was denied, and transubstantiation considered as no better than a novel doctrine. He made it appear, that Christ only commanded his followers to keep the feast of the eucharist, in remembrance of his last supper with them. That as Christ broke bread, and drank wine with his disciples in a friendly manner, before he was dragged to prison, to judgment, and to execution, consequently, his followers should observe it as a feast of unity to the end of the world.

Dr. Taylor, after being interrogated by the chancellor for a considerable time, was at length committed to prison.

Bigotry has no feeling. Persecution knows no end. While he was in prison, he spent the greatest part of his time in prayer, in reading the sacred scriptures, and in exhorting the poor prisoners, confined with him, to a sense of their duty.   The prison in which Dr. Taylor was confined, was that commonly called the king's Bench ; and there he met with that holy and pious man Bradford, whose affinity in religious sentiments contributed to mitigate his sufferings.   If two virtuous or pious persons are of the same opinion, and under the same circumstances, they generally feel for each other.   This was the case with Dr. Taylor and Bradford; for, no sooner did they meet each other in prison, than they blessed God who had brought them together, to suffer for the truth of the gospel.

After Dr. Taylor had lain a considerable time in prison, he was cited to appear at Bow-church, in Cheapside, to answer to the dean of the arches, why he had married a wife.   To cite a prisoner to appear before a judge, is only a piece of solemn mockery, and such as is practised by the Spanish inquisition.   But the popish clergy seem to be wholly directed by hypocrisy.

When he was brought before the dean of the arches, he defended marriage in such a masterly manner, that the dean would not venture to pronounce a divorce, but only deprived him of his benefice.   He was then remanded to prison, and kept there above a year and a half; when he and several others were brought to be examined before the chancellor.

Gardner asked him, whether he adhered to the form of religion, as established by king Edward VI ?   Whether he approved of the English book of common prayer ? Whether he was married ? and many other questions.   To all these, Dr. Taylor gave clear and satisfactory answers, justifying his conduct; but these were not sufficient, seeing his death was resolved on.

Concerning marriage, Dr. Taylor proved, not only from the sacred scriptures, but likewise from the primitive writers, that the clergy were not prohibited from it. As he was a learned civilian, and a canonist, he proved from the Justinian institutions, that all oaths of celibacy were then condemned, and the priests were exhorted to marry.   Nay, so strict was the emperor in this particular, that if a man made over a legacy to his wife, on condition of her not marrying again, the will was to be void.

He added further, that it was contained in the pandects, that if a man had a woman a slave, and made her free on condition she should never marry, yet she might marry, and her former master should not be permitted to reclaim her. It was the more necessary to quote the pandects, because they were written in the sixth century; and although many abuses had then crept into the church, yet celibacy was not in the number.

The next time, he was brought before the chancellor, was in company with L. Saunders, already mentioned, and Bradford, whom we shall take notice of afterwards. Dr. Taylor was charged with heresy by the chancellor, and the other bishops who were present. He acknowledged, that he abhorred all the popish doctrines of the church of Rome ; that the pope was antichrist ; that to deny the clergy the privilege of marriage, was the doctrine of devils. That there were but two sacraments in the New Testament ; that the mass was idolatry, the body of Christ being in heaven ; and last of all, that he would abide by these sentiments to the last, being convinced that they were consistent with the doctrines laid down by Christ and his apostles.

One may easily imagine what would be the consequences of such a free and open declaration. A papist could not bear to hear his favourite notions thus called in question, and even condemned as idolatry ; especially as it was the queen's religion, and the chancellor was her favourite.

The chancellor then pronounced sentence on him, and he was taken to a prison in Southwark, called the Clink, where he remained till night, and was then sent to the Compter in the Poultry. Here he remained seven days; when Bonner, bishop of London, with others, came to the said Compter to degrade him, bringing with them the popish habits.*

---

* Superstition had been brought to such a height, in the reign of Henry I. that the clergy got themselves exempted from corporal punishments; but his grandson Henry II, in the constitutions of Clarendon, got it ordained, that

In the execution of this ceremony, though of a very serious nature, Dr. Taylor turned one part of it to ridiculous contempt. The bishop commanded him to put on the vestments, but this he refused. Bonner then ordered his servants to force them on him; and when they had dressed him, he walked about the room, with his hands by his sides, saying, " look at me, my lord, am not I like a very pretty fool?" and speaking to the other priests who were present, he said, " what say you, my masters, supposing I was to walk into Cheapside with all this trumpery, would not the boys laugh at me?"

The last part of the ceremony of degradation, is for the bishop to strike the person degraded on the breast; but Bonner's chaplain advised him not to strike Dr. Taylor, for he would surely strike again.

The bishop therefore contented himself with pronouncing a curse upon Dr. Taylor; to which, the doctor answered, you may curse as long as you please, but I am confident God will support me. I have the witness of a good conscience, that I am standing in defence of the truth; whereas you dare not say that you are doing so, but I will pray for you.

When he was brought up to his chamber, he told Bradford, that he had made the bishop of London afraid; " for (said he) his chaplain advised him not to strike me, lest I should strike him again, which I made him believe I would, although I never intended to do so."

To strike an enemy is strictly forbidden in the gospel; but had even Dr. Taylor been so unguarded as to strike the bishop, it could only have been imputed to the ignorance which at that time prevailed, even over the minds of pious men.

The night after he was degraded, his wife, with his son Thomas, came to see him; and such was the good nature of the keeper, that he permitted them to go into his apartment to sup with him, Thus he found a great difference between the keeper of the bishop's prison, and the

the clergy should suffer the same punishments as the laity; and, therefore, the clergy, that it might not be said that a priest suffered death, always degraded him before execution.

keeper of the Compter. The bishop's keepers were ever cruel, blasphemous, and tyrannical, like their master; but the keepers of the king's prisons, for the most part, shewed as much favour as could be granted, to those whom they had in custody. John Hull, the servant, came with the wife and son of Dr. Taylor; and, at their first coming in, they all kneeled down and prayed.

After supper, the doctor walked two or three times across the room, blessing God that he had singled him out to bear witness to the truth, as it is in Jesus; that he had thought him worthy to suffer for his name sake; and, turning to his son, he said, " my dear son, God Almightly bless you, and give his holy spirit, to be a true servant of Christ; to hear his word, and constantly to stand by the truth all thy life long: and, my son, see that thou fear God always: flee from all sin and wicked living: be virtuous: attend closely to your book, and pray to God sincerely. In all things that are lawful, see that thou be obedient to thy mother: love her and serve her: be ruled and directed by her now in thy youth, and follow her good counsel in all things. Beware of lewd company, of young men that fear not God, but indulge their vain appetites and lusts. Fly from whoredom, and abhor all filthy living; remembering that I, thy father, am to die in defence of holy marriage. Another day, when God shall bless thee, love and cherish the poor people, and count that thy chief riches is to be rich in alms; and when thy mother is far advanced in years, forsake her not, but provide for her according to her abilities, and see that she want for nothing. And God will bless thee, and give thee long life upon earth, and prosperity; for which now, upon my knees, I pray through the merits of Jesus Christ."

Then turning to his wife, he said, " my dear wife, continue steadfast in the faith, fear, and love of God. Keep yourself undefiled from popish idolatries and superstition. I have been unto you a faithful yoke-fellow, and so have you been unto me; for the which, I pray God to reward you, and doubt not, my dear, but he will reward you. Now the time is come, that I shall be taken from you, and you discharged of the wedlock bond towards me: therefore, I will give you my counsel, that I think most expedient for you. You are yet a child-bearing woman; and, therefore, it will be most convenient for you to marry; for, doubtless, you will not of yourself be able to support our dear children, nor be out of trouble, till you be married. Therefore, as soon as providence shall point out some pious, honest man, who, you think, will support the poor children, be sure to marry him, and live in the fear of God; but, by all means, avoid idolatry and superstition."

Having said these words, he fell down and prayed for his family; and then he gave his wife an English prayer book, as set forth by king Edward VI. and to his son Thomas, he gave a Latin book, containing a collection of sentiments from the writings of the primitive fathers, relating to the courage and constancy of the ancient martyrs.

The next morning, which was the fifth day of the month called February, the sheriff of London, attended by his officers, came to the Compter, and took Dr. Taylor to the Woolpack, near Aldgate; and this was only two in the morning. His wife, having some suspicion that he was to be taken out that morning, waited all night in the church of St. Botolph, near Aldgate, having with her a poor orphan girl, whom the doctor had brought up, and one of her own children. When the sheriff and his company came opposite Botolph church, the orphan girl cried out, " O, my dear father; mother, mother, here is my father led out." Then Taylor's wife cried out, " Rowland! Rowland! where art thou?" for, the morning was extremely dark. To this, Dr. Taylor answered, " here I am, but I am confined." The sheriff's officers wanted to hurry him away; but the sheriff who had more humanity, ordered them to let him speak to his wife.

She then came to him, when taking his wife and daughter, with the orphan girl, by the hands, he kneeled down, and prayed with them; which, when the sheriff, and the other people present saw, they shed tears. Prayers being over, he rose up, and taking his wife by the hand, bade her have comfort, for he had a clear conscience.

'God," said he, " will provide a father for my children, but let them be steadfast in the faith." To which, his wife answered, " God be with you, my dear Rowland, and I will, with his grace, meet you at Hadley."

He was then put into a chamber, with four of the yeomen of the guard, and the sheriff's officers. As soon as he entered the chamber, he fell down, and gave himself wholly up to prayer. There the sheriff seeing his wife, told her, that she must not speak to her husband; but that she might go to his house, and he would provide her, so as she should not want for any thing. To this, she answered, that she would rather go to her mother's house, and two officers were sent to conduct her thither.

This part of the sheriff's conduct seems to have arisen from principles of humanity ; for, what man can see a wife and children weeping beside a father and husband, condemned for a disputable offence, without shedding a tear of compassion ?

Dr. Taylor remained at the Woolpack till eleven in the forenoon, when the sheriff of Essex came to receive him, and they prepared to set out on horseback. As they came out of the inn, John Hull, his old servant, whom we have mentioned before, was there waiting, having with him Dr. Taylor's son Thomas. John lifted up the boy that he might see his father, and then set him on the horse before him. Dr. Taylor taking off his hat, said, " good people, this is my son, begotten in lawful wedlock, and I bless God for lawful matrimony." He then lifted up his eyes towards heaven, and prayed for his son ; laid his hat upon the boy's head, and blessed him. After this, he delivered him to John Hull, whom he shook by the hand, and said, " thou hast been the faithfulest servant I ever had."

The procession then set out on the Essex road, but when they came near Brentwood, one Arthur Taisie, who had been formerly a servant with Dr. Taylor, not knowing he had been condemned, came up and shook hands with him, for he thought he had been at liberty. The sheriff told him, that he was not, but that he was his prisoner.

When they arrived at Brentwood, they made a close hood for Dr. Taylor, having two holes for his eyes, and one for his mouth, to breathe at. They did this, that no man might know him, or speak to him; which practice they frequently used with others.

All the way, Dr. Taylor was as joyful as if he had been going to take the possession of an estate; and, indeed, how could it be otherwise? He knew he was suffering for the faith, and that the truth was able to support him.

At Chelmsford, they were met by the sheriff of Suffolk, who was to take him into that county to be executed. While they were at supper, the sheriff of Essex laboured earnestly with him to return to the popish religion. He told him, "that as he was a man of universal learning, so his death would be a great loss to the nation." The sheriff, whatever his own opinions were, said a great deal to Dr. Taylor; and falling before him on his knees, with tears running down his cheeks, earnestly begged of him to recant his opinions, and be reconciled to the church, promising that he, and all his friends would procure his pardon. But his reply shewed that he was steadfast and immoveable.

The sheriff, and his companions, that heard him, were amazed at his constancy; for the nearer his sufferings approached, the more he was strengthened to endure them.

When he came within two miles of Hadley, he desired to alight from his horse; which done, he leaped two or three times, as men do at country scenes of diversion. The sheriff being surprised, asked him, what he meant by acting in that manner? His answer was, "good Mr. Sheriff, I am almost at home." When he was arrived at Aldham Common, the place where he was to be burnt, he lifted up his eyes to heaven, and thanked God that the last struggle was come, and he hoped he should be enabled to go through with it.

He tore the hood from his face, that he might be seen by the numerous spectators, many of whom had formerly been his parishioners. He then began to speak to the people who were praying for him; but the officers thrust sticks into his mouth, and threatened to cut his tongue out, unless he would promise to keep silence.

When he had prayed, he kissed the stake, and set himself into a barrel filled with pitch, which had been placed for that purpose. Fire being set to the pitch, Dr. Taylor continued praying in the most devout manner, till one of the officers, more humane than the rest, knocked out his brains with a halbert; which put an end to his misery.

Dr. Taylor was not only a pious man, but he had been, for his knowledge of the canon and civil laws, long esteemed as the glory of Cambridge. He had, from his distinguished abilities, confuted the chancellor in his arguments concerning the marriage of the clergy; and, indeed, in all other respects, he was so well acquainted with the ancient fathers, that he was, with great propriety called, "The Walking Library." But no mercy is shewn, where religious rancour takes place. There is something in all such persecutions, that shuts up the bowels of compassion, even towards the nearest relations. Civil persecutors may have some compassion, but those who persecute from erroneous notions of religion, are generally strangers to every tender sensation.

The Martyrdom of Thomas Tomkins.

THIS person was by trade a weaver, and lived with great reputation, in the parish of St. Leonard, Shoreditch. Being accused of heresy, he was summoned before that merciless persecutor, bishop Bonner, who confined him, with many others, in his palace at Fulham.

During his imprisonment, he was treated by the bishop in a manner not only unbecoming a prelate, but a man. He several times beat him with a distinguished cruelty, and tore the greatest part of his beard from his face, for no other reason, but his not assenting to the doctrine of transubstantiation.

2 x

Another instance of this cruel bishop's inhumanity to Tomkins, was exhibited before several persons who came to visit him. The bishop finding him inflexible, took hold of him by the wrist, and held his hand over the flame of a wax candle, in order, if possible, to make him deviate from those uncorrupted truths of the gospel he had so strongly preserved. This punishment Tomkins submitted to, with great fortitude, till the veins burst; and water issuing from the hand, flew into the face of a by-stander, who was so affected, that he requested the bishop to forbear, saying, he had sufficiently punished the prisoner.

A few days after this, Tomkins was brought before the bishop, at his consistory court at St. Paul's, to whom he delivered the following articles of confession in writing, sealed up, and signed with his own hand.

" I Thomas Tomkins, of the parish of St. Leonard, Shoreditch, in the diocess of London, having confessed, and declared openly, heretofore, to Edmund Bonner, bishop of London, mine ordinary, that my belief hath been, many years past, and is at this present, that the body of our Saviour Jesus Christ is not truly, and in very deed, in the sacrament of the altar, but only in heaven; and so in heaven, that it cannot now indeed be really and truly in the sacrament of the altar."

" And moreover, having likewise confessed and declared to my said ordinary openly many times, that although the church, called the Catholic church, hath allowed, and doth allow the mass and sacrifice made and done therein, as a wholesome, profitable, and godly thing; yet my belief hath been many years past, and is at this present, that the said mass is full of superstition, plain idolatry, and unprofitable for the soul; and so I have called it many times, and take it at this present."

" Having also confessed and declared to my said ordinary, that the sacrament of baptism ought to be only in the vulgar tongue, and not otherwise ministered; and also, without such ceremonies as are generally used in the Latin church, and otherwise not to be allowed."

" Finally, being often and many times called before my said ordinary, and talking withal, touching all my said confessions and declarations, both by my said ordinary, and divers other learned men, as well his chaplains as others, and counselled by them all to embrace the church, and to recant mine error, in the premises which they told me was plain heresy, and manifest error ; do testify and declare hereby, that I do and will continually stand to my said confession, declaration, and belief, in all the premises, and every part thereof; and, in no wise, recant, or go from any part of the same. In witness whereof, I have subscribed and passed this writing, this 26th of September, 1554.

THOMAS TOMKINS."

Bishop Bonner, and the rest of the tribunal, strongly pressed Tomkins to recant his errors, and return to the mother-church ; but he only answered, " I was born and brought up in ignorance till of late years ; and now I know the truth, I will continue therein unto death."

Finding him inflexible, they declared him a heretic, and ordered the sheriff of London, who attended, to conduct him immediately to Newgate. Here he remained till the 16th of the month called March, 1555, when he was conducted to Smithfield, and there burnt, triumphing in the midst of the flames, and adding to those martyrs who had preceded him, through the path of the fiery trial to the realms of immortal glory.

The Martyrdom of William Hunter.

THIS pious young man, was the son of poor, but honest and religious parents, who trained him up in the doctrines of the reformation ; and, when at a proper age, put him apprentice to one Thomas Taylor, a silk-weaver, in Coleman-street, London.

On the accession of queen Mary, orders were issued to the priests of every parish, to summon all their parishioners to recieve the communion at mass the Easter following, when young Hunter, who was then only nineteen years of age, refusing to obey the summons, was threatened with being brought before the bishop to answer for his disobedience.

In consequence of this, his master, fearful of incurring ecclesiastical censure, desired he would leave him, at least for a time; upon which, he quitted his service, and went to his father at Brentwood, in Essex. .

During his stay here, he one day went into the chapel, and seeing the bible lay on the desk, he opened it, and began to read. Being observed by an officer of the bishop's court, he severely reprimanded him, and said, " why meddlest thou with the bible? understandest thou what thou readest? canst thou expound the scriptures?" To.which, Hunter replied, " I do not presume to do it; but finding the bible here, I read it for my comfort and edification."

The officer then informed a neighbouring priest of the liberty Hunter had taken in reading the bible, who immediately sent for him, and chastised him, saying, " sirrah, who gave thee leave to read the bible and expound it?" He answered, as he had done to the officer; and on the priest's saying, it became him not to meddle with the scriptures, he frankly declared his resolution to read them as long as he lived. The priest upbraided him as a heretic; but he boldly denied the charge. Being asked his opinion concerning the corporal presence in the sacrament, he replied, that he esteemed the bread and wine but as figures, and looked upon the sacrament as an institution in remembrance of the death and sufferings of our Lord and Saviour Jesus Christ. On this, the priest openly declared him a heretic, and threatened to complain of him to the bishop.

· A neighbouring justice having heard that young Hunter maintained heretical principles, sent for his father to inquire the particulars. The old man told him, that his son had left him, and that he knew not whither he was gone. The justice, not believing what he said, threatened to commit him to prison, unless he would immediately cause his son to be apprehended, and brought before him. To this he replied, with tears in his eyes, " would you have me seek out my son to be burned ?"

The old man, however, was obliged to go, (or at least pretended to do so) in quest of his son; when meeting him by accident, he asked his father if he was seeking for him ; to which the old man answered with tears, he was; and that it was by order of the justice, who threatened to put him in prison. The son, to secure his father from any danger on his account, said, he was ready to accompany him home, which he accordingly did.

The next day, young Hunter was apprehended by the constable of the parish, who put him in the stocks for twenty-four hours, and then took him before the justice. On his arrival, the justice called for a bible, turned to the sixth chapter of St. John, and desired him to give his opinion of the meaning of it, as it related to the sacrament of the altar.

Hunter gave the same explanation as he had done to the priest ; and persisting in his denial of the corporal presence in the eucharist, the justice upbraided him with heresy, and wrote an account of his conduct to the bishop of London.

In consequence of this, young Hunter was summoned to appear at the consistory court held at St. Paul's. He accordingly attended at the time appointed, when he was severely reproved for having fallen from the Catholic faith, and was exhorted to return to the same.

To this, he boldly answered, that he had not fallen from the Catholic faith, but believed and confessed it with all his heart.

He was then desired by the bishop to recant what he had said concerning the sacrament of the altar ; but he declared, that by the help of God, he would still continue to persist in that faith he had hitherto maintained.

Being urged still further, and promised, that if he would recant, he should go home unhurt, he said to the bishop, " my lord, if you will let me alone, and leave me to my own conscience, I will return to my father, and dwell with him, or else with my master again, and will keep my opinion to myself."

The Bishop answered, "I am content, so that thou wilt go to church, receive, and be confessed."

This, Hunter peremptorily refused; upon which, after several farther efforts to bring him over, the bishop ordered him to be put in the stocks, where he continued two days and nights, having only a crust of brown bread, and a cup of water, given to him for refreshment.

At the expiration of the two days, the bishop went to him, and finding the bread and water lay by him untouched, he ordered some of his servants to take him out of the stocks, and let him breakfast with them; but as he was deemed a heretic, they would not comply with the bishop's request.

After this, he was repeatedly brought before the bishop, who, sometimes by soothing him, and sometimes by threats, endeavoured to bring him to a recantation; but all his efforts proved ineffectual. In consequence of this, the persecuting prelate passed sentence on him, which was, that he should be removed to Newgate for a time, from whence he should be removed to Brentwood; "where (said the bishop) thou shalt be burned."

A few days after this, the bishop sent for him again, and promised him preferment, if he would recant, to which, he replied, " my lord, I thank you for your great offer; but if you cannot enforce my recantation from scripture, I cannot in my conscience, turn from God for the love of the world; for I count all things but dross for the love of Christ."

He was then carried back to Newgate; and, in a few days, removed to Brentwood, where he was confined in an inn till the day of his execution. During this time, he was visited by many of his neighbours and acquaintances, all of whom he exhorted to beware of popish superstition and idolatry.

On the morning of the 27th of the month called March, 1555, the sheriff gave orders for the necessary preparations to be made for his execution. In the mean time, the sheriff's son, who was his friend, visited him at the inn, and encouraged him not to fear the men who were making preparations for his death ; to whom, he said, that thank God, he was not the least intimidated ; for that he had cast up his account, and knew well the happy consequences that would attend his strict adherence to the cause of Christ.

A short time after this, he was led from the inn to the stake, between one of the sheriff's officers, and his brother Robert. In their way, he was met by his father, who, with tears flowing from his eyes, said to him, " God be with thee, son William."

When he arrived at the place of execution, he kneeled on a fagot, and repeated the 51st psalm, till he came to these words : " The sacrifices of God are a broken spirit : a broken and a contrite heart, O God, thou wilt not despise." He was then interrupted by one of the officers, who told him the translation was wrong, the words being an humble spirit : but he said, the translation was a contrite heart, on which, he was told, that the heretics translated books as they pleased.

The sheriff then produced him a letter from the queen, containing his pardon, if he would recant ; but he refused life on those terms, went up to the stake, and was chained to it, saying to the spectators : " Good people, pray for me, and make quick dispatch : pray for me, while you see me alive, and I will pray for you."

He then took a fagot, and embraced it in his arms ; and, on a priest's offering him a book, said, " Away, thou false prophet : beware of him, good people, and come away from their abominations, lest ye be partaker of their plagues."

As soon as the fire was kindled, our martyr gave his prayer-book to his brother, who, to encourage him, reminded him of the passion of his dear Redeemer, and bade him be of good cheer : to which, he replied, " I fear neither torture nor death : Lord Jesus, receive my departing spirit !" The fire burning rapidly, he was soon consumed, yielding up his life, with patience and humility, to him who gave it ; and in testimony of the truth of that God, who cannot change, but whose word is the same yesterday, to day, and for ever.

The next that suffered were Higbed and Canston, both of Essex, two men so fervent for religion, that in these blind and idolatrous times, they could not lie long hid in obscurity, but were constrained to bear their testimony, though at the loss of their lives.

Bonner perceiving these were men of repute in their country, and such as were called gentlemen, he took the more pains to bring them off their profession ; and went to Colchester himself to seek to reclaim them ; sometimes using fair promises, and flattering enticements, at other times threatening them with high words, to terrify them. At last, seeing them both constant and immoveable in their zeal for their religion, he caused them and some others, apprehended in that country, at the same time, and for the same cause, to be brought up to London, where they were committed close prisoners ; and were first privately examined by the bishop and his chaplain, and urged, by all means, to forsake their opinions. But when the bishop saw that way would work no alteration, he caused them to be brought to open examination, at the consistory at St. Paul's, the seventeenth day of the month called February, 1555 ; where being further pressed to recant of the errors which they said were held, and to return to the unity of the church ; but they still refusing ; a great list of articles was delivered them, and their answers thereunto required of them the next day.

At the second time of their public appearance and trial, their answers were read ; and Canston being first called, was exhorted again to be comfortable to the unity of the church ; into which, they said, they were ready to receive him : he replied, " you lay snares and gins to catch us, but, mark, what measure you meet shall be measured to you again."

Then Higbed was called ; to whom the like persuasions were used, but to as little purpose as the other ; for he told them, he had been sixteen years in the mind he was then in, and should not alter now.

At their last appearance before them, the prisoners declared (calling God to record) that their persisting in that steadfastness, was not in wilfulness, as some might judge, but for conscience sake. " For," said they, " we sought the Lord, that we might do nothing contrary to his blessed word ; and in that he hath shewed his power in our weakness, we cannot but praise him, unto whom, we give thanks, through Christ Jesus our Lord."

When they had thus spoken, the bishop began to pronounce the sentence against Canston ; to whom, Canston said, it was a rash judgment, without love and mercy. Then was sentence also pronounced against Higbed : and both were delivered to the sheriffs, who sent them to Newgate, where they remained fourteen days, continually praising God, not so much concerned at their afflictions, as rejoiced in their consolations, praying, and earnestly desiring, they might persevere to the end, to the praise of the eternal God, and comfort of the brethren.

The fourteen days being expired, they were, by four o'clock in the morning, led from Newgate to Aldgate ; and there delivered to the sheriff of Essex, who conveyed them to the places where they were executed, viz. Higbed to Hornden on the hill ; and Thomas Canston to Rayleigh ; where they both, with great constancy, finished their testimonies in the fire, greatly rejoicing, and giving the glory to God.

The Martyrdom of William Pigot, Stephen Knight, and John Lawrence ; the two former Laymen, and the latter a Priest.

THESE three pious christians having been pointed out by the emissaries of Bonner and Gardner, information was given to those savage prelates, that they maintained religious opinions contrary to the doctrine and practice of the holy mother-church. In consequence of this, they were all three summoned to appear before bishop Bonner, at his consistory court in London, where they were severally questioned concerning their faith of the coporal presence in the sacrament.

Having respectfully answered and subscribed, that they were not substantially, but figuratively, the body and blood of Christ in that holy ordinance, they were severely reprimanded by the court, admonished to recant their heretical opinions, and for that time dismissed.

A few days after, they were again examined concerning the same tenet, when they made the like declaration as before ; in consequence of which, the bishop addressed himself to the two laymen, and, with an affected concern for their spiritual and temporal interests, warmly exhorted them to reject their heresies, and not expose themselves to death here, and damnation hereafter, by obstinately persisting in disobedience to the holy see : but these plain and honest christians were too well grounded in the doctrines of Christ's pure gospel, to be moved from their adherence to the true faith. They, therefore, told the bishop, that they could not recant consistently with the dictates of their own consciences, nor would they abjure the opinions to which they had subscribed.

After this, bishop Bonner entered into argument with Lawrence, the priest, alone ; and having demanded of what order he was, he answered, that he was admitted to priest's orders eighteen years past ; that he was some time a black friar ; and that he was betrothed to a maid, whom he intended to marry.

The bishop then asked him his opinion of the corporal presence in the sacrament : to which, he replied, that it was an institution of our blessed Lord, in commemoration of his death and sufferings ; and that those were greatly deceived, who believed that his body was verily present in the same, saying, that he had long before ascended into heaven, and was placed at the right hand of the glorious majesty of the Father.

Lawrence was, for the present, dismissed ; but a few days after, he, Pigot, and Knight, were again summoned before the bishop, who, with his usual hypocrisy, exhorted them to recant, embrace the Roman catholic faith, and not be the wilful cause of their own destruction. But no arguments could induce them to recede in a single point ; all of them declaring, they would abide by their opinions, because they were founded on the word of God ; whereas the other was merely of human invention.

From this frank declaration, bishop Bonner proceeded to pass sentence on them as irreclaimable heretics; and then degraded Lawrence with the usual ceremonies. After which, they were all three delivered to the sheriff, who conducted them to Newgate.

On the 28th of the month called March, 1555, (the day appointed for the execution of Pigot and Knight) they were removed early in the morning to the respective places destined for their execution, the former at Braintree, and the latter at Malden, in Essex. When Knight arrived at the stake, he kneeled down, and, with an audible voice, said the following prayer :

" O Lord Jesus Christ! for whose love, I leave willingly this life, and desire rather the bitter death of thy cross, with the loss of all earthly things, than to the blasphemy of thy most holy name, or to obey men in breaking thy holy commandment. Thou seest, O Lord, that where I might live in wordly wealth to worship a false God, and honour thine enemy, I choose rather the torment of the body, and the loss of this life ; and have counted all things but vile dust and dung, that I might win thee ; which death is dearer unto me, than thousands of gold and silver. Such love, O Lord, hast thou laid up in my breast, that I hunger for thee, as the deer that is wounded desireth the foil. Send thy holy comforter, O Lord, to aid, comfort, and strengthen this weak piece of earth, which is empty of all strength of itself. Thou rememberest, O Lord, that I am but dust, and able to do nothing that is good ; therefore, O Lord, as of thine accustomed goodness and love, thou hast invited me to this banquet, and accounted me worthy to drink of thine own cup among thine elect ; even so give me strength, O Lord, against this thine element which, as to my sight, it is most irksome and terrible, so to my mind, it may at thy commandment (as an obedient servant) be sweet and pleasant ; that through the strength of thy holy spirit, I may pass through the rage of this fire into thy bosom, according to thy promise, and for this mortal, receive an immortal, and for this corruptible, put on incorruption. Accept this burnt sacrifice and offering, O Lord, not for the sacrifice, but for thy dear Son's sake, my Saviour, for whose testimony, I offer this free-will offering, with all my heart, and with all my soul. O heavenly Father, forgive me my sins, as I forgive all the world. O sweet Son of God my Saviour, spread thy wings over me. O blessed and Holy Ghost, through whose merciful inspiration, I am come hither, conduct me into everlasting life. Lord, into thy hands, I commend my spirit. Amen."

Both these martyrs suffered with amazing fortitude and resignation, proving to the spectators, that, as is the day of the sincere believer, so likewise shall be his strength.

The next day, John Lawrence suffered at Colchester. He was carried to the place of execution in a chair, (being unable to walk, from the pressure of the irons with which his legs were bound, and the weakness of his body from want of proper nourishment while in prison). The chair was fastened to the stake, and he sat in it, for some time, with great composure, praying to God to enable him to undergo the fiery trial; at length, the fagots were lighted and he triumphantly expired in the cause of his glorious master, in sure and certain hope of an eternal existence in heaven.

The Martyrdom of Dr. Robert Farrar, bishop of St. David's.

THE emissaries of the persecuting bishops had for some time, fixed their eyes on this worthy and pious prelate, who not only in the former reign, but also after the accession of Mary, had been particularly zealous in promoting the reformed doctrines, and exploding the errors of popish idolatry. Information of this being given to the bishop of Winchester, (who was then likewise lord chancellor) Dr. Farrar, with several others, was summoned to appear before him, and the other commissioners, appointed for the abominable work of massacreing protestants.

After some previous harangue, the bishop formally told him, that the queen and parliament had restored religion to the state in which it was at the beginning of the reign of Henry VIII, that he was in the queen's debt, but her majesty would cancel the same, and re-admit him to her favour, if he would return to the holy catholic church.

Undismayed by this information, Dr. Farrar answered, that, with respect to the debt, he submitted it to the lord treasurer; but his lordship might well remember, that, upon two former occasions, he had solemnly sworn never to acknowledge the papal jurisdiction over the realm of England; and, therefore, it was needless to rehearse what he had already so peremptorily declared.

After a long debate, Gardner sternly demanded, if he would recant, and acknowledge the papal supremacy; to which, Farrar, with a resolution becoming a true christian and worthy bishop, expressed a degree of contempt, that his lordship should even think he would recede from an oath he had made to his maker: an oath he could not break, consistent with his duty to God, and his regard to the interest of the reformed religion in his native country.

The ambitious Gardner was so highly incensed at this spirited behaviour in Dr. Farrar, that, according to his inhuman custom, he treated him with scurrility, calling him froward knave, and telling him, that he should know his fate in a short time. To this, Farrar coolly replied, that he would ever readily obey his summons, but would never retract what he had solemnly sworn, at the instigation of him, or any other man whatever.

The examination being over, Dr. Farrar was ordered to Newgate, where he was a short time confined, and then sent into Wales, there to receive his sentence of condemnation.

On his arrival at Carmarthen, he was delivered to the sheriff of the county, who took him before Henry Morgan, then bishop of St. David's, and Constantine, the public notary, by whom he was committed to the custody of the keeper of Carmarthen jail.

A few days after ' is commitment to that prison, he was sent for by bishop Morgan, who exhorted him to recant; on condition of which, he assured him of the queen's clemency, as well as preferment to an office of dignity in the church. But our martyr was inflexible : he would not listen to any proposals derogatory to the oath he had taken ; upon which, bishop Morgan asked him the two following questions:

1. " Whether he believed the marriage of priests, allowed by the laws of the holy church ?

2. " Whether he believed, that in the blessed sacrament of the altar, after the words of consecration duly pronounced by the priests, the very body and blood of Christ are really and substantially contained, without the substance of bread and wine ?"

Dr. Farrar refused to answer to these questions, unless the bishop produced a commission, authorizing him to ask them ; upon which, he was remanded to prison.

At length, after various disputes with bishop Morgan, he appealed from him, as an incompetent judge, to cardinal Pole ; notwithstanding which, sentence was pronounced against him as a heretic, and he was delivered over to the secular power, having been previously degraded by Morgan.

Thus, for his steadfast adherence to the uncorrupted doctrines of the reformation, and resolute denial of the papal jurisdiction in these realms, was Dr. Farrar condemned, degraded, and delivered up to the secular power; and, on the eve of the day called Passion Sunday, in the bloody year 1555, was executed in the market-place of Carmarthen, amidst a numerous crowd of spectators.

The following circumstance is an evincing proof what constancy and resolution this good man possessed, and how determined he was to retain those religious principles to the last, which, during his life, he had so strongly adhered to.

The son of a person of distinction visiting him, a few days before his execution, and lamenting the cruel fate that awaited him, the doctor told him, that if he saw him once stir in the pains of burning, he might then give no credit to his doctrine, but look upon it as the effects of enthusiasm.

He resolutely fulfilled his promise, and greatly surprised his friend, who came to condole his fate ; for he stood motionless in the midst of the flames, holding both his hands till they were burnt to the stumps ; at which time, one of the officers struck him on the head with a staff, and put a period to his life.

The sufferings and Martyrdom of Rawlins White, a poor Fisherman, of South-Wales.

To such a height did the rage and malice of popish persecutors arrive, during this reign, that they not only vented their fury on men of eminence and learning, who espoused the protestant cause, but the meanest and most ignorant of the people, who would not submit to the papal yoke, were arraigned at their bloody tribunal, and put to death for no other cause but that of professing the truth expounded in the scriptures.

Rawlins White (the poor man whose sufferings we are going to relate) had been so attentive to the preaching of the gospel during the late reign, that he attained to a very competent knowledge of the holy scriptures, and became a zealous assertor of the protestant doctrines, having wholly renounced the superstition and idolatry of the popish religion, and conformed to the public worship of God, according to the English common prayer-book then set forth.

Being thus converted to the true faith of Christ, he took great pains to instruct his son in the same, causing him to read a portion of holy scripture every night and morning, till he likewise became well grounded in the principles of true religion, as contained in the gospel.

White was not only desirous of acquiring saving knowledge himself, but also of communicating it to others ; insomuch that he took every opportunity of visiting his neighbours, endeavouring to instruct those, whom he found desirous of obtaining the knowledge of the truth.

He continued to practise those devout and holy exercises in a public manner, till the death of king Edward, when popery being restored, and the pure religion discouraged and restrained, he used to meet privately with his friends, pray, and encourage them to hold fast to the truth.   At length, he was apprehended, by one of the officers of the town, on a suspicion of heresy, who taking him before the bishop of Landaff, he was, by that prelate, committed to prison.

During his confinement, several of his friends sent him money privately ; and he was visited by many, whom he instructed in the faith of Christ, and exhorted to beware of popish emissaries, as of wolves in sheep's clothing.

After a long imprisonment, the bishop of Landaff summoned White to appear before him ; and endeavoured to bring him over to the popish idolatry and superstition ; but all his exhortations proving ineffectual, he told him in anger, that he must come to a resolution either to recant his heretical opinions, or endure the rigour of the law against those who maintained tenets repugnant to the doctrines of the holy see.

On the day appointed for his examination, the bishop, in the presence of his chaplains, and many of the neighbours, assembled in the chapel, declared that White was known not only to maintain heretical principles himself, but to inculcate the same amongst his acquaintance. Then addressing himself to White, he told him, that he had frequently, since his first warning, both there and in his house, been admonished to relinquish his heretical tenets, and yet had always turned a deaf ear to the most salutary advice.   He added, that, out of clemency, they had once more sent for him, mildly to endeavour to bring him to an humble sense of his errors, and assure him, that, upon due penitence for the crimes he had committed, both against God and the law of his sovereign. they were disposed to shew him mercy : but that, if in spite of the royal clemency, and abomination of the reverend fathers, he obstinately persisted in his heresies, they were determined to execute on him the utmost rigour of the law, as a most damnable heretic.

White, without the least sign of fear at the peremptory declaration of the bishop, told his lordship, that he blessed God he was a christian, and held no doctrines contrary to the divine mind and will as revealed in the scriptures of truth : if he did, he begged to be convinced of the same out of the divine word, to which he determined ever most implicitly to conform.

After much exhortation, the bishop assured him, that if he would not recant, he must condemn him as a heretic. To which, White replied, that he might proceed as he thought proper, but that he could not condemn him as a heretic, as he did not maintain any opinion that was not supported by the word of God.

The bishop then desired the people present to join with him in prayer, that it would please God to turn White's heart, and bring him to the acknowledgment of the true religion.

Our martyr applauded this behaviour of the bishop as becoming his profession, assuring him, that, if their request was agreeable to the divine will, God would, doubtless, hear and grant the same : and that, while he was praying to his God, he (White) would pray to his God, who he knew would hear and perform his desire.

Accordingly, they all went to prayer ; which being finished, the bishop asked him, how he found himself disposed in his mind ? He replied, the very same as before.

The bishop, incensed that no change could be wrought upon him, was ready to have read the sentence, but he was advised first to say mass ; during which ceremony, White standing at the door of the choir, cried out to the populace, "bear witness, that I bow not to this idol," (meaning the host, which the priest held over his head.)

Mass being performed, he was again warmly admonished to recant, but all exhortation was ineffectual. The bishop, therefore, read the definitive sentence, after which, he was carried to Cardiff, and imprisoned in a place called Cockmarel, a most filthy and loathsome dungeon, where he continued till the writ of his execution came from London.

Upon the day appointed for terminating his life, which was on the 30th of the month called March, 1555, he was brought from prison; and in his way to the place appointed for the bloody scene, met his wife and children, wringing their hands, and most bitterly lamenting his approaching fate. This affecting sight drew tears from his eyes; but soon recollecting himself, and striking his breast with his hand, he said, "ah! flesh, stayest thou me? wouldst thou fain prevail? well, do what thou canst: by God's grace, thou shalt not get the victory."

As soon as he arrived at the stake, he fell on his knees, and kissed the earth, saying, "earth to earth, and dust to dust; thou art my mother, to thee I must return."

When he was fastened to the stake, and the straw, reeds, and wood were placed around him, a priest appointed for the purpose, stood up and harangued the spectators, who were exceedingly numerous, it being market-day.

The priest having finished his discourse, in which he inveighed against the opinion of the protestants concerning the sacrament of the altar, our martyr rebuked him, proved his doctrine to be false, and cited, as his authority those words of our Lord, "do this in remembrance of me."

The fire being kindled, he was soon surrounded by the flames, in the midst of which, this good old man (for he was sixty years of age) held up his hands till the sinews shrunk, crying earnestly, "O Lord, receive my soul! O Lord, receive my spirit!" The flames were so vehement about his legs, that they were almost consumed, before the upper part of his body caught the fire; notwithstanding which, he bore his sufferings with the greatest composure and resignation, cheerfully resigning his soul into the hands of him who gave it, in sure and certain hopes of being hereafter rewarded with a crown of eternal life.

The persecution and martyrdom of George Marsh, a minister of the gospel.

THIS eminent and pious divine was descended from poor, but honest and religious parents, who educated him from his earliest years, in the principles of the reformed religion ; so that when he arrived at manhood, he was well versed in the doctrines of the pure gospel of Christ.

At the first set off in life, he followed the business of farming ; and, by his honest endeavours, maintained his family with decency and reputation for some years : but on the decease of his wife, being disposed to study, he placed his children with his father, quitted his farm, and went to Cambridge, where he made such a progress in literature, that he soon entered into holy orders.

He officiated as curate in several parishes in the county of Lancaster ; kept a school at Dean ; and was a zealous promoter of the true religion, as well as a vigorous opposer of the idolatries of the church of Rome, during the reign of king Edward VI. But when popery raised its destructive head, he, among many others, became the object of its persecution, as one that propagated doctrines contrary to the infallible church, and therefore liable to the severest censure and punishment.

Marsh, on hearing that search was made after him, absconded for some time, and in his retirement, often deliberated with himself, whether he should fly abroad to save his life, or surrender himself up, in order to ward off the mischief which threatened his mother and brother, who were supposed to have concealed him from the persons employed to search out heretics.

During this unsettled state of his mind, he consulted with his friends, and earnestly sought direction of God, that he might be guided in the way, which most conduced to his glory, and his own spiritual and eternal interest.

At length, thinking that flight would evince cowardice in the best of causes, he determined, by the grace of God, to abide by the consequences, and, acccordingly, surrendered himself to the earl of Derby at his seat at Latham, in the county of Lancaster.

When he was brought into the earl's presence, he was charged with propagating heresy, and sowing sedition amongst the people ; but he denied the charge, and declared, that he preached no other doctrine than what was contained in the word of God, and that he always enforced allegiance to his sovereign, according to the will of God.

Being asked to deliver a summary of his belief, he declared, that he believed in God the Father, Son, and Holy Ghost, according to the creeds of the apostles, the council of Nice, and the saints Athanasius, Austin, and Ambrose.

A Romish priest, who was present, then proceeded to inquire his opinion concerning the favourite tenet of the church of Rome, relating to the sacrament. Marsh answered in general, that he believed whosoever received the holy sacrament of the body and blood of Christ, according to his own appointment, did eat and drink his body and blood, with all the benefits arising from the same, because our Lord was ever present at his own ordinances.

This general reply not appearing satisfactory, they descended to particulars, and peremptorily demanded his opinion, whether or not the elements were changed into the very body and blood of Christ after consecration.— Our martyr briefly observed, that what he believed he had already declared, and desired them not to propose to him such hard and unprofitable questions, in order to endanger his life, and, as it were, to suck from him his very blood.

Incensed at this reply, the earl told him, that instead of seeking his destruction, he meant to preserve his life in this world, and secure his happiness in that which is to come, by converting him from damnable errors and heresies, and bringing him over to the holy mother-church out of which there was no salvation.

After many questions and exhortations, finding he still persevered in the faith which opposed that of the infallible church, the earl gave him pen and ink, and ordered him to write down his belief concerning the sacrament of the altar; and, on his writing just what he had before delivered, he was commanded to be more particular, when he wrote only the following words : " further I know not."

This resolute behaviour exposed him to the keenest resentment of his popish persecutors, who committed him to prison, and suffered no one to come near him, but the keeper, who brought him daily the scanty allowance of the place.

Various attempts were made, during his confinement, to bring him to a recantation ; but as he still remained fixed and determined in his faith, they administered to him the four following articles, to which, the earl declared, if he would not subscribe, he should be sent to the county gaol, and proceeded against with the utmost severity :

" 1. Whether the mass now used, in the church of England, was according to Christ's institution, and with faith, reverence, and devotion, to be heard and seen ?

" 2. Whether Almighty God, by the words pronounced by the priest, did change the bread and wine, after the words of consecration, into the body and blood of Christ, whether it were received or reserved ?

" 3. Whether the lay-people ought to receive but under the form of bread only, and that the one kind was sufficient for them ?

" 4. Whether confession to the priest now used in England, was godly and necessary ?

Having retired for some time to consider of these articles, he returned, and delivered his opinion of them as follows :

The first he absolutely denied.

The second he answered in the very words he had before written.

With respect to the third, he declared, that lay-people, according to the institution of Christ, ought to receive under both kinds, and that, therefore, to receive under one kind only was not sufficient.

To the last he observed, that though auricular confession was a good means to instruct ignorant people, it was not necessary to salvation, because not commanded by God.

To these points he added, that his faith in Christ, founded on the infallible word of the only living and true God, he never would deny at the instance of any living creature, or through fear of any punishment whatsoever; and moreover desired of the earl, that his friends might be permitted to see him during his confinement.

In a few days, he was committed to Lancaster gaol, laid in irons, and arraigned at the bar with the common felons, where they endeavoured to extort from him information of several persons in that country, whom they suspected of maintaining heretical opinions; but no means could prevail with him to utter a word that might endanger the lives or liberties of his faithful brethren in Christ.

He was severely reprimanded for reading aloud to the people (who flocked every morning and evening under the prison window) the litany and prayers of the reformed church, together with select passages of holy writ in the English tongue, which they termed preaching, and, therefore, deemed criminal.

After remaining some weeks in confinement at Lancaster, he was removed to Chester, and placed in the bishop's liberty, where his lordship frequently conferred with him, and used his utmost endeavours to bring him to an acknowledgment of the corporal presence in the sacrament of the altar, the mass, confession, and, in short, all the tenets and practices of the church of Rome.

When the bishop found he would not assent to a single point, he remanded him to prison; and, in a few days, summoned him before him in the cathedral church of Chester, where, in the presence of the mayor, chancellor, and principal inhabitants of that city, both laity and clergy, he caused him to take a solemn oath, to answer truly to such articles as might be alleged against him.

After he was sworn, the chancellor accused him of having preached and published most heretically and blasphemously, within the parishes of Dean, Eccles, Berry, and many other parishes within the bishop's diocess, directly against the pope's authority, the catholic church of Rome, the mass, and the sacrament of the altar, with many articles.

To all these charges, Marsh answered in brief, that he had neither heretically nor blasphemously preached or published against any of the articles, but as occasion served; and as his conscience obliged him to maintain the truth, as declared in God's word, and as all then present had acknowledged in the preceding reign.

Being examined as to every particular article, he modestly answered, according to the doctrine publicly taught in the reign of king Edward VI.

After a confinement of three weeks longer in prison, Marsh was again brought into the cathedral, where the chancellor made a formal harangue on the bishop's care of his flock, in order to prevent infection from scabby sheep, and the like; which ended, the former articles were propounded to him; and to which he severally answered in the negative.

Being charged with having declared, that the church and doctrine taught and set forth in king Edward's time, was the true church; and that the church of Rome is not the true catholic church: he acknowledged the declaration, and ratified it by a repetition.

Several persons present taking occasion to ask him, (as he denied the bishop of Rome's authority in England,) whether Linus, Anacletus, and Clement, who were bishops of Rome, were not good men; he replied in the affirmative, but reminded them, that they claimed no more authority in England than the archbishop of Canterbury doth in Rome.

As this observation highly reflected on the validity of the papal supremacy, the bishop was so incensed, that he gave Marsh very abusive language, calling him a most damnable, irreclaimable, and unpardonable heretic.

In return for this, Marsh mildly expostulated with the bishop, telling him, if he could be persuaded, in his own conscience, that the articles proposed to him were founded on God's word, he would gladly yield in every point; declaring, that he held no heretical opinion, but utterly abhorred every kind of heresy; and then called all present to bear witness, that, in the articles of religion, he held no other opinion than what was by law established, and publicly taught in England, at the death of king Edward the sixth ; and that, in such religion and doctrines, by the grace of God, he would stand, live, and die.

He was then, for the last time, asked, whether he would stand to the same, being full of heresies, or forsake them, and return to the catholic church ? and on his heartily declaring he would continue steadfast and immoveable in the faith of God's word, nor ever return to any church that was not founded on scripture authority, the bishop began to read his sentence of condemnation, but was interrupted by the chancellor, in order to give him yet an opportunity of recanting.

He resolutely withstood the earnest entreaties of several people, who desired him to accept of the proffered mercy; nor could even the repeated exhortations of the bishop and chancellor prevail with this eminent servant of Christ, to deny his Lord and master, and submit to the usurpation of cruel, tyrannical men.

All endeavours proving ineffectual, the bishop proceeded in passing sentence, which being ended, Marsh was delivered up to the sheriffs, who conveyed him to the North-gate prison, where he was confined in a dungeon till the day of his execution.

On the 4th of the month called April, 1555, this firm believer was led to the place appointed for the bloody scene, amidst a crowd of lamenting spectators. It was near a village called Spital-Boughton, at a small distance from Chester. As soon as he arrived at the place, the chamberlain of that city shewed him a box, containing the queen's pardon, on condition that he would recant. Our martyr coolly answered, that he would gladly accept the same, (for he loved the queen) but as it tended to pluck him from God, who was King of kings, and Lord of lords, he could not receive it on such terms.

Then turning to the spectators, he told them the cause of the cruel death which awaited him, and exhorted them to remain steadfast in the faith of Christ ; which done, he kneeled on the ground, directed his prayer to God, for strength equal to the fiery trial, arose, and was chained to the stake, having a number of fagots under him, and a cask full of pitch and tar hanging over his head.

The fire being kindled, he suffered, for a considerable time, the most exquisite torture, his flesh being so broiled, and puffed up, that those who stood before him could not see the chain with which he was fastened. At length, with the utmost fortitude, he spread forth his arms, and said, with a voice to be universally heard by the spectators, "Father of heaven, have mercy upon me." Soon after which, he yielded up his spirit into the hands of him who gave it.

Thus died, in confirmation of the gospel of Christ, a sincere believer, raising, by his patient resignation, the wonder and astonishment of all that saw him suffer, the greater part of whom cried out with ecstasy, "of a truth, God is with him."

This pious christian, during the course of his confinement, wrote the particulars of his respective examinations before his bloody persecutors; as also a great number of letters to different people, among which, we shall copy the following:

A letter from George Marsh, to several of his friends, immediately after the close of his last examination.

"HERE you have, dearly beloved friends in Christ, the chief and principal articles of christian doctrine, briefly touched, which heretofore I have both believed, professed, and taught, and as yet do believe, profess, and teach; and am surely purposed, by God's grace, to continue in the same until the last day. I do want both time and opportunity to write out, at large, the probations, causes, parts, and effects of those articles; which, whoso desireth to know, let them read over the common places of the pious, learned men, Philip Melancthon, and Erasmus Sarcerius, whose judgment, in these matters of religion, I do chiefly follow and lean unto. The Lord give us understanding in all things, and deliver us from this evil world, according to his will and pleasure, and bring us again out of this hell of affliction, into which, it hath pleased the merciful Lord to throw us down : and deliver us out of the mouth of the Lion, and from all evil doing, and keep us unto his everlasting and heavenly kingdom.   Amen.

" Though satan be suffered, as wheat, to sift us for a time, yet our faith faileth not through Christ's aid, but that we are, at all times, able and ready to confirm the faith of our weak brethren, and always ready to give an answer to every man that asketh us a reason of the hope that is in us, and that with meekness and reverence, having a good conscience ; and whereas they backbite us as evil-doers, they may be ashamed, forasmuch as they have falsely accused our good conversation in Christ. I thought myself now, of late years, for the cares of this life, well settled with my loving and faithful wife and children, and also well quietted in the peaceable possession of that pleasant Euphrates, I do confess it : but the Lord, who worketh all things for the best to them that love him, would not there leave me, but did take my dear and beloved wife from me ; whose death was a painful cross to my flesh.

" Also, I thought myself now, of late years, well placed under my most loving and most gentle Laurence Saunders, in the cure of Langhton. But the Lord, of his great mercy, would not suffer me long there to continue (although for the small time I was in this vineyard, I was not an idle workman).   But he hath provided me, I perceive it, to taste of a far other cup ; for by violence hath he yet, once again, driven me out of that glorious Babylon, that I should not taste too much of her wanton pleasures, but with his most dearly beloved disciples, to have my inward rejoicing in the cross of his son Jesus Christ. The glory of whose church, I see it well, standeth not in the harmonious sound of the bells and organs, nor yet in the glittering of mitres and copes, neither in the shining of gilt images and lights (as the blind papists do judge it) but in continual labours, and daily afflictions, for his name sake.

" God, at this present, here in England, hath his fan in hand, and after his great harvest, whereinto these years

past he hath sent his labourers, is now sifting the corn
from the chaff, and purging his floor, and ready to gather
the wheat into his garner, and burn up the chaff with un-
quenchable fire.

"Take heed, and beware of the leaven of the scribes,
and of the sadduces; I mean the erroneous doctrines of
the papists, which, with their glosses, deprave the scriptures; for, as the apostle St. Peter doth teach us, "there
shall be false teachers amongst you, who privily shall bring
in damnable heresies: and many shall follow their pernicious ways, by reason of whom the way of truth shall be
evil spoken of, and through covetousness, shall they, with
feigned words, make merchandise of you:" and Christ
earnestly warneth us, to "beware of false prophets, which
come to you in sheep's clothing, but inwardly they are
ravening wolves. Ye shall know them by their fruits."
The fruits of the prophets are their doctrine. In this
place, are we christians taught, that we should try the
preachers, and others that come under a colour, to set
forth true religion unto us; according to the saying of
St. Paul, "prove all things, hold fast that which is good."
Also the evangelist St. John, saith, "believe not every
spirit, but try the spirits, whether they are of God; because many false prophets are gone out into the world."
Therefore, if thou wilt know the true prophets from the
false, try their doctrine by the true touchstone, which is
the word of God: and as the pious Bereans did, search
ye the scriptures, whether those things which be preached unto you, be even so or not; or else by the outward
conversation of them, ye may easily be deceived."

A letter from George Marsh to a friend unknown.

"GRACE be with you, and peace be multiplied in the
knowledge of God, and Jesus the Lord.

"After hearty commendations, and thanks to you, not
only for your large token, but much more for your loving letters, full of consolation to me, as touching my person, to you unknown: these shall be to certify you, that I

rejoice greatly in the Lord, when I do perceive how my sweet Saviour Christ doth stir up the minds, not only of my familiar friends in time past, but also of sundry and divers, heretofore unto me unknown and unacquainted, to bear part with me in this my painful and costly imprisonment, sending me things not only necessary for this present life, but also comfortable letters, encouraging and exhorting me to continue grounded and established in the faith, and not to be moved away from the hope of the gospel, whereof, according to my small talent, I have been a minister ; and daily I call and cry unto the Lord, in whom is all my trust.   And without whom, I can do nothing : that he, which hath begun a work in me, would vouchsafe to go forth with it until the day of Jesus Christ, being surely certified in my conscience of this, that he will so do, forasmuch as he hath given me, that not only I should believe on him, but also suffer for his sake. The Lord strengthen me, with his holy spirit, that I may be one of the number of those blessed, which enduring to the end shall be saved.

" And whereas you say, that my suffering of persecution with Christ is a thing to you most comfortable, I make answer, that in all mine adversity and necessity, nothing on your behalf is greater consolation unto me, than to hear of the faith and love of others, and how they have good remembrance of us always.   For my trust in the Lord is, that this my business shall happen to the furtherance of the gospel ; and that you will be none of those forgetful and hypocritical hearers, whereof some being but way-side hearers, the devil cometh, and taketh away the word out of their hearts, lest they should believe and be saved, (but let prayer be made without ceasing, by the congregation unto God for them) ; and, no doubt, God will, to your consolation, gloriously deliver, by one means or other, his oppressed. Only tarry ye the Lord's leisure: be strong : let your hearts be of good comfort : and wait ye still for the Lord. He tarrieth not that will come: look for him, therefore ; and faint not, and he will never fail you.   Yours,

GEORGE MARSH."

The Martyrdom of William Flower, who, for striking a Priest, had his right hand cut off, and was afterwards burnt, for his steadfast adherence to the truth.

WILLIAM FLOWER was born at a place called Snow-hill, in the county of Cambridge. He was, educated in the Roman catholic persuasion; and being brought up to the church, when, at a proper age, he was admitted into orders, and became a professed monk in the abbey of Ely.

After residing some time in the monastery, he threw off the monkish habit; became a secular priest; returned to the place of his nativity; and officiated for some years, in a clerical capacity.

In process of time, on a serious review of the sacred scriptures, and candid comparisons of them with the doctrines and practices of the Romish church, he began to doubt of the authenticity of the latter; and, on a farther inspection, finding them wholly repugnant to the word of God, and founded on the mere inventions of men, he abjured them, and earnestly embraced the doctrines of the reformation.

After having thus departed from the Romish church, he came to London, and took up his residence at Lambeth, where he married, and kept a school for his livelihood.

Going one day from Lambeth to Westminster, he went into St. Margaret's church, at the time that mass was performing. As he refused to kneel at the elevation of the host, he was severely reprimanded by the priest; at which, Flower was so irritated, that he struck him on the head, the priest having, at the same time, in his hand a chalice, containing some consecrated wafers.

As his behaviour, on this occasion, proceeded rather from rash zeal than well-grounded knowledge, he submitted himfelf to the award of bishop Bonner, willing to endure, for his folly, whatever punishment he should think proper to inflict.

The bishop would have mitigated his punishment for the crime he had committed on the priest, if he would have subscribed to the popish faith ; but that he would not consent to, on any terms whatever ; in consequence of which, he was committed a prisoner to the Gate-house.

After remaining some time in prison, he was brought before the bishop, who administered to him, on oath, several articles. But not answering satisfactorily to these, he was committed to the Fleet-prison, when he was brought before the warden, and found guilty of abusing a priest in the duty of his office, and also of maintaining damnable heresies.

He was again brought before the bishop, who used the most forcible arguments to induce him to recant ; but these all proving ineffectual, he asked him, if he knew any matter, or cause, why sentence should not be pronounced against him as a heretic ? To which, he answered, " I have nothing at all to say, for I have already said unto you all that I had to say ; and that I have said, I will not go from : and, therefore, do what you will."

The bishop then proceeded to the sentence, condemning and excommunicating him as a heretic ; after which, he was degraded, and delivered over to the secular power.

The 24th of the month called April, was the day appointed for his execution, and the place St. Margaret's church yard, Westminster. On the morning of the fatal day, he was led to the stake, amidst a prodigious number of spectators. Immediately on his arrival at the place, he kneeled down, and prayed to God, acknowledging his faith, as follows :

" O Eternal God, most mighty and merciful Father, who has sent down thy Son upon the earth, to save me, and all mankind ; who ascended up into heaven again, and left his blood upon the earth behind him, for the redemption of our sins, have mercy upon me, have mercy upon me, for thy dear son our Saviour Jesus Christ's sake, in whom, I confess only to be all salvation and justification, and that there is no other means, nor way, nor holiness, in which, or by which, any man can be saved in this world. This is my faith, which I beseech all men here to bear witness of."

He then repeated the Lord's Prayer very deliberately, and with an audible voice; after which, he arose, and prepared himself for undergoing the destined punishment.

A Romish priest, who was present, desired him to recant his heresy, and thereby save his life : to whom, he said, "sir, I beseech you, for God's sake, to be contented; for that I have said, I have said ; and I trust to the living God; he will give me his holy spirit to continue to the end."

He then desired all the world to forgive him, whom he had offended, as he, from his heart forgave all the world.

This done, he was chained to the stake, and his left hand fastened to his side. The other hand, with which he had struck the priest, was then held up, and cut off, the blood plentifully gushing from the wrist; which punishment he bore without the least apparent emotion. The fagots were then piled round him, and being immediately kindled, he cried out with a loud voice, "O the Son of God, have mercy upon me ; O the Son of God, receive my soul." These words he repeated three times, when the violence of the smoke took away his speech ; but he still shewed the spectators, that he was not yet deprived of life, by holding up the arm from whence the hand had been cut, with the other, as long as he was able. There not being a sufficiency of fagots, he underwent great torture, the lower parts being consumed a considerable time before the others were scarcely affected. At length, however, they finished his miseries, by striking him a violent blow on the head, which brought the upper part of him into the fire ; and, in this dreadful manner, he yielded up his life.

The sufferings and Martyrdom of John Cardmaker, Priest; and John Warne, Upholder.

JOHN CARDMAKER was educated in the Romish religion ; and, for some years, was a friar of the order of St. Francis. After the dissolution of religious houses by Henry VIII, he attended with such diligence to the preaching and writing of pious, learned divines, that he became a convert to the protestant faith, obtained a living in the reformed church, and was an eminent preacher of the gospel.

In the reign of Edward VI, he was appointed reader at St. Paul's, and prebendary of Wells, in which functions, he continued indefatigable, till the accession of queen Mary, when he was apprehended, together with the bishop of Wells, and committed to the Fleet, though the laws of king Edward were then in full force.

When the papal supremacy and jurisdiction prevailed in England, and bishops had authority, by virtue of the statute, *ex officio*, to proceed against heretics, Cardmaker was removed from the Fleet to the Compter, where he contracted an acquaintance with Laurence Saunders, (already mentioned) by whom he was animated and encouraged to continue steadfast in his faith and profession.

In process of time, he was summoned to appear before the arrogant and cruel Bonner, who alleged against him divers charges, which, with Cardmaker's answers, were as follows :

1. That after his professing the Roman catholic religion, and entering into holy orders, he took a wife, and had by her a female child, thereby breaking his vow, and the order and ordinance of the church.

The first part of this charge he allowed, but denied his having broken any vow by his marriage ; because he was allowed to marry, both by the laws of the realm, and also by the laws of the church of England.

2. That he believed and taught, and did still believe, that in the sacrament of the altar, under the visible signs, that is, under the forms of bread and wine, there is really and truly the true and natural body of our Saviour Christ.

He replied, that he had believed and taught it as contained in this article, but he did not then so believe and teach.

3. That the belief of the catholic church is, that having the body and blood of Christ really and truly contained in the sacrament of the altar, is to have, by the omnipotent power of Almighty God, the body and blood of Christ there invisibly, but really present under the same sacrament, and to make thereby a new God, or a new Christ, or a new body of Christ.

The whole of this he denied.

4. That it may stand well together, the faith of the Catholic church is, that the body of Christ is visibly and truly ascended into heaven, and there is, in the visible form of his humanity; and yet the same body in substance, is invisibly and truly contained in the sacrament of the altar.

All this he denied as absurd and unscriptural.

5. That Christ, at his last supper, taking bread into his hands, breaking, and giving it to his apostles, saying, "take eat, this is my body," did institute a sacrament there, willing that his body, really and only, should be contained in the said sacrament; no substance of bread and wine there remaining.

To the first part, he assented, but denied the latter part; and to these his answers, he subscribed his name.

For persisting in these answers, he was condemned and sent to Newgate, where he was visited by a messenger, from the council, to know whether or not he would recant.

He told the messenger, that since God, of his mercy, had opened his eyes to see his eternal truth, he had called upon his name, to give him his grace to understand his word, and was determined, by the aid of the same grace, to continue steadfast in the same.

After some debate, concerning the corporeal presence in the sacrament of the altar, the messenger, finding Cardmaker inflexible in his opinion, departed, and acquainted the council with the result of his message.

John Warne, fellow-martyr with Cardmaker, was by trade an upholder, and lived with great credit and reputation, being a very pious and conscientious man.

As all who professed the protestant faith, in these persecuting times, were liable, not only to molestation in the performance of religious duties, but also to be arraigned at the bloody tribunal of the relentless Bonner; Warne, among the rest, was suspected of heresy, brought before the bishop, and had the following articles laid to his charge :

1. That he believed, that in the sacrament, called the sacrament of the altar, there is not the very, true, and natural body of our Saviour Christ in substance, under the forms of bread and wine.

2. That he believed, that after the words of consecration spoken by the priest, there is not (as the church of England doth believe and teach) the body of Christ, but that there doth only remain the substance of material bread, as it is before the consecration, and that the said bread is no ways altered and changed.

3. That he believed, that if the Catholic church doth believe and teach, there is in the mass (now used in England, and in other places of christendom) a sacrifice, wherein there is a sacrament concerning the body and blood of Christ, really and truly, then that belief and faith of the church are nought, and against God's truth and the scripture.

4. That neither in lent past, nor any time since the queen's reign, he had been at church, nor had heard mass, nor had been confessed, nor had received the sacrament of the altar ; and said, that he was not sorry for the same, because his conscience was not defiled, as it would otherwise have been.

Warne underwent several examinations, in the presence of different persons, on these articles ; at all of which, he declared, that he did believe and confess the same to be true.

At length, the bishop of London having frequently warned him to abjure his heretical tenets, and return to obedience to the church of Rome, but all without effect, the definitive sentence was pronounced, when he was delivered up to the sheriffs, and sent to Newgate.

While these two martyrs were in prison, some of the popish emissaries had spread a report that they intended to recant, which occasioned the following letter.

A letter from J. Cardmaker to his friend.

"THE peace of God be with you. You shall right well perceive that I have not gone back, as some men do report of me, but am as ready to give my life, as many of my brethren that are gone before, although by a policy I have a little prolonged it, and that for the best, as already it appeareth unto me, and shall shortly appear unto all. That day that I recant any point of doctrine, I shall suffer twenty kinds of death, the Lord being mine assistant, as I doubt not but he will. Commend me to my friend, and tell him no less. This the Lord strengthen you, me, and all his elect. My riches and poverty are as they were wont to be, and I have learned to rejoice in poverty, as well as riches, for that I account now to be very riches. Thus, fare ye well in Christ. Salute all my brethren, in my name. I have conferred with some of my adversaries, learned men, and I find that they be but sophists and shadows."

On the 30th of the month called May, 1555, these two martyrs were conducted under a strong guard, from New-gate to Smithfield, the place appointed for their execution.

As soon as they arrived at the stake, Warne began his prayer, which having finished, he prepared himself for the fiery trial. While Warne was at prayers, Cardmaker was discoursing with the sheriffs, insomuch that the friends of the reformation feared he would recant; but these apprehensions soon subsided; for, after his conference with the sheriffs, and a short prayer, he courageously went to the stake, took his fellow-sufferer by the hand, comforted him, and cheerfully submitted to be bound.

When the people beheld this, they were greatly rejoiced, as it totally removed their fearful apprehensions that they would recant; and they exclaimed, with the most distinguished satisfaction, "God be praised, the Lord strengthen you; the Lord Jesus receive your spirits."

The executioner having set fire to the fagots, they burnt with great rapidity; and the two martyrs soon passed through the flames, to enjoy the crown of triumph and victory, prepared for the true soldiers of Christ in his blessed kingdom.

On the same day that these two martyrs suffered in Smith-field, John Orderly, and John Simpson, were burnt in Es-sex ; the former at Rayleigh, and the latter at Rochford.

The Life and Martyrdom of Thomas Hawkes.

THOMAS HAWKES was the son of reputable and pious parents, who gave him a good education, and brought him up in the reformed religion. He strictly adhered to his religious principles ; so that finding the gospel, after the death of king Edward, began to decline, (especially among great families, in one of which he lived) he quitted his ser-vice, and returned home, where he hoped quietly to en-joy the worship of God, according to the dictates of his own conscience.

In these expectations, however, he soon found himself disappointed. As there were now popish emissaries in ev-ery corner, lying in wait to give information if any one was only suspected of favouring the doctrines of reformation, Hawkes was apprehended, and brought before the earl of Oxford, (in whose service he had formerly lived) for be-ing unfounded in religion, and contemning the sacraments of the church, in that he had kept a son unbaptized three weeks, because he would not suffer him to be baptized af-ter the popish manner.

The earl referred him to bishop Bonner, to whom having written that he had refused to have his child bap-tized, according to the order of the church now in use, he left him to his lordship's discretion.

When Hawkes was brought before the bishop, he was asked the cause of keeping the child unbaptized so long ; to which, he returned for answer, that he was bound to do nothing contrary to the word of God.

The bishop then urged, that baptism being a sacrament contained in the word of God, and incumbent on every christian, he was, consequently, criminal in denying, or not conforming to the same. To this, he said, that he, by no means, denied God's institution, but men's invention therein; such as the use of oil, cream, spittle, salt, candle, &c.

After much debate on the subject, the bishop asked him, if he would have his child baptized according to the service-books, set out in the reign of Edward VI. To which, he replied, that it was the very thing he desired from his soul.

This was, however, mere equivocation to learn his sentiments, for it appeared in the sequel, that Bonner's drift was to compel him to submit to the superstitions of the church of Rome, which, however, with all his artifice, he was not able to effect.

The bishop, with several others, held various conferences with Hawkes, concerning his belief of the corporeal presence in the sacrament of the altar, the mass, the holy creed, holy water, and other ceremonies of the church of Rome; but these also he rejected, as he had done that of baptism, because they were contrary to the word of God, by which alone, he was determined to be guided and directed in all matters of faith and religion; nay, he boldly told them all, that he would not credit them in any thing, but what they could prove from the holy scripture.

At length, Bonner, finding he could by no means prevail with him to recant his opinions, and submit to the church of Rome, sent him prisoner to the Gate-house, in Westminster, commanding the keeper to confine him closely, and not permit any person to converse with him.

During his confinement, various methods were used to bring him over to recant, such as conversation, reading to him, taking 'him to hear sermons, and the like; but all proved ineffectual; his constant answer, to all who spoke to him on that subject, being, "I am no changling."

Bonner, incensed at his steadfastness, told him, he should find him no changling neither, and immediately went out, and wrote the following paper:

"I Thomas Hawkes do hereby confess and declare, before my ordinary, Edmund Bonner, bishop of London, that the mass is abominable, detestable, and full of all superstition; and also concerning the sacrament of the body and blood of Christ, (commonly called the sacrament of the altar) that Christ is in no part thereof, but only in heaven. This I have believed, and this I do believe."

Bonner ordered Hawkes to subscribe to this paper; but he refused to set his name to what he had not written himself; upon which, the haughty prelate struck him on the breast, declaring, at the same time, that he would severely chastise all such proud and disobedient knaves.

A few days after this, the bishop summoned him, with several others, to appear publicly in the consistory court at St. Paul's where the several articles alleged against him, together with the bill of confession, were read to him; to all which, he firmly abided.

They then strongly exhorted him to recant, that they might not be obliged to pass the solemn sentence upon him. To which, he cheerfully replied, that if he had a hundred bodies, he would suffer them all to be torn to pieces, rather than abjure the faith of Christ's gospel.

On his thus steadfastly persevering in the faith which he professed, the bishop read the sentence of condemnation against him, and five others; after which, he was sent back to prison, where he remained till the month called June following, when he was delivered into the hands of lord Rich, who caused him to be conveyed to Chelmsford, and from thence to Coxall, in Essex, where he was burnt on the 10th of the same month.

Hawkes gave many pious exhortations, and godly admonitions to his friends who came to visit him; and several of them requesting, if it was possible, that he would shew them some token, by which might appear the possibility of burning without repining, he promised, by the help of God, to shew them that the most exquisite torments were to be endured in the glorious cause of Christ, and his gospel, the comforts of which were able to lift the believing soul above all that men or devils can inflict.

Accordingly, it was agreed between them, that if the rage of pain was tolerable, he should lift up his hands towards heaven, before he gave up the ghost.

A short time after this agreement, he was led to the place of execution, where, being fastened to the stake with a chain, he addressed the multitude, and especially lord Rich, reasoning with him on the iniquity and dreadful consequences of shedding the innocent blood of the saints.

Having fervently prayed to Almighty God, the flames were kindled around him, and he continued in them so long that his speech was taken away by their violence ; his skin was contracted, and the spectators thought he was dead, when, on a sudden, and contrary to all expectation, this eminent and zealous servant of God, mindful of the promise he had made to his friends, held his hands flaming over his head, and, as if in an ecstasy of joy, clapped them thrice together.

The astonished multitude testified their approbation of his faith and patience ; and his friends, to whom he made the promise, were exceedingly confirmed in the most holy faith, by being eye-witnesses to the power of divine strength, which is able to support the servants of God, under every trial that may befal them, for the sake of the truth, as it is in our blessed Redeemer.

While he was in confinement, he wrote a great number of letters to different people, and, among them, one to his wife, which so strongly displays the tender husband, and pious christian, that we shall preserve a copy of it.

A letter from Thomas Hawkes to his wife.

" GRACE be with you, and peace from God the Father, and from our Lord Jesus Christ, who gave himself for our sins, to deliver us from this present evil world, through the good will of God our Father, to whom be praise for ever and ever. Amen.

" My dear yoke-fellow in the Lord, forasmuch as the Lord hath not only called me to work in his vineyard, but hath also fulfilled his good work in me, (I trust to his glory, and to the comfort of all those that look for his coming) I thought it my duty, dear yoke-fellow, to write unto you some lessons out of God's book; and if you will direct yourself thereafter, doubt not of it but God, who refuseth none that will come unto him with their whole heart, will assist you with his holy spirit, and direct you in all his ways, to his honour and glory, who grant it for his mercy sake. Amen.

" First, I exhort you to fear God ; to serve and honour his holy name ; to love him with all your heart, soul, and mind ; to believe faithfully all his promises ; to lay sure hold upon them, that in all your troubles, whatsoever they are, you may run straight to the mercy of God, and he will bring you out of them : keep you within his wings ; then shall you be sure that neither devil, flesh, nor hell, shall be able to hurt you.

" But take heed ; if you will not keep his holy precepts and laws, and, to the uttermost of your power, call for the help of God to walk in the same, but will leave them, and run to all abominations with the wicked world, and do as they do ; then be sure to have your part with the wicked world, in the burning lake that never shall be quenched. Therefore, beware of idolatry, which doth, most of all, stink before the face of Almighty God, and was, by all good men, most detested from the beginning of the world. For which, what kingdoms, nations, and realms, God hath punished with most terrible plagues, with fire, brimstone, hunger, sword, pestilence, &c. to the utter subversion of them, it is manifestly to be seen through the whole bible. Yea, his own peculiar people, whom he had done so much for, when they fell from him, and went and served other gods, contrary to his commandment, he utterly destroyed and rooted them out from off the earth. Again, how he has preserved those that abhor superstition and idolatry, and that have only taken hold upon God with their whole heart, to serve him, to love him, and to fear him, &c. it is most manifestly to be seen, even from the beginning, out of what great dangers he hath always delivered them : yea, when all hope of deliverance was past as touching their expectation, even then, in the sight of all his enemies, would he work his godly will and purpose, to the utter amazement and destruction of all those that were his manifest enemies.

" Further, I exhort you, in the bowels of Christ, that you will exercise and be steadfast in prayer ; for, prayer is the only means to pierce the heavens, to obtain, at the hand of God, whatsoever we desire, so that it be asked in faith. Oh, what notable things do we read in the scriptures, that have been obtained through fervent prayer! We are commanded to call upon him for help, aid, and succour, in necessities and troubles ; and he hath promised to help us. Again, they that will not call upon him with their whole heart, but upon other dead creatures, in whom there is no help, (for there was none found worthy to open the book, but only the lamb Christ, which was killed for our sins), I say, who that will refuse his help, must even, by the the terrible judgments of God, come utterly to confusion ; as it hath, and is daily manifest to be seen. And whatsoever you desire of God in your prayer, ask it for Jesus Christ's sake, for whom, and in whom, God hath promised us to give all things necessary. And though that which we ask, come not at the first and second calling, yet continue still knocking, and he will, at length, open his treasures of mercy, so that ye shall be sure to obtain : for he hath so promised, if ye continue in faith, hoping surely in him. These former lessons, with all such instructions as I have told you by my mouth, I do wish that you would most earnestly learn ; and then, I doubt not, but God, who is the giver of all grace, will assist you in all your doings, that you may be found worthy of his kingdom, which is prepared through Christ.

" Further, whereas it pleased God to send us children, my desire is, that they may be brought up in the fear of God, and in his laws. And this is to certify you, that you deliver, in any wise, my eldest son to Mr. Throgmorton, who, upon his good-will, hath promised me to bring him up, according to my desire; and I trust, as God hath put into his heart. See, therefore, that you deliver him, in any wise, without delay ; and as for the other, if you shall seem to be burdened with him, (which I think nature will not suffer) my desire is, that he be brought up in the fear of God, the uttermost of your endeavour, with some honest man that hath the fear of God before his eyes ; and let us give thanks unto God, who hath given them us, beseeching him that they may be counted worthy to be of that flock that shall stand on the right hand of the majesty of God, when he shall judge the world.   Amen.

"Yet once again, I warn you, that you continue in fervent prayer, as I said before; then shall you be sure, that God, even of his own mercy, according as he hath promised, will be an husband unto you, and provide better for you than ever I was able to do ; yea, he will cause all men that fear him to pity you, to help you, to succour you in all your necessities, so that if any do you wrong, he will be avenged on them.   Moreover, I wish you to keep company with those, of whom you may learn to come to a more perfect knowledge in God ; and, I doubt not, but God will provide that such will be glad to receive you if you shall profess, and go forward in his truth.

" Finally, and to make an end, I desire you, that you take heed with whom you couple yourself.   See that he be a man that feareth God, loveth his laws, and will walk in the same to the utmost of his power ; such a one as can be content to love you, and to care for you.   Take heed, he be no brawler, no drunkard, no wicked person, not given to filthiness, no worldling, no dicer, nor carder. In fine, no filthy person, but chuse you such a one, as God may be glorified in both your lives.   And again, on your part, love him, serve him, obey him in all godliness, as long as God shall give you life in this world.   Then shall ye both be sure to obtain that kingdom which God the Father hath prepared, and Jesus Christ obtained for you, that never shall have an end, where I trust to abide your coming.   Amen.

By your husband,

THOMAS HAWKES."

The sufferings and Martyrdom of Thomas Watts, a linen draper, of Billericay, in Essex.

THOMAS WATTS was born of reputable and pious parents, in the county of Essex. He was educated in the reformed religion, and, during the reign of Edward VI, was a zealous professor of the protestant faith. On the accession of queen Mary to the throne, apprehending he should be troubled, if not persecuted, on account of his following a religion contrary to that which was then introduced, he relinquished business, sold his goods, and disposed of his substance to his wife and children.

As he lived in the county of Essex, he came under the cognizance of lord Rich, before whom he was brought, and by whom he was demanded the reason of his disobeying the queen's laws, absenting himself from church, neglecting the mass, and setting up unlawful conventicles, contrary to her majesty's command.

Watts replied, with composure, that if he had offended against the law, he was subject to the penalty of the law; upon which, a justice of the peace then present, inquired of him, from whom he had imbibed his new-fangled religion? Watts upbraided the justice with hypocrisy, reminding him, that in the days of the late king, no one inveighed more strenuously against the Romish doctrines than himself, pronouncing the mass to be abominable, earnestly exhorting none to believe therein, and that their belief should be only in Christ; nay, adding further, that whosoever should introduce any strange notion here, should be deemed a traitor, and punished as such.

The justice reviled Watts as an insolent, lying knave, and persuaded the sheriff not to pay any regard to what he had said.

Soon after this, information was given to bishop Bonner, that Thomas Watts maintained, inculcated, and encouraged heretical opinions. In consequence of this, he was brought into the consistory court in London, and there examined, concerning the discourse he had with lord Rich, and other commissioners, at Chelmsford, when he publicly related the truth ; after which, the following articles were alleged against him, requiring, according to the custom of the court, a particular answer to each article.

1. It was alleged against him, that he did not believe in the sacrament of the holy Catholic church, as the Catholic church of Rome, and other churches, members of the same, have believed and taught, but despised the same.

To this, he answered, that he believed in all the sacraments, according to Christ's institution, but not according to the church of the bishop of Rome ; that he believed according to the preaching of several ministers of the gospel, who preached the word of God truly and sincerely.

2. That he believed, and taught others, that the substance of material bread and wine, do not remain in the sacrament of the altar after consecration.

To this, he replied, that he believed, that Christ's body is now in heaven, and no where else ; and that he never would believe, that Christ's body was in the sacrament.

3. That he believed the mass to be abominable.

To this, he frankly answered in the affirmative, declaring that he would never recant his opinion.

4. That he believed, that confession to a priest was not necessary.

To this, he said, he did not believe, that the priest could absolve him of his sins ; but allowed, that it was good to ask spiritual advice of the priest.

5. That in the open sessions, he confessed, that he had refused to come to the church to hear mass, and receive the sacrament of the altar ; because, according to the service of the church, set out in the days of king Edward the sixth, such duties were deemed abominable, heretical, and schismatical ; that he declared, that all that was done in the church on the accession of her majesty, was abominable, heretical, schismatical, and unscriptural ; and also, that he uttered before the com-

missioners, other erroneous and arrogant words, to the injury of his soul, and bad example of the people present.

To this, he answered, without the least attempt to evade, that he declared his opinion, as in the article above-mentioned, and begged of God that he might live and die in that faith.

These, and other articles of less moment, were read to him, and his answers minuted down; after which, the bishop used the most forcible arguments to bring him to a denial of (what he called) his errors, and to be obedient to the holy mother-church.

Watts, however, remaining inflexible, and beseeching God that he might be enabled to hold out to the end, in the true faith of Christ, sentence of condemnation was pronounced against him, and he was delivered up to the sheriffs of London, who conducted him to Newgate.

On the 9th of the month called June, he was carried from Newgate to Chelmsford, his execution being appointed at that place on the 11th .On the same evening, he was conveyed there, he was in company with Thomas Hawkes, and others; and they all joined together in the most fervent prayer.

The day before his execution, he was visited by his wife, and six children, whom he addressed in the following manner:

"My dear wife, my good children, the time of my departure is at hand; therefore, henceforth I know you no more; but as the Lord hath given you unto me, so I give you again unto the Lord, whom I charge you to obey and fear. Beware that ye turn not to this abominable popery, as a testimony against which, I shall shortly, by God's grace, shed my blood. Let not the murdering of God's saints cause you to recant, but take occasion thereby, more earnestly, to contend for the faith once delivered to the saints. My dear children, I trust God will be a merciful father unto you."

This affecting address struck such an impression on two of his children, that they desired to be burned with him. So sympathetic a feeling, from such tender

branches, for a time, discomposed our martyr, the man
giving way to the parent; but, after having a little recovered himself, he embraced them with all the tenderness of a dying father, took his leave, and was led to the
stake, where he quietly yielded up his spirit into the
hands of him that gave it, saying, " into thy hands, O
God, I commend my spirit."

Such was the attachment of this steadfast believer to
the cause of his dear Lord and Master, that the most
moving spectacle of his disconsolate wife, and six innocent babes, could not in the least stagger his resolution;
but he persevered against all worldly considerations, being animated so to do, by an assurance of an immortal
crown of glory in his Redeemer's kingdom.

About the same time that Watts suffered, three others
shared the same fate, for their adherence to the truth of
the gospel; namely, Nicholas Chamberlain, weaver;
Thomas Osmond, fuller; and William Bamford, weaver. The first of these was burnt at Colchester, on the
14th of the month called June; the second suffered the
next day at Maningtree; and the third the following day
at Harwich.

The sufferings and deaths of John Bradford, a divine; and John Leafe, an apprentice.

THE first of these martyrs was born at Manchester,
where he received an education sufficiently liberal to
qualify him for the more exalted office of life, having obtained to a considerable knowledge in classical and math-
ematical literature.

On his arrival at years of maturity, having some distinguished friends, by their interest, he became secretary
to sir John Harrington, who was treasurer to Henry VIII.

After having been in this office for some time, being
of a studious turn of mind, he quitted it, and went to
Cambridge, where he made such great improvements,
that in the space of one year, that university conferred

on him the degree of master of arts; soon after which, he was admitted to a fellowship in Pembroke college.

At this time, there was at Cambridge one Martin Bucer, a zealous advocate for the reformed religion.— This person discovered a great regard for Bradford, and persuaded him to follow those studies which most conduced to qualify him for the work of the ministry.

Bradford having that diffidence of himself, which is generally the attendant on real merit, excused himself from taking upon him that important office, as not being sufficiently qualified; but Bucer, at length, brought him to consent to enter on the solemn work, and he was ordained a deacon, by Dr. Ridley, bishop of London, who made him prebendary of St. Paul's; where, in rotation, he preached for three years, the true gospel of Christ: namely, the doctrines of salvation by faith, and repentance unto life, together with the necessity of a life of holiness, as the evidence of that faith, at the end of which, the protestant cause suffered a violent shock, in the death of the pious young king.

After the accession of queen Mary, Bradford continued his course of preaching, till he was obstructed by the following incident.

In the first year of the reign of that princess, Bonner, then bishop of London, ordered Bourn, a canon of St. Paul's, and afterwards bishop of Bath, to preach a sermon, wherein he took occasion from the gospel of the day to justify Bonner, then restored to his bishopric, in preaching on the same text that very day four years, and enforcing doctrines, for which, according to the terms of the preacher, he was thrown into the Marshalsea, and there kept prisoner during the time of king Edward VI.

These words occasioned great murmurings amongst the people; nay, so incensed were they, that one of them threw a dagger at the preacher, and threatened to drag him from the pulpit, insomuch that he was obliged to withdraw, and desired Bradford to advance, and endeavour to appease the people, who were so tumultuous, that they could not be quelled even from the authority of the lord-mayor.

As soon as Bradford ascended the pulpit, the people shouted, "God save thy life, Bradford;" and then quietly attended to his discourse, in which, he reproved them for their disorderly behaviour, and exhorted them to peace and tranquillity; on which, after he had finished, they peaceably dispersed.

In the afternoon of the same day, Bradford preached at Bow-church, when he took occasion to rebuke the people for their tumultuous behaviour at St. Paul's in the morning.

Three days after this incident, he was summoned before the queen, and her council, and there charged as the cause of the late riot about Bourn's preaching at St. Paul's, though he was the very person that preserved him from the outrage of the people, and appeased the tumult.

He was also accused of preaching to the people at Bow-church, though he then warmly exhorted them to peace. But nothing that he could allege, in vindication of his innocence, availed; for he was committed to the tower, on a charge of sedition, because they found he was a popular man, and greatly caressed by the people.

He was confined above a year and six months, till the popish religion was restored by act of parliament.— He then took occasion to examine himself concerning his faith, because he could not speak against the doctrine of the church of Rome, without incurring much danger; whereas, while the laws of king Edward were unrepealed, he might freely speak according to the dictates of his own conscience, and the rules of God's most holy word.

The principal articles alleged against Bradford were, his denying the doctrine of transubstantiation, or the corporeal presence of Christ in the sacrament; and asserting, that wicked men did not partake of Christ's body in the said sacrament.

Several bishops, and other learned men, were appointed to confer with him; but their arguments had no weight, because they were not founded on scripture, but human tradition.

As Bradford would not admit of any tenets, or practices, but what were contained in the scripture, he was deemed a heretic, first excommunicated, then condemned, and committed to the custody of the sheriffs of London, by whom he was conducted, the night before his execution, to the prison of Newgate ; and, the following day, brought to the stake, with the martyr who succeeds in the order of this catalogue.

John Leafe was an apprentice to a tallow-chandler, and, at the age of nineteen years, on an information laid against him of heresy, was committed to the Compter, by the aldermen of the ward in which he lived.

After being some time confined in that prison, he was brought before bishop Bonner, and by him examined concerning his faith in the sacrament of the altar, and other points ; to all which, he answered, in such a manner as gave little satisfaction to the tyrannical bishop.

A few days after this, he underwent another examination ; but his answers being the same as before, he was condemned, and delivered over to the secular power, for not believing that the bread and wine in the sacrament, by the words of consecration, are changed into the very body and blood of Christ, really and substantially.

After his condemnation, the bishop sent two bills to him, the one containing a recantation, and the other his confession. The messenger, after reading the former to him, (for he could neither read nor write himself) asked, if he would sign it ; to which, without the least hesitation, he answered in the negative. He then read to him his confession, when he immediately took a pin, and pricking his hand, sprinkled the blood upon the bill, desiring the messenger to shew the bishop that he had already signed it with his blood.

When these two martyrs were conducted to the place of execution, (which was Smithfield) Bradford fell prostrate on one side of the stake, and Leafe on the other. In this position, they continued praying for some minutes, till Bradford was desired by the sheriff to make an end, and arise, the multitude of people being very great.

On this notice, they both arose ; and, after Bradford had made a short harangue to the people, they were both fastened to the stake, and the reeds and fagots placed around them.   2 Q

Being thus prepared, Bradford, lifting up his eyes and hands to heaven, exclaimed, "O England, England, repent thee of thy sins! beware of antichrist; beware of idolatry; take heed they do not deceive you." Then turning to young Leafe, who was to suffer with him, he said, "be of good comfort, brother, the time of our deliverance is at hand." The young man said, "Lord Jesus, receive our departing spirits."

The fire was then put to the fagots, and they both endured their sufferings with the utmost composure and resignation, reposing an unshaken confidence in that blessed Redeemer, who died to save mankind.

While Bradford was in prison, he employed his time in writing various comfortable treatises, addressed to the advocates of the reformation. He also wrote pious letters to the city of London, the university of Cambridge, and the towns of Lancashire and Cheshire, besides many others to his private friends and acquaintances. Among the latter, we shall preserve the following:

A Letter from J. Bradford to certain pious persons, encouraging them to prepare themselves to bear the cross with patience.

"GRACIOUS God, and most merciful Father, for Jesus Christ's sake, thy dearly beloved Son, grant us thy mercy, grace, wisdom, and holy spirit, to counsel, comfort, and guide us in all our thoughts, words, and works, to thy glory, and everlasting joy and peace for ever. Amen.

"In my last letter, you might perceive my conjecturing to be no less towards you than I have now learned. But, my dearly beloved, I have learned none other thing than what I before told you would come to pass, if ye cast not away that which ye have learned. I do appeal to both your consciences, whether I speak truth herein, as well of my telling (though not so often as I might and should, God forgive me) as also of your learning. Now God will try you, to make others learn by you, that which ye learned by others, and by them which have suffered this day, you might learn, (if already you had not learned) that life and honour are not to be regarded more than God's commandment. They, in no point, for all that ever their ghostly fathers could do, having Dr. Death to take their part, would consent, or seem to consent to the popish mass, and papistical god, otherwise than they had received in the days of our late king. And this their faith they have confessed with their deaths, to their great glory, and all our comforts, if we follow them : but to our confusion, if we start back from the same. Wherefore, I beseech you to consider, as well to praise God for them, as to go the same way with them if God please.

" Consider not the things of this life, which is a very prison to all God's children ; but the things of everlasting life, which is our very home. But, to behold this, ye must open the eyes of your mind, of faith, I should have said, as Moses did, who chose rather to suffer affliction with the people of God, than to possess the riches of Egypt, and the treasures of Pharaoh's court. Your house, home, and goods, yea life and all that ever ye have, God hath given you as love-tokens, to admonish you of his love, and to win your love to him again. He will try your love, whether ye set more by him than by his tokens. If ye, for the sake of his tokens, that is, your house, home, goods, yea life, will go with the world rather than lose them, then be assured, your love, as he cannot but espy it to be strumpet's love, so will he cast it away with the world. Remember, that he who will save his life, shall lose it, if Christ be true ; but he who adventureth, yea, loseth his life for the gospel's sake, the same shall be sure to find it eternally.— Do not ye know, that the way to salvation is not the broad way which many run in, but the straight way in which now few walk.

" Before persecution came, men might partly have stood in a doubt by the outward state of the world with us, (although, by God's word, it was plain) which was the highway, (for there were as many that pretended the gospel as popery) but now the sun is risen, and the wind bloweth ; so that the corn, which has not taken fast root, neither can nor will abide ; and, therefore, ye may easily see the strait way, by the small number of passengers.   Who will now adventure their goods, and life, for the sake of Christ, who gave his life for our sakes ? We are now become gergesites, that would rather lose Christ than our swine.   A wife is proved faithful, when she rejecteth and withstandeth other suitors.   A faithful christian is then found so to be, when his faith is assaulted.

" If we are neither able nor willing to forsake this world for God's glory, and the gospel's sake, ere long shall we be obliged to leave it for nature's sake.   Die ye must once, and leave all ye have, (God only knoweth how soon) whether ye will or not ; and seeing you cannot avoid it, why will ye not voluntarily do it for God's sake ?

" If ye go to mass, and do as most part doth, then may ye live quietly, and at rest ; but if ye refuse to go thither, then ye shall go to prison, lose your goods, leave your children comfortless, yea, lose your life also.   But, my dearly beloved, open the eyes of your faith, and consider the shortness of this life, that it is even as a shadow and as a smoke.   Again, consider how intolerable the punishment of hell-fire is, and that how endless.   Last of all, look on the joys incomprehensible, which God hath prepared for all them, world without end, who lose either life, land, or goods, for his name's sake, and then reason thus ; if we go to mass, the greatest enemy that Christ hath, though for a little time we shall live in quiet, and leave to our children something to live upon hereafter, yet we shall displease God, fall into his hands, (which is horrible to hypocrites) and be in wonderful hazard of falling from eternal joy into eternal misery, first of soul, and then of body, with the devil, and all idolaters.

" Again, we shall want peace of conscience, which surmounteth all the riches of the world ; and for our children, who knoweth whether God will visit our idolatries on them in this life ? Yea, our house and goods, and even our lives, are in danger of being lost by many casualties ; and when God is angry with us, he can, when he pleases, send one means, or other, to take all from us for our sins, and to cast us into greater trouble, who will not come into some little for his sake.

" On this sort, reason with ourselves, and then, doubtless, God will work otherwise with you, and in you, than ye are aware of. Where now ye think yourselves unable to abide persecution, be most assured, that if you earnestly purpose not to forsake God, that he will make you so able to bear his cross, that you shall rejoice therein. " God is faithful, (saith St. Paul) who will not suffer you to be tempted above that you are able ; but will, with the temptation, also make a way to escape, that ye may be able to bear it." Think how great a benefit it is, if God will make you worthy of his honour, to suffer loss of any thing for his sake. He might justly inflict most grievous plagues upon you, and yet now he will correct you with that rod, whereby ye shall be made like to his Christ, that ye may forever reign with him. Suffer yourselves, therefore, now to be made like to Christ, for else ye shall never be made like unto him. The devil would gladly have you now to overthrow that, which ye have a long time, steadfastly professed. O, how would he triumph, if he could win his purpose ! O, how would the papists triumph against God's gospel in you ! O, how would you confirm them in their wicked popery ! O, how would the poor children of God be discomforted, if you should go to mass, and other idolatrous service, and do as the world doth !

" Hath God delivered you from labour to serve him so ? Hath God miraculously restored you to health, from your grievous agues, for such a purpose ? Hath God given you such blessings in this world, and good things all the days of your life hitherto, and now, of equity, will ye not receive at his hands, and for his sake, some evil ? God forbid ; I hope better of you. Use prayer ; and cast your care upon God ; commit your children into his hand ; give to God your goods, bodies, and lives, as he hath given them, or rather lent them, to you. Say, with Job, God hath given, and God hath taken away, his name be praised for ever. Cast your care upon him, I say, for he is careful for you ; and take it amongst the greatest blessings of God, to suffer for his sake. I trust he hath kept you hitherto to that end.

" And I beseech thee, O merciful Father, for Jesus
Christ's sake, that thou wouldst be merciful unto us ;
comfort us with thy grace, and strengthen us in thy truth,
that in heart we may believe, and in tongue boldly confess thy gospel, and to thy glory and our eternal salvation, Amen.   Pray for me, and I, by God's grace, will do
the same for you.

JOHN BRADFORD."

*A farewell letter from J. Bradford to his Mother, a short
time before he was burnt.*

" GOD's mercy, and peace in Christ, be more and
more perceived of us, Amen.
" My most dear mother, in the bowels of Christ, I
heartily pray and beseech you to be thankful for me unto
God, who now taketh me unto himself.   I die not as a
criminal, but as a witness of Christ, for the truth of
whose gospel, I have hitherto confessed. I thank God,
both by preaching and imprisonment, and now I am willing to confirm the same by fire.   I acknowledge that
God might justly have taken me hence for my sins,
(which are many, great and grievous ; but the Lord, for
his mercy in Christ, I hope, hath pardoned them all) but
now, dear mother, he taketh me hence by this death, as a
confessor and witness, that the religion taught by Christ
Jesus, the prophets, and the apostles, is God's truth.—
The prelates in me do persecute Christ, whom they hate,
and his truth, which they will not abide, because their
works are evil.   They do not care for the light, lest men
thereby should discover their darkness.   Therefore, my
dear mother, give thanks to God for me, that he hath
made the fruit of your womb to be a witness of his glory,
and attend to the truth, which I have truly taught out of
the pulpit of Manchester.   Use often and continual prayer to God the Father, through Jesus Christ.   Hearken to
the scriptures, and serve God according to them, and not
according to the custom : beware of the Romanish religion in England ; defile not yourself with it : carry the

cross of Christ as he shall lay it upon your back : forgive them that kill me : pray for them, for they know not what they do : commit my *cause to God our Father : be mindful of both your daughters, and help them as well as you can.

" I send all my writings to you and my brother Roger : do with them as you will, because I cannot as I would, he can tell you more of my mind. I have nothing to give you, or to leave behind me for you : only I pray to God, my Father, for Christ's sake, to bless you, and keep you from evil. May he make you patient and thankful, that he will take the fruit of your womb to witness his truth; wherein I confess to the whole world, I die, and depart this life, in hope of a much better : which I look for at the hands of God my Father, through the merits of his dear Son Jesus Christ.

" Thus, my dear mother, I take my last farewell of you in this life, beseeching the Almighty and eternal Father, by Christ, to grant us to meet in the life to come, where we shall give him continual thanks, and praise for ever and ever. Amen.

Your son, in the Lord,
JOHN BRADFORD."

June 24, 1555.

The persecutions and sufferings of Margaret Polley, widow, the first female Martyr in England.

INFORMATION being given against Margaret Polley, to Maurice, bishop of Rochester, her ordinary, and diocessan, she was brought before him, when his lordship, according to the pontifical solemnity of the church of Rome, rose from his chair, and, in solemn parade, harangued her as follows :

" We Maurice, by the sufferance of God, bishop of Rochester, proceeding of our mere office in a cause of heresy, against thee, Margaret Polley, of the parish of Popingberry, in our diocess and jurisdiction of Rochester, do lay, and object against thee, all and singular the ensuing articles.

" To these, all and singular, we require of thee a true, full, and plain answer, by virtue of thine oath thereupon to be given."

The oath being administered by the official, the bishop looked steadfastly at the woman, and demanded of her a peremptory answer to each of the following articles.

1. Are not those heretics, who maintain and hold other opinions than our holy mother and catholic church doth ?

Ans. They are, indeed, heretics, and grossly deceived, who hold and maintain doctrines contrary to the will of God, contained in the holy scriptures, which I sincerely believe were written by holy men, immediately taught and instructed by the Holy Ghost.

2. Do you hold and maintain that, in the sacrament of the altar, under the form of bread and wine, there is not the very body and blood of Christ, and that the said body is verily in heaven only, and not in the sacrament ?

Ans. What I have learned from the holy scriptures, those living oracles of God, I do, and will steadfastly maintain, viz. that the very body which was crucified for the very sins of all true believers, ascended into heaven, and is there placed at the right hand of the majesty on high ; that such body has ever since remained there, and therefore cannot, according to my belief, be in the sacrament of the altar.

I believe that the bread and wine in the sacrament, are to be received as symbols and representatives of the body and blood of Christ, but not as such really and substantially.

I think, in my weak judgment, that it is not in the power of any man, by pronouncing words over the elements of bread and wine, to transubstantiate them into the real body and blood of Christ.

In short, it is my belief, that the eucharist is only a commemoration of the death of our Saviour, who said, " as oft as ye do this, do it in remembrance of me."

These pertinent and frank replies greatly provoked the haughty prelate, who exclaimed against the woman as an obstinate heretic, and, after much scurrilous language, told her, she was a silly woman, and knew not what she said, and that it was the duty of every christian to believe as the mother-church hath and doth teach.

The bishop then asked her the following question : " Will you, Margaret Polley, recant the error which you maintain, be reconciled to the holy church, and receive the remission of sins ?" To which, she replied, " I cannot believe otherwise than I have spoken, because the practice of the church of Rome is contrary not only to reason, and my senses, but also to the word of God."

Immediately on this reply, the bishop pronounced sentence of condemnation against her ; after which, she was carried back to prison, where she remained daily celebrating the praises of God for upwards of a month.

She was a woman in the prime of life, pious, charitable, humane, learned in the scriptures, and beloved by all with whom she was acquainted.

When the day arrived appointed for her execution, she was conducted from the bishop's prison at Rochester, to Tunbridge, where she was burned, sealing the truth of what she had testified with her blood, and shewing that the God of all grace, out of the weakest vessel, can give strength, and cause the meanest instruments to magnify the glories of his redeeming love.

On the same day that Margaret Polley suffered, one Christopher Wade, a weaver of Dartford, in Kent, who had likewise been condemned by bishop Maurice, shared the same fate, and at the same place ; but they were executed separately, he first submitting to the dreadful sentence.

About the same time, John Bland, John Frankesh, Nicholas Sheterden, and Humphrey Middleton, were all burnt together at Canterbury. The two first were ministers and preachers of the gospel, the one being rector of Adesham, and the other vicar of Rolvindon, in Kent. They all resigned themselves to their fate with christian fortitude, fervently praying to God to receive them into his heavenly kingdom.

The persecutions and Martyrdoms of John Launder, and Dirick Carver.

JOHN LAUNDER, of Godstone, in Surry, husbandman; and Dirick Carver, of Brighthelmstone, in Sussex, brewer, were apprehended in the dwelling-house of the latter, as they were at prayers, and sent up to the queen's council at London, where being examined, and not giving satisfactory answers to the questions proposed, they were committed prisoners to Newgate, to wait the leisure, and abide the determination of the cruel and arrogant bishop Bonner.

Launder, on his examination, confessed, that the occasion of his being at Brighthelmstone, was to transact some business for his father; and that hearing Carver was a great promoter of the doctrines of the reformation, he went to his house in order to join in prayer to God, with the pious christians who resorted thither, on which, he was apprehended by Gage, the officer appointed for that purpose.

He also confessed, that there is here on earth one whole and universal catholic church, the members of which are dispersed throughout the world; that he believed the same church doth set forth and teach only two sacraments, which are, Baptism and the Lord's Supper; that whosoever doth teach, or use any more sacraments, or any other ceremonies, he doth abhor them from the bottom of his heart.

He further said and believed, that all the service, sacrifices, and ceremonies, now used in this realm of England, and in other parts of the world, where they are used after the same manner, are erroneous, contrary to Christ's institution, and the determination of Christ's catholic church, whereof he believed himself to be a member.

He also confessed and believed, that in the sacrament, called the sacrament of the altar, there are not really and truly contained, under the forms of bread and wine, the very natural body and blood of Christ in substance; but that, when he did receive the material bread, he received the same in remembrance of Christ's death and passion, and no otherwise.

Moreover, he confessed, said, and believed, that the mass used in the realm of England, or elsewhere, in Christendom, is abominable, and directly against God's word, and his catholic church ; and that there is nothing said or used in it, good or profitable ; for though the *gloria in excelsis*, "the creed and pater-noster," and other parts of the mass, are good in themselves. yet being used amongst other things that are superstitious, they become corrupt. Lastly, he confessed and believed, that auricular confession is not necessary to be made to any priest, or to any other creature, but every person ought to confess his sins to God alone, because no person has any authority to absolve any man from his sins.

Having openly acknowledged and maintained these opinions, in the bishop's consistory court, and refusing to recant, he was condemned, and delivered over to the secular power.

Dirick Carver, being examined by bishop Bonner, concerning his faith in the sacrament of the altar, the mass, auricular confession, and the religion then taught and set forth in the church of England, delivered the following, as his invariable tenets, because founded on the infallible word of the only living and true God.

To the first point, he declared, that he had and did believe, that the very substance of the body and blood of Christ is not in the sacrament of the altar ; and that there is no other substance remaining in that sacrament, after the words spoken by the priest, but the substance of bread and wine.

As to the mass, he believed there was no sacrifice in it, nor any salvation for a christian, except it was said in the mother-tongue, that he might understand it.

With respect to auricular confession, he believed that it was necessary to apply to a priest for spiritual counsel; but that the absolution of the priests. by the imposition of hands was not profitable to salvation ; acknowledging, at the same time, that he had not been confessed, nor received the sacrament since the coronation of the queen.

Concerning the last point, he declared it as his opinion and belief, that the faith and religion then taught, and set forth, were not agreeable to God's word, and that bishop Hooper, Cardmaker, Rogers, and other pious men, who were lately burned, were sound divines, and preached the true doctrine of Christ.

Being farther examined, he confessed, that since the queen's coronation he had the bible and psalter read in English divers times, at his house in Brighthelmstone ; and that, about twelve months then past, he had the English litany said in his house, with other prayers in English.

After these examinations, he was strongly persuaded to recant, but this he peremptorily refused ; on which, sentence of condemnation was passed on him at the same time as on Launder ; and the time of his execution was fixed for the 22d of the month called July, at Lewes, in Sussex.

On his arrival at the stake, he kneeled down and prayed ; and, when he had finished his prayers, he arose, and addressed the spectators as follows :

" Dear brothers and sisters, bear witness, that I am come to seal with my blood the gospel of Christ, because I know that it is true. Many of you know, that the gospel hath been truly preached to you here in Lewes, and now it is not so preached ; and because I will not here deny God's gospel, I am condemned to die."

On this, the sheriff said, " if thou dost not believe in the pope, thou art damned, body and soul." But our martyr pitied his blindness, and begged of God to forgive his errors.

Being then fastened to the stake, and the fire kindled round him, he patiently submitted to his fate, and expired, calling out, " O Lord, have mercy upon me ! Lord Jesus, receive my spirit !"

His fellow-martyr, John Launder, was burnt the following day at Steyning ; where he cheerfully gave up his life to that God, from whose hands he had received it.

The sufferings and deaths of John Denley, John Newman, and Patrick Packingham.

As Denley and Newman were travelling together into Essex, on a visit to some friends, they were accidentally met by Tyrrel, a justice of the peace for the said county, who suspecting them of heresy, caused them to be apprehended, and searched ; and, at the same time, took from Denley a confession of his faith in writing, concerning the sacrament of the altar, together with certain notes collected from the holy scriptures.

The justice immediately sent them to London, and with them a letter to be presented to the queen's council, together with the papers he found on the former.

On their being brought before the council, they were admonished and desired to yield obedience to the queen's laws ; but this advice proving ineffectual, their examination was referred to Bonner, bishop of London.

On the 28th of the month called June, 1555, Denley and Newman, together with Patrick Packingham, (who had been apprehended two days before) were brought before Bonner, at his palace in London.

The bishop having examined the two former upon their confessions, and finding them inflexibly to adhere to the same, he used his customary exhortation; on which, Denley said, " God save me from your counsel, and keep me in the mind I am in ; for that which you count heresy, I take to be the truth."

Bonner then ordered them to appear in the bishop's consistory court, where the following articles were jointly and severally exhibited against them :

1. That they were now in the diocess of London, and under the jurisdiction of the bishop of London.

These they acknowledged to be true.

2. That they had not, nor did believe, that there is a oatholic church of Christ here on earth.

This they severally denied ; for that they did believe the holy catholic church, which is built upon the foundation of the prophets and apostles, Christ being the head ; and that where two or three are gathered together in

Christ's name, they are the members of the said holy catholic church, which is dispersed throughout the world; which church doth preach God's word truly, and doth also minister the two sacraments, Baptism, and the Supper of the Lord, according to his blessed word.

3. That each of them had not, nor did believe, that this church of England is any part, or member of the said catholic church.

They severally answered, that they did believe, that this church of England, using the faith and practice that are now used, is no part or member of the aforesaid holy catholic church, but is the church of antichrist, the bishop of Rome being the head thereof.

4. That they had believed, and did believe, that the mass, now used in the church of England, was abominable, and blasphemy against God's word.

They answered in the affirmative.

5. That they had believed, and did believe, that auricular confession, now used in the realm of England, was not profitable, but contrary to God's word.

To this, they all answered in the affirmative.

6. That they had believed, and did believe, that absolution given by the priest, and hearing confession, are not good, nor allowable by God's word, but contrary to the same.

To this, they answered, that remission of sins is only to be obtained from God, through the blood of Jesus Christ.

7. That they had believed, and did believe, that the christening of children, as it is used now in the church of England, is not good nor allowable by God's word. Likewise, the confirming of children, the giving of orders, the saying mattins and vespers, the anointing or oiling of sick persons, and the making holy bread and holy water, with other rites of the church.

To this, they replied, that the christening of children, or the sacrament of baptism, is altered and changed ; for John the Baptist used nothing but preaching the word and water, as appears from Christ's desiring to be baptized by him ; for we do not read that he asked for any cream, or oil, or spittle, or wax, or salt, but used merely water ; nor was this water consecrated.

8. That they had believed, and did believe, that there are but two sacraments in Christ's catholic church, the sacrament of baptism, and the sacrament of the altar.

To this, they briefly replied, that they believed no more, except they would make the rainbow a sacrament ; for there is no sacrament but hath a promise annexed to it.

The bishop then stated one article to Packingham alone, which was, that he, Patrick Packingham, being of the age of twenty-one years at least, did irreverently stand in the great chapel, having his cap on his head during the time of mass, on the 23d of the month called June ; that he refused holy bread, and holy water at the priest's hands, thereby contemning and despising both the mass, holy water, and holy bread.

This article he ackowledged to be true.

On the 5th of the month called July, the bishop proceeded in the usual form, against these three persons, in his consistory court at St. Paul's. After various articles and answers were publicly read, they were exhorted to recant ; and both promises and threats were used by Bonner, in order to prevail with them ; but, on their remaining steadfast in their faith and profession, they were all condemned as heretics, and delivered into the custody of the sheriffs of London, who conducted them to Newgate, where they were kept till writs were issued for their respective executions.

Denley was ordered to be executed at Uxbridge, where, being conveyed, on the day appointed, he was chained to the stake ; and, when the flames began to be powerful, he expired in the midst of them, singing a psalm to the praise of his Redeemer. A popish priest, who was present at his execution, was so incensed at his singing, that he ordered one of the attendants to throw a fagot at him, which was accordingly done, and he received a violent fracture in his skull, which, with the fire, soon deprived him both of speech and life.

A few days after, Packingham suffered at the same place ; but Newman was executed at Saffron-Walden, in.

Essex.   They both died with great fortitude and resignation, cheerfully resigning their souls into the hands of him who gave them, in full expectation of receiving crowns of glory in the heavenly mansions.

The Martyrdoms of William Coker, William Hooper, Henry Lawrence, Richard Collier, Richard Wright, and William Steer, all inhabitants of the county of Kent, who were burnt together at Canterbury, on the 31st of the month called August, 1555.

INFORMATION having been given, at the same time, against these six persons, they were all brought before Dr. Richard Thornton, suffragan of Canterbury, and bishop of Dover ; Dr. Horpsfield, archdeacon, Richard Fawcet, and Robert Collins, of the spiritual court of Canterbury ; when divers articles were respectively exhibited against them ; to all which, they answered, as men determined to adhere to the truth of the gospel they had professed.

Being again brought before the above persons, they were further examined, and the substance of their respective answers was as follows :

William Coker declared, he would answer no otherwise than as he had done before.   Being offered six days respite to consider of it, he refused to accept their indulgence; in consequence of which, he immediately received sentence of death.

William Hooper, at first, seemed to assent to the faith and determination of the Roman catholic church ; but, on serious reflection, he retracted, and firmly professed his faith in the pure gospel of Christ, as well as renounced the errors of popery.   He was, therefore, immediately sentenced to be burned.

Henry Lawrence, who was next examined, denied auricular confession, and refused to receive the sacrament of the altar, because the order of the holy scripture was changed in the order of the said sacrament.

Being charged with not taking off his cap when the suffragan mentioned the sacrament, and reverenced the same, he said, there was no need for him so to do.

Being likewise asked concerning the verity of the sacrament given to Christ's disciples, he affirmed, that even as Christ gave his body to his disciples, so likewise Christ himself said, he was a door, &c. adding, moreover, that as he said before, so he still said, that the sacrament of the mass is an idol, and no resemblance of Christ's passion.

Being required to subscribe to these articles, he wrote under the bill of examination as follows: " ye are all of antichrist, and him ye follow." He was then prevented from speaking farther, and sentence of condemnation was pronounced on him in the usual form.

Richard Collier, being examined with respect to the sacrament of the altar, answered, he did not believe there was the real and substantial body and blood of Christ, but only bread and wine; and that it was most abominable, detestable, and wicked, to believe otherwise. In consequence of which, he also received sentence of death.

Richard Wright being asked by the judge, what he believed of the real presence in the sacrament, answered that, touching the sacrament of the altar and the mass, he was ashamed to speak of it; nor would he, therefore, by any means allow it. In consequence of which, he likewise received sentence of condemnation.

William Steer. the last examined, was required by the judge to answer the articles laid before him. But he denied the judge's authority, for which, he was deemed guilty of denying the authority of the queen. He also observed, that Thomas Cranmer, archbishop of Canterbury, then in prison, was his diocessian; and, therefore, required Dr. Thornton to shew his authority from the archbishop, or otherwise he would deem it invalid.

With respect to the sacrament of the mass, he said, as he found not the popish belief contained in the scriptures, he entirely disbelieved it; in consequence of

2 s

which, he received the same sentence with his fellow-prisoners.

These six men being thus condemned for professing the truth of Christ's gospel, were immediately delivered over to the secular power. They continued in prison, consoling each other daily in prayer, till the 31st of the month called August, the day appointed for their execution, when they were conveyed to Canterbury, and there led to the stakes, of which there were three two of them chained to each. They all joyfully yielded up their lives as sacrifices to God, in testimony of their regard to the word of truth, which abideth to all eternity.

The Persecution and Martyrdom of George Tankerfield, a cook, and citizen of London.

GEORGE TANKERFIELD was brought up by his parents in the popish religion, to which he zealously adhered till the beginning of the reign of queen Mary, when the horrid cruelties exercised on those who dissented from that church, so strongly impressed his mind, that he began to detest, and openly exclaim against the principles of that religion he had hitherto professed, which, on examination, he found contrary to the divine mind and will, as contained in the sacred word.

This excited the astonishment of his acquaintances, and raised the resentment of the popish faction, especially those who were interested in its restoration; insomuch, that Sir Roger Cholmondeley, and Dr. Martin, two of the queen's commissioners for ecclesiastical affairs, dispatched a yeoman to Tankerfield's house, in order to apprehend and bring him before them.

Tankerfield being absent, when the yeoman came in quest of him, it was pretended, that he was wanted to serve up a dinner at the house of lord Paget. When he came home, his wife told him, that he was required to attend at a banquet; to which he replied, "a banquet, woman; but such a banquet as will not be pleasing to the flesh."

The next day, he was seized by a constable, and committed to Newgate ; and, after being confined there some time, he was brought before, and repeatedly examined by bishop Bonner, and others, concerning divers articles and tenets of religion. He was chiefly required to give his opinion concerning auricular confession, the popish sacrament of the mass, and other ceremonies.

In answer to the first of these, he said, he had not confessed to any priest for several months, and that he would not be confessed by any priest hereafter, because he found no such duty commanded in the word of God, which he now took as his only guide in all matters of religion.

With respect to the sacrament, commonly called the sacrament of the altar, he declared, he did not believe, that in the said sacrament, there was the real body and blood of Christ, because the body of Christ was ascended into heaven, and there sat at the right hand of God the Father.

To the last point, he answered, that the mass then used in the Church of England, was full of idolatry, abomination, and wholly inconsistent with the word of God ; adding that there were but two sacraments in Christ's church ; namely, baptism and the Lord's supper.

The bishop, after this confession, in his usual manner, exhorted him to recant his opinions, declaring them to be damnable heresies ; but Tankerfield assured the bishop, that he would persist in his belief till it should be proved erroneous from scripture authority, being regardless of the tenets of the greatest prelate upon earth, if not founded on the word of eternal truth, declaring at the same time, that the arbitrary commissioners for ecclesiastical affairs condemned persons without proving any thing against them.

Bonner, with an affected concern for his interest, temporal, and eternal, used many enticing words to bring him to the mother-church ; but our martyr boldly told him, without the least reserve, that the church, of which the pope is supreme, is no part of Christ's catholic church ; and pointing to the bishop, he said, " good people, beware of him, and such as he is, for these be they that deceive you."

The bishop was so enraged at this resolute behaviour, that he proceeded to read the sentence of condemnation ; immediately after which, Tankerfield was delivered over to the secular power.

The place allotted for his execution, was St. Alban's, in Hertfordshire, whither being conveyed on the day appointed, he, with patience and constancy, resigned his life into the hands of that God who gave it, as a testimony of the truth of his holy word, which had been able to make him wise unto salvation.

The Martyrdom of Elizabeth Warne, Widow.

THIS pious woman, and steadfast believer in the pure gospel of Christ, (according to the dying request of her husband, who, some time ago, had sealed the truth with his blood) persisted in worshipping God according to the dictates of her own conscience, and the form she conceived was contained in the divine command.

Information being given against her, she was apprehended in a house in Bow-church-yard, in company with several others, who were assembled for prayer and other spiritual exercises; and, with them, was sent to the Compter, from whence, she was committed to Newgate.

She had been but a few days confined, before she was sent for by the queen's commissioners, who, after some examination, gave her up to the bishop of London.

The chief article alleged against her, by Bonner, was, her not believing the real presence in the sacrament of the altar. She was also accused of absenting herself from church, speaking against the mass, despising the ceremonies of the holy mother-church, &c.

To these accusations, she gave such answers as highly offended the bishop, who warmly exhorted her to recant her erroneous and heretical opinions. She replied, " do with me what you will ; for, if Christ was in an error, then I am in an error."

On this peremptory declaration, she was condemned as a heretic, delivered to the sheriff of London, and conducted to Newgate.

When the day appointed for her execution arrived, she was carried from Newgate to Strafford-le-bow, where she suffered martyrdom for the cause of Christ and his gospel, following her husband through the path of a fiery trial, to the heaven of rest that awaits all the disciples of our blessed and glorious Redeemer.

The Martyrdom of Robert Smith.

THIS martyr was originally educated in the Roman catholic religion ; but having for some time enjoyed a place under the Provost of Eaton college, he was converted to the true faith by the preaching of several reformed ministers in that learned seminary.

As he was known to profess the protestant religion, he was, on the accession of queen Mary, deprived of his post in the college, and soon after sent up prisoner to the bishop of London, by whom, he was committed to Newgate, after being examined by him divers times, at his palace, and in other places.

Being questioned by the bishop concerning auricular confession, he declared, he had never been confessed since he arrived at years of discretion, because he never thought it needful, nor commanded of God to confess his faults to any of that sinful number called priests.

The bishop then inquired how long it was since he had received the sacrament of the mass, and what was his opinion concerning the same.

To this, he replied, that he had never received the same, since he arrived at years of discretion, nor, by the grace of God, ever would ; neither did he esteem it in any point necessary, because it was not God's ordinance, but rather set up in mockery of God, and to deprive him of the honour which is his due.

Being questioned concerning his belief in the corporeal presence in the sacrament, after the words of consecration pronounced by the priest, he replied, "I have once told you, that it was not God's ordinance, much less can it be God, or any part of his substance, but only mere bread and wine, and to be received in a figurative sense alone ; adding further, that if he could prove from scripture, that it was the very body, he would believe it, but till then, he should esteem it a detestable idol, not God, but contrary to God and truth."

This answer so irritated the haughty prelate, that he greatly reviled Smith ; but his passion abating. he afterwards examined him in milder terms, and coolly inquired his opinion concerning the catholic church.

Smith replied, "I believe there is one catholic church, or congregation of the faithful, which (as the apostle saith) is built upon the prophets and apostles, Christ Jesus being the chief corner-stone. I also believe, that this church, in all words and works, maintaineth the word of God, and bringeth the same for her authority ; of this church, I am assured, that by grace, I am made a member."

He was then examined concerning holy bread, holy water, and other ceremonies of the church ; but these points he denied as unscriptural ; and persisting in his opinions, notwithstanding the repeated admonitions of the bishop, he was summoned to appear at the consistory court, where having made the same confession as before, sentence of condemnation was passed upon him, and he was delivered over to the secular power.

After the cruel sentence was passed, Smith remonstrated with the lord-mayor, sheriffs, and others who were present on the occasion, on the iniquity of their procedures, which were contrary to all laws, human and divine ; but the general cry was, " away with the heretic, away with the heretic." He then addressed himself to the spectators in the following manner :

" Ye have seen and heard, my friends, the great injury I have this day received ; and ye are all witnesses, that we have referred the equity of our cause to the book of God, which appeal not being admitted, we are condemned unheard."

Turning to the mayor, he said, "though, my lord, you have here exercised your authority unjustly, and will not attend the cry of the poor, I commit my cause to that God who judgeth aright, and will render unto every man according to his deeds; that God, at whose awful bar, both you and I must stand without respect or authority, and where sentence will be passed without partiality, bigotry, or caprice, and according to the eternal laws of infallible truth."

After this, he was carried back to Newgate, where he was closely confined till the 8th of the month called August, which was appointed for his execution. On the morning of that day, he was conducted, under a proper guard, to Uxbridge, and there led to the stake. He bore his punishment with the most amazing fortitude, in full hopes, that he was giving up a temporary existence for one that would be immortal.

Smith had received a very liberal education; and, during the time of his imprisonment, he wrote a great number of treatises, letters, &c He had a good turn for poetry, in which, several of his compositions were formed. Among the number of his writings, we shall preserve the following:

The substance of an epistle, written by Robert Smith, to the persecuted flock of Christ.

"To all which love God unfeignedly, and intend to lead a godly life, according to his gospel, and to persevere in his truth unto the end, grace and peace from God the Father, and from our Lord Jesus Christ, Amen.

"Be not afraid, most dearly beloved, in our Saviour Jesus Christ, at these most perilous days, wherein, by the suffering of God, the prince of darkness is broken loose, and rageth in his members against the elect of God, with all cruelty, to set up again the kingdom of antichrist, against whom, see that ye be strong in faith, to resist his most devilish doctrines, with the pure gospel of God, arming yourselves with patience, to abide whatsoever shall be laid to your charge for the truth's sake, knowing that thereunto you are called, not only to believe in him, but also to suffer for him. Oh! how happy are ye, that, in the sight of God, are counted worthy to suffer for the testimony of Christ. Quit, therefore, yourselves, Oh, my loving brethren, and rejoice in him for whom ye suffer ; for, unto you do remain the unspeakable joys, which neither the eye hath seen, nor the ear hath heard, neither the heart of man is able to comprehend in any wise. Be not afraid of the bodily death ; for your names are written in the book of Life ; and the prophets do record, that, in the sight of the Lord, precious is the death of his saints. Watch, therefore, and pray that ye be not prevented in the day of temptation. Now cometh the day of your trial, wherein the waters rage, and the stormy winds blow. Now shall it appear, whether you have builded upon the fleeting sand, or upon the unmoveable rock Christ, which is the foundation of the prophets and apostles, whereon every house that is builded, groweth into an holy temple of the Lord, by the mighty working of the holy Ghost. Now approacheth the day of your battle, wherein it is required, that you shew yourselves the valiant soldiers of Christ Jesus, with the armour of God, that ye may be able to stand fast against the crafty assaults of the devil. Christ is your captain, and you are his soldiers, whose cognizance is the cross, to the which, he willingly humbled himself, even unto the death, and thereby spoiled his enemies, and now he triumphs over them, in the glory of his Father, making intercession for them, that do here remain to suffer the afflictions, that are to be fulfilled in his mystical body. It behoveth, therefore, every one, that will be accounted his scholar, to take up his own cross, and follow him, as you have him for example ; and I assure you, that he being on your side, nothing shall be able to prevail against you ; and that he will be with you even to the world's end. You have his promise in the 28th of Matthew. He will go forth with his host as a conqueror, to make a conquest.

He is the man that sitteth on the white horse crowned with immortality; and ye, brethren, are his fellowship, whereof he is the head. He hath your hearts in his hand. As a bow bent after his godly will, he shall direct the same, according to the riches of his glory, into all spiritual and heavenly cogitation. He is faithful, and will not suffer you to be further assaulted, than he will give you strength to overcome: and, in the most danger, he will make a way that you may be able to bear it. Shrink not, therefore, dear hearts, when ye shall be called to answer for the hope that is in you; for we have the comforter, even the spirit of truth, which was sent from the heavens to teach us.— He shall speak in us: he shall strengthen us. What is he then, that shall be able to confound us? Nay, what tyrant is he that boasteth himself of his strength to do mischief, whom the Lord shall not, with his spirit, by the mouth of his servants, smite? Yea, suddenly will the Lord bring down the glory of the proud Philistines, by the hands of his servant David. Their strength is in shield and spear; but our help is in the name of the Lord, which made both heaven and earth. He is our buckler, and our wall, a strong tower of defence. He is our God, and we are his people. He shall bring the counsels of the ungodly to nought. He shall take them in their own net.— He shall destroy them in their own inventions. The right hand of the Lord shall work this wonder. His power is known amongst the children of men. Their fathers have felt it, and are confounded. In like manner, shall they know that there is no counsel against the Lord: when their secrets are opened to the whole world, and are found to be against the living God, work they ever so craftily, build they ever so strongly, yet down shall their Babel fall, and the builders themselves shall then be scattered upon the face of the earth, as accursed of God. The just shall see this, and be glad, and praise the name of the Lord, that so marvelleously hath dealt with his servants, as to bring their enemies under their feet. Then shall the fearful seed of Cain tremble and quake. Then shall the mocking Ishmaelites be cast out of the door. Then shall the proud Nemborth see his labour lost. Then shall the beast

2 т

of Babylon be trodden under foot. Then shall the scribes and pharisees, for madness, fret and rage. Then shall their painted wisdom be known for extreme folly. Then shall the bloody dragon be void of his prey. Then shall the whore of Babylon receive double vengeance. Then shall they scratch their crowns, for the fall of their mistress harlot, whom they now serve for filthy lucre, when no man shall buy their wares any more. Then shall the popish priesthood cry, with care, even when the Lord shall help his servants, which day is not far off, wherein the kingdom of antichrist shall have an end, and never rise any more; in the mean time, abide in certain and sure hope, cleaving unto the promises of God, which in their own time shall be fulfilled. What better quarrels can you have to give your lives for, than the truth itself? That man that giveth his life for the truth, taketh the readiest way to life. He that hath the pope's curse for the truth, is sure of Christ's blessing. Well then, my brethren, what shall now let, but that you go forwards as ye have begun? Nay, rather run with the runners, that ye may obtain the appointed glory. Hold on the right way. Look not back. Have the eye of your heart fixed upon God; and so run that you may get hold of it. Cast away all your worldly pelf, and worldly respects, as the favour of friends, the fear of men, sensual affection, respect of person, honour, praise, shame, rebuke, wealth, poverty, riches, lands, possessions, carnal fathers and mothers, wife and chilrden, with the love of your own selves; and in respect of that heavenly treasure you look for. Let all these be denied and utterly refused of you, so that, in no condition, they do abate your zeal, or quench your love towards God. In this case, make no account of them, but rather repute them as vile, in comparison of everlasting life.— Away with them as thorns that choke the heavenly seed of the gospel, where they be suffered to grow; they are burdens of the flesh, which encumber the soul. Exchange them, therefore, I beseech you, for advantage. Doth not he gain, that findeth heavenly and immortal treasure, for earthly and corruptible riches? Loseth that man any thing, who of his carnal father and mother is forsaken, when, therefore, he is received of God the Father, to be his child and heir in Christ? Heavenly for earthly, mortal for immortal, transitory for things permanent, is great gain to a christian conscience.

" Therefore, as I began, I exhort you in the Lord not to be afraid. Shrink not, my brethren : mistrust not God : be of good comfort : rejoice in the Lord : hold fast your faith : and continue to the end.   Deny the world, take up the cross, and follow him who is your leader, and is gone before.   If you suffer with him, you shall reign with him. What way can you glorify the name of your heavenly Father better, than by suffering death for his Son's sake ? What a spectacle shall it be to the world, to behold so godly a fellowship as you servants of God ? In so just a quarrel, as the gospel of Christ is, with so pure a conscience, so strong a faith, and so lively a hope, to offer yourselves to suffer most cruel torments at the hands of God's enemies ; and so to end your days in peace, to receive, in the resurrection of the righteous, life everlasting.

" Be strong, therefore, in your battle, the Lord God is on our side ; and his truth is your cause, and against you be none but the enemies of the cross of Christ, as a serpent and his seed, the dragon with his tail, the marked man of the beast, the offsring of the pharisees, the congregation malignant, the generation of vipers and murderers, as their father the devil hath been from the beginning. To conclude, such are they as the Lord God hath always abhorred, and in all ages resisted and overthrown.   God, from whom nothing is hid, knoweth what they are.   He that searcheth the hearts of men, hath found out them to be crafty, subtle, full of poison, proud, disdainful, stiff-necked, devourers, and barkers against the truth, filthy and shameless.— And, therefore, doth the spirit of God, by the mouths of his holy prophets and apostles, call them by the names of foxes, serpents, cockatrices, lions, leopards, bulls, bears, wolves, dogs, swine, beasts ; teaching us thereby to understand that their natural inclination is to deceive, poison, and destroy, as much as in them lies, the faithful and elect of God ; but the Lord, with his right arm, shall defend his little flock against the whole rabble of these worldlings, which have conspired against him. He hath numbered all the hairs of his children's heads, so that not one of them shall perish without his fatherly will. He keepeth the sparrows, much more will he preserve them whom he hath purchased with the blood of the immaculate Lamb. He will keep them until the hour appointed, wherein the name of God shall be glorified in his saints. In the mean time, let them work their wills, let them envy, let them blaspheme, let them curse, betray, whip, scourge, hang, and burn; for, by this means, God will try his elect, as gold in the furnace. And, by these fruits, shall they also bring themselves to be known what they be; for as he that, in suffering patiently for the gospel of God, is thereby known to be of Christ, even so also is the persecutor of him known to be a member of antichrist. Besides this, their extreme cruelty shall be a means the sooner to provoke God to take pity upon his servants, and to destroy them that so tyrannously treat his people, as we may learn by the histories, as well in the bondage of Israel under Pharaoh in Egypt, as in the miserable captivity of Judah in Babylon, where, when the people of God were in most extreme thraldom, then did the Lord stretch forth his mighty power to deliver his servants. Though God, for a time, suffered them to be exalted in their own pride, yet shall they not escape his vengeance.

" To conclude, my brethren, I commit you to God and the power of his word, which is able to establish you in all truth. His spirit be with you, and work alway, that ye may be mindful of your duties towards him, whose ye are, both body and soul, whom see that ye love, serve, dread, and obey, above all worldly powers; and for nothing under the heavens, defile your conscience before God: dissemble not with his word: God will not be mocked. Nay, they that dissemble with him, deceive themselves, such shall the Lord deny, and cast out at the last day; such, I say, as bear two faces in one head; such as play on both hands; such as deny the known truth; such as obstinately rebel against him; all such, with their partakers, shall the Lord destroy. God defend you from all such, and make you perfect unto the end, and your sorrow shall be turned into joy."

A letter from Robert Smith to his wife.

" SEEK first to love God, dear wife, with your whole heart, and then it shall be easy to love your neighbour.

" Be friendly to all creatures, and especially to your own soul.

" Be always an enemy to the devil, and to the world, but especially to your own flesh.

" Hearing of good things, join the ears of your head and heart together.

" Seek unity and quietness with all men, but especially with your conscience ; for it will not easily be entreated.

" Love all people, but especially your enemies.

" Hate the sins that are past, but especially those to come.

" Be as ready to further your enemy, as he is to hinder you, that you may be the child of God.

" Defile not that which Christ hath cleansed, lest his blood be laid to your charge.

" Remember that God hath hedged in your tongue with the teeth and lips, that it might speak under correction.

" Be ready, at all times, to look at your brother's eye, but especially in your own eye : for, he that warneth others of what he himself is guilty, doth give his neighbour the clear wine and keepeth the dregs to himself.

" Beware of riches and worldly honour ; for, without understanding, prayer, and fasting, it is a snare. and also poverty, all which are like to consuming fire, of which, if a man take a little, it will warm him, but if he take too much, will consume him : for it is hard for a man to carry fire in his bosom, and not be burnt.

" Shew mercy to the saints for Christ's sake, and Christ shall reward you for the saints' sake. Among all other prisoners, visit your own : for it is enclosed in a perilous prison.

" If you will love God, hate evil, and you shall obtain the reward of well doing.

" Thus, fare you well, good Anne. Have me heartily commended to all that love the Lord unfeignedly. I beseech you, have me in your prayer, while I am living ; and

I am assured, the Lord will accept it.   Bring up my children, and yours, in the fear of God, and then shall I not fail, but receive you together in the everlasting kingdom of God, into which I hope to go.

Your husband,

ROBERT SMITH."

About the same time that Smith was burnt, three others, who had been condemned by bishop Bonner, shared the same fate : namely, Stephen Harwood, Thomas Fust, and William Hale.   The first of these suffered at Stratford, near Bow ; the second at Ware ; and the third at Barnet.

The persecution and Martyrdom of Robert Samuel, a Minister of Bradford in Suffolk.

ROBERT SAMUEL was a very pious man, and an eminent preacher of the gospel, according to the principles of the reformation, during the reign of Edward VI.   He attended his charge with indefatigable industry, and by his preaching and living recommended and enforced the truth of the gospel.

Soon after the accession of queen Mary, he was turned out of his living, and retired to Ipswich ; but he could not withstand using his utmost efforts to propagate the reformed religion, and, therefore, what he was denied doing in public, he did in private.

While he was spending his time in this christian manner, the queen commanded the commissioners for ecclesiastical affairs, to publish an order, that all priests who had been married in the days of king Edward, should put away their wives, and be compelled again to chastity, (as their hypocritical term expressed it) and a single life.

This order, Samuel could by no means obey ; because, he knew it to be abominable, and contrary to the law of Christ, and to every tie, social and humane.   Therefore, determining with himself, that God's laws were not to be violated for the traditions of men, he still kept his wife at

Ipswich, and omitted no opportunity of instructing his christian friends in the neighbourhood.

At length, his conduct reaching the ears of Foster, a justice of peace in those parts, every artifice was used by that popish bigot to apprehend Samuel, who was taken into custody by some of his myrmidons, when on a visit to his wife at Ipswich.

Being taken before Foster, he was committed to Ipswich goal, where he conversed and prayed with many of his fellow-sufferers, during his confinement in that place.

In a short time, he was removed from Ipswich, to Norwich, where Dr. Hopton, the persecuting bishop of that diocess, and Dunning the chancellor, exercised on him the most intolerable cruelties.

In order to bring Samuel to recant, they confined him in a close prison, where he was chained to a post in such a manner, that standing only on tiptoe, he was, in that position, forced to sustain the weight of his body.

To aggravate this torment, they kept him in a starving condition twelve days, allowing him no more than two bits of bread, and three spoonfuls of water, each day, which was done in order to protract his misery, till they could invent new torments, to overcome his patience and resolution.

These inhuman proceedings brought him to so shocking a state, that, ready to perish with thirst, he would often gladly have drank his own water; but his body was so parched, that he emitted not a single drop of urine.

At length, when all the tortures, that these savages could invent, proved ineffectual ; and nothing could induce our martyr to deny his great Lord and Master, he was condemned to be burned ; an act less cruel than what he had already suffered.

On the 31st of the month called August, 1555, he was led to the stake, where he declared to the people around him, what cruelties he suffered during the time of his imprisonment, but that he had been enabled to sustain them all by the consolation of the divine spirit, with which he had been daily visited.

As this eminent martyr was leading to execution, a young woman, who had belonged to his congregation, and received the benefit of his spiritual discourses, came up to him, and, as the last token of respect, cordially embraced him. This being observed by some of the blood-thirsty papists, diligent inquiry was made for her the next day, in order to bring her to the stake, but she happily eluded their search, and escaped their cruel intentions.

Before he was chained to the stake, he exhorted the spectators to avoid idolatry, and hold fast to the truth of the gospel ; after which, he kneeled down, and, with an audible voice, said the following prayer :

" O Lord, my God and Saviour ; who art Lord in heaven and earth, maker of all things, visible and invisible, I am the creature, and work of thy hands : Lord God, look upon me and others thy people, who, at this time, are oppressed by the worldly-minded for thy law's sake ; yea, Lord, thy law itself is now trodden under foot, and men's inventions exalted above it ; and, for that cause, do I, and many of thy creatures, refuse the glory, praise, and conveniencies of this life, and do chuse to suffer adversity, and to be banished, yea, to be burnt, with the books of thy word, for the hope-sake that is laid up in store. For, Lord, thou knowest, if we would but seem to please men in things contrary to thy word, we might, by their permission, enjoy these advantages that others do, as wife, children, goods, and friends ; all which, I acknowledge, to be thy gifts, given to the end I should serve thee. And now, Lord, that the world will not suffer me to enjoy them, except I offend thy laws, behold, I give unto thee my whole spirit, soul, and body ; and lo, I leave here all the pleasures of this life, and do now leave the use of them, for the hope-sake of eternal life purchased in Christ's blood, and promised to all them that fight on his side, and are content to suffer with him for his truth, whensoever the world and the devil shall persecute the same.

" O Father, I do not presume to come unto thee, trusting in mine own righteousness ; no, but only in the merits of thy dear Son my Saviour. For which excellent gift of salvation, I cannot worthily praise thee, neither is my sacrifice worthy, or to be accepted with thee, in comparison of our bodies mortified, and obedient unto thy will : and now, Lord, whatsoever rebellion hath been, or is found in my members against thy will, yet do I here give unto thee my body to the death, rather than I will use any strange worshipping, which, I beseech thee, accept at my hand for a pure sacrifice. Let this torment be to me the last enemy destroyed, even death, the end of misery, and the beginning of all joy, peace, and solace : and when the time of resurrection cometh, then let me enjoy again these members then glorified, which now be spoiled and consumed by the fire. O Lord Jesus, receive my spirit into thy hands. Amen."

When he had finished his prayer, he arose, and being fastened to the stake, the fagots were placed round him, and immediately lighted. He bore his sufferings with a courage and resolution truly christian, cheerfully resigning this life of care and trouble in exchange for another, where death shall be swallowed up in victory, where tears shall be wiped away from all eyes, and an eternity employed in singing the praises of that grace, which has brought the redeemed of the Lord through much tribulation, and advanced them to mansions at the right hand of God, where are pleasures for evermore.

As he was a faithful pastor over his flock during his life, so he was resolved they should not forget him after his death, as appears by the following composition, which he wrote during his confinement.

A letter of exhortation from R. Samuel, to some of the Congregation over whom he presided.

" A MAN knoweth not his time ; but as a fish is taken with the angle, and as the birds are caught with the snare, so are men caught and taken in the perilous time when it cometh upon them. The time cometh ; the day draweth near. Better it were to die (as the preacher saith) than to live and see the miserable works which are done under the sun.

"Alas! for this sinful nation, a people of great iniquity, corrupting their ways. They have forsaken the Lord; they have provoked the holy one of Israel to anger, and are gone backward. Who now liveth not in such security and rest, as though all dangers were clean over-past? Yea, who liveth not now in such felicity, worldly pleasures, and joys, wholly seeking the world, providing, and craftily shifting for the earthly clod and carnal appetite, as though sin were clean forgotten, overthrown, and devoured?

"We might now worthily, dear christians, lament and bewail our heavy estate, miserable condition, and sorrowful chance; yes, I say, we might well accuse ourselves, and, with Job, curse these our turbulent, wicked, and bloody last days of this world, were it not that we both see and believe, and find in God's sacred book, that God hath reserved a remnant in all ages, I mean the faithful, as many as have from the beginning of the world exercised, with divers afflictions and troubles, cast and dashed against all perils and dangers, as the very dross and outcasts of the earth, and yet will in no wise halt between God and Baal. Christ will not part spoil with his mortal enemy the devil: he will have all, or lose all; he will not permit the devil to have the service of the body, and he to stand contented with the heart and mind; but he will be glorified both in your bodies and your spirits, which are his, as St. Paul saith, 1 Cor. vi. For he hath made, bought all, and dearly paid for all, as St. Peter saith. With his own immaculate body, hath he clean discharged your bodies from sin, death, and hell, and, with his most precious blood, paid your ransom, and full price, once for all, and for ever.

"Now, what harm, I pray you, or what loss sustain you by this? Why are ye, O vain men, more afraid of Jesus, your gentle Saviour, and his gospel of salvation, than of a legion of cruel devils, going about, with false delusions, utterly to destroy you both soul, and bodies? Think you to be more sure than under your captain Christ? Do you promise yourselves to be more quiet in Satan's service, than in Christ's religion? Esteem you more these transitory and pernicious pleasures, than God and all his heavenly treasures? O palpable darkness, horrible madness, and wilful blindness, without comparison, too much to be suffered any longer! We see, and will not see; we know, and will not know; yea, we smart, and will not feel, and that our consciences well know. O miserable souls, which would, for foolish pleasures, lose the royal kingdom, and permanent joys of God, with the everlasting glory which he hath prepared for them that truly love him, and renounce the world! The children of the world live in pleasure and wealth, and the devil, who is their god, and prince in this world, keepeth their wealth which is proper unto them, and letteth them enjoy it. But let us which be of Christ, seek and inquire for heavenly things, which, by God's promise and mercy in Christ, shall be peculiar unto us. Let carnal people pass for things that be pleasant for the body, and do appertain to this transitory life : " yet shall they once (as the kingly prophet saith) run about the city of God, to and fro, howling like dogs, desiring one scrap of the joys of God's elect ;" but all too late, as the rich glutton did.

" Let us, therefore, press for those things that do pertain to the spirit, and are celestial. We must be here (St. Paul saith) not as inhabiters, and home-dwellers, but as strangers ; not as strangers only, but after the mind of Paul, as painful soldiers appointed by our governor of darkness of this world, against spiritual craftiness in heavenly things. The time is come ; we must to it ; the judgment must begin first at the house of God. Began they not first with the green and sappy tree ? And what followed then on the dry branches ? Jeremy speaking in the person of God, saith, " in the city, wherein my name is invocated, will I begin to punish," but as for you (meaning the wicked) shall you be innocents, and not once touched ? Nay, the dregs of God's wrath, the bottom of all sorrows, are reserved unto them in the end : but God's house-hold shall drink the flower of the cup of mercy. Wherefore, we ought not to be dismayed, or discourage ourselves, but rather be of good comfort ; not sorrowful, but joyful, in that God of his goodness will vouchsafe to take up his beloved children, to subdue our sinful lusts, our wretched flesh and blood unto his glory, the promoting of his holy word, and edifying of his church. What, if the earthly house of this our habitation, 2 Cor. v. (St. Paul, meaning the body) be destroyed ! we know assuredly we have a building not made with hands, but everlasting in heaven, with such joys as faith taketh not, hope toucheth not, and charity apprehendeth not. They pass all desires and wishes.—— Obtained they may be by Christ, esteemed they cannot be. Wherefore, the more affliction and persecution the word of God bringeth, the more felicity and greater joy abide in heaven. But worldly peace, idle ease, wealthy pleasure, and this present and pleasant transitory life and felicity, which the ungodly foolish imagine to procure unto themselves, by persecuting and thrusting away the gospel, shall turn unto their own trouble, and, at last, unto horrible destructions, and dire change of realms and countries ; and after this life, if they repent not, unto their perpetual misery. For they had rather, with Nabal, and his temporal pleasures, descend to the devil, than with Christ, and his bodily troubles, ascend into the kingdom of God his Father. "But an unwise man (saith the psalmist) comprehendeth them not, neither doth the foolish understand them ;" that is, these bloody persecutors grow up and flourish like the flowers and grass in the field. But unto this end, do they so flourish, that they may be cut down, and cast into the fire forever. For, as Job saith, "their joy lasteth but the twinkling of an eye," and death shall lie gnawing upon them as doth the flock upon the pasture ; yea, the cruel worm, late repentance (as St. Mark saith) shall lie gnawing, tormenting, and accusing their wretched conscience for evermore.

"Let us, therefore, good christians, be constant in obeying God rather than men. For although they slay our sinful bodies (yea, rather our deadly enemies) for God's truth ; yet they cannot do it, but by God's will, to his praise and honour, and to our eternal joy and felicity.

These are the days of vengeance, saith St. Luke, that all
things written may be fulfilled. Now, therefore, saith God,
by the mouth of his prophet, "I will come unto thee,
and will send my wrath upon thee." Upon thee, I say,
O England, and punish thee, according to thy ways, and
reward thee after all thine abomination! Thou hast kindled the fire of God's wrath, and hast stirred up the coals.
For thou wast once enlightened, and hadst tasted of
heavenly gift, and wast become partaker of the Holy
Ghost, and hadst tasted of the good word of God: yea,
it is yet in thy mouth, saith the prophet. Alas, O England, thou knowest thy Lord and master's will, but didst
not do it! thou must, therefore, says he, suffer many
stripes, and many sharp strokes.

"Let the enemies of Christ, and all unbelievers, look
to be tormented and vexed, without hope of God's mercy, who know not God in Christ to be their very righteousness, their life, their own salvation, and alone Saviour, nor believe in him.

"But we are the children of saints, and look for another life, which God shall give to all them who change
not their faith, and shrink not from him. Rejoice, therefore, ye christian afflicted brethren, for they cannot take
our souls and bodies out of the hands of the Almighty,
which are kept as in the bosom of our most loving Father; and, if we abide fast in Christ, and turn not away,
surely we shall live for ever. Christ affirmeth the same,
saying, "my sheep hear my voice, I know them, they
hearken unto me, and to no strangers, and I give them
everlasting life: for they shall not be lost, and no man
shall pluck them out of my hands:" no, nor yet this flattering world, with all its vain pleasures, nor any tyrant,
with his threats, can once move them out of the way of
eternal life. What consolation, or comfort, can we have
more pleasant and effectual than this? God is on our side,
and fighteth for us. As the world can do nothing against
his might, neither in putting away or diminishing from
his glory, nor putting him from his celestial throne; so
neither can it hurt any of his children without his good
will: for we are members of his body, of his flesh, and

of his bones, and as dear to him as the apple of his eye.
Let us, therefore, with earnest faith, lay fast hold on the
promises in the gospel, and let us not be separated from
the same by temptation. tribulation, or persecution.

" Let us consider the truth of God to be invincible and
immutable, promising and giving us, his faithful soldiers,
life eternal.   It is he only that hath reserved it for us:
it is his only benefit, and of his only mere mercy, and unto him only must we render thanks.   Let not, therefore,
the vain fantasies and dreams of men, and foolish
gaudy toys of the world, nor the crafty delusions of the
devil, drive, and separate us from our hope of the crown
of righteousness, that is laid up in store for us against the
last day.   O, that happy and joyful day, I mean, to the
faithful, when Christ, by his covenant, shall grant and
give unto them that overcome, and keep his words to the
end. that they may ascend and sit with him. as he ascended and sitteth on the throne with his Father ! the same
body and soul that are now with Christ afflicted, shall
then with Christ be glorified : now in cruel hands, a
sheep appointed to die ; then sitting at God's table with
Christ in his kingdom, as God's honourable and dear
children ; where we shall have heavenly riches for earthly poverty ; fulness of the presence of the glory of God,
for hunger and thirst ; celestial joys in the company of
angels, for sorrows, troubles, and cold irons ; and life
eternal for bodily death.   O happy souls ! O precious
death, and evermore blessed, right dear in the eyes of
God ! to you the spring of the Lord shall ever be flourishing.   Then (as saith Isaiah) the Redeemer shall return,
and come again into Sion ; praising the Lord, and eternal
mercies shall be over their heads : they shall obtain
mirth and comfort ; sorrow and wo shall be utterly vanquished.   Yes, I am he, saith the Lord, that in all things
giveth you everlasting consolation.   To whom, with the
Father and the Holy Ghost, be glory and praise for ever.
Amen.

ROBERT SAMUEL."

About the time that Samuel suffered, several others shared the same fate, for adhering to the principles of the reformed religion.

William Allen, a labouring man, was burnt at Walsingham, in Norfolk.

Thomas Cobb, a butcher, suffered at Thetford, in the same county.

Roger Coo, an ancient man of independence, was burnt at Yexford, in Suffolk.

Four others also suffered about the same time at Canterbury, viz. George Cotmer, Robert Streater, Anthony Burward, and George Brodridge ; all of whom bore their punishment with christian fortitude, glorifying God in the midst of the flames.

The sufferings and Martyrdoms of Robert Glover, and Cornelius Bongey, both of the city of Coventry.

At the time Robert Glover was apprehended, he lay sick at the house of his brother John Glover, who had secreted himself, on account of a warrant being issued to bring him before his ordinary, on a suspicion of heresy.

Though Glover was in great danger from the indisposition of his health, yet such was the brutality of the popish emissaries, that they took him out of his bed, and carried him to Coventry gaol, where he continued ten days, though no misdemeanor was alleged against him.

When the ten days were expired, in which he suffered great affliction from his illness, he was brought before his ordinary, the bishop of Litchfield and Coventry, who told him that he must submit to ecclesiastical authority, and stand reproved for not coming to church.

Glover assured his lordship, that he neither had, nor would come to church, so long as the mass was used there, to save five hundred lives, challenging him to produce one proof from scripture to justify that idolatrous practice.

After a long altercation with the bishop, in which, Glover both learnedly and judiciously defended the doctrines of the reformation, against the errors and idolatries of popery, and evinced that he was able to give a reason for the faith he professed, he was remanded back to Coventry gaol, where he was kept close prisoner, without a bed, though much indisposed; but nevertheless, the divine comforts enabled him to sustain such cruel treatment without repining, till, at length, he was permitted to provide himself with that necessary convenience.

From Coventry, he was removed to Litchfield, where he was visited by the chancellor and prebendaries, who exhorted him to recant his errors, and be dutiful to the holy mother-church; but he refused to conform to that, or any other church, whose doctrines and practices were not founded on scripture authority, which he determined to make the sole rule of his religious conduct.

After this visit, he remained alone eight days, at the expiration of which, he was again brought before the bishop, who inquired how his imprisonment agreed with him, and warmly entreated him to become a member of the mother-church, which had continued many years; whereas the church, of which he had professed himself a member, was not known but in the time of Edward VI.

With respect to the inquiry, our martyr was silent, treating it with that contempt which such mean behaviour in a prelate deserved, but told his lordship, that he professed himself a member of that church, which is built on the foundation of the apostles and prophets, Jesus Christ himself being the chief corner-stone : and then quoted that well-known passage in the epistle of St. Paul to the Ephesians. This church, added he, hath been from the beginning, though it bore no pompous shew before the world, being, for the most part, under crosses and afflictions, despised, rejected, and persecuted.

After much debate, in which, Glover cited scripture for whatever he advanced, to the confusion and indignation of the haughty prelate, he was commanded, on his obedience, to hold his peace, as a proud and arrogant heretic.

Glover then, with a spirit becoming a man and a christian, told the bishop, he was not to be convinced by insolent and imperious behaviour, but by sound reasoning, founded on scripture; desiring, at the same time, that he would propound to him some articles ; but the bishop chose to decline that method of proceeding, till he should be summoned to the consistory-court, dismissing him with an assurance, that he should be kept in prison, and there have neither meat nor drink, till he recanted his heresies.

Our martyr heard the cruel words with patience and resignation, lifting up his heart to God, that he might be enabled to stand steadfast in the faith of the glorious gospel.

When he was brought into the consistory-court, the bishop demanded of him, how many sacraments Christ had instituted to be used in his church? He replied, two, Baptism, and the Lord's Supper, and no more.

Being asked, if he allowed confession, he answered in the negative.

With respect to the real presence in the sacrament of the altar, he declared, that the mass was neither sacrifice nor sacrament, because they had taken away the true institution ; and when they should restore it, he would give his judgment concerning Christ's body in the sacrament.

After several other examinations, public and private, he was condemned as a heretic, and delivered over to the secular power.

Cornelius Bongey, (who was apprehended much about the same time as Glover, and suffered with him) was examined by Randolph, bishop of Litchfield and Coventry, and the following articles alleged against him :

1. That he did hold, maintain, and teach in the city of Coventry, that the priest hath no power to absolve a sinner from his sins.

2 x

2. That he asserted, there were in the church of Christ but two sacraments, Baptism and the Lord's Supper.

3. That in the sacrament of the popish altar, there were not the real body and blood of Christ. but the substance of bread and wine, even after consecration.

4. That for the space of several years, he did hold and defend, that the pope is not the head of the visible church on earth.

Bongey acknowledged the justness of these allegations, and protested that he would hold fast to them so long as he lived ; in consequence of which, he also was delivered over to the secular power.

On the 20th of the month called September, 1555, these two martyrs were led to the stake at Coventry, where they both yielded up their spirits to that God who gave them, hoping, through the merits of the great Redeemer, for a glorious resurrection to life immortal.

John and William Glover, brothers to Robert, were sought after by the popish emissaries, in order to be brought to the stake, but they eluded their searches, and happily escaped. However, the resentment of the popish persecutors did not cease here, for after their deaths, the bones of one were taken up and dispersed in the highway; and the remains of the other were deposited in a common field.

The Martyrdoms of William Wolsey, and Robert Pigot, both of the Isle of Ely, in the county of Cambridge.

INFORMATION being laid against these two persons by the popish emissaries, they were sought after, and soon apprehended. William Wolsey was first taken ; and, being brought before a neighbouring justice, was bound over to appear at the ensuing sessions, to be holden for the Isle of Ely. But, a few days after, he was taken into custody, and committed to Wisbeach gaol, there to remain till the next assizes for the county.

During his confinement here, he was visited by the chancellor of Ely, who told him, that he was out of the pale of the catholic church, and desired that he would not meddle any more with the scriptures than became a layman.

After a short pause, Wolsey addressed the chancellor as follows : " Good doctor, what did our Saviour mean, when he said, Matt. xxiii. But wo unto you, scribes and Pharisees, hypocrites ! for ye shut up the kingdom of heaven against men : for ye neither go in yourselves, neither suffer ye them that are entering to go in."

Robert Pigot was apprehended, and brought before Sir Clement Hyam, judge, who reproved him severely for absenting himself from church. The reason he assigned for his absence was, that he deemed the church a congregation of believers, assembled together for the worship of God, according to the manner laid down in his most holy word ; and not a church of human invention, founded on the whimsical fancy of fallible men.

In consequence of this answer, he was with Wolsey, committed to prison, where they both remained, till the day appointed for their execution.

During their confinement, several of the neighbours came to visit them, among whom, was Peter Valerices, a Frenchman, chaplain to the bishop of Ely, who thus addressed them : " My brethren, according to mine office, I am come to talk with you, for I have been almoner here these twenty years and more; wherefore, my brethren, I desire you to take it in good part. I desire not to enforce you from your faith, but I require and desire you, in the name of Jesus Christ, that you stand to the truth of his gospel, and his word ; and I beseech Almighty God, for his Son's sake, to preserve both you and me in the same unto the end, for I know not, brethren, how soon I may be in the same case with you."

This address, being so different from what was expected, drew tears from all who were present, and greatly comforted our martyrs.

On the 9th of the month called October, Pigot and Wolsey were brought before Dr. Fuller the chancellor, and other commissioners for ecclesiastical affairs, who laid several articles to their charge, but particularly that of the sacrament of the altar.

When that article was proposed, they jointly declared the sacrament of the altar was an idol, and that the real body and blood of Christ were not present in the said sacrament; and, to this opinion, they said they would stand, though at the peril of their lives, being founded on the authority of God's word, which enjoined the worship of the supreme God alone.

After this declaration, they were exhorted by Dr. Shaxton, one of the commissioners, to consider of the danger of continuing in that belief, and recant the same, lest they should die here, and perish hereafter; adding, that he had believed as they did, but was now become a new man in point of faith.

This not having any effect, Dr. Fuller upbraided Wolsey with obstinacy and fool-hardiness; but endeavoured to sooth Pigot into compliance, desiring one of the attendants to write to the following purport:

" I Robert Pigot do believe, that after the words of consecration spoken by the priest, there remain no more bread and wine, but the very body and blood of Christ, substantially the self-same that was born of the Virgin Mary."

It was then read to Pigot; and his answer being required, he briefly said, " sir, that is your faith, but never shall be mine, till you can prove it from scripture."

These two martyrs thus persevering in the faith of the pure gospel, sentence of death was passed, and they were both ordered to be burned as heretics.

On the 16th of the month called October, 1555, the day appointed for their execution, they were conducted to the stake, amidst the lamentations of great numbers of spectators. Several English translations of the New Testament being ordered to be burned with them, they took each one of them in their hands, lamenting, on the one hand, the destroying so valuable a repository of sacred truth, and glorying, on the other, that they were deemed worthy of sealing the same with their blood.

They both died in the triumph of faith, magnifying the power of divine grace, which enables the servants of God to glory in tribulation, and count all things but as dross, for the excellency of the knowledge of Christ their Redeemer.

The lives, sufferings, and Martyrdoms of Hugh Latimer, bishop of Worcester ; and Nicholas Ridley, bishop of London.

HUGH LATIMER was born of mean parents, at Thirkeston, in Leicestershire, about the year 1475, who gave him a good education, and sent him to Cambridge, where he shewed himself a zealous papist, and inveighed much against the reformers, who, at that time, began to make some figure in England. But conversing frequently with Thomas Bilney, the most considerable person at Cambridge of all those who favoured the reformation, he saw the errors of popery, and became a zealous protestant.

Latimer being thus converted, laboured, both publicly and privately, to promote the reformed opinions, and pressed the necessity of a holy life, in opposition to those outward performances, which were then thought the essentials of religion. This rendered him obnoxious at Cambridge, then the seat of ignorance, bigotry, and superstition. However, the unaffected piety of Bilney, and the cheerful and natural eloquence of honest Latimer, wrought greatly upon the junior students, and increased the credit of the protestants so much, that the popish clergy were greatly alarmed, and according to their usual practice called aloud for the secular arm.

Under this arm, Bilney suffered at Norwich : but his sufferings, far from shaking the reformation at Cambridge, inspired the leaders of it with new courage. Latimer began to exert himself more than he had yet done ; and succeeded to that credit with his party, which Bilney had so long supported. Among other instances of his zeal and resolution in this cause, he gave one which was very remarkable : he had the courage to write to the king (Henry VIII) against a proclamation, then just published, forbidding the use of the bible in English, and other books on religious subjects. He had preached before the king once or twice at Windsor ; and had been taken notice of by him in a more affable manner, than that monarch usually indulged towards his subjects. But whatever hopes of preferment his sovereign's favour might have raised in him, he chose to put all to the hazard, rather than omit what he thought his duty. His letter is the picture of an honest and sincere heart : he concludes in these terms :

" Accept, gracious sovereign, without displeasure, what I have written. I thought it my duty to mention these things to your majesty. No personal quarrel, as God shall judge me, have I with any man : I wanted only to induce your majesty to consider well, what kind of persons you have about you, and the ends for which they counsel. Indeed, great prince, many of them, or they are much slandered, have very private ends. God grant your majesty may see through all the designs of evil men, and be in all things equal to the high office, with which you are intrusted. Wherefore, gracious king, remember yourself; have pity upon your own soul, and think that the day is at hand, when you shall give account of your office, and the blood which hath been shed by your sword : in the which day, that your grace may stand steadfastly, and not be ashamed, but be clear and ready in your reckoning, and have your pardon sealed with the blood of our Saviour Christ, which alone serveth at that day, is my daily prayer to him, who suffered death for our sins. The spirit of God preserve you."

Lord Cromwell was now grown up into power, and being a favourer of the reformation, he obtained a benefice in Wiltshire for Latimer, who immediately went thither and resided, discharging his duty in a very con-

scientious manner, though persecuted much at the same
time, by the Romish clergy; who, at length, carried their
malice so far as to obtain an archiepiscopal citation for
his appearance in London. His friends would have had
him fly; but their persuasions were in vain. He set
out for London in the depth of winter, and under a severe
fit of the stone and colic; but he was most distressed at
the thoughts of leaving his parish exposed to the popish
clergy. On his arrival at London, he found a court of
bishops and canonists ready to receive him; where, instead of being examined, as he expected, about his sermons, a paper was put into his hands, which he was ordered to subscribe, declaring his belief in the efficacy of
masses for the souls in purgatory, of prayers to the dead
saints, of pilgrimages to their sepulchres and relics, the
pope's power to forgive sins, the doctrine of merit, the
seven sacraments, and the worship of images; which,
when he refused to sign, the archbishop, with a frown,
begged he would consider what he did. "We intend
not (said he) Mr. Latimer, to be hard upon you; we
dismiss you for the present; take a copy of the articles;
examine them carefully, and God grant, that at our next
meeting, we may find each other in better temper."

The next, and several succeeding meetings, the same
scene was acted over again. He continued inflexible,
and they continued to distress him. Three times,
every week, they regularly sent for him, with a view either to draw something from him by captious questions,
or to tease him at length into compliance. Tired out
with this usage, after he was summoned at last, instead
of going, he sent a letter to the archbishop, in which,
with great freedom, he told him, "that the treatment
he had lately met with, had fretted him into such a disorder as rendered him unfit to attend that day; that, in
the mean time, he could not help taking this opportunity
to expostulate with his grace for detaining him so long
from his duty; that it seemed to him most unaccountable, that they, who never preached themselves, should
hinder others; that, as for their examination of him, he
really could not imagine what they aimed at; they pre-

tended one thing in the beginning, and another in the progress; that if his sermons were what gave offence, which he persuaded himself were neither contrary to the truth, nor to any canon of the church, he was ready to answer whatever might be thought exceptionable in them; that he wished a little more regard might be had to the judgment of the people; and that a distinction might be made between the ordinances of God and man; that if some abuses in religion did prevail, as was then commonly supposed, he thought preaching was the best means to discountenance them; that he wished all pastors might be obliged to perform their duty; but that, however, liberty might be given to those who were willing; that as to the articles proposed to him, he begged to be excused subscribing to them; while he lived, he never would abet superstition; and that, lastly, he hoped the archbishop would excuse what he had written; he knew his duty to superiors, and would practise it; but in that case, he thought a stronger obligation laid upon him."

The bishops, however, continued their persecutions, but their schemes were frustrated in an unexpected manner. Latimer being raised to the see of Worcester, in the year 1533, by the favour of Ann Boleyn, then the favourite wife of Henry, to whom, most probably, he was recommended by lord Cromwell, he had now a more extensive field to promote the principles of the reformation, in which he laboured with the utmost pains and and assiduity. All the historians of those times mention him as a person remarkably zealous in the discharge of his new office; and tell us, that in overlooking the clergy of his diocess, he was uncommonly active, warm, and resolute, and presided in his ecclesiastical court with the same spirit. In visiting, he was frequent and observant; in ordaining, strict and wary; in preaching, indefatigable; and in reproving and exhorting, severe and persuasive.

In 1536, he received a summons to attend the parliament and convocation, which gave him a further opportunity of promoting the work of reformation, whereon his heart was so much set. Many alterations were made in religious matters, and a few months after, the bible was translated into English, and recommended to a general perusal, in October, 1537.

Latimer, highly satisfied with the prospect of the times, now repaired to his diocess, having made a longer stay in London than was absolutely necessary. He had talents, but he pretended to have none for the state affairs. His whole ambition was to discharge the pastoral functions of a bishop, neither aiming to display the abilities of a statesman, nor those of a courtier. How very unqualified he was to support the latter of these characters, the following story will prove. It was the custom in those days for the bishops to make presents to the king on New-year's day, and many of them would present very liberally, proportioning their gifts to their expectancies. Among the rest, the bishop of Worcester, being then in town, waited upon the king, with his offering; but, instead of a purse of gold, which was the common oblation, he presented a New Testament, with a leaf doubled down in a very conspicuous manner, to this passage ; " whoremongers and adulterers God will judge."

In 1539, he was summoned again to attend the parliament. The bishop of Winchester, Gardner, was his greatest enemy ; who, upon a particular occasion, when the bishops were with the king, kneeled down and solemnly accused bishop Latimer of a seditious sermon preached at court. Being called upon by the king, with some sternness to vindicate himself, Latimer was so far from denying and palliating what he had said, that he boldly justified it ; and turning to the king, with that noble unconcern, which a good conscience inspires, " I never thought myself worthy, said he, nor did I ever sue to be a preacher before your grace ; but I was called to it, and would be willing, if you mislike it, to give place to my betters : for I grant, there may be many more worthy the room than I am. And if it be your grace's pleasure to allow them for preachers, I can be content to bear their books after them. But, if your

2 Y

grace allow me for a preacher, I would desire you to give me leave to discharge my conscience, and to frame my doctrine according to my audience. I had been very dolt indeed to have preached so at the borders of your realm, as I preach before your grace." The greatness of his answer baffled his accuser's malice. The severity of the king's countenance changed into a gracious smile, and the bishop was dismissed with that obliging freedom, which this monarch never used but to those he esteemed.

However, as the bishop could not give his vote for the act of the six papistical articles, drawn up by the duke of Norfolk, he thought it wrong to hold any office in a church, where, such terms of communion were required; and, therefore, he resigned his bishopric, and retired into the country, where he purposed living a sequestered life. But, in the midst of his security, an unhappy accident carried him again into the tempestuous weather, which was abroad. He received a bruise by the fall of a tree, and the contusion was so dangerous, that he was obliged to seek out for better assistance than could be afforded him by the unskilful surgeons of those parts. With this view, he repaired to London, where he had the misfortune to see the fall of his patron, lord Cromwell: a loss which he was soon made sensible of. For Gardner's emissaries quickly found him out in his concealment, and something which he had been heard to say, against the six articles, being alleged against him, he was sent to the tower; where, without any judicial examination, he suffered through one pretence or another, a cruel imprisonment for the remaining six years of king Henry's reign.

On the death of Henry, the protestant interest revived under his son Edward; and Latimer, immediately upon the change of government, was set at liberty. An address was made by the protector, to restore him to his bishopric. The protector was very willing to gratify the parliament, and proposed the resumption of his bishopric to Latimer; who now thinking himself unequal to the weight of it, refused to resume it, choosing rather to ac

cept an invitation from his friend archbishop Cranmer,
and to take up his residence with him at Lambeth; where
his chief employment was to hear the complaints, and redress the grievances of the poor people ; and his character, for services of this kind, was so universally known,
that strangers from every part of England would resort to
him.

In these employments, he spent more than two years,
during which time, he assisted the archbishop in compo-
sing the homilies, which were set forth by authority,
in the first year of king Edward.   He was also appointed to preach the lent sermons before the king, which office he also performed during the three first years of his
reign.

Upon the revolution, which happened at court, after
the death of the duke of Somerset, he retired into the
country, and made use of the king's licence as a general
preacher in those parts, where he thought his labours
might be most serviceable.

He was thus employed during the remainder of that
reign, and continued the same course, for a short time,
in the beginning of the next ; but, as soon as the re-in-
troduction of popery was resolved on, the first step towards it was the prohibition of all preaching, and licensing
only such as were known to be popishly inclined.   The
bishop of Winchester, who was now prime-minister,
having proscribed Latimer from the first, sent a message
to cite him before the council.   He had notice of this design some hours before the messenger's arrival, but he
made no use of the intelligence.   The messenger found
him equipped for his journey, at which expressing his
surprise, Latimer told him, that he was as ready to attend
him to London, thus called upon to answer for his faith,
as ever he was to take any journey in his life : and that
he doubted not, but that God, who had enabled him to
stand before two princes, would enable him to stand before a third.   The messenger then acquainting him, that
he had no orders to seize his person, delivered a letter,
and departed.   However, opening the letter, and finding it a citation from the council, he resolved to obey it,

and set out immediately. As he passed through Smithfield, he said, cheerfully, "this place of burning hath long groaned for me." The next morning, he waited upon the council, who having loaded him with many severe reproaches, sent him to the tower, from whence, after some time, he was removed to Oxford.

Nicholas Ridley, bishop of London, received the earliest part of his education at Newcastle-upon-tyne, from whence, he was removed to the university at Cambridge, where his great learning, and distinguished abilities, so recommended him, that he was made master of Pembroke-hall, in that university.

After being some years in this office, he left Cambridge, and travelled into various parts of Europe for the advancement of knowledge. On his return to England, he was made chaplain to king Henry VIII, and bishop of Rochester, from which he was translated to the see of London by king Edward VI.

In private life, he was pious, humane, and affable; in public, he was learned, sound, and eloquent; diligent in his duty, and very popular as a preacher.

He had been educated in the Roman catholic religion, but was brought over to that of the reformed, by means of reading Bertram's book on the sacrament; and he was confirmed in the same, by frequent conferences with Cranmer and Peter Martyr, so that he became a zealous promoter of the reformed doctrines and discipline during the reign of king Edward.

On the accession of queen Mary, he shared the same fate with many others who professed the truth of the gospel. Being accused of heresy, he was first removed from his bishopric, then sent prisoner to the tower of London, and afterwards to Bocardo prison, in Oxford; from whence, he was committed to the custody of Irish, mayor of that city, in whose house he remained, till the day of his execution.

On the 30th of September, 1555, these two eminent prelates were cited to appear before the divinity-school at Oxford,

Agreeable to this citation, they both appeared on the day appointed.

Dr. Ridley was first examined, and severely reprimanded, by the bishop of Lincoln, because, when he heard the cardinal's grace, and the pope's holiness mentioned in the commission, he kept on his cap. The words of the bishop were to this effect : " Mr. Ridley, if you will not be uncovered, in respect to the pope, and the cardinal his legate, by whose authority we sit in commission, your cap shall be taken off."

The bishop of Lincoln then made a formal harangue, in which, he entreated Ridley to return to the holy mother-church, and insisted on the antiquity and authority of the see of Rome, and of the pope, as the immediate successor of St. Peter.

Dr. Ridley, in return, strenuously opposed the arguments of the bishop, and boldly vindicated the doctrines of the reformation.

After much debate, the five following articles were proposed to him, and his immediate and explicit answers required.

1. That he had frequently affirmed, and openly maintained and defended, that the true natural body of Christ, after consecration of the priest, is not really present in the sacrament of the altar.

2. That he had often publicly affirmed, and defended, that in the sacrament of the altar, remaineth still the substance of bread and wine.

3. That he had often openly affirmed, and obstinately maintained, that in the mass, is no propitiatory sacrifice for the quick and dead.

4. That the aforesaid assertions have been solemnly condemned by the scholastical censure of this school, as heretical, and contrary to the catholic faith, by the prolocutor of the convocation-house, and sundry learned men of both universities.

5. That all and singular the premises are true, and notoriously known, by all near at hand, and in distant places.

To the first of these articles, Ridley replied, that he believed Christ's body to be in the sacrament, really, by grace and spirit effectually, but not so as to include a lively and moveable body under the forms of bread and wine.

To the second he answered in the affirmative.

Part of the fourth he acknowledged, and part he denied.

To the fifth, he answered, that the premises were so far true, as his replies had set forth. Whether 'all men spake evil of them he knew not, because he came not so much abroad to hear what every man reported.

He was then ordered to appear the following day in St. Mary's church, in Oxford, to give his final answer; after which, he was committed to the custody of the mayor.

When Latimer was brought into court, the bishop of Lincoln warmly exhorted him to return to the unity of the church, from which he had revolted.

The same articles which were proposed to Dr. Ridley, were read to Latimer; and he was required to give a full and satisfactory answer to each of them.

His replies not proving satisfactory to the court, he was dismissed; but ordered to appear in St. Mary's church, at the same time with Dr. Ridley.

On the day appointed, the commissioners met, when Dr. Ridley being first brought before them, the bishop of Lincoln stood up, and began to repeat the proceedings of the former meeting, assuring him that he had full liberty to make what alterations he pleased in his answers to the articles proposed to him, and to deliver the same to the court in writing.

After some debate, Dr. Ridley took out a paper, and began to read; but the bishop interrupted him, and ordered the beadle to take the writing from him. The doctor desired permission to read on, declaring the contents were only his answers to the articles proposed; but the bishop and others, having privately reviewed it, would not permit it to be read in open court.

When the articles were again administered, he referred the notary to his writing, who set them down according to the same.

The bishop of Gloucester affecting much concern for Dr. Ridley, persuaded him not to indulge an obstinate temper, but recant his erroneous opinions, and return to the unity of the holy catholic church.

Ridley coolly replied, he was not vain of his own understanding, but was fully persuaded, that the religion he professed was founded on God's most holy and infallible church; and, therefore, he could not abandon or deny the same, consistent with his regard for the honour of God, and the salvation of his immortal soul.

He desired to declare his reasons, wherefore, he could not, with a safe conscience, admit of the popish supremacy, but his request was denied.

The bishop finding him inflexible in his faith, according to the doctrine of the reformation, thus addressed him: " Dr. Ridley, it is with the utmost concern, that I observe your stubbornness and obstinacy, in persisting in damnable errors and heresies; but, unless you recant, I must proceed to the other part of my commission, though very much against my will and desire."

Ridley not making any reply, sentence of condemnation was read; after which, he was carried back to confinement.

When Latimer was brought before the court, the bishop of Lincoln informed him, that though they had already taken his answers to certain articles alleged against him, yet they had given him time to consider on the same, and would permit him to make what alterations he should deem fit, hoping, by that means, to reclaim him from his errors, and bring him over to the faith of the holy catholic church.

The articles were again read to him, but he deviated not, in a single point, from the answers he had already given.

Being again warned to recant, and revoke his errors, he refused, declaring, that he never would deny God's truth, which he was ready to seal with his blood. Sentence of condemnation was then pronounced against him, and he was committed to the custody of the mayor.

A few days after this, they were both solemnly degraded by the bishop of Gloucester, and the vice-chancellor of Oxford; after which, they were delivered over to the secular power.

The 16th of October, 1555, was the day appointed for their execution, and the place Town-ditch, behind Baliol college.

Latimer went to the stake in an humble, plain lay-dress, and Dr. Ridley in his ecclesiastical habit, which he wore when a bishop. They embraced each other on the melancholy occasion; and Dr. Ridley encouraged his fellow-labourer, and fellow-sufferer, in the cause of Christ, to be of good cheer, assuring him, that God would assuage the fury of the flames, or enable them to endure them.

Our martyrs then kneeled down, and, with great earnestness, prayed to Almighty God to enable them to sustain the fiery trial that awaited them.

When they arose from prayer, one of the popish priests, in an occasional sermon, upbraided them with heresy and departure from the church of Christ. Dr. Ridley was desirous of vindicating himself from the aspersion of the priest, but was denied that liberty, and commanded to prepare immediately for the fire, unless he would recant, and abjure his heretical opinions; without hesitation, therefore, he took off his clothes, distributed them among the populace, and together, with Latimer, was chained to the stake.

Latimer soon expired, crying, "O Father of heaven, receive my soul." But Ridley, by reason of the fire burning low, and not flaming about his body, endured the most exquisite torture, leaping in the fire, and begging for Christ's sake, that the flames might surround him; till, at length, some of the spectators having taken off part of the fagots, the fire had vent, and the bag of gunpowder that was fastened to his neck exploded, after which, he was not seen to move, but fell down at the feet of his fellow-sufferer.

Thus, did these two pious divines, and steadfast believers, testify, with their blood, the truth of the everlasting gospel, upon which depends all the sinner's hope of salvation.

Latimer, at the time of his death, was in the eightieth year of his age, and preserved the principles he had professed with the greatest magnanimity. He had naturally a happy temper, formed on the principles of true christianity. Such was his cheerfulness, that none of the accidents of life could discompose him : such was his fortitude, that not even the severest trials could unman him. He had a collected spirit, and, on no occasion, wanted a resource. He could retire within himself, and hold the world at defiance.

And as danger could not daunt, so neither could ambition allure him. Though conversant in courts, and intimate with princes, he preserved, to the last, (a rare instance of moderation !) his primeval plainness. In his profession, he was indefatigable ; and, that he might bestow as much time as possible on the active part of it, he allowed himself only those hours for his private studies, when the busy world is at rest, constantly rising, at all seasons of the year, by two in the morning. How conscientious he was in the discharge of the public parts of his office, we have many examples. No man could persuade more forcibly ; no man could exert, on proper occasions, a more commanding severity. The wicked, in whatever station, he rebuked with censorian dignity, and awed vice more than the penal laws.

As to his sermons, which are still extant, and of which, an edition was published upwards of twenty years, they are, indeed, far enough from being exact pieces of composition ; yet his simplicity and familiarity, his humour and drollery, were well adapted to the times ; and his oratory, according to the mode of eloquence at that day, was exceedingly popular. His action and manner of preaching too, were very affecting ; and no wonder ; " for he spoke immediately from his heart." His abilities, however, as an orator, made only an inferior part of his character as a preacher. What particularly reccommends him, is, that noble and apostolic zeal which he continually exerted in the cause of truth.

Ridley was no less indefatigable in promoting the reformed religion, than his fellow-sufferer Latimer. He was naturally of a very easy temper, and distinguished for his great piety and humanity to the distressed. He persevered to the last, in that faith he professed, and cheerful-

2 z

ly resigned his life in defence of the truth of the gos. pel.

Both these worthy prelates, during their confinement, employed their time in writing various pieces to propagate that gospel to which they had so strictly adhered. They also wrote great numbers of letters to their respective friends and particular acquaintances.

Among the pieces written by Dr. Ridley, was a farewell address to the university of Cambridge, and particularly to the members of Pembroke-Hall, of which he had been master. He also wrote addresses, of the same nature, to the cities of Rochester, (the see of which he had some time held) Westminster, and London. But as all these are too tedious to be here inserted, we shall only preserve the following extract from the last.

" O London, London, to whom now may I speak in thee, or whom shall I bid farewell? Shall I speak to the prebendaries of Paul's? Alas! all that loved God's word, and where the true setters forth thereof, are now (as I hear say) some burnt and slain, some exiled and banished, and some confined in hard prison, and appointed daily to be put to the most cruel death, for Christ's gospel-sake. As for the rest of them, I know they could never brook me well, nor could I ever delight in them.

" Shall I speak to the see thereof, wherein of late, I was placed almost, and not fully, the space of three years? But what may I say to it, being (as I hear say I am) deposed and expulsed by judgment, as unjust usurper of that room? O judgment! judgment! Can this be just judgment, to condemn the chief minister of God's word, the pastor and bishop of the diocess, and never bring him into judgment, that he might have heard what crimes were laid to his charge, nor ever suffer him to have any place, or time, to answer for himself? Thinkest thou, that hereafter, when true justice shall have place, this judgment can ever be allowed, either of God or man? Well, as for the cause, or whole matter of my deposition, and the spoil of my goods, which thou possessest yet, I refer it unto God, who is a just judge; and I beseech God, if it be his pleasure, that which is but my personal wrong, be not laid to thy charge in the latter day ; this only I can pray for.

"O thou wicked and bloody see, why dost thou set up again many altars of idolatry, which, by the word of God, were justly taken away ? Why dost thou daily delude thy people, masking in thy masses, instead of the Lord's holy Supper, which ought to be common, as well (saith Chrysostom, yea the Lord himself) to the people, as to the priest ? How darest thou deny the people of Christ, contrary to his express commandment in the gospel, his holy cup ? Why babblest thou to the people, the common prayer in a strange tongue, wherein St. Paul commandeth, in the Lord's name, that no man should speak before the congregation, except it should be by and by declared in their common tongue, that all might be edified ? Nay, hearken thou whorish bawd of Babylon, thou wicked limb of antichrist, thou bloody wolf, why slayest thou down, and makest havoc of the prophets of God ? Why murderest thou, so cruelly, Christ's poor silly sheep, which will not hear thy voice, because thou art a stranger, and will follow none other but their own pastor Christ, his voice ? Thinkest thou to escape, or that the Lord will not require the blood of his saints at thy hands ? Thy God, which is the work of thy hands, and, whom thou sayest thou hast power to make ; that thy deaf and dumb god, I say, will not, indeed, nor can, (although thou art not ashamed to call him thy maker) make thee to escape the revenging hand of the high and Almighty God. But, be thou assured, that the living Lord, our Saviour and Redeemer, who sitteth on the right hand of his Father in glory, he seeth all thy wicked ways, and cruelty, done to his dear members, and he will not forget his holy ones, and his hands (O thou whorish drab) shalt thou never escape. Instead of my farewell to thee, now I say, fie upon thee, fie upon thee, filthy drab, and all thy false prophets.

"Yet thou, (O London) I may not leave thee thus. Although thy episcopal see, now being joined in league with the seat of Satan, thus hath now both handled me and the saints of God ; yet I do not doubt, but in that great city there may be many pious mourners, who do daily mourn for that mischief, and who never did, nor shall, consent to that wickedness, but do detest and abhor it as the ways of Satan. But these privy mourners here I will pass by, and bid them farewell with their fellows hereafter, when place and occasion shall more conveniently require. Among the worshipful of the city, and especially which were in office of mayoralty, yea, and in other cities also, (whom now to name it is not necessary) in the time of my ministry, which was from the latter part of Sir Rowland Hill's year, unto Sir George Barnes's year, and a great part thereof, I do acknowledge, that I found no small humanity and gentleness, as I thought: but (to say the truth) that I do esteem, above all other, for true christian kindness, which is shewed in God's cause, and done for his sake. Wherefore, O Dobs, Dobs alderman and knight, thou, in thy year, didst win my heart for evermore, for that honourable act, that most blessed work of God, of the erection and setting up of Christ's holy hospital, and truly religious houses, which by thee, and through thee, were begun. For thou, like a man of God, when the matter was moved for the relief of Christ's poor silly members to be holpen from extreme misery, hunger, and famine; thine heart, I say, was moved with pity, and as Christ's high honourable officer in that cause, thou calledst together thy brethren, the aldermen of the city, before whom thou breakedst the matter for the poor; thou didst plead their cause, yea, and not only in thine own person, thou didst set forth Christ's cause, but to further the matter, thou broughtest me into the council-chamber of the city, before the aldermen alone, whom thou hadst assembled there together to hear me speak what I could say, as an advocate, by office and duty, in the poor men's cause. The Lord wrought with thee, and gave thee the consent of thy brethren; whereby the matter was brought to the common-council, and so to the whole body of the city: by whom, with an uniform consent, it was committed to be drawn, ordered, and devised by a certain number of the most witty citizens, and politic; endued, also with godliness, and with ready hearts to set forward such a noble act, as could be chosen in all the whole city ; and they, like true and faithful ministers, both to their city, and their master Christ, so ordered, devised, and brought forth the matter, that thousands of silly poor members of Christ, which else, for extreme hunger and misery, should have famished and perished, shall be relieved, holpen, and brought up, and shall have cause to bless the aldermen of that time, the 'common-council, and the whole body of the city ; but especially thee, O Dobs, and those chosen men, by whom this honourable work of God was begun and wrought, and that so long, throughout all ages, as that godly work shall endure ; which I pray Almighty God may be ever, unto the world's end.   Amen.

" And thou, O Sir George Barnes, the truth is to be confessed to God's glory ; and to the good example of others, thou wast in thy year, not only a furtherer and continuer of that, which, before thee, by thy predecessor, was well begun, but also didst labour so to have perfected the work, that it should have been an absolute thing, and perfect spectacle of true charity and godliness unto all christendom.   Thine endeavour was to have set up an house of occupations, both that all kind of poverty, being able to work, should not have lacked, whereupon profitably they might have been occupied to their own relief, and to the profit and commodity of the commonwealth of the city, and also to have retired thither the poor babes brought up in the hospitals, when they had come to a certain age and strength, and also all those which, in the hospital aforesaid, had been cured of their diseases.   And to have brought this to pass, thou obtainedst, not without great diligence and labour, both of thee and of thy brethren, and of that godly king Edward, that christian and peerless prince's hand, his princely palace of Bridewell, and what other things to the performance of the same, and under what condition, is not unknown.   That this thine endeavour hath not had like success, the fault is not in thee, but in the condition and state of the time, which the Lord of his infinite mercy, vouchsafe to amend, when it shall be his gracious will and pleasure.

" Farewell now, all ye citizens that be of God, of what state and condition soever ye be.   Undoubtedly, in London, you have heard God's word truly preached.   My heart's desire, and daily prayer shall be for you, as for whom, for my time, I know to my Lord God I am accountable ; that ye never swerve, either for loss of life, or worldly goods, from God's holy word, and yield unto antichrist : whereupon must needs follow the extreme displeasure of God, and the loss both of your bodies and souls, into perpetual damnation for evermore.

" Thus, fare ye all well.   I pray God give you understanding of his blessed will and pleasure, and make you to believe and embrace the truth.   Amen."

A few days after Latimer and Ridley suffered, three others shared the same fate, for professing the truth of the gospel.   Their names were, John Webb, George Roper, and Gregory Parke.

They were all burnt in one fire at Canterbury, most patiently enduring their torments, accounting themselves happy and blessed of the Lord, that they were made worthy to suffer for the gospel of their Redeemer.

The bloody transactions of the year 1555, were terminated in the death of John Philpot, who, after a long confinement, during which, he underwent various examinations, was at length, brought to the stake in Smithfield, on the 18th of the month called December, where he patiently resigned his soul into the hands of him who gave it. He was a very learned man, and pious christian ; and during his confinement, wrote a great number of letters to his friends, and others ; as also a variety of treatises on that religion, in defence of which, he gave up his existence in this mortal world.   Among his various writings, was the following :

A prayer to be said at the stake, by all those whom God shall account worthy to suffer for his sake.

" MERCIFUL God and Father, to whom our Saviour Christ approached in his fear and need, by reason of death, and found comfort. Gracious God, and most bounteous Christ, on whom, Stephen called in his extreme need, and received strength. Most benign holy spirit, which in the midst of all crosses of death, didst comfort the apostle St. Paul, with more consolations in Christ, than he felt sorrows and terrors, have mercy upon me, a miserable, vile, and wretched sinner, who now draws near the gates of death, deserved both in soul and body eternally, by reason of manifold, horrible, old, and new transgressions, which in thine eyes, O Lord are open and known. O, be merciful unto me, for the bitter death and bloodshedding of thine own only Son Jesus Christ ! and though thy justice doth require (in respect of my sins) that now thou shouldst not hear me, measuring me, in the same measure I have measured thy majesty, contemning thy daily calls ; yet let thy mercy, which is above all thy works, and wherewith the earth is filled ; let thy mercy, I say, prevail towards me, through, and for the mediation of Christ our Saviour ; and for whose sake, in that it hath pleased thee to bring me forth now as one of his witnesses, and a record bearer of thy verity and truth taught by him, to give my life therefore (to which dignity I do acknowledge, dear God, that there was never any so unworthy and so unmeet, no not the thief then hanged with him on the cross.) I most humbly, therefore, pray thee, that thou wouldst, accordingly, aid, help, and assist me with thy strength and heavenly grace, that, with Christ thy Son, I may find comfort, with Stephen, I may see thy presence, and gracious power ; with Paul, and all others, who, for thy name's sake, have suffered afflictions and death, I may find so present with me thy gracious consolations, that I may, by my death, glorify thy holy name, propagate and ratify thy verity, comfort the hearts of the heavy, confirm thy church in thy truth, convert some that are to be converted, and so depart forth of this miserable world, where I do daily heap sin upon sin, and so enter into the fruition of thy blessed mercy ; whereof now give, and increase in me, a lively trust, sense, and feeling, where, through the terrors of death, the torments of fire, the pangs of sin, the darts of satan, and the horrors of hell, may never depress me, but may be driven away through the working of that most gracious spirit; which now plenteously endue me withal, that through the same spirit, I may offer (as I now desire to do in Christ by him) myself wholly, soul and body, to be a lively sacrifice, holy and acceptable in thy sight. Dear Father, whose I am, and always have been, even from my mother's womb, yea even before the world was made, to whom I commend myself, soul and body, family and friends, country, and all the whole church, yea even my very enemies, according to thy good pleasure ; beseeching thee entirely to give, once more, to this realm of England, the blessing of thy word again, with godly peace, to the teaching and setting forth of the same. O dear Father, now give me grace to come unto thee. Purge, and so purify me by this fire, in Christ's death and passion, through thy spirit, that I may be a burnt-offering of a sweet smell in thy sight, who livest and reignest with the Son and the Holy Ghost, now and for ever more, world without end. Amen.

The persecutions and sufferings of Thomas Whittell, priest; Bartlet Green, John Tudson, John Went, Thomas Brown, Isabel Fostel, and John Lashford ; all of whom were burnt together in Smithfield, for professing the truth of the gospel.

THE popish emmissaries having laid informations against these seven persons, they were all apprehended ; and being brought before bishop Bonner, at his consistory-court in St. Paul's church, the following articles were exhibited against them, after the usual introductory parade, the substance of which is thus expressed :

" These articles and every part and parcel of them, we Edmund Bonner, by the permission of God, bishop of London, do object and minister unto thee, Thomas Whit-

tell, &c. of our mere office, for thy soul's health, and reformation of thine offences or misdemeanors, admonishing
thee, in virtue of obedience, and under the pains, both of
the censures of the church, and the laws of the realm, to
answer fully, plainly, and truly to the same.''

1. Whether you, and each of you, do believe there is a
catholic church?

To this, they replied in the affirmative ; but Tudson and
Brown added further, that the church of England, as it
was at present used, was not part of the true catholic
church.

2. That there are in the church seven sacraments.

To this, they answered in the negative, declaring they
acknowledged only two sacraments in Christ's catholic
church, baptism, and the supper of the Lord.

Went and Tudson affirmed, that the sacrament of the
altar, then used, was an idol, and consequently no sacrament.

3. That they were first baptized in the faith of the catholic church, professing, by their godfathers, their faith in
the same.

They all confessed, they were baptized in the faith of
Christ, and of the church then used ; but that afterwards,
during the reign of king Edward VI, hearing the gospel
preached, and the great truths of the same opened and
explained, they followed the forms and doctrines then used
and set forth.

4. That they, for the space of certain years, did ratify and
allow, and not depart from any part of the profession of the
same church, in which they were baptized.

To this article, they all assented ; but John Went added, moreover, that about seven years past, being then
twenty years old, he began to dislike certain ceremonies
used in the church of England, and did at present dislike
the same, though his godfather and godmother promised
for him to the contrary.

Tudson also declared, that nine years ago, being then
about eighteen years old, he disapproved the doctrines and
ceremonies then taught and set forth in the church of England excepting the time of king Edward, when the gos-

3 A

pel was truly preached ; but that the religion set forth in the present reign, was not agreeable to God's word, nor the true catholic church, instituted by Christ and his apostles.

Isabel Foster declared, in answer to this fourth article, that she continued in the same faith and religion, in which she was baptized, after she came to years of discretion, till the reign of king Edward VI, at which time, hearing the gospel fully and faithfully preached, she received and embraced the doctrines then taught and set forth.

5. That they, of late years, have swerved, and gone away, and spoken against the profession of the same church of England, at least some part thereof, especially the sacrifice of the mass, the sacrament of the altar, and the authority of the church of Rome.

This they all acknowledged, but Whittell added to the general confession, that he had swerved not in the whole, but in part, not from the whole catholic church, but from the church of Rome, in speaking against the mass, the sacrifice thereof, and the supremacy of the pope.

Joan Lashford also declared, that she never heretofore swerved from any part of Christ's catholic faith and religion ; but that, from the time she was eleven years of age, she disliked the sacrifice of the mass, the sacrament of the altar, and the authority of the papal see, as well as the doctrines and practices of the same, because they were contrary to God's holy word, and the religion contained in the gospel.

6. That they refused to be reconciled to the unity of the church of Rome.

This they all acknowledged, because that church, and its doctrines, and practices, were contrary to the unity of Christ's word, and the true catholic faith.

Bartlet Green added, that he was contented to be reconciled to the unity of Christ's catholic church, but not to the church of Rome.

7. That they refused to come to hear mass, and to receive the said sacrament, calling it an idol.

This, also, they confessed to be true, assigning, as a reason, that the mass, with the sacrament thereof, as then used and set forth in the church of England, was dissonant and disagreeable to the word, and preaching of the gospel.

Went farther observed, that the mass, which he called the Lord's supper, as then used in the church of England, was full of idolatry, and against God's word; and that he much repented his having been present at the same, through fear of persecution, since the queen's coronation.

Isabel Foster confessed, she had not heard mass, nor received the sacrament, but refused coming into the place where it was admnistered, because she knew there was no such sacrament founded on the word of God.

Being asked her belief concerning the same, she declared, there were only material bread, and material wine, and not the real substance of the body and blood of Christ in the same sacrament, as she had been taught to believe by the ministers of the gospel in time of king Edward VI, when she believed the word of God was preached in its purity.

8. That they were sent by the commissioners to the bishop to be examined and imprisoned.

Generally granted.

9. That all and singular the premises have been, and are true, and manifest; and that they are of the diocess and jurisdiction of London.

Generally granted.

Such was the general examination of these persons in the consistory-court of the bishop of London. We shall now proceed to a more minute and circumstantial relation of the particulars of each, individually considered.

Thomas Whittell was a married priest, and an eminent and laborious minister of the gospel, in the county of Essex, during the reign of Edward VI: but, on the accession of queen Mary, he was deprived of his living, and wandered from place to place, preaching in private as often as opportunity afforded.

In process of time, he was apprehended by one of the popish emissaries, who, amongst many others, made a trade of informing against heretics (as they were then called) and brought before the bishop of Winchester, who being at that time indisposed, he was referred to the bishop of London. When he appeared before his lordship, he asked him, if he would have come to mass that morning, if he had been sent for?

Whittell replied, he would have obeyed the summons of his lordship, though he had no veneration for the mass.

Bonner was so incensed at this reply, that striking him with his fist on his face, he said, " Villain, thou shalt be fed with bread and water."

The bishop afterwards employed a neighbouring priest to tamper with Whittell, promising him considerable preferment in the church, if he would recant his erroneous opinions, and acknowledge the papal supremacy; but Whittell assured the priest, that he thought he held nothing but the truth, and, therefore, he could not so slightly abjure the same.

A paper to the following purport was then read to him, in order for his subscribing the same:

" I Thomas Whittell, priest, of the diocess of London, acknowledge and confess with my mouth, agreeing with my heart, before you, reverend father in God, Edmund, by the grace of God, bishop of London, my ordinary, that I do detest and abhor all manner of heresies and errors against the sacrament of the altar, or any of the sacraments of the church; which heresies and errors have heretofore been condemned, in any wise by the Catholic church: and I do protest and declare, by these presents, that I do both now hold, observe, and keep in all points, the Catholic faith, and belief of Christ's church, according as this church of England, being a member of the said Catholic church, doth now profess and keep, and, in no wise, to swerve or decline from the said faith during my natural life, submitting myself wholly and fully to you, reverend father, my said ordinary, in all such things concerning my reformation and amendment at all times ; in witness whereof, I have hereunto subscribed my name."

To this bill, Whittell, at the instigation of the popish emissary, and through fear of punishment, subscribed his name ; and the priest left him for that night, with a promise of his liberty in the morning.

But when our martyr came to reflect seriously on his conduct in abjuring the truth of God's most holy word, and denying his great Lord and Master, Jesus Christ, the sole head of the church malitant, and triumphant, he suffered inconceivable horrors of conscience, insomuch that, bereft of sleep, he threw himself on the ground, and, during the whole night, deplored his backsliding, and treachery to a merciful Saviour and Redeemer ; nor could he eat, or enjoy any comfort of life, till he sent for the priest, told him the horrors that had wrung his soul, and tore his name from the paper he had subscribed.

His troubled mind was now at rest ; and though he had no prospect before him but the flames and certain death, he triumphed in what he had done, determining to live and die in the faith of Christ, and not retract the same on the severest penalty ; and he was enabled, by the grace of God, to abide by the resolution ; for he was soon after brought into the bishop's court, and again examined ; when, holding fast to the truth of the gospel, he received sentence of death.

Barlet Green was descended from a good family, and educated at the university of Oxford ; where, by reading the divinity lectures of Peter Martyr, he obtained a sound knowledge of the christian faith, and became a zealous professor of the pure gospel of Christ.

After leaving the university, he became a member of the Temple society, and applied himself to the study of the common law, though he neglected not the scripture, in which, he much delighted.

The first cause of suspicion that Green deviated from the church of Rome, arose from a letter he wrote to one of his fellow students at Oxford, who had fled beyond sea, on account of his religion. This letter was an answer to one he had received from his friend, in which, he was desired to inform him concerning the truth of a report, which had been propagated, that the queen was dead.

The letter being intercepted, was much aggravated by the queen's council, as having a treasonable meaning; on which, Green was taxed with having been the author of some printed questions, that were lately dispersed in the city, and, on that suspicion, committed to the Fleet.

Although, on examination, no part of the charge could be proved, they still detained him, in order to propose some questions relative to religion, and thereby inveigle him into confessions that might afford them an opportunity of persecuting him as an enemy to the principles of the Romish persuasion.

This artful procedure had the desired effect; for though they could not persecute him on the charge alleged, they inferred from the very correspondence, that he maintained opinions contrary to the holy mother church, and committed him, on mere presumption, to the tower.

After they had confined him some time, they sent him to the bishop of London, and a letter with him, acquainting the bishop, that he was erroneous in his religious principles, and desiring that he might be treated accordingly.

The bishop, in the presence of several other prelates, the archdeacon and dean, treated Green with much respect, and inquired the cause of his imprisonment.

Our martyr informed the bishop, that he was confined on account of a letter he had written to an intimate friend, whose name was Gorden, though he had made proper submission.

Though Bonner, at first, treated him with affected tokens of respect, yet he appeared desirous of adding him to the number martyred by the Roman church; for when he had vindicated himself from the charge brought against him, he asked him, if, since he was a prisoner, he had not spoken, or written, against the real presence of

Christ in the sacrament of the altar ? Green desired the bishop not to put new questions to him, as he was cleared of the old ; upon which, a lawyer present assured him, that though he was cleared of treason, yet, if during his confinement, he had maintained heretical opinions, his ordinary had a right to proceed against him on that account.

One Chadrey, a priest. being sent for, asserted, that, in the presence of the Lieutenant of the tower, Green had spoken against the real presence and the sacrifice of the mass, and averred, that the chuch of Rome was the church of antichrist.

Being asked by the bishop, if the charge was true, and if he would defend the same by scholastic reasoning, he replied, that he had not presumption enough to make such an attempt before so learned a body ; but that he was satisfied. in his own mind, concerning those points, which were sufficient for his salvation.

The lawyer then took Green aside, and desired him not to oppose the judgment of so many learned men, and indeed the whole church ; but to conform to the doctrines and ceremonies of the same, as of undoubted authority, and indisputable validity.

This effort, however. not proving effectual, the bishop used the most soothing means to give Green over to the popish cause. He invited him to sup at his own table, lodge in his palace, and accept of other distinguishing tokens of respect. From hence, the artful prelate took occasion to ask him, why he departed from the literal sense of the words in the sacrament, where Christ says, " this is my body ?"

Green endeavoured to evade the answer, but being pressed by the bishop, replied, he was inclined to reject the literal sense, from the manner of speaking, from the circumstance itself, and by comparing it with other passages of scripture, allowing that Christ took bread, and affirmed it to be his body, though he could not understand the affirmation as literal, but as figurative, in the same manner, as when Christ is called a door, a vine, a way, &c.

Our martyr was for the present dismissed, but afterwards was sent for, and examined by the bishop, and several others; when he continued steadfast in his faith, notwithstanding the strongest persuasions, and most delusive arguments, were used to make him recant.

All endeavours thus failing, he was summoned to appear at the consistory court, where he underwent an examination concerning the articles already mentioned.

The following are the particular answers he gave to the articles proposed to him, as drawn up by the bishop's register, at the command of his lordship.

That neither in the time of king Edward the sixth, after the mass by him was put down, nor in the time of queen Mary, when the mass was restored again, he hath heard any mass at all; but he saith, that in the reign of the said queen's majesty, he, the said Bartlet, at two several times, on two Easter-days, in the chamber of John Pulline, one of the preachers in king Edward's time, in the parish of St. Michael's, Cornhill, in the diocess of London, did receive the communion with the said Pulline, and Christopher Goodman, some time reader of the divinity lecture in Oxford, now gone beyond the sea; and the second time, with the said Pulline, and one Runneger, master of arts, of Magdalen college, in Oxford.

And this examinant saith, that, at both the said communions, he, and the others before-named, did take and receive bread and wine; which bread and wine, he saith, were used there by the said Pulline, only reading the words of the institution expressed in the book of communion. In which receiving and using, this examinant saith, that he and others aforesaid, did receive the sacrament of the Lord's supper; and that they received material bread and material wine, no substance thereof changed, and so no real presence of the body and blood of Christ being there, but only grace added thereto.

And this examinant saith, that he hath heretofore, during the reign of the queen's majesty aforesaid, refused, and so doth now refuse to come and hear mass, and to receive the sacrament of the altar, as they are now used and ministered in the church of England, because he saith, that concerning the mass, he cannot be persuaded in his conscience, that the sacrifice pretended to be in the same, is agreeable to God's word, or maintainable by the same; or that, without deadly offence, he can worship the body and blood of Christ, which is pretended to be there.

And, as concerning the sacrament of the altar, this examinant saith, that he heretofore, during the said reign, had refused, and now doth refuse to receive the same, as it is now used in the church of England, because it is not usual, according to the institution of Christ, both in a strange tongue, and also not ministered in both kinds; and besides, that, contrary to God's word, it is taught, that the thing there ministered is to be adored as the real and true body of Christ.

And furthermore, this examinant saith, that during the said reign, he hath not confessed to the said priest, nor received the absolution at his hand, because he is not bound, by God's word, to make auricular confession.

Bartlet Green.

Many lucrative offers were made him, during his confinement, if he would conform to the church of Rome; but he rejected them all with a christian disdain, fully resolved not to commit an act, on any terms, so repugnant to the dictates of his conscience.

As he lived, so he died, becoming a follower of Christ, resigning himself up to the cruelty of his tormentors, and patiently submitting to his lot of trial here, in order to appear hereafter as gold ten times purified in the fire, and made meet to partake of the inheritance of the saints in light.

Thomas Brown resided in the parish of St. Bride's, Fleet-street, and, at the instigation of the constable of the parish, was brought before the bishop of London, for absenting himself from church. After his first examination, he was dismissed, but, in a few days, received a summons to attend the bishop at his palace in Fulham.

3 B

Here he underwent another examination by his lordship, and others, concerning his faith ; when he gave answers to all their questions, in a manner that was consistent with the principles of a strenuous advocate for the truth of the gospel.

On the close of this second examination, he was again dismissed for the present, but required by the bishop to attend mass the next day at the palace. Instead of obeying this order, he retired to an adjacent field, where he kneeled down, and prayed in private. Information of this being given to the bishop, he was highly incensed, as he imputed our martyr's conduct to an impious contempt of the mass.

Being brought before the bishop, a third time, his lordship told him, he had taken much pains to reclaim him, and yet he had reported that he sucked his blood. To this, our martyr replied, that he was, indeed, a blood-sucker; but, if he could prove him guilty of heresy from scripture, he would conform to the church of Rome. That he condemned him because he would not confess and believe the bread in the sacrament of the altar (as he called it) to be the body of Christ, therefore, he shed his blood ; and not only his, but that of many of the queen's loyal subjects, for which, he must answer at a more just and impartial tribunal than that of his bloody consistory.

After this reply, he was condemned, delivered over to the secular power, and committed to Newgate.

John Tudson was brought before the cruel and arbitrary Bonner, to be proceeded against according to ecclesiastical law, for not conforming to the holy mother church.

The bishop, after repeated examinations, publicly condemned him in the consistory court of London, for adhering to doctrines he had been taught by the preachers in the time of king Edward the sixth.

He persisted steadfastly in his faith, and courageously suffered in the cause of the gospel.

John Went, and Isabel Foster, underwent the same trial, and were condemned to suffer the same fate.

Joan Lashford had attended her father-in-law, John Warne, and her own mother, Elizabeth Warne, when they were confined under condemnation for heresy; for which, as we have already observed, they were both burned.—This giving suspicion, that she was one of the obnoxious persons in those days called heretics, she was brought before Bishop Bonner, and by him examined and condemned.

On the 27th of the month called January, 1556, these seven believers in, and faithful servants of Christ, were conducted from Newgate to Smithfield, there to endure the last torments that could be inflicted on them by their cruel persecutors. They all went with great cheerfulness, singing hymns to the praise of their Redeemer, both in the way to, and at the place of execution. Bartlet Green, in particular, frequently repeated the following lines :

O Christ, my God, sure hope of health,
  Besides thee have I none :
The truth I love, and falsehood hate,
  Be thou my guide alone.

They were chained to three different stakes, but consumed together in one fire, freely yielding up their lives in testimony of the truth, and sealing with their blood, the doctrines of that gospel they had so zealously supported.

Two of these worthy martyrs, namely, Thomas Whittell, and Bartlet Green, wrote a great number of letters, to their friends and acquaintances, during their confinement; among which, as mementos, we shall preserve one of each.

Bartlet Green had been educated at the university, and afterwards studied the law in the temple, where he gave a loose to the follies and vanities of the young men of that age. In the course of some time, he was sensibly convinced of the impropriety of his conduct, and heartily bewailed, that he had not sooner amended. This appears evident from the following epistle, which he wrote a

short time before his death, and left in a book belonging
to Bartram Crolthrop, one of his most intimate acquaintances :

" Two things have very much troubled me whilst I
was in the temple, pride and gluttony ; which, under
the colour of glory and good fellowship, drew me almost
from God. Against both, there is one remedy, by earnest prayer, and without ceasing. And forasmuch as
vain glory is so subtle an adversary, that almost it woun-
deth deadly, ere ever a man can perceive himself to be
smitten ; therefore, we ought so much the rather, by
continual prayer, to labour for humbleness of mind.
Truly gluttony beginneth under a charitable pretence of
mutual love and society, and hath in it most unchari-
tableness. When we seek to refresh our bodies, that
they may be the more apt to serve God, and perform our
duties towards our neighbours, then stealeth it in as a
privy thief, and murdereth both body and soul, that now
it is not apt to pray, or serve God, apt to study or labour
for our neighbour. Let us, therefore, watch and be sober : for our adversary, the devil, walketh about, like a
roaring lion, seeking whom he may devour. And remember, what Solomon saith, " a patient man is better
than a strong warrior ; and he that conquereth his own
stomach, is better than he that conquereth towns and
cities."

BARTLET GREEN."

" Agreement of minds, joining in unity of faith, and
growing up in charity, is true and steadfast amity. Farewell, my Bartram, and remember me, that we may be
like to meet together hereafter. Farewell. At Newgate, January 20, 1556. Set sober love against hasty
wrath.

BARTLET GREEN."

A Letter from Thomas Whittell, to Filles and Cutbert, two of his particular friends : written a short time before his death.

" My dear and well beloved brethren in Christ, Messrs. Filles and Cutbert, I wish you all welfare of soul and body. Welfare of soul is repentance of sin, faithful affiance in Christ Jesus, and godly life. Welfare to the body is the health of the same, with all necessary things for this life. The soul of man is immortal, and, therefore, ought to be well kept, lest immortality of joy should turn to immortality of sorrow. As for the body, be it ever so well kept, and much made of, yet shortly, by nature, will it perish and decay : but those that are ingrafted and incorporated into Christ by true faith, feeling the motion of God's holy spirit, as a pledge of their election and inheritance, exciting and stirring them not only to seek heavenly things, but also to hate vice, and embrace virtue, will not only do these things, but also, if need require, will gladly take up their cross, and follow their captain, their king, and their Saviour Jesus Christ, (as his poor afflicted church of England now doth) against that false and antichristian doctrine and religion now used, and especially that blasphemous mass wherein Christ's supper, and holy ordinance, are altogether perverted and abused, contrary to his institution, and to Paul's proceedings : so that, that which they have in their mass is neither sacrament of Christ, nor yet sacrifice for sin, as the priests falsely pretend. It is a sacrament, that is, as St. Augustine saith, " a visible sign of invisible grace," when it is administered to the communicants, according to Christ's example, and as it was, of late years, in this realm. And as for sacrifice, there is none to be made now for sin : " for Christ, with one sacrifice, hath perfected for ever those that are sanctified."

" Beware of false religion, and men's vain traditions, and serve God with reverence and godly fear, according to the doctrine of his gospel ; whereto cleave ye, that ye may be blessed, though of wicked men you are hated and accused. Rather drink of the cup of Christ, with his church, than of the cup of that rose-coloured whore of Babylon, which is full of abominations. Rather strive ye to go to Heaven by the path which is strait to the flesh and blood, with the little flock, than to go in the wide way, following the enticements of the world and the flesh, which lead to damnation.

"Like as Christ suffered in the flesh, saith St. Peter, so arm ye yourselves with the same mind : for Christ suffered for us, leaving us an example to follow his footsteps. Blessed are they that suffer for his sake ; great is their reward in Heaven. He that overcometh, saith St. John, Rev. 2, 3, shall eat of the tree of life ; he shall have a crown of life, and not be hurt of the second death : he shall be clothed with white array, and not be put out of the book of life ; yea, I will confess his name, saith Christ, before my Father, and before his angels, and he shall be a pillar in the house of God, and sit with me on my seat. And thus, I bid you farewell, mine own brethren, and dear fellows in Christ ; whose grace and peace be always with you. Amen.

THOMAS WHITTELL."

Four days after the before-mentioned seven martyrs suffered in Smithfield, five others were burnt at Canterbury. Their names were, John Lodmas, Ann Albright, Joan Cotmer, Agnes Snoth, and Joan Sole.

These five steadfast servants of God, and willing followers of Christ, were bound together at two stakes, rejoicing in the flames, and chaunting hallelujahs to God and the Lamb, who had given them the victory over their enemies, and a good hope, through grace, that when this earthly tabernacle was dissolved, they should have a house, not made with hands, but eternal in the heavens.

An account of the life, sufferings, and Martyrdom of Thom-
as Cranmer, the first Protestant Archbishop of Canter-
bury, who was burnt at Oxford, on the 21st of the month
called March, 1556.

THIS eminent prelate was born at Aslacton, in Notting-
hamshire, on the 2d of the month called July, 1489. His
family was ancient, and came in with William the conqueror. He was early deprived of his father Thomas
Cranmer, Esq. and, after no extraordinary education,
was sent by his mother to Cambridge, at the age of fourteen, according to the custom of those times.

Having completed his studies at the university, he took
the usual degrees, and was so well beloved, that he was
chosen fellow of Jesus college ; soon after which, he became celebrated for his great learning and abilities.

In 1521, he married, by which he forfeited the fellowship
of Jesus college ; but his wife dying in child-bed, within
the year, he was re-elected. This favour he most grate-
fully acknowledged, and chose to decline an offer of a much
more valuable fellowship in cardinal Wolsey's new seminary, at Oxford, rather than relinquish friends who had treated
him with the most distinguished respect.

In 1523, he commenced doctor of divinity ; and, being
in great esteem for theological learning, he was chosen divinity lecturer in his own college, and appointed, by the
university, one of the examiners in that science. In this
office, he principally inculcated the study of the holy scriptures, then greatly neglected, as being indispensably necessary for the professors of that divine knowledge.

The plague happening to break out at Cambridge,
Cranmer, with some of his pupils, removed to Waltham-
abbey, where, falling into company with Gardner and Fox,
one the secretary, the other almoner of king Henry VIII,
that monarch's intended divorce of Catharine his queen,
the common subject of discourse in those days, came upon
the carpet ; when, Cranmer advising an application to our
own, and to the foreign universities, for their opinion in
the case, and giving these gentlemen much satisfaction,
they introduced him to the king, who was so pleased with

him, that he ordered him to write his thoughts on the subject, made him his chaplain, and admitted him into that favour and esteem, which he never afterwards forfeited.

In 1530, he was sent by the king, with a solemn embassy, to dispute on the subject of the divorce at Paris, Rome, and other foreign parts. At Rome, he delivered his book, which he had written in defence of the divorce, to the pope, and offered to justify it in a public disputation : but, after various promises and appointments, none appeared to oppose him ; while in private conferences, he forced them to confess, that that marriage was contrary to the law of God. The pope constituted him penitentiary general of England, and dismissed him. In Germany, he gave full satisfaction to many learned men, who were before of a contrary persuasion : and prevailed on the famous Osander (whose niece he married while there) to declare the king's marriage unlawful.

During the time he was abroad, the great archbishop Warham died. Henry, convinced of Cranmer's merit, determined that he should succeed him ; and commanded him to return for that purpose. He suspected the cause, and delayed : he was desirous, by all means, to decline this high station : for he had a true and primitive sense of the office. But a spirit, so different from that of the churchmen of his times, stimulated the king's resolution ; and the more reluctance Cranmer shewed, the greater resolution Henry exerted. He was consecrated in the month called March 30, 1533, to the office ; and though he received the usual bulls from the pope, he protested, at his consecration, against the oath of allegiance, &c. to him. For he had conversed freely with the reformed in Germany ; had read Luther's books : and was zealously attached to the glorious cause of reformation.

The first service he did the king, in his archiepiscopal character, was pronouncing the sentence of his divorce, from queen Catharine : and the next, in joining his hands with Anne Boleyn, the consequence of which marriage was the birth of Elizabeth, to whom he stood godfather.

As the queen was greatly interested in the reformation, the friends to that good work began to conceive high hopes; and, indeed, it went on with desirable success. But the fickle disposition of the king, and the fatal end of the unhappy Anne, for a while, alarmed their fears: though, by God's providence, without any ill effects. The pope's supremacy was universally exploded; monasteries, &c. destroyed, upon the fullest detection of the most abominable vices, and inordinances: that valuable book of "The erudition of a christian man," was set forth by our great archbishop, with public authority: and the sacred scriptures, at length, to the infinite joy of Cranmer, and the worthy lord Cromwell, his constant friend and associate, were not only translated, but introduced into every parish. The translation was received with inexpressible joy; every one, that was able, purchased it, and the poor flocked greedily to hear it read: some persons in years, learned to read on purpose, that they might peruse it: and even little children crowded with eagerness to hear it! we cannot help reflecting, on this occasion, how much we are bound to prize this sacred treasure, which we enjoy so perfectly: and how much to contend against every attempt of those enemies and that church, which would deprive us of it, and again reduce us to legends and schoolmen, to ignorance and idolatry.

Cranmer, that he might proceed with true judgment, made a collection of opinions from the works of the ancient fathers and later doctors; of which, bishop Burnet saw two volumes in folio; and it appears, by a letter of lord Burleigh's, that there were then six volumes of Cranmer's collections in his hands. A work of incrediblel abour, but vast utility.

A short time after this, he gave a shining proof of his sincere and disinterested constancy, by his noble opposition to what are commonly called king Henry's six bloody articles.* However, he weathered the storm; and pub-

* By these, none were allowed to speak against transubstantiation on pain of of being burned as heretics, and forfeiting their goods and chattels, as in case of treason. It was also thereby made felony, and forfeiture of lands and goods,

lished, with an incomparable preface, written by himself, the larger bible; six of which, even Bonner, then newly consecrated bishop of London, caused to be fixed for the perusal of the people, in his cathedral of St. Paul's.

The enemies of the reformation, however, were restless: and Henry, alas! was no protestant in his heart. Cromwell fell a sacrifice to them; and they aimed every possible shaft at Cranmer. Gardner, in particular, was indefatigable: he caused him to be accused in parliament, and several lords of the privy council, moved the king to commit the archbishop to the tower. The king perceived their malice; and one evening, on pretence of diverting himself on the water, ordered his barge to be rowed to Lambeth side. The archbishop, being informed of it, came down to pay his respects, and was ordered, by the king, to come into the barge and sit close by him. Henry made him acquainted with the accusations of heresy, faction, &c. which were laid against him; and spoke of his opposition to the six articles. The archbishop modestly replied, that he could not but acknowledge himself to be of the same opinion, with respect to them; but was not conscious of having offended against them. The king then putting on an air of pleasantry, asked him, if his bed-chamber could stand the test of these articles? The archbishop confessed, that he was married in Germany, before his promotion; but assured the king, that on the passing of that act, he had parted with his wife, and sent her abroad to her friends. His majesty the king was so charmed with his openness and integrity, that he discovered the whole plot that was laid against him; and gave him a ring of great value to produce upon any future emergency.

A few days after this, Cranmer's enemies summoned him to appear before the council. He accordingly attended, when they suffered him to wait in the lobby, amongst the footmen, treated him, on his admission, with haughty contempt, and would have sent him to the tower. But

---

to defend the communion in both kinds, or marriage of the clergy, or of those who had vowed celibacy: or to speak against private masses and auricular confession.

he produced the ring; and gained his enemies a severe reprimand from Henry, and himself the highest degree of security and favour.

On this occasion, he shewed that lenity and mildness for which, he was always so much distinguished : he never persecuted any of his enemies. But, on the contrary, freely forgave even the inveterate Gardner, on his writing a supplicatory letter to him for that purpose. The same lenity he shewed towards Dr. Thornton, the suffragan of Dover, and Dr. Barber, who, though entertained in his family, entrusted with his secrets, and indebted to him for many favours, had ungratefully conspired with Gardner to take away his life.

When Cranmer first discovered their treachery he took them aside into his study, and telling them, that he had been basely and falsely accused by some, in whom he had always reposed the greatest confidence, desired them to advise him how he should behave himself towards them. They not suspecting themselves concerned in the question, replied, that such vile, abandoned villains, ought to be prosecuted with the greatest rigour; nay, deserved to die, without mercy. At this, the archbishop, lifting up his hands to Heaven, cried out, " merciful God ! whom may a man trust ?" And then taking out of his bosom the letters, by which he had discovered their treachery, asked them, if they knew those papers ? When they saw their own letters produced against them, they were in the utmost confusion , and falling down upon their knees, humbly sued forgiveness. The archbishop told them, " that he forgave them, and would pray for them ; but that they must not expect him ever to trust them for the future."

He was condemned for treason, and pardoned; but, to gratify Gardner's malice, and her own implacable resentment against him for her mother's divorce, Mary gave orders to proceed against him for heresy. His friends, who foresaw the storm, had advised him to consult his safety, by retiring beyond sea ; but he chose rather to continue steady to the cause, which he had so nobly supported hitherto ; and preferred the probability of sealing his testimony with his blood, to an ignominious and dishonourable flight.

The tower was crowded with prisoners; insomuch that Cranmer, Ridley, Latimer, and Bradford, were all put into one chamber; which they were so far from thinking an inconvenience, that, on the contrary, they blessed God for the opportunity of conversing together; reading, and comparing the scriptures, confirming themselves in the true faith, and mutually exhorting each other to constancy in professing it, and patience in suffering for it. Happy society! blessed martyrs! rather to be envied, than the purpled tyrant, with the sword deep-drenched in blood, though encircled with all the pomp and pageantry of power!

In the month called April, 1554, the archbishop, with bishops Ridley and Latimer, was removed from the tower to Windsor, and from thence to Oxford, to dispute with some select persons of both universities. But, alas! what farces are disputations, where the fate of men is fixed, and every word is misunderstood! And such was the case here: for, on the 20th of the month called April, Cranmer was brought to St. Mary's, before the queen's commissioners, and refusing to subscribe to the popish articles, he was pronounced a heretic, and sentence of condemnation was passed upon him. Upon which, he told them, that he appealed from their unjust sentence to that of the Almighty; and that he trusted to be received into his presence in heaven for maintaining the truth, as set forth in his most holy gospel.

After this, his servants were dismissed from their attendance, and himself closely confined in Bocardo, the prison of the city of Oxford. But this sentence being void in law, as the pope's authority was wanting, a new commission was sent from Rome, in 1555; and in St. Mary's church, at the high altar, the court sat, and tried the already-condemned Cranmer. He was here well nigh too strong for his judges; and, if reason and truth could have prevailed, there would have been no doubt, who should have been acquitted, and who condemned.

In the month called February, following, a new commission was given to bishop Bonner and bishop Thirlby, for the degradation of the archbishop. When they came down to Oxford, he was brought before them ; and after they had read their commission from the pope, (for not appearing before whom in person, as they had cited him, he was declared contumacious, though they themselves had kept him a close prisoner) Bonner, in a scurrilous oration, insulted him in the most unchristian manner, for which, he was often rebuked by bishop Thirlby, who wept, and declared, it the most sorrowful scene he had ever beheld in his whole life. In the commission, it was declared, that the cause had been impartially heard at Rome ; the witnesses on both sides examined, and the archbishop's counsel allowed to make the best defence for him they could.

At the reading of this, the archbishop could not help crying out, " good God ! what lies are these ; that I, being continually in prison, and not suffered to have counsel or advocate at home, should produce witnesses, and appoint my counsel at Rome ! God must needs punish this shameless and open lying !"

When Bonner had finished his invective, they proceeded to degrade him ; and that they might make him as ridiculous as they could, the episcopal habit, which they put on him, was made of canvas and old rags. Bonner, in the mean time, by way of triumph and mockery, calling him Mr. Canterbury, and the like.

He bore all this treatment with his wonted fortitude and patience ; told them " the degradation gave him no concern, for he had long despised those ornaments :" but when they came to take away his crosier, he held it fast, and delivered his appeal to Thirlby, saying, " I appeal to the next general council."

When they had stripped him of all his habits, they put on him a poor yeoman-beadle's gown, thread-bare and ill-shaped, and a townsman's cap ; and, in this manner, delivered him to the secular power to be carried back to prison, where he was kept entirely destitute of money, and totally secluded from his friends. Nay, such was the iniquity of the times, that a gentleman was taken into custody by Bonner, and narrowly escaped a trial, for giving the poor archbishop money to buy him a dinner.

Cranmer had now been imprisoned almost three years, and death should have soon followed his sentence and degradation : but his cruel enemies reserved him for greater misery and insult. Every engine that could be thought of, was employed to shake his constancy ; but he held fast to the profession of his faith. Nay, even when he saw the barbarous martyrdom of his dear companions, Ridley and Latimer, he was so far from shrinking, that he not only prayed to God to strengthen them, but, also, by their example, to animate him to a patient expectation and endurance of the same fiery trial.

The papists, after trying various severe ways to bring Cranmer over, without effect, at length determined to try what gentle methods would do. They accordingly removed him from prison to the lodgings of the dean of Christ-church, where they urged every persuasive and affecting argument to make him deviate from his faith ; and, indeed, too much melted his gentle nature, by the false sunshine of pretended civility and respect.

The unfortunate prelate, however, withstood every temptation, at which, his enemies were so much irritated, that they removed him from the dean's lodgings to the most loathsome part of the prison in which he had been confined, and then treated him with uncommon severity. This was more than the infirmities of so old a man could support : the frailty of human nature prevailed ; and he was induced to sign six different recantations, drawn from him by the malice and artifice of his enemies.

This, however, did not satisfy them. They were determined not to spare his life. Nothing less than his death could satiate the gloomy queen, who said, that " as he had been the promoter of heresy, which had corrupted the whole nation, the abjuration, which was sufficient in other cases, should not serve his turn ; for she was resolved he should be burned." Accordingly, she sent orders to Dr. Cole, to prepare a sermon on the occasion of his death, which was fixed to be on the 21st of the month called March.

The archbishop had no suspicion that such would be his fate, after what he had done; but he soon found his mistake.

The papists, determined to carry their resentment to the most extravagant length, thought to inflict a farther punishment on him, by obliging him to read his recantation publicly in St. Mary's church; and on this, they proposed to triumph in his death: but their base intentions were happily frustrated.

On the morning of the day appointed for his execution, he was conducted between two friars to St. Mary's church. As soon as he entered, Dr. Cole mounted the pulpit, and the archbishop was placed opposite to it, on a low scaffold, a spectacle of scorn and contempt to the people.

Cole magnified his conversion as the immediate work of God's inspiration; exhorted him to bear up with resolution against the terrors of death; and, by the example of the thief on the cross, encouraged him not to despair, since he was returned, though late, into the bosom of the church. He also assured him, that dirges and masses should be said for his soul in all the churches of Oxford.

As soon as the archbishop perceived, from Cole's sermon, what was the bloody decree, struck with horror at the base inhumanity of such proceedings, he gave, by all his gestures, a full proof of the deep anguish of his soul.

At length, being called upon by Cole to declare his faith and reconciliation with the catholic church, he rose with all possible dignity; and, while the audience was wrapped in the most profound expectation, he kneeled down, and repeated the following words:

" O Father of Heaven! O Son of God, Redeemer of the world! O Holy Ghost! proceeding from them both; three persons, and one God, have mercy upon me, most wretched and miserable sinner! I, who have offended both Heaven and earth, and more grievously than any tongue can express, whither then may I go, or where shall I fly for succour? To Heaven, I may be ashamed to lift up my eyes; and in earth, I find no refuge; what shall I then do? Shall I despair? God forbid! O good God, thou art merciful! and refusest none who come to thee for succour: to thee, therefore, do I run: to thee do I humble myself, saying, O Lord God, my sins are great, but yet have mercy upon me, for thy great mercy! O God, the Son, thou wast not made man, this great mystery was not wrought for few, or small offences! nor didst thou give thy Son unto death, O God the Father, for our little and small sins only, but for all the greatest sins of the world: so the sinner return unto thee, with a penitent heart, as I do here at this present; wherefore, have mercy upon me, O Lord! whose property is always to have mercy: for although my sins be great, yet thy mercy is greater! I crave nothing, O Lord! for my own merits, but for thy name's sake, that it may be glorified thereby, and for thy dear Son, Jesus Christ's sake, and now, therefore, Our Father, &c."

. He then rose up, exhorted the people to a contempt of this world, to obedience to their sovereign, and to mutual love and charity. He told them, that being now on the brink of eternity, he would declare unto them his faith, without reserve or dissimulation: he then repeated the apostle's creed, and professed his belief thereof, and of all things contained in the Old and New Testament.

By speaking thus in general terms, the attention of the audience was kept up; but amazement continued that attention, when they heard him, instead of reading his recantation, declare his great and unfeigned repentance, for having been induced to subscribe the popish errors: he lamennted, with many tears, his greivous fall, and declared that the hand which had so offended, should be burned before the rest of his body.

He then renounced the pope in most express terms, and professed his belief concerning the eucharist to be the same, with what he had asserted in his book against Gard-ner.

This was a great disappointment to the papists : they made loud clamours, and charged him with hypocrisy and falsehood : to which, he meekly replied, " that he was a plain man, and never had acted the hypocrite, but when he was seduced by them to a recantation."

He would have gone on further, but Cole cried, " stop the heretic's mouth, and take him away."

Upon this, the monks and friars rudely pulled him from the scaffold, and hurried him away to the stake, (where Ridley and Latimer had before been offered up) which was at the north of the city, in the ditch opposite Baliol college.

But, if his enemies were disappointed by his behaviour in the church, they were doubly so by that at the stake. He approached it with a cheerful countenance ; prayed, and undressed himself ; his shirt was made long, down to his feet, which were bare, as was his head, where a hair could not be seen. His beard was so long and thick, that it covered his face with wonderful gravity ; and his rever-end countenance moved the hearts both of friends and enemies.

The friars tormented him with their admonitions ; while Cranmer gave his hand to several old men, who stood by, bidding them farewell.

When he was chained to the stake, and the fire kin-dled, he seemed superior to all sensation but that of piety. He stretched out the offending hand to the flame, which was seen burning for some time before the fire came to any other part of his body ; nor did he draw it back, but once to wipe his face, till it was entirely consumed : saying often, " this unworthy hand, this hand hath offended;" and, raising up his eyes to heaven, he expired, with the dying prayer of St. Stephen in his mouth, " Lord Jesus, receive my spirit !"

He burned, to all appearance, without pain or motion ; and seemed to repel the torture by mere strength of mind, shewing a repentance and fortitude, which ought to can-cel all reproach of timidity in his life.

3 D

Thus died archbishop Cranmer, in the sixty-seventh year of his age, and the twenty-third of his primacy ; leaving an only son, of his own name, behind him.

He was a man, naturally of a mild and gentle temper ; not soon provoked, and yet so easy to forgive, that it became a kind of proverb concerning him, " do my lord of Canterbury a shrewd turn, and he will be your friend as long as you live."

His candour and sincerity, meekness and humility, were admired by all who conversed with him : but the queen could not forgive his zeal for the reformation, nor his divorce of her mother, and therefore, she brought him to the stake ; which has justly numbered him amongst the noblest martyrs who suffered for the truth of the gospel.

He may truly be ranked with the greatest primitive bishops, and the fathers of the very first class, who were men as well as himself ; and, therefore, if in a scrutiny of theirs, or of his character, some infirmities and imperfections may appear, we may learn to make a wise and moral improvement by them. His learning was great, and his endeavour to encourage it greater. To him, under God, we are indebted for the great blessing we enjoy of reformation, of which, he was the pillar and ornament : and, while we repeat the liturgy, and hear the bible in our congregations, so long shall we venerate the name of archbishop Canmer.

Cranmer's labours were well seconded by Ridley, Latimer, and Hooper, who were his fellow-martyrs in the cause of reformation : but the characters of this illustrious quadriumvirate differed one from the other. Cranmer was most respected ; Latimer was most followed ; Ridley best esteemed ; and Hooper most beloved. The art and address of Cranmer, proved a happy balance to the zeal of Latimer ; while the relaxed notions of Hooper, were tempered by the virtue and wisdom of Ridley.

Cranmer, during his imprisonment, wrote a great number of letters to different persons, whom he knew to be professors of Christ's gospel. Amongst, these we shall preserve the following :

A letter from archbishop Cranmer, to —— Wilkinson, exhorting her to fly in the time of persecution.

" THE true comforter in all distress, is only God, through his Son Jesus Christ; and whosoever hath him, hath company enough, if he were in a wilderness all alone; and he that hath twenty thousand in his company, if God be absent, is in a miserable wilderness and desolation.— In him is all comfort, and without him is none. Wherefore, I beseech you, seek your dwelling there, where you may truly and rightly serve God, and dwell in him, and have him ever dwelling in you. What can be so heavy a burden as an unquiet conscience, to be in such a place as a man cannot be suffered to serve God in Christ's religion? If you be loth to depart from your kindred and friends, remember that Christ calleth them his mother, sisters, and brothers, that do his Father's will. Where we find, therefore, God truly honoured according to his will, there we can lack neither friend nor kindred.

" If you be loth to depart for the slander of God's word, remember that Christ, when his hour was not yet come, departed out of his country into Samaria, to avoid the malice of the scribes and pharisees; and commanded his apostles, if they were pursued in one place, they should fly to another. And was not Paul let down by a basket out at a window, to avoid the persecution of Aretas? And what wisdom and policy he used, from time to time, to escape the malice of his enemies, the acts of the apostles do declare. And, after the same sort, did the other apostles, albeit, when it came to such a point, that they could no longer escape danger of the persecutors of God's true religion, then they shewed, themselves, that they flying before came not of fear, but of godly wisdom to do more good; and that they would not rashly, without urgent necessity, offer themselves to death, which had been but a temptation of God. Yea, when they were apprehended, and could no longer avoid, then they stood boldly to the profession of Christ; then they shewed how little they passed of death; how much they feared God more than men ; how much they loved and preferred the eternal life to come above this short and miserable life.

" Wherefore, I exhort you, as well by Christ's command-ment, as by the example of him and his apostles, to with-draw yourself from the malice of yours and God's ene-mies, into some place where God is most purely served ; which is no slandering of the truth, but a preserving of yourself to God, and the truth, and to the society, and comfort of Christ's little flock. And that you will do, do it with speed, lest, by your own folly, you fall into the persecutor's hands. And the Lord send his holy spirit to lead and guide you wheresoever you go ; and all that be godly will say, Amen."

The Martyrdoms of Agnes Potten, and Joan Trunchfield ; who were both burnt together at Ipswich, in Suffolk.

THESE two advocates and sufferers for the pure gospel of Christ, lived in the town of Ipswich, in the county of Suffolk. Being both apprehended on an information of heresy, they were brought before the bishop of Norwich ; who examined them concerning their religion in general, and their faith in the corporeal presence of Christ, in the sacrament of the altar in particular.

With respect to the latter article, they both delivered it as their opinion, that in the sacrament of the Lord's Sup-per, there was represented the memorial only of Christ's death and passion, saying, that, according to the scriptures, he was ascended up into Heaven, and sat at the right hand of God the Father ; and, therefore, his body could not be really and substantially in the sacrament.

A few days after this, they were again examined by the bishop, when both of them still continuing steadfast in the profession of their faith, sentence was pronounced a-gainst them as heretics, and they were delivered over to the secular power.

On the day appointed for their execution, which was in the month called March, 1556, they were both led to the stake, and burnt in the town of Ipswich. Their constancy was admired by the multitude who saw them suffer; for as they undressed and prepared themselves for the fire, they earnestly exhorted the people to believe only in the unerring word of the only living and true God, and not regard the devices and inventions of men.

They both openly declared, that they despised the errors and superstitions of the church of Rome, and most patiently submitted to the acute torments of devouring flames, calling upon the God of their salvation, and triumphing in being deemed worthy to suffer for the glorious cause of Jesus Christ, their Lord and master.

The persecution and Martyrdoms of Richard Spurg, Thomas Spurg, John Cavill, and George Ambrose, laymen; and Robert Drake, and William Tims, ministers.

THESE six pious christians resided in the county of Essex, and diocess of London. Being accused of heresy, they were all apprehended, and sent by lord Rich, and other commissioners, at different times, to bishop Gardner, lord Chancellor of England; who, after a short examination, sent the four first to the Marshalsea prison in the Borough, and the two last to the king's bench, where they continued during the space of a whole year, till the death of bishop Gardner.

When Dr. Heath, archbishop of York, succeeded to the chancellorship, four of these persecuted brethren, namely, Richard and Thomas Spurg, John Cavill and George Ambrose, weary of their tedious confinement, presented a petition to the lord chancellor, subscribing their names, and requesting his interest for their enlargement.

A short time after the delivery of this petition, sir Richard Read, one of the officers of the court of chancery, was sent by the chancellor to the Marshalsea to examine them.

Richard Spurg, the first who passed examination, being asked the cause of his imprisonment, replied, that he, with several others, being complained of, by the minister of Bocking, for not coming to their parish church, to lord

Rich, was thereupon sent up to London by his lordship, to be examined by the late chancellor.

He acknowledged, that he had not been at church since the English service was changed into Latin (except on Christmas day was twelve months) because he disliked the same, and the mass also, as not agreeable to God's holy word.

He then desired, that he might be no farther examined concerning this matter, until it pleased the present chancellor to inquire his faith concerning the same, which he was ready to deliver.

Thomas Spurg, on his examination, answered to the same effect with the other, confessing that he absented himself from church, because the word of God was not then truly taught, nor the sacraments of Christ duly administered, as prescribed by the same word.

Being farther examined, touching his faith in the sacrament of the altar, he said, that, if he stood accused in that particular, he would answer as God had given him knowledge, which he should do at another opportunity.

John Cavill, likewise agreed in the chief particulars with his brethren ; but farther said, the cause of his absenting himself from the church was, that the minister there had advanced two doctrines, contrary to each other ; for, first, in a sermon he delivered when the queen came to the crown, he exhorted the people to believe the gospel, declaring it to be the truth ; and, if they believed it not, they would be damned; and that, secondly, in a future discourse, he declared that the New Testament was false in forty places, which contrariety gave him much disgust, and was among other things the cause of his absenting himself from church.

George Ambrose answered to the same effect, adding moreover, that after he had read the late bishop of Winchester's book, entitled, *De Vera Obedientia*, with bishop Bonner's preface thereunto annexed, both inveighing against the authority of the bishop of Rome, he esteemed their principles more lightly than he had done before.

Robert Drake was a minister of Thundersly, in Essex, to which living, he had been presented by lord Rich, in the reign of Edward VI, when he was ordained priest by Dr. Ridley, then bishop of London, according to the reformed English service for ordination.

On the accession of queen Mary to the throne of England, he was sent for by Gardner, bishop of Winchester, who demanded of him, whether he would conform, like a good subject, to the laws of the realm then in force. He answered, that he would abide by those laws that were agreeable to the law of God; upon which, he was immediately committed to prison.

William Tims was a deacon and curate of Hockley, in Essex, in the reign of Edward VI, but being deprived of his living, soon after the death of that monarch, he absconded, and privately preached in a neighbouring wood, whither many of his flock attended to hear the word of God.

In consequence of these proceedings, he was apprehended by one of the constables, and sent up to the bishop of London, by whom he was referred to Gardner, bishop of Winchester, and lord-chancellor, who committed him to the king's Bench prison.

A short time after his confinement, he (with the others before mentioned) was ordered to appear before the bishop of London, who questioned them in the usual manner, concerning their faith in the sacrament of the altar.

Tims answered, that the body of Christ was not in the sacrament of the altar, really and corporeally, after the words of consecration spoken by the priest; and that he had been a long time of that opinion, ever since it had pleased God, of his infinite mercy, to call him to the true knowledge of the gospel of his grace.

On the 28th of the month called March, 1556, these six persons were all brought into the consistory-court, in St. Paul's church, before the bishop of London, in order to be examined, for the last time; who assured them, that if they did not submit to the church of Rome, they should be condemned for heresy.

The bishop began his examination with Tims, whom he called the ringleader of the others. He told him, that he had taught them heresies, confirmed them in their erroneous opinions, and endeavoured, as far as in him lay, to render them as abominable as himself ; with many other accusations equally false and opprobrious.

He was then asked by the bishop, what he had to say in his own vindication, in order to prevent him from proceeding against him as his ordinary. To which, he replied as follows :

" My lord, I am astonished, that you should begin your charge with a falsehood ; you aver, that I am the ringleader of the company now brought before you, and have taught them principles contrary to the Romish church, since we have been in confinement ; but the injustice of this declaration will soon appear, if you will inquire of these my brethren, whether, when at liberty, and out of prison, they dissented not from popish principles as much as they do at present ; such inquiry, I presume, will render it evident, that they learned not their religion in prison.

" For my own part, I declare, I never knew them, till such time as I became their fellow-prisoner : how then could I be their ring-leader and teacher ? With respect to the charge alleged against me, a charge which you endeavour to aggravate to the highest degree, whatever opinion you maintain concerning me, I am well assured, I hold no other religion than what Christ preached, the apostles witnessed, the primitive church received, and of late the apostolical and evangelical preachers of this realm have faithfully taught, and for which you have cruelly caused them to be burnt, and now seek to treat us with the like inhuman severity. I acknowledge you to be my ordinary."

The bishop, finding it necessary to come to a point with him, demanded, if he would submit himself to the holy mother-church, promising, that if he did, he should be kindly received ; and threatening, at the same time, that if he did not, judgment should be pronounced against him as a heretic.

In answer to this, Tims told his lordship, he was well persuaded, that he was within the pale of the catholic church, whatever he might think ; and reminded him, that he had most solemnly abjured that very church to which he since professed such strenuous allegiance ; and that, contrary to his oath, he again admitted, in this realm, the authority of the pope, and was, therefore, perjured and and forsworn in the highest degree. He also recalled to his memory, that he had spoken with great force and perspicuity against the usurped power of the pope, though he afterwards sentenced persons to be burnt, because they would not acknowledge the pope to be the supreme head of the church.

To this, Bonner sternly demanded, what he had written against the church of Rome ?

Tims pertinently answered, " my lord, the late bishop of Winchester, wrote a very learned treatise, entitled, *De vera Obedientia*, which contains many solid arguments against the papal supremacy : to this book, you wrote a preface, strongly inveighing against the bishop of Rome, reproving his tyranny and usurpation, and shewing that his power was ill-founded, and contrary both to the will of God, and the real interest of mankind."

The bishop, struck with the poignancy of this reproof, evasively told him, that the bishop of Winchester wrote a book against the supremacy of the pope's holiness, and he wrote a preface to the same book, tending to the same purpose : but that the cause of the same arose not from their disregard to his holiness, but because it was then deemed treason by the laws of the realm to maintain the pope's authority in England.

He also observed, that at such time, it was dangerous to profess to favour the church of Rome, and, therefore, fear compelled them to comply with the prevailing opinions of the times : for if any person had conscientiously acknowledged the pope's authority in those days, he would have been put to death : but that since the queen's happy accession to the throne, they might boldly speak the dictates of their consciences ; and farther reminded him, that as my lord of Winchester was not ashamed to recant his errors at St. Paul's cross, and that he himself had done the same, every inferior clergyman should follow the example of his superiors.

3 E

Tims, still persisting in the vindication of his own conduct, and reprehension of that of the bishop, again replied, " my lord, that which you have written against the supremacy of the pope may be well proved from scripture to be true; that which you now do is contrary to the word of God, as I can sufficiently prove."

Bonner, after much further conversation, proceeded to form of law, causing his articles, with the respective answers to each, to be publicly read in court.

Tims acknowledged only two sacraments, Baptism and the Lord's Supper; commended the bishop of Winchester's book, *De vera Obedientia*, and the bishop of London's preface to the same. He declared, that the mass was blasphemy of Christ's passion and death; that Christ is not corporeally but spiritually present in the sacrament, and that as they used it, it was an abominable idol.

Bonner exhorted him to revoke his errors and heresies, conform to the church of Rome, and not abide so strenuously by the literal sense of the scripture, but use the interpretation of the fathers.

Our martyr frankly declared, he would not conform thereunto, notwithstanding the execrations denounced against him by the church of Rome, and demanded of the bishop what he had to support the doctrine of the real presence of Christ in the sacrament of the altar, but the bare letter of scripture?

On the bishop's replying, the authority of the holy catholic church, Tims informed him, that he had the popish church, for which he was perjured and forsworn, declaring that the see of Rome was the see of antichrist, and, therefore, he would never consent to yield obedience to the same.

The bishop, finding Tims so inflexible in his adherence to the faith, professed that every attempt to draw him from it was vain and fruitless, read his definitive sentence, and he was delivered over to the secular power.

Bonner then used the same measures with Drake as he had done with Tims; but Drake frankly declared, that he denied the church of Rome, with all the works thereof, even as he denied the devil, and all his works.

The bishop, perceiving all his exhortations fruitless, pronounced sentence of condemnation, and he was immediately delivered into the custody of the sheriffs.

After this, Thomas and Richard Spurg, George Ambrose, and John Cavill, were severally asked, if they would forsake their heresies, and return to the catholic church. They all refused consenting to the church of Rome ; but said, they were willing to adhere to the true catholic church, and continue in the same.

Bonner then read their several definitive sentences, after which, he committed them to the custody of the sheriffs of London, by whom they were conducted to Newgate.

On the 14th of the month called April, 1556, the day appointed for the execution, they were led to Smithfield, where they were all chained to the same stake, and burnt in one fire, patiently submitting themselves to the flames, and resigning their souls into the hands of that glorious Redeemer, for whose sake, they delivered their bodies to be burned.

Tims, during his imprisonment, wrote a great number of letters and epistles to his friends and brethren in the cause of Christ ; among which, we shall preserve the following :

A letter from William Tims, to his friends in Hockley.

" THE grace of God the Father, through the merits of his dear Son Jesus, our Lord and only Saviour, with the continual aid of his holy and mighty spirit, to the performance of his will, to our everlasting comfort be with you, my dear brethren, both now and evermore. Amen.

" My dearly beloved, I beseech God to reward the great goodness that you have shewed unto me, sevenfold into your bosoms ; and as you have always had a most godly love unto this word, even so I beseech him to give you grace to love your own souls, and then, I trust, you will flee from all those things that should displease our good and merciful God, and hate, and abhor all the company of those that would have you to worship God, any otherwise than is contained in his holy word. And beware of those masters of idolatry that is, these papistical priests. My dear brethren, for the tender mercy of God, remember well what I have said unto you, and also written, which I am now ready to seal with my blood. I praise God that ever I lived to see the day, and blessed be my good and merciful God, that ever he gave me a body to glorify his name. And, dear hearts, I do now write unto you for none other cause, but to put you in remembrance that I have not forgotten you, to the end that I would not have you forget me, but to remember well what I have simply, by word of mouth, and writing, taught you. Which, although it were not simply done, yet truly, as your own conscience beareth me record; and, therefore, in any case take good heed, that you do not that thing which your own conscience doth condemn. Therefore, come out of Sodom, and go to heaven-ward, with the servants and martyrs of God, lest you be partakers of the vengeance of God that is coming upon this wicked nation, from which the Lord God defend you, and send us a joyful meeting in the kingdom of heaven : unto which, God bring you all, Amen. Thus now, I take my leave of you for ever in this world, except I be burned amongst you, which thing is uncertain unto me as yet.

By me,
Your poorest and most
Unworthy brother in Christ,
W. TIMS."

Newgate, April 12.

The examinations and Martyrdoms of Joan Beach, widow, of Turnbridge ; and John Harpole, of the city of Rochester.

INFORMATION being laid against these two persons for heresy, they were apprehended, and, by the magistrates of the respective places where they lived, committed to prison. After being some time in confinement, they were separately examined before Maurice, bishop of Rochester, their diocessian.

Joan Beach was first taken before the bishop for examination, when the following articles were exhibited against her:

1. That living in the parish of Tunbridge, she belonged to the diocess of Rochester.

This she granted.

2. That all people who preach, teach, believe, or say otherwise, or contrary to their mother, the holy catholic church, are excommunicated persons and heretics.

This she acknowledged to be true, but added withal, that nevertheless, she believed not the holy catholic church to be her mother, but believed only the Father of Heaven, to be her Father.

3. That she had affirmed, and did affirm, maintain, and believe, contrary to the said mother church of Christ, that in the blessed sacrament of the altar, under form of bread and wine, there are not the very body and blood of our Saviour Christ in substance, but only a token and memorial thereof; and that the very body and blood of Christ are in Heaven, and not in the sacrament.

4. That Christ being in Heaven, could not be in the sacrament.

To this, she answered, that she had, and did verily believe, hold, and affirm, in the sacrament of the altar, under the forms of bread and wine, there were not the very blood of our Saviour in substance, but only a token and remembrance of his death to the faithful receiver, and that his body and substance are only in Heaven, and not in the sacrament.

5. That she had been, and then was, among the parishioners of Tunbridge, noted and strongly suspected of being a sacramentary and an heretic.

To this, she answered, that she did not know how she had been, or was reputed amongst the parishioners of Tunbridge, nor was their opinion of any avail to her immortal state.

The bishop finding her inflexible in the faith she professed, strongly urged her to preserve her life by renouncing her errors; which she peremptorily refusing, he pronounced sentence on her, and she was delivered over to the secular power.

John Harpole, being next examined before the same bishop, articles of a similar nature were exhibited against him, as his fellow sufferer, Joan Beach.

His answers to all of them were much to the same import with hers: upon which, the bishop pronounced sentence of death on him in the usual form.

These two faithful followers of Christ, were burnt together in one fire, in the city of Rochester, about the latter end of the month called April, 1556. They embraced each other at the stake, and cheerfully resigned their souls into the hands of their Redeemer; after repeatedly singing hallelujahs to the praise and glory of his name.

The persecution and sufferings of Christopher Lister, John Mace, John Spencer, Simon Joyn, Richard Nichols, and John Hammond; who were all burnt together at Colchester, in Essex, for professing the truth of the gospel.

THESE six persons being all apprehended on a charge of heresy, were brought before bishop Bonner, at his palace, at Fulham; where articles were exhibited against them of the same nature, and in the usual form, as those against others on the like occasion.

1. To the first article, namely, that there was one holy catholic church on earth, in which the religion and faith of Christ are truly professed, they all consented and agreed; but John Spencer added, that the church of Rome was no part of Christ's catholic church.

2. To the second, concerning the seven sacraments, they answered, that in the true catholic church of Christ, there are but two sacraments, baptism and the Lord's supper.

3. To the third, they unanimously agreed and confessed, they were baptized in the faith and belief of the catholic church, and that their godfathers and godmothers had promised and professsed for them, as contained in the article administered.

4. To the fourth article, concerning their continuance in the faith and profession in which they were baptized, they agreed, that they did so continue ; Nichols observed, that he had more plainly learned the truth of his profession, by the doctrine set forth in the days of king Edward VI, that thereupon he had built his faith, and would continue the same, by the grace of God, to his life's end.

5. Concerning swerving from the catholic faith, they declared, that they had not swerved, nor departed in the least from the faith of Christ.

They unanimously confessed, that they had disapproved of, and spoken against the sacrifice of the mass, and the sacrament of the altar, affirming, that they would not come to hear, nor be partakers thereof ; that they had believed, and then did believe, that they were set forth and used contrary to God's word and glory.

They granted also, that they had spoken against the usurped authority of the bishop of Rome, who was an oppressor of the holy church of Christ, and ought not to have any power in England.

6. Concerning their reconciliation to the unity of the church ; they said, that they never refused, nor did then refuse to be reconciled to the unity of Christ's catholic church ; but declared, they had, and then did, and would forever hereafter, refuse to come to the church of Rome, or to acknowledge the authority of the papal see ; but did utterly abhor the same for rejecting the book of God, the bible, and setting up the mass, with other ridiculous and antichristian ceremonies.

7. That disapproving the mass and sacrament of the altar, they had refused to come to the parish church, &c.

This they all granted, and Simon Joyn added moreover, that the cause wherefore he refused to be partaker of their trumpery, was, because the commandments of God were there broken, and Christ's ordinances changed, and the bishop of Rome's ordinance put up in their stead.

Christopher Lister affirmed, that in the sacrament of the altar, there is the substance of bread and wine, as well after the words of consecration as before, and that there are not in the same, the very body and blood of Christ, really, substantially, and spiritually, by faith in the faithful receiver, and that the mass is not a propitiatory sacrifice for the quick and dead, but mere idolatry and abomination.

They then said, that they were sent to Colchester prison, by the king and queen's commissioners, because they would not come to their parish churches : that what was contained in the premises was true ; and that they belonged to the diocess of London.

On the close of this examination, the bishop dismissed them, but ordered them to attend again in the afternoon. This order they obeyed, when the articles and answers of the first examination were read to them ; and they resolutely persisted in the profession they had made.

After various endeavous to bring them to recant, without the least effect, sentence of death was pronounced against them, and they were all delivered over to the secular power.

The writ for their execution being made out, they were removed to Colchester, where, on the 28th of the month called April, 1556, they were fastened to two stakes, and burnt in one fire. They all cheerfully met their fate, giving glory to God in the midst of the flames, and encouraging others, for the truth of the gospel, to follow their example.

The Martyrdoms of Hugh Laverock, an old decrepit man ; and John Apprice, a blind man.

THE former of these martyrs was by trade a painter, and lived in the parish of Barking, in Essex. At the time of his apprehension, he was in the 68th year of his age, and very helpless from the natural infirmities of life. Being, however, accused of heresy by some of the popish emissaries in his neighbourhood, he, with his fellow-sufferer, was taken before Bonner, to be examined with respect to their faith.

The bishop laid before them the same articles as mentioned in the former lives; and they returned answers to the same effect with other advocates for the truth of the gospel.

On the 9th of the month called May, 1556, they were both brought into the consistory-court at St. Paul's, where their articles and answers were publicly read; after which, the bishop endeavoured to persuade them to recant their opinions concerning the sacrament of the altar.

Hugh Laverock declared, that by the grace of God, he would stand to the profession he had already made, for he could not find the least authority in the word of God, for approving the doctrine of the corporeal presence in the sacrament.

The bishop then addressed himself to John Apprice, and demanded what he had to say in his defence? The honest blind man answered the haughty prelate, that the doctrine he set forth and taught was so conformable to the world, that it could not be agreeable to the scriptures of God; and that he was no member of the catholic church of Christ, seeing he made laws to kill men, and made the queen his executioner.

The first examination being over, they were, for the present, dismissed, but ordered to appear the next day at the bishop's palace, at Fulham. Being accordingly conducted there, the bishop, after some discourse with them, and finding them steadfast in their faith, pronounced the definitive sentence; when, being delivered over to the secular power, they were committed to Newgate.

On the 15th of the month called May, they were conveyed to Stratford-le-bow, the place appointed for their execution.

As soon as they arrived at the stake, Laverock threw away his crutch, and thus addressed his fellow-sufferer : "John Apprice, be of good comfort, brother ; for my lord of London is our good physician ; he will cure us both shortly, thee of thy blindness, and me of my lameness."

These two steadfast believers in Christ were both chained to one stake. They endured their sufferings with great fortitude, and cheerfully yielded up their lives, in testimony of the truth of their blessed Redeemer.

The sufferings and Martyrdoms of Catharine Hutt, Joan Hornes, and Elizabeth Thackvill.

THESE three pious women being apprehended on suspicion of heresy, were carried before sir John Mordaunt and Edmund Tyrrel, Esqrs. justices of the peace for the county of Essex, who sent them prisoners to the bishop of London, for not conforming to the order of the church, and not believing the real presence of Christ's body in the sacrament of the altar.

Being brought before the bishop, he exhibited to them the articles usual on the occasion ; to which, they answered as follows :

To the first, concerning their belief, that there was a Catholic church of Christ upon earth, they all assented.

To the second, relating to the seven sacraments, they said, they did not understand properly what they were.

To the third, concerning their baptism, they replied, they believed they were baptized, but knew not what their godfathers and godmothers promised for them.

To the fourth, about their continuance in the same faith, into which they were baptized, until they arrived at the age of fourteen years, or the age of discretion, without disapproving of the same ; they granted it to be true.

To this article, Catharine Hutt observed, that at that time, she did not understand what she professed.

Joan Hornes added, that in the days of king Edward VI, she learned the faith that was then set forth, and still continued in the same; and would, with God's assistance, continue the remainder of her life.

To the fifth article, concerning the mass, and the sacrament of the altar, they said, they could discern no excellence in the mass, nor could they believe but that Christ's natural body was in Heaven, and not in the sacrament of the altar.

Concerning the see of Rome, they acknowledged no supremacy in the same, nor would they adhere to it.

To the sixth article, on their reconciliation to the church of Rome, they refused to be reconciled to the same.

The seventh, on their disapproving the service of the church, and not frequenting their parish church, they acknowledged to be true.

Catharine Hutt alleged, as the cause of her absenting herself from church, that she neither approved the service in Latin, the mass, mattins, or even song; nor were the sacraments used and administered according to God's word. She declared moreover, that mass was an idol, neither were the body and blood of Christ in the sacrament of the altar, as they compelled persons to believe.

To the eighth article, they declared, that they were all sent up to the bishop of London, by sir John Mordaunt and Edmund Tyrrel, Esqrs. justices of the peace for the county of Essex, because they could not believe the presence of Christ's body in the sacrament of the altar, and for absenting themselves from their parish church.

To the ninth article, that they were of the diocess of London, they all assented, except Catherine Hutt, who said, she was of the parish of Bocking, in Essex, which is of the particular jurisdiction of Canterbury, and not under that of the diocess of London.

On the 13th of the month called April, they were again brought before the bishop: and the respective articles, with their answers, publicly read in court, in order to their final judgment.

Catharine Hutt, being first examined, was required to declare her opinion of the sacrament of the altar, and to return to the catholic faith. To this, she replied, that the sacrament, as enforced by the papists, was not truly God, but a dumb god, made with men's hands; upon which, she received sentence of death.

Joan Hornes was next examined, and being charged, that she did not believe the sacrament of Christ's body and blood, to be Christ himself, said, if you can make your god shed blood, or shew any sign of a true, living body, then will I believe you : but it is bread as to the substance, and that which you call heresy is the manner in which I trust to serve my God to the end of my life.

Concerning the bishop and see of Rome, I detest them as abominations, and desire ever to be delivered from the same.

In consequence of these answers, sentence of condemnation was immediately pronounced on her.

Elizabeth Thackvill continuing steadfast in her former confessions, and refusing to recant, shared the same fate with the other two ; when they were all delivered over to the secular power, and committed to Newgate.

On the 16th of the month called May, the day appointed for their execution, they were conducted to Smithfield, where being all fastened to one stake, and the fagots lighted, their bodies were soon consumed, after they had recommended their spirits into the hands of that God, for the truth of whose word, they joyfully suffered death, in hopes of obtaining life everlasting.

On the same day these three were executed in Smithfield, two others suffered at Gloucester, namely, Thomas Drowry, a blind boy ; and Thomas Croker, a bricklayer.

They both submitted to their fate with great fortitude and resignation, cheerfully yielding up their souls to him who gave them.

The examinations and sufferings of Thomas Spicer, John Denny, and Edmund Poole, all of the county of Suffolk.

THESE three persons were apprehended by the justices of the county in which they lived, and committed to prison, for not attending mass at their parish church.

After being sometime in confinement, they were brought before the chancellor of Norwich, and the register, who sat at the town of Beccles, to examine them with respect to their faith. The articles alleged against them were as follows :

1. That they believed not the pope of Rome to be the supreme head immediately under Christ, of the universal catholic church.

2. That they believed not holy bread and holy water, ashes, palms, and other like ceremonies, used in the church to be good and laudable for stirring up the people to devotion.

3. That they believed not after the words of consecration spoken by the priest, the very natural body of Christ, and no other substance of bread and wine, to be in the sacrament of the altar.

4. That they believed it to be idolatry to worship Christ in the sacrament of the altar.

5. That they took bread and wine in remembrance of Christ's passion.

6. That they would not follow the cross in procession, nor be confessed to a priest.

They all acknowledged the justness of these articles, in consequence of which, they were condemned by the chancellor, who first endeavoured to reclaim them from their opinions, and bring them over to the church of Rome ; but all his admonitions and exhortations proving ineffectual, he pronounced sentence on them, and they were immediately delivered into the hands of the high-sheriff for the county of Suffolk.

On the 21st of the month called May, 1556, these three pious christians were led to the stake in the town of Beccles, amidst a great number of lamenting spectators. As soon as they arrived at the place of execution, they devoutly prayed, and repeated the articles of their faith. When they came to that article concerning the holy catholic church, sir John Sillard, the high-sheriff, thus addressed them : " that is well said, sirs ; I am glad to hear you say, you believe the catholic church ; this is the best expression I ever heard from you yet."

To this, Pool answered, that though they believed the catholic church, yet they believed not in their popish church, which is no part of Christ's catholic church, and, therefore, no part of their belief.

When they arose from prayer, they went joyfully to the stake, and being chained to it, and the fagots lighted, they praised God with such cheerfulness in the midst of the flames, as astonished the numerous spectators.

Soon after they were fastened to the stake, several bigotted papists called to the executioner to throw fagots at them, in order to stop their mouths ; but our martyrs disregarding their malice, boldly cofessed the truth with their latest breath, dying, as they had lived, in certain hopes of a resurrection to life eternal.

The Martyrdoms of Thomas Harland, John Oswald, Thomas Abington, and Thomas Read, who were all burnt together at Lewes, in Sussex.

THE popish emissaries having laid informations, against these four persons, they were all apprehended on suspicion of heresy, and immediately sent to London, to be examined by Bonner, bishop of that diocess, relative to their faith.

Thomas Harland being first examined, the bishop objected to his conduct in not attending his parish church : to which, he answered, that since the mass was restored, he never chose to hear the same, because it was in Latin, which he did not understand, and, therefore, could not reap any benefit thereby.

John Oswald refused to answer any objection, till his accusers were brought face to face before him ; nevertheless, he declared, that he was not to be awed into any concessions by fear of fire and fagot ; but as the faithful ministers of the gospel of Christ, during the reign of king Edward VI, had suffered and gone before him, he was ready to suffer and follow after them, and would count it his glory and honour so to do.

The other two, Abington and Read, said, they abjured all popish superstitions and errors, and that they would ever hold fast to the faith, as it was the pure gospel of Christ.

The bishop finding them all resolute, and that they were determined to adhere to their religious opinions, after endeavouring to prevail on them to recant, passed sentence of condemnation on them, and they were immediately delivered over to the secular power.

After a long confinement in the king's bench prison, they were all sent down to Lewes, in Sussex, where, on the 16th of the month called June, 1556, they were burned together in one fire, praising God for enabling them to bear, with fortitude, the punishment allotted them for professing the truth of his most holy word.

On the 20th of the same month, two others suffered at the same place, namely, Thomas Wood, minister ; and Thomas Mills.

They both died with christian fortitude, rejoicing and praising God, that he had numbered them among those who freely gave up their miserable existence here, for the truth of the gospel, in hopes of obtaining an everlasting inheritance in the heavenly mansions.

The sufferings and Martyrdoms of Henry Wie, William Hollywell, Ralph Jackson, Laurence Pern, John Derifall, Thomas Bowyer, George Searls, Lyon Couch, Henry Adlinton, John Routh, Edmund Hurst, Elizabeth Peper, and Agnes George, who were all burnt together at Stratford-le-bow, near London.

THESE thirteen persons were apprehended in the different places, where they lived, the greater part of them being inhabitants of the county of Essex ; and were sent, at various times, up to London, to be examined by bishop Bonner, concerning thier religious principles.

On the 9th of the month called June, they were all brought together before Dr. Darbyshire, the bishops chancellor, who, in form of law, administered to them the following articles :

1. That there is on earth a catholic church, wherein the religion of Christ is truly professed.

To this, they all answered in the affirmative ; but added, that they believed the true faith of Christ was, wherever the word of God was truly preached.

2. That there were seven sacraments.

They all answered in the negative ; some affirmed, that in the church of Christ, there were only two sacraments, viz. baptism, and the Lord's supper ; others desired to believe as the scriptures taught them ; and others refused to reply, not properly understanding these points.

3. That they were baptized in the faith of the catholic church, professing, by their godfathers, &c. the religion of Christ, and to renounce the devil and all his works, &c.

To this, they all assented without exception.

4. That when they came to years of discretion, they did not depart from the said profession and faith, and did not disapprove any part thereof for several years.

The greater part of them answered in the affirmative. One of the women added, that in the days of king Edward VI, she departed from her old faith and religion, and embraced the gospel of Christ, as it was then taught and set forth.

5. That of late, they had swerved from their former catholic faith, and had spoken against the mass, the sacrament of the altar, and authority of the papal see.

This, upon the whole, they confessed to be true.

One of them said, the mass was of such a nature, that he could not, in his own conscience, believe it to be authorized from God. Another observed, that for nine or ten years past, he could not approve the mass, nor the sacrament of the altar, because they could not be proved from the scripture of truth ; declaring, at the same time, that at the age of fourteen, he had taken an oath against the authority of the papal see, and would, by the **grace of God, abide** firmly by the same.

6. That they refused to be reconciled to the unity of the church, or to confess the lawfulness of the papal see.

To this article, they all, except two, answered in the affirmative. Those who refused, said, they did not understand the import of the same. The two women added, they refused to be reconciled to the faith and religion that were then used in the realm of England, though they never refused to be reconciled and brought to the unity of the catholic church of Christ.

7. That disapproving the service of the church, they refused to come to their parish churches, denied the bodily presence of Christ in the sacrament, called the mass an abomination, &c.

This was answered, in general, in the affirmative ; but one denied, that he called the mass an abomination, or an idol : another, though he granted the article, confessed his infirmity, that he went to his parish church, and received it before he was put into prison.

8. This article related to their being brought before the commissioners, and by them sent to the bishop of London ; to which, they answered in the following order :

Edmund Hurst, Ralph Jackson, and George Searls, answered in the affirmative.

Henry Wie said, that he was brought before several justices of the peace, in Essex, concerning one Highted, his late master, and thereupon committed to Colchester castle, and from thence, sent to London, to the bishop, for farther examination.

William Hollywell made the like confession, excepting the circumstance of Highted.

John Derifall said, he was called before lord Rich, and Midmay of Chelmsford ; and by them sent to the bishop of London to be farther examined.

Thomas Bowyer, said, he was brought before one Wiseman, of Falstead; and by him sent to Colchester castle; and from thence, to the bishop of London, to be further examined.

3 G

Lyon Couch said, that he was three times brought before the king and queen's commissioners, and by them sent to the bishop of London.

Henry Adlinton said, that coming to Newgate to speak with one Gratwick, prisoner there for the testimony of Jesus Christ, he was apprehended and brought before Dr. Story, and by him sent to the bishop of London.

Agnes George said, that she was committed to prison in Colchester by Maynard, an alderman of the town, for refusing to go to church, and by him sent to the bishop of London.

Elizabeth Peper said, that she was apprehended by two constables and an alderman, for refusing to come to church, and by them sent to the bishop of London to be farther examined.

9. That they believed the premises to be true, as confessed above, and that they were of the diocess of London.

This was generally agreed to. Elizabeth Peper added, she was of the town of Colchester; and Agnes George said, she was of the parish of Barefold.

These thirteen persons being thus examined by the bishop of London's chancellor, in open court, persisting in their answers, and refusing to recant, or be reconciled to the church of Rome, had sentence of condemnation pronounced against them; and being delivered over to the secular power, were all sent to Newgate.

Three others were also condemned to die at the same time : but, before the day appointed for their execution, a reprieve was sent them by cardinal Poole.

Soon after the condemnation of these pious christians, Dr. Fecknam, dean of St. Paul's, told the audience, in his sermon, that they held as many tenets as there were faces among the whole ; which being represented to them, they drew up the following confession of their faith, to which, they respectively subscribed their names :

1. " There are but two sacraments in Christ's church, that is, the sacrament of Baptism, and the Lord's Supper. For, in these is contained the faith of Christ's church ;

that is, the two testaments, the law and the gospel. The effect of the law is repentance, and the effect of the gospel, remission of sins.

2. " We believe there is a visible church, wherein the word of God is preached, and the holy sacrament truly administered, visible to the world, although it be not credited, and by the death of saints confirmed, as it was in the time of Elias the prophet, as well as now.

3. " The see of Rome is the see of antichrist, the congregation of the wicked &c. whereof the pope is head under the devil.

4. " The mass is not only a profanation of the Lord's Supper, but also a blasphemous idol.

5. " God is neither spiritually nor corporeally in the sacrament of the altar, and there remaineth no substance in the same, but only the substance of bread and wine.

"For these, the articles of our belief, we being condemned to die, do willingly offer our corruptible bodies to be dissolved in the fire, all with one voice assenting and consenting thereunto, and, in no point, dissenting or disagreeing from any of our former articles."

Early in the morning of the 28th of the month called June, 1556, being the day appointed for their execution, they were conducted from Newgate to Stratford-le-bow, the place allotted for them to confirm that faith they had professed, and to which they had so strenuously adhered.

On their arrival at the destined place, the sheriff made use of a stratagem to bring them over to the Romish faith. He divided them into two companies, and placed them in separate apartments. This done, he visited one company, and told them the other had recanted, by which, their lives would be saved ; and exhorted them to follow their example, and not cast themselves away by their own mere obstinacy.

But this scheme failed in its effect ; for they told the sheriff, that their faith was not built on man, but on Christ crucified.

The sheriff, finding his project fail with the first party to whom he applied, had recourse to the same with the others, admonishing them to recant like wise men, and not be guilty of destroying themselves by their own bigotry and prejudice.

But they answered to the same effect as their brethren had done before, assuring the sheriff, that their faith was not built on man, but on Christ, and his infallible word.

They were then brought from their different apartments, and all led together to the place of execution, where they embraced each other ; and, after praying in the most fervent manner, prepared themselves for their fate.

These thirteen steadfast believers in Christ were chained to different stakes, but all burnt together in one fire, shewing such love to each other, firm faith in their Saviour and Redeemer, Jesus Christ, that the concourse of spectators, assembled on the occasion, were astonished at the undaunted behaviour of so many poor innocents, thus patiently enduring the acutest torments, rather than comply with the errors and superstitions of the church of Rome.

The sufferings and Martyrdoms of Robert Bernard, Adam Foster, and Robert Lawson, who were burnt at St. Edmund's Bury, in Suffolk.

THE first of these martyrs was a poor labourer, and lived in the parish of Frasden, in the county of Suffolk. Being apprehended by the constable of the parish for not going to church, he was brought before Dr. Hopton, bishop of Norwich, who inquired of him, whether he had been with a priest at Easter to confess, or whether he had received the sacrament of the altar.

To these questions, Bernard frankly replied, " No, I have not been with the priest, nor confessed myself unto him ; but I have confessed my sins unto Almighty God, and, I trust, he hath forgiven me ; wherefore, I need not go to the priest for such matters, as he cannot forgive his own sins."

The bishop, after using various arguments to go to confession without effect, pronounced him a heretic ; on which, Bernard said, " my lord, it grieveth me not one whit to be called a heretic by you, for so your forefathers called the prophets and apostles of Christ long before this time."

Incensed at this abrupt reply, the bishop arose, and bade Bernard follow him. He then went to the sacrament of the altar, to which he kneeled and prayed, and severely reproved Bernard for not doing the same : but our martyr told him, he knew no authority for such behaviour in the word of God.

The bishop then addressing him, pointed to the pix over the altar, in which the wafer or host is kept, and said, " why, lewd fellow, whom seest thou yonder ?" " nobody, my lord," replied Bernard. " Seest thou not thy Maker, varlet ?" demanded the prelate. " My maker!" returned the countryman; " no, I see nothing but a few clouts hanging together in a heap."

This answer so irritated the bishop, that he commanded the gaoler to take him away, and lay irons enough on him, declaring that he would reduce him to subjection before he had done with him.

The next day, he was again brought before the bishop, who asked him, if he retained the same opinions as he professed yesterday. To which, Bernard replied, "yes my lord, I remember myself well, for I am the same man to day that I was yesterday, and hope I shall remain steadfast to the end of my life in the principles I have professed."

One of his lordship's attendants being desirous of examining Bernard himself, advised the bishop to avoid giving himself any further trouble, by committing his examination to him. Having obtained permission so to do, he took Bernard to an inn, where several popish emissaries were assembled. They first used many fair words, and alluring promises, to persuade him to abjure what they called his heretical opinions. This, however, not taking effect, they threatened him with whipping, the stocks, and burning; but all to no purpose. He told them,

" friends, I am not better than my master, Christ, and
the prophets, whom your forefathers served after this
sort ; and I, for his sake, am content to suffer the like at
your hands, if God should so permit, trusting that he will
strengthen me in the same, according to his promise, and
and that of his ministers."

After this declaration, they took him back to the bishop, who, according to the usual form of proceeding in
the court, condemned him as a heretic, and he was delivered over to the secular power.

Adam Foster lived in the parish of Mendlesham, in the
county of Suffolk.   He was apprehended in his own
house by two constables, at the command of a neighbouring justice, for absenting himself from mass, and
not receiving the sacrament at Easter.   Being taken before the bishop of Norwich, who examined him concerning his religious principles, and finding him steadfast in
his faith, according to the doctrines set forth in the days
of king Edward VI, he condemned him as a heretic, and
he was delivered to the secular power.

Robert Lawson, by trade a linen-draper, was apprehended on the same account as the two former ; and being brought before sir John Tyrrel, he committed him to
the prison of Eye, in Suffolk.   After laying there a short
time, he was conducted to the bishop of Norwich for examination, when holding fast to the principles he had
professed, and withstanding every effort made use of by
the bishop to bring him to recant, he was deemed a
heretic, received sentence of death, and was delivered
into the hands of the sheriff, in order for execution.

On the 30th of the month called June, 1556, these three
soldiers of Christ were conducted to St. Edmund's Bury,
in Suffolk, where being all fastened to one stake, they
made a most triumphant exit, and died in full assurance
of happiness hereafter, giving glory to that God who had
enabled them to undergo their sufferings for his name's
sake.

About the same time these three suffered, there was
one John Fortune, a blacksmith, of the parish of Mendlesham, in Suffolk, who was several times examined

by the bishop of Norwich, and others, about the mass, the sacrament of the altar, and other points of the Romish religion, which he refuted by texts quoted from scripture. His sentence of condemnation is recorded in the bishop's register; but whether it was ever carried into execution, we are not informed.

The persecutions and sufferings of Julius Palmer, fellow of Magdalen-College, Oxford; John Gwin, and Thomas Askine, who suffered Martyrdom at Newbury, in Berkshire.

JULIUS PALMER was the son of a respectable merchant, and born in the city of Coventry, in the county of Warwick. He received his first education at the free school of that place; after which, he was sent to Oxford, where, in process of time, he obtained a fellowship in Magdalen college, in that university.

As he was brought up a zealous papist, he refused to conform to the service of the church, as practised in the time of king Edward VI, for which, he was expelled the college; and, for some time, he kept a school in the city of Oxford.

On the accession of queen Mary, the visitors went to Magdalen college, to displace such us refused to be of the popish religion. Palmer availed himself of this opportunity; and, by close application himself, joined to the interest of his friends, he was reinstated in his fellowship.

During the time of his expulsion from the college, he used frequently to converse with some of his acquaintance who were protestants; and, being by them advised to study the scriptures, he began to entertain doubts concerning the truth of several Romish doctrines, and would often ask questions on that subject.

His sincere attachment to the principles he professed, (though opposite in their nature at different periods,) was the cause of his expulsion in the days of king Edward VI, and his troubles in the reign of queen Mary; for, had he been a dissembler, he might have retained his fellowship under the reign of the former, and escaped death under that of the latter.

When the persecution raged in the beginning of the reign of queen Mary, he inquired, very particularly, into the cause of persons being apprehended, the nature of the articles upon which they were condemned, the manner of their treatment, and their behaviour at the time of their suffering. Nay, so desirous was he of knowing this, that he sent over one of his pupils from Oxford to Gloucester, to see the whole form of bishop Hooper's execution, and bring him a minute account of the bloody transaction.

Before he had imbibed well grounded notions of the gospel of Christ, and the pure uncorrupted worship of God, he was inclined to think, that very few would undergo the fiery trial for the sake of their profession; but, when experience proved to him the cruelties which the papists inflicted, and the protestants endured; when he had been present at the examination of bishops Ridley and Latimer, and had seen them burnt at Oxford, as well as been an eye-witness to their faith, patience, and fortitude, these scenes converted him absolutely from popery; and, on his return from the execution, he was heard to utter these expressions amongst his friends; " O raging cruelty! O barbarous tyranny!"

From that very day, he applied himself most assiduously to learn the truth of God's word; and, to that end, borrowed Peter Martyr's commentary on the Corinthians, and read many other well-written treatises on religion, till, at length, he became as zealous an asserter of the protestant cause, as he before had been an obstinate opposer of it.

He now began to form excuses and pretences for absenting himself from mass, and other popish services and ceremonies; but, finding that his absence on these occasions, incurred the suspicions of many, and disapprobation of the president of the college, to avoid expulsion, which might be attended with danger, and to preserve his conscience inviolate, he resigned his fellowship.

On his leaving the college, his friends procured him the place of teacher to the grammar school at Reading, in Berkshire, where he was received by those who loved the gospel of Christ, both on account of his eminent learning, and his zealous adherence to the truth.

In process of time, some hypocritical professors of the reformed religion, insinuated themselves into his confidence, with a design to learn his religious principles.—Their disingenuous stratagem succeeded to their wishes; for, as he was a man of an open, unreserved temper, he freely declared his sentiments, which those snakes reported to his enemies, who thereupon caused his library to be searched for heretical books; and finding some of his writings, both in Latin and English, that inveighed against popish cruelty, they threatened to lay this discovery before the queen's commissioners, unless he would quietly resign his school to a friend of theirs, and depart.

Palmer, fearful of death, complied with their unjust proposal, and departed from Reading, leaving behind him all his goods, with a quarter's salary that was due to him.

Being thus destitute of a livelihood, he went to Evesham, in Worcestershire, where his mother lived, in order to obtain from her a legacy, which his father had bequeathed him four years before.

As soon as he saw his mother, he implored her blessing on his bended knees; but, she having been informed, by his brother, of the cause of his resignation, and the business of his visit, hastily exclaimed, "thou shalt have Christ's curse and mine, whithersoever thou goest."

Julius, at first, stood amazed at so unexpected and heavy a curse from his own mother; but, after he had recollected himself a little, he said, " O mother, your own curse you may give me, which God knoweth I never deserved; but God's curse you cannot give me, for he hath already blessed me."

His bigotted mother said, "thou wentest from God's blessing, when thou wast banished for an heretic from thy fellowship at Oxford, and, for the like knavery, hast thou been expelled from Reading too."

3 H

"Alas! mother, returned Julius, my case has been misrepresented to you, for I was not expelled from the college at Oxford, but freely I resigned my fellowship there. Heretic I am none, for I oppose not the true doctrine of Christ, but defend it to my utmost power."

His mother then vehemently declared, that he believed not as his father and forefathers had done, but according to the new doctrine, taught and set forth in the days of king Edward VI, which is damnable heresy.

In answer to this, he confessed, he believed the doctrine that was publicly set forth in the reign of king Edward VI. He also affirmed it to be truth, and that, instead of being new, it was as old as Christ and his apostles.

The mother, incensed at this frank declaration of his principles, ordered him to depart the house, nor ever more esteem her as his mother, informing him, at the same time, that he had no property there, either in money or goods, as his father bequeathed nothing to heretics.

Our martyr, as became a true follower of the blessed Jesus, when he was reviled, reviled not again, but committed his cause to him, who judgeth righteously. On leaving his bigotted mother, he thus addressed her : "mother, you have cursed me, I beseech God to bless you, and prosper your undertakings as long as you live."

This pathetic address, attended with flowing tears, in some degree, moved her compassion ; and, on his leaving the room, she threw a piece of gold after him, saying, "keep that to make thee a true man."

Palmer being thus repulsed by his mother, on whom he relied as his only friend, as well as disregarded by his brother, was destitute of all help, and knew not what steps to take in order to obtain subsistence.

At length, he thought of returning privately to Magdalen college, depending on the confidence of a few friends he had in that house. He accordingly went thither ; and, through the interest of Allen Cope, a fellow of the same, he obtained a recommendation to a school in Gloucestershire.

He had not proceeded far on his journey to that place, before he altered his resolution, and determined to go privately to Reading, to try if he could obtain his salary that was due, and, at the same time, dispose of the goods he had left there.

No sooner had he arrived at Reading, than his old enemies got knowledge of it, and consulted in what manner they should proceed against him.

In a short time, it was concluded amongst them, that one Hampton, who had formerly professed himself a protestant, (but was, in reality, a time-server) should visit under colour of friendship, to learn the cause of his return.

Hampton traitorously went, when Palmer, with his usual sincerity, and openness of soul, disclosed the whole design, which the other immediately related to the confederates, who caused him to be apprehended that very night, by the officers appointed for the purpose, requiring him, in the queen's name, quietly to surrender himself.

Palmer was then carried to prison, where he remained ten days in the custody of an unmerciful keeper; at the expiration of which time, he was brought before the mayor of Reading, and charged with the following crimes:

1. That he said, the queen's sword was not put into her hand to execute tyranny, and to kill and murder the true servants of God.

2. That her sword was too blunt towards the papists, but too sharp towards the true christians.

3. That certain servants of sir Francis Knowles, and others, resorting to his lectures, fell out among them, and had almost committed murder; therefore, he was a sower of sedition, and a procurer of unlawful assemblies.

4. That his landlady had written a letter to him, which they had intercepted, wherein she requested him to return to Reading, and sent her commendations by token, that the knife lay hid under the beam, whereby they inferred, that she had conspired with him against her husband.

5. That they once found him alone with his said landlady, by the fireside, the door being shut, thereby suspecting him of incontinency with her.

Three men, who were suborned for the purpose by, one of the confederates, swore these things against him before the mayor, who thereupon sent him to the cage, to be an open spectacle of contempt to the people.

The same villain also spread a report, that he was thus punished for the most enormous crimes and misdemeanors, which had been fully proved against him.

After he had been thus unjustly exposed to public shame, the mayor sent for him to answer for himself, concerning what was laid to his charge.

He fully overthrew all the evidence, by proving the letter said to have been written to him by his landlady, to be of their own forging ; and, in the most incontestable manner acquitted himself of all the other crimes laid to his charge.   The mayor was confounded, to think he should have given such credit to his persecutors ; and though he did not choose to discharge him immediately, yet he thought of doing it as soon as a convenient opportunity should offer.

While Palmer was in prison, he was visited by one John Galant, a true professor of the gospel, who said to him, " O Palmer ! thou hast deceived many men's expectations; for, we hear that you suffer not for righteousness' sake, but for thy own demerits."

Palmer replied, " O brother Galant, these be the old practices of that fanatical brood : but, be you well assured, and God be praised for it, I have so purged myself and detected their falsehood, that, from henceforth, I shall be no more molested therewith."

When his enemies found, they had miscarried in their plot against him, they determined to accuse him of heresy. This was accordingly done, in consequence of which, he was taken before the mayor, and Bird, the bishop of Salisbury's official, in order to give an account of his faith, and to answer to such information as might be laid against him.

In the course of his examination, they gathered from him sufficient grounds to proceed against him.   Articles were accordingly drawn up, and sent to Dr. Jeffrey, at Newbery, who was to hold his visitation there on the Thursday following.

The next day, Palmer was conducted to Newbery, together with one Thomas Askine, who had been for some time imprisoned on account of his religion. Immediately on their arrival, they were committed to the Blind-house prison, where they found one John Gwin, who was confined there for no other reason but professing the truth of the gospel.

On the 10th of the month called July, 1556, a place being prepared in the parish church of Newbery, to hold the consistory-court, Dr. Jeffrey, representative of the bishop of Sarum, Sir Richard Abridge, John Winchom, Esq. and the minister of Inglefield, repaired thither, as commissioners appointed for the purpose.

After the prisoners were produced, the commission read, and other things passed, according to the usual form, Dr. Jeffrey, in the presence of several hundred spectators, called to Palmer, and asked, if he was the writer of a two-penny pamphlet that had been lately published ?

Having some altercation about this affair, in which, Palmer answered in his own behalf with great force and propriety, the doctor rising from his seat, said to him, " Mr. Palmer, we have received certain writings and articles against you from the right worshipful the mayor of Reading, and other justices, whereby we understand, that being brought before them, you were convicted of certain heresies.

1. " That you deny the supremacy of the pope's holiness.

2. " That you affirm there are but two sacraments.

3. " You say, that the priest sheweth up an idol, at mass, and, therefore, you went to no mass since your first coming to Reading.

4. " You hold there is no purgatory.

5. " You are charged with sowing sedition, and seeking to divide the unity of the queen's subjects."

Several books and pamphlets were then produced ; and Palmer being asked, if he was the author of them, replied in the affirmative, declaring at the same time, that they contained nothing but what was founded on the word of God.

Jeffrey then reviled him, declaring that such opinions were dictated by no good spirit, and that he was very wicked in slandering the dead, and railing at a catholic and learned man living.

Palmer replied, if it be a slander, he slandered himself, for I do but report his own writings, and expose absurdities therein contained ; and I esteem it not railing to inveigh against Annas and Caiaphas, being dead.

The doctor, incensed at this reply, assured him, that he would take such measures, as should compel him to recant his damnable errors and heresies ; but Palmer told him, that although of himself he could do nothing, yet if he, and all his enemies, both bodily and ghostly, should exert their efforts, they would not be able to effect what they desired, neither could they prevail against the mighty powers of divine grace, by which, he understood the truth, and was determined to speak it boldly.

After much farther discourse, the minister of Inglefield pointed to the pix over the altar, saying to Palmer, " what seest thou there?" To which, he replied, " a canopy of silk, embroidered with gold."

" But what is within ?" demanded the priest. " A piece of bread in a cloth," replied our martyr.

The priest then upbraided him as a vile heretic, and asked him, if he did not believe that those who receive the holy sacrament of the altar, do truly eat Christ's natural body.

He answered, " if the sacrament of the Lord's Supper be administered as Christ did ordain it, the faithful receivers do, indeed, spiritually and truly eat and drink in it Christ's body and blood.

On being asked, if he meant with the holy mother-church, really, carnally, and substantially ? He declared, " he could not believe so absurd and monstrous a doctrine."

After this, the court was adjourned, when one of the justices took Palmer aside, and, in the presence of several persons, exhorted him to revoke his opinions, and thereby preserve his life ; promising him, at the same time, if he would conform to the church, to take him into his family as his chaplain, and give him a handsome salary, or, if he chose not to resume the clerical function, to procure him an advantageous farm.

Palmer heartily thanked him for his kind offer, but assured him, that he had already renounced his living in two places, for the sake of Christ and his gospel, and was ready to yield up his life in defence of the same, if God, in his providence, should think fit to call him to it.

When the justice found he could, by no means, bring him to a recantation, he said, " well Palmer, I perceive that one of us two must be damned ; for we are of two faiths, and there is but one faith that leads to life and salvation."

Palmer observed, on the occasion, that it was possible they might both be saved, for that as it had pleased a merciful God to call him at the third hour of the day, that is, in the prime of life, at the age of twenty-four years, so he trusted, that in his infinite goodness, he would graciously call him at the eleventh hour of his old age, and give him an eternal inheritance among the saints in light.

After much conversation had passed, and many efforts were tried in vain, Palmer was remanded to prison ; but the other men, John Gwin, and Thomas Askine, were brought into the consistory-court, received their definitive sentence, and were delivered over to the secular power, to be burned as heretics.

Though the particular examinations and answers of these two martyrs are not recorded, there is no doubt, but they were of the same faith, and equally steadfast in it, as their fellow-sufferer Palmer ; but they were very illiterate, from whence, it is supposed, their examination was short, they not having a capability of making any defence.

The next morning, the commissioners required Julius Palmer to subscribe to certain articles which they had gathered from his answers, (with the addition of those odious epithets and terms, horrid, heretical, damnable, and execrable doctrines) which, when he had read, he refused to subscribe, affirming, that the doctrines which he held

and professed, were not such, but agreeable to, and founded on the word of God.

Jeffrey, being now greatly incensed, Palmer consented
to subscribe, provided they would strike out those odious
epithets; upon which, they gave him a pen, and bade
him do as he pleased, when he made such alterations as
he thought proper, and then subscribed.

Having thus set his hand to the articles which they had
drawn up, they asked him, if he would recant; but he peremptorily refusing, they pronounced sentence against him,
and he was delivered over to the secular power.

While he was in prison, he gave great comfort to his
two fellow-sufferers, and strongly exhorted them to hold
fast to the faith they had professed. On the morning
of their execution, about an hour before they were led
to the stake, he addressed them in words to the following
effect:

"Brethren, be of good cheer in the Lord, and faint not;
remember the words of our Saviour Christ, who saith,
'happy are ye, when men shall revile and persecute you for
my sake: rejoice, and be exceeding glad, for great is your
reward in heaven.' Fear not them that kill the body, but
are not able to hurt the soul; God is faithful, and will not
suffer us to be tempted above what we are able to bear.
We shall end our lives in the fire, but exchange them for
a better life: yea, for coals, we shall receive pearls; for
God's spirit certifieth our spirit, that he hath prepared
for us blissful mansions in heaven for his sake, who suffered for us."

These words not only strengthened and confirmed the
resolution of his two weak brethren, but drew tears from
many of the multitude.

When they were brought by the high-sheriff and constables of the town to the sand-pits, (the place appointed
for their execution) they fell on the ground; and Palmer,
with an audible voice, repeated the 31st psalm; but the
other two made their prayers secretly to Almighty God.

When Palmer arose from prayer, there came behind
him two popish priests, exhorting him to recant and save
his soul.

Our martyr exclaimed, " away, away, and tempt me no longer! Away! I say from me, all ye that work iniquity, for the Lord hath heard the voice of my tears."

When they were chained to the stake, Palmer thus addressed the spectators: " good people, pray for us, that we may persevere to the end, and, for Christ's sake, beware of popish teachers, for they deceive you."

As he spoke this, one of the attendants threw a fagot at him, which striking him on the face, caused the blood to to gush from three several places ; but this cruel behaviour escaped not the notice or resentment of the sheriffs, who not only upbraided his cruelty, but manfully retaliated the injury on the man, who had thus insulted suffering innocence.

When the fire was kindled, and began to reach their bodies, they lifted up their hands towards heaven, and cheerfully, as though they felt not much pain, said, " Lord Jesus, strengthen us! Lord Jesus, assist us! Lord Jesus, receive our souls!" and thus, they continued without any struggling, till they ended their mortal lives, and exchanged a scene of exquisite pain, for an everlasting habitation in the heavenly mansions.

About the same time the above three persons suffered at Newbery, three women were burnt in the island of Guernsey, whose names were, Catharine Cawches, the mother ; Guillemine Gilbert, and Perotine Massey, her daughters.

Their execution was attended with distinguished marks of cruelty, but they bore all with a fortitude that evinced their steadfast faith in him who died for all mankind. They were fastened to different stakes, the mother being placed in the middle, the elder daughter on her right hand, and the younger on the left. They were first ordered to be strangled, but the fagots being immediately lighted, the ropes with which they were fastened, gave way before they were deprived of life. Perotine, the elder daughter, being pregnant, the intense heat of the devouring flames occasioned her womb to burst, and, from within her body, was forced the innocent babe alive. It was a fine male infant, and being by a spectator of this scarce to be paralleled

3 t

scene, snatched from the fire, and laid on the grass, it was, as soon as the bailiffs, &c. came to the knowledge of the fact, most inhumanly ordered to be cast into the flames, where, with its hapless mother, it miserably perished, being, as it may not be improperly termed, baptized in its innocent blood, born and dying a martyr. Such was the Herodian cruelty of these persecuting times, when reason was influenced by bigotry, and humanity sacrificed to erroneous conceptions!

In the same month that these suffered, two men and a woman were burnt at Greenstead, in Sussex, and one man in the town of Leicester. The names of the three former were, Thomas Dungate, John Foreman, and Mary Tree. And that of the latter, Thomas Moor.

They all bore their sufferings with great fortitude, and cheerfully resigned their souls into the hands of that God who gave them, as a testimony of their faith in the truth of his most holy gospel.

The examination, condemnation, and martyrdom of Joan Waste, a poor blind woman, who was burnt in the town of Derby.

THIS poor woman, during the time of king Edward VI, used to frequent the church to hear divine service in the vulgar tongue, together with homilies and sermons, by which means, she became confirmed and established in the principles of the reformed religion.

Having purchased a New Testament in English, she applied to an old man, whom she paid for reading such passages as she directed him; by which means, she became so well versed in the holy scriptures, that she could repeat entire chapters by heart; and, by citing proper texts of scripture, would reprove the errors in religion, as well as the vicious customs and practices that prevailed in those days.

Thus, did this pious woman increase in the knowledge of God's word, leading a life of exemplary godliness, without molestation, or any kind of interruption, during the reign of king Edward.

But, on his demise, and the introduction of popery, with the accession of queen Mary, because she continued steadfast in the profession of that faith she had embraced from the knowledge of the divine word, and refused to communicate with those who maintained contrary doctrines, she was brought before Dr. Ralph Bayn, bishop of Litchfield and Coventry, and Dr. Draycott, the chancellor, as one suspected of heresies, and by them committed to Derby prison.

She was divers times privately examined by Peter Finch, the bishop's official; and afterwards brought to public examination before the bishop, his chancellor, and several more of the queen's commissioners; when the following articles were alleged against her.

1. That she held the sacrament of the altar to be only a memorial, or representation of Christ's body, and material bread and wine; and that it ought not to be reserved from time to time, but immediately received.

2. That she held, that in receiving the sacrament of the altar, she did not receive the same body that was born of the virgin Mary, and suffered on the cross for the redemption of mankind.

3. That she held, that Christ, at his last supper, did not only bless the bread which he had then in his hands, but was blessed himself; and that, by virtue of the words of consecration, the substance of the bread and wine was not converted, nor turned into the substance of the body and blood of Christ.

4. That she granted, she was of the parish of Allhallows, in Derby, and that all and singular the premises are true.

To these respective articles, she answered, that she believed just as much as the holy scriptures taught her, and according to what she had heard preached by many pious and learned men; some of whom suffered imprisonment, and others death, for the same doctrine.

Among others, she mentioned Dr. Taylor, and asked, if they would follow his example in testimony of their doctrine? Which, unless they were willing to do, she desired for God's sake, they would not trouble her, (being a poor, blind, and illiterate woman) declaring at the same time, she was ready to yield up her life in defence of that faith she had publicly professed.

The bishop and his chancellor, urged many arguments in proof of the doctrine of the real presence in the sacrament of the altar, demanding why Christ was not as able to make the bread his body, as to turn water into wine, to raise Lazarus from the dead, and the like, threatening her, at the same time, with imprisonment, torments, and death.

The poor woman, terrified at these threatenings, told the bishop, if he would, before that company, take it upon his conscience, that the doctrine which he would have her to believe, concerning the sacrament, was true ; and that he would, at the awful tribunal of God, answer for her therein, (as Dr. Taylor, in several sermons, had offered) she would then further answer them.

The bishop, declaring that he would, the chancellor said to him, " my lord, you know not what you do ; you may, in no case, answer for a heretic."

The bishop, struck by this interposition of the chancellor, demanded of the woman, whether she would recant or not, and told her, she should answer for herself.

This honest christian finding, at length, they designed but to prevaricate, told his lordship, that if he refused to take upon himself to answer to the truth of what they required her to believe, she would answer no farther, but desired them to do their pleasure.

In consequence of this, sentence of death was pronounced against her, and she was delivered to the sheriff, who immediately conducted her to the prison of Derby.

On the first of the month called August, 1556, the day appointed for her execution, she was led to the stake. Immediately on her arrival at the fatal spot, she kneeled down, and, in the most fervent manner, repeated several prayers she had been accustomed to use, and desired the spectators to pray also for her departing soul. Having finished her prayers, she arose, and was fastened to the stake; when, the fagots being lighted, she called on the Lord to have mercy upon her, and continued so to do, till the flames deprived her both of speech and life. And thus, did this poor woman quit this mortal stage, to obtain a life of immortality, the sure and certain reward of all those who suffered for the sake of the true gospel of their blessed Redeemer.

On the 8th of the month called September, one Edward Sharp was burnt at Bristol; and, on the 25th of the same month, a young man, by trade a carpenter, suffered at the same place.

The day preceding the last martyrdom, John Hart, a shoe-maker, and Thomas Ravendale, a currier, were burnt at Mayfield, in Sussex; and, on the 27th of the same month, one John Horn, and a woman, suffered at Wotten-Underedge, in Gloucestershire.

All these martyrs submitted to their fate, with the most christian fortitude, giving glory to God for having numbered them among the followers and advocates of his most holy gospel.

The last we find recorded, who suffered for the truth of the gospel, in the bloody year, 1556, were five persons (confined, with many others, in Canterbury castle) who were cruelly starved to death. Their names were as follows :

William Foster, Alice Potkins, and John Archer, condemned; John Clark, and Dunstan Chittenden, not condemned.

The cruel usage these unhappy persons suffered from their unfeeling persecutors, is displayed in a letter written by one of them, and thrown out of the window of the prison; of which, the following is an exact copy :

"Be it known unto all men that shall read, or hear read, these our letters, that we, the poor prisoners of the castle of Canterbury, for God's truth, are kept, and lie in cold irons; and our keepers will not suffer any meat to be brought to us to comfort us. And, if any man do bring us any thing, as bread, butter, cheese, or any other food, the said keeper will charge them that so bring us any thing, except money or raiment, to carry it them again; or else, if he do receive any food of any for us, he doth keep it for himself, and he and his servants do spend it, so that we have nothing thereof; and thus, the keeper keepeth away our victuals from us : insomuch, that there are four of us prisoners here for God's truth, famished already ; and thus it is his mind to famish us all : and we think he is appointed thereunto by the bishops and priests, and, also, by the justices, so to famish us ; and not only us of the said castle, but, also, all other prisoners, in other prisons, for the like cause, to be also famished : notwithstanding, we write not these our letters, to that intent, we might not afford to be famished for the Lord Jesus' sake, but for this cause and intent, that they, having no law to famish us in prison, should not do it privily, but that the murderers' hearts should be openly known to all the world, that all men may know of what church they are, and who is their father.   Out of the castle of Canterbury."

Among the others confined with these five, were ten men, who, having been examined by Dr. Thornton, suffragan of Dover, and Nicholas Harpsfield, archdeacon of Canterbury, were sentenced to be burnt.   They had been confined a considerable time, but their sentence was, at length, put into execution ; and they were the first who opened the bloody transactions of the year 1557. Their names were as follows :

Stephen Kemp, of Norgate ;   William Waterer, of Beddingden ;   W. Prowting, of Thornham ; W. Lowick, of Cranbroke ;   Thomas Hudson, of Salenge ; William Hay, of Hithe ;   Thomas Stephens, of Beddingden ; John Philpot, Nicholas Final, and Matthew Bradbridge, of Tenterden.

The six first were burnt at Canterbury, on the 15th of the month called January, 1557.

Stephens and Philpot suffered, the next day, at Wie. And Final and Bradbridge, the day after, at Ashford.

They all bore their sufferings with christian fortitude, happily rejoicing that their troubles were drawing to an end, and that they should leave this world, to be transplanted to that where the weary are at rest.

Notwithstanding the number of sacrifices that had been made in various parts of the kingdom, since the accession of queen Mary, in order to indulge the bigotry of that infatuated princess, yet they were far from being at an end. Naturally disposed to tyranny, and encouraged in her blood-thirsty principles, by Bonner, bishop of London, she determined to compel all her subjects, who differed from herself in religious sentiments, either to submit to her maxims, or fall victims to her unsatiated revenge.

To facilitate this horrid intention, in the beginning of the month called February, 1557, she issued the following proclamation, which was, in a great measure, promoted by bishop Bonner, whose cruel soul, in conjunction with hers, thirsted after the blood of those who thought not as they did.

A bloody Commission, issued by King Philip, and Queen Mary, to persecute the poor Members of Christ.

" PHILIP and Mary, by the grace of God, king and queen of England, &c. ' To the right reverend Father in God, our right, trusty, and well-beloved counsellor, Thomas, bishop of Ely ; and to our right, trusty, and well-beloved William Windsor, knight, lord Windsor, Edward North, knight, lord North ; and to our trusty and well-beloved counsellor, J. Bourn, knight, one of our chief secretaries, J. Mordant, knight, Francis Englefield, knight, master of our wards and liveries, Edward Walgrave, knight, master of our great wardrobe, Nicholas Hare, knight, master of the rolls, Thomas Pope, knight, Roger Cholmley, knight, Richard Rede, knight, Rowland Hill, knight, William Rastal, serjeant at law, Henry Cole, clerk, dean of St. Paul's, William Roper, and Ralph Cholmley, Esqrs. William Cook, Thomas Martin, John Story, and John Vanghan, doctors of the law, greeting.

" Forasmuch as divers, devilish, and slanderous persons have not only invented, bruted, and set forth divers false rumours, tales and seditious slanders against us, but also, have sown divers heresies, and heretical opinions, and

set forth divers seditious books, within this our realm of
England, meaning thereby to stir up division, strife, contention, and sedition, not only amongst our loving subjects, but also, betwixt us and our said subjects, with
divers other outrageous misdemeanors, enormities, contempts, and offences, daily committed and done, to the
disquieting of us and our people : we, minding the due
punishment of such offenders, and the repressing of such
like offences, enormities, and misbehaviours from henceforth, having special trust and confidence in your fideli-
ties, wisdoms, and discretions, have authorized, appointed, and assigned you to be our commissioners ; and, by
these presents, do give full power and authority unto you,
and three of you, to inquire, as well by the oaths of
twelve good and lawful men, as by witnesses, and all
other means and politic ways you can devise, of all and
singular heretical opinions, lollardies, heretical and seditious books, concealments, contempts, conspiracies, and
all false rumours, tales, seditions, and slanderous words, or
sayings, raised, published, bruted, invented, or set forth
against us, or either of us, or against the quiet govern-
ance and rule of our people and subjects, by books, lies,
tales, or otherwise, in any county, key, bowing, or other place or places, within this our realm of England,
or elsewhere, in any place or places, beyond the seas,
and of the bringers in, utterers, buyers, sellers, readers, keepers, or conveyers of any such letter, books,
rumour, and tale ; and of all and every their coadjutors,
counsellors, comforters, procurers, abettors, and main-
tainers, giving unto you, and three of you, full power
and authority, by virtue hereof, to search out, and take
into your hands and possesions, all manner of heretical
and seditious books, letters, and writings, wheresover
they, or any of them shall be found, as well in printers,
houses and shops, as elsewhere, willing you, and every of
you, to search for the same, in all places, according to
your discretions.

" And, also, to inquire, hear, and determine, all and
singular enormities, disturbances, misbehaviours, and
negligences, committed in any church, chapel, or other

hallowed places, within this realm ; and, also, for and concerning the taking away, or withholding any lands, tenements, goods, ornaments, stocks of money, or other
things belonging to every of the same churches and
chapels, and all accounts and reckonings concerning the
same.

" And, also, to inquire and search out all such persons
as obstinately do refuse to receive the blessed sacrament of
the altar, to hear the mass, or to come to their parish
churches, or other convenient places appointed for divine
service ; and all such as refuse to go on procession, to
take holy bread, or holy water, or otherwise do misuse
themselves in any church, or other hallowed places,
wheresoever any of the said offences have been, or hereafter shall be committed, within this our said realm.

" Nevertheless, our will and pleasure are, that when,
and as often as any person, or persons, hereafter being
called or convened before you, do obstinately persist, or
stand in any manner of heresy, or heretical opinion, that
then ye, or three of you, do immediately take order, that
the same person, or persons, so standing, or persisting,
be delivered and committed to his ordinary, there to be
used, according to the spiritual and ecclesiastical laws.

" And, also, we give unto you or three of you, full
power and authority, to inquire and search out all vaga-
bonds, and masterless men, barrators, quarrellers, and
suspected persons, abiding within our city of London,
and ten miles compass of the same, and all assaults and
affrays done and committed within the same city and
compass.

" And, further, to search out all wastes, decays, and
ruins of churches, chancels, chapels, personages, and
vicarages, in the diocess of the same, being within this
realm, giving you, and every of you, full power and
authority, by virtue hereof, to hear and determine the
same, and all other offences and matters above specified
and rehearsed, according to your wisdoms, consciences,
and discretions, willing and commanding you, or three of
you, from time to time, to use and devise all such politic
ways and means, for the trial and searching out of the

premises, as by you, or three of you, shall be thought most expedient and necessary : and, upon inquiry, and due proof had, known, perceived, and tried out, by the confession of the parties, or by sufficient witnesses before you, or three of you, concerning the premises, or any part thereof, or by any other ways or means requisite, to give and award such punishment to the offenders, by fine, imprisonment, or otherwise ; and to take such order for redress and reformation of the premises, as to your wisdoms, or three of you, shall be thought meet and convenient.

"Further, willing and commanding you, and every three of you, in case you shall find any person, or persons, obstinate or disobedient, either in their appearance before you, or three of you, at your calling or assignment, or else in not accomplishing, or not obeying your decrees, orders, and commandments, in any thing or things, touching the premises, or any part thereof, to commit the same person, or persons, so offending, to ward, there to remain, till by you, or three of you, he be discharged or delivered, &c."

Account of twenty-two persons, viz. fourteen men, and eight women, who were all apprehended at Colchester, for professing the truth of the gospel, and brought together from thence to London, to be examined by bishop Bonner.

THE bloody proclamation before mentioned, which was issued on the 8th of the month called February, 1557, gave the new inquisition an opportunity of extending their horrid ravages ; so that persecution universally prevailed, and most of the gaols in the kingdom were crowded with prisoners.

The rage of persecution was particularly prevalent, in and about the town of Colchester, insomuch that twenty-three persons were apprehended together, of which number, only one escaped ; the others being sent up to London, in order to abide by the award of a most bloody tribunal. They consisted of fourteen men and eight women, who were fastened together, with a chain placed between them, each holding the same in their hands and being at the same time tied separately with a cord round the arm. On their entrance into the city, they were pinioned, and, in that manner, conducted to Newgate.

Before we proceed to relate farther particulars relative to these innocent and persecuted people, it may not be improper, in order to give the reader a just idea of that detested persuasion which can justify such horrid cruelty and injustice, to lay before our readers a transcript of the popish commissary's letter to bishop Bonner on this occasion. It was as follows:

The Commissary's letter to Bonner, bishop of London.

" AFTER my duty done in receiving and accomplishing your honourable and most loving letter, dated the 7th of August, be it known unto your lordship, that the 28th of August, the lord of Oxenford, lord Darcy, H. Tyrel, A. Brown, William Bendelows, E. Tyrel, R. Weston, R. Appleton, published their commission, to seize the lands, tenements, any goods of the fugitives, so that the owners should have neither use nor advantage thereof, but by inventory remain safe in keeping, until the cause were determined.

" And, also, there was likewise proclaimed the queen's warrant, for the restitution of the church goods within Colchester, and the hundreds thereabout, to the use of God's service. And then were called the parishes particularly, and the heretics partly committed to my examination. And that divers persons should certify me of the ornaments of their churches, betwixt this and the justices next appearance, which shall be on Michaelmas next. And the parishes, which had presented at two several times, to have all ornaments with other things, in good order, were exonerated for ever, till they were warned again, and others to make their appearance from time to time. And those names blotted in the indenture, were indicted for treason, fugitives, or disobedients, and were put forth by Mr. Brown's commandment. And, before the sealing, my lord Darcy said unto me apart, and Mr. Bendelows, that I should have sufficient time to send unto your lordship ; yea, if need were, the heretics to remain in durance, till I had an answer from you, yea, till the lord legates graces commissioners come into the country.

" And Mr. Brown came unto my lord Darcy's house and parlour, belonging unto Mr. Barnaby, before my said lord, and all the justices, and laid his hand on my shoulder, with a smiling countenance, and desired me to make his hearty commendations to your good lordship, and asked me, if I would : and I said, yea, with a good will. Wherefore, I was glad, and thought that I should not have been charged with so sudden carriage.

" But, after dinner, the justices counselled with the bailiffs, and with the gaolers, and then after took me unto them, and made collation of the indentures, and sealed them ; and then Mr. brown commanded me, this afternoon, being the 30th of August, to go and receive my prisoners by and by. And then, I said, it is an unreasonable commandment, for that I have attended on you here these three days, and this Sunday early, I have sent home my men. Wherefore, I desire you to have a convenient time appointed, wherein I may know, whether it will please my lord, my master, to send his commissioners hither, or that I should make carriage of them unto his lordship. Then Mr. Brown said, we are certified that the council have written to your master to make speed, and to rid these prisoners out of hand : therefore, go, receive your prisoners in haste. I answered, sir, I shall receive them within these ten days. Then Mr. Brown said, the limitation lieth in us, and not in you, wherefore, get you hence.

" I replied, sir, ye have indicted and delivered me by this indenture, whose faith or opinions, I knew not, trusting that ye will grant me a time to examine them, lest I should punish the catholics. Well, said Mr. Brown, for that cause, ye shall have time betwixt this and Wednesday. And, I say unto you, Mr. Bailiffs, if he do not receive them at your hands on Wednesday, set open your door, and let them go.

" Then I said, my lord, and masters all, I promise to discharge the town and country of these heretics within these ten days. The lord Darcy answered, commissary, we do and must all agree in one. Wherefore, do ye receive them on or before Wednesday.

To which, I replied, my lord, the last I carried, I was going betwixt the castle, and St. Catharine's chapel, two hours and a half, and in great press and danger : wherefore, this may be to desire your lordship, to give in commandment unto Mr. Sayer, my baliff, here present, to aid me through his liberties, not only with men and weapons, but that the town-clerk may be ready there with his book to write the names of the most busy persons ; and this upon three hours' warning ; all which, both my lord and Mr. Brown commanded.

" The 31st of August, William Goodwin, of Muchbirch, husbandman, this bringer, and Thomas Alsey of Copford ; your lordship's apparator of your consistory in Colchester, covenanted with me, that they should hire two other men at the least ; whereof one should be a bow-man, to come to me the next day, about two of the clock in the afternoon, so that I might recite this bargain before Mr. Archdeacon ; and pay the money, that is fory-six shillings and eight pence. Wherefore, they should then go forth with me unto Colchester, and, on Wednesday, efore three of the clock, in the morning, receive there at my hand within the castle and mote-hall, fourteen men and eight women, bound with cords and fetters, and drive, carry, or lead, and feed with meat and drink, as heretics ought to be found continually, unto such time that the said Goodwin and Alsey shall cause the said two and twenty persons to be delivered unto my lord of London's officers, and within the safe keeping of my said lord, and then to bring unto me again the said fetters with a perfect token of, or from my said lord, and then this covenant is void, or else, &c."

" Mr. Bendelows said unto me, in my lord of Oxenford's chamber, at the king's head, after I had said mass before the lords, that, on the morrow, after holy-rood day, when we shall meet at Chelmsford, for the division of these lands, I think, Mr. Archdeacon, you, and Mr. Smith shall be fain to ride with certain of the jury to those portions and manors in your part of Essex ; and, in like case, divide yourselves, to tread and view the ground with the quest, or else I think they will not labour the matter, and so do you say, unto Mr. Archdeacon."

" Alice, the wife of William Walley, of Colchester, hath submitted herself, abjured her erroneous opinions, asked absolution, promised to do her solem n penance in her parish church at St. Peter's, on Sunday next, and to continue a Catholic and a faithful woman, as long as God shall send her life. And, for these covenants, her husband standeth bound in five pounds. Which Alice is one of the nine women of this your indenture, and she is big with child. Wherefore, she remaineth at home, and this done in the presence of the baliffs, alderman, and town clerk. And because Mr Brown was certified there was no curate at Lexdon, he inquired who was the former ? The answer was made, sir Francis Jobson. Who is the parson ? They of the questmen answered, sir Roger Ghostlow. When was he with you ? Not these fourteen years. How is your cure served ? Now and then. Who is the patron ? My lord of Arundel. And, within short time after, Sir Francis Jobson came with great courtesy unto my lord Darcy's place. And, of all gentlemen about us, I saw no more come in."

" Sir Robert Smith, priest, sometime canon of Bridlington, now canon of Appledoore, in the wild of Kent, came to Colchester, the 28th day of August, with his wife big with child, of late divorced, taken on suspicion, examined by the lords ; and Mr. Brown told me, that they have received letters from the detachment of certain persons, especially of one priest, whose name is Pullen, (but his right name is Smith) doubting this priest to be the said Pullen, although neither he, nor his wife, would confess the same."

" Wherefore, he lieth still in prison ; but surely this is not Pullen. If it please your lordship to have in remembrance, that the householder might be compelled to bring every man his own wife to her own seat in the church, in the time of divine service, it would profit much.

" And, also, there be yet standing hospitals, and others of like foundation, about Colchester, which I have not known to appear at any visitation, as masters and lazars of St. Mary Magdalene, in Colchester, the proctor of St. Catharine's chapel in Colchester, the hospital or breadhouse of the foundation of the lord H. Harney in Laermarny, the hospital and beadman of Little Horsley.

" Thus, presuming on your lordship's goodness, I am more than bold to trouble you with this worldly business, beseeching Almighty God to send your honourable lordship a condign reward.

" We found a letter, concerning the marriage of priests, in the hands of the aforesaid sir Robert Smith. Also, I desired Mr. Brown, the doer of all things, to require the audience to bring in their unlawful writings or books, who asked me, if I had proclaimed the proclamation ? I said yea. Then he said openly upon the bench, that they should be proclaimed once every quarter. And then take the constables and officers, and they alone take and punish the offenders accordingly.

By your poor Beadman,
JOHN KINGSTON, Priest.

Easthrop, this 30*th day of August.*"

An Indenture made between the Lords and Justices within specified, and Bonner's Commissary, concerning the delivery of the prisoners before-mentioned.

" THIS indenture made the nineteenth of August, in the third and fourth years of the reign of our sovereign lord and lady Philip and Mary, by the grace of God, king and queen of England, Spain, France, both Sicilies, Jerusalem, and Ireland, defenders of the faith, archdukes of Austria, dukes of Burgundy, Millain, and Brabant, counties of Hasburgh, Flanders, and Tyrol, between the right honourable lord John de Vere, earl of Oxford, lord high chamberlain of England, Thomas lord Darcy of Chich, Henry Tirel, knight, Anthony Brown, the king and queen's serjeant at law, William Bendelows, serjeant at law, Edmund Tirel, Richard Weston, Roger Appleton, Esqrs. justices of oyer and terminer, and of the peace, within the said county of Essex, to be kept, of the one party; and John Kingston, clerk, bachelor at law, commissary to the bishop of London, of the other party, witnesseth, that Ro. Coleman, of Walton, in the county of Essex, labourer—Joan Winseley, of Horseley, Magna, in the said county, spinster—Stephen Glover, of Rayley, in the county aforesaid, glover—Richard Clerke, of Much-Holland, in the said county, mariner—William Maunt, of Much-Bentley, in the said county, husbandman—Thomas Winseley, of Much-Horseley, in the said county, sawyer—Margaret Field, of Ramsey, in the said county, spinster—Aliace Munt, of Much-Bentley, in the said county, spinster—Agnes Whitlock, of Dover-court, in the said county, spinster—Rose Allin, of the same county, spinster—Richard Bongoer, of Colchester, in the said county, currier—Richard Atkin, of Halstead, in the said county, weaver—Robert Barcock, of Wiston, in the county of Suffolk, carpenter—Richard George, of Westbarhoult, in the county of Essex, labourer—Richard Jolly, of Colchester, in the said county, mariner—Thomas Firefanne, of the same town and county, mercer—Robert Debnam, late of Debnam, in the said county, weaver—Cicely Warren, of Cocksail, in the said county, spinster—Christian Pepper, widow, of the same town and county—Allin Sampson, and Alice, the wife of William Wallis, of Colchester, spinster—William Bongeor, of Colchester, in the said county, glazier—being indicted of heresy, are delivered to the said John Kingston, clerk, ordinary to the bishop of London, according to the statute in that case provided.

In witness whereof, to one part of this indenture remaining with the said earl, lord, and other the justices, the said ordinary hath set to his hand and seal ; and to the other part remaining with the said ordinary, the said earl, lord, and other the justices, have set to their several hands and seals, the day and year above-written.

" Oxenford, Thomas Darcy, Henry Tyrel, Anthony Brown, William Bendelows, Edmund Tyrel, Richard Weston, Roger Appleton."

The twenty-two persons before-mentioned, sent from Colchester to London, were, at length, brought before bishop Bonner, who examined them separately with respect to their faith ; but he did not choose to proceed against them, till he had sent the following letter to cardinal Pole :

A Letter from Bishop Bonner to Cardinal Pole.

" May it please your grace, with my most humble obedience, reverence, and duty, to understand, that going to London, upon Thursday last, and thinking to be troubled with Mr. German's matter only, and such other common matters as are accustomed, enough to weary a right strong body, I had the day following, to comfort my stomach withal, letters from Colchester, that either that day, or the day following, I should have sent there twenty-two heretics, indicted before the comissioners ; and, indeed, so I had, and compelled to bear their charges, as I did of the others ; a sum of money that I thought full evil bestowed. And these heretics, notwithstanding they had honest catholic keepers to conduct and bring them up to me, and, in all the way from Colchester to Stradford-bow, did go quietly and obediently, yet coming to Stratford, they began to take heart of grace, and to do as they pleased themselves, for they began to have their guard which generally increased, till they came to Aldgate, where they were lodged, Friday night.

" And albeit, I took order, that the said heretics should be with me early on Saturday morning, to the intent they might quietly come, and be examined by me ; yet it was between ten and eleven of the clock before they would

come, and no way would they take but through Cheapside, so that they were brought to my house with a thousand persons. Which thing I took very strange, and
spake to sir John Gresham, then being with me, to tell
the mayor and the sheriffs, that this thing was not well
suffered in the city. These naughty heretics, all the
way they came through Cheapside, both exhorted the
people to their part, and had much comfort from the
promiscuous multitude; and, being entered into my
house, and talked withal, they shewed themselves desperate, and very obstinate; yet I used all the honest
means I could, both of myself and others, to have won
them, causing divers learned men to talk with them; and
finding nothing in them but pride and wilfulness, I
thought to have them all hither to Fulham, and here to
give sentence against them. Nevertheless, perceiving,
by my last doing, that your grace was offended, I thought
it my duty, before I any farther proceeded herein, to ad-
vertise first your grace hereof, and know your good pleasure, which I beseech your grace I may do by this trusty
bearer. And thus, most humbly, I take my leave of
your good grace, beseeching Almighty God, always to
preserve the same. At Fulham, A. D. 1557.

" Your grace's most bounden beadsman, and servant,
EDMUND BONNER."

From the contents of this letter, we evidently see the
persecuting spirit of the blood-thirsty Bonner, who was
manifestly desirous of glutting himself with the massacre of those innocent persons.

Cardinal Pole, though a papist, was a man of moderation and humanity, as appears, not only by his endeavour
to mitigate the fury of Bonner, but also by several of his
letters directed to archbishop Cranmer, as well as many
complaints alleged against him to the pope, for his lenity
towards the heretics.

Nay, so incensed was his holiness at his proceedings,
that he ordered him up to Rome, and would have proceeded against him most rigorously, had not queen Ma-

ry interposed in his behalf, and warded off the danger that threatened him.

It was shrewdly suspected, that the cardinal, a short time before his coming from Rome to England, began to favour the opinion and doctrine of Luther.

But, to return to the immediate account of our martyrs, who would certainly have all suffered, had it not been for the interposition of cardinal Pole.

It would exceed the limits of our work, and be tedious to the reader, were we minutely to relate the articles that were respectively administered to each, and their several answers to the same. We shall, therefore, confine ourselves to that of the Lord's Supper, on which they were principally examined.

General confession of these persons, concerning the sacrament of the Lord's Supper.

" WHEREAS Christ, at his last supper, took bread, and, when he had given thanks, he brake it, and gave it to his disciples, and said, ' take, eat, this is my body.' And likewise took the cup, and thanked, &c. We do understand it to be a figurative speech, as the common manner of his language was in parables, and dark sentences, that they which were carnally-minded, should see with their eyes, and not understand ; signifying this, that as he did break the bread among them, being but one loaf, and they all did partake thereof, so we, through his body, in that it was broken and offered on the cross for us, are all partakers thereof; and his blood cleanseth us from our sins, and hath pacified God's wrath towards us, and made the atonement between God and us, if we walk henceforth in the light, even as he is in the true light.

" And that he said further, ' do this in remembrance of me' ; it is a memorial and token of the suffering and death of Jesus Christ : and he commanded it for this cause, that the followers of Christ should come together to shew his death, and to thank him for his benefits, and magnify his holy name ; and so to break bread, and drink the wine, in remembrance that Christ had given his body, and shed his blood for us.

"Thus, you may well perceive, though Christ called the bread his body, and wine his blood, yet it followeth not, that the substance of his body should be in the bread and wine, as divers places in scripture are spoken by the apostles, in like phrase of speech, as in John xv. 'I am the true vine.' Also in John x. 'I am the door.' And as it is written in the ninth chapter to the Hebrews, and in Exodus xxiv. how Moses took the blood of calves, and sprinkled both the book, and all the people, saying, ' this is the blood of the covenant or testament.' And, also, in the fifth chapter of Ezekiel, how the Lord said unto him, concerning the third part of his hair, say, ' this is Jerusalem,' &c.

"Thus, we see how the scriptures speak in figures, and ought to be spiritually examined, and not as they would have us to say, that the bodily presence of Christ is in the bread, which is a blasphemous understanding of the word, and contrary to the holy scriptures.

"Also, we see, that great idolatry is sprung out of the misunderstanding of the words of Christ, ' this is my body,' and yet daily springeth to the great dishonour of God; so that men worship a piece of bread for God; yea, and hold that to be their maker."

After this confession of their faith and doctrine was written and exhibited, they also drew up a letter in form of a short supplication, or rather an admonition to the judges and commissioners, requiring that justice and judgment, after the rule of God's word, might be administered unto them. The copy of the letter is as follows:

A supplication of the prisoners to the Judges.

"To the right honourable audience, before whom our writings and the confession of our faith shall come; we poor prisoners, being fast in bonds upon the trial of our faith, which we offer to be tried by the scriptures, pray most heartily, that, forasmuch as God hath given you power and strength over us as concerning our bodies, under whom we submit ourselves as obedient subjects in all things, yet being officers and rulers of the people, may execute true judgment, keep the laws of righteousness, govern the people, and defend the cause of the poor and helpless.

" God, for his Son Jesus Christ's sake, give you the wisdom and understanding of Solomon, David, Hezekiah, Moses, with divers other most virtuous rulers, by whose wisdom and godly understanding, the people were justly ruled and governed in the fear God, all wickedness was by them overthrown and beaten down, and all godliness and virtue did flourish and spring. O God, which art the most high, the creator and maker of all things, and of all men, both great and small, and carest for all alike, who dost try all men's works and imaginations, before whose judgment-seat shall come both high and low, rich and poor ; we most humbly beseech thee, to put into our rulers' hearts the pure love and fear of thy name, that even as they themselves would be judged, and as they shall make answer before thee, so they may hear our causes, judge with mercy, and read over these our requests and confessions of our faith, with deliberation, and a godly judgment.

" And, if any thing here seemeth to you to be erroneous or disagreeing with the scripture, if it shall please your lordships to hear us patiently which do offer ourselves to be tried by the scriptures, thereby to make answer ; and, in so doing, we poor subjects being in much captivity and bondage, are bound to pray for your noble estate and long preservation."

Notwithstanding the request of those men was so just, and their doctrine so sound, yet the bishop, and the other judges, would have passed sentence on them, had it not been for cardinal Pole, and some others, who thought the putting to death so many together would produce a cabal among the people. It was therefore decreed, that they should make submission, or confession, such as they would themselves and be discharged. This they readily agreed to ; and their submission was made in the following form :

The submission or confession of the aforesaid prisoners.

" BECAUSE our Saviour, at his last supper, took bread, and when he had given thanks, he brake it, and gave it unto his disciples, and said, ' take, eat, this is my body which is given for you, this do in remembrance of me.'   Therefore, according to the words of our Saviour Jesus Christ, we do believe in the sacrament to be spiritually Christ's body.   And, likewise, he took the cup, gave thanks, and gave it to his disciples, and said, ' this is my blood of the New Testament which is shed for many.'

" Therefore, likewise, we do believe, that it is spiritually the blood of Christ, according as his church doth administer the same.   Unto which catholic church of Christ, we do in like, as in all other matters, submit ourselves, promising therein to live as it becometh good christian men, and, herein this realm, to behave ourselves as becometh faithful subjects unto our most gracious king and queen, and to all other superiors, both spiritual and temporal, according to our bounden duties."

The whole twenty-two persons brought from Colchester, respectively subscribed their names to this submission ; as did also six others who had been apprehended in London, and were brought with them for their examination.   The names of the whole were as follows :

John Atkin, Allin Sympson, Richard George, Thomas Firefanne, W. Maunt, Richard Jolly, Richard Gratwicke, Thomas Winseley, Richard Rothe, Richard Clerke, Stephen Glover, Robert Coleman, Thomas Merse, William Bongeor, Robert Barcock, Margaret Hyde, Elyn Euring, Christian Pepper, Margaret Field, Alice Munt, Joan Winseley, Cicely Warren, Rose Allin, Ann Whitlocke, George Barker, John Saxby, Thomas Locker, and Alice Locker.

In consequence of this submission, they were all immediately set at liberty ; though several of them were afterwards apprehended, and put to death.   One of the women, namely, Margaret Hyde, escaped their resentment but a short time, being one in the list we have next to mention, who suffered for the truth of the gospel.

The sufferings and Martyrdoms of Thomas Loseby, Henry Ramsey, Thomas Thyrtell, Margaret Hyde, and Agnes Stanley, who were all burnt together in Smithfield.

THE popish emissaries having laid information against these five persons, they were all apprehended ; and, being examined by several justices of the county of Essex, in which they resided, were by them sent up to the bishop of London, for examination. On their arrival, the bishop referred them to the chancellor, who, after propounding to them the articles, usual on the occasion, in the diocess of London, committed them all to Newgate.

After being imprisoned about three months, by order of the chancellor, they were summoned to appear before the bishop himself, when the following singular articles were exhibited against them :

1. That they thought, believed, and declared, within some part of the city and diocess of London, that the faith, religion, and ecclesiastical service here observed and kept, as it is in the realm of England, was not a true and laudable faith, religion, and service, especially concerning the mass and the seven sacraments, nor were they agreeable to God's word ; and, that they could not, without grudging and scruple, receive and use it, nor conform themselves unto it, as other subjects of this realm customarily have done.

2. They had thought, &c. that the English service, set forth in the time of king Edward the sixth, in this realm of England, was good, godly, and catholic, in all points, and that it alone ought here in this realm to be received, used, and practised, and none other.

3. They had thought, &c. that they were not bound to their parish church, and there to be present at mattins, mass, even-song, and divine service.

4. They had thought, &c. that they were not bound to come to procession to the church, upon times appointed, and to go in the same, with others of the parish, singing or saying the accustomed prayers used in the church, nor to bear a taper or candle, on Candlemasday, nor take ashes on Ash-Wednesday, nor bear palms on Palm-Sunday, nor to creep to the cross upon days accustomed, nor to receive

holy water and holy bread, or to accept or allow the ceremonies and usages of the church, after the manner in which
they were then used in this realm.

5. That they had thought, &c. that they were not bound,
at any time, to confess their sins to any priest, and to receive absolution at his hands as God's minister, nor to receive, at any time, the blessed sacrament of the altar, especially as it is used in the church of England.

6. That they had thought, &c. that in matters of religion
and faith, they were bound to follow and believe their own
consciences only, and not credit the determination and common order of the catholic church, and see of Rome, nor
any member thereof.

7. That they had thought, &c. that the fashion and manner of christening infants, are not agreeable to God's word,
and that none can be effectually baptized, and therefore saved, except they are arrived to years of discretion to believe
themselves, and willingly accept, or refuse, baptism at his
pleasure.

8. That they had thought, &c. that prayers to saints, or
prayer for the dead, were not available, nor allowable by
God's word; and that souls departed this life do immediately go to heaven or hell, or else do sleep till the day of doom;
so that there is no place of purgation at all.

9. That they had thought, &c. that all those, who in the
time of king Henry VIII, or in the time of queen Mary,
the present sovereign of England, had been burned as heretics, were no heretics, but faithful, sincere christians ; especially Barnes, Garret, Jerome, Frith, Rogers, Hooper,
Cardmaker, Latimer, Taylor, Cranmer, Ridley, &c. and
that they did allow and approve all their opinions, and disapproved their condemnations and burnings.

10. That they had thought, &c. that fasting and prayers
used in the church of England, and the appointing a day
for fasting and abstaining from flesh upon fasting days, especially in the time of Lent, are not laudable nor allowable,
by God's word, and that men ought to have liberty, all
times, to eat all kind of meat.

11. That they had thought, &c. that the sacrament of
the altar is an idol ; and to reserve, keep, and honour it, is

idolatry and superstition, as were also the mass and elevation of the sacrament.

12. That they had thought, &c. that they were not bound to be convened before an ecclesiastical judge, concerning matters of faith, nor to make answer at all, especially upon oath on a book.

The first, second, third, fourth, fifth, eighth, and ninth, they granted, in general, excepting that they denied the souls departed to sleep till the day of judgment, as mentioned in the eighth article.

With respect to the sixth article objected to them, they thought themselves bound to believe the true catholic church, so far as it instructed them according to God's holy word, but not to follow the determinations of the superstitious church of Rome.

Concerning the eighth and twelfth articles, they denied that they ever maintained any such absurd opinions, but granted that man of himself, without the aid and assistance of God's spirit, had no power to do any thing acceptable in the sight of God.

To the tenth article, they answered, that true fasting and prayer used, according to God's word, were allowable, and approved in his sight ; and, that by the same word, every faithful man may eat all meats, at all times, with thanksgiving to God for the same.

Having given these answers, they were dismissed, and conveyed to their respective places of confinement, where they remained till they were again brought before the bishop, who made no other inquiry, than whether they would abjure their heretical opinions ; and, on their refusal, again dismissed them.

At length, they were brought into the public consistory-court at St. Paul's, and severally demanded what they had to allege, why sentence of condemnation should not be pronounced against them.

Thomas Loseby being first questioned, thus replied, " God give me grace to withstand you, your sentence, and your law, which devours the flock of Christ ; for I perceive death is my certain portion, unless I will consent to believe in that accursed idol the mass."

3 M

Thomas Thyrtell being next examined, said, "my lord, if you make me a heretic, you make Christ and the twelve apostles all heretics; for I hold one and the same faith with them, and I will abide in that faith, being assured that it will obtain for me everlasting life."

Henry Ramsey, being required to recant, answered, "my lord, would you have me abjure the truth; and, for fear of death here, forfeit eternal felicity hereafter?"

Margaret Hyde, being questioned, replied, "my lord, you have no cause to pronounce sentence against me, for I am in the true faith, nor will ever forsake it; and I wish I was more confirmed in it than I am."

Agnes Stanley, the last examined, said, "My lord, I would suffer every hair of my head to be burned, before I would renounce the faith of Christ, and his holy gospel."

The court now broke up, but was convened again in the afternoon, when the prisoners appeared, and were again severally examined.

Thomas Loseby being first called upon, his articles and answers were read; after which, many attempts were made to bring him to a recantation; but he persisted in his faith, declaring that he hoped he had the spirit of God, which had led him into all truth. His sentence of condemnation was therefore pronounced, and he was delivered to the custody of the sheriff, in order for execution.

Various arguments were used by the bishop to bring over Margaret Hyde; but she declared, she would not depart from what she said upon any penalty whatever; and added, that she would gladly hear his lordship instruct her from some part of God's word, and not talk to her concerning holy bread and holy water, which was no part of God's word.

The bishop, finding her resolute, pronounced sentence on her, and she was delivered over to the secular power.

Agnes Stanley was also admonished to return to the communion of the holy mother-church; but she continued steadfast in her faith, declaring she was no heretic, and that those who were burned, as the papists said, for heresy, were true martyrs in the sight of God. In consequence of this, she likewise received sentence of death, and was committed to the care of the sheriff.

Thomas Thyrtell being asked, what he had to allege, answered, " my lord, I will not hold with those idolatrous opinions you would inculcate ; for, I say, the mass is idolatry, and I will abide by the faith of Christ as long as I live."

He was then proceeded against in the same manner as the former.

Henry Ramsey, who was last called, being asked, whether he would stand by his answers as the rest had done, or recant and become a new member of the church, replied, " I will never abjure my religion, in which I will live, and in which I will die."

Their examination being closed, and sentence of death passed on them all, they were immediately conducted to Newgate, where they continued till the 12th of the month called April, 1557. On the morning of that day, they were conducted to Smithfield, the place appointed for their execution, where, being fastened to two stakes, they were burnt in one fire, praising God as long as they had the power of speech, and cheerfully giving up their lives in testimony of the truth of the gospel.

The examination and persecution of Stephen Gratwick, who, with William Morant, and John King, suffered Martyrdom in St. George's Fields, in the county of Surry.

STEPHEN GRATWICK being informed against by some of the popish emissaries, on a suspicion of heresy, was apprehended, and being carried before a justice of the peace, was committed to the Marshalsea-prison, where he continued for a considerable time.

At length, he was brought before Dr. White, bishop of Winchester, in St. George's church, Southwark, in order to answer such questions as he should state, relative to his religious opinions.

The bishop first asked him, if he would revoke the heresies which he had maintained and defended within his diocess; when Gratwick answering in the negative, he administered the usual articles, desiring him to give an ample answer to each.

These articles being read, Gratwick replied, " my lord, these articles are of your making, and not of mine ; nor have I had any time to examine them ; therefore, I desire the liberty of lawful appeal to mine ordinary, having no concern with you."

During his examination, the bishop of Rochester, and the archdeacon of Canterbury, arrived ; when, on a consultation about the present case, it was agreed to introduce a person to represent the ordinary ; which being done, Gratwick desired leave to depart, but the counterfeit ordinary insisted on his being detained ; that he was justly summoned before those lords, and him, on trial of his faith; and that, if he would confess the truth, he should be quietly dismissed, and allowed full liberty.

Gratwick told him, that he would turn his own argument upon him ; for Christ came before the high-priest, scribes, and pharisees, bringing the truth with him, being the very truth himself; yet both he and his truth were condemned, and had no avail with them ; the apostles, likewise, and all the martyrs that died since Christ, did the same.

The bishop of Winchester then asked his opinion concerning the sacrament of the altar ; to which, he replied, " my lord, I do verily believe, that in the sacrament of the Lord's Supper, truly administered in both kinds, according to the institution of Christ, unto the worthy receiver, he eateth mystically, by faith, the body and blood of Christ."

The bishop of Rochester observed, that this definition was a mere evasion of the principal points ; for that he separated the sacrament of the altar from the Supper of the Lord, intimating thereby, that the former was not the true sacrament ; and also condemned their method of administering it in one kind, as well as hindered the unworthy receiver to eat and drink the body and blood of Christ, which, if duly weighed, were points of the highest importance, though he had craftily evaded them.

Having entered into closer examination concerning this matter, the counterfeit ordinary ordered the articles to be read again; and Gratwick refusing to make any reply, was threatened with sentence of excommunication; on which, he thus addressed himself to his examiners:

"Since you thirst for my blood, before you are glutted with the same, permit me a word in my own cause. On Sunday, my lord of Winchester, I was before you, who took occasion to preach from these words of St. James: 'If any man among you seem to be religious, and bridleth not his tongue, but deceiveth his own heart, this man's religion is vain.' From these words, my lord, by wrested inferences, you slandered us poor prisoners, upbraiding us with the title of Arians, Herodians, Sacramentaries, and Pelagians. When we stood up to speak in vindication of ourselves, you threatened to cut out our tongues, and caused us to be dragged out of the church by violence; nevertheless, I will abide by the truth to the end of my life."

The incensed prelate, after various endeavours, by threats and promises, to bring him to a recantation without effect, pronounced sentence of condemnation upon him; and he was delivered over to the sheriff, who immediately conducted him to the Marshalsea-prison. Here he remained, till the latter end of May, 1557, when he was brought to the stake in St. George's Fields, and cheerfully resigned up his soul into the hands of him who gave it.

William Morant, and John King, suffered with him; but we have no account on record relative to their examination.

*The Martyrdoms of Alice Bendon, John Fishcock, Ni-
cholas White. Nicholas Pardue, Barbara Finall, Mary
Bradbridge, and Amos Wilson, who were all burnt
together in the city of Canterbury.*

ALICE BENDON was the wife of Edward Bendon, of
the parish of Stablehurst, in the county of Kent. Being brought before a magistrate, on an information of
heresy, she was asked, why she absented herself from
the church ? To which, she replied, because there was
much idolatry practised there against the honour and
glory of God.

In consequence of this answer, she was committed to
Canterbury castle ; but her husband making interest for
her enlargement, she was ordered to appear before the
bishop of Dover, who asked her, if, in condition she
was released, she would go to church ? To this, she
gave no satisfactory answer, notwithstanding which, the
bishop gave her liberty.

On her arrival at home, her husband admonished her
for her conduct, and advised her to go to church with
him ; but this she absolutely refused ; on which, she
was again apprehended, and taken before sir John
Gifford, who committed her to her former place of confinement.

In consequence of this, her husband made a second
application for her discharge, to the bishop of Dover ;
but, in this, he failed, the bishop telling him, she was a
most obstinate, irreclaimable heretic ; and, therefore, he
could not release her.

Her husband then informed his lordship, that, if he
could keep her brother, Roger Hall, from her, she
would conform to the mother-church ; whereupon, she
was removed to another prison, and charge given, that,
if her brother came to visit her, he should be apprehended.

She continued some time in this place, without her
brother's knowledge, though he sought diligently to find
her at the hazard of his life.

In process of time, he accidentally found her out, by hearing her voice as he passed by the prison window, when she was repeating a psalm, and bemoaning herself; but, fearing to go to her in a public manner, he found a method of conveying to her some money and sustenance, by means of a long stick, which reached to the window of the prison.

In this prison, she continued nine weeks, without seeing any one but her keeper, lying in her clothes upon straw, and having but three farthings a day, in bread, allowed for her subsistence, with no other liquor to drink but water.

This hard usage brought upon her a complication of disorders, insomuch that she could not walk without the greatest pain.

After being some time confined in this loathsome prison, the bishop summoned her before him, and asked her, if she would go to church, promising her great favours, if she would be reformed, and return to the holy mother-church.

To this, she answered, " I am verily persuaded, by the great severity which you have used towards me, that ye are not of God, neither can your doings be godly; and I see, that you seek my utter destruction."

She then shewed them how miserable and lame she was from lying so long on the cold ground, in that filthy prison, where she was deprived of the necessaries of life.

After this, the bishop caused her to be removed from thence to the prison, at the West-gate in Canterbury, where she had better usage, and continued till the latter end of April following, when she, and the rest of the prisoners, being brought before the commissioners, were severally examined; and, on persisting in those principles which their persecutors deemed heresy, they received sentence of excommunication, were delivered to the sheriffs, and sent back to prison.

Here they continued till the 19th of the month called June, when they were all seven brought to the place of execution.

Alice Bendon behaved remarkably courageous on this melancholy occasion, setting an example to her fellow-martyrs, who kneeled down, joined together in prayer, and behaved with such zeal and affection, as excited the esteem of their very enemies.

Having finished their devotions, and mutual salutations, they were chained to several stakes; and being encompassed with the flames, they quietly yielded up their souls to the Lord, in hopes of a joyful resurrection to life eternal.

The Martyrdoms of Richard Woodman, George Stevens, William Maynard, Alexander Hosman, Thomasin Wood, Margery Morris, James Morris, Dennis Bongess, Ann Ashdon, and Mary Groves, who were all burnt together at Lewes, in the county of Sussex.

THOUGH these ten persons all suffered together, yet we do not find any other particulars relative to either, except Richard Woodman, who was a considerable merchant in the parish of Warbleton, in the county of Sussex, and whose troubles arose from the following incident:

There was one Fairbank, who, for some time, had been a married priest, and served the cure of Warbleton, where he often persuaded the people not to credit any doctrine but that which he preached, and which was then taught and set forth in the days of king Edward the sixth; but, in the beginning of the reign of queen Mary, Fairbank deserted his reformed principles, and favoured the Romish tenets; upon which, Woodman upbraided him with inconstancy and cowardice, and reminded him how differently he then preached from what he had formerly done.

In consequence of this open and frank behaviour, he was apprehended; and being brought before several of the justices of the peace for the county of Sussex, was committed to the King's-Bench prison, where he remained a considerable time.

At length, Woodman, and four other prisoners, were brought together, to be examined by Bonner, bishop of London, who, after asking them some questions, desired they would be honest men, and profess themselves members of the true catholic church, which was built upon the apostles and prophets, Christ being the head of the same. To this, they all said, that they were members of the true church, and determined, by God's grace, to continue in the same; upon which, they were all discharged.

Woodman had not long returned home, before a report was spread, that he had conformed to the church of Rome; but he vindicated himself from that aspersion in several companies; in consequence of which, complaint was made to sir John Gage, who issued warrants for apprehending him.

As he was one day employed in his ordinary occupation, three men came to him from the queen's chamberlain, arrested him in her majesty's name, and told him, he must go with them before their lord.

The surprise of the action put him into great consternation; and he desired to go home, in order to put on a dress suitable to appear in before his superiors.

When he came to his house, he demanded of the men that arrested him, to shew their warrant, that he might know the cause wherefore he was apprehended, and be better prepared to answer for himself when he should come before their master.

The men, not having any warrant, were startled at his demand; and Woodman severely reprimanded them for offering to take him without. "I heard (said he) there were several warrants out against me; but they were called in as soon as I had satisfied the commissioners by letter, that I was not guilty of the things laid to my charge; therefore, set your hearts at rest, for I will not go with you, without a warrant, unless you force me, which do at your peril."

On their leaving his house, he called them back, and told them, if they would produce a warrant, he would go with them freely. One of them said, he would fetch

one that was left in his house ; but, while he was gone,
Woodman escaped, and absented himself from home
three days, during which, they searched his house sev.
eral times, but could not find him.

Woodman, finding his enemies thus resolute on his
destruction, prepared himself a convenient cottage in a
wood, near his house, where he had pen and ink, a bible, and such necessaries as he had occasion for, daily
brought him.

His absence soon produced a report, that he had left
the kingdom ; in consequence of which, his enemies
ceased to search for him ; and he embraced this opportunity of visiting his friends and brethren ; after which,
he went over to Flanders ; but not approving of so re-
mote a situation from his family, he soon returned to
England.

When it was known, that he was come home, the
priest that was curate of the parish, and other popish emissaries, procured warrants to apprehend him. They
often searched his house for that purpose, but could not
find him ; for he had artfully contrived a secret place
which they could not discover.

At length, through the treachery of his father, and
one of his brothers, (whom he had told of his hiding-
place, and they having great part of his substance, both land
and money, in their hands) his house was beset in the
night, which, as soon as he discovered, he ran out bare-
foot, but unhappily treading upon some stones, he fell
down, and being seized, was sent prisoner to London.

On the 14th of the month called April, 1557, he was
brought befor Dr. Christopherson, bishop-elect of Chichester, who told him, he was sorry to see him on the
present occasion, as he heard, that he was a man greatly
esteemed in the country where he lived, for his probity
and charity; and, at the same time, advised him seriously to
consider his present situation, and not to think himself
wiser than all the realm, assuring him, that he meant to
do him much service.

Woodman replied, that so far from esteeming himself wiser than all the realm, he was disposed to learn

of every man that could teach him the truth ; and, that with respect to the general esteem in which he was held by his neighbours, he had ever endeavoured to maintain a conscience void of offence. "As for my wife and children, (said he) they are all in God's hand, and I have them all as though I had them not, according to the words of St. Paul ; but had I ten thousand pounds in gold, I would forego it all, rather than displease my God."

When the bishop informed him, that the sheriff applied to him out of respect to his character, he replied, that he thought proper to appeal to his ordinary ; " for (said he) they seek most unrighteously to shed my blood, and have laid many unjust things to my charge. If you can prove, from the word of God, that any of my religious principles are false, I am willing to renounce the same, and stand here desirous of being reformed."

After this, several divines conversed with him on the sacrament of the altar, purgatory, and other popish topics ; when Woodman confuted his opponents with great energy and propriety, asserting, and proving, from scripture, that there were but two sacraments ordained by Christ, and observed by him, and his immediate disciples and apostles.

Being required, by the bishop of Chichester, to relate a plain and full account of his belief concerning the sacrament of the altar, he made this explicit confession : " I do believe, that if I came to receive the sacrament of the body and blood of Christ, truly ministered, believing that Christ was born for me, and that he died on the cross for me, and that I shall be saved from my sins by his blood, and receive the sacrament in that remembrance, then I believe, that I do receive the whole Christ mystically, by faith."

A few days after this, Woodman was privately examined by lord Montague's chaplain, who made use of many arguments to bring him over to the Romish faith ; but all his efforts were ineffectual ; for Woodman would not yield to any thing that was not founded on the authority of sacred writ.

After some time, our martyr was again brought before the bishop of Winchester, in St. George's church, Southwark, where several gentlemen and clergy were present, and examined concerning the cause of his imprisonment : to which, he replied, it was for speaking to the curate of his parish in the pulpit, and not for heresy.

Being asked, what he had to allege in vindication of himself from that charge, he cited the following words of the statute :

" Whoso doth interrupt any preacher, or preachers, lawfully authorized by the queen's majesty, or by any other lawful ordinary, that all such shall suffer three months' imprisonment for so doing; and, furthermore, be brought to the quarter-sessions, and being sorry for the same, shall be released upon his good behaviour, for one whole year."

He then observed, that he had not so offended against the statute ; for the person to whom he spoke, was not lawfully authorized, as he had not put away his wife ; and, consequently, according to the law then in force, he had no right to preach.

On the 15th of the month called June, Woodman was again brought before the bishop of Winchester, in St. Saviour's church, Southwark, in the presence of the archdeacon of Canterbury, Dr. Langdall, and several other dignitaries.

The bishop of Winchester, producing some writings, asked, if they were his ? to which, he replied in the affirmative ; but refused to answer to the articles he might exhibit against him, because he was not of his diocess, though he was then in it ; consequently, he had nothing to do with him, who was not his ordinary.

After some dispute, the bishop peremptorily asked him, if he would become an honest man, and conform to the holy mother-church ? To which, Woodman replied, that no person could, with justice, object to his character ; and that he was surprised he should charge him with heresy, as the bishop of London had discharged him of all matters that were laid against him on that head.

The bishop then observed, that when he was released, perhaps those things were not laid to his charge ; and that, therefore, they were now objected to him, because he was suspected of being a heretic.

Woodman, at length, consented to answer to the several articles exhibited against them, which having done, he distinctly rehearsed the articles of his belief in the following form :

"I believe in one God, the Father Almighty, maker of heaven and earth, and of all things visible and invisible. And in one Lord, Jesus Christ, my Saviour, very God, and man. I believe in God, the Holy Ghost, the comforter of all God's chosen people, and that he is equal with the Father and the Son. I believe the true catholic church, and all the sacraments that belong thereto."

Being farther asked, concerning his belief in the sacrament of the altar, he told them, he would answer no farther questions, because he perceived they sought to shed his blood.

As the bishop of Chichester was not yet consecrated, he would not undertake, judicially to examine Woodman, and therefore submitted the whole to the bishop of Winchester, who, after many other questions, and farther arguments to bring him over to recant, at length pronounced sentence of condemnation against him ; and he was accordingly delivered over to the secular power.

About a fortnight after this, Woodman was conveyed to Lewes, in Sussex, together with his fellow martyrs, concerning whose examinations (as we have already observed) there is not any thing recorded, except that they were all condemned for heresy a few days after their apprehension.

On the 22d of the month called July, 1557, these ten steadfast believers in Christ, were led to the place of execution ; and, being chained to several stakes, were all consumed in one fire. They died with becoming fortitude and resignation, committing their departing spirits into the hands of that Redeemer, who was to be their final judge, and who, they had reason to hope, would usher them into the realms of bliss, with "come ye blessed of my Father, inherit the kingdom prepared for you from the foundation of the world."

Extract of a letter of Richard Woodman's, to one Roberts, of Hawkhurst.

"GRACE, mercy, and peace from God the Father, and from his Son our only Saviour, Jesus Christ, by the operation and working of the Holy Ghost, be multiplied plentifully upon you, dear sister, that you may the more joyfully bear the cross of Christ that you are under, to the end, to your only comfort and consolation, and to all our brethren and sisters in those parts that love our Lord unfeignedly, certifying you, that I, and all my brethren with me, are joyful, praised be God, looking daily to be dissolved from these our mortal bodies, according to the good pleasure of our heavenly Father, praising God also for your constancy and kindness, shewed unto God's people in this troublesome time of persecution. Blessed are the merciful, for they shall obtain mercy. The fruits always declare what the tree is; for a good man and woman, out of the good treasure of their hearts, bring forth good fruits.

"Wherefore, dear sister, let our faith be made manifest to the world by our deeds; and, in the midst of a crooked and perverse nation, as St. Paul saith, let your light shine as in a dark place.

"O dear hearts! now is the gospel of God overwhelmed with many black and troublesome clouds of persecution, for the which cause, very few go about to have their eyes made clear by the true light of the gospel, for fear of losing their treasures of this world, which are but vain, and shall perish.

"Let us not, therefore, be like unto them which light their candle, and put it under a bushel, but let us set our candle upon a candlestick, that it may give light unto all them that are in the house; that is to say, let all the people of the household of God see our good works, in suffering all things patiently that shall be laid upon us for the gospel sake, if it be death itself; for Christ died for us, leaving us an example, that we should follow his steps. And as he hath given his life for us, so ought we to give our lives for the defence of the gospel, to the comfort of our brethren.

"How is it then, that some will say, that their faith is good, and yet they do all the deeds of antichrist, the devil? St. Paul saith, to believe with the heart justifieth, and to confess with the mouth maketh a man safe. Here may all see, that no man or woman can have a true faith, unless they have deeds also ; and he that doubteth, is like the waves of the sea, tossed about of the wind, and can look for no good thing at the Lord's hands. Now is the acceptable time that Christ spoke of, yea, even now is the axe put to the root of the tree, that so every tree that bringeth not forth good fruit, must be hewn down, and cast into the fire.

"Now is the Lord come with his fan in his hand, to try the wheat from the chaff ; the wheat he will gather into his barn, and the chaff he will burn. Now is the time come that we must go to meet the bridegroom with oil in our lamps. We are also bidden to the feast ; let us make no excuses ; our master hath delivered talents unto us. Now is the Lord come to see, if there be any fruit upon his trees, if he find none, he will serve us as he did the wild fig-tree, that is, never fruit shall grow on him more. If we go to meet the bridegroom, without oil in our lamps, and should go to buy, the doubt is, we should be served as the foolish virgins were, to whom, God said, depart, I know you not. If we use not our talents well, they shall be taken from us, and given to others ; and all such unprofitable servants shall be cast into hell, where shall be weeping and gnashing of teeth.

"May not all people now perceive, that this is the time that our master Christ speaketh of, that the father should be against the son, and the son against the father, and one brother against another, that the brother shall deliver the brother to death ; yea, and that the wicked shall say all manner of wicked sayings against us for his name sake, the which I have found by experience. I praise God that gave me strength to bear it.

" I have no mistrust, but that the world shall see and know my blood shall not be dear in my own sight, whensoever it please God to give my adversaries leave to shed it. I do earnestly believe, that God, which hath begun this good work in me, will perform it to the end; for, when I have been in prison, sometimes wearing bolts and shackles, lying on the bare ground, and sometimes sitting in the stocks, and bound with cords, that my body was swelled, and I like to be overcome with pain, sometimes lying in the woods and fields, wandering to and fro, brought before justices, sheriffs, lords, doctors, and bishops; called dog, devil, heretic, whoremonger, traitor, thief, deceiver, and such like. Yea, even they that did eat of my bread, that should have been most my friends by nature, have betrayed me; yet, for all this, I praise God, that hath separated me from my mother's womb. All this that hath happened unto me, hath been easy; for I praise God, they are not able to prove one tittle of their sayings to be true, but that way which they call heresy, I serve my Lord God; and, at all times, before whomsoever I have been brought, God hath given me mouth and wisdom, against which, my adversaries have not been able to resist. Wherefore, dear sister, be of good comfort, with all your brethren and sisters, and take no thought what you shall say; for it shall be given you the same hour according to the promises, as I have always found, and as you and all others of God's elect shall well find, when the time is full come. And whereas I and many others have hoped, that this persecution would have been at an end ere this time, now I perceive God will have a further trial, to root out all dissemblers, that no man should rejoice in himself, but he that rejoiceth should rejoice in God; wherefore, if prophecy should fail, and tongues should cease, yet love must endure, for fear hath painfulness, but a perfect love casteth out all fear, which love I have no mistrust, but God hath poured it upon you so abundantly, that nothing in the world shall be able to separate you from God, neither high nor low, rich nor poor, life nor death, shall be able to put you from Christ, but by him I trust you shall enter into New-Jerusalem, there to live for ever."

The Martyrdom of John Hullier, minister, who was burnt at Cambridge.

JOHN HULLIER was descended of reputable parents, who, after giving him a liberal education at a private school, sent him to Eaton college, from whence, according to the rules of that foundation, he was elected to the King's college, at Cambridge.

After he had been at college about three years, he was admitted to a fellowship, and obtained a curacy at Babram, a village, about three miles from Cambridge. He had not been long here before he went to Lynn, where he had several debates with the papists, who reporting his principles to Dr. Thurlby, bishop of the diocess, he sent for him, and, after a short examination relative to his faith, committed him to the castle of Cambridge.

A short time after this, he was cited to appear at St. Mary's church, before several doctors both of law and divinity, by whom, he was reprimanded for opposing the doctrines of the church of Rome, and maintaining and defending those set forth in the days of king Edward VI.

His examination being finished, he was required to recant his erroneous opinions; which peremptorily refusing, he was degraded, condemned, and delivered over to the secular power, who immediately divested him of all his books, papers, and writings.

On the day appointed for his execution, he was conducted to the stake without the town, at a place called Jesus Green, near Jesus college, where, having made the necessary preparations on the melancholy occasion, he desired the spectators to pray for him, and to bear witness that he died in the faith of Christ, sealing the same with his blood. He likewise assured them, that he died in a good cause, for the testimony of the truth, and that there was no other rock, but Jesus Christ, to build upon, nor any hope of salvation, but through his death and sufferings.

One of the proctors of the university, and some of the fellows of Trinity college, were offended at his address to the people, and reproved the mayor for giving him liberty to speak. To this, our martyr made no reply; when being chained to the stake, he earnestly called upon God for his grace and support, to enable him to undergo the fiery trial.

As soon as the fagots were lighted, a number of books were thrown into the midst of them ; and, among the rest, a communion book, which our martyr catching, joyfully read in it, till the flames and smoke prevented him from seeing. He then prayed with a loud voice, holding the book as long as he was able, and praising God for sending it to him as a comforter in his last moments.

After the spectators thought he had been dead, he suddenly uttered, " Lord Jesus, receive my spirit," and then quietly expired.

His death was greatly lamented by many of the spectators, who prayed for him, and expressed their grief by floods of tears, he having been a man of eminent piety, and the most exemplary virtue.

The Martyrdoms of Simon Miller, and Elizabeth Cooper, who were burnt together in the city of Norwich.

Simon Miller was an eminent merchant in the town of Lynn-Regis. He was a godly man, zealous for the truth of the gospel, and averse to the popish religion.

Having occasion to go to Norwich on business, while there, he inquired of some people coming out of church from the popish service, where he might go and receive the communion, which being reported to chancellor Dunning, he ordered him to appear before him. This summons he readily obeyed, when the chancellor asked him several questions, to which, answering agreeable to the dictates of his conscience, he was committed prisoner to the bishop's palace.

After being sometime in confinement, he obtained permission to go home, in order to settle his worldly concerns. On his return, he was again examined by the chancellor, who required him to recant his opinions, and return to the holy mother-church ; but Miller remaining inflexible in his faith and profession, he was condemned as a heretic, and delivered over to the secular power.

Elizabeth Cooper (his fellow-martyr) was the wife of a tradesman in Norwich. She had formerly been prevailed on to recant the protestant, and embrace the Romish religion : but, being troubled in her conscience for so doing, she went one day to St. Andrew's church, where, in the presence of a numerous audience, she stood up, and publicly revoked her recantation. For this, she was immediately apprehended, and committed to prison. The next day, she was brought before the bishop, when persisting in her faith, she was condemned as a relapsed person, and delivered to the sheriff for execution.

On the 30th of the month called July, 1557, they were both led to the stake in a hollow without the city, near Bishopsgate. As soon as the fagots were lighted, Elizabeth Cooper expressed some fear ; but, being encouraged by the advice and example of her fellow-martyr, she remained fixed ; and they both cheerfully resigned their souls into the hand of him who gave them.

The sufferings and Martyrdoms of William Bongeor, Thomas Benhote, William Purchase, Agnes Silverside, Helen Ewring, Elizabeth Folk, William Munt, John Johnson, Alice Munt, and Rose Allen, who were all burnt on the same day, at Colchester, in Essex.

On the 7th of the month called March, 1357, about two o'clock in the morning, Edmund Tyrrell, (who was a descendant of that family who murdered king Edward V. in the tower of London) assisted by the bailiff of the hundred, two constables, and a great number of other attendants, went to the house of William Munt, farmer, at Much-Bently, in Essex ; and, after alarming the family, told Munt, that he and his wife must both go with him to Colchester castle.

This sudden surprise greatly affected his wife, who, after she had a little recovered herself, desired of Tyrrell, that her daughter might be permitted to fetch her something to drink before she went with him. This being granted, Tyrrell took the opportunity of advising the daughter, as she passed by him, to give her father and mother better counsel, and admonish them to behave more like good christians, and members of the catholic church.

The daughter replied, they had the holy ghost for their instructer, and, therefore, needed no other. This answer greatly irritated Tyrrell, who, after using many harsh words, assured her, he was now convinced of the absolute necessity of calling such heretics to immediate account.

Tyrrell, from the most abusive language, proceeded to the most cruel behaviour; and, in order to try if she could bear burning, took the girl by the wrist, and held the lighted candle under her hand, burning it across the back till the sinews cracked; frequently exclaiming, during the barbarous operation, " why, thou whore, wilt thou not cry?" This she endured with the utmost patience, telling the villain, if he thought proper, he might then begin at her feet and proceed to the head; for that, he that prompted him to the work would one day pay him his wages.

Tyrrell then seized William Munt, Alice his wife, and Rose Allen, their daughter, and immediately conducted them to Colchester castle, together with John Johnson, whom they took in their way, in consequence of an information that had been laid against him for heresy.

They, also, the same morning, apprehended the six others who suffered with them, namely, William Bongeor, Thomas Benhote, William Purchase, Agnes Silverside, Helen Ewring, and Elizabeth Folk; but not chusing to place those with the rest, they sent them prisoners to Mote-hill.

After they had been confined a few days, they were all brought together before several justices of the peace, priests, and officers, (amongst whom were Kingston the commissary, and Boswell the bishop of London's secretary) with many others, in order to be examined relative to their faith.

The first person called on was William Bongeor, who being examined concerning his faith in the sacrament, replied, that what they termed the sacrament of the altar was bread, is bread, and remaineth bread, and was not in the least holier for the consecration. This he affirmed, and at the same time protested against all the popish doctrines in general; upon which, he immediately received sentence of condemnation.

Thomas Benhote, also, denied the sacrament of the altar, and abjured the errors of the Romish church.

William Purchase declared, that when he received the sacrament of the altar, he received the bread in an holy use, and both bread and wine as such, but in remembrance of Christ's death and passion.

Agnes Silverside said, she approved not of the popish consecration, nor any of the pageant absurdities and superstitions of the church of Rome, which was the church of antichrist.

Helen Ewring, also, renounced all the doctrines and practices set forth by the church of Rome.

Elizabeth Folk being asked, whether she believed the presence of Christ's body to be in the sacrament of the altar, really and substantially? replied, she believed it was a substantial and a real lie.

The commissioners being incensed at so abrupt a reply, asked her, whether, after consecration, there remained not the body and blood of Christ in the sacrament? She answered, that before consecration, and after, it was bread, and that what man blessed without God's word, was accursed and deemed abominable by that word.

They then examined her relative to her confession by a priest, of going to church, to hear mass, of the authority of the bishop of Rome, &c. Unto all which, she answered, that she would neither use, nor frequent any of them, by the grace of God, but did utterly detest them from her very heart and soul.

In consequence of this, sentence of condemnation was passed upon her; immediately after which, she kneeled down, lifted her eyes and hands to heaven, and, in an audible voice, praised God, that she was deemed worthy to suffer for the testimony of Christ, praying, at the same time, for her persecutors.

William Munt being asked his opinion concerning the sacrament of the altar, said, it was a most abominable idol; and that, if he should observe any part of the popish superstition, he should displease God, and bring a curse upon himself; and, therefore, for fear of the divine vengeance, he would not bow down to an idol.

John Johnson answered to the same effect with Munt; but added, that, in receiving the sacrament, according to Christ's institution, he received the body of Christ spiritually.

Alice Munt renounced all popish error and superstition, and continued steadfast in the profession of the true faith of Jesus Christ.

Rose Allen who was last called, being examined concerning auricular confession, hearing mass, and the seven sacraments, answered, that they were an abomination in the eyes of the Lord, and that she would, therefore, for ever reject them. She, likewise, told them, that she was no member of their church, for they were the members of antichrist, and would have the reward of antichrist, if they repented not.

In consequence of this, sentence was then read against her; and she, and the rest, were all delivered over to the secular power.

Bishop Gardner having an account transmitted to him of the condemnation of these ten innocent persons, for the alleged crime of heresy, sent down a warrant for their being burned, and fixed the time on the 2d of the month called August.

As the prisoners were confined in different places, it was resolved by the officer, that part of them should be executed in the former, and the rest in the latter part of that day. Accordingly, William Bongeor, William Purchase, Thomas Benhote, Agnes Silverside, Helen Ewring, and Elizabeth Folk, were brought early in the morning to the place appointed for them to suffer, where every thing was prepared for the bloody catastrophe.

When our martyrs arrived at the spot, they kneeled down, and humbly addressed themselves to Almighty God, though they were interrupted by their popish enemies.

After they had done praying, they arose, were fastened to the stakes, and all burnt in one fire. They died with amazing fortitude and resignation, triumphing in the midst of the flames, and exulting in hopes of the future glory that awaited their departure from a sinful world.

In like manner, in the afternoon of the same day, William and Alice Munt, Rose Allen, and John Johnson, were brought to the same place where their fellow-martyrs had suffered in the morning. As soon as they arrived at the fatal spot, they all kneeled down, and for some time prayed with the greatest fervency. After prayers, they arose, and cheerfully submitted to be fastened to the stakes. They earnestly prayed to God to enable them to endure the fiery trial, exhorted the people to beware of idolatry, and, with their latest breath, confessed the faith of Christ crucified, whom to know is eternal life, and for whom to die is the glory of his chosen people.

The Martyrdom of Richard Crashfield, who was burnt at Wymondham, in Norfolk.

THE popish emissaries having laid an information against this pious man, he was apprehended on suspicion of heresy, and was brought before chancellor Dunning, who examined him concerning the ceremonies of the church, whether he believed them to be good and godly?

Crashfield replied, he believed as many of them as were founded on the word of God, and authorized by the practice and example of Christ and his apostles.

The chancellor then particularly examined him concerning the corporeal presence in the eucharist : to which, Crashfield said, he believed Christ's body was broken by him upon the cross, and his blood shed for his redemption, of which, bread and wine are a perpetual remembrance, the pledge of God's mercy, and the seal of his promise to those who faithfully believe in his most holy gospel.

Crashfield was then dismissed for the present, and sent back to prison ; but, the next day, he was again brought before the chancellor, who asked him, if he still persisted in his heretical opinions ?

On his replying in the affirmative, and confirming the same, by his answers to other questions and articles proposed to him, the chancellor stood up, and in form required him to turn from his wicked errors and damnable heresies, and not be an example of impiety and obstinacy, adding, through his presumptuous reading, he persuaded silly women to embrace his errors at the hazard of their souls, and promising him mercy on his compliance with these terms.

Our martyr boldly maintained his faith in the pure doctrines and uncorrupted ceremonies of the church of Christ, telling the arrogant chancellor, that it was of God, whom he had offended, that he craved mercy, and not of him who was a sinner-like himself, and therefore incapable of dispensing forgiveness, or giving any satisfaction to his precious soul.

At length, the chancellor finding him inflexibly attached to his opinions and principles, in order to obtain pretence for condemning him, asked, when he was last at his parish church ? and, on his answering, that it was two years past, the chancellor told him, he stood excommunicated, and was consequently condemned as a heretic.

Crashfield not making any reply, sentence of death was passed on him, and he was delivered to the sheriff of the county in order for execution.

A few days after his condemnation, he was brought to the stake, where, in the presence of numerous spectators, with great patience and constancy, he yielded up his soul to God, in testimony of the truth of his most holy word, in hopes of enjoying an everlasting habitation in the heavenly mansions.

The sufferings and Martyrdom of Joice Lewis, who was burnt at Litchfield, in Staffordshire, for professing the truth of the Gospel.

In the beginning of the reign of queen Mary, Joice Lewis went to church, heard mass, was confessed, and attended to all the ceremonies of the Romish church, till at length it pleased God, by the preaching of a protestant minister, to convince her of her errors, and convert her to the true faith of the gospel of Christ.

What greatly contributed to her conversion was, the burning of a faithful servant of God at Coventry. She inquired into the cause of that cruel affair; and being told, it was because he would not receive the mass, she began to entertain doubts concerning the truth of the religion she professed, and accordingly applied for satisfaction to one Glover, who had suffered much himself for his steadfast attachment to the truth of Christ's gospel.

This good man pointed out to her the errors of the Romish church, proving them to be antiscriptural and antichristian, and advising her to make the word of God her constant study, and regulate her faith and practice by that alone.

J. Lewis immediately took his advice, and gave herself up to prayer, and acts of benevolence; determined, by the grace of God, both to do and believe what she was enjoined by the word of God:

Being one day urged by her husband to go to church, when the holy water was spread about, she turned her back on it, and highly expressed her displeasure. This being observed by several of the congregation, an accusation was, the next day, laid against her, before the bishop of Litchfield, for despising the sacrament of the church.

The bishop sent an officer to summon her to appear before him; but, when the summons was delivered to her husband, he threatened the officer, unless he immediately withdrew.

This treatment being reported to the bishop, he ordered both Lewis and his wife to appear before him; when, after a short examination, he dismissed the husband, on his begging pardon for his conduct, and offered forgiveness to her for the offence she had committed at the church, on the same terms. But she courageously told him, that by refusing holy water, she had not offended God, or any of his laws.

Though the bishop was greatly offended at this reply, yet as she was a person of considerable repute, he did not proceed immediately against her, but gave her a month to consider of it, binding her husband in an hundred pounds bond, to bring her again to him at the expiration of that time.

When the period fixed was nearly arrived, many of their friends advised her husband, by all means, not to deliver her up, but to convey her to some retirement, saying, he had better sustain the loss of an hundred pounds, than be instrumental to his wife's destruction.

To these remonstrances, the unnatural husband replied, he would not forfeit his bond for her sake; and, accordingly, when the time was expired, he delivered her to the bishop, who still finding her resolute, committed her to a loathsome prison.

She was several times examined by the bishop, who reasoned with her on her not coming to mass, receiving the sacrament, and sacramentals of the holy church: to this, she replied, that she found not those things in God's words, which he so much urged and magnified as necessary, to salvation, adding, that if those things were founded on God's word, she would receive them with all her heart.

The bishop told her, if she would believe no more than was in scripture, she was a damnable heretic; and, after much farther discourse with her, pronounced sentence against her as an irreclaimable heretic.

After her condemnation, she remained a whole year in confinement, when, at length, the writ for her execution arriving, she sent for several of her friends to advise her how to behave herself, that her death might redound to the glory of God, and the establishment of his people; declaring, at the same time, that she feared not death, when she thought on her Saviour Christ.

The night before she suffered, two priests visited her, and desired to hear her confession, but she rejected their request with disdain.

In the morning of the 10th of September, 1557, she was conducted to the place of execution by the two sheriffs, and a strong guard. As soon as she arrived at the stake, she kneeled down, and prayed most earnestly to God, beseeching him to abolish the idolatrous mass, and deliver the kingdom from popery; to which, one of the sheriffs, and many of the spectators, cried, Amen.

When she was chained to the stake, she appeared not in the least afraid of the horrid punishment that awaited her; but, on the contrary, wore a calm and pleasing countenance; and, when the fagots were lighted, she lifted up her hands and eyes to heaven, in which posture, she quietly resigned her soul into the hands of her blessed Redeemer; for whose most holy word, she patiently suffered here, in full hopes of everlasting life in the realms above.

The Martyrdoms of Ralph Allerton, James Awstoo, Margery Awstoo, his wife, and Richard Roth, who were all burnt together at Islington, near London.

RALPH ALLERTON, being informed against by several bigotted papists in the neighbourhood where he lived, was apprehended on suspicion of heresy; and, after undergoing a short examination before a magistrate, was committed to prison.

A few days after, he was brought before lord Darcy, who accused him of not only absenting himself from church, but also that, by preaching, he had persuaded others to follow his example.

To this, Allerton made the following confession : that coming to his parish church, and finding the people sitting there, some gazing about, and others gazing on unprofitable subjects, he exhorted them to pray, meditate on God's word, and not sit idle ; to which, they willingly consented ; and, after prayer, he read a chapter to them out of the New Testament. This he continued to do, for some time, till he was informed, his proceedings were contrary to law, as he was neither priest nor minister ; upon which, he desisted.

He likewise confessed, that he was taken up for reading in the parish of Welley ; but, when those that apprehended him understood he had read but once, and that it was an exhortation to obedience, they let him go ; after which, being afraid, he kept in woods, barns, and solitary places, till he was apprehended.

After this examination, the lord Darcy sent him to London to the queen's commissioners, by whom, he was referred to bishop Bonner, who persuaded him publicly to recant his profession at St. Paul's church, and then dismissed him ; whereupon, he returned into the country.

He was greatly troubled in his conscience for what he had done, earnestly repented of the same, and openly professed the faith he had shamefully revoked, till Thomas Tye, priest of the parish, (who had been a professor of the truth, but was now a persecutor) caused him to be apprehended, and again brought up to the bishop of London.

When he came before the bishop, he asked him the cause of his being brought, telling him, he believed he was wrongfully accused, unless he had dissembled.

Allerton told him, that he was not guilty of what was laid to his charge, and desired to know his accusers, and the particulars of his accusation, in order that he might be able to defend himself.

In answer to this request, the bishop told him, that if he had not dissembled, he needed not to be afraid, or ashamed ; and urged him to tell him, if he dissembled in his former recantation.

Allerton replied, " if my accusers are not produced before you, my conscience will constrain me to accuse myself; for, I confess, I have most grievously offended God by my dissimulation, when I was last before your lordship, for which, I am now heartily concerned."

When the bishop inquired the cause of his dissembling, he replied, " My lord, if your lordship remembers, I set my hand to a certain writing, the contents of which were, that I did believe in all things as the catholic church teacheth, &c. in which, I did not disclose my mind, but most shamefully dissembled, as I made no distinction between the true church and the false one."

Being called upon to declare what he thought to be the true church, he would not allow the church of Rome to be so; but said, that on the contrary, those christians who were persecuted by the Romish church, were members of the true catholic church of Christ. Upon which, the bishop called him heretic, and sent him to the Little-ease prison, at Guildhall, in London.

After being confined there a whole day, the bishop again sent for him; and, in the presence of the dean of St. Paul's, and the chancellor of the diocess, produced some writings, which Allerton acknowledged to be his. The bishop then asked, if he had been at mass since he was last before him; to which, he answered in the negative, declaring that he had neither been at mass, mattins, nor any other strange worshipping of God.

The chief person that appeared against him in the court, was Thomas Tye, the priest of the parish, who affirmed, that he was a seditious person, and had stirred up great strife in the neighbourhood where he lived.

This, with other complaints, being alleged against him, he was sent to prison again, and, in a short time, brought before the queen's council, who demanded of him whether he believed, that after the words of consecration spoken by the priest, there remained no bread, but the very body of our Saviour Jesus Christ, God, and man, and no other substance under the form of bread.

On Allerton's demanding scripture proof for this doctrine of transubstantiation, the bishop asked him, if Christ did not say, " this is my body ?" adding, " wilt thou deny these words of our Saviour Christ, or was he a dissembler ?" " No, my lord, (replied our martyr) Christ is true, and all men are liars ; yet I must refuse to understand the words of our Saviour so fantastically as you teach or take them, for then we should agree with the heretics called Nestorians, who denied that Christ had a true natural body. This, methinks, you do, my lord, if you affirm his body to be there, because you then affirm his body to be fantastical, not natural ; and therefore look well to it for God's sake."

The bishop, after severely reprimanding him for what he had said, dismissed him for the present, and he was re-conducted to prison.

On the 15th of the month called May, he was brought before bishop Bonner, at his palace in London, where the following articles were exhibited against him. :

1. That he was of the parish of Much-Bently, in Essex, and of the diocess of London.

2. That on the 10th of January last past, Mr. John Mordant, preaching at St. Paul's, London, the said Ralph Allerton did there openly submit himself to the church of Rome, with the rites and ceremonies thereof.

3. That he did consent and subscribe, as well unto the submission, as also to one other bill, in which he granted, that if he should, at any time, turn again unto his former opinions, it should then be lawful for the bishop to denounce and adjudge him as a heretic.

4. That he had subscribed to a bill, wherein he affirmed, that in the sacrament, after the words of consecration be spoken by the priest, their remain still material bread and material wine ; and that he believed, that the bread is the bread of thanksgiving, and the memorial of Christ's death ; and that, when he received it, he received the body of Christ spiritually in his soul, but material bread in substance.

5. That he had openly affirmed, and also advisedly spoken, that which is contained in the said former fourth article last before specified.

6. That he had spoken against the bishop of Rome, with the see and church of the same; and also against the seven sacraments, and other ceremonies and ordinances of the same church, used then within this realm.

7. That he had allowed and commended the opinions and faith of Messrs. Cranmer, Ridley, Latimer, and others, of late burnt within this realm, and believed their opinions to be good and godly.

8. That he had divers times affirmed, that the religion used within this realm, at the time of his apprehension, was neither good nor agreeable to God's word, and that he could not conform himself thereunto.

9. That he had affirmed, that the book of common prayer, set forth in the reign of king Edward VI. was, in all parts, good and godly: and, that the said Ralph, and his company, being prisoners, did daily use among themselves, in prison, some part of the same book.

10. That he had affirmed, that if he were out of prison, he would not come to mass, mattins, nor even-song, nor bear taper, candle, nor palm, nor go in procession, nor would receive holy water, holy bread, ashes, or pix, nor any other ceremony used within this realm.

11. That he had affirmed, that if he were at liberty, he would not confess his sins to any priest, to receive absolution of him, nor yet would receive the sacrament of the altar, as it was then used.

12. That he had affirmed, that praying to saints, and prayers for the dead, were neither good nor profitable; and that a man is not bound to fast and pray, but at his own will and pleasure; neither that it is lawful to reserve the sacrament, nor to worship it.

13. That the said Ralph Allerton hath, according to these affirmations, abstained and refused to come unto his parish church, ever since the 10th of January last, or to use, receive, or allow any ceremonies, sacraments, or other rites then used in the church.

To these articles, our martyr, in general, answered in the affirmative, objecting only to that clause in the 12th, ' that a man is not bound to fast and pray, but at his own will and pleasure;" and confessed, at the same time, that he had neither fasted nor prayed so frequently as was his duty to have done.

Many arguments were used by Dr. Derbyshire, the bishop's chancellor, and others, to bring Allerton to a recantation; but, all proving ineffectual, he was sent back again to prison.

A few days after, he, with his fellow-martyrs, was ordered to appear before bishop Bonner, at his palace at Fulham, where, in his private chapel, he judicially propounded to them divers articles, the particulars of which were addressed to Ralph Allerton, in the following form.

"Thou, Ralph Allerton, canst not deny but that the information given against thee, and remaining now in the acts of this court of thine ordinary Edmund Bonner, bishop of London, was, and is, a true information."

The substance of the information was this:

That one Lawrence Edwards had a child unchristened, and Tye, the curate, asked him, why his child was not baptized? Edwards replied, it should be baptized when he could find one of his own religion.

Tye, told him, he had imbibed those notions from some busy people, who go about to spread heresy. Edwards acknowledged he had, telling him, at the same time, if his doctrine was better, he would receive it. He then produced Allerton, to whom the curate said, if he had instructed Edwards, it was against God's commandments to enter into the church. On this, Allerton thus addressed the people who were present. "O good people, now is fulfilled the saying of the priest and prophet Esdras, viz. The fire of a multitude is kindled against a few, they have taken away their houses, and spoiled their goods. Which of you have not seen this day? Who is here among you that seeth not all these things done upon this day? The church, unto which they call us, is the church of antichrist, a persecuting church."

This was the cause of his being apprehended, and sent up to the bishop of London.

He was also charged with writing several letters, and other things, which were found on him in prison. He confessed, when they were produced, that he had written them, and that they were intended to be sent to some persons that were in the prison for the sake of the gospel, at Colchester, where they were afterwards burnt.

Allerton was then dismissed, and the examination deferred to the afternoon, when several other articles were objected to him ; but these being mostly false, he refused to answer. He granted, indeed, that he disapproved of the mass and other ceremonies, that were contrary to the express word of God.

When the decree of pope Innocent III, concerning the sacrament of the altar, was read to him by the bishop, he declared, he regarded it not, nor was it necessary that any man should believe it.

When Bonner asked him, what he had to allege, why sentence of condemnation should not be passed upon him, he briefly answered, " my lord, you ought not to condemn me as a heretic, for I am a good christian : but do as you have determined, for I perceive that right and truth are suppressed, and cannot now appear upon earth."

In consequence of this answer, Allerton was condemned as a heretic, and immediately delivered over to the secular power.

James Awstoo, and Margery, his wife, were next examined, when the bishop, among other things, asked the former, if he had been confessed in Lent, and whether he had received the sacrament at Easter ?

Awstoo replied, he had been confessed by the curate of Allhallows, Barking, near the tower of London ; but that he had not received the sacrament of the altar, because he detested it as an abominable idol.

The bishop then asked Margery, his wife, if she approved of the religion then used in the church of England ? She replied in the negative, affirming it to be corrupt and antiscriptural ; and that those who conformed to it, were influenced rather by fear, than a conviction that it was founded on the word of God.

3 Q

Being required, by the bishop, to go to church, hear mass, and pray for the prosperity of the queen, she declared her abhorrence of mass, and that she would not come into any church where there were idols.

The bishop then made use of the most forcible arguments to induce them to recant; but they both persisted in their faith and profession, and in renouncing all popish doctrines and practices; in consequence of which, they separately received sentence of condemnation, and were delivered into the hands of the sheriff, in order for execution.

Richard Roth, the last examined, was strongly urged by the bishop to acknowledge the seven sacraments, as also the corporeal presence in the eucharist. But he briefly told him, that if those doctrines were taught in the holy scriptures, he would believe them; if otherwise, he must reject them.

Being examined more particularly concerning the sacrament of the altar, and other points, he plainly declared, that, in that ceremony, there were not the very body and blood of Christ; but that it was a dead god, and the mass was abominable, and contrary to God's holy word and will, from which faith and opinion, he was determined, through the strength of divine grace, never to depart.

He was afterwards accused of being an encourager of heretics, and that he had written divers letters to certain persons who were burnt at Colchester; the latter of which, he frankly acknowledged.

Being asked his opinion of Ralph Allerton, he answered, that he esteemed him as a sincere servant of God; and that, if hereafter, at any time, he should be put to death for his faith and religion, he believed he would die a martyr for the cause of Christ, and the truth of his gospel.

He was then asked, if he approved of the order and rites of the church at that time used in England? To which, he answered in the negative, declaring that he utterly abhorred them. In consequence of which, he received sentence of death, and was immediately delivered to the sheriff, in order for execution.

On the 17th of September, 1557, these four steadfast believers in Christ were conducted by the sheriff, and his attendants, to Islington, (the place appointed for their execution) where they were fastened to two stakes, and consumed in one fire. They all behaved in a manner truly consistent with their situation, and as became the real followers of Jesus, cheerfully resigning up their souls in testimony of the truth of his most holy word.

The persecution and deaths of John Hallingdale, William Sparrow, and Richard Gibson, who were all burnt together in Smithfield.

INFORMATIONS having been laid against these three persons, on suspicion of heresy, they were all apprehended ; and, after being confined for some time, were at length brought together to be examined before Bonner, bishop of London, when articles were exhibited against each separately, and their respective answers required thereunto.

The first person examined was John Hallingdale, against whom, the following articles were exhibited.

1. That the said John Hallingdale is of the diocess of London, and subject to the bishop of London's jurisdiction.

2. That the said John, before the time of the reign of Edward the Sixth, late king of England, was of the same faith and religion that were then observed, believed, taught and set forth here in this realm of England.

3. That during the reign of the said Edward the Sixth, late king of England, upon the occasion of the preaching of certain ministers in that time, he did not abide in his former faith and religion, but did depart from them, and so did, and doth continue, till this present day, and so determineth to do (as he saith) to his life's end.

4. That the said John Hallingdale hath thought, believed, and spoken, divers times, that the faith, religion, and ecclesiastical service, received, observed, and now used in this realm of England, are not good and laudable, but

against God's commandment and word; especially concerning the mass and the seven sacraments: and that the said John will, in no wise, conform himself to the same, but speak and think against it during his natural body.

5. That the said John absenteth himself continually from his own parish church of St. Leonard, neither hearing mattins, mass, nor even-song; nor yet confessing his sins to the priest, or receiving the sacrament of the altar at his hands, or in using other ceremonies, as they are now used in the churches and realm of England: and, as he remembereth, he never came but once, into the parish church of St. Leonard, and careth not (as he saith) if he never come there any more, the service being as it is there at present, and so many abuses being there, as he saith there are, especially the mass, the sacraments, the ceremonies, and service set forth in Latin.

6. That the said John, when his wife, called Alice, was brought to bed of a man-child, caused the said child to be christened in English, after the same manner and form in all points, as were used in the time of king Edward the Sixth, aforesaid, and caused it to be called Joshua; and would not have the said child christened in Latin, after the form and manner now used in the church and realm of England; nor will have it, by his will (as he saith) confirmed by the bishop.

The particulars stated in all these articles, our martyr acknowledged to be just; and said, he would not, on any condition whatever, revoke his answers.

The bishop then asked him, whether he did firmly believe, that in the sacrament, commonly called the sacrament of the altar, there are really and truly the very body and blood of our Saviour Christ, or not? To which, Hallingdale made answer, that he neither in the time of king Edward IV. nor at present, did believe, that, in the said sacrament, there are really the body and blood of Christ: for, if he had so believed, he would (as others had done) have received the same, which he did not, because he had believed, and then did believe, that the very body of Christ is only in heaven, and no where else.

He likewise said, that Cranmer, Latimer, Ridley, Hooper, and many others, who had been lately burned for heretics, were far otherwise, as they all preached the true gospel. That, on their preaching, he grounded his faith and conscience, according to the saying of St. John, in the 18th chapter of his Revelation, that the blood of the prophets and of the saints, and of all that were slain, upon earth, was founded in the antichristian church; by which, is understood, that church whereof the pope is head.

After this examination, he was re-conducted to prison; and, the next day, brought again before the bishop, who used his utmost endeavours to prevail on him to recant; but, finding them all ineffectual, he read the sentence of condemnation, and he was immediately delivered over to the secular power.

The articles exhibited against William Sparrow, were the following :

1. That thou, William Sparrow, wast, in times past, detected and presented lawfully unto thine ordinary, the bishop of London, called Edmund, who also is now thine ordinary, and of the said diocess : and thou wast presented and detected unto him for heresy, errors, and unlawful opinions, which thou didst believe, set forth, and hold.

2. That thou, before thy said ordinary, didst openly and judicially confess the said heresies, errors, and unlawful opinions, as appeareth plainly in the acts of the court made before thine ordinary.

3. That thou, after the premises, didst make thy submission in writing, and didst exhibit and deliver the same as thy deed to thy said ordinary, openly confessing and recognizing thy heresies, errors, and unlawful opinions, and thine offences, and translations in that behalf.

4. That thou, after the premises, didst promise unto thy said ordinary, voluntarily, and of thy own accord, that always, after the said submission, thou wouldst in all points; conform thyself unto the common order of the catholic church, observed and kept here in this realm of England, and, in no wise, fall again into heresies, errors, or unlawful opinions.

5. That thou, since thy said submission, hast willingly fallen into certain heresies, and errors, and hast holden and set forth divers unlawful opinions, to the very great hurt of thy own soul, and also to the great hinderance and loss of divers others, especially against the sacrament of the catholic church.

6. That thou, since the said submission, hast willingly gone about divers places within the diocess of London, and sold divers heretical, erroneous and plasphemous ballads, and wast apprehended and taken with the ballads about thee, and committed to prison.

To these respective articles, Sparrow gave the following answers.

To the first, second, third, and fourth articles, he answered affirmatively.

To the fifth article, he answered, that if he had spoken against the sacrament of the altar, &c. he had spoken but the truth.

To the sixth, he answered, that he granted it; adding, that he did sell the ballads then shewn and read before him, and that the same contained God's holy word.

After this examination, he was sent back to prison; but, in the afternoon of the same day, he was again brought before the bishop, who charged him with his former submission.

To this charge, he answered, "I am very sorry, that I ever made it; for it was the worst deed I ever did."

The bishop then told him, that he went to church, and there was confessed, and heard mass.

This, Sparrow acknowledged, and that it was with a troubled conscience. And added, "that which you call the truth, I do believe to be heresy."

Bonner then charged him with the contents of the fifth article; to which, he answered, that he had done as was contained in that article, and so he would again, were he at liberty.

Being then asked by the bishop, whether he would persist and continue in the same; he answered, that he would not go from his opinion: and added, "that which you call heresy is good and godly; and, if every hair of my head were a man, I would burn them all, rather than go from the truth."

After this, the bishop endeavoured to prevail on him to recant, saying, that on those conditions, he should be dismissed; but Sparrow continuing resolute in his faith and opinions, the bishop proceeded to read the sentence of excommunication against him, and he was condemned as a heretic; after which, he was delivered into the hands of the sheriff, and by him again conducted to prison.

The misfortunes of Richard Gibson arose from his doing a singular piece of service to one, with whom he was particularly acquainted. This person was arrested for debt, when Gibson being surety for him, his friend treacherously fled, and he not not being able to discharge the debt, was thrown into the Poultry-compter, where he remained upwards of two years.

When he was about to be released, some litigious and bigotted papist laid an accusation against him, to the bishop of London, of heresy, because he had never confessed, nor received the sacrament of the altar, while he was in confinement.

In consequence of this, he was ordered to appear before the bishop, who examined him concerning his faith and religion. At first, he seemed to make a certain submission, which was recorded in the bishop's register: but this not appearing sufficiently satisfactory, the following articles were exhibited against him.

1. That the said Richard Gibson, prisoner in the Compter in the Poultry, in the diocess of London, hath, otherwise than became a faithful christian, and a good subject in this realm of England, behaved himself, in words and deeds, in divers conditions and points, contrary to the order, religion, and faith of Christ's catholic church, and contrary to the order of this realm, to the pernicious and evil example of the inhabitants of the city of London, and the prisoners of the prison of the said Compter in the Poultry, and greatly to the hurt and damage of his own soul; offending, especially in the articles following: by reason whereof, the said Richard Gibson was and is, in the jurisdiction of the said bishop of London, and subject to the

said jurisdiction, to make answer to his offences and transgressions underwritten, according to the order of the law.

2. That the said Richard Gibson hath irreverently spoken against the pope, and see, and church of Rome ; and likewise against the the whole church of this realm of England ; and against the seven sacraments of the catholic and whole church of christendom ; and against the articles of the christian faith, here observed in this realm of England; and against the commendable and laudable ceremonies of the catholic church.

3. That the said Richard Gibson hath commended, allowed, defended, and liked, Cranmer, Latimer, and Ridley ; and, also, other heretics here in this realm of England, according to the ecclesiastical laws condemned for heretics ; and, also, all their heretical, erroneous, damnable, and wicked opinions, especially against the sacrament of the altar, and the authority of the pope and see of Rome, with the whole religion thereof.

4. That the said Richard Gibson hath comforted, aided, assisted, and maintained, both by words and otherwise, heretics and erroneous persons, or at least suspected and infamed of heresies and errors condemned by the catholic church, to continue in their heretical and erroneous opinions aforesaid, favouring and counselling the same unto his power.

5. That the said Gibson hath affirmed and said, that the religion and faith commonly observed and kept, and used now here in this realm of England, are not good nor laudable, nor in any wise agreeable unto God's word and commandment.

6. That the said Richard Gibson hath affirmed, that the English service, and the books commonly called the books of communion, or common-prayer, here set forth in this realm of England, in the time of king Edward the Sixth, were, in all parts and points, good and godly, and the same only, and no other, ought to be observed and kept in this realm of England.

7. That the said Gibson hath affirmed, that if he may at once be out of prison, and at liberty, he will not come to

come to any parish church, or ecclesiastical place, to hear the mattins, mass, or even-song, or any divine service, now used in this realm of England, nor come to the procession upon times and days accustomed, nor bear at any time any taper or candle, or receive pix, at mass-time, nor to receive holy water, nor holy bread, nor observe the ceremonies or usages of the catholic church here observed and kept commonly in this realm of England.

8. That the said Gibson hath affirmed, that he is not bound at any time, though he have liberty, and the presence of a priest, convenient and meet, to confess his sins to the said priest, nor to receive absolution at his hands, nor to receive of him the sacrament, called the sacrament of the altar, after such form as is now used within the realm of England.

9. That the said Richard Gibson hath affirmed, that prayer unto saints, or prayers for the dead, are not laudable, or profitable ; and that no man is bound, at any time, or in any place, to fast or pray, but, only at his own will and pleasure ; and that it is not lawful to reserve, or keep, the said sacrament of the altar.

Gibson having answered these respective articles, was dismissed for the present ; but the next day, was again brought before the bishop for a farther examination.

Several questions were put to him, but he refused answering to either, saying, the bishop of London was not his ordinary.

His last examination was at the bishop's consistory-court, where Bonner, after some discourse, asked, if he knew any cause, why sentence should not be pronounced against him ? To which, he told the bishop, he had not any thing against him for which he might justly condemn him.

The bishop then told him, that men said, he was an evil man.

Gibson replied, " yea, my lord, and so may I say of you also."

After this, sentence of condemnation was read; at the end of which, he said, " blessed am I, that I am cursed at our hands."

3 R

He was then delivered to the sheriff, who conducted him to prison, in order for execution.

On the 18th of the month called November, 1557, these three faithful servants of Christ were conducted under a proper guard, to Smithfield, where they were all fastened to one stake. After they had, for some time, fervently prayed to God to enable them to endure the fiery trial, the fagots were lighted, and they all cheerfully resigned their souls into the hands of him who gave them.

The sufferings and Martyrdoms of John Rough, minister, and Margaret Maring, who were both burnt together in Smithfield.

JOHN ROUGH was a native of Scotland, and born of reputable and pious parents. Being deprived of his right of inheritance to certain lands by some of his kindred, he was so irritated, that, though very young, he entered himself a member of the order of Black Friars, at Stirling, in Scotland.

Here he continued upwards of sixteen years, when the earl of Arran, then regent of Scotland, and afterwards duke of Hamilton, taking a liking to him, applied to the archbishop of St. Andrew's to dispense with his professed order, that he might serve him as his chaplain.

The archbishop readily granting the earl's request, Rough was disengaged from his monastic order, and continued chaplain to his patron about a year; when it pleased God to open his eyes, and give him some knowledge of the truth of the gospel.

At this time, the earl sent him to preach in the county of Ayre, where he continued about four years, during which time, he discharged the duties of his office with the strictest diligence.

On the death of the cardinal of Scotland, he was sent for to officiate at St. Andrew's, for which, he had a pension allowed him from king Henry VIII.

After being some time in this situation, he began to abhor the idolatry and superstition of his own country ; and, when he found, that on the accession of Edward VI. there was free profession of the gospel in England, he left his situation, and went first to Carlisle, where he was appointed preacher, as also to Berwick, and Newcastle-upon-Tyne, by the duke of Somerset, protector to the young king.

A short time after this, he married, and the archbishop of York gave him a benefice near the town of Kingston upon Hull, which he enjoyed till the death of the king.

On the accession of queen Mary, when the religion was altered, and persecution took place in all parts of the kingdom, Rough fled with his wife, into the Low-Countries, and took up his residence at a place called Norden. Here he maintained himself by knitting and selling caps and hose, till the month of October, 1557, when, wanting yarn, and other necessaries for his trade, he embarked for England, and arrived in London on the 10th of November following.

Soon after his arrival, he was informed, there was a private congregation of religious people in a certain part of the city, which having found out, he joined them, and was elected their minister.

In this office, he continued for some time, till, at the instigation of Roger Serjeant, a hypocrite and false brother, on the 13th of December, he, together with one Cuthbert Simpson, deacon of the aforesaid congregation, was apprehended by the vice-chamberlain of the queen's household, at the Saracen's-Head, in Islington, where the congregation had assembled for the purpose of performing their usual worship; and, to avoid suspicion, it had been given out, that their meeting was to hear a play.

Rough and Simpson were both conducted by the vice-chamberlain, to the queen's council, who charged them with assembling to celebrate the communion of the Lord's supper. After a long examination, Simpson was, for the present, dismissed, but Rough was sent prisoner to Newgate.

On the 18th of December, bishop Bonner ordered Rough to be brought before him, at his palace in London, to examine him concerning his religious faith; when the following articles were exhibited against him:

1. That thou, John Rough, didst directly speak against the seven sacraments used commonly and reverently, as things of estimation and great worthyness in the Catholic church; and, also, didst reprove and condemn the substance of the altar, affirming, that in the same, are not really and truly the very body and blood of Christ; and that confession to the priest, and absolution given him (by the minister of Christ) for sins, are not necessary nor available in any wise.

2. Thou hast misliked and reproved the religion and ecclesiastical service, as it is now used in this realm: and hast allowed the religion and service used in the latter years of king Edward the sixth; and so much as in thee lieth, hast, by word, writing, and deed, set forward, taught, and preached the same openly; and, in sundry places, affirmed, that the said English service, and doctrine therein contained, are agreeable, in all points, to God's word, and to the truth; condemned utterly the Latin service now used in the queen's reign; and induced others, by thine example, to do the same.

3. Thou hast, in sundry places within this realm, commended and approved the opinion and doctrine of Thomas Cranmer, late archbishop of Canterbury, Nicholas Ridley, and Hugh Latimer, concerning the sacrament of the altar; affirming, that in the sacrament, there remained, after the words of consecration, material bread, and material wine, without any transubstantiation.

4. That thou hast, in sundry places of this realm, since the queen's reign, ministered and received the communion, as it was used in the late days of king Edward VI. and thou knowest, or credibly hast heard of divers, that yet do keep books of the said communion, and use the same in private houses, out of the church, and are of opinion against the sacrament of the altar.

5. Thou dost know, and hast been conversant with all, or a great part of such Englishmen, as have fled out of the realm; and hast consented and agreed with them in their opinions, and hast succoured, maintained, and

helped them ; and hast been a conveyor of their seditious letters and books into this realm.

6. That thou, in sundry places of this realm, hast spoken against the pope of Rome, and his apostolic see, and hast plainly contemned and despised the authority of the same, misliking, and not allowing the faith and doctrine thereof, but directly speaking against it ; and, by thine example, hast induced others, the subjects of this realm, to speak and to do the like.

7. That thou hast said, that thou hast been at Rome, and tarried there about thirty days, or more, and that thou hast seen little good, or none, there, but very much evil. Amongst the which, thou sawest one great abomination, that is to say, a man (or the pope) that should go on the ground, to be carried upon the shoulders of four men, as though he had been God, and no man. Also, a cardinal to have his harlot riding openly behind him. And, thirdly, a pope's bull, that gave express licence to have and use their stews, and to keep open bawdry, by the pope's approbation and authority.

8. That thou, since thy last coming into England, from parts beyond sea, hast perniciously allured and comforted divers of the subjects of this realm, both young and old, men and women, to have and use the book of communion set forth in this realm in the latter days of king Edward VI. and hast also thyself read and set forth the same, causing others to do the like, and to leave off their coming to their parish churches, to hear the Latin service now used.

9. That thou, the third Sunday of Advent, the 12th of December, 1557, wast apprehended at the Saracen's-Head at Islington, in the county of Middlesex, and diocess of London, by the queen's vice-chamberlain, with one Simpson, a tailor, and Hugh, a hosier, and divers others there assembled, under the colour of hearing a play, to have read the communion-book, and to have used the accustomed fashion, as was in the latter days of king Edward VI.

To these respective articles, Rough answered as follows :

To the first, he said, that he had spoken against the number of the said sacraments, being fully persuaded that there are only two sacraments, to wit, baptism and the supper of the Lord ; and, as for the other five, he denied them to be sacraments, and, therefore, had spoken against them.

With respect to the sacrament of the altar, (which he called the supper of the Lord) he confessed, that he had spoken and taught, that, in the said sacrament, there are not really and substantially the very body and blood of Christ ; but that the substance of both bread and wine remains in that sacrament, without any change being made to it by consecration.

Concerning the confession of sins, he said, he thought it necessary, provided the offence was done to the priest, but if it was done to any other, then it was, not necessary to make any confession to the priest ; but to endeavour to obtain a proper reconciliation with the party offended.

To the second article, he answered, that he did, and had before misliked the order of the Latin service then used, and also did allow the service used in the latter part of king Edward's reign ; for that the holy scripture hath taught the same ; and, therefore, he granted that he did teach, and set forth the said English service, as in the said article was objected.

The third he granted, saying, that he had approved of the doctrine of the parties mentioned, as agreeable to God's word ; and they were godly, learned men, and such as had perfect understanding, as in the contents of the same article.

To the fourth article, he answered, that he did well like the communion used in king Edward's days ; but said, that he had not ministered, nor received the same in England, since the queen's reign, nor yet knew any that had the books thereof ; but, on the other side the sea, he knew many that had these books, and that there also he had received the communion in sundry places.

To the fifth article, he confessed, that he had been familiar with many English men and women in Friesland, and agreed with them in opinion; as Story, Thomas Young, George Roo, and others, to the number of one hundred persons, who fled thither on account of their religion, using the same as was set forth in the reign of the good king Edward VI; but otherwise he denied the contents of the article.

The sixth and seventh articles, he acknowledged to be both true.

To the eighth article, he answered, that since his last coming into England, (which was about the 10th of November) he had, in sundry places, in the suburbs of London, prayed and read such prayers and service as are appointed in the book of communion, and had desired others to do the like, both men and women, whom he knew by sight, but not by name. However, he did not cause any to withdraw themselves from the Latin service; but only said, that it was better to pray in a tongue they understood, than in one they did not.

To the ninth article, he confessed, that at the time, and place mentioned, he was present to hear divine service, and there was apprehended by the queen's vice-chamberlain, with one Simpson, a tailor, and one Hugh, a hosier, with divers others, both men and women, whose names he knew not; and, by the said vice-chamberlain, was brought before the council, who sent him to Newgate, from whence he was, soon after, brought before the bishop of London; but otherwise he denied the contents of this article.

After Rough had given these answers to the respective articles exhibited against him, he was dismissed for the present; but re-conducted to his place of confinement.

On the 20th of December, he was brought to the consistory-court at St. Paul's, before Dr. Bonner, bishop of London, the bishop of St. David's, Dr. Fecknam, abbot of Westminster, and others, in order to undergo a final examination.

After various methods used by the court to persuade him to recant, without effect, Bonner read the articles, with his answers, before-mentioned. He then charged him with marrying, after having received priestly orders;

and that he had refused to consent to the Latin service then used in the church.

Rough answered, their orders were of none effect, and that the children he had by his wife were legitimate. With respect to the Latin service then used, he said, he utterly detested it, and that if he was to live as long as Methuselah, he would never go to church to hear the abominable mass.

In consequence of this declaration, the bishop proceeded to the ceremony of degradation, exempting him from all the benefits and privileges of their church; after which, he read the sentence of condemnation; and Rough being delivered to the sheriff, was, by him, reconducted to Newgate, there to remain till the time appointed for his execution.

Margaret Maring, belonged to a private congregation in London, where Rough used to officiate. She was apprehended and brought before the bishop of London, who, after examination, sent her prisoner to Newgate. She was afterwards brought before the bishop, a second and third time, and, after a further examination, and using various arguments to prevail on her to recant, without effect, she was delivered to the sheriff for execution, who re-conducted her to Newgate.

On the 22d of December, 1557, she, with her fellow-martyr, John Rough, was conducted, by the proper officers, to Smithfield, where they were both fastened to one stake, and burnt in the same fire. They both behaved themselves with true christian fortitude, and cheerfully gave up their lives, in testimony of the truth of that gospel, which was professed by him from whom they hoped to receive an eternal reward in his heavenly kingdom.

The deaths of these two martyrs closed the horrid and bloody transactions of the year, 1557. We shall now proceed to a relation of those that occurred in the succeeding year, which happily, by the queen's death, put an end to human sacrifices in this kingdom.

The sufferings and Martyrdoms of Cuthbert Simpson, Hugh Fox, and John Davenish, who were all burnt together in Smithfield.

THESE three persons were apprehended together at Islington, at the same time with John Rough, and, being brought before the queen's council, were committed to different prisons.

Cuthbert Simpson, who was deacon of the same congregation of which Rough was pastor, was committed prisoner to the Tower, where he was examined by the recorder of London, and one Cholmley, who commanded him to declare what persons he had called upon, or summoned, to come to the English service; but he peremptorily told them, he would not comply with their request.

They then ordered him to be put to the rack, on which he laid, in great agonies, upwards of three hours. While he was in the most excruciating torments, they asked him the same question as they had done before, and he made the same answer. He was then loosed from the rack, and conducted to the room appointed for his confinement.

Soon after, he was again brought to the room in which he had been racked, when the recorder of London, and the lieutenant of the Tower, once more desired him to confess; but still he refused, saying, he was determined not to satisfy them.

They then tied his two fore-fingers together, with a small arrow between them: this done, they drew the arrow backward and forward so quick, that the blood followed, and the arrow broke; after which, they racked him twice, and then conducted him to his dungeon.

About ten days after this, the lieutenant asked him again, if he would confess what had been repeatedly asked by himself, and the recorder? to which, Simpson answered, that he would say no more than he had said.

He was afterwards taken before the bishop of London for further examination.

Hugh Fox, and John Davenish, were next examined.

3 s

Their respective answers being all written down, they were afterwards read to them; when, they persisting and continuing steadfast in their faith and opinions, the bishop pronounced the difinitive sentence; and they were all delivered over to the secular power.

While Cuthbert Simpson was in the consistory-court, bishop Bonner took particular notice of him to the people. "Ye see," said he, "this man, what a personable man he is; and I tell you, that if he were not an heretic, he is a man of the greatest patience that ever came before me. He hath been twice racked in one day in the Tower, and also, in my house, he hath felt much sorrow, and yet I never saw his patience broken."

. On the 28th of the month called March, 1558, these three steadfast believers in Christ were conducted by the sheriffs, and their proper officers, to Smithfield, where they were all fastened to one stake, and burnt in the same fire. They behaved with true christian fortitude to the last, praising and glorifying God, that he had enabled them to go through the horrid punishment allotted them, for no other reason but their strict adherence to the truth of his most holy gospel.

About this time, one William Nicoll, of Haverford-West, in Pembrokeshire, was apprehended for speaking disrespectfully of the church of Rome; and being condemned as a heretic, was burnt in said town, on the 9th of the month called April, 1558. But the particulars of his examination, &c. are not recorded.

The persecutions and Martyrdoms of William Seaman, Thomas Carman, and Thomas Hudson, who were all burnt together at Norwich.

WILLIAM SEAMAN was a husbandman, of a religious turn of mind, and a strict professor of the truth of the gospel. He was betrayed into the hands of the popish emissaries by the perfidy of a neighbour; and being taken before Sir John Tyrrel for examination, he committed Seaman to prison; and, the next day, he was sent to Dr. Hopton, bishop of the diocess, who, after a short examination, passed sentence of condemnation on him, and he was delivered over to the secular power.

Thomas Carman, who had been apprehended a short time before, was brought before the bishop, for examination, on the same day; when, asserting the cause of Christ with no less warmth than the former, he was consigned to the same inhuman and merciless punishment.

Thomas Hudson, was by trade a glover, and lived at the town of Aildesham, in Norfolk. Though destitute of any education in his younger years, yet, by his diligence and love of the gospel, as preached in the days of king Edward, he had learned to read, became well versed in the sacred book of God, and grounded in the faith once delivered to the saints.

Disapproving the doctrines and practices set forth under the reign of queen Mary, he absented himself from his native place, went into Suffolk, and there continued travelling from one part to another, as occasion required.

On the 19th of the month called May, 1558, these three steadfast believers in Christ were conducted to the place appointed for their execution, called Lollard's Pit, without Bishopsgate, at Norwich. As soon as they arrived at the fatal spot, they all kneeled down, and severally offered up their prayers to God, to enable them to undergo, with christian fortitude, the fiery trial that awaited them, and they all cheerfully resigned their souls into the hands of that God who had protected and supported them under their sufferings for his name's sake.

About the same time these three men were burnt at Norwich, three others suffered at Colchester; namely, William Harris, Richard Day, and Christian George.

They all willingly submitted to their fate, and cheerfully resigned up their lives in testimony of the truth of the gospel.

The persecution and sufferings of William Fetty, a lad of twelve years of age, who was so barbarously scourged in bishop Bonner's palace in London, that it occasioned his death.

IF dying innocently in the cause of Christ, and his religion, constitutes the character of a martyr, no one can be more entitled to a place in our catalogue than this youth, who was unmercifully scourged to death, at the instigation of the relentless and cruel Bonner:

Among those who were persecuted and imprisoned for the profession of Christ's gospel, and yet delivered by the providence of God, was John Fetty, the father of the lad under consideration. He had been accused, by his own wife, to the minister of the parish in which he lived, of absenting himself from church, the sacrament of the altar, confession, and other ceremonies; for neglect of which, he was apprehended by one of the officers employed for that purpose. He was afterwards released. But was again apprehended, and carried before Sir John Mordaunt, one of the queen's commissioners, by whom, after examination, he was sent to Lollard's Tower*, where he was put into the stocks, and had a dish of water set by him, with a stone in it, to point out to him, that it was the chief substance he might expect to receive.

After he had been in prison for the space of fifteen days, (the greatest part of which time he was kept in the

---

* Lollard's Tower was a large, detached room, belonging to bishop Bonner's palace, in London, and formed as a prison of the most gloomy nature. It was set apart for the punishment of protestants, (called Lollards) who were brought before him on an accusation of heresy, and who were here subjected to various tortures, at the discretion of that biggotted and merciless tyrant. The most common punishment inflicted was, setting them in the stocks, some of whom were fastened by the hands, and others by the feet. They were, in general, permitted to sit on a stool, but, to increase the punishment, some were deprived of that indulgence, so that lying with their backs on the ground, their situation became exceeding painful. In this dungeon, and under these tortures, they were kept, some for several days, and others for weeks, without any other sustenance than bread and water; and to add to their affliction, they were prohibited from being seen by their relations, or friends. Many of those who had tender constitutions, fell under the conflict; but those who were otherwise, escaped, and lived to execrate the name of their inhuman persecutor.

stocks, sometimes by one leg, and sometimes by the other) William Fetty, one of his sons, came to the bishop's palace, in order to obtain permission to see him.

When he arrived there, one of the bishop's chaplains asked him his business ; the boy replied, he wanted to see his father, at the same time, shedding tears, and expressing the greatest unhappiness. The chaplain asked, who was his father; and, when the boy told him, he pointed towards Lollard's Tower, intimating, that he was there confined.

The chaplain then told him, his father was a heretic ; to which, the boy (who was of a bold and forward spirit, and had been instructed by the father in the reformed religion) answered, " my father is no heretic : but you have Balaam's mark."

On this, the incensed priest took the boy by the hand, and led him to a large room in the palace, where he scourged him in the most severe and unmerciful manner; after which, he ordered one of his servants to carry him in his shirt to his father, the blood running down to his heels.

As soon as he saw his father, he fell on his knees, and craved his blessing. The poor man, beholding his child in so dreadful a situation, exclaimed, with great grief, " alas ! son, who hath thus cruelly treated you?" the boy replied, " seeking to find you out, a priest, with Balaam's mark, took me into the bishop's house, and treated me in the manner you see."

The servant then seized the boy with great wrath, and dragging him from his father, led him back to the place where he had been scourged by the priest. Here he was kept three days, in the course of which, his former punishment was several times repeated, though not in so severe a manner as before.

At the expiration of that time, Bonner, in order to make some atonement for this cruel treatment of the boy, and to appease the father, determined to release both of them. He, therefore, ordered the latter to be brought before him, in his bed-chamber, early in the morning.

When the poor man came before the bishop, he said, " God be here, and peace." To which, the bishop replied, " that is neither God speed, nor good-morrow." ·

One of the bishop's chaplains standing by, reviled Fetty for the speech he had made ; when he, after looking about, and spying a bundle of black beads, and a small crucifix, said, " as Christ is here handled, so you deal with Christ's chosen people."

The bishop was so enraged at this, that he called him a vile heretic, and said, " I will burn thee, or I will spend all that I possess." However, in a little time, his passion cooled, and thinking of the consequences that might arise. from scourging the child, he ordered them both to be discharged.

The father immediately went home with his son ; but the poor boy, from an extraordinary effusion of blood, and a mortification which ensued, died a few days after, to the great grief of his persecuted and indulgent parent.

The old man remained, without farther persecution, during the residue of his life, often praising God for delivering him out of the hands of his enemies.

The Martyrdoms of Robert Mills, Stephen Cotton, Robert Dines, Stephen Wight, John Slade, and William Pikes, who were all burnt together at Brentford, in Middlesex.

THESE six men were apprehended, with several others, in a close near Islington, where they had assembled to pay their devotions to their Maker ; and, being taken before a magistrate, were committed to prison on suspicion of heresy.

A few days after their apprehension, they were brought before Dr. Thomas Derbyshire, the bishop of London's chancellor for examination.

After which, they were re-conducted to prison, but ordered to appear on the 11th of the month called July, at the consistory-court at St. Paul's. Accordingly, on that day, they were brought before the bishop and his chancellor, by the latter of whom, they were asked, if they would turn from their opinions against the holy mother-church ; and, if not, whether they would shew cause why sentence of condemnation should not be pronounced against them. To this, they all answered, that they would not go from the truth, nor any part of the same on any conditions whatever.

· The chancellor then dismissed them, but ordered, that they should appear again before him the next day, in the afternoon, to hear the definitive sentence pronounced, agreeable to the ecclesiastical law then in force.

They were accordingly brought at the time appointed, when the chancellor sat as judge, accompanied by sir Edward Hastings, and sir Thomas Cornwallis. The chancellor used his utmost endeavours to prevail on them to recant their opinions ; but they all proved ineffectual. He, therefore, read the sentence of condemnation ; and they were delivered over to the sheriffs, who conducted them to prison, in order for execution.

The chancellor, having condemned these six innocent persons, sent a certificate of their condemnation to the lord chancellor's office, from whence, the next day, a writ was issued for their being burnt at Brentford.

On the 14th day of the month called July, 1558, they were conducted by the sheriffs, and their attendants, from Newgate, to the place appointed for their execution. As soon as they arrived at the fatal spot, they all kneeled down, and, for some time, prayed in the most fervent manner. After this, they arose, and, undressing themselves, went cheerfully to the stakes, of which, there were three in number, though all consumed in the same fire. Being bound to the stakes, and the fagots lighted, they all quietly yielded up their souls to that God, for whose gospel they suffered, and whose heavenly mansions they were in hopes of inheriting.

A few days after the execution of the before mentioned six martyrs at Brentford, seven others, apprehended with them, at the same time and place, were burnt in Smithfield ; namely, Henry Pond, Rainhold Eastland, Robert

Southam, Matthew Ricarby, John Floyd, John Holiday, and Roger Holland.

In the beginning of the month called August, four men were burnt at St. Edmund's Bury, in Suffolk. Their names were John Cooke, Robert Miles, Alexander Lane, and James Ashley.

The persecution and sufferings of Cicely Ormes, who was burnt at Norwich.

THIS woman was one of the spectators at the burning of Simon Miller, and Elizabeth Cooper (before mentioned) ; and was apprehended for saying, she would pledge them of the cup of which they drank, viz. success to the true cause of Christ, and destruction to the usurpation of papists.

This poor woman had been before apprehended, and, after being some time confined, by the advice of her friends, and fearing the horrors of death, she recanted, and thereby obtained her liberty. But she could not enjoy a moment of peace after : she, therefore, abjured the abominable errors she had confessed, and determined to adhere inviolably to the true gospel of Christ.

On the 23d of September, 1558, she was conducted to the usual place of execution for martyrs, without Bishopsgate. As soon as she arrived at the stake, she kneeled down, and, after making her fervent prayers to God, thus addressed the spectators :

" Good people, I believe in God the Father, God the Son, and God the Holy Ghost : this I do not, nor will recant ; but I renounce from the bottom of my heart, the principles and practices set forth by the church of Rome, and never will have to do with them, by the grace of God, to my life's end.

" I would not have you think, good people, that I expect to be saved, because I offer myself here unto death for the truth's sake ; no, I trust for acceptance with God, justification in his sight, and eternal redemption on the merits and passion of Jesus Christ alone."

After this, she embraced the stake, and said, " welcome, the cross of Christ."

Being fastened, and the fagots lighted, she spoke, with an audible voice, these words : " my soul doth magnify the Lord, and my spirit rejoiceth in God my Saviour." These were the last words she was heard to say ; for the fire burning rapidly, she soon gave up the ghost, quietly resigning her life in testimony of the truth of God's most holy word.

The Martyrdoms of Alexander Gouch, and Alice Driver, who were burnt together at Ipswich, in Suffolk.

THESE two persons having been suspected of heresy, were apprehended, and after a short examination relative to their religious sentiments, were committed to Melton gaol.

After undergoing another examination separately, they, for their steadfastness in their faith and opinion, received sentence of condemnation as heretics, and were delivered to the secular power to be put to death.

On the 4th of November, 1558, they were taken from the gaol to Ipswich, escorted by the high-sheriff and his officers, and accompanied by a prodigious number of spectators.

When they came to the stake, they sang psalms together, then kneeled down, and fervently prayed for some time ; at which, the sheriff was so offended, that he ordered the bailiffs to interrupt them, and desire they would make an end.

On this, Gouch arose, and said, "do, Mr. Sheriff, let us pray a little while, for we have but a short time to live here." But this was forbidden ; and the bailiffs, were ordered immedately to prepare them for the fire.

Without farther delay, they were fastened to the stake, when many of the spectators shook them by the hands, notwithstanding the sheriff threatened them for their presumption. The fagots being lighted, they joyfully resign-

3 T

ed up their souls to God, their last words being, " into thy hands, O Lord, we commit our spirits."

About the same time, and for the same cause, three men were burned at St. Edmund's Bury, in Suffolk, viz. Philip Humphrey, John David, and Henry David, his brother. But the particular account of their examinations and deaths is not recorded.

The sufferings and Martyrdom of Elizabeth Prest, who was burnt at Exeter.

THIS poor woman was the wife of a labouring man, and lived at a small village near the town of Launceston, in Cornwall. Her husband, and three children, were zealous papists ; and she would frequently rebuke them for their superstition ; but he, being the superior, forced her sometimes to go to church, to follow in procession, and to conform to the Romish ceremonies.

Being greatly afflicted at the thoughts of doing that which was so much against her inclination, she prayed to God for his assistance, took courage, and left her husband and family.

For some time, she travelled from one place to another, maintaining herself by labour and spinning. But, at length, she returned to her husband ; a few days after which, she was accused of heresy by some of her neighbours ; and being apprehended, was sent to Exeter, to be examined by Dr. Troublevile, then bishop of the see.

After this, she was dismissed for the present, and sent back to prison; but, in a few days, she was again brought before the bishop, who finding her still obstinate, and that all his endeavours to alter her opinion were ineffectual, he read the dreadful sentence of condemnation; at the close of which, she said, " I thank thee, my Lord, my God ; this day have I found that which I have long sought."

Between the time of her condemnation and execution, she was visited by several priests, who used the most forcible arguments to prevail on her to recant, promising that, on those conditions, her life should be saved. She replied, "No; that I will not. God forbid that I should lose the life eternal, for this carnal and short life. I will never turn from my heavenly husband, to my earthly husband; from the fellowship of angels, to mortal children: and, if my husband and children be faithful, then am I theirs. God is my father, God is my mother, God is my sister, my brother, my kinsman. God is my friend most faithful."

On the day appointed for her death, she was delivered to the sheriff, who, with his officers, conducted her to the place of execution, without the walls of Exeter, called Southenkey.

Being fastened to the stake, and the fagots lighted, she repeatedly cried out, "God, be merciful to me a sinner." And, in a short time, quietly resigned her soul, into the hands of him who gave it.

The Martyrdoms of John Cornford, of Wortham, Christopher Brown, of Maidstone, John Herst, of Ashford, Alice Snoth, and Catharine Knight, alias Tinley, an aged woman.

THESE five were the last that suffered martyrdom in the reign of queen Mary, who died on the 17th of November, 1558, in the 43d year of her age, and the 6th of her reign.

The matter why they were judged to the fire, was for believing the body not to be in the sacrament of the altar, unless it be received; saying, moreover, that we receive another thing also, besides Christ's body, which we see, and is a temporal thing, according to St. Paul, "The things that be seen, be temporal," &c.

Item, For confessing, that an evil man doth not receive Christ's body, "Because no man hath the Son, except it be given him of the Father."

Item, That it is an idolatry, to creep to the cross, and St. John forbidding it, saith, "Beware of images."

Item, For confessing, that we should not pray to our lady, and other saints, because they be not omnipotent.

For these, and other such like articles of christian doctrine, were these committed to the fire. Against whom, when the sentence should be read, and they excommunicated, after the manner of the papists, John Cornford, stirred with a vehement spirit, of the zeal of God, proceeding in a more true excommunication against the papists, in the name of them all, pronounced sentence against them, in these words, as follows :

" In the name of our Lord Jesus Christ, the Son of the most mighty God, and by the power of his holy Spirit, and the authority of his holy catholic and apostolic church, we do here give into the hands of satan, to be destroyed, the bodies of all those blasphemers and heretics, that do maintain an error against his most holy word, or do condemn his most holy truth for heresy, to the maintenance of any false church or feigned religion, so that by this, thy just judgment, O most mighty God, against thy adversaries, thy true religion may be known to thy great glory and our comfort, and to the edifying of all our nation. Good Lord, so be it, Amen."

These godly martyrs, in their prayer which they made before their martyrdom, desired God, that their blood might be the last that should be shed, and so it was.

Besides the martyrs above named, there were several others imprisoned in divers parts of the realm, whereof some were but newly taken and not yet examined, some examined, but not condemned, and others were both examined and condemned, but, for lack of the writ, escaped.

There were others, also, condemned, and the writ also was brought down for their burning ; and yet, by the deaths of the chancellor, the bishop, and queen Mary, happening together about one time, their lives were preserved.

To relate all those cases of persecution and suffering, with the particular circumstances attending them, would extend beyond the limits of the present work : we shall therefore omit them, refering the reader to the authentic records, where they may be found, particularly to Fox's Book of Martyrs.

It may, however, be acceptable to our readers to hear the names of the principal sufferers, who, although their lives were not sacrificed to the severities and malice of their persecutors, yet endured no little scourging and suffering, and evinced, by their patience and steadfast perseverence, that their non-compliance was purely in obedience to the will and requisition of their Lord and master.

The following is a list of some of them :

John Hunt, Richard White, Richard Wilmot, Thomas Fairfax, Thomas Green, James Harris, Robert Williams, William Living and his wife, John Lithal, Elizabeth Young, Elizabeth Lawson, Thomas Christenmass, William Watts, Alexander Winhurst, John Davis, ——— Roberts, Anne Lucy, Edward Bennet, Jeffry Hurst, William Wood, Thomas Horton, Thomas Sprat, John Cornet, Thomas Bryce, Gertrude Crokhay, Thomas Rose, Richard Burtic and Catharine his wife, Dr. Ægido, Dr. Constantine, and William Lithgow.

A SHORT ACCOUNT OF THE PERSECUTIONS IN
IRELAND, DISTINGUISHED IN THE ENG-
LISH ANNALS BY THE NAME OF THE
IRISH MASSACRE.

THOUGH the various attempts made by the Irish against
the English, usually go under the denomination of rebellion, yet they more properly deserve the epithet persecution, as all their destructive efforts were particularly levelled at the protestants only, whom they were determined, if
possible, totally to extirpate from the kingdom. They
had, indeed, heretofore miscarried ; but they, at length,
hit upon a project, that succeeded to their wishes, and produced a catastrophe that will remain memorable to the
latest posterity.

A short time before the horrid conspiracy broke out,
which we are now going to relate, the papists of Ireland,
had presented a remonstrance to the lords-justices of that
kingdom, demanding the free exercise of their religion,
and a repeal of all laws to the contrary ; to which, both
houses of parliament in England solemnly answered, that
they would never grant any toleration to the popish religion in that kingdom.

This farther irritated the papists to put in execution the
diabolical plot concerted for the destruction of the protestants ; and it failed not of the success wished for by its
malicious and rancorous projectors.

The design of this horrid conspiracy was, that a general insurrection should take place at the same time
throughout the kingdom ; and that all the protestants,
without exception, should be murdered. The day fixed
for this horrid massacre, was, the 23d of October, 1641 ;
and the chief conspirators, in the principal parts of the
kingdom, made the necessary preparations for the intended conflict.

The conspirators were in arms all over the kingdom
early in the morning of the day appointed, and every protestant who fell in their way, was immediately murdered.

No age, no sex, no condition was spared. The wife weeping for her butchered husband, and embracing her helpless children, was pierced with them, and perished by the same stroke. The old, the young, the vigorous, the infirm, underwent the same fate, and were blended together in one common ruin. In vain, did flight save from the first assault : destruction was every where let loose, and met the hunted victims at every turn. In vain, was recourse had to relations, to companions, to friends : all connexions were dissolved, and death was dealt by that hand, from which protection was implored and expected. Without provocation, without opposition, the astonished English, living in profound peace, and, as they thought, full security, were massacred by their nearest neighbours, with whom they had long maintained a continual intercourse of kindness and good offices. Nay, even death was the slightest punishment inflicted by these monsters in human form : all the tortures which wanton cruelty could invent, all the lingering pains of body, the anguish of mind, the agonies of despair, could not satiate revenge excited without injury, and cruelty derived from no cause whatever. Depraved nature, even perverted religion, though encouraged by the utmost licence, cannot reach to a greater pitch of ferocity than appeared in those merciless barbarians. Even the weaker sex themselves, naturally tender to their own sufferings, and compassionate to those of others, here emulated their robust companions in the practice of every cruelty. The very children, taught by example, and encouraged by the exhortations of their parents, dealt their feeble blows on the dead carcasses of the defenceless children of the English.

Nor was the avarice of the Irish sufficient to produce the least restraint on their cruelty. Such was their frenzy, that the cattle they had seized, and by rapine made their own, were, because they bore the name of English, wantonly slaughtered, or, when covered with wounds, turned loose into the woods, there to perish by slow and lingering torments.

The commodious habitations of the planters were laid in ashes, or levelled with the ground. And where the wretched owners had shut themselves up in the houses, and were preparing for defence, they perished in the flames, together with their wives and children.

Many were put to deaths of the most horrid nature, and such as could have been invented only by demons instead of men.

Some of them were laid with the centre of their backs on the axle-tree of a carriage, with their legs resting on the ground, on one side, and their arms and head on the other. In this position, one of the savages scourged the wretched object on the thighs, legs, &c. while others set on furious dogs, who tore to pieces the arms and upper parts of the body ; and, in this dreadful manner, were they deprived of their existence.

Great numbers were fastened to horses tails ; and, the beasts being set on full gallop by their riders, the wretched victims were dragged along till they expired.

Others were hung on lofty gibbets, and a fire being kindled under them, they finished their lives, partly by hanging, and partly by suffocation.

Nor did the more tender sex escape the least particle of cruelty, that could be projected by their merciless and furious persecutors. Many women, of all ages, were put to deaths of the most cruel nature. Some in particular were fastened with their backs to strong posts, and being stripped to their waists, the inhuman monsters cut off their breasts with shears, which, of course, put them to the most excruciating torments ; and, in this position, they were left, till, from the loss of blood, they expired.

Such was the savage ferocity of these barbarians, that even unborn infants were dragged from the womb to become victims to their rage. Many unhappy mothers, who were near the time of their delivery, were hung naked on the branches of trees, and their bodies being cut open, the innocent offspring were taken from them, and thrown to dogs and swine. And, to increase the horrid scene, they would oblige the husband to be a spectator before he suffered himself.

A SHORT ACCOUNT OF THE MASSACRE IN FRANCE.

In the year, 1572, a massacre took place in Paris, soon after Henry, king of Navarre, was married to Margaret, sister to the king of France.

This was called, not a marriage of individuals, but a marriage between the churches of the Roman Catholics and the Protestants.

A few hours previous to the massacre, the young duke of Guise, who was to be principally intrusted in the affair, called together the French and Swiss officers, and told them, "that the time was come in which the king was to be revenged of the protestants; the beast is caught (said he) let him not therefore escape; your triumph will be glorious, your victory easy, and the spoils great." The duke of Guise then sent to the provost of the city, and commanded him to assemble the aldermen of the respective wards, that they might be ready to receive the king's commands: when they met together, the same orders were given to them as to the officers; and they were told, that the signal for beginning the bloody business, was to be the ringing of a bell in the Louvre; and the tokens, by which to know each other, were to be white crosses on their hats.

The dreadful hour arrived, and the fatal bell was rung, about twelve o'clock at night, on the eve of the 24th of the month called August, A. D. 1572; the signal being thus given, the duke of Guise hastened to Coligni's house, at the head of a body of troops, and joined Cossen, who, with his guard, it was pretended, went to defend the admiral. They knocked violently at Coligni's door, when Labonnous, one of his servants, immediately opened it, and was instantly stabbed by Cossen. A number of troops, with Cossen at the head of them, then entered the house; but the duke of Guise remained in the court-yard. The assassins ranged through the several apartments, murdered all they met, and at length came to Coligni's chamber. That brave devoted martyr, when he saw them, said, " I have long prepared myself for death, and now, that I shall find it, commend my soul to the Almighty God." A German

3 σ

soldier, named Besme, first wounded him; after which, Cossen, and several others, completed the murder. The duke of Guise, called out from below, " Is the business done ?" The murderers replied, it was; and, to convince him, threw the body out of the window. The corpse was then treated with great indignity; and a person belonging to the duke of Nevers, cut off the head, and carried it to the king. The cruel monarch appeared pleased with the sight, and the bloody minded queen-mother ordered it to be embalmed, and sent as a present to the pope. The headless corpse was dragged about the streets, with great indignity, for several days, indecently mangled, and then hung upon a gibbet, with the shoulders downwards. This was the end of one of the greatest men France ever produced; who, by a glorious martyrdom, concluded a life spent in the service of the Almighty.

The attendants and domestics of the king of Navarre, and the young prince of Conde, were basely butchered, and the streets of Paris streamed with protestant blood. In some measure, to palliate their cruelties, the Roman catholics, while they were murdering the innocent people, cried out, " Vile wretches, this is for wanting to overturn the constitution of your country; this is for conspiring to murder the king." Rank, sex, or age, was no protection; nobles sunk beneath the daggers of ruffians; the tears of beauty made no impression on the hearts of bigotry; the silver hairs of venerable age, and the piteous cries of helpless infancy, were alike disregarded. Superstition steeled the hearts of the papists against the ties of humanity; and infatuation directed the sword of false zeal, to pierce the bosoms of piety and innocence. The lamentations of distress, the shrieks of terror, and the groans of the dying, were music to the ears of the furious murderers: they enjoyed the horrors of slaughter, and triumphed over the mangled carcasses of those whom they had butchered.

Upon this dreadful occasion, swords, pistols, muskets, cutlasses, daggers, and other instruments of death, had been put into the hands of above sixty thousand furious and bigotted papists, who now, in a frantic manner, ran up and down the streets of Paris, uttering the most horrid blasphemies, and committing the most inhuman barbarities. It is almost beyond the power of imagination to paint, or of language to describe, the cruelties that were acted on that fatal night, and the two succeeding days. The infirm were murdered in the bed of sickness; the aged stabbed while tottering on their crutches; children snatched from their mothers, and tossed on the points of of spears; infants strangled in their cradles; pregnant women ripped open; and men indiscriminately murdered by various means. The confusion and horrors of the scene were dreadful indeed; oaths, shoutings, shrieks, and the discharge of fire-arms, were heard in all quarters; houses were defiled with the blood of their owners; the streets strewed with carcasses; and the waters of the Seine appeared of a crimson colour, from the number of mangled bodies which had been thrown into that river.

Three hundred and fifty protestants were confined in a place called the Archbishop's Prison. To this place, a number of soldiers repaired, picked their pockets of what money they had, took from them such garments as they thought proper to appropriate to their own uses, and then drawing their swords, cut them to pieces without the least remorse.

After the massacre had subsided, the inhuman assassins paraded the streets, boasting, that they had died their white cockades red, with the blood of hugonots. The inhabitants of the villages which lay below Paris, on the borders of the Seine, were astonished to see the number of dead bodies that floated down the stream; and even some of the Roman catholics were so much touched with compassion, as to exclaim, " it surely could not be men, but devils, in their appearance, who have transacted these cruelties." The pope's legate, soon after, gave all who were concerned in these murders, a general absolution, which plainly evinces, that the Roman catholics themselves thought these transactions criminal.

Occurrences supplementary to the Massacre in Paris.

IT was represented to the king by his council, that the massacre would be ineffectual, if it did not extend to every part of the kingdom ; for though all the protestants of Paris were murdered, yet if any were suffered to live in other parts of France, they would again increase in numbers, and spread to the metropolis. This occasioned the massacre to become more general, for the king sent orders to all parts of the nation to put the protestants to death.

At Meaux, the king's attorney, Cosset, having received the bloody mandate, ordered a number of ruffians to attend him at seven o'clock in the evening. At the appointed time, he commanded the city gates to be shut, and all the protestants seized. This was immediately executed ; many were murdered that night, and about two hundred of the principal persons were confined till the next day. On the ensuing morning, Cosset, and his murderers, went to the prison, and having a list of protestants' names, called them one by one, and murdered them as they answered to the call. They then plundered the houses of those they had murdered, divided the spoils, gave an entertainment upon the occasion, and concluded the evening with illuminations.

At Troyes, the protestants were all seized, and put into dungeons. The provost then commanded the common executioner to go and murder them all. Shocked, however, at the inhumanity of the thing, the executioner had spirit enough to refuse, with this remarkable expression : " my office obliges me to execute none but such as are legally condemned." But this did not save the protestants for the provost engaged the gaoler to perform what the executioner had refused. They were all accordingly murdered, and their bodies buried in pits, dug on purpose, within the prison.

At Orleans, the massacre continued for a week, and a prodigious number of men, women, and children, were murdered ; the general cry being, "kill the hugonots, and take the spoil." Some, who were weak enough to apostatize from their faith to save their lives, had weapons put into their hands, and were compelled to kill those of the religion they had forsaken, or to be murdered themselves; the Roman catholics crying, in derision, all the time, " smite'em, smite'em; were they not your holy brothers and sisters ?"

At Lyons, all the protestants' houses were plundered, and the slaughter was almost incredible. At Rouen, six thousand were massacred. At Thoulouse, about three hundred were martyred upon the occasion. Many were drowned at Angiers; and several were butchered at Bordeaux; though happily, at the latter place, several got expeditiously on board a ship, and escaped to England.

These barbarities inflamed such protestants as escaped, rather with rage than terror: their irreconcilable hatred to the court, supplied them with fresh vigour, and the spirit of revenge increased their strength. The king, under whose influence this dreadful havoc had been committed, never enjoyed his health after, but died in about two years, his blood gushing daily through the pores of his skin; so that he expired, as it were, weltering in his own gore.

> Fear haunts the guilty mind with horrid views,
> And Providence the murderer pursues;
> Those, by whose means the innocent are slain,
> Shall live detested, and expire in pain.

A SHORT ACCOUNT OF THE RISE, PROGRESS, &c. OF THE INQUISITION.

WHEN the reformed religion began to diffuse the gospel light throughout Europe, pope Innocent the Third, entertained great fear for the Romish church. Unwilling that the spirit of free inquiry should gain ground, or that the people should attain more knowledge than the priests were willing to admit, he determined to impede, as much as possible, the progress of reformation. He accordingly instituted a number of inquisitors, or persons who were to make inquiry after, apprehend, and punish heretics, as the reformed were called by the papists.

Courts of inquisition were now erected in several countries ; but the Spanish inquisition became the most powerful, and the most dreadful of any. Even the kings of Spain themselves, though arbitrary in all other respects, were taught to dread the power of the lords of the inquisition ; and the horrid cruelties they exercised compelled multitudes, who differed in opinion from the Roman catholics, carefully to conceal their sentiments.

The pope now thought proper to give the inquisitors the most unlimited powers, as judges delegated by him, and immediately representing his person : they were permitted to excommunicate, or sentence to death, whom they thought proper upon the most slight information of heresy. They were allowed to publish crusades against all whom they deemed heretics, and to enter into leagues with sovereign princes, to join those crusades with their forces.

In 1244, their powers were farther increased by the emperor Frederick the Second, who declared himself the protector and friend of all the inquisitors, and published two very cruel edicts, viz.

1. That all heretics, who continued obstinate, should be burnt.

2. That all heretics who repented, should be imprisoned for life.

The officers of the inquisition are, three inquisitors or judges, a fiscal proctor, two secretaries, a magistrate, a messenger, a receiver, a gaoler, an agent of confiscated possessions, several assessors, counsellors, executioners, physicians, surgeons, door-keepers, familiars, and visiters, who are are all sworn to secrecy.

The principal accusation against those who are subject to this tribunal, is heresy, which comprises all that is spoken, or written against any of the articles of the creed, or the traditions of the Romish church. The other articles of accusation are, renouncing the Roman catholic persuasion, believing that persons of any other religion may be saved, or even admitting that the tenets of any but papists are, in the least, reasonable or proper. We shall mention two other things which incur the most severe punishments, and shew the inquisitors, at once, in an absurd and tyrannical light, viz. Disapproving any action done by the inquisition, or disbelieving any thing said by an inquisitor.

The grand article, heresy, comprises many subdivisions : and, upon a suspicion of any of these, the party is immediately apprehended. Advancing an offensive proposition ; failing to impeach others who may advance such ; contemning church ceremonies ; defacing idols ; reading books condemned by the inquisition ; lending such books to others to read ; deviating from the ordinary practices of the Romish church ; letting a year pass without going to confession ; eating meat on fast-days ; neglecting mass ; being present at a sermon preached by a heretic ; not appearing when summoned by the inquisition ; lodging in the house of, contracting friendship with, or making a present to, a heretic ; assisting a heretic to escape from confinement, or visiting one in confinement ; are all matters of suspicion, and prosecuted accordingly. Nay, all Roman catholics were commanded, under pain of excommunication, to give immediate information, even of their nearest and dearest friends, if they judge them to be what were called heretics, or any ways inclined to heresy.

The inquisition likewise takes cognizance of such as are accused of being magicians, soothsayers, witches, wizards, blasphemers, common swearers : and of such as read, or even possess the Bible in the common language, the Talmud of the jews, or the Alcoran of the mahometans.

Upon all occasions, the inquisitors carry on their processes with the utmost severity, and punish those who offend them, with the most unparalleled cruelty. A protestant has seldom any mercy shewn him; and a jew who turns christian, is far from being secure; for, if he is known to keep company with another new-converted jew, a suspicion immediately arises, that they privately practise together, some jewish ceremonies; if he keeps company with a person who was lately a protestant, but now professes popery, they are accused of plotting together; but if he associates with a Roman catholic, an accusation is often laid against him for only pretending to be a papist, and the consequence is, a confiscation of his effects as a punishment for his insincerity, and the loss of his life if he complains of ill usage.

Death is usually the portion of a prisoner, the mildest sentence being imprisonment for life; yet the inquisitors proceed by degrees, at once subtle, slow, and cruel. The gaoler, first of all, insinuates himself into the prisoner's favour, by pretending to wish him well, and advise him well, and, among other hints falsely kind, tells him to petition for a hearing.

When the person impeached is condemned, he is either severely whipped, violently tortured, sent to the galleys, or sentenced to death: and, in either case, his effects are confiscated. After judgment, a procession is performed to the place of execution, which ceremony is called an auto de fe, or act of faith.

The following is an account of an auto de fe, performed at Madrid, in the year 1682.

The officers of the inquisition, preceded by trumpets, kettle-drums, and their banner, marched on the 30th of the month called May, in cavalcade, to the place of the great square, where they declared by proclamation, that on the 30th of the month called June, the sentence of the prisoners would be put in execution.

There had not been a spectacle of this kind at Madrid for several years before, for which reason it was expected, by the inhabitants, with as much impatience as a day of the greatest festivity.

On the day appointed, a prodigious number of people appeared, dressed as splendidly as their respective circumstances would admit. In the great square, was raised a high scaffold; and thither, from seven in the morning till the evening, were brought criminals of both sexes: all the inquisitions in the kingdom sending their prisoners to Madrid.

Of these prisoners, twenty men and women, with one renegado mahometan, were ordered to be burned; fifty jews and jewesses, having never before been imprisoned, and repenting of their crimes, were sentenced to a long confinement, and to wear yellow caps; and ten others indicted for bigamy, witchcraft, and other crimes, were sentenced to be whipped, and then sent to the galleys: these last wore large paste-board caps, with inscriptions on them, having a halter about their necks, and torches in their hands.

The whole court of Spain was present on this occasion. The grand inquisitor's chair was placed in a sort of tribunal, far above that of the king. The nobles here acted the part of the sheriff's officers in England, leading such criminals as were to be burned, and holding them when fast bound with thick cords. The rest of the criminals were conducted by the familiars of the inquisition.

Among those who were to suffer, was a young jewess, of exquisite beauty, and but seventeen years of age. Being on the same side of the scaffold where the queen was seated, she addressed her, in hopes of obtaining a pardon, in the following pathetic speech: " Great queen! will not your royal presence be of some service to me, in my miserable condition ? Have regard to my youth; and oh ! consider, that I am about to die for professing a religion imbibed from my earliest infancy !" Her majesty seemed greatly to pity her distress, but turned away her eyes, as she did not dare to speak a word in behalf of a person who had been declared a heretic.

Now, mass began, in the midst of which, the priest came from the altar, placed near the scaffold, and seated himself in a chair prepared for that purpose.

3 x

The chief inquisitor then descended from the amphitheatre, dressed in his cope, and having a mitre on his head. After bowing to the altar, he advanced towards the king's balcony, and went up to it, attended by some of his officers, carrying a cross and the gospels, with a book containing the oath by which the kings of Spain oblige themselves to protect the catholic faith, to extirpate heretics, and to support, with all their power, the prosecutions and decrees of the inquisition.

On the inquisitor's approach, and presenting this book to the king, his majesty rose up, bareheaded, and swore to mantain the oath, which was read to him by one of his counsellors: after which, the king continued standing till the inquisitor was returned to his place; when the secretary of the holy office mounted a sort of pulpit, and administered the like oath to the counsellors and the the whole assembly. The mass was begun about twelve at noon, and did not end till nine in the evening, being protracted by a proclamation of the sentences of the several criminals, which were all separately rehearsed aloud one after the other.

After this, followed the burning of the twenty-one men and women, whose intrepidity in suffering that horrid death, was truly astonishing: some thrust their hands and feet into the flames with the most dauntless fortitude; and all of them yielded to their fate with such resolution, that many of the amazed spectators lamented that such heroic souls had not been more enlightened.

The king's near situation to the criminals rendered their dying groans very audible to him. He could not, however, be absent from this dreadful scene, as it is esteemed a religious one; and his coronation oath obliges him to give a sanction by his presence to all the acts of the tribunal.

EPISCOPACY.

On queen Elizabeth's accession to the throne, in 1558, the parliament restored the tenths to the crown; and the protestant religion was again established. The bishops refusing the oath of supremacy, were removed, and others put in their stead. About the beginning of this queen's reign, arose a people professing the pure religion, and allowing of nothing but what was taken out of the scriptures. They, moreover, openly condemned the received discipline of the church of England, with the liturgy and calling of the bishops, as savouring too much of the Romish religion. They declared it to be an impious thing to hold any doctrine common with the church of Rome, and were very zealous to have the church of England reformed in every point, according to the church of Geneva.

These dissenters were first known by the name of Puritans, and afterwards by that of protestant non-conformists.

They soon became very numerous, crying down the ecclesiastical form of government, as a thing polluted with Romish dregs, printing books to the same effect, and refusing to go to the public worship, as was then used; whereupon, many endeavours were used to suppress them, and the law was commanded to be put in execution, which required uniformity, and the books written by the Puritans to be delivered into the bishops' hands, on pain of imprisonment. By these courses of persecution and force, they were kept down for a time, the archbishop of Canterbury using his utmost endeavours to settle an uniformity, in ecclesiastical discipline, according to the laws, which he saw lay gasping, if the Puritans increased, and thereupon provided articles for all ministers to subscribe ; but he found great opposition or disturbance in this his design, both at home and abroad ; for one Robert Brown, a young man of Cambridge, from whom a people called Brownists took their name, and one Richard Harrison, a school-master, set forth books in Zealand, and dispersed them over England, condemning the church of England for no church. These books were by authority prohibited, and several of the chief of these Brownists were executed at Bury, in Suffolk.

Before giving an account of the execution of those persons, we shall insert their complaint to the parliament, relating their hard usage in prison.

" *The humble, most earnest, and lamentable complaint and supplication of the persecuted and prescribed church, and servants of Christ, falsely called Brownists, unto the high court of parliament.*

" THE most high God, possessor of heaven and earth, bringeth at this present before your lordships and wisdoms (right honourable) his own cause, his own people (his own sworn, and most treacherous enemies) together with the most shameful usage of his truth and servants, that ever hath been heard of in the days of Sion's professed peace and tranquillity.

" His cause and people he offereth unto your consideration and defence, in our profession and persons. His enemies and their outrage against his truth and servants in the persons and bloody proceedings of the prelates of this land, and their accomplices.

" We profess the same faith, and truth of the gospel with her majesty, which your honours, this whole land, and all the reformed churches under heaven, this day, do hold and maintain. We go beyond them (being our only fault, even in the judgment of our tyrannical and most savage enemies) in the detestation of all popery, that most fearful antichristian religion, and draw nearer, in some points, by our practice unto Christ's holy order and institution. This is our faith, this is our cause (right honourable) yea, the Lord's cause in our sinful hands.

" For the profession and maintenance of which faith, the fore named enemies of God detain in their hands within the prisons, about London (not to speak of other gaols throughout the land) about threescore and twelve persons, men, women, young, and old, lying in cold, in hunger, in dungeons, and in irons; of which number, they have taken the Lord's day last, being the 3d day of the 4th month, 1592, about sixteen persons hearing the word of God truly taught, praying and praising God for his favours shewed unto us, unto her majesty, your honours, and this whole land, and desiring our God to be merciful to us, unto our gracious prince and country. Being employed in these holy actions, and no other (as the parties, who disturbed them can testify) they were taken in the very place where the persecuted church and martyrs were enforced to use the like exercise in queen Mary's days.

" The former number are now unbailable, committed by the prelate or bishop of London, unto whose close (for the most part) several prisons, as Bridewell, Limbo or Dungeon in Newgate, the Fleet, the Marshalsea, the Compters, the Clink, the Gatehouse, the White-Lion, c. wherein we willingly acknowledge the lot and inheritance in this life, of our forefathers and brethren, the holy martyrs of the former age, and the entailed acellama, or bloody succession of the see of London, and that whole lineage. Well, here our brethren lie (how long, Lord, holy and true, thou knowest!) in dungeons, in hunger, in cold, in nakedness, and all outward distress; for these bloody men will allow them neither meat, drink, fire, lodging, nor suffer any whose hearts the Lord would stir up for their relief, to have any access unto them, purposing belike, to imprison them unto death, as they have done seventeen or eighteen others, in the same noisome gaols, within these six years. The husband and wife being now taken by them, they permit not to be in the same, but have sent them to be close kept in other prisons. What the poor family doth at home, in the mean time, your lordships may consider, and justly pity. Some of this company had not one penny about them, when they were sent to close prison, nor any thing, being abroad (which is the case of most of them, if not all) to procure themselves and their poor families any maintenance, save only their handy labours and trades, whereby it is come to pass, that these enemies of God, do not only starve and undo a number of men in the prisons, but even a lamentable company of poor orphans and servants abroad; their unbridled slanders; their lawless privy searches; their violent breaking open and rifling of our houses; their lamentable and barbarous usages of women and young children, in these hostile assaults; their uncontroled thievery; robbing and taking away of whatsoever they think meet from us in this case; their unappeased and merciless pursuit of us from our houses, trades, wives, children, especially from the holy society of the saints and church of God, we are enforced to omit, lest we should be over-tedious to your lordships; but their dealing this way towards us is so woful (right honourable) as we may truly demand with grief of heart, whether the foreign enemy, or our native countrymen, do possess and bear rule over us in our dear and native country?

"Their whole dealing herein is most barbarous, most inhuman, but especially most unchristian, and such as exceeds the cruelty of the heathen and popish professed tyrants, and persecutors. The records of the heathen persecutions under Nero, Trajan, Decius, Galienus, Maximinian, &c. can scarce afford us any examples of the like cruelty and havoc; for the heathen Romans would murder openly and professedly. These godless men have put the blood of war about them, in the day of the peace and truth, which this whole land professeth to hold with Jesus Christ, and his servants. Bishop Bonner, Story, and Weston, dealt not after this sort; for those whom they committed close, they would also either feed, or permit to be fed by others, and they brought them in short space openly into Smithfield to end their misery, and to begin their never ending joy. Whereas Bishop Elmar, Dr. Stanhope, and Mr. justice Young, with the rest of that persecuting and blood-thirsty faculty, will do neither of these. No felons no murderers, no traitors in this land, are so dealt with.

"There are many of us, by the mercies of God, still out of their hands. The former holy exercise and profession, we purpose not to leave, by the assistance of God. We have as good warrant to reject the ordinances of antichrist, and labour for the recovery of Christ's holy institutions, as our fathers and brethren, in queen Mary's days, had to do the like; and we doubt not, if our cause was truly known unto her majesty and your wisdoms, but we should find greater favour than they did, whereas our estate now is far more lamentable.

"And, therefore, we humbly and earnestly crave of her majesty and your lordships, both for ourselves abroad, and for our brethren now in miserable captivity, but just and equal trial, according unto her majesty's laws. If we prove not our adversaries to be in a most pestilent and godless course, both in regard of their offices, and their proceedings in them, and ourselves to be in the right way, we desire not to have the benefit of her majesty's true and faithful subjects, which, of all earthly favours, we account to be one of the greatest. Are we malefactors? Are we any wise undutiful unto our prince? Maintain we any errors? Let us then be judicially convicted thereof, and delivered to the civil authority; but let not these bloody men both accuse, condemn, and closely murder after this sort, contrary to all law, equity, and conscience, where they alone are the plaintiffs, the accusers, the judges, and the executioners, of their most fearful and barbarous tyranny.

They should not, by the laws of this land, go any further in cases of religion, than their own ecclesiastical censure, and then refer us to the civil power. Their forefathers, Gardner, Bonner, and Story, dealt thus equally, and we crave but this equity. Oh! let her excellent majesty, our sovereign, and your wisdoms, consider and accord unto this our just petition; for streams of innocent blood are like to be spilt in secret by these bloodthirsty men, except her majesty and your lordships do take order with their most cruel and inhuman proceedings.

" We crave for all of us but the liberty either to die openly, or to live openly, in the land of our nativity. If we deserve death, it beseemeth the majesty of justice not to see us closely murdered; yea, starved to death with hunger and cold, and stifled in loathsome dungeons. If we be guiltless, we crave but the benefit of our innocence, viz. That we may have peace to serve our God and our prince in the place of the sepulchre of our fathers.

" Thus, protesting our innocence, complaining of violence and wrong, and crying for justice on the behalf, and on the name of that righteous judge, the God of equity and justice, we continue our prayers unto him for her majesty and your honours, whose hearts we beseech him to incline towards this our most equal and just suit, through Christ Jesus our Lord."

Besides many that finished their days in loathsome prisons, there were five condemned and executed, sealing their testimonies with their blood. Their names were Elias Thacker, John Copping, Henry Barrowe, John Greenwood, and John Penry; of whom we shall now insert a farther account.

Two ministers of the Brownist persuasion were condemned and put to death, in the summer of 1583, for nonconformity, viz. Elias Thacker, hanged at St. Edmund's Bury, June 4th, and John Copping, two days after. Their indictments were for spreading certain books, seditiously penned by Robert Brown, against the Book of Common Prayer, established by the laws of this realm. The sedition charged upon Brown's book was, that it subverted the constitution of the church, and acknowledged her majesty's supremacy civilly, but not otherwise, as appears by the report which the judges sent to court viz. that the prisoners, instead of acknowledging her majesty's supremacy in all causes, would allow it only in civil. This the judges took hold of, to aggravate their offence to the queen, after they had passed sentence upon them, on the late statute of the 23d Eliz. against spreading seditious libels, and for refusing the oath of supremacy. Copping had suffered a long and illegal imprisonment from the bishop of his diocess : his wife being brought to bed while he was under confinement, he was charged with not suffering his child to be baptized ; to which he answered, that his conscience could not admit it to be done with god-fathers and god-mothers, and he could get no preacher to do it without. He was accused further with saying, the queen was perjured, because she had sworn to set forth God's glory directly, as by the scriptures are appointed, and did not ; but these were only circumstances, to support the grand charge of sedition, in spreading Brown's book. However, it seemed a little hard to hang men for spreading a seditious book, at a time when the author of that very book [Brown] was pardoned and set at liberty. Both the prisoners died by their principles ; for though Dr. Still, the archbishop's chaplain, and others, travelled and conferred with them, yet at the very hour of their death, they remained immoveable ; they were both found in the doctrinal articles of the church of England, and of unblemished lives. One Wilsford, a layman, would have suffered with them, but upon conference with secretary Wilson, who told him the queen's supremacy might be understood, only of her majesty's civil power over ecclesiastical persons, he took the oath, and was discharged.

Barrowe was apprehended at the Clink-prison, in Southwark, where he was sent to visit his brother Greenwood. He was carried immediately to Lambeth, where the archbishop would have examined him upon the oath *ex officio*, but he refused to take it, or to swear at all, upon the bible ; but (says he) by God's grace, I will answer nothing but the truth. So the archbishop took a paper of interrogatories into his hand, and asked him,

1. Whether the Lord's prayer might be used in church? He answered, that in his opinion it was rather a summary than a form, and not finding it used by the apostles, he thought it should not be constantly used by us.

2. Whether forms of prayer may be used in the church? He answered, that none such ought to be imposed.

3. Whether the common prayer be idolatrous, or superstitious? He answered, that in his opinion, it was so.

4. Whether the sacraments of the church are true sacraments and seals of the favour of God? He answered, he thought, as they were publicly administered, they were not.

5. Whether the laws of the church were good? He answered, that many of them were unlawful and antichristian.

6. Whether the church of England is a true church? He answered, that as it was now formed, it was not; yet that there are many excellent, good christians of it.

7. Whether the queen be supreme governor of the church, and may make laws for it? He answered, that the queen was the supreme governor of the church, but might not make laws other than Christ had left in his word.

8. Whether a private person may reform, if the prince neglects it? He answered, that no private persons might reform the state, but they are to abstain from unlawful things commanded by the prince.

9. Whether every particular church ought to have a presbytery? He answered in the affirmative.

After this examination, he was remanded to close prison, and denied a copy of his answers, though he earnestly desired it.

Greenwood, the minister, was examined after the same manner before the archbishop of Canterbury, the bishops of London and Winchester, the lords chief justices, the lord chief baron, and the master of the rolls. He had interrogatories put to him as Barrowe had, but refused to swear, and made much the same answer with the other. At length, on the 21st of the month called March,

o

1592, they, together with Saxio Bellot, Gent. Daniel Studley, girdler, and Robert Bowlle, were indicted at the sessions house, Old-Bailey, upon the statute of 23d Eliz. for writing and publishing sundry seditious books and pamphlets, tending to the slander of the queen and government; when they had only written against the church; but this was the archbishop's artful contrivance, to throw off the odium of their death from himself to the civil magistrate; for, as the reverend and learned Hugh Broughton observes, " though Barrowe and Greenwood were condemned for disturbance of the state; yet this would have been pardoned, and their lives spared, if they would have promised to come to church." Upon their trial, they behaved with constancy and resolution, shewing no token of recognition (says the attorney) nor prayer for mercy : they protested their inviolable loyalty to the queen, and obedience to her government; that they never wrote, nor so much as intended any thing against her highness, but only against the bishops and the hierarchy of the church; which was apparent enough. However, the jury brought them all in guilty. Bellot desired a conference, and, with tears confessing his sorrow for what he had done, was pardoned. Bowlle and Studley being looked upon only as accessaries, though they continued firm, declaring their unshaken loyalty to the queen, and refusing to ask for mercy, were reprieved, and sent back to prison; but Barrowe and Greenwood were to be made examples. Sentence of death being passed upon them, March 23, sundry divines were appointed to pursuade them to recant; who not succeeding, they were brought in a cart to Tyburn, on the last of March, and exposed under the gallows for some time to the people, to see, if the terrors of death would affright them; but remaining constant, they were brought back to Newgate, and on the sixth of April, 1592, carried a second time to Tyburn, and executed. At the place of execution, they gave such testimonies of their unfeigned piety towards God, and loyalty to the queen, praying so earnestly for her long and prosperous reign, that when Dr. Reynolds, who attended them, reported their behaviour to her majesty, she repented that she had yielded to their death.

About six weeks after this, the reverend John Penry or Ap-Henry, a Welsh divine, was executed for the same crime, in a cruel and inhuman manner. He was a pious and learned man, well disposed to religion, (says Strype) but mistaken in his principles, and hot in his temper; a zealous reformer, and a declared enemy of the archbishop. He was born in the county of Brecknock, and educated first at Cambridge, and afterwards at St. Alban's-Hall, Oxford, where he proceeded M. A. 1586, and entered into holy orders, being well acquainted with arts and languages. He preached in both universities with applause, and afterwards travelling into Wales, was the first, as he said, that preached the gospel publicly to the Welsh, and sowed the good seed among his countrymen. In the year 1588, he published a view of such public wants and disorders, as are in her majesty's country of Wales, with a humble petition to the high court of parliament for their redress: wherein is shewed, not only the necessity of reforming the state of religion, among that people, but also, the only way in regard of substance, to bring that reformation to pass. He also published an exhortation to the governors and people of her majesty's country of Wales, to labour earnestly to have the preaching of the gospel planted among them. Printed 1588.

It was never known before this time, that a minister and a scholar was condemned to death for private papers, found in his study; nor do I remember more than once since that time, in whose case it was given for law, that *scribere est agere*, that to write has been construed an overt-act; but Penry must die, right or wrong; the archbishop was the first man who signed the warrant for his execution, and after him, Puckering and Popham. The warrant was sent immediately to the sheriff, who the same day erected a gallows at St. Thomas Waterings; and, while the prisoner was at dinner, sent his officers to bid him make ready, for he must die that afternoon; accordingly, he was carried in a cart to the place of execu-

tion. When he came thither, the sheriff would not suffer
him to speak to the people, nor make any profession of
his faith towards God, or his loyalty to the queen, but
ordered him to be turned off in a hurry, about five
o'clock in the evening, May 29th, 1593, in the 34th year
of his age.

The court being struck with this behaviour of the
Brownists, began to be ashamed of hanging men for
sedition against the state, who died with such strong professions of loyalty to the queen and government, and
therefore could suffer only for the cause of religion.. This
raised an odium against the bishops and high commissioners, who, all men knew, were at the bottom of these
proceedings. It is said the queen herself was displeased
with them, when she heard of the devotion and loyalty of
the sufferers. It was therefore resolved, to proceed for
the future, on the late statute of the 31st Eliz. to retain
the queen's subjects in their obedience; and, instead of
putting the Brownists to death, to send them into banishment. Upon this statute, Johnston, pastor of the
brownist-church, was convicted, and all the gaols were
cleared for the present; though the commissioners took
care, within the compass of another year, to fill them
up again.

Queen Elizabeth died in the year 1602, in the 70th
year of her age, and 45th of her reign; and was succeeded by king James I. who ascended the English
throne, the succeeding year, having reigned in Scotland
from his infancy.

The Puritans suffered greatly also in the reign of
king James, who, in his speech to the parliament, in the
year 1620, said, " As touching religion, laws enough
are made already. It stands in two points, persuasion
and compulsion: men may persuade, but God must
give the blessing. Jesuits, priests, puritans, and sectaries, erring both on the right hand, and left hand, are
forward to persuade unto their own ends, and so ought
you the bishops, in your example and preaching; but
compulsion to obey is to blind the conscience."

These people presented the following address to the king and parliament, relating the great oppressions they were under.

"*To our sovereign lord the king's most excellent majesty, together with the honourable nobility, knights, and burgesses, now assembled at the high-court of parliament.*

" MAY it please your majesty, honours, worships, graciously to respect the humble suit of God's poor afflicted servants, and well-affected loyal subjects to your highness and honours : we are many of us constrained to live in exile out of our native country, others detained in prisons, all of us in some affliction, which the prelates and clergy of this land have inflicted upon us for our faith in God, and obedience to the gospel of our Lord Jesus Christ. We have never to this day been convinced of heresy, error, or crime, for which we should sustain the great calamities we have endured. The grounds of christian religion, professed and maintained in this land, and other churches round about, we also with one heart and spirit assent unto and possess : enemies we are to all popery, anabaptistery, or other heresy, schism, rebellion, treason, or faction, and whatsoever else is contrary to the wholesome doctrine of the gospel, or the prosperity and good estate of this realm; our only desire is to serve God, as that we may please him with reverence and fear, abstaining and keeping our souls and bodies from all remnants of the Roman religion, idolatry, imposition, and vain will-worship, of what sort soever : we witness against the unlawful pompous hierarchy and priesthood of this nation, as utterly disagreeing from the Testament of Christ, and ministry there appointed, in their offices, callings, administrations, and lord-like livings and maintenance; against the confuse, profane and irreligious multitude of all sorts of vicious livers, baptized into, and retained in the body of the church of England, without voluntary profession of, and holy walking in the faith of the gospel ; against their manner of worship and service, by reading prayers out of a book, instead of true spiritual invocation on the name of the Lord; and briefly, against all their popish abuses and relics of the man of sin whatsoever; and because this our testimony maketh against the irregular authority of the prelates, reproveth their evil actions, and disapproveth their pomp, stateliness, rich revenues, stipends, &c. therefore have they in all hostile manner set themselves against us, persecuting us unto bands, exile, and death itself, reproaching us as Schismaticks, Donatists, Brownists, seditious persons, &c. though they could never convince us of these, or any the like crimes; and though we have not ceased, neither by God's grace will cease, to wish and produce good to their souls and bodies in the Lord: now, therefore, our humble request is unto your majesty, honours, and worships, that notwithstanding these differences, we may be suffered to return into our native country, there to live in peace, practising the faith of Christ, which we profess, and have long since set forth to the view of the world in our public confession, wherein none hitherto have shewed us any error; and seeing the people of other nations are by your majesty and honours suffered in this realm, though differing from the ecclesiastical state of the same, we hope that your highness's natural and loyal subjects may find like favour at your hands; for although we cannot but hold and witness the truth of God against the corruptions remaining, yet hold we in no wise lawful for ourselves, or any subjects, to attempt the reforming or abolishing of these, or any the like abuses; for God hath committed the sword into your majesty's hand alone; who in his time will persuade (we trust) your royal heart to fulfil his will, and execute his judgments upon the remainders of the spiritual Babylon, which will turn to as great honour to God, honour to your majesty, and good of this realm, as the abolishing of abbots, monks, friars, mass, images, &c. hath turned heretofore.

"So the Lord of lords, and Ruler of the earth, will establish your crown and kingdom unto length of days; and howsoever this our suit will be regarded, we will not cease in all places of our pilgrimage, to pray for and procure the good of your majesty, your honours, worships, and all our country, whom God Almighty bless with long life and happy days on earth, and crown with everlasting glory in the highest heavens, Amen."

In the year, 1604, in this king's reign, four persons were banished out of England, after they had suffered three months' imprisonment, for no other cause than separating themselves from the church of England, refusing to communicate, join, or partake with the same in their public ministry and worship, reputing many corruptions to be still remaining amongst them, which were derived from popery.

PERSECUTIONS

IN

GREAT-BRITAIN AND AMERICA,

AFTER THE MIDDLE OF THE SEVENTEENTH CENTURY.

ABOUT the middle of the seventeenth century, much persecution and suffering were inflicted on a sect of protestant dissenters, commonly called Quakers: a people which arose at that time in England; some of whom sealed their testimony with their blood.

For an account of the above people, see Sewel's, or Gough's History of them.

The principal points in which their conscientious non-conformity rendered them obnoxious to the penalties of the law, were,

1. Their christian resolution of assembling publicly for the worship of God, in a manner most agreeable to their consciences.

2. Their refusal to pay tithes, which they esteemed a Jewish ceremony, abrogated by the coming of Christ.

3. Their testimony against wars and fighting, the practice of which, they judged inconsistent with the command of Christ: "Love your enemies," &c. Mat. v. 44.

4. Their constant obedience to the command of Christ: "Swear not at all," &c. Mat. v. 34.

5. Their refusal to pay rates or assessments for building and repairing houses for a worship which they did not approve.

6. Their use of the proper and scriptural language, of "thou," and "thee," to a single person : and their disuse of the custom of uncovering their heads, or pulling off their hats, by way of homage to man.

7. The necessity many found themselves under, of publishing what they believed to be the doctrine of truth ; and sometimes even in the places appointed for the public national worship.

Their conscientious non-compliance in the preceding particulars, exposed them to much persecution and suffering, which consisted in prosecutions ; fines ; cruel beatings, whippings, and other corporeal punishments ; imprisonment ; banishment ; and even death.

To relate a particular account of their persecutions and sufferings, would extend beyond the limits of this work : we shall therefore refer, for that information, to the histories already mentioned, and more particularly to Besse's Collection of their sufferings ; and shall confine our account here, mostly to those who sacrificed their lives, and evinced, by their disposition of mind, constancy, patience, and faithful perseverance, that they were influenced by a sense of religious duty.

Numerous and repeated were the prosecutions against them ; and sometimes for transgressions or offences, which the law did not contemplate or embrace.

Many of the fines and penalties exacted of them, were not only unreasonable and exorbitant, but as they could not consistently pay them, were sometimes distrained to several times the value of the demand ; whereby many poor families were greatly distressed, and obliged to depend on the assistance of their friends.

Numbers were not only cruelly beaten and whipped in a public manner, like criminals, but some were branded, and others had their ears cut off.

Great numbers were long confined in loathsome prisons ; in which, some ended their days, in consequence thereof.

Many were sentenced to banishment ; and a considerable number were transported. Some were banished on pain of death ; and four were actually executed by the hands of the hangman, as we shall here relate, after inserting copies of some of the laws of the country where they suffered.

"At a General Court held at Boston, the 14th of Oct. 1656.

" WHEREAS, there is a cursed sect of heretics, lately risen up in the world, which are commonly called quakers, who take upon them to be immediately sent from God, and infallibly assisted by the Spirit, to speak and write blasphemous opinions, despising government, and the order of God, in the church and commonwealth, speaking evil of dignities, reproaching and reviling magistrates and ministers, seeking to turn the people from the faith, and gain proselytes to their pernicious ways : this court taking into consideration the premises, and to prevent the like mischief, as by their means is wrought in our land, doth hereby order, and by authority of this court, be it ordered and enacted, that what master or commander of any ship, bark, pink, or catch, shall henceforth bring into any harbour, creek, or cove, within this jurisdiction, any quaker or quakers, or other blasphemous heretics, shall pay, or cause to be paid, the fine of one hundred pounds to the treasurer of the country, except it appear he want true knowledge or information of their being such ; and, in that case, he hath liberty to clear himself by his oath, when sufficient proof to the contrary is wanting : and, for default of good payment, or good security for it, shall be cast into prison, and there to continue till the said sum be satisfied to the treasurer as aforesaid. And the commander of any catch, ship, or vessel, being legally convicted, shall give in sufficient security to the governor, or any one or more of the magistrates, who have power to determine the same, to carry them back to the place whence he brought them ; and, on his refusal so to do, the governor, or one or more of the magistrates, are hereby empowered to issue out his or their warrants to commit such master or commander to prison, there to continue, till he give in sufficient security to the content of the governor, or any of the magistrates, as aforesaid. And it is hereby further ordered and enacted, that what quaker soever shall arrive in this country from foreign parts, or shall come into this jurisdiction from any parts adjacent, shall be forthwith committed to the house of correction; and, at their entrance to be severely whipped, and by the master thereof be kept constantly to work, and none suffered to converse or speak with them, during the time of their imprisonment, which shall be no longer than necessity requires. And it is ordered, if any person shall knowingly import into any harbour of this jurisdiction, any quakers' books or writings, concerning their devilish opinions, shall pay for such book or writing, being legally proved against him or them, the sum of five pounds; and whosoever shall disperse or conceal any such book or writing, and it be found with him or her, or in his or her house, and shall not immediately deliver the same to the next magistrate, shall forfeit or pay five pounds, for the dispersing or concealing of any such book or writing. And it is hereby further enacted, that if any person, within this colony, shall take upon them to defend the heretical opinions of the quakers, or any of their books or papers, as aforesaid, if legally proved, shall be fined for the first-time forty shillings; if they shall persist in the same, and shall again defend it the second time, four pounds; if notwithstanding they shall again defend and maintain the said quakers' heretical opinions, they shall be committed to the house of correction till there be convenient passage to send them out of the land, being sentenced by the court of Assistants to banishment. Lastly, it is hereby ordered, that what person or persons soever, shall revile the persons of the magistrates or ministers, as is usual with the quakers, such person or persons shall be severely whipped, or pay the sum of five pounds.

" This is a true copy of the court's order, as attests

" EDWARD RAWSON, Sec."

"At a General Court held at Boston, the 14th *of Oct.* 1657.

" As an addition to the late order, in reference to the coming or bringing of any of the cursed sect of the quakers into this jurisdiction, it is ordered, that whosoever shall from henceforth bring, or cause to be brought directly or indirectly, any known quaker or quakers, or other blasphemous heretics, into this jurisdiction, every such person shall forfeit the sum of one hundred pounds to the country, and shall by warrant from any magistrate be committed to prison, there to remain till the penalty be satisfied and paid ; and if any person or persons, within this jurisdiction, shall henceforth entertain and conceal any such quaker or quakers, or other blasphemous heretics, knowing them so to be, every such person shall forfeit to the country forty shillings for every hour's entertainment and concealment of any quaker or quakers, &c. as aforesaid, and shall be committed to prison as aforesaid, till the forfeiture be fully satisfied and paid. And it is further ordered, that if any quaker or quakers shall presume, after they have once suffered what the law requires, to come into this jurisdiction, every such male quaker shall, for the first offence, have one of his ears cut off, and be kept at work in the house of correction, till he can be sent away at his own charge; and for the second offence, shall have his other ear cut off : and every woman quaker, that has suffered the law here, that shall presume to come into this jurisdiction, shall be severely whipped, and kept at the house of correction at work, till she be sent away at her own charge, and so also for her coming again, she shall be alike used as aforesaid. And for every quaker, he or she, that shall a third time herein again offend, they shall have their tongues bored through with an hot iron, and be kept at the house of correction close to work, till they be sent away at their own charge. And it is further ordered, that all and every quaker arising from among ourselves, shall be dealt with, and suffer the like punishment as the law provides against foreign quakers.

"EDWARD RAWSON, Secr."

" An Act made at a General Court, held at Boston, the 20th of October, 1658.

" WHEREAS, there is a pernicious sect, commonly called quakers, lately risen, who by word and writing have published and maintained many dangerous and horrid tenets, and do take upon them to change and alter the received laudable customs of our nation, in giving civil respect to equals, or reverence to superiors; whose actions tend to undermine the civil government, and also to destroy the order of the churches, by denying all established forms of worship, and by withdrawing from orderly church fellowship, allowed and approved by all orthodox professors of truth, and instead thereof, and in opposition thereunto, frequently meeting by themselves, insinuating themselves into the minds of the simple, or such as are least affected to the order and government of church and commonwealth, whereby divers of our inhabitants have been infected, notwithstanding all former laws, made upon the experience of their arrogant and bold obtrusions, to disseminate their principles amongst us, prohibiting their coming into this jurisdiction, they have not been deterred from their impetuous attempts to undermine our peace, and hazard our ruin.

" For prevention thereof, this court doth order and enact, that every person or persons, of the cursed sect of the quakers, who is not an inhabitant of, but is found within this jurisdiction, shall be apprehended without warrant, where no magistrate is at hand, by any constable, commissioner, or select man, and conveyed from constable, to constable, to the next magistrate, who shall commit the said person to close prison, there to remain (without bail) until the next court of Assistants, where they shall have legal trial. And being convicted to be of the sect of the quakers, shall be sentenced to banishment, on pain of death. And that every inhabitant of this jurisdiction, being convicted to be of the aforesaid sect, either by taking up, publishing, or defending the horrid opinions of the quakers, or the stirring up mutiny, sedition, or rebellion against the government, or by taking up their abusive and destructive practices, viz. denying civil respect to equals and superiors, and withdrawing from the church assemblies; and instead thereof, frequenting meetings of their own, in opposition to our church order; adhering to, or approving of any known quaker, and the tenets and practices of quakers, that are opposite to the orthodox received opinions of the godly; and endeavouring to disaffect others to civil government and church order, or condemning the practice and proceedings of this court against the quakers, manifesting thereby their complying with those, whose design is to overthrow the order established in church and state: every such person, upon conviction before the said court of Assistants, in manner aforesaid, shall be committed to close prison for one month, and then, unless they choose voluntarily to depart this jurisdiction, shall give bond for their good behaviour, and appear at the next court, where, continuing obstinate, and refusing to retract and reform the aforesaid opinions, they shall be sentenced to banishment, upon pain of death. And any one magistrate upon information given him of any such person, shall cause him to be apprehended, and shall commit any such person to prison, according to his discretion, until he come to trial as aforesaid."

It appears there were also laws passed in both of the then colonies of New-Plymouth and New-Haven, and in the Dutch settlement at New-Amsterdam, now New-York, prohibiting the people called quakers, from coming into those places, under severe penalties; in consequence of which, some underwent considerable suffering.

The two first that sealed their testimony with their blood, were William Robinson, merchant, of London, and Marmaduke Stevenson, a countryman of Yorkshire. These coming to Boston, in the beginning of September, were sent for by the court of Assistants, and there sentenced to banishment, on pain of death. This sentence was passed also on Mary Dyar, mentioned hereafter, and Nicholas Davis, who were both at Boston. But William Robinson, being looked upon as a teacher, was also condemned to be whipped severely ; and the constable was commanded to get an able man to do it.   Then Robinson was brought into the street, and there stripped ; and having his hands put through the holes of the carriage of a great gun, where the gaoler held him, the executioner gave him twenty stripes, with a three-fold cord whip. Then he and the other prisoners were shortly released, and banished ; which, that it was for no other reason but their being quakers, may appear by the following warrant.

" You are required by these, presently to set at liberty William Robinson, Marmaduke Stevenson, Mary Dyar, and Nicholas Davis, who, by an order of the court and council, had been imprisoned, because it appeared by their own confession, words, and actions, that they are quakers ; wherefore, a sentence was pronounced against them, to depart this jurisdiction, on pain of death ; and that they must answer it at their peril, if they, or any of them, after the 14th of this present month, September, are found within this jurisdiction, or any part thereof.

                                   " EDWARD RAWSON.
" Boston, September 12, 1659."

Though Mary Dyar and Nicholas Davis left that jurisdiction for that time, yet Robinson and Stevenson, though they departed the town of Boston, could not yet resolve (not being free in mind) to depart that jurisdiction, though their lives were at stake.   And so they went to Salem, and some place thereabout, to visit, and build up their friends in the faith.   But it was not long before they were taken, and put again into prison at Boston, and chains locked to their legs.   In the next month, Mary Dyar returned also.   And as she stood before the prison, speaking with one Christopher Holder, who was come thither to inquire for a ship bound for England, whether he intended to go, she was also taken into custody.   Thus, they had now three persons, who, according to their sanguinary law, had forfeited their lives.   And, on the 20th of October, these three were brought into the court, where John Endicot and others were assembled.   And being called to the bar, Endicot commanded the keeper to pull off their hats ; and then said, that they had made several laws to keep the quakers from amongst them ; and neither whipping, nor imprisoning, nor cutting off ears, nor banishing upon pain of death, would keep them from amongst them. And further, he said, that he or they, desired not the death of any of them. Yet, notwithstanding, his following words, without more ado, were, "Give ear, and harken to your sentence of death." W. Robinson then desired that he might be permitted to read a paper, giving an account of the reason why he had not departed that jurisdiction. But Endicot would not suffer it to be read, and said in a rage, "You shall not read it, nor will the court hear it read." Then Robinson laid it on the table.

The following is a copy of it.

"On the 8th of the eighth month, 1659, in the after part of the day, in travelling between Newport in Rhode-Island, and Daniel Gold's house, with my dear brother, Christopher Holden, the word of the Lord came expressly to me, which did fill me immediately with life and power, and heavenly love, by which he constrained me, and commanded me to pass to the town of Boston, my life to lay down, in his will, for the accomplishing of his service, that he had there to perform, at the day appointed. To which heavenly voice, I presently yielded obedience, nor questioned the Lord, how he would bring the thing to pass, being, I was a child, and obedience was demanded of me by the Lord, who filled me with living strength and power, from his heavenly presence ; which, at that time, did mightily overshadow me, and my life at that time, did say Amen, to what the Lord required of me, and had commanded me to do ; and willingly I was given up, from that time to his day, the will of the Lord to do and perform, whatever became of my body. For the Lord had said unto me, ' My soul shall live in everlasting peace, and my life shall enter into rest, for being obedient to the God of my life." I being a child, durst not question the Lord in the least,

4 A

but rather willing to lay down my life, than to bring dishonour to the Lord.   And as the Lord made me willing,
dealing gently and kindly with me, as a tender father by a
faithful child, whom he dearly loves, so the Lord did deal
with me, in ministering his life unto me, which gave and
gives me strength to perform what the Lord required of
me, and still as I did, and do stand in need, he ministered
and ministereth more strength and virtue, and heavenly
power and wisdom, whereby I was, and am made strong
in God, not fearing what man shall be suffered to do unto
me, being filled with heavenly courage, which is meekness and innocence, for the cause is the Lord's that we go
in, and the battle is the Lord's ; and thus saith the Lord of
hosts, the mighty and the terrible God, " Not by strength,
nor by might, nor by power of man, but by my Spirit,"
saith the Lord of hosts ; " I will perform what my mouth
hath spoken, through my servants, whom I have chosen,
mine elect, in whom my soul delighteth." Friends, the
God of my life, and the God of the whole earth, did lay
this thing upon me, for which I now suffer bonds near unto
death.   He, by his almighty power and everlasting love,
constrained me, and laid this thing upon me ; and, truly, I
could not deny the Lord, much less resist the Holy One
of Israel.   Therefore, all who are ignorant of the motion
of the Lord, in the inward parts, be not hasty in judging
in this matter, lest ye speak evil of the thing ye know not.
But, of a truth, the Lord God of heaven and earth, commanded me by his Spirit, and spake unto me by his Son,
whom he hath made heir of all things, and in his life I live,
and in it I shall depart this earthly tabernacle, if unmerciful men be suffered to take it from me.   And herein I
rejoice, that the Lord is with me, the ancient of days, the
life of the suffering seed, for which I am freely given up,
and singly do I stand in the will of God ; for, to me, to live
is Christ, and to die, is gain : and truly, I have great desire and will herein, knowing that the Lord is with me,
whatever ignorant men shall be able to say against me ;
for the witness of the Spirit I have received, and the presence of the Lord and his heavenly life doth accompany
me, so that I can say, in truth, and from an upright heart,

blessed be the Lord God of my life, who hath counted me worthy, and called me hereunto, to bear my testimony against ungodly and unrighteous men, who seek to take away the life of the righteous, without a cause, as the rulers of Massachusetts-Bay do intend, if the Lord stop them not from their intent. Oh! hear, ye rulers, and give ear and listen, all ye that have any hand herein, to put the innocent to death, for in the name, and fear, and dread, of the Lord God, I here declare the cause of my staying here amongst you, and continuing in the jurisdiction, after there was a sentence of banishment upon pain of death, as ye said, pronounced against me, without a just cause; as ye all know, that we that were banished, committed nothing worthy of banishment, nor of any punishment, much less banishment upon pain of death. And now, ye rulers, ye do intend to put me to death, and my companion, unto whom the word of the Lord came, saying, " Go to Boston with thy brother, William Robinson." Unto which command he was obedient, who had said unto him, " he had a great work for him to do." Which thing is now seen, and the Lord is now a doing of it; and it is in obedience to the Lord, the God of the whole earth, that we continued amongst you, and that we came to the town of Boston again, in obedience to the Lord, the Creator of heaven and earth, in whose hand your breath is; and will ye put us to death for obeying the Lord, the God of the whole earth? Well, if ye do this act, and put us to death, know this, and be it known unto you all, ye rulers and people, within this jurisdiction, that whosoever hath a hand therein, will be guilty of innocent blood: and not only upon yourselves, will ye bring innocent blood, but upon the town, and the inhabitants thereof, and every where within this jurisdiction, that had the least hand therein. Therefore be instructed, ye rulers of this land, and take warning betimes, and learn wisdom, before it be hid from your eyes.

" Written in the common gaol, the 19th of the eighth month, 1659, in Boston, by one who feareth the Lord, who is by ignorant people called a Quaker, and unto such am I only known by the name of William Robinson, yet a new name have I received, which such know not."

Robinson desiring again that the paper might be read, that so all that were present might hear it, it was denied him, and Endicot said, ‘W. Robinson, hearken to your sentence of death ; you shall be had back to the place from whence you came, and from thence to the place of execution, to be hanged on the gallows till you are dead.’   This sentence was not altogether unexpected by W. Robinson ; for it was four months now that he had believed that this would be his fate.

Robinson being taken away, M. Stevenson was called, and Endicot said to him, ‘ If you have any thing to say, you may speak.’   He knowing how they dealt with his companion, was silent, though he had also written in prison a paper, containing the cause of his being come there ; but he kept it with him, and found afterwards occasion to deliver it to somebody.   Then Endicot pronounced sentence of death against him, saying, ‘ M. Stevenson, you shall be had to the place from whence you came, and from thence to the gallows, and there to be hanged till you are dead.’

After this, he was taken away, and Mary Dyar was called : to whom Endicot spoke thus : ‘ Mary Dyar, you shall go to the place from whence you came, (to wit the prison) and from thence to the place of execution, and be hanged there until you are dead.’   To which she replied, ‘ The will of God be done.’   Then Endicot said, ‘ Take her away, marshal.’   To which she returned. ‘ Yea, joyfully I go.’   And in her going to the prison, she often uttered speeches of praise to the Lord ; and, being full of joy, she said to the marshal, he might let her alone, for she would go to the prison without him.   To which he answered, ‘ I believe you, Mrs. Dyar ; but I must do what I am commanded.’   Thus she was led to prison, where she was kept a week, with the two other her companions, that were also condemned to die.

The paper of Marmaduke Stevenson, mentioned before, which he gave forth after he had received sentence of death, was thus :

“ In the beginning of the year 1655, I was at the plough, in the east part of Yorkshire, in Old England, near the place where my outward being was, and as I walked after the plough, I was filled with the love and presence of the living God, which did ravish my heart when I felt it ; for it did increase and abound in me like a living stream, so did the love and life of God run through me like precious ointment, giving a pleasant smell, which made me to stand still ; and as I stood a little still, with my heart and mind stayed on the Lord, the word of the Lord came to me in a still small voice, which I did hear perfectly, saying to me, in the secret of my heart and conscience, ' I have ordained thee a prophet unto the nations.' And at the hearing of the word of the Lord, I was put to a stand, being that I was but a child for such a weighty matter.   So at the time appointed, Barbadoes was set before me, unto which I was required of the Lord to go, and leave my dear and loving wife, and tender children : for the Lord said unto me immediately by his spirit, that he would be as a husband to my wife, and as a father to my children, and they should not want in my absence, for he would provide for them when I was gone.   And I believed that the Lord would perform what he had spoken, because I was made willing to give up myself to his work and service, to leave all and follow him, whose presence and life is with me, where I rest in peace and quietness of spirit (with my dear brother) under the shadow of his wings, who hath made us willing to lay down our lives for his own name sake, if unmerciful men be suffered to take them from us ; and if they do, we know we shall have peace and rest with the Lord for ever in his holy habitation, when they shall have torment night and day. So, in obedience to the living God, I made preparation to pass to Barbadoes, in the fourth month, 1658.   So, after I had been some time on the said island in the service of God, I heard that New England had made a law to put the servants of the living God to death, if they returned after they were sentenced away, which did come near me at that time ; and as I considered the thing, and pondered it in my heart, immediately came the word of the Lord unto me, saying, " Thou knowest not but that thou mayest go thither." But I kept this word in my

heart, and did not declare it to any until the time appointed.
So, after that, a vessel was made ready for Rhode Island,
which I passed in.   So, after a little time that I had been
there, visiting the seed which the Lord hath blessed, the
word of the Lord came unto me, saying, " go to Boston
with thy brother William Robinson." And at his command I was obedient, and gave up myself to do his will,
that so his work and service may be accomplished : for
he hath said unto me, that he hath a great work for me to
do ; which is now come to pass : and for yielding obedience to, and obeying the voice and command of the
everliving God, who created heaven and earth, and the
fountains of waters, do I, with my dear brother, suffer
outward bonds near unto death.   And this is given forth
to be upon record, that all people may know, who hear
it, that we came not in our own wills, but in the will of
God.   Given forth by me who am known to men by the
name of

'   MARMADUKE STEVENSON,

  " But have a new name given me, which the world
knows not of, written in the Book of Life.   •

  " Written in Boston prison, in the 8th month, 1659."

Mary Dyar being returned to prison, wrote the following letter, which she sent to the rulers of Boston.

To the General Court in Boston.

  " Whereas, I am by many charged with the guiltiness
of my own blood ; if you mean, in my coming to Boston, I am therein clear, and justified by the Lord, in
whose will I came, who will require my blood of you,
be sure, who have made a law to take away the lives of
the innocent servants of God, if they come among you,
who are called by you, cursed quakers ; although I say,
and am a living witness for them and the Lord, that he
hath blessed them, and sent them unto you ; therefore
be not found fighters against God, but let my counsel and
request be accepted with you, to repeal all such laws, that

truth, and the servants of the Lord, may have free passage among you; and you be kept from shedding innocent blood, which I know there are many among you would not do, if they knew it so to be; nor can the enemy that stirreth you up, thus to destroy his holy seed, in any measure countervail the great damage that you will, by thus doing, procure. Therefore, seeing the Lord hath not hid it from me, it lieth upon me, in love to your souls, thus to persuade you. I have no self-ends the Lord knoweth; for if my life were freely granted by you, it would not avail me, nor could I expect it of you, so long as I should daily hear or see the sufferings of these people, my dear brethren, and the seed, with whom my life is bound up; as I have done these two years, and now it is like to increase, even unto death, for no evil doing, but coming among you. Was ever the like laws heard of among a people that profess Christ come in the flesh? And have such no other weapons but such laws to fight against spiritual wickedness withal, as you call it? Wo is me for you! Of whom take ye counsel? Search with the light of Christ in you, and it will shew you of whom, as it hath done me and many more, who have been disobedient and deceived, as now ye are: which light, as you come into, and obeying what is made manifest to you therein, you will not repent that you were kept from shedding blood, though it were by a woman. It is not mine own life I seek (for I choose rather to suffer with the people of God, than to enjoy the pleasures of Egypt) but the life of the seed, which I know the Lord hath blessed, and therefore seeks the enemy thus vehemently to destroy the life thereof, as in all ages he ever did. O harken not unto him, I beseech you, for the seed's sake, which is one in all, and is dear in the sight of God, which they that touch, touch the apple of his eye, and cannot escape his wrath; whereof I having felt, cannot but persuade all men that I have to do withal, especially you who name the name of Christ, to depart from such iniquity as shedding blood, even of the saints of the Most High. Therefore, let my request have as much acceptance with you, if ye be christians, as Esther's had with

Ahasuerus, whose relation is short of that that is between christians; and my request is the same that her's was: and he said not that he had made a law, and that it would be dishonourable for him to revoke it; but when he understood that those people were so prized by her, and so nearly concerned her, as in truth these are to me, you may see what he did for her. Therefore, I leave these lines with you, appealing to the faithful and true witness of God, which is one in all consciences, before whom we must all appear; with whom I shall eternally rest, in everlasting joy and peace, whether you will hear or forbear. With him is my reward, with whom to live is my joy, and to die is my gain, though I had not your forty-eight hours warning, for the preparation of the death of Mary Dyar.

' And know this also, that if through the enmity you shall declare yourselves worse than Ahasuerus, and confirm your law, though it were but by taking away the life of one of us, that the Lord will overthrow both your law and you, by his righteous judgments and plagues poured justly upon you, who now whilst ye are warned thereof, and tenderly sought unto, may avoid the one, by removing the other. If you neither hear, nor obey the Lord nor his servants, yet will he send more of his servants among you, so that your end shall be frustrated, that think to restrain them ye call cursed Quakers, from coming among you by any thing you can do to them. Yea, verily, he hath a seed here among you, for whom we have suffered all this while, and yet suffer; whom the Lord of the harvest will send forth more labourers to gather, out of the mouths of the devourers of all sorts, into his fold, where he will lead them into fresh pastures, even the paths of righteousness, for his name's sake. Oh, let none of you put this good day far from you, which verily in the light of the Lord I see approaching, even to many in and about Boston, which is the bitterest and darkest professing place, and likely so to continue so long as you do as you have done, that ever I heard of. Let the time past therefore suffice, for such a profession as brings forth such fruits as these laws are. In love and in the spirit of meekness I again beseech you, for I have no enmity to the persons of any ; but you shall know, that God will not be mocked ; but what ye sow, that shall ye reap from him that will render to every one according to the deeds done in the body, whether good or evil. Even so be it, saith ' MARY DYAR.'

A copy of this was given to the general court after Mary Dyar had received the sentence of death, about the 8th or 9th month, 1659.

The day appointed to execute the bloody sentence was the 27th of Oct. when, in the afternoon, the condemned prisoners were led to the gallows, by the marshal Michaelson, and captain James Oliver, with a band of about two-hundred armed men, besides many horsemen; as if they were afraid that some of the people would have rescued the prisoners: and that no actors on the stage might be wanting, the priest Wilson joined the company, and when the court deliberated how to deal with the Quakers, said, ' hang them, or else,' (drawing his finger athwart his throat) as if he would have said, ' dispatch them this way.' Now the march began, and a drummer going next before the condemned, the drums were beaten, especially when any of them attempted to speak. Glorious signs of heavenly joy and gladness were beheld in the countenances of these three persons, who walked hand in hand, Mary being the middlemost; which made the marshal say to her, who was pretty aged, and stricken in years, ' are not you ashamed to walk thus hand in hand between two young men ?' ' No', replied she, ' this is to me an hour of the greatest joy I could enjoy in this world. No eye can see, nor ear can hear, no tongue can utter, and no heart can understand, the sweet incomes, or influence, and the refreshings of the spirit of the Lord, which now I feel.' Thus going along, W. Robinson said, ' this is your hour, and the power of darkness.' But presently the drums were beaten ; yet shortly after, the drummers leaving off beating, Marmaduke Stevenson said, ' this is the day of your visitation, wherein the Lord hath visited you.' More he spoke, but could not be understood, by

4 B

reason of the drums being beaten again.   Yet they went on with great cheerfulness, as going to an everlasting wedding feast, and rejoicing that the Lord had counted them worthy to suffer death for his name's sake.

When they came near the gallows, they took leave of each other with tender embraces, and Robinson went cheerfully up the ladder, and then said to the people, 'this is the day of your visitation, wherein the Lord hath visited you : this is the day the Lord is risen in his mighty power, to be avenged on all his adversaries.' He also signified, that he suffered not as an evil doer, and desired the spectators, to mind the light that was in them ; to wit, the Light of Christ, of which he testified, and was now going to seal it with his blood.   This so incensed the envious priest, that he said, ' hold thy tongue, be silent, thou art going to die with a lie in thy mouth.'   The rope being now about his neck, the executioner bound his hands and legs, and tied his neckcloth about his face : which being done, Robinson said, ' now ye are made manifest ;' and the executioner being about turning him off, he said, ' I suffer for Christ, in whom I live, and for whom I die.' He being turned off, Marmaduke Stevenson stept up the ladder, and said, ' be it known unto all this day, that we suffer not as evil doers, but for conscience sake.' And when the hangman was about to turn him off, he said, ' This day shall we be at rest with the Lord :' and so he was turned off.

Mary Dyar seeing her companions hanging dead before her, also stept up the ladder ; but after her coats were tied about her feet, the halter put about her neck, and her face covered with a handkerchief, which the priest Wilson lent the hangman, just as she was to be turned off, a cry was heard, ' stop, for she is reprieved.' Her feet then being loosed, they bade her come down. But she, whose mind was already as it were in heaven, stood still, and said, she was there willing to suffer as her brethren did, unless they would annul their wicked law.   Little heed was given to what she said, but they pulled her down, and the marshal and others taking her by the arms, carried her to prison again. That she thus was freed of the gallows this time, was at the intercession of her son, to whom it seems they could not then resolve to deny that favour. She now having heard why she was reprieved, wrote the next day, being the 28th of October, the following letter to the court.

The 28th of the 8th month, 1659.

' Once more to the general court assembled in Boston, speaks Mary Dyar, even as before. My life is not accepted, neither availeth me, in comparison of the lives and liberty of the truth and servants of the living God, for which in the bowels of love and meekness I sought you ; yet, nevertheless, with wicked hands have you put two of them to death, which makes me to feel, that the mercies of the wicked is cruelty. I rather choose to die than to live, as from you, as guilty of their innocent blood : therefore, seeing my request hindered, I leave you to the righteous judge, and searcher of all hearts, who, with the pure measure of light he hath given to every man to profit withal, will in his due time let you see whose servants you are, and of whom you have taken counsel, which I desire you to search into : but all his counsel hath been slighted, and you would none of his reproofs. Read your portion, Prov. i. 24 to 32. For verily the night cometh on you apace, wherein no man can work, in which you shall assuredly fall to your own master. In obedience to the Lord, whom I serve with my spirit, and pity to your souls, which you neither know nor pity, I can do no less than once more warn you, to put away the evil of your doings ; and kiss the son, the light in you, before his wrath be kindled in you ; for where it is, nothing without you can help or deliver you out of his hand at all ; and if these things be not so, then say there hath been no prophet from the Lord sent amongst you ; though we be nothing, yet it is his pleasure, by things that are not, to bring to nought things that are.
" When I heard your last order read, it was a disturbance unto me, that was so freely offering up my life to him

that gave it me, and sent me hither so to do, which obedience being his own work, he gloriously accompanied
with his presence, and peace, and love in me, in which I
rested from my labour, till by your order and the people,
I was so far disturbed, that I could not retain any more
of the words thereof, than that I should return to prison,
and there remain forty and eight hours ; to which I submitted, finding nothing from the Lord to the contrary,
that I may know what his pleasure and counsel is concerning me, on whom I wait therefore, for he is my life,
and the length of my days ; and as I said before, I came
at his command, and go at his command.

' MARY DYAR.'

The magistrates now perceiving that the putting William Robinson and Marmaduke Stevenson to death, caused great discontent among the people, resolved to send
away Mary Dyar, thereby to calm their minds a little. And
so she was put on horseback, and by four horsemen conveyed fifteen miles towards Rhode-Island, where she was
left with a horse and a man, to be conveyed the rest of
the way; which she soon sent back, and so repaired home.
Mary Dyar, being come to Rhode-Island, went from
thence to Long-Island, where she staid the most part
of the winter : and then coming home again, she was
moved to return to the bloody town of Boston, whither
she came on the 21st of the third month, in the year 1660,
and on the 31st she was sent for by the general court.
Being come, the governor John Endicot said, ' are you
the same Mary Dyar that was here before ?'   And it
seems he was preparing an evasion for her, there having
been another of that name returned from Old England.
But she was so far from disguising, that she answered un-
dauntedly, ' I am the same Mary Dyar that was here the
last general court.'   Then Endicot said, ' you will own
yourself a Quaker, will you not ?   To which Mary Dyar
said, ' I own myself reproachfully called so.'   Then the
jailor, (who would also say something) said, 'she is a vagabond.'   And Endicot said, the sentence was passed upon
her the last general court, and now likewise ; ' you must

return to the prison, and there remain till to-morrow at nine o'clock ; then from thence you must go to the gallows, and there to be hanged till you are dead.' To which Mary Dyar said, ' this is no more than what thou saidst before.' And Endicot returned, ' but now it is to be executed ; therefore prepare yourself to-morrow at nine o'clock.' She then spoke thus : ' I came in obedience to the will of God the last general court, desiring you to repeal your unrighteous laws of banishment on pain of death, and that same is my work now, and earnest request ; although I told you, that if you refused to repeal them, the Lord would send others of his servants to witness against them.' Hereupon Endicot asked her, whether she was a prophetess ? And she answered, ' she spoke the words that the Lord spoke in her ; and now the thing was come to pass.' And beginning to speak of her call, Endicot cried, ' away with her ; away with her.' So she was brought to the prison house where she was before, and kept close shut up until the next day.

About the appointed time the marshal Michaelson came, and called her to come hastily ; and coming into the room where she was, she desired him to stay a little ; and speaking mildly, said, she should be ready presently. But he being of a rough temper, said he could not wait upon her, but she should now wait upon him. One Margaret Smith, her companion, being grieved to see such hard-heartedness, spoke something against their unjust laws and proceedings : to which he said, ' you shall have your share of the same.' Then Mary Dyar was brought forth, and with a band of soldiers led through the town, the drums being beaten before and behind her, and so continued, that none might hear her speak all the way to the place of execution, which was about a mile. With this guard she came to the gallows, and being gone up the ladder, some said to her, that if she would return, she might come down and save her life. To which she replied, ' nay, I cannot, for in obedience to the will of the Lord I came, and in his will I abide faithful to the death.' Then captain John Webb said, that she had been there before, and had the sentence of banishment upon pain of death, and had broken the law in coming again now; and therefore was guilty of her own blood. To which she returned, 'nay, I come to keep blood-guiltiness from you, desiring you to repeal the unrighteous and unjust law of banishment upon pain of death, made against the innocent servants of the Lord ; therefore my blood will be required at your hands, who wilfully do it : but for those that do it in the simplicity of their hearts, I desire the Lord to forgive them. I came to do the will of my Father, and in obedience to his will, I stand even to death. Then priest Wilson said, ' Mary Dyar, O repent, O repent, and be not so deluded, and carried away by the deceit of the devil.' To this Mary Dyar answered, ' Nay, man, I am not now to repent.' And being asked by some, whether she would have the elders pray for her, she said, ' I know never an elder here.' Being further asked whether she would have any of the people to pray for her ? She answered she desired all the prayers of the people of God. Thereupon some scoffingly said, ' It may be she thinks there is none here.' She looking about, said, ' I know but few here.' Then they spoke to her again, that one of the elders might pray for her. To which she replied, ' Nay, first a child, then a young man, then a strong man, before an elder in Christ Jesus.' After this she was charged with something which was not understood what it was, but she seemed to hear it ; for she said, ' it is false, it is false ; I never spoke those words.' Then one mentioned that she should have said she had been in paradise. To which she answered, ' yea I have been in paradise several days.' And more she spoke of eternal happiness, into which she was now to enter. In this well disposed condition she was turned off, and died a martyr of Christ, being twice led to death, which the first time she expected with undaunted courage, and now suffered with christian fortitude.

William Leddra, who was banished from Boston on pain of death, was under such necessity of conscience, that he could not forbear returning thither ; where he came about the conclusion of the foregoing year ; but was soon taken prisoner, and being fastened to a log of wood,

was kept night and day locked in chains, in an open prison, during a very cold winter.

On the 9th of the first month of this year, he was
brought into the court of Assistants, with his chains and
log at his heels. And he asking the gaoler, when he intended to take off the irons from his legs; the gaoler
roughly answered, 'when thou art going to be hanged.'
W. Leddra then being brought to the bar, it was told him
by the rulers, speaking of their law, that he was found
guilty, and that he was to die. He said, 'what evil
have I done?' The answer was, his own confession was as
good as a thousand witnesses. He asked, what that was?
To which they answered, that he owned these quakers
that were put to death, and that they were innocent. Besides that, he would not put off his hat in court, and that
he said 'thee' and 'thou.' Then said William to them,
'you will put me to death for speaking English, and for
not putting off my clothes.' To this major-general Denison returned, 'a man may speak treason in English.'
And William replied, 'is it treason to say thee and thou,
to a single person?' But none answered only Simon
Broadstreet, one of the court, asked him, 'whether he
would go for England?' To which he answered, 'I
have no business there.' Hereupon, Broadstreet, pointing to the gallows, said, 'then you shall go that way.'
To which William returned, 'what! will ye put me to
death for breathing in the air in your jurisdiction? and for
what you have against me, I appeal to the laws of England
for my trial; and if by them I am guilty, I refuse not to
die.' Of this no notice was taken, but instead thereof,
they endeavoured to persuade him to recant of his error
(as they stiled it) and to conform; to which, with a grave
magnanimity he answered, 'what! to join with such
murderers as you are? Then let every man that meets me
say, lo! this is the man that hath forsaken the God of his
salvation.'

Whilst the trial of W. Leddra was thus going on, Wenlock Christison, who was already banished upon pain of
death, came into the court. This struck a damp upon
them, insomuch that for some space of time there was

silence in the court: but at length one of the bloody council cried, ' here is another, fetch him up to the bar.' Which the marshal performing, the secretary Rawson, said, ' is not your name Wenlock Christison?' ' yea,' said Wenlock. ' Well,' said the governor, John Endicot, ' what dost thou here? wast thou not banished upon pain of death?' To which Wenlock answered, ' yea, I was.' And to the question, ' what dost thou here then?' He answered, ' I am come here to warn you that you should shed no more innocent blood; for the blood that you have shed already, cries to the Lord God for vengeance to come upon you.' Whereupon it was said, ' take him away gaoler.'

It having been told W. Leddra, at the last general court he had liberty given to go for England, or to go out of their jurisdiction; and that promising to do so, and come there no more, he might save his life; he answered, ' I stand not in my own will, but in the will of the Lord: if I may have my freedom, I shall go, but to make you a promise, I cannot.' But this was so far from giving consent, that they proceeded to pronounce sentence of death against him; which being done, he was led from the court to the prison again, where the day before his death he wrote the following letter to his friends:

" Most dear and inwardly beloved:

" The sweet influences of the morning star, like a flood distilling into my innocent habitation, hath so filled me with the joy of the Lord, in the beauty of holiness, that my spirit is as if it did not inhabit a tabernacle of clay, but is wholly swallowed up in the bosom of eternity, from whence it had its being.

" Alas, alas, what can the wrath and spirit of man, that lusteth to envy, aggravated by the heart and strength of the king of the locusts, which came out of the pit, do unto one that is hid in the secret places of the Almighty? Or, unto them that are gathered under the healing wings of the Prince of Peace? under whose armour of light they shall be able to stand in the day of trial, having on the breastplate of righteousness, and the sword of the Spirit, which

is their weapon of war against spiritual weakness, princi-
palities, and powers, and the rulers of the darkness of this
world, both within and without! Oh, my beloved! I have
waited as a dove at the windows of the ark, and have stood
still in that watch, which the master (without whom I
could do nothing) did, at his coming, reward with the fulness of his love, wherein my heart did rejoice, that I might
in the love and life of God, speak a few words to you, sealed with the spirit of promise, that the taste thereof might
be a savour of life, to your life, and a testimony in you of
my innocent death : and if I had been altogether silent,
and the Lord had not opened my mouth unto you, yet he
would have opened your hearts, and there have sealed my
innocency with the streams of life, by which we are all
baptized into that body which is in God ; whom, and in
whose presence there is life ; in which, as you abide, you
stand upon the pillar and ground of truth : for, the life being the truth and the way, go not one step without it, lest
you should compass a mountain in the wilderness ; for
into every thing there is a season.

" As the flowing of the ocean doth fill every creek and
branch thereof, and then retires again towards its own being and fulness, and leaves a savour behind it, so doth the
life and virtue of God flow into every one of your hearts,
whom he hath made partakers of his divine nature ; and
when it withdraws but a little, it leaves a sweet savour behind it, that many can say, they are made clean through
the word that he hath spoken to them : in which innocent
condition, you may see what you are in the presence of
God, and what you are without him. Therefore, my dear
hearts, let the enjoyment of the life alone, be your hope,
your joy and consolation, and let the man of God flee those
things that would lead the mind out of the cross, for then
the savour of the life will be buried : and although some
may speak of things that they received in the life, as
experiences, yet the life being veiled, and the savour that
it left behind washed away by the fresh floods of temptation, the condition that they did enjoy in the life, boasted
of by the airy thing, will be like the manna that was gath-

ered yesterday, without any good scent or savour. For, it was only well with the man while he was in the life of innocency; but being driven from the presence of the Lord, into the earth, what can he boast of? And although you know these things, and (many of you) much more than I can say; yet, (for the love and zeal I bear to the truth and honour of God, and tender desire of my soul to those that are young, that they may read me in that from which I write, to strengthen them against the wiles of the subtil serpent that beguiled Eve) I say, stand in the watch within, in the fear of the Lord, which is the very entrance of wisdom; and the state where you are ready to receive the secrets of the Lord: hunger and thirst patiently, be not weary, neither doubt. Stand still and cease from thy own working, and in due time thou shalt enter into the rest, and thy eyes shall behold thy salvation, whose testimonies are sure, and righteous altogether: let them be as a seal upon thine arm, and as jewels about thy neck, that others may see what the Lord hath done for your souls; confess him before men, yea before his greatest enemies; fear not what they can do unto you: greater is he that is in you, than he that is in the world: for he will clothe you with humility, and in the power of his meekness you shall reign over all the rage of your enemies in the favour of God; wherein as you stand in faith, ye are the salt of the earth; for many seeing your good works, may glorify God in the day of their visitation.

"Take heed of receiving that which you saw not in the light, lest you give ear to to the enemy. Bring all things to the light, that they may be proved, whether they be wrought in God; the love of the world, the lust of the flesh, and the lust of the eye, are without the light, in the world; therefore, possess your vessels in all sanctification and honour, and let your eye look at the mark: he that hath called you is holy: and if there be an eye that offends, pluck it out and cast it from you: let not a temptation take hold, for if you do, it will keep from the favour of God, and that will be a sad state; for, without grace possessed, there is no assurance of salvation; by grace you are saved;

and the witnessing of it is sufficient for you, to which I re-
commend you all, my dear friends, and in it remain,

"Your brother,

"WILLIAM LEDDRA.

"Boston Gaol, the 13th of the first month, 1660-61."

The next day after this letter was written, the execution of W. Leddra, was performed, which was on the
14th of the First month.   After the lecture was ended,
the governor John Endicot came with a guard of soldiers
to the prison, where W. Leddra's irons were taken off,
with which he had been chained to a log both night and
day during a cold winter ; and now they were knocked
off, according to what the jailor once said, as hath been
related before.   William then having taken his leave of
Wenlock Christison, and others then in bonds, when
called, went forth to the slaughter,   incompassed with
a guard to prevent his speaking to his friends ; which
Edward Wharton, an inhabitant of Salem, and also banished on pain of death, seeing, and speaking against, one
amongst the company said, ' O Edward, it will be your
turn next ?'   To which captain Oliver added, ' if you
speak a word I'll stop your mouth.'   Then W. Leddra
being brought to the foot of the ladder, was pinioned,
and as he was about to ascend the same, he took leave
of his friend E. Wharton, to whom he said, ' all that
will be Christ's disciples, must take up the cross.'   He
standing upon the ladder, somebody said, ' William, have
you any thing to say to the people ? Thereupon he spoke
thus :   ' For the testimony of Jesus, and for testifying
against deceivers, and the deceived, I am brought here
to suffer.'   This took so much with the people, that it
wrought a tenderness in many. But to quench this, priest
Allen said to the spectators, ' people, I would not have
you think it strange to see a man so willing to die ; for
that's no new thing.   And you may read how the apostle
said, that some should be given up to strong delusions,
and even dare to die for it.' But he did not say where the
apostle speaks so, neither have I found it any where in
holy writ ; though I know that Paul saith, Rom. v. 7,

" Peradventure for a good man some would even dare to
die." But it seems it was sufficient for Allen, if he could
but render Leddra odious ; who however continued
cheerful : for as the executioner was putting the halter
about his neck, he was heard to say, ' I commit my
righteous cause unto thee, O God.' The executioner
then being charged to make haste, W. Leddra, at the
turning off the ladder, cried, " Lord Jesus, receive my
spirit ;" and so he was turned off, and finished his days.
The hangman cut down the dead body, and lest it should
be as barbarously used as those of William Robinson and
Marmaduke Stevenson (which none holding when cut
down, fell to the ground to the breaking of W. Robinson's skull) Edward Wharton, John Chamberlain, and
others, caught the body in their arms, and laid it on the
ground, till the hangman had stript it of its clothes ; who
having done so, said, that he was a comely man, as indeed he was. The body being stript, William's friend took
it, laid it in a coffin, and buried it. For farther confirmation of what hath been related, the following letter of
one of the spectators, that was there accidentally, may
be added :

" Boston, March, 26, 1661.

" On the 14th of this instant, here was one William
Leddra, which was put to death. The people of the town
told me, he might go away if he would : but when I made
farther inquiry, I heard the marshal say, that he was
chained in prison, from the time he was condemned, to
the day of his execution. I am not of his opinion : but
yet truly me thought the Lord did mightily appear in
the man. I went to one of the magistrates at Cambridge,
who had been of the jury that condemned him, (as he
told me himself) and I asked him by what rule he did it ?
He answered, that he was a rogue, a very rogue. But what
is this to the question, (I said) where is your rule ; he said,
he had abused authority. Then I goes after the man, and
asked him, whether he did not look on it as a breach of
rule to slight and undervalue authority ? And I said that
Paul gave Festus the title of honor, though he was a
heathen. (I do not say these magistrates are heathens),

I said then. When the man was on the ladder, he looked on me, and called me friend, and said, know, that this day I am willing to offer up my life for the witness of Jesus. Then I desired leave of the officers to speak, and said, Gentlemen I am a stranger both to your persons and country, and yet a friend to both : and I cried aloud, for the Lord's sake, take not away the man's life ; but remember Gamaliel's counsel to the jews. If this be of man, it will come to nought, but if it be of God, ye cannot overthrow it : but be careful ye be not found fighters against God. And the captain said, ' why had you not come to the prison ?' The reason was, because I heard the man might go if he would ; and therefore I called him down from the tree, and said, ' come down William, you may go away if you will.' Then captain Oliver said, ' it was no such matter ;' and asked what I had to do with it ? and besides, bade me begone : and I told him I was willing ; for I cannot endure to see this, I said. And when I was in the town, some did seem to sympathize with me in my grief. But I told them, that they had no warrant from the word of God, nor precedent from our country, nor power from his majesty, to hang the man. I rest,

" Your friend,

" THOMAS WILKIE."

" To Mr. George Lad, master of the America,
of Dartmouth, now at Barbadoes."

William Leddra being thus dispatched, it was resolv-ed to make an end also of Wenlock Christison. He therefore was brought from the prison to the court at Boston, where the governor John Endicot, and the deputy governor Richard Billingham, being both present, it was told him, ' unless you renounce your religion, you shall surely die.' But instead of shrinking, he said, with an undaunted courage, ' nay, I shall not change my religion, nor seek to save my life ; neither do I intend to deny my master ; but if I lose my life for Christ's sake, and the preaching of the gospel, I shall save my life.' This noble resolution gave such a check to his persecutors, that they did not then go on with the trial, but sent him away to prison again.   And it being said by somebody, that William Leddra was dead, a certain person said to Wenlock, 'O thy turn is next.' To which he gravely replied, 'the will of the Lord be done,' shewing thereby his entire resignation.

Being now locked up again in prison, he was kept there till about the fourth month : but then the court being set, a spirit of confusion appeared there, and a division among several of the members ; for though the greatest part were for taking the same course with him, as with those that were already put to death, yet several would not consent to it.   And as natural occurrences sometimes cause reflections among observing people, so it happened here ; For during their deliberations how to deal with Wenlock Christison, which lasted for the space of two weeks, the sun in the firmament shown not, a thing at that season somewhat extraordinary; which gave occasion for some to say, that the sun abhorring this bloody business, hid itself from them.   But after many debates, the sanguinary council at length agreed, and Wenlock was brought to the bar, where the governor, John Endicot, asked him what he had to say for himself, why he should not die ?   He answered, 'I have done nothing worthy of death ; if I had, I refuse not to die.'   To this another said, 'thou art come among us in rebellion, which is as the sin of witchcraft, and ought to be punished.'   Hence it appears, how perversely these blood-thirsty persecutors applied the holy scriptures to their cruel ends, and so made a wrong use of the prophet Samuel's words to Saul ; to which false conclusion Wenlock answered, 'I came not among you in rebellion, but in obedience to the God of heaven, not in contempt of any of you, but in love to your souls and bodies ; and that you shall know one day, when you and all men must give an account of the deeds done in the body. Take heed (thus he went on) for you cannot escape the righteous judgments of God.'   Then said major-general Adderton, 'you pronounce woes and judgments, and those that are gone before you pronounced woes and judgments ; but the judgments of the Lord God are not come upon us as yet.' So insolent and hardhearted may man become, as not to stick even to defy the Most High. Adderton, received this answer from Wenlock: ' Be not proud, neither let your spirits be lifted up; God doth but wait till the measure of your iniquity be filled up, and that you have run your ungodly race; then will the wrath of God come upon you to the utmost. And as for thy part, it hangs over thy head, and is near to be poured down upon thee, and shall come as a thief in the night, suddenly, when thou thinkest not of it.'

Then Wenlock asked, ' by what law will ye put me to death ?' The answer was, ' we have a law, and by our law, you are to die.' ' So said the jews of Christ (replied Wenlock) we have a law, and by our law he ought to die. Who empowered you to make that law ?' To which one of the board answered, ' we have a patent, and are the patentees; judge whether we have not power to make laws.' Hereupon Wenlock asked again, 'how, have you power to make laws repugnant to the laws of England ?' ' No,' said the governor. ' Then (replied Wenlock) you are gone beyond your bounds, and have forfeited your patent : and that is more than you can answer. Are you (asked he) subjects to the king, yea, or nay ?' ' What good will that do you ?' replied the secretary. ' If you are (answered Wenlock) say so; for in your petition to the king, you desire that he would protect you, and that you may be worthy to kneel among his loyal subjects.' To which one said, ' yea, we are so.' ' Well (said Wenlock) so am I, and for any thing I know, am as good as you, if not better; for if the king did but know your hearts as God knows them, he would see that they are as rotten towards him, as they are towards God. Therefore seeing that you and I are subjects to the king, I demand to be tried by the laws of my own nation.' It was answered, 'you shall be tried by a bench and a jury :' for it seems they began to be afraid to go on in the former course of trial, without a jury, this being contrary to the laws of England. But Wenlock said, ' that is not the law, but the manner of it : for I never heard nor read of any law that was in England to hang quakers.' To this the governor replied, ' that there was a law to hang jesuits.' To which Wenlock returned, ' if you put me to death, it is not because I go under the name of a jesuit, but of a quaker : therefore I appeal to the laws of my own nation.' But instead of taking notice of this, one said, that he was in their hands, and had broken their law, and they would try him. Wenlock still appealed to the laws of his own nation : yet the jury being called over, went out, but quickly returned, and brought him in guilty. Whereupon the secretary said, ' Wenlock Christison, hold up your right hand.' ' I will not, said Wenlock, I am here and can hear thee.' Then the secretary cried, ' Guilty or not guilty ?' ' I deny all guilt, replied Wenlock, for my conscience is clear in the sight of God.' But the governor said, ' the jury hath condemned thee.' Wenlock answered, ' the Lord doth justify me ; who art thou that condemnest ?'

They then voted as to the sentence of death, but were in a manner confounded, for several could not vote him guilty of death. The governor seeing this division, said, ' I could find in my heart to go home :' being in such a rage, that he flung something furiously on the table ; which made Wenlock cry, ' it were better for thee to be at home than here, for thou art about a bloody piece of work.' Then the governor put the court to vote again ; but this was done confusedly, which so incensed the governor, that he stood up and said, ' you that will not consent, record it : I thank God I am not afraid to give judgment.' Thus we see that to be drunk with blood, doth not quench the thirst after blood ; for Endicot, the governor, seeing others backward to vote, precipitately pronounced judgment himself, and said, ' Wenlock Christison, harken to your sentence : you must return to the place from whence you came, and from thence to the place of execution, and there you must be hanged until you are dead, dead, dead.' To which Wenlock said, ' the will of the Lord be done, in whose will I came amongst you, and and in whose counsel I stand, feeling his eternal power, that will uphold me unto the last gasp.' Moreover he cried thus: 'known be it unto you all, that if ye have power to take my life from me, my soul shall enter into everlasting rest, and peace with God, where you yourselves shall never come. And if ye have power to take my life from me, the which I do question, I do believe you shall never more take quakers' lives from them: note my words; do not think to weary out the living God, by taking away the lives of his servants. What do you gain by it? For the last man that you have put to death, here are five come in his room. And if ye have power to take my life from me, God can raise up the same principle of life, in ten of his servants, and send them among you in my room, that you may have torment upon torment, which is your portion; for there is no peace to the wicked, saith my God.' The holy confidence with which he utttered these words, shewed, and the sequel made it appear plain, that something supernatural was contained in them: and it is remarkable, that among the imprisoned quakers, there were then several that had been banished on pain of death; and among these, also Elizabeth Hooten; and Edward Wharton staid in his habitation, contrary to his sentence of banishment.

Wenlock, having received sentence of death, was again brought to prison, where having been detained five days, the marshal and a constable came to him, with an order from the court, for his enlargement, with twenty-seven more of his friends, then in prison, for their testimony to he truth, saying, they were ordered by the court to make him acquainted with their new law. 'What means this?' said Wenlock: 'have ye a new law?' 'Yes,' said they. 'Then ye have deceived most people,' said Wenlock. 'Why?' said they. 'Because,' said he, 'they did think he gallows had been your last weapon. Your magistrates said, that your law was a good and wholesome law, made or your peace, and the safeguard of your country. What! are your hands now become weak? The power of God is over you all.'

Thus the prison doors were opened, and Wenlock, with twenty-seven more of his friends, as aforesaid, set at iberty, save that two of them, viz. Peter Parson, and Judith Brown, being stripped to the waist, and fastened to a cart's tail, were whipped through the town of Boston, with twenty stripes apiece.

Now, though not long after, an order came from the king, as will be seen anon, whereby these persecutors were charged to desist from putting the quakers to death, yet it seems they had got some scent of the king's displeasure, who had a mind to stop their bloody career: for having got a book written by George Bishop, containing a relation of cruel persecution in New-England, he read a passage concerning major-general Denison, who, to put off those that complained of their wicked proceedings, said, 'this year ye will go to complain to the parliament, and the next year they will send to see how it is; and the third year the government is changed.' He took much notice of this, and calling to the lords to hear it, said, 'Lo! these are my good subjects of New-England; but I will put a stop to them.'

It was not long before an opportunity offered; for, the news of William Leddra's death being come into England, with an information of the danger that others were in, of going the same way, their friends took it so to heart, especially Edward Burrough, that having got audience of the king, he told to him, there was a vein of innocent blood opened in his dominions, which, if it was not stopped, would overrun all. To which the king replied, 'but I will stop that vein.' Then Burrough desired him to do it speedily; 'for we know not,' said he, 'how many, may soon be put to death.' The king answered, 'as soon as you will. Call (said he to some present) the secretary, and I will do it presently.' The secretary being come, a mandamus was forthwith granted. A day or two after, going again to the king, to desire dispatch of the matter, the king said, he had no occasion, at present, to send a ship thither; but if they would send one, they might do it as soon as they could. E. Burrough then asked the king, if it would please him to grant his deputation to one called a quaker, to carry the mandamus to New-England. The king answered, 'yes, to whom you will.' Whereupon, E. Burrough named one Samuel Shattock, who being an inhabitant of New-

England, was banished on pain of death, if ever he returned thither. And the king accordingly granted the deputation to him, with full power to carry the mandamus, which was as followeth :

"CHARLES R.

"Trusty and well beloved, we greet you well. Having been informed that several of our subjects amongst you, called quakers, have been, and are imprisoned by you, whereof some have been executed, and others, (as hath been represented unto us) are in danger to undergo the like : we have thought fit to signify our pleasure in that behalf for the future ; and do hereby require, that if there be any of those people called quakers, amongst you, now already condemned to suffer death, or other corporal punishment, or that are imprisoned, and obnoxious to the like condemnation, you are to forbear to proceed any farther therein : but that you forthwith send the said persons (whether condemned or imprisoned) over into this our kingdom of England, together with the respective crimes or offences laid to their charge ; to the end, that such course may be taken with them here, as shall be agreeable to our laws, and their demerits. And for so doing, these our letters shall be your sufficient warrant and discharge.

"Given at our court, at Whitehall, the 9th day of
September, 1661, in the 13th year of our reign.

'By his majesty's command,
                    "WILLIAM MORRIS."

The Superscription was :
To our trusty and well-beloved John Endicot, Esq. and
to all and every other the governor, or governors,
of our plantations of New-England, and of all the
colonies thereunto belonging, that now are, or hereafter shall be ; and to all and every the ministers and
officers of our said plantations and colonies whatsoever, within the continent of New-England.'

This mandamus to the rulers of New-England, being obtained, as hath been said, quick dispatch was thought necessary to send it thither. And Samuel Shattock being impowered by the king to carry it, an agreement was made with one Ralph Goldsmith, who was master of a good ship, and also one of those called quakers, for three hundred pounds (goods or no goods) to sail in ten days. He then immediately made all things ready to set sail, and with a prosperous gale, arrived in about six weeks time, before the town of Boston, in New-England, upon a first day of the week. The townsmen seeing a ship come into the bay, with English colours, soon came on board, and asked for the captain. Ralph Goldsmith then told him, he was the commander. Then they asked him whether he had any letters; and he said, 'yes.' Whereupon they asked, if he would deliver them; but he said, 'no, not to day.' So they went ashore, and reported there was a ship full of quakers, and that Samuel Shattock was among them, who they knew was, by their law liable to be put to death, for coming in again after banishment: but they knew not his errand nor authority.

All being thus kept close, and none of the ship's company suffered to go on shore that day; next morning Samuel Shattock, the king's deputy, and Ralph Goldsmith, the commander of the vessel, went on shore; and sending the men that landed them, back to the ship, they two went through the town, to the governor John Endicot's door, and knocked. He sending a man to know their business, they sent him word their business was from the king of England, and that they would deliver their message to none but the governor himself. Thereupon they were admitted to go in, and the governor came to them, and commanded Shattock's hat to be taken off, and having received the deputation and the mandamus, he laid off his hat, and ordered Shattock's hat to be given him again; he looked upon the papers, and then going out, went to the deputy-governor, and bid the kings deputy, and the master of the ship follow him. Being come to the deputy governor, and having consulted with him about the matter, he returned to the two aforesaid persons, and said, ' we shall obey his majesty's command.' After this the master of the ship gave liberty to the passengers to come ashore, which they did, and met together with their friends of the town, to offer up praises to God for this wonderful deliverance.

Now, for as much as several of their friends were yet in prison at Boston, the following order was given forthwith by the council not long after :

"*To William Salter, keeper of the prison, at Boston.*

"You are required by authority, and order of the general court, forthwith to release and discharge the quakers, who at present are in your custody. See that you do not neglect this.

"By order of the court,

"EDWARD RAWSON, Sec.

"Boston, 9th Dec. 1661."

They then consulted what to do, that they might not incur the king's displeasure ; and it was agreed to send a deputation to him. First, colonel Temple was sent to acquaint the king, with their having set the quakers at liberty ; and he was followed, not long after, by the chief priest, John Norton, and Simon Broadstreet one of the magistrates.

It appears by an application to king James the second, in the year 1685, that there were, in England and Wales, 1460 of the people called quakers, prisoners ; some under sentence for premunire ; some for refusing to swear ; some under fines on the act of banishment ; and others on writs of excommunication ; besides above 320, who died prisoners ; of whom, 100 were judged to have died in consequence of their long confinement and hard usage.

After king James' declaration for liberty of conscience ; after the passing of the act of toleration, in the reign of king William and queen Mary, in 1689 ; and after the act, that the solemn affirmation and declaration of the people called quakers, should be accepted instead of an oath, in

the usual form, passed 1696, these people were greatly re-
leived from the frequent persecutions and great sufferings
to which they had been exposed.

Notwithstanding the great exemption and relief which
they experienced from the above acts, the laws still stand
open against them, and are frequently enforced, particularly for not complying with military regulations, and for
refusing to pay tithes ; on both of which accounts, there
have continued to be frequent instances, not only of some
who have been prosecuted and distrained from, but of
others, who have been cast into prison, where they have
sealed their testimonies with their lives.

PERSECUTED

BY

THE MAHOMETANS.

The Martyrdom of Abdallah. *

Two mahometans of Arabia, persons of consideration in their own country, have been lately converted to the christian faith. One of them has already suffered martyrdom, and the other is now engaged in translating the scriptures, and in concerting plans for the conversion of his countrymen. The name of the martyr was Abdallah; and the name of the other, who is now translating the scriptures, is Sabat; or, as he is called since his christian baptism, Nathaniel Sabat. Sabat resided in my house, some time before I left India, and I had from his own mouth, the chief part of the account, which I shall now give to you. Some particulars I had from others. His conversion took place after the martyrdom of Abdallah, ' to whose death he was consenting:' and he related the circumstances to me with many tears.

Abdallah and Sabat were intimate friends, and being young men of family in Arabia, they agreed to travel together, and to visit foreign countries. They were both zealous mahometans. Sabat is son of Ibrahim Sabat, a noble

* This account is taken from a sermon, preached at Bristol, England, in 809, for the benefit of the "Society for Missions to Africa and the East," y Claudius Buchanan, L. L. D. from India.

family, of the line of Beni-Sabat, who trace their pedigree to Mahomet. The two friends left Arabia, after paying their adorations at the tomb of their prophet, at Mecca, and travelled through Persia, and thence to Cabul. Abdallah was appointed to an office of state, under Zemaun Shah, king of Cabul ; and Sabat left him there, and proceeded on a tour through Tartary.

While Abdallah remained at Cabul, he was converted to the christian faith, by the perusal of a Bible (as is supposed) belonging to a christian from Armenia, then residing at Cabul.* In the mahometan states, it is death for a man of rank to become a christian. Abdallah endeavoured for a time to conceal his conversion, but finding it no longer possible he determined to flee to some of the christian Churches, near the Caspian sea. He accordingly left Cabul in disguise, and had gained the great city of Bochara, in Tartary, when he was met in the streets of that city by his friend Sabat, who immediately recognized him. Sabat had heard of his conversion and flight, and was filled with indignation at his conduct. Abdallah knew his danger, and threw himself at the feet of Sabat. He confessed that he was a christian, and implored him, by the sacred tie of their former friendship, to let him escape with his life. " But, sir," said Sabat, when relating the story himself, " *I had no pity*. I caused my servants to seize him, and I delivered him up to Morad Shah, king of Bochara. He was sentenced to die, and a herald went through the city of Bochara, announcing the time of his execution. An immense multitude attended, and the chief men of the city. I also went and stood near to Abdallah. He was offered his life, if he would abjure Christ. The executioner stood by him with his sword in his hand. 'No,' said he (as if the proposition was impossible to be complied with) ' I cannot abjure Christ.' Then one of his hands was cut off at the wrist. He stood firm, his arm hanging by his side with but little motion. A physician, by desire of the king, offered to heal the wound, if he would recant. He made no answer, but looked up steadfastly towards

* The Armenian christians in Persia, have among them a few copies of the Arabic Bible.

heaven, like Stephen, the first martyr, his eyes streaming with tears, He did not look with anger towards *me*. He looked at me, but it was benignly, and with the countenance of forgiveness. His other hand was then cut off. But, sir,' said Sabat, in his imperfect English, ' he never *changed*, he never *changed*. And when he bowed his head to receive the blow of death, all Bochara seemed to say, ' what new thing is this ?''

Sabat had indulged the hope, that Abdallah would have recanted, when he was offered his life ; but, when he saw that his friend was dead, he resigned himself to grief and remorse. He travelled from place to place, seeking rest, and finding none. At last, he thought that he would visit India. He accordingly came to Madras, about five years ago. Soon after his arrival, he was appointed by the English government a mufti, or expounder of mahometan law ; his great learning, and respectable station in his own country, rendering him eminently qualified for that office. And now, the period of his own conversion drew near. While he was at Visagapatam, in the Northern Circars, exercising his professional duties, Providence brought in his way a new Testament in Arabic.* He read it with deep thought, the Koran lying before him. He compared them together, and at length, the truth of the word of God fell on his mind, as he expressed it, like a flood of light.

* One of those copies sent to India, by the " Society for Promoting Christian Knowledge."

4 E

EXAMPLES

OF

THE JUST JUDGMENTS OF GOD

ON

PERSECUTORS, &c.

TO WHICH IS ANNEXED,

A CHRISTIAN PLEA AGAINST PERSECUTIONS FOR THE

CAUSE OF CONSCIENCE.

"Now I say unto you, refrain from these men, and let them alone; for if his counsel, or this work, be of men, it will come to nought; but if it be of God, ye cannot overthrow it; lest haply, you be found even to fight against God."

Acts v. 38, 39.

EXAMPLES

OF

THE JUST JUDGMENTS OF GOD

ON

PERSECUTORS, &c.

ALTHOUGH the long-suffering and merciful God, does not immediately enter into judgment on such as have, in the most flagrant manner, violated his holy laws, yet there are numerous instances, even in this life, where we may read in legible characters, his displeasure marked with dreadful afflictions on stubborn offenders.

Many examples may be produced, both from sacred and profane history, wherein severe and awful judgments have been poured down on the heads of hardened persecutors ; some of the most distinguished of which, we shall lay before our readers.

In the Old Testament, we may read what befel Cain, Ishmael, Joseph's brethren, Pharaoh, Ahab, Saul, Jezebel, Joash, Haman, Nebuchadnezzar, the presidents and princes of Media and Persia, and many others: and, in the New-Testament, we find how it fared with Herod, Judas, Pilate, &c.

King Antiochus, sirnamed Epiphanes, a great persecutor of the Jews, who committed great evils at Jerusalem, and took all the vessels of gold and silver that were therein, and sent to destroy the inhabitants of Judea, without a cause ; and as himself confessed, who, in a proud and insolent manner, protested he would make Jerusalem a common burying-place, and the streets thereof run with the blood of God's people, was by God's just judgment, plagued with a grievous sickness, having a remediless pain in his bowels, and an intolerable torment in his inward parts : his body bred abundance of worms, which continually crawled out of the same ; yea, he so rotted above ground, that by reason of an intolerable stink, no man could endure to come near him, neither could he, himself, endure the same ; but, in a flood of extreme misery, ended his days, which as he confessed, came upon him for the evil aforesaid.   See the life of Judas Maccabees, in *Clarke's Martyrol.* p. 13, as also the *First Book of Maccabees,* chap. i. x. and chap. vi. viii. &c.

Herod (called the great) who, that he might kill Christ, sent and slew all the children in Bethlehem, and the coasts thereof, from two years old and under, and who afterwards, as history relates, being given up of God to wickedness, slew his own wife, children, nearest kins-folks, and familiar friends, was smitten of God with a grievous sickness, like a fire in his inward parts ; and rotting in his bowels, &c. an abundance of worms swarmed out of him, while yet alive ; a violent cramp seized him, and being in dreadful anguish, he sought to destroy himself, but was prevented by his friends ; and so at length, in extreme misery, he ended his wretched life.   See *Clarke's Gen. Martyrol.* p. 26.

Judas Iscariot betrayed his Lord and Master, for the love of money.   Read his fate in *Mat.* xxvii. 3, 4, 5.

Pilate, under whom Christ was crucified, in the days of Tiberius Nero, then emperor, through the just punishment of God, was first apprehended and accused at Rome ; deposed ; and then banished to the town of Lyons, and at length killed himself. *Acts and Mon.* p. 50.

Caiphas, who sat upon the judgment-seat, and condemned Christ, was, in the reign of the emperor, Caesar Caligula, removed from the high-priest's office, and did not long after escape with his life.   *ibid.*

Tiberius Caesar, who was called Tiberius Nero, in whose reign, and government Christ himself suffered, was poisoned to death.   *ibid.*

Caesar Caligula, emperor of Rome, who wished that all the people of Rome had but one neck, that he might at pleasure destroy them at once, was slain when he had reigned but four years.   *ibid.*

Claudius Nero, of whom it is said, that he ruled thirteen years, with no little cruelty to the Christians, was, in the end, slain.   *ibid.*

Certain men of the Jewish nation, informers, had accused the martyr Simon (son of Cleophas, and reputed nephew to Christ) for being a christian, and one of the stock of David, against whom Trajanus, the emperor, had given forth a commandment 'that whosoever could be found of the stock of David, he should be inquired out, and put to death ; of which stock, upon inquiry, these his accusers, were found to be, and so right justly were put to execution themselves, which sought the destruction of another; though not long after, the good man Simon, after he had been scourged many days, bearing it with singular constancy, when he was an hundred and twelve years old, was crucified and put to death, finishing his course in the Lord. *Acts and Mon.* p. 65, 66.

Three other wicked, evil disposed persons (informers) seeing the soundness, grave, constant, and virtuous life of Narcissus, then bishop of Jerusalem, aged an hundred and sixty three years, accused him of some great crime, that he was clear of, and having laid it to his charge, they, the better to make their accusation seem more probable before the people, binding it with a great oath, one wishing to be destroyed by fire, if he said not true ; the other to be consumed with a grievous sickness ; the third, to loose both his eyes, if they did lie : Narcissus, although having his conscience clear, yet not able, being but one man, to withstand their accusations, bound with such oaths, gave place, and removed himself from the multitude into a solitary desert, by himself, where he continued many years ; in the mean time, the first, by casualty, was burnt, with all his family and goods ; the second was seized with a dreadful sickness, whereof he died ; and the third, confessed his fault, and repented of the same, yet he lost the sight of both his eyes ; and thus was their false perjury punished ; and Narcissus, after long absence, returned home again, and was, by this means, both cleared of the fact, and received into his bishoprick again. *Acts and Mon.* p. 80.

Antiohcus, tormentor and executioner of extreme torments, (under Alexander Severus, the emperor and persecutor of the christians) upon a young youth, called Agapitus, of the age of fourteen years, who suffered Martyrdom for not sacrificing to idols, after he had been assailed with sundry torments, viz. first, with whips scourged, then hanged by the feet, after having hot water poured upon him, at last, cast to wild beasts ; with all which torments, he could not be hurt ; finally, with the sword was beheaded. This said Antiochus, in executing the aforesaid torments, suddenly fell down from his Judicial seat, crying out, ' that all his bowels burned within him,' and so gave up the ghost. *Hen. de Erfordia*, lib. 6. ch 29. *Acts & Mon.* page 85.

What can be more striking, on this subject, than the miserable end of the emperor Nero, that bitter persecutor of christianity, whose agonies were so great, from the shocking barbarity with which he was treated, even by his own subjects, that he, in vain, implored to be eased, by death, from his sufferings ; and when he could find neither friend nor enemy, to grant even this request, he added the crime of suicide to his enormous vices, and unlamented, perished by his own hand. *Southwell's New Book of Martyrs*, p. 462.

In a word, if histories speak true, few or none of the persecuting Roman emperors, died in their beds.

Decius, the persecutor, being overcome in war, to avoid his enemies' hands, he leaped with his horse into a whirlpool, and was drowned *Clarke's Gen. Martyrol.* p. 54.

Valerianus, the emperor, and persecutor of the christians, was taken prisoner of the Persians, when he was seventy years of age, and Saphores, the king of the Persians, used him for his horse block ; for whensoever the king was minded to mount his horse, openly, in the sight of his people, Valerianus, the quondam emperor, was brought forth instead of a block, for the king to tread upon his back, in mounting his horse ; and, in the end, he was condemned to be slain, and powdered with salt, for a perpetual monument of his own wretchedness. *Acts & Mon.* p. 105. *ex Euseb.*

The two emperors, Dioclesian, and Maximinian, rigid enemies to the christian faith, after abdicating, through vexatious circumstances, their thrones, both died unhappily : the latter, in particular, in his attempting to restore himself, unnaturally falling by the means of his own son Maxentius, who likewise came to as untimely an end as his parent, being drowned, in the prime of his life, and the very meridian of his sins and impieties. *Southwell's New Book of Martyrs*, p. 462.

The example of the emperor Maximinus, another persecutor of Christ's church, deserves recital. Soon after his setting forth his impious decrees, against the unoffending christians, which were engraved in brass, he was, by the just judgments of the Most High, afflicted with a dreadful and unnatural disease, having lice, and other shocking vermine, crawling from his very entrails, in so terrible a manner, as to render abortive every method to afford him relief ; and attended with so horrid a putrescent stench, that for several days before his death, no persons would hazard their lives to give him the least assistance. *ib.*

To leave the Roman history, and turn our eyes on transactions nearer the present period, let us take notice of the hand of God on Sigusmund, emperor of Germany, for his unjustifiable treatment of John Huss, and Jerome of Prague. After the martyrdom of those eminent lights of the reformation, by his orders, nothing he took in hand succeeded, but a series of the most unhappy events attended him and his family, which, in one generation, became extinct: he, in his wars, was ever the loser, and his empress, Barbara, turned out so infamously lewd, as to be a lasting infamy to her family, and a disgrace to her sex. *ib.*

In the reign of Henry II. of France, the chancellor, Oliver, who, at the instigation of cardinal Lorain, brother to that implacable enemy of the gospel, the duke of Guise, had stretched the authority of the laws, to bring many worthy persons to utter destruction, for their adherence to the truth; this unjust judge, being struck with great remorse and self conviction of his misdeeds, fell sick, and so great were the horrors of his tormented conscience, for his cruel decrees against the righteous, that he could not rest day or night, for the torture of his wounded mind, but shortly expired, horribly shrieking out, with a loud cry, in his last moments, 'Oh! cardinal, thou wilt make us all be damned,' with which words, he gave up the ghost. *ibid.*

Neither did the cardinal himself, nor his brother, the duke of Guise, long triumph in the success of their bloody machinations, as the former shortly after died, and the latter fell a sacrifice to the daggers of his exasperated countrymen. *ibid.*

Hoimeister, an arch papist, and a chief pillar of the pope's antichristian doctrine, as he was proceeding on his journey to Ratisbon, to be present at a council held there, and to defend the Romish superstitions against the defenders of Christ's gospel, was prevented from executing his impious purpose, being suddenly seized in his progress, near the city of Ulmes, with an extreme illness, of which he almost instantly expired, in great agonies, crying out in the most horrid manner. *ibid.*

The following tragedy, which happened in the university of Louvaine, will likewise exemplify our subject: a learned person in the above seminary, who was reader of divinity to the monks of St. Gertrude, and had violently maintained the corrupt errors of popery, at length falling extremely ill, and perceiving no hopes of recovery, he regretted, with the greatest perturbation of mind, his manifold sins, but more particularly his having so warmly espoused the cause of idolatry, &c. in opposition to the divine truths of the gospel; an offence, he said, of so heinous a nature, as to be too great to expect God's pardon. Continually repeating this terrible expression, he expired in all the horrors of desperation. *ibid.*

Jacob Latomus, who was president of a college, at Louvaine, is another instance of the dreadful judgments of God, on persons offending against his most holy word. Latomus went to Brussels, to make a long oration against the reformed religion, and to indicate popery, which he did before the emperor; but so little

4 r

to the purpose, as to verify the common observation, 'that a bad advocate does much more harm than good to any cause.' The Romish clergy, and indeed the whole court, seem to have been of this opinion. He returned to Louvaine, despised and ridiculed by those, who plainly saw he had vainly attempted to defend a train of absurdities, which required the utmost sophistry to vindicate; and, whether it might proceed from the mortification he felt, at the indifferent reception his pious falsehoods met with at Brussels, or whether his own conscience plainly pointed out to him his impious conduct (the latter, indeed, seems to be more probably the case) he, very soon after his return, fell into an open fury of madness, at the very instant he was giving his public lectures, and was forced to be conveyed, raving with lunacy, to a close room, and fastened down therein; and from that period, to his last breath, his whole cry was, " that he was damned and rejected of God, and that there was no hope of salvation for him, because he had, against the positive conviction of his own conscience, withstood the truth of God, and Christ's holy word;" and thus shortly ended his wretched life, with all the violence of the most furious insanity.   *ibid*, p. 463.

Ponchet, archbishop of Tours, made application to have a court erected, called *Chamber Ardent*, wherein to condemn the protestants to the flames; but soon after obtaining permission to execute his cruel intentions, he was struck with a disease, called the fire of God, which began at his feet, and ascended upwards with so tormenting a burning, that he was obliged to have one member cut off after another, and thus miserably ended his days.

The legate and chancellor Du Pratt, who was the first that opened to the parliament of Paris, the knowledge of heresies, and gave out the first commissions to put the faithful to death, soon after died, at his house, at Natoillet, swearing, and horribly blaspheming God. After his death, his stomach was found to be pierced and gnawed asunder with worms.   *ibid.*

Queen Mary, whose vehement zeal for establishing popery in England, and in whose reign, the blood of so many martyrs was spilled, did not prosper in her undertakings; but, through a series of losses and disappointments, in state affairs, as also, being forsaken by her husband, Philip, of Spain, with whom she promised herself much happiness, after a short and wretched reign of five years, four months, and eleven days, ended her life, as owned by herself, of that corrosive and mental torture, a broken heart.

The fatal day, on which Ridley and Latimer suffered at Oxford, the old duke of Norfolk paid a visit to bishop Gardner, at his house in London, in consequence of his being invited to dine with him, at that time. But so eager was this bloody prelate to glut his ears with the news of the absolute destruction of those two pious sufferers, that he postponed his usual time of dining, saying, "he would not eat till he received positive assurance of the execution of the barbarous sentence, he knew was to be put in practice that day at Oxford."

Accordingly, as soon as the messenger arrived, which was not till four o'clock, and had given him the assurance of his cruel wishes being completed, he ordered dinner to be ushered in, and sitting down to it with great apparent satisfaction, said, "now, my lord duke, we can set down to refresh ourselves with pleasure." But observe the hand of God on this impious priest; no sooner had he swallowed a few morsels, but he was suddenly seized with so violent a fit of illness, that he was obliged to be taken from table, and from that moment to the last of his life, never was free from the greatest misery and torture; for fifteen days and nights did he languish, never being able, either by urine, or any other means, to evacuate, which caused such a terrible inflammation in his body, as if he were, in a manner, burning alive. By the raging fire in his intestines, his body was miserably swoln and black; his tongue thrust at last out of his mouth: he expired, a shocking spectacle, and with a most nauseous and undurable effluvia: a proper end to so inhuman a persecutor of the righteous. *Southwell's New Book of Martyrs,* p. 464.

Doctor Dunning, chancellor of Norwich, a bloody man, who condemned several innocent persons, in the midst of his rage died suddenly (as it is said) sitting in his chair.

The like judgment fell upon bishop Thornton, Suffragan of Dover, who, after he had exercised great cruelty in persecuting, at length, upon a Sunday (so called) looking upon his men, playing at bowls, fell suddenly in a palsy, and being had to bed, was put in mind to remember God; "yea," said he, "so I do, and my lord cardinal too," and so died.

After he was dead, the cardinal ordained another bishop, in his room, who being at Greenwich, after he had received the cardinal's blessing, going down a pair of stairs from the chamber, he fell down and broke his neck: to these examples, also, may be added, the terrible judgment of God upon the parson, at Crundall, in Kent, who having received the pope's pardon from cardinal Poole, coming home to his parish, exhorted the people to receive the same, saying, "that he now stood as clear in his conscience, as when he was first born, and mattered not if he died the same hour he spoke it:" Whereupon, being suddenly stricken by the hand of God, and leaning a little on the one side, he immediately shrunk down in the pulpit, and so was found dead, not speaking one word more.

Not long before the death of queen Mary, died suddenly, Doctor Jeffery, Chancellor of Salisbury, who, not long before his death, had caused above ninety persons to be summoned to appear before him, to the end he might examine them, by inquisition, concerning their religion, but by the providence of God, he was prevented from executing the evil, he intended against them, for in the midst of his buildings, he was taken away by the mighty hand of God.

One Woodrove, who was sheriff of London, rejoiced much at the death of the innocent, and was very cruel in his office; for when one Rogers was going in a cart towards Smithfield, to be burnt, and, in the way, his children being brought to him, because the cartman stopped his cart, that he might speak to them, he caused the cartman's head to be broken: but what happened? Within a week after, this sheriff coming out of his office, he was suddenly smitten by the hand of God, the one half of his body being benumbed; and lay bed-ridden, and in this infirmity, he continued seven or eight years, till his dying day.

Alexander, the keeper of Newgate, a cruel enemy of those that lay there for religion, died very miserably, being so swelled that he was more like a monster than a man, and so rotten within, that no man could abide the smell of him; this cruel wretch, to hasten the poor lambs to the slaughter, would go to Bonner, Story, Cholmley, and others, crying out, " rid my prison, rid my prison, I am too much pestered with these heretics."

James, the son of the said Alexander, having left unto him, by his father, great substance, within three years, wasted all to nought, and when some marvelled how he spent those goods so fast; " Oh!" said he, " evil gotten, evil spent:" And shortly after, as he went to Newgate market, fell down suddenly, and there wretchedly died.

John Peter, son-in-law to this Alexander, a horrible blasphemer of God, and no less cruel to the said prisoners, commonly, when he would affirm any thing, were it true or false, used to say, " if it be not true, I pray God I rot e're I die ;" accordingly, he did rot away, and so died most miserably.

The sudden death of many more persecutors, might be mentioned, who were cut off in this queen's time, and before; but by what is inserted may be seen, that the Lord was against those persecuting priests and bishops.

John Endicot, governor of Massachusetts colony, a principal promoter of the persecution there; soon after he had signed a warrant for the barbarous whipping of Edward Wharton, was visited with a filthy and loathsome disease, of which he died. It was observed, that at the time when this governor lay on his death-bed, the common executioner, or hangman, who, by his commands, had imbrued his hands in the blood of the innocent, was also cut off, and died in great horror of mind, and torment of body. Their deaths thus concurring, were remarked by some, who said, "who would have thought the head and tail should go so near together." *Besse's Collection of the Sufferings of the Quakers, vol. 2, p. 280.*

Humphrey Adderton, who, at the trial of Wenlock Christison, did, as it were, bid defiance to heaven, by saying to Wenlock, "you pronounce woes and judgments, and those that are gone before you, pronounced woes and judgments; but the judgments of the Lord God are not come upon us yet," was suddenly surprised. He was an officer, or major of the soldiery, and having been, on a certain day, exercising his men with much pomp and ostentation, he was returning home in the evening, near the place where they usually loosed the quakers from the cart, after they had whipped them, his horse, suddenly affrighted, threw him with such violence that he instantly died, his eyes being dashed out of his head, and his brains coming out at his nose, his tongue hanging out at his mouth, and the blood running out at his ears. Being taken up and brought into the court-house, the place where he had been active in sentencing the innocent to death, his blood ran through the floor, exhibiting to the spectators a shocking instance of the divine vengeance against a daring and hardened persecutor, thus made a fearful example of that divine judgment, which, when forewarned of, he had openly despised, and treated with disdain. *ibid.*

John Norton, one of their chief priests, a principal exciter of the magistrates to persecute the innocent, and put them to death, was cut off by a sudden and unexpected stroke, for having been at his worship in the forepart of the day, and intending to go thither again in the afternoon, as he was walking in his own house, he was observed to fetch a great groan, and leaning his head against the chimney-piece, was heard to say, "the hand, or judgment, of the Lord is upon me," and so sunk down, and spake no more, and had fallen into the fire, had not an ancient man, then present, prevented it. *ibid.*

John Danfort, a member of their church, and a captain of their castle at Boston, as he lay, in the heat of the day, upon his bed, was struck dead in a strange manner, by lightning. *ib.*

John Webb, who, with armed men, led Mary Dyer to her execution, as he, with others, were busy in killing a whale, was, on a sudden, after a strange manner, carried into the sea and drowned. *ibid.*

Timothy Dalton, a persecuting priest at Hampton, and his brother Philemon, both inveterate opposers of the people called quakers, were soon taken away ; the said Philemon was killed by the fall of a tree on his leg, and the other by another visitation. This priest had called it blasphemy to say, " the light within was the light of Christ." *ibid.* p. 271.

Captain Johnson, who led forth William Leddra to be put to death, was afterwards taken with a distemper which deprived him of his reason and understanding as a man. *ibid.*

Marshal Brown, of Ipswich, a rapacious plunderer of the quakers' goods, was soon after cast upon a bed of languishing, where he lay in great affliction of body, and horror of conscience, and so departed this life. *ibid.*

Edward Norris, a priest at Salem, who excited the rulers and people there against the innocent, saying, " what they did to the quakers was not persecution but prosecution ;" at a time when he was vindicating the proceedings against them, in a sermon to the people, was suddenly struck dumb in his pulpit, and after a short time, died. *ibid.*

Priest Mitchel, of Cambridge, soon after he had endeavoured to stir up the rulers there to persecution, was smitten by the hand of the Lord ; and it was related of him, that his tongue, while he was yet alive, was turned exceeding black in his mouth ; and in that condition, he died. *ibid.*

Richard Bellingham, who violently prosecuted this people even to death, having completed the measure of his iniquity, ended his government with his life, being bereft of his understanding, and dying distracted. *ibid.*

Samuel Archer, a marshal in Salem, who had frequently taken away the quakers' goods, to defray his master's reckoning at the tavern, was suddenly removed and cut off. *ibid.*

Many other particular persons, who had been noted instruments in carrying on the work of persecution, were afterwards observed to fall under several calamitous disasters and casualties, which were esteemed by those who knew them, as tokens of the divine displeasure manifested against them, by reason of the particular share of guilt which their personal concern in shedding innocent blood had brought upon them. *ib.*

But if we extend our observations yet farther, and take a view of that terrible scene of judgment and calamities, which, for many years, after the putting those innocent martyrs to death, fell upon the inhabitants of this province in general, we shall shall have reason to conclude, that as there was a concurrence of the magistrates, priests, and many of the people, in making and executing those laws, by which the innocent were devoted to destruction, their general guilt might draw down a decree of the divine vengeance upon them, and that the variety of heavy judgments which followed were of the Lord, who ordaineth his arrows against the persecutors. *ibid.*

Their own Historian, Cotton Mather, in his History of New-England, says, in book I, page 27:

"For now more than twenty years, the blasting strokes of Heaven upon the secular affairs of this country have been such, as rather to abate, than enlarge the growth of it."

Page 29. "The many calamities which have ever since been wasting the country, have so nipt the growth of it, that its latter progress hath held no proportion with what was from the beginning."

Page 31. "There have been several years wherein the terrible famine hath terribly struck the town in the face. The angel of death hath often shot the arrow of death into the midst of the town. The small-pox hath especially four times been a great plague upon us. Never was any town under the copes of heaven more liable to be laid in ashes, either through the carelessness or wickedness of them that sleep in it."

Page 32. "Ten times hath the fire made notable ruins among us, and our good servant been almost our master."

Page 38. "Ah! Boston! thou hast seen the vanity of all worldly possessions. One fatal morning, which laid fourscore of thy dwelling-houses, and seventy of thy ware-houses in a ruinous heap, not nineteen years ago, gave thee to read it in fiery characters: and an huge fleet of thy vessels, if they were all together, that have miscarried in the late war, has given thee to read more of it."

Chap. 2. He tells how the consuming wrath of God is every day on the young men, saying, "New-England has been like a tottering house, the very foundations of it have been shaking, the house thus oversetting, by the wrath of God, hath been like Job's house, 'it falls upon the young men, and they are dead:' The disasters on our young folks have been so multiplied, that there are few parents among us, but what will go with wounded hearts down unto their graves: their daily means are, "Ah! my son, cut off in his youth! my son! my son!"

Book V. chap. i. p. 85. "By land, some of the principal grains, especially our wheat and our pease, fell under an unaccountable blast, from which we are not yet even unto this day delivered: and besides that constant frown of heaven upon our husbandry, recurring every year, few years have passed wherein either worms, or droughts, or some consuming disasters, have not befallen the labour of the husbandmen. By sea, we were visited with multiplied shipwrecks ; enemies preyed upon our vessels and our sailors ; and the affairs of the merchant were clogged with losses abroad, or fires breaking forth in the chief seats of trade at home, wasted their substance, with yet more costly desolations : nor did the land and sea more proclaim the controversy of our God against us, than that other element of the air, by the contagious vapours, whereof several pestilential sicknesses did some times become epidemical among us : yea, the judgments of God having done the first part of the moth upon us, proceeded then to do the part of a lion in lamentable wars, wherein the barbarous Indians cruelly butchered many hundreds of our inhabitants, and scattered whole towns with miserable ruins."

Page 87. " The scourges of Heaven were employed upon the churches of New-England for their miscarriages ; and they were sorely lashed with one blow after another."

Page 88. " That God hath a controversy with his New-England people is undeniable; the Lord having written his displeasure in dismal characters against us ; though personal afflictions do oftentimes come only or chiefly for probation ; yet as to public judgments, it is not wont so to be, especially when, by a continued series of providence, the Lord doth appear and plead against his people, 2 *Sam*. xxi. 11. as with us it hath been from year to year. Would the Lord have whetted his glittering sword, and his hand have taken hold on judgments? Would he have sent such a mortal contagion, like a besom of destruction, in the midst of us? Would he have said, " sword, go through the land, and cut off man and beast ?" Or, would he have kindled such devouring fires, and made such fearful desolations in the earth, if he had not been angry ? It is not for nothing, that the merciful God, who doth not willingly afflict nor grieve the children of men, hath done all these things unto us; yea, and with a cloud hath covered himself, that our prayer could not pass through."

Much more might be extracted from the above book, of the sore afflictions of New-England, but our limits will not allow their insertion.

A CHRISTIAN PLEA AGAINST PERSECUTION

CAUSE OF CONSCIENCE.

PERSECUTION for the cause of conscience, is against the doctrine of Jesus Christ, the Saviour of the world, the King of kings, and Lord of lords; it is against scripture, reason, experience, and the testimony of many eminent men, princes and learned authors.

Christ commanded, that the tares and wheat should be let alone in the world, and not plucked up until the harvest, which is the end of the world. *Mat.* xiii.

Christ also commandeth, that they that are blind, should be let alone, referring their punishment unto the falling into the ditch. *Mat.* xv.

Again, he reproved his disciples, who would have had fire come down from heaven, and devour those Samaritans, who would not receive him, in these words, "ye know not what manner of spirit ye are of; for the Son man is not come to destroy men's lives, but to save them." *Luke,* ix. 55, 56.

The prophets foretold, that "in the last days it shall come to pass, that the mountain of the house of the Lord shall be established in the top of the mountains, and it shall be exalted above the hills; and people shall flow unto it. And many nations shall come, and say, come, let us go up to the mountain of the Lord, and to the house of the God of Jacob; and he will teach us of his ways, and we will walk in his paths: for the law shall go forth of Zion, and the word of the Lord from Jerusalem. And he shall judge among many people, and rebuke strong nations afar off; and they shall beat their swords into plough-shares, and their spears into pruning hooks: nation shall not lift up a sword against nation, neither shall they learn war any more." *Micah,* iv. 1, 2, 3.

4 G

" The weapons of our warfare are not carnal." 2 *Cor.* x. 4.

And he chargeth straitly (that his disciples should be so far from persecuting those that would not be of their religion) that when they were persecuted, they should pray; when they were cursed, they should bless, &c. *Mat.* v. And the reason seems to be, because they who now are tares, may hereafter become wheat: they who are now blind, may hereafter see; they that now resist him, may hereafter receive him; they that are now in the devil's snare, and oppose the truth, may hereafter come to repentance; and they that are now blasphemers and persecutors (as Paul was) may, in time, become faithful as he; they that are now idolatrous, as the Corinthians once were, may hereafter become true worshippers as they: 1 *Cor.* vi. 9. They that are now no people of God, nor under mercy (as the saints sometimes were, 1 *Pet.* ii. 20) may hereafter become the people of God, and obtain mercy as they.

Some come not till the eleventh hour: if those that come not till the last hour should be destroyed, because they come not at the first, they would thereby be prevented and never come. *Mat.* xx. 6.

King James, in his speech to the parliament, 1609, saith, "It is a sure rule in divinity, that God never loves to plant his church by violence and bloodshed; and that it is usually the condition of christians to be persecuted, but not to persecute."

Again, he saith, page 4, speaking of the papists; "I have good proof, that I intended no persecution against them for conscience cause."

And in the same king's Exposition of *Rev.* 20, printed 1588, he writes thus: "Compassing of the saints, and besieging of the beloved city, declareth unto us a certain note of a false church to be persecution; for they come to seek the faithful; the faithful are them that are sought; the wicked are the besiegers, the faithful are the besieged."

And the king of Bohemia hath thus written: "And notwithstanding the success of the latter times (wherein sundry opinions have been hatched about the subject of religion) may make one clearly discern with his eye, and as it were to touch with his finger, that according to the truth of the scripture, and a maxim heretofore maintained, by the ancient doctors of the church, that men's consciences ought in no sort to be violated, urged, or constrained; and whensoever men have attempted any thing, by this violent course, whether openly, or by secret means, the issue hath been pernicious, and the cause of great and wonderful innovations in the principalest and mightiest kingdoms and countries of all christendom."

And, further, he saith: " So that once more we do profess before God, and the whole world, that from this time forward we are firmly resolved, not to persecute or molest, or suffer to be persecuted or molested. any person whomsoever, for matter of religion; no, not those who profess themselves to be of the Romish church, neither to trouble nor disturb them in the exercise of their religion, so they live conformable to the laws of the states, &c."

Hilary against Auxentius, saith thus: " The christian church doth not persecute, but is persecuted. And lamentable it is to see the folly of these times, and the foolish opinion of this world, in that men think by human aid to help God, and with worldly pomp and power to undertake to defend the christian church. I ask the bishops, what help used the apostles in publishing the gospel? With the aid of what power did they preach Christ, and convert the heathen from their idolatry to God? When they were in prisons, and lay in chains, did they praise and give thanks to God for any dignities or favours received from the court? Or, do you think that Paul went about with regal mandates, or kingly authority, to gather and establish the church of Christ? Sought he protection from Nero Vespatian?

" The apostles wrought with their hands for their own maintenance, travelling by land and water, from town to city, to preach Christ; yea, the more they were forbidden, the more they taught and preached Christ; but now, alas! human help must assist and protect the faith, and give the same countenance too: and, by vain and worldly honours, do men seek to defend the church of Christ, as if he, by his power, were unable to perform it.

" The church, formerly, by enduring misery and imprisonment, was known to be a true church. The pretended church now does terrify others by imprisonment, banishment and misery, and boasteth that she is highly esteemed of the world; whereas, the true church cannot but be hated of the same."

Turtul. ad Scapulam—" It agreeth both with human reason and natural equity, that every man worship God uncompelled; neither beseemeth any religion to compel another to be of their religion, which willingly and freely should be embraced, and not by constraint; forasmuch as the offerings were required of those that freely, and of good will offered, and not from the contrary."

Jerom in Proaem. lib. 4. in Jeremiam—" Heresy must be cut off with the sword of the spirit: let us strike through, with the arrows of the spirit, all sons and disciples of misled heretics ; that is, with testimonies of the scriptures ; the slaughter of heretics is by the word of God."

Brentius, upon the first of the Corinthians, chap. 3—" No man hath power to make or give laws to christians, whereby to bind their consciences ; for willingly, freely and uncompelled, with a ready desire and cheerful mind, must those that come ¡un unto Christ."

Luther, in his books of the Civil Magistrate, saith, " The laws of the civil magistrates' government extend no further than over the body or goods, and to that which is external, for over the soul God will not suffer any man to rule, only he himself will rule there ; wherefore, whosoever doth undertake to give laws unto the souls and consciences of men, he usurpeth that government himself, which appertaineth unto God, &c."

Therefore, upon 1 Kings, v. he saith, " In the building of the temple, there was no sound of iron heard, to signify, that Christ will have in his church a free and willing people, not compelled and constrained by laws and statutes."

Again, he saith upon Luke xxii.—" It is not the true catholic church, which is defended by the secular arm, or human power, but the false and feigned church, which, although it carries the name of a church, yet it denies the power thereof."

It is no prejudice to a kingdom or commonwealth, if liberty of conscience be suffered to such as fear God.

Abraham abode among the Canaanites a long time, yet contrary to them in religion. *Gen.* xiii.

Again, he sojourned in Gerar ; and king Abimelech gave him leave to abide in his land, *Gen.* xx. 15.

Isaac also dwelt in the same land, yet contrary in religion, *Gen.* xxvi.

Jacob lived twenty years in one house with his uncle Laban, yet differed in religion, *Gen.* xxxi.

The people of Israel were about four hundred and thirty years in that infamous land of Egypt, and afterwards seventy years in Babylon ; all which time they differed in religion from the state. *Exod.* xii. and 2 *Chron.* xxxvi.

Come to the time of Christ, when Israel was under the Romans, where lived divers sects of religion, as Herodians, Scribes and Pharisees, Sadduces, Libertines, Thudians, and Samaritans, besides the common religion of the Jews, Christ, and his apostles ; all which differed from the common religion of the state, which was like the worship of Diana, which almost the whole world then worshipped. *Acts,* xix. 20.

All these lived under the government of Cæsar, (being nothing hurtful to the commonwealth) giving unto Cæsar that which was his ; and for their religion and consciences towards God, he left them to themselves, as having no dominion over their souls and consciences ; and when the enemies of truth raised up any tumults, the wisdom of the magistrate most wisely appeased them. *Acts* xviii. 14, and xix. 35.

That famous lawyer Coke saith, in regard to men's being obliged to accuse or purge themselves by oaths, " the oath *ex officio*, is an invention of the devil, to cast the souls of miserable people into hell."

" Let the judges," saith Tindall, " judge and condemn the trespasses under lawful witnesses, and not break up into the consciences of men, afer the example of Antichrist's disciples, and compel them either to forswear themselves, or to testify against themselves ; which abomination, saith he, our prelates learned of Caiaphas, Mat. xxvi. saying to Christ, ' I adjure, or charge thee in the name of the living God, that thou tell us whether thou be Christ, the Son of the living God." *Valq. Coniro illustraes, p.* 124. *num.* 27.

Jer. Tayler, chaplain in ordinary to king Charles, in his book, entitled, 'A Discourse of the Liberty of Prophesying,, says, " as contrary as cruelty is to mercy, as tyranny is to charity ; so is war and bloodshed to the meekness and gentleness of the christian religion.

" Although we must contend earnestly for the faith, yet, this contention must be with arms fit for the christian warfare, the sword of the spirit, the shield of faith, &c. but not with other arms ; for a churchman must not be a striker, for the weapons of our warfare are nor carnal, but spiritual.

" If the persons be christians in their lives, and christians ain their professions ; if they acknowledge the eternal son of God for their master, and Lord, and live in all relations as becomes persons making such professions, why then should I hate such persons whom God loves, and who love God, who are partakers of Christ, and Christ hath a title to them, who dwell in Christ, and Christ in them, because their understandings have not been brought up like mine, have not had the same masters, they have not met with the same books; have not the same opinions that I have, and do not determine their school questions to the same sense of my sect or interest ?

" I earnestly contend, that another man's opinion shall be no rule to mine ; and that my opinion shall be no snare and prejudice to myself; that men use one another so charitably, that no error or violence tempt men to hypocrisy ; this very thing being one of the arguments I used to persuade permissions, lest compulsion introduce hypocrisy, and make sincerity troublesome, &c.

" From the dictates of holy scriptures, it is observable, that this, with its appendant degrees, I mean, restraint of prophesying, imposing upon other men's understandings, being masters of their consciences, and lording it over their faith, came in with the retinue and train of antichrist, as other abuses and corruptions of the church did, by reason of the iniquity of the times, and the cooling of the first heats of christianity, and the increase of interest, and the abatements of christian simplicity, when the church's fortune grew better, and her sons grew worse, and some of her fathers worst of all.

" All wise princes, till they were overborne with faction, and solicited by peevish persons, gave toleration to differing sects.

" And the experience which christendom hath had in this last age, is argument enough, that toleration of differing opinions, is so far from disturbing the public peace, or destroying the interest of princes and commonwealths, that it doth advantage the public ; it secures the peace, because there is not so much as the pretence of religion left to such persons, to contend for, it being already indulged to them.

" And, indeed, there is great reason for princes to give toleration to disagreeing persons, whose opinions cannot by fair means be altered ; for if the persons be confident, they will serve God according to their persuasions ; and if they be publicly prohibited, they will privately convene, and then all those inconveniencies and mischiefs, which are arguments against the permission of conventicles, are arguments for the public permissions of differing religions, &c. they being restrained, and made miserable, endears the discontented persons and makes more hearty and dangerous confederations."

" The duke of Savoy, repenting of his war, undertaken for religion, against the Piedmontans, promised them toleration, and was as good as his word,: as much is done by the nobility of Polonia. So that the best princes and the best bishops gave toleration and impunities : (and it is known, that the first persecution of disagreeing persons, was by the Arians, by Circumcellians, and Donatics, and from them they of the church took example, &c.) And, among the Greeks, it became a public and authorized practice, till the question of images grew hot and high ; for then the worshippers of images, having taken their example from the empress Irene, who put her son's eyes out for making an edict against images, began to be as cruel as they were deceived, especially being encouraged by the pope of Rome, who then blew the coals to some purpose.

I may, upon this occasion, mention as a remarkable circumstance, that, till the time of Justinian, the emperor,

A. D. 325, the Catholics and Novatians had churches indifferently permitted even in Rome itself, but the bishops of Rome, whose interest was much concerned in it, spoke much against it, and laboured for the eradication of the Novatians; and, at last, when they got power into their hands, they served them accordingly. But, it is observed by Socrates, that when the first persecution was made against them at Rome, by pope Innocent the first, at the same instant, the Goths invaded Italy, and became lords of all, it being just in God, &c.

And I have heard it observed as a blessing upon St. Austin, who was so merciful to erring persons, as, the greatest part of his life, to tolerate them, and never endure that they should be given over to the secular power to be killed; that the very night the Vandals set down before his city of Hippo, to besiege it, he died, and went to God; being taken from the miseries to come.

Let all errors be as much, and as zealously suppressed as may be, but let it be done by such means as are proper instruments of their suppression, by preaching and disputation, by charity and sweetness, by holiness of life, assiduity of exhortation, by the word of God, and prayer.

For these ways are most natural, most prudent, most peaceable and effectual, only let not men be hasty, in calling every disliked opinion by the name of heresy; and when they have resolved that they will call it so, let them use the erring person like a brother, not beat him like a dog, or convince him with a gibbet, or vex him out of his understanding or persuasion.

Chrysostomus said, 'it is not the manner of the children of God to persecute others to death about their religion; but it hath been, and is their condition, to be put to death themselves for the testimony of the truth. Moreover (said he) the shedding of blood about religion is an evident token of antichrist." *Relig. Uris. p.* 192.

Haywardus said, 'that the best writers of that time did agree in one opinion, with Tertulliano, Lactantio, Cassidoro, and Josephus, &c. that people must persuade men to embrace religion with reason, and not compel them by violence.

" I have, for a long season, determined (said one of the kings of France) to reform the church, which, without peace, I cannot do, for it is impossible to reform or convert people by violence.'

" I am king as a shepherd (said he) and will not shed the blood of my sheep; but will gather them through the mildness and goodness of a king, and not through the power of tyranny. And I will give them that are of the reformed religion, liberty to live and dwell free, without being examined, perplexed, molested, or compelled to any thing contrary to their consciences; for they shall have the free exercise of their religion, &c." *Vide Chron. Vande Underg.* 2. *deel. p.* 1514.

Luther said, ' that the hypocrite's church was to be known by its manners, whose image and sign was Esau, yet she boasted of God, and would be accounted his church, but lived wholly according to the world. Further (said he) the true church is not defended by a fleshly arm, which wicked bishops especially use, and cry unto.' *Thesau. p.* 622.

Calvin said, ' that the apostle gave to understand, that to exercise authority over one's faith, was in no wise just, nor tolerable : yea, it is tyranny in the church ; for faith ought to be free from all subjection of men.'

Several of the priests in the Low countries requested of the prince and states, that they would introduce ordinances and discipline according to their opinions ; but the prince and states rejected their requests, esteeming them prejudicial both to religion and policy, when they observed the divers opinions that were among the people ; concluding, it was the best way to preserve unity among the people, to give liberty to all : Anno. 1608. *Edict.* fol. 27.

Constantius, the emperor, said, ' that it was enough that he preserved the unity of the faith, that he might be excusable before the judgmentseat of God ; and that he would leave every one to his own understanding, according to the account he will give before the judgmentseat of Christ. Hereto may we stir up people, not compel them ; beseech them to come into the unity of the christians, but to do violence to them, we will not in any wise.' *Sabast. Frank. Chron.* fol. 127.

Those princes that have ruled by gentleness and clemency, added to justice, and have exercised moderation and meekness towards their subjects, always greatly prospered and reigned long.

But, on the contrary, those princes that have been cruel, unjust, perfidious, and oppressors of their subjects, have soon fallen, they and their estate into danger, or total ruin.

Veritus, said, "seeing Christ is a lamb, whom you profess to be your head and captain, then it behoveth you to be sheep, and to use the same weapons which he made use of, for he will not be a shepherd of wolves, and wild beasts, but only of sheep ; wherefore, if you lose the nature of sheep, and be changed into wolves, and wild beasts, and use fleshly weapons, then will you exclude yourselves out of his calling, and forsake his banner, and then will he not be your captain."

Stephanus, king of Poland, said, 'it belongeth not to me to reform the conscience. I have always gladly given that over to God, which belongeth to him, and so shall I do now ; and also for the future, I will suffer the weeds to grow until the time of harvest; for I know that the number of believers are but small; therefore, he said, when some were proceeding in persecution, 'ego sum rex populorum ; non conscientiarum ;' that is, 'I am the king of the people, not of their consciences.' He also affirmed, that religion was not to be planted with fire and sword. *Chron. Van. de Rel. Urijh.* 2 *deel.*

Tindal said, 'the New Testament of Christ suffered no law of compelling, but alone of persuading and exhorting.' *Fox's Acts and Mon.* p. 1338.

The prince of Orange testified, *Anno.* 1579, 'that it was impossible that the land should be kept in peace, except there was a free toleration in the exercise of religion.'

'Where hast thou ever read, in thy days (said *Mento*) in the writings of the apostles, that Christ or the apostles ever cried out to the magistrates, for their power, against them that would not hear their doctrine, or obey their words? I know certainly, said he, that where the magistrate shall banish with the sword, there is not the right knowledge, spiritual word, nor church of Christ : it is *invocare brachium seculare.*'

'It is not christian like, but tyrannical,' said D. Philipson, 'to banish and persecute people about faith and religion, and they that so do, are certainly of the pharisaical generation, who resisted the Holy Ghost.'

Erasmus, said, 'that though they take our money and goods, they cannot therefore hurt our salvation ; they afflict us much, with prisons, but they do not thereby separate us from God.' *In de Krijdges wrede,* fol. 63.

Lucernus said, 'he that commandeth any thing, wherewith he bindeth the conscience, this is an antichrist.' *In de Benuse disp.* fol. 71.

King Charles the first, in his book known by the name of 'The Royal Portrait,' writes as followeth :

Page 67. In his prayer to God, he saith, 'thou seest how much cruelty among christians is acted, under the colour of religion ; as if we could not be christians, unless we crucify one another.'

Page 28. 'Make them at length seriously to consider, that nothing violent and injurious can be religious.'

Page 70. 'Nor is it so proper to hew out religious reformations by the sword, as to polish them by fair and equal disputations, among those that are most concerned in the differences, whom, not force, but reason ought to convince.

4 H

'Sure, in matters of religion, those truths gain most upon men's judgments, and consciences, which are least urged with secular violence, which weakens truth with prejudices.'

Page 115. ' It being an office, not only of humanity, rather to use reason than force, but also of christianity to seek peace, and ensue it.

Page 91, 92. 'In point of true conscientious tenderness, I have often declared, how little I desire my laws and sceptre should intrench on God's sovereignty, who is the only king of men's consciences.

Page 123. ' Nor do I desire any man should be further subject unto me, than all of us may be unto God.

Page 76. ' The enjoining of oaths, upon people, must needs, in things doubtful, be dangerous, as in things unlawful damnable.'

To his son, the prince of Wales, he says, page 165, ' My counsel and charge to you is, that you seriously consider the former real, or objected miscarriages, which might occasion my troubles, that you may avoid them.

' Beware of exasperating any factions, by the crossness and asperity of some men's passions, humours and private opinions, employed by you, grounded only upon differences in lesser matters, which are but the skirts and suburbs of religion, wherein a charitable connivance, and christian toleration often dissipate their strength, when rougher opposition fortifies, and puts the despised and oppressed party into such combinations, as may most enable them to get a full revenge on those they count their persecutors, who are commonly assisted by that vulgar commiseration, which attends all that are said to suffer under the notion of religion.

Page 116. ' Take heed, that outward circumstances and formalities of religion devour not all.

Page 164. ' Your prerogative is best shewed and exercised in remitting, rather than exacting the rigour of the laws, there being nothing worse than legal tyranny.

Page 234. ' The best government and highest sovereignty you can attain unto, is to be subject to God, that the sceptre of his word and Spirit, may rule in your heart.

Page 241. ' Always keep up solid piety, and those fundamental truths, which mend both the hearts and lives of men, with impartial favour and justice.

Page 242. ' My charge and counsel to you is, that as you need no palliations for any design, so that you study really to exceed in true and constant demonstrations of goodness, piety and virtue (towards the people) even all these men that make the greatest noise and ostentations of religion, so you shall neither fear any detection (as they do who have but the mask of goodness) nor shall you frustrate the just expectations of your people.'

In his prayer, page 1, of the same book, he says, 'O never suffer me for any reason of state, to go against the reason of conscience, which is highly to fight against thee, the God of reason, and judge of our consciences.

Page 121. 'Break in sunder, O Lord, all violent confederations to do wickedly and injuriously.

Page 136. 'Thou, O Lord, shalt destroy them that speak lies; the Lord will abhor both the bloodthirsty and deceitful men.

Page 164. 'Church affairs should be managed neither with tyranny, parity, nor popularity; neither people oppressed.

Page 171. 'Oh, thou that art the God of reason and peace, soften our hearts; and persuade us to accept of peace with thyself, and both to secure and preserve peace among ourselves, as men and christians: condemn us not to our passions, which are destructive both of ourselves and others; clear up our understandings to see thy truth, both in reason, as men, and in religion, as christians.'

FINIS.

TO THE SUBSCRIBERS.

In presenting this work to Subscribers, the Publisher returns his acknowledgments to them, for their liberal patronage ; and he flatters himself, from the care taken to do justice to the subject, that it will give general satisfaction ; and not, as has too often been the case, add another to the list of impositions. It was his intention to particularize the ministers (a large number having added their names to the list) and the society to which they belonged, but some of the subscriptions being returned without those distinctions, it was thought proper to omit the rest.

Some names are probably incorrectly spelled, owing to the illegible manner in which they were written. As there are a number of places of the same name, in different states, it is very likely, some will be found in a state to which they do not belong. And there being some subscription lists not yet returned, will account for the omission of such names as are not inserted

SUBSCRIBERS' NAMES.

Robert Smith, Secretary of State to the United States.
Gabriel Duval, Comptroller.
Daniel D. Tompkins, Governor of the State of New-York.
De Witt Clinton, late Mayor of the city of New-York.

VERMONT.

Silas Bingham
Eleazer Barrow, jr.
Wm. Campbell
David Dickinson
Philip Davis
John Ferguson
Wm. G. Hooker
Richard Hall, jun.
Joseph Huntington
Thomas A. Merrill
Solomon Miller
Ephraim Miller
Timothy Matthews
Artemas Nixon
Chauncey Pier
Lemuel Peet
Warner Pierce
Jabez Rogers, jun.
Samuel Swift
Peter Starr
Clark Stephens
C. Starksborough
Jacob Tucker
Enoch Woodbridge
Richard Worth
Wm. Worth
James M. Young

MASSACHU-SETTS.

James Alley
Benj. Alley, 3d
Timothy Alley
Samuel Alley
Zachariah Awill
Joseph Alley
Lewis Alley
David Adams
Wm. B. Abbott
Silas Arnold
David Aldrich
Joseph Andrus
Samuel Arms
Elias Arnold
Anthony H. Adams
Thomas Baldwin
Jonathan Buffum
Robert Brookhouse
John Brown
Edward Brown
Benj. Beckford
Jonathan Bright
Isaac Bassett
John Bailey
William Brown
Jehemiah Bassett
William Breed
Thomas B yd
John Broadhead

Jonathan Boyce
I. Bull
Asa Breed, jun.
Fred. Burchstead
Amos Breed, jun.
Peter Barry
James Bickford
Micajah Burrill
Amos Breed
Thos. Bowlin, jun.
John Binbeck
B. Broudin
Prudence Bordman
John Beers
Samuel Baxter
Francis Blanchard
Ebenezer Brede
—Anna Brede
M. R. Bartlett
Andrew Bordman
Charles Brookett
S. Bingham
James Brown
James Beret
Joseph Brown
Ebenezer Blue
Chs. Baldwin
G. T. Bulkeley
Daniel Boynton
Henry K. Brown
Joshua K. Bulkely
Rufus Bradly
Luther Burtlett
Saml. N. Barker
James Burroughs
Reuben Bacon
George Beckwith
Wm. Basery
Robert F. Barnard
Luther Beoper
Lemuel Bullard
P. E. Braudin
Eion Bradley
Tillotson Bronson
Elijah Bryan
Bond & Bull
Ezekiel Bradley
Anthony Bristol
Lewis Buston
J. Buckingham
Alice M. Cooley
Benjamin Cande
Andrew Cro kett
Abijah Chase
John Clarke
Micajah Cullins
Moses Conner
Isaiah Chase
Charles Chase
—Phebe Chase
Joseph Cornier
David Curtin

Nathaniel Collins
Enoch Curtin
Samuel Collins
Abigail Curtin
Saml. Collins, jun.
Stephen Collins
Jacob Chase
Lawson Caryl
Joseph Clay
William Collice
John Canfield
William Chadwell
Ambrose Collins
James Chotler
Edward Casey
Nathan Caltin
Henry Crittenton
Joseph Croset
Jeremiah Colegrove
James Cumming
Preserve Carter
Addison Cowles
Abijah Cornwell
Nathan Clark
Amos Clark
Enoch Dow
Robert Delan
John Dunkley
Elijah Downing
Josiah Dunham
Cyrus Dean
Timothy Davis
James Dane
Joseph Dane
N. Dillingham
Sylv. Dummick
J. Decolt. & Co.
John Dickinson
Bradick Danporth
Joseph Darley
Erasmus Dewy
Saml. Dernion
John Day
Daniel Dewey
—Amanda Davidson
Wm. Durand
Joseph Fikley
Brown Emerson
David Eldridge
Joseph Eustice
Ezekiel Estes
William Estes
Samuel Evelith
Asa Ellis
Elisha Ely
Leveus Eddy
Gaius Fenn
Joseph Fuller, 3d
Oliver Fuller
Rufus Farnam
—Sarah Flagg
Wm. Fitzgerald

Oramel Fanning
Eldad Francis
Thomas Fary
Henry Frost
James Francis
John Foot
—Susan Fowler
Jer. Goodhue
H. B. Gram
Zacheus Green
Abraham Grant
Richard Gridley
Varnum Gardner
Levi Glover
Robert Green
Wm. Griswold
Thomas Gold
Titus Goodman
Justin Griswold
Eli Green
Wm. Gorban
Samuel W. Heath
Josh. Huntington
Daniel Hopkins
Joseph Hart
Wm. Hunt
Barnabus Harick
Wm. Harker
Samuel D. How
Freeman Hearsey
Epes Maskill
Amos Harrington
Robert Hartshorn
T. Hancock
William Hilliard
Jonathan Hager
Phineas B. Hovey
Samuel Hastings
Jonas Holden
John Houghton
John Hayden
John P. Hilge
—Isabella Hovey
Thomas Hovey
Alvon Hyde
Ransom Hinman
Abm. Howland
Theodore Hinedale
Nathaniel Harris
George Hodge
George Holloway
Moses Hallock
Eleazer Hamlin
Lemuel Higgin
Edmund Ingalls
David Ingersoll
Thomas Ives
Ephraim Jaudon
Joseph Jackson
Jones & Arnold
Joseph Jeffery
John Jebine

John L. Johnson
Benjamin Johnson
Humph. S. Johnson
Richard Johnson
Samuel Johnson
Ezra Johnson
Uriel Josephs
Ebenezer Jenkins
Daniel James
Oliver Jewett
Aaron Jaqua
James Jacklin
Stephen James
W. P. Kentisbess
Lemuel King
Michael Kindlen
Richard Knight
Andrew Kennedy
Martin Kellogg
Philo Kibborn
John Kinney
George Knig
Oliver Kellogg
—Mary Kellogg
Affia Kellogg
Nehemiah Kellogg
Ezra Kimberly
Noah Kelsey
Charles Lowell
—Susan Low
John Lummins
Nathaniel Lewis
John Lindsley
Nathl. Livermore
John Luthie
Mat. R. Lanckton
Edward Lenard
Benj. Lapham
Thomas L adletter
Elisha Latimer
Wm. Lusk
Benj. Lovejoy
D. Leavenworth
Samuel Mewer
John L. Moulton
John Mower
Ezra Mudge
Timothy Munro
Josiah Moore
Royal Morse
James Munro
Chester Munger
Gamaliel Merritt
Frederick Manson
Abel Mack ntire
Eli Maynard
George Martin
Ebenr. Mansfield
—Sarah L. Munro
Wm. V. N. Morris
—Jesse Mann
Thomas Melody

SUBSCRIBERS' NAMES.

D. M'Fairlind, jr.
Stephen Mead
Abm. Merriman
Pharah Newhall
Winthrop Newhall
Abijah Newhall
Samuel Neal
Timothy Newhall
Aaron Newhall
Levi Nye
Aaron Newell
David Noble
Timothy Northam
Deodatus Noble
John Nichols, jun.
John Nichols
James Odell
Gaml. W. Oliver
Henry Oliver
Wm. Oliver
Vious Osborn
Jeremiah Peabody
Benj. Pickering
Nathan Peabody
David Perkins
Saml. Punchered
Oliver Peabody
George Pierce
Walter Phillips
James Pratt
Benj. H. Phillips
Jonathan Phillips
James Purinton
John Purinton
Abijah Purinton
John Pearson
Joseph Phipps
Jonathan Phillips
Josiah Parks
Charles Parks
John Phelps
Daniel Peponn
David Perry
Ths. Punderson, jr.
Lemuel Pomeroy
Philow Pnetibone
Josiah B. Prescott
Eli Porter
Samuel Porter
C. Penniman
Nathan Pierson, jr.
Henry Pierson
James Pierson
Nathan Pierson
Howel Pierson
David Perry
Moses Pinley
James C. Peneroy
Azariah Pratt
Robert L. Potter
George Pinchon
Martin Ritter
Peter G. Robbins
Thomas Reed
John Richards, jr.
John Ross
David Russel
William Russel
Henry Rice
Oliver Robbins
Abeland Reynolds
Abraham Reed
Moses Reed
Josiah Q. Robinson
Joseph Raymond
Abm. Rockwell
J. W. Robins
John B. Root
Simuel Stanwood
Joseph Scates
T. Symonds
Wm. Stickney

Enoch Stickney
Nebemiah Sibbe
Andrew Seaston
John Stowel
Nathan Shed
Wm. Smith
Henry Sanford
Stephen Shelton
Preserved Sprague
Franklin Sawyer
Moses Swift
Roswell Slocking
Abner Stevens
Amos Squiere
Thomas Stebbins
David Staples
Samuel Smith
Jesse Sabin
Wm. Starkweather
Davie Smith
Amos Shepardson
Amasa Shattuck
Timothy Saunders
Daniel Smith, jun.
Benjamin Smith
Daniel Stow
Justus Smith
John J. Suins
Stephen Sibby
Henry Silsbe
Daniel Silsbe
Henry Silsbe, jun.
John Twombley
John Tarbell
Jethro Thatcher
Henry Taylor
Joseph Tucker
Giles Tinker
Wm. Towner
Josiah Talmage
Caleb Thurston
Joseph C. Turner
Erastus Tracy
Saml. M. Thurston
Jabez Turner
Hugh Umprey
Daniel Webb
Samuel Worcester
Stephen Webb
Nathl. W. Williams
Philip Wells
John Waters
Holder Wheeler
Wm. B. Whitney
Samuel L. West
David Williams
John West
David Webb
John Walton
Nathl. Woodward
John Wion
Joseph Whiton
Ebenezer West
Abel West
Peter Werden
Elisha Wells
John Waterman
George Whitman
John Whipple
John P. Whitmore
Simeon Warner
Dennis Wood
Henry Wisnell
John Williams
Stephen Washburn
James Warner
Robert Watson
Wm. Wainwright
Dudley Woodworth
John Whiting
J. Whittleres, jun.
Daniel Young

Williams College,
President,
Ebenr. Fitch, D. D.
Tutors,
C. Dewy, A. M.
J. Nelson, A. B.
C. Bushnell, A. B.
Students,
W. H. Abercrombie
James C. Allen
Solomon M. Allen
Chas. A. Baldwin
Charles F. Bates
Henry J. Blake
Job Clark
Elam Clark
John C. Clark
Harvey Coe
Elisha Cook
Lewis Dickinson
Abner A. De Wolf
Jonathan Eastman
William Eaton
Justin Edwards
Cor. B. Everest
Salmin Giddings
Hiram Hinsdell
Wm. D. Hornett
Elisha Hubbard
Calvin Hubbell
Caleb Hustin
Charles Jenkins
H. Judd
Silas Jones
Cyrus Joy
Henry Knapp
Charles Larned
Samuel S. Lewmin
Nich. M. Masters
Saml. M. Mackay
Wm. H. Maynard
Philip V. N. Morris
James Nash
Ariel Otis
Job Pierson
Amatus Robins
Moses D. Robinson
Chas. F. Sedgwick
Geo. B. Swildon
Wm. B. Stow
E. M. Townsend
Wm. Twining
S. Van Rensselaer
A. D. Vanderburg
Abm. P. Vosbarg
Moses Warren
Jon. Windward
Cyrus Yale

R. ISLAND.

W. Aran, jun.
Alin L. Almy
William Almy
Christopher Arnold
Joseph Anthony
James Anthony
Geo. L. Atwell
David Atwood
Saml O. Auchmuty
Christopher Almy
Samuel Allen
Samuel Albro
Elijah Burlingham
Jabez Boss
Lloyd Beal
Peter Barker
Eliza Brmon
Samuel Brown
Benj. C. Brown
Martin Benson
Moses Brown

Arnold Buffum
Obadiah M. Brown
Allen Brown
David Benedict
Israel Bullock
Jabez Brown
Wheaton Bragg
Cors. G. Bowler
Ichabod Brown
Nicholas Brown
Ebenezer Burges
Lewis Bosworth
Masa Bassett
Robert S. Babcock
Henry Beverly
Joseph La Bruce
David Buffum
Calvin Barlow
Samuel Brown
D. Coggeshall
Samuel Carr, jun.
Benjamin U. Carr
Saml. C. Caulking
Geo. Champlin
James M. Casin
John Cross
Nathaniel Crocker
Chauncey Cooley
Benjamin Corlam
Peter Carpenter
Samuel Carlisle
Wm. Church
Shubael Cady
Ward Cowing
Robert Cochran
Henry Clark
David Curtis
C. Childs
Joseph Cornell
Thomas Cony
John Cowen
John Carpenter, jr.
Floide Colhoun
Henry Y. Cranston
Elisha Chase
Wm. P. Cara
F. Coggeshall
James Coggeshall
Geo. Clark, jun.
James Center
Wm. Card
John Cross
John C. Chester
Wait Clarke
Resolved Carr
Lemuel Chester
Ruth Chase
Elisha Dyer
Golden Dearah
Oliver Dyer
Simon Dean
Henriet. C. Downle
Nehemiah Dodge
David Delano
James R. Ducray
John W. Davis
Th. Dennis, jun.
Robert Dennis
Horatio S. Dexter
Thomas Earnsley
Clark Edwards
Caleb Earl
Moses Eldy
John Easton
Michael Eddy
John Earl
James Fenner
Catharine Field
Richard M. Field
James Field
J. Frazer
Mat. Gategoal

Benj. Greene
Joseph A. Guthrow
Geo. Gavit, 2d
Mary M. Gray
Stephen Gano
Jonathan Going
John Goss
Zephaniah Graves
Allen Gladding
Benj. C. Grafton
John H. Greene
Benj. Gorham
Seneca Greene
Wm. C. Greene
Nich. R. Gardner
Albert W. Gardner
Henry Gardner
George Gavit
John Randy
Thomas Hazard
Benjamin Hall
N. Hoppin & Son
Martha Hill
Seneca Hammond
Thomas Hopkins
Stephen Harris
Josiah Humphreys
John Hawkins
John Hall
Wm. Hardin
Richard Hardin
Silas Hall, jun.
John Hall
Chs. E. Hoskins
Dennis Holland
John Irish
B. Ingraham
Jacob Ide, jun.
Benjamin Jones
Paul Jewett
Benj. James
Wm. Jenkins
Thomas Jones
Hervey Jenks
Jer. F. Jenkins
Evan M. Johnson
James B. Kennedy
Peleg Kaighn
John Lyon
James Livingston
Josh. H. Langley
Josiah Lawson
Lucy Ann Lippott
Josh. H. Langley
Joseph Lee
Joseph Lyndon
Samuel Lee
Nathl. Lyndon
Benj. Malliken
Thomas Messer
Lewis Maxson
Silas Maxson
Asa Messer
Joseph R. Mason
Henry S. Mansfield
Saml. B. Martin
David March
Isaac Manchester
Josiah Munro
Thos. H. Mumford
Samuel Merwin
Wm. Munro
Joanna P. Be Mort
Simeon Martin
Lewis Maxson
Silas Maxson
Wm. S. Nichols
John T. Nichols
Joseph Oatley
Mary Olney
Wm. Potter
Thomas Perry

26

SUBSCRIBERS' NAMES.

David Peck
Alvin Park
Walter Paine
John Perrin
Joshua Perry
Earl Potter
Joseph S. Pettes
James B. Philips
Prudence Peckham
William Prior
Joseph Pendleton
Mat. Robinson
Henry Russell
Susanna Raymar
Thomas Raynolds
John Richmond
Charles Roley
P. P. Remmington
John Reed
Daniel V. Ross
Eleazer Reed, jun.
Thomas Sherman
Jer. T. Sherman
Wm. Sayer
Christoph. Starkey
John A. Shaw
Abiat Sherman
Mary Searle
Richard Smith
O. Starkweather
Saml. S. Stillwell
Barnabas Sterre
Joseph Simmons
Sylvester Sprague
Abm. Sherman
Job Shearman
James Sheffield
Wm. Stillman
Joseph Stillman
James Sayer
James Sutton
Eleazer Tribute
E. Thompson
Peter Taylor
John Taylor
Barailla M. Taylor
Ichabod Taylor
Wm. Vernon
Th. M. Venson
Joshua Vose
Benj. Wightman
Stephen Wilcox
James Wilson
Stephen Wardwill
Wm. Woodward
Thomas Williams
Peter Wheelock
Saml. N. Warner
James Wakefield
Thomas Williams
John Ward
Saml. Whitehorne
G. G. Whitehorne
David Williams
Stephen Wilcox
Wm. Wilbers
John Young
Daniel Young
Joseph G. Young
J. Yeomans

CONNECTICUT.

Jane Atwater
Chauncey Arnold
Benjamin Agnes
Levi Arnold
Charles Atwater
Mes. Angier, jun.
Wm. C. Atwater
Timothy Allen
Nathaniel Adams

Nathan Aldrich
Ezekiel E. Achun
Lucius Atwater
Elnathan Atwater
David Atwater
John C. Bull
P. B. Boyce
Joseph Barber
Joseph Bishop
Eli Barns
Nancy Bellomy
Horace Beach
Sherman Blair
Stephen Bristol
W. Surdick
John Beatty
Elijah Beebe
David U. Bentley
Moses Benjamins
Jeremiah Brown
Joshua P. Burnham
Elisha Babcock
Martha Bigelow
Elizabeth Bolles
Eleazer Badger
Caleb Bacon
Daniel Baldwin
Charles Bostwick
Wm. Barns
Jarod Bradley
Beriah Bradley
Nathan Brers
Abel Burritt, jun.
Samuel Barnet
A. F. Bradford
Samuel Beckwith
Joshua C. Burton
John Bell
Henry Burdick
John Brush
Nehemiah Bradley
Theodore Burrell
Wm. Bordman
Martin Benson
Josiah Buckwith
Samuel Bishop
John Bell
John Chester
Edward B. Cook
Alerius Bull
George Chandler
Charles Carew
Nathl. Chapman
L. H. Cobb
Benj. Cranston
Christopher Cok
Alpheus Chapman
Aaron Chapin
Corning & Bulkley
Cynthia Church
George Catlin
Joseph Coe
John Carrington
Peter W. Clark
John Cook, jun.
Wm. Crocker
Alfred Cowles
Elijah Cowles
Zenn Cowles
Daniel Clark
Nathl. Clack
Jonathan Coryt
David Coe
Seth Doud
John Davis
Thomas Dougal
John Dennison
B. Davison, jun.
Nehemiah Dodge
John G. Davis
Daniel Danforth
Rebekah Dunning

Samuel Driggs
Grace Dougal
John Daggett
Elijah Davis
William Daggett
Raphael Dickinson
Zina Doolittle
George Dour
James R. Dodge
Charles Dayton
S. Dibble
Geo. Durwell
Charles Deway
Stephen Deway
John Day
Benj. Douglas, jr.
Charles Denison
Zebulon Ely
Benjamin Ells
Ezra S. Ely
George Elliott
Thomas Ells
Isaac Frost
L. Fndick
Dennis Fanning
John Forsyth
Asa Farwell
Cole C. Filly
Alanson Ford
Joseph French
Abm. C. Fowler
Peter Farnam
Richard Ferrin
Ezekiel Fuller
H. Grannis
Lydia Goddard
George Gordon
Th. H. Goddard
Dl. P. Gladding
R. J. Goodman
John Graves, 2d
James Gilbert
George Griswold
Newman Greenleaf
Joshua A. Gone
Elias Gilbert
Amos Goodsell
Leveret Gorham
Jacob Goodsell
Paul C. Grimball
Jona. Goodrich
Moses Goodman
Charles Gilbert
Seth Goodman
John Garnis
Saml. Goodyear
Charlotte Glenny
John Hinscale
Ch. Nequembourg
J. W. Harrison
Dl. B. Hempsted
James N. Hyde
Sally Huntington
Elizabeth Holbrook
Theo. Humphreys
Sarah Hawks
Ephraim Hollister
Maria Hopkins
Catharine Hopkins
James Harrison
Benj. D. Hubbard
Norman Hayden
Stephen Higgins
Harley Hooker
James S. Huggins
Sidney Hull
Eben. Huggins, jr.
Eli Hotchkiss
Ezra Hotchkiss
Timothy Hall
Wyllys Hotchkiss
Eli Hotchkiss

L. T. P. Huntington
O. Holme
Ariel Hancock
Isaac Hunt
John Hannah
Asa Hitchcock
Allen Hurd
Henry Haugh
Dustin Heckuff
Abel Hyde
David Harris
Lathrop Holmes
Salmon Hunt
Decius Humphreys
Sophia Humphreys
Reuben Hills
Hannah Hart
Roger Hooker
Daniel Hart
Daniel D. Hart
Jesse Hart
Andrew Hull
Samuel Hull
Polly Hart
Josephus Hotchkys
John Hyde
John How
James Hitchcox
Samuel Higby
Abm. Horsford
Francis Reare
Joseph Huntington
Levi Ives
Eli Ives
Enoch Ives
George Irish
Richard Imlay
Reuben E. Ives
Stephen Ives
Martha Ingersoll
Amos Johnson
Levi C. Judson
N. Jackson
Jones & Dunn
Peter Johnson
Simeon Jones
Isaac Jones
Walter King
Andrew Kingsbury
Forbes Kyle, jun.
Linus Kimberly
J. Kinne
Philo Kibbern
John Kinney
Charles B. Lines
Amos Leich
Gerard Lathrop
Saml. L. Luckwood
James Low
Samuel Langdon
Nehemiah Lovell
John Longworthy
Benjamin Lines
Joshua Lovell
Josiah Laurence
Roswell Lee
Elisha Leer
James Loomis
Roger Leonard
Rhoda Lewis
Nancy Lewis
Ezekiel Lovejoy
Lorram Loomis
Clarissa Morgan
Esther Morgan
Thankful Morgan
Samuel Min, jun.
Hosea Min, jun.
Medad Meeker
Andrew Mark
George Miles
Abel M'Ewen

John M'Catty
Michael Mulvy
Ebenezer Moore
Samuel Meswin
E. W. Morse
Eneas Munson
Asa M'Nell
Charles Marshall
James Merriman
Abm. Merriman
Benj. Maxam
Darius Mason
Joel Mills
Thomas Mather
John Mix
Titus Moss
H. Mulford
Henry May
Josiah Myrick
Seth Marshall
A. Miller
George Nichols
Samuel Nevins
Birdsey Norton
Wm. Noyes, jun.
Myron Norton
Edward Nichol
Thomas Noyers, 2d
Jedediah Norton
Wm. Orshall
David L. Ogden
Nathl. Olmstead
David L. Perkins
Eleazer Porter
Wm. Parker
Gad Peck
L. Peck
Joseph Potter
Geo. L. Perkins
Augustus Perkins
Nathan Perkins
Antonly Phelps
C. L. Porter
Walter Phelps
Ruth Patten
John Payne
Prime & Bradley
Levi Parrot
Hezekiah Pierpont
Timothy Plant
Peter H. Pond
J. R. Peck
Avery Preston
Wm. Peckham
Jacob Penuyer
Samuel Pardee
Daniel Patchen
Nathaniel Peck
Zilpha Pardee
David Parsons
Joel Pomeroy
Joseph Put
Serina Pittibone
Otis Preston
Sidney Porter
Daniel Pratt
S. Potter
N. Phelps
Orren Pearl
Seth Peck
P. W. Perit
Hezekiah Peck
Michael Peck, jun.
Caleb P. Pitkin
Jos. J. Prudden
Catharine Pond
Baldwin, Pond &Co
Eleazer Pardee
Jona. Phillips, jun.
Warner Pierce
Solomon Philips
Jonas Powel

SUBSCRIBERS' NAMES

Samuel Penoyer
Abm. Pierce
Th mas Pierce
Joseph Pierce
Jonathan Palmer
Henry Roberts
Mat. F. Russell
Josiah Rogers
Reuben Rice
Nancy Rhodes
Gurdon C. Robins
Geo. S. Rathbone
Wi throp Roberts
G. N. Raymond
Henry Rositor
Jacob Rockwell
Thomas Rhodes
John Robertson
Milo Root
Sarah Root
Abiram Ring
Gideon Roberts
Elijah Rogers
Sylvester Roper
Nathaniel Roper
Amos Roberts
Timothy Stillman
Wm. Shelden
Charles Seabury
Rachel Starr
I. B. Sheffield
Jonathan Sizer
John Starry
Smith & Brumley
Spencer & Gilman
Henry Shepard
John H. Stone
Wm. Shepard
Moses Stewart
Samuel Spalding
Wm. Scott
Samuel Sacket
John Skinner
James Stillman
G. Schellenger
Wm. Stone
Gad Stanley
David Smith
Alex. Skinner
Ethan Smith
Louis Seymour
Timothy Sedgwick
Wm. Sedgwick
Pomroy Strong
Norris Stanley
Ebenezer Scott
Da iel Smith
Samuel Slater
Whiting Stanley
Wm. Sm th
Strong Miles, & Co.
Joseph Shove
Patty Seely
Samuel Seely
J. S. T. Sutton
Daniel Sutton
Wm. Ta'cott
Samuel Tripp
John Tyler
Jonathan Truman
David Thomas
Solomon Taylor
Henry Trowbridge
Wm. Townsend
Wm. Trowbridge
W. E. Thompson
Amos Treat
Jonathan Taylor
Wm. A. Taylor
Joha. Thompson
Daniel Tillotson
J. Thompson, jun

Rachel Todd
Elijah Treat
Avis Turner
Hez. P. Ufford
Isaac Upson
Thomas Upford
George White
Luzon Whitney
Samuel West
Saml. Whittemore
Alvan Wilcox
Henry Ward
James B. Weight
Jacob Ward
James White
Wm. Wait
Amos Wheeler
Solomon Winegen
H. E. Wilder
B. R. Wilson
Daniel Werrel
Noadiah Woodruff
Polly Whitman
Luke Wadsworth
Benj. Wheeler
Henry Whitman
Z. Whiting
Simon Waterman
Sophiah Woodruff
Joel Welton
Barnab. Woodcock
Abm. H. D. White
Benj. Whiting
John Whiting

NEW-YORK.

Priscilla Akerly
William Acheson
John Allen
Will am Allen
Joseph Atkins
John A. Anderson
Philip I. Amigh
Peter G. Amigh
John G. Amigh
R. Adriance
Jacob Adriance
Peter Angevine
John Anthony
Jared Andreuss
John Allen jun.
John Ayers jun
John Anderson
William Anthony
Ashbel H. Andrews
Peter Abbey
Riley Allcox
Alanson Austin
John Abeel
Mary Ashley
Ames Corwin
Richard Allison
James Allison
Robert Anderson
Alexan. Anderson
John Ayrs
Wm. Anthony
James Anderson
David Andress
Enos Alley
Royal Aldridge
Stephen Allen
Elizabeth Avery
Jesse Adams
Stephen Anderson
Israel Anderson
David Adee
Josiah Archer
James Angevine
Elisha Allen
Ju. Abercrombie

Jeremiah Anderson
Samuel Adams
Richard Alley
Reuben Abby
James Abbots
William Ashley
Hobby Adee
Alice Abbate
Garret Adriance
Ezekiel Angell
Jediah Allen
John I. Allen
Nathaniel Arnold
George Angevine
Philip Allen
Benj. B. Adams
Elijah I. Abbatt
John Adamson
Frederick Austin
Obadiah Andrus
Moses Austin
Asa Andrews
Robert Abbott
Jacob Badgley
Daniel Boyd
John Birdsall
James Bingham
James Brooks
Henry Burdan
Jonathan Brooks
Jared Beach
Thomas Bloodgood
Betts & Thomas
John M. Bruce
Robert Bruce
L. S. Burling
Jeremiah Barnhart
Robert Blair
Stephen S. Band
Lewis Barrett
Absalom Barrett
Nicholas Baker
Daniel Butler
Luther Brownill
R. V. D. Burgh
Amos T. Boyan
John Brill
Peter Brill jun.
Villeros Bees
Elisha Boulding
George Brinkerhoff
Nathaniel Berry
Underhill Budd
Benjamin Bowne
Joseph Burroughs
John N. Baley
Andrew Broomfield
Robert R. Brett
John Bedford
James Brownfield
N. Barton
Hugh Buchanan
William Beatty
John Brown
Thomas Bradshaw
John M Bradford
John Boardman
Robert R. Brower
Robert Boyd
Jacob Rarney
M. & I. Batcheldre
N. R. Bassett
Elisha Brunson
James Brown
Joseph Reintnal
Gad R. Bennet
Jacob Bishop
Edmund N. Bush
Harris Burr
Blamel Burr
Eliza Burr

Amorilles Burr
Anna Beach
Wm. Brown
D. Brooks
Daniel Burton
John Buchannan
Moses Burt
Luther Babbit
James M'Bean
John Brown
William Beaty
William Burger
James Bell
Patrick Blain
W. H. Bridges
John Boaldman
Cornelius Bogardus
David Boyd
Daniel Bull
Zina Beardsley
Cadwalader Bull
Wm. Bookstaver
David Belknap
Anth Burrows
John Bowen
Abm. Beach
Wm. O'Brien
Edm. D. Barry
Freeman Bishop
Anna Bancker
Robert Buwne
Thomas Buckley
S. A. Burtus 25 cop.
Abraham Bell
G. Bruce
Christian Beewer
Petr Bertrand
Wm. S. Burling
Jacob Barker
Joseph Bonnel
James Brown
Thomas Brown
Amos Bruod
Juda Bruce
Wm. Brien
Wm. S. S. Banker
Ch. D. Bevoise
Alice Bloomfield
James Brown, jun.
William Buutre
Wm. W. Berwick
Jacob Browner
John A. Blauvelt
Abm. Rogers
Caleb W. Baldwin
David Brown
Simon Baker
Frederick Biemlee
Henry Bartholf
James Bartholf
Thomas Belch
John Berry
Edmund Barford
John Barrow
Wm Beaty
St. N. Byard
James Billens
Theodocius Barton
Isaac Blauvelt
John Blades
James Bord
Peter Boyd, jun.
Nathl. Brown
Gilbert Budd
Thomas Brown
Parthena Brown
John Barbes
William Burling
Samuel Burling
Richard Burling
Stephen Barnes
Jonah Brundage

Henry Belding
John Barker
Elisha Brewster
Joseph Bodd
Henry Barker
Obadiah Bustwick
Daniel Bonnett
Peter Bonnett
Stephen Bates
John Bonnett
R mson Burton
Willett Bowne
Ann Bowne
James Byrd
Lester Beebee
James Bettine
Thomas Bidell
Isaac Bishop
Bedjamin Briggs
Jeremiah Bedell
Caleb Braley
Valentine Baker
George Blsom
Luke W. Barton
Alarcus Bull
John Brown
Isaac Belknap
Benjamin Busling
Mary C. Bowman
James Barnes
Jonathan Birdsall
Solomon Birdsall
Wm. Baker
Wm. Bedell, jun.
Wm. Birdsall
Henry Barmore
Abraham Bedell
David Bedell
Cornelius Brown
Caleb Brown
Samuel Bushnell
Stephen Brown
Abel Bowen, jun.
Benj. Boyce
Luther Bingham
Francis Bunker
Richard Barnes
Truman Buckney
Asa Bement
Ashbel Byington
Reuben Barlow
Jared Braley
Nathaniel Bishop
Wm. Barber
Cyprian Branch
Thomas Bachus
J. W. Brewster
Nathaniel Barker
Pearsall Brown
Samuel Belden
John Barwght jun.
John B. dle
Wm. Bell
Henry Boremus
Wm. Baker
Caleb Birnham
Isaac Boyce
Thomas Benham
Ebenezer Boyce
Francis Bowman
Jonathan Burt
Salmin Boswick
George Barker
Amos Beeker
Abner Burnham
Abm. Bleeker
Steph. Band
Kellogg Berry
Edmund Bement
Seth Barde
Nathaniel Barr
William Birdsall

Nathaniel Bird
Joseph Barns
E. & I. Barns
W. Boughton
John J. Blauvelt
Corns. J. Blauvelt
Samuel Bushnell
B. B. Blidenburgh
Daniel Brown
William Barnes
John Buckhout
Samuel Belknap
Charles Belknap
David Belknap
C. Blauvelt
Nicholas Blauvelt
Daniel Blauvelt
Dowe Blauvelt
Jonathan Bates
William Bowron
John V. Bartow
Cornelius Cruger
Abraham Cross
Zeno Carpenter
Millard Codington
Margaret Carr
William Cornwell
Peter Croger
John Cashear
Wm. Callahan
John Cole
William Corlies
Henry Cole
William Chambers
Robert S. Clark
D. A. Cumming
Henry Covert
Timothy Cheesman
A. Cairns
Benj. Carpenter
Andrew Cropsey
Stephen Coles
A. H. Conklin
Nath. Chittenden
Ebenezer Cary
John Cooper
Reed Crandle
Major Clark
James Cooper
Thomas Coleman
Henry N. Clark
Reuben Clark
Francis Clark
Nathan Clark
William Clark
James Cromwell
H. Conklin
David Clark
Archibald Combs
James Combs
John Clor
Jason Cande
Thomas Carvon
Amhurst Crane
Rodolphus Crane
John Clark
James Carmichael
Walter Clark
Joel Clement
Robert Cameron
James Coe
Humphrey Clark
Benj. Collier
Jonathan Clark
Alexander Caruth
S. Cuggeshall
John Collings
Alexander Combs
Daniel Cornell
Ezra Conklin
Jesse Conklin
A. Cunningham

Jesse Carpenter
David Clark
Charles Chandler
Stephen Crane
William Codington
Christian Christ
T. Carpenter
Townsend & Fuller
Charles Campbell
Joseph Clement
Samuel Carman
George Coldwell
Ezekiel Cooper
George Cock
Samuel Campbell
Benjamin Crane
25 copies.
Collins & Perkins
50 copies
Robt. H. Cumming
Josiah Cox
Chr. Cogwise
Henry Covenhoven
Henry Cole
Amos Corning
Thomas Coles
James Carson
Jacob Carle
Henry Carpenter
R. & I. Calwon
Eli Chapin
David Cole
Thomas Cock
Joseph Craig
Mary Cottela
John Clough
John Cruger
Moses Coe
Geo. Corlies
Israel Corse
James Cheetham
Daniel Cocker
Frederick Cursor
David V. Cott
Joseph Cromwell
R. Chamberlain
Elizabeth Coles
Wm. H. Cornell
Stephen Cornell
Philip Caverly
John W. Cornell
Benjamin Cornell
Thomas Cornell
Thomas I. Cornell
Elisha Carpenter
Jacob Carpenter
Wm. Carpenter
John Carpenter
Thomas Carpenter
Isaac Carpenter
Joseph Cornwall
John Cromwell
Allen Crosman
Nathaniel C. Clark
Thomas Clapp
Benj. Carpenter
Hacaliah Carhart
Reuben Coe
Josiah Carpenter
Samuel Carpenter
Crawford & Sniffin
Hannah Carpenter
Jona. Carpenter
Elijah Culner
Allen Clapp
John Clapp
Henry Cornell
Joshua Cornell
Benj. Cock
Oli. Cheesborough
Caleb Carman
James Corvel

Mary Clews
James Coleman
Merrit Coleman
R. Crommeline
Elijah Crane
Charles B. Coffin
Saml. Chadayne
Levi Carpenter
R. Carpenter
Joshua Carpenter
James Carpenter
Benj. Carpenter
Josiah Cock
William Cole
Stephen Carpenter
Abm. Cornell
Daniel Chichester
Ichabod Cue
Benjamin Cady
Nathan Coleman
Eunice Cuffin
Thaddeus Coleman
Samuel Crandel
Barnabas Coleman
Ezekiel Clark
Stephen Crundel
Matthew Cadwell
Francis Clark
Timothy Crundell
Oliver Collins
Ward Coxon
Nathan Croswell
Samuel Cogswell
Nathan Chapin
Darius Carroll
Jabez Colt
Samuel Curtis
Wm. Constable
Joshua Collins
Joshua Collins, jr.
John Conner
William Creed
Th. Cassey, jun.
John P. Clark
Wm. Cronkhite
Murray L. Cutter
Gifford Collins
Solomon Cook
Silas Calkins
Eliphalet Clark
Israel Camp
Jonathan Clawson
Daniel Clark
Samuel Canfield
J. Canfield
Joseph Crane
James Collins
T. Chittenden, jr.
Nathaniel Cowles
John Cushiner
John Cashaw
Reuben Close
Peter N. Card
Noah Cock
Benj. H. Cunklin
Amos Cock
David Cole
Jacobus D. Clark
Thomas Comstock
Gilbert Carpenter
Robert Carpenter
Levi Cock
Peter Dewitt, jun.
Cynthy Dally
Oliver De Lancey
Justis Dearman
Thomas Dawson
John Dewitt
Matt. Daniel, jun.
Ann Day
Benj. De Forest
A. De Forest

Benjamin Dyer
Dunn & Rothry
Abraham Demarest
Moses Dean
William Donington
George Duryea
Stephen Dorlon
John Duffield
Jonas Denton
David D. Long
Tamar Dennis
Jonathan Dennis
John Dennis
T. E. Doughty
John Doughty
Wm. Doughty
Thomas Doughty
Jacob Doughty
Cornell Doughty
James Durland
Gilbert Denniston
Daniel Dean
Simeon Dewitt
Ephraim Dewitt
Philip W. Deforest
Nathaniel Davis
John F. Doty
James Daniel
Andrew Delamane
William Dunlap
William Delvin
William H. Duree
Peter Dean
David G. Drake
Daniel Denton
Bowdewine Decker
William Decker
George Davidson
E. Duyckinck 50 c.
Benj. Demarest
Henry Dean
Joseph Dorrnin
Francis Doremus
Robert Dingee
Wm. Dealing
James Donaldson
John Darby
Abm. De Bunn
Francis Davis
Jacob Day
Thomas Davis
Wm. Donald
Joseph Drinker
Thomas Doxie
Abm. Duryea
John Derrig
Elizabeth Doty
N. Davenport
Jarvis Dusenberry
Henry Disbrow
Samuel Deall
Samuel Dick
Benjamin Drake
Henry Dickinson
Isaac Dickinson
Geo. Dillingham
Alex. Dennison
John Dubois
Chs. Dusenberry
James Divens
Abigail Dwight
John Dresser
Samuel Dewy
John Darrow
Peter P. Dox
Jonathan Dean
Allen Doughty
Matthew Dubois
Samuel Doughty
Wm. Doughty
Silas Downing
Gilbert Dean

E. Delavergne
A. Doughty
Azariah Darrow
James Dakin
Jeremiah Doty
David Dakin
Geo. Dour
Jas. R. Dodge
Martin Doughty
Hugh M. Donald
Joseph Dean 3 cop.
Gilbert Dean
William Egbert
Cath. A. Eldridge
Adam Empie
John H. Emigh
Jesse Everett
Abraham Eights
Peter E. Elmendorf
Eb. S. Edgarton
Daniel Edge
Enos Egerton
William Elliot
Edward Ely
John English
John Ebbetts
William Edgar
James M. Elliott
Daniel Edwards
Effingham Embre
John Everitt
John J. Everts
Stephen Ely
William Ely
John A. Elliott
Campbell & Elliott
Samuel S. Elliott
Eli Ensign
Thomas Eckerson
Luke Eckerson
Nicholas H. Emigh
David Fish
Nathaniel Fish
William Flagler
John Funck
Isaac Frost
Zacharias Flagler
Philip Flagler
Harmony Forman
John Fryer
Benj. W. Ford
Grove Foot
Robert Forester
Jabez Foot
Alex. Ferguson
Charles Fowler
Elijah Fowler
Robert Forrest
Samuel Falconer
Gerge Ferguson
Alexander Fairly
Th. Folherbame
John Ford
Benjamin Ferris
James Fennel
John Fuller
Henry Fisk
Samuel Frost
Sands Ferris
John Feaks
Hannah Fisher
Clorator Franklin
York Fleminter
John Flandra
Jas. Flandrau, jr.
Joshua Fowler
Aaron Field
William Field
Mercey Field
Uriah Field
Josiah Field
George Freeman

Robert Field	Tempe Green	Richard Harris	Thomas Havens	Charles Kniffin
Abigail Fowler	Elizab. Governeur	Jesse Hallock	Richard Harcourt	Frederick Knapp
Elijah Fisher	David Gladd	Richard Hallock jr.	Alexander Hunter	Patty King
Saml. W. Fisher	Joseph Gunn	Elisha Hammond	Adam Hibler	John Keache
David Falconer	Robert Grant	Joseph Horton	Charlotte Hopkins	James Kane
Samuel Fisher	Gilbert Griffin	Samuel Holstead	Richard Harding	S. Kellogg
George Farrington	Zophar Griffin	Henry Hunter	Samuel Haviland	George Knower
John L. Fonda	Jesse Griffin	Winthrop Hoag	John Hayt	Nathaniel King
Walker Farrington	Elisha Gregory	Abraham Hoag	William Howel	John Kuling
John Flewellen	Arnold Gates	Fred. Harrison	D. Hathaway	John Keachie
Robert Flewellen	Charles Gillet	Thomas Hicks	Elliot Hopkins	Larius Kingsbury
Peter Ferris •	River Green	Arcovester Hamlin	Christian Huston	Josiah Kirbel
Obed W. Folger	John Griswold	Zebina Handerson	James Hazen	G. A. Kuypers
Gideon R. Fitch	Isaac Gilbert	Abm. Holdridge	Nathaniel Harcourt	Eli Knapp
Abel Fitch	Levi Goodrich	W. Hoffman	Thaddeus Hait	Maria Kidney
Isaac Flagler	Arthur N. Gladd	Jonathan Hoag	Henry Howard	James Ketcham
Jesse Fleet	John B. Gay	Elijah Hulbert	Jeremiah Haxton	Edward Kermeyt
Prior Frost	Wm. Germona	John S. Hopkins	Peter Hall	Richard Kaven
John Ferguson	Peter Germond	Amos P. Hall	Benjamin Hall	Jonah Kellogg
Richard Grant	Luther Gay	Luke Hill	William G. Hall	Israel Ketcham
Thomas Gardner	D. Green	Joseph Howland	Stephen Halsted	Nehemiah Knight
James Greaton	Morris German	Justus Hinman	William Haxton	Roswell Kinne
Elizabeth Gipson	Hez. Goodman	John Honxey	Edward Hunting	Caleb Kirby
John Geib, jun,	John Giles	Augustin Hayden	Ephraim Hough	Abm. Kniffen
James Geery	Esther Goodrich	John Hagerman	Isaac Hurton	Daniel Knowlton
Samuel Gunton	James Graham	William Holden	James Hudge	Benj. Lowerre
William Gidney	Edmund Griswold	Leonard Herrick	Garret Hyer	John Lush
George Green	Juliana Goldsmith	N. B. Hubbell	A. Hun	James H. Lyon
Cyrus Gage	Thomas Green	Joseph E. Haff	Amos P. Hall	Wm. D. Luzell
S. Gildersleeve	Andrew Gregg	Richard Haight	R. Henry	Michael Lowber
I. W. Green	John H. Hobert	Ebenezer Haight	Arthur Hotchkiss	John R. Lawrence
John Gidley	William Higgins	David Haight	George Humphrey	Dickson Lewis
John Green	Horace Rinsdale	Obadiah Haight	John Hackney	Thomas Lincoln
Joseph Green	Adrian Hageman	John Haight, jun.	William Hegartis	Joseph Labbrey
Hugh Gregg	Richard Hatfield	Robert Haight	Harriet Hillhouse	William Lockwood
Andrew Grey	Jabez Halsey	Roswell Herrick	Pelatiah Hayden	A. Lefoy
John Gifford	James Hewart	Charles Howland	Andrew Herren	John Lefferts
Alexander Grant	Valentine Hicks	Jeremiah Howland	James Hawkins	Valentine Lewis
John W. Gilchrist	John S. Hunn	William Hutching	George Howell	Macajah Lewis
John Gray	Wager Hull	James Holmes	John G. Hurton	Peter Losing
E. W. & W. W. Groesbuck	Ann Hendricks	Leonard Haight	James Hark	Joseph Lancaster
	Samuel Hicks	Ebenezer Hurd	John Insley	Henry Lossing
John H. Goryway	Whitehead Hicks	Isaac Kuestis	Jona. Ingersull	Thomas Lamorrow
Garret Gates	James Hallett	Rinard Hopper	Robert Jameson	Saunders Lansing
Henry Guest, jun.	John Hunn	Henry Hendrix	Sylvanus Jenkins	Jacob Lansing, jr.
Anthony Groesbeck	J. W. Hawkshurst	Zebulon Houston	Eliza Jumel	Henry R. Lansing
Wm. D. Gilberry	Uriah Hill	John Hudson	Th. L. Jackson	P. Lansing
Stephen Gellitt	Robert Hawke	Abm. A. Herring	Peter Jay	Isaac Lobagh
Denison Giles	Townsend Hubbs	Caleb Horton	Peter Jones	Thomas Little
Thomas Gifford	Thomas Hubbs	Gilead Honeywell	Zophar Jones	Elias Lasill
John Giffen	Samuel Hubbs	Sanford Hoag	Elizabeth Jenkins	Josiah Leonard
Joshua Goldsmith	John C. Holmes	Walter Haight	Eunice Jenkins	Levy Leray
Joseph Gregg	William Hyde	Eliab Hoag	Thomas Jenkins	Isaac Ledyard
William Grant	Richard Hunt	John Hoag	Stephen James	Robert Lleague
John Griscom	Lott Hunt	James Haight	Winton Jenks	Thomas Liddle
Joseph Ganity	Stephen Hunt	James Hunter	Lewis Johnson	William Lander
Archibald Gracie	Oliver Hoffman	Moses Haight	John Johnson	John Liddle
Robert Godron	Ben. Haviland	Ludlow Haight	David Jacobs	E. Y. Langworthy
Isaac Grimshaw	Ira Holmes	Isaac Hutchinson	David Jacocks	Samuel Lee
John Gilmore	James Hawkshurst	Mott Hicks	Joseph Jacocks	George Leslie
Frederick Graham	Christopher Hubbs	William Harrison	Wm. T. Jacocks	James Little
Samuel Glean	John Horton	Cath. Harrison	Townsend Jackson	William Lawrence
Robet Gowan	Philemon Halsted	Henry Hinsdale	Jacobus Jersey	Charles Lindsey
James Green	Ezekiel Halsted	Jacob Hallock	Abigail Jones	I. H. Livingston
Daniel Garthwait	Wm. Haviland	John Hull, jun.	Stephen Jarvis	William Lawson
John B. Gillespie	Thomas Huggeford	Robert Hunt	Jabez Jackson	Hezekiah Lord
Frederick Guion	Jeremiah Horton	Thomas Holmes	Henry Johnson	R. R. Lawrence
Elias Guion, jun.	Daniel Haight	David Hains	P. Johnson	John B. Lansing
Elijah Grerion	Abraham Horton	Sarah Hunt	Joseph I. Jackson	B. Livingston
Gilbert Griffin	Abijah Haviland	Thomas Humphres	William Jackson	D. Lynch
Joseph Griffin	Daniel Haight	Gilbert Hathaway	Cornelius Jacobs	Nicholas Low
Benjamin Griffin	Joseph Hatfield	Halsted & Horton	John Jarvis	Samuel Lyons
William Gray	Gilbert Hatfield	Ezekiel Halsted	Isaac Johnson	Anthony Lockman
Solomon Gedney	Richard Hatfield	Joshua Hatfield	Davey Joyce	Wm. L. Lawrence
Isaac Gedney	John Horton	Jonathan Hogeland	Lydia Judson	John Lenon
Jonathan Gedney	Timothy Hunt	James Hipwell	Benj. Jackson	John Lee
John Griffin	Israel Hunt	Humphry Howland	John Johnson	Th. T. Loomis
James Griffin	A. B. Haviland	Samuel Hake	Michael A. Jones	Robert Lane
Barth. Griffin	John M. Hewitt	Seth Hast	Clulow Jackson	Garret Lozier
Mary Griffin	Nathaniel Holley	Benj. D. Hasbrook	David King	George Lewis
Seaman Germond	Roe Haviland	Foster Hallock	Daniel Keyt	Abm. D. Lent
	Stephen Hoxie	Joseph Horton	David R. Keyt	Daniel Latting

SUBSCRIBERS' NAMES.

Wm. Leggett	John Millery	Whiting Mann	Joanna Pearce	Elijah Peck
Eliza Lewis	Andrew M'Torbie	John Mehund	John Perrot	A. E. Peters
Peter Lorillard	John M'Thie	Abraham Morey	William Prince	Henry Pearsall
David Laforge	John M'Farland	James Morey	James Purdy	John Pearsall
Gilbert Lewis	James Maxwell	Thomas Mygate	Peter Pettet	Chester Parsons
Aug. Lawrence	John Maxwell	Phineas Martin	Francis Pill	James Pugsley
John Le Count	Thomas M'Clump	John Myer	David Purdy, jun.	Elihu Paine
Edward Lee	John Milmie	John Myer, jun.	Samuel Peters	Ann Quimby
John Lawrence	George M'William	Edom Myer	Thorn Pudney	Peter Queaureau
Samuel Lyon	Peter M'Intosh	Garret Myer	Robert Palmer	Luke C. Quick
Andrew Lyon	David C. Miller	Samuel Mott	Winslow Page	H. Quackenbush
Hyatt Lyon	Samuel Miller	Samuel Meeker	David Peryn	Nicholas Rome
Th. P. Lawrence	John Molther	Jesse Merritt	Eleazar Platt	John B. Reynolds
Joseph Lawrence	Alex. M'Leod	Tripp Mosher	E. Pemberton	Stewart Robinson
Henry Lawrence	R. Milledoler	Gideon Mott	Giles W. Porta	Simon Richardson
Walker Lyon	Edward Madan	Hugh Montgomery	Thomas Paskel	Abraham Remson
Edw. Lawrence	John M'Intire	Peter Mirest	Andrew Proudfit	Richard Risley
Benjamin Lisk	Collin M'Arthur	James D. Mirest	Moses Platt	William Rague
John Loines	Th. M'Creem	Jacobus D. Mirest	Jesse Potter	Francis Raymond
Samuel Logan	John Moneypenny	David B. Mirest	William Priestly	Robert Raymond
James Lyon	Phineas Mundy	Caleb Merritt	John Polly	William Ray
Henry Ludlow	Charles Miller	Jesse Marshall	Daniel Puppeno	Anthony Rawling
Jedediah Lincoln	William Martin	William Mathews	John Piersonde	William Reynolds
Henry Loortaken	Ephraim Marsh	Gideon Nichols	Robert Perry	R. N. Roerkrans
James Loss	John Moore	William Nichols	Wm. Parkinson	Hezekiah Rodgers
Thomas Lake	Garret Myer	Freelove Nichols	Phinehas Peek	Griffen Reynolds
David Lawton	Eleanor Moore	John Noxin	Thomas Pope	Roland Ricketton
Wm. Lathrop	Chris. Merkles	Isaac Nelson	Albert Picket	Harmech Roswell
Hez. O. Lathrop	P. M'Donough	Samuel Niles	Robert Perine	Micah Rogers
Mary M'Creed	Aaron Marsh	J. Nelson, 2 cop.	Mary Prowitt	Richard Rapalye
Robert Moore	David P. Mandevill	Charles Newbold	Silas Pearsall	Benj. Rogers
Hugh M'Lead	John Mustard	John Nicoll	William Pleas	Henry Reynolds
Aaron Morehouse	James Mills	Aaron Nash	Aaron H. Palmer	James Rodgers
Neil A. M'Kinnon	John M'Mullen	John Negus	Joshua Pine	John Randel
Jacob Miller	Joseph Meeks	James Nimmo	William Poynts	Silas Reynolds
Mary M'Cammon	Richard Mott	Patrick Niblo	John Pease	James Rogers
Jonathan Mundon	Adam Mott	Ebenr. Nickerson	Philip Pell	James Ross
George Moalder	William Mead	George Newbold	Lewis Pintard	Margaret Ross
James M'Carter	Ann Maria Marsh	James Nash	William Pinkney	Augustine Rogers
Daniel Murray	Samuel Mott	Robert Nesbit	Micajah Pinkney	Martha Rogers
Richard Mabbatt	Abijah Morgan	Richard Newal	James Pine	John B. Romeyn
Charles Millard	John Metritt, jun.	Nicholas Nelson	David Purdy	S. N. Rowan
Charles Merritt	Andrew Merritt	Cornelius Newland	Nathaniel Penfield	John Rodgers
Peter M'Lees	Jane Miller	Zadock Newbury	James Pelham	Moses Rogers
Adam Montross	Isaiah Maynard	William Niles	Letty Purdy	George Randall
Increase Mills, jr.	Joseph Merritt	Mary Nash	Jesse Park, jun.	William Robertson
James Mailler	James Merritt	Ebenezer Noyes	Timothy Park	Micajah Reynolds
Andrew M'Kearlie	Wm. Marthews	Robert Newby	Tamazin Peck	John R. B. Rodgers
John M'Ke	James M'Gowan	Ebenezer Nish	Roger Purdy	Edward Riley
Gilbert M'Master	Charles M'Donald	Henry Northrop	Elijah Purdy, jun.	David Rice
Thos. M'Clumpha	Caleb Merritt	Ann Nelson	Asber Pike	David Romaine
Alexander Miller	Arch. M'Donald	Josiah Osborn	William Purdy	Lathieo Rodney
Fred. G. Mayer	Benj. Maitland	John M. Ogden	John Poillon	Elias Ring
John M'Comb	James Morgan	Nehemiah Oakley	Hannah Pugsley	Simeon Romaine
John M. Michael	Robert Morrell	Richard H. Osborn	Joseph Pell	Wm. Rosegrant
David Mason	Nehemiah Merrill	J. L. Ostrander	Samuel Parsons	Robert Robertson
David M'Kinstry	John S. Myers	William Owen	Edmund Pearsall	Jasper E. Ruckle
John Morrell	Jesse Makeel	David Olmstead	Prior & Dunning	Peter Robertson
Selah Mapes	Peter Miller	Ottis & Miller	100 copies	William Rees
N. G. Minturn	Nathaniel Montross	Jacob Oakley	Thomas Pearsall	Daniel Rapelye
Saml. M'Kenny	Thomas Mosher	Peter Obert	George Parke	Stephen Robins
Stephen M'Crane	Jacob Makell	Thomas Oliver	James Palmer	Samuel Robins
John M'Coun, jun.	Nathaniel Merritt	Joel Osborn	Gilbert Pugsley	John Rushmore
Cyrus Mann	Samuel Meker	James Oakley	Joshua Pierce	William Renoud
Eliphalet Mott	Hannah M'Colon	Sarah Oakley	Joshua Pitney	Stephen Renoud
Wm. 1. M'Cartie	Lydia Mann	William Oakley	William Powel, jr.	Daniel Rodgers
William Marvin	Conklin Miller	Daniel Odell	Solomon Philips	Caleb Russell
Mathu & Thorn	Richard Macy	Melancton Osborn	Warner Pierce	Ezekiel Robins
Samuel M'Elroy	Robert Macy	Nathaniel Owen	Nathan Potter	Joseph Reynolds
Samuel Morris	John Macy	C. Onderdonk	Richard Prior	Sylvester Roe
Joshua Marsh	Joseph M'Knowen	Daniel Ogden	Benjamin Peck	Joshua N. Rice
Willard Miller	C. M'Kinstry, jun.	Benj. Price	Adriel Pease	Thaddeus Reed
George M'Queen	David E. M'Kinstry	Samuel G. Pearsall	Wm. Penniman	Oliver Riggles
George M'Gowen	Consider Morgan	Mary Pell	George H. Paldock	David Rogers
James Murray	Anne Morgan	John Post	Hepzibeth Pettys	John Rogers
Lydia Moore	Dexter Mason	Robert Prevost	David Plumb	James Reynolds
John M'Clumpha	James Marbey	Jane Pierry	David Pratt	James Renaus
John M'Collum	Stephen Marshall	John Pope	Judah Paddock	Calvin Reid
Malcum M'Farlin	Caleb Master	William Pearsall	Daniel Power	Jacob Rundal
Alexander Murray	James Marshall, jr.	Jane Price	Oliver Partridge	Eliakim Reed
John M'Masters	John M'Donald	Richard Palmer	Steph. P. Partridge	M. A.
John M'Geach	Ebenezer Mott	John Patterson	Silas Pigoon	

Joseph Reynolds
Rinear Ramson
Isaac Ramson
Jarvis Bogers
Benj. S. Reeve
George Strebeck
James Smith
William Smith
David Smith
John W. Starman
Strong Sturges
T. & J. Swords, 30 copies.
Samuel Sharp
John Sprowl
Henry Smith
Robert Sands
C. Stewart
William Sperry
John Stewart
Seger & Souther-land
Isaac Sherwood
Jeremiah Shotwell
John Shotwell
Aaron Smith
A. R. Stephens
Richard Speaight
James Sherwood
C. Stonehouse
Wm. T. Slocum
Miles Sweeney
John W. Scout
Joseph Shutwell
Alex. Saunders
Samuel Sherman
Joshua Sands
Isaac Simonson
Abraham Seacor
Matson Smith
Andrew Smith
Erving Smith
Nathan Stilwell
David Seaman
Oliver Secor
Jesse Sutton
James Sivers'
Abel Smith
William Sutton
Jared Strong
Benj. S. Stewart
Neil. Sherewood, jr
Fred. Schureman
F. Sheereman, jun.
Elizabeth Shute
James Seacord, jun.
David Seacord
Thomas Shute
James Somerville
Robert Sneden
Thos. R. Starkins
Josiah Straro
Clerk Stephens
James Smith
Benjamin Show
William Seymour
David Sands 2 cop.
D. Stringham
John Sheffield
Robert Sutton
John Sutton
Thos. Seymour
Elizabeth Starkey
Alexander Smith
Henry P. Skinner
John Starr, jun.
Silvanus Seeby
John M. Sanford
John Slocome
Smith & Furman, 26 copies
George B. Sharp

Tunis Slingerland
Barnett B. Speere
Garret Sickels
James Scott
Burdet Stryker
Selah Smith
James H. Spice
Isaac Smith
Joseph P. Smith
Ozias Smith
Othniel Smith
E. Sturtevant
William Standley
Jacob Smith
Charlotte Smith
Andrew F. Smuck
Henry Saunders
Jonas Secor
Catharine Sickles
Isaac Sharpless
James Spurce
Cath. Sutlipp
Sann Smith
David Stewart
John K. Simonson
James Searing
William Sopho
Nathaniel Sellick
Wm. Sharp
Judah Swizth
Abraham Summers
John C. Stogiboum
John Swift
Jehoiakim Skinkle
Harvy Sadd
C. Sturtevant, jun.
Henry D. Sedgwick
Mitten Seward
Ephraim G. Swift
Levi Shepherd
Peter Stringham
Ostrom Shepherd
James Sweet
Henry Swift
Albert Seaman
Smith & Dutcher
Jer. Shearman
Libbeus Swift
Darius Sweet
Wm. Southerland
Hugh Shearman
Wm. Sherwond
Amos Sanford
Cyrus Swan
Josiah Stebbins
John W. Smith
A. Sterling
Armenia Swift
Ephraim Smith
Samuel Stanford
Samuel Strong
Treadwell Scudder
Wm. H. Smith
David Staples, jun.
Nathaniel Shield
Lewis Stebbins
Philip Sickler
A. Stoutenburgh
E. Shearman
Thomas L. Storm
Nathan Serwood
W. Seward, juu.
Nathaniel Sackett
A. Southerland
William Smith
Caleb Sutton
Abraham Schultz
D. Southerland, jr.
D. Sayre
Samuel Sackett
Robert Simmons
John Stilman

James Stillwell
James Strange
Hannah Spencer
Ezra St. John
Francis Sea
Stephen Sellick
Edward Southwick
Samuel Scobey
Samuel Sexsey
Thomas Skelding
Renselaer Schuyler
Joseph Smith
Daniel Shields
Thomas Stewart
William Strong
Robert Sempson
David Stewart
John Shilling
John Smealie
Daniel Stewart
Samuel Smith
Munson Smith
Cyrus Stebbens
R. Schermerhorn
Joseph Shurtliff
Thaddeus Seely, jr.
Henry Seely
Isaac Satterly
Abraham Stickney
Benj. Strong
Jonathan Shepher
Ann Smith
Solomon Smith
Eben Smith
Aaron Sergeant
Selah Strong
Moses Shay
John Stoutenburgh
Willet Seaman
Thomas Tuthill
Joshua Terry
Tooker & Conklin
James H. Todd
John Tinkey
Joseph Taylor
S. Truwridge
James Tittlare
N. Taylor
Thomas Tucker
Gilbert Thorn
Stephen Titus
Obadiah Townsend
Samuel Thorn
Benj. Townsend
Joseph Tice
John Townsend
William Talman
Wm. Titus, 9 cops.
Z. Townsend
James Thorn, jun.
John Taylor
David Thomas
Jacob Ten Eyke
Richard S. Treat
A. Ten Broock
J. & L. Towsend
Platt Titus
Taft & Mead
Sarah Tupper
Sally Tibbits
Sarah Tibbits
Isaac Thrall
Andrew Tracy
Samuel Tuthill
Wm. Townsend
John Towpley
Michael M. Titus
Richard Titus
J. Tiebout 25 cop.
Abraham Taylor
Thomas Tom
James Tillery

John Townsend
William Townsend
John Taylor
Thomas Turnbull
William Taylor
Peter S. Titus
John Totten
Robert Tolerton
Samuel Titus
Richard Townsend
George Townsend
Joshua Titus
John Titus
Charity Tilford
Thomas Theall
Catharine Thomas
Geo. W. Tompkins
Noah Tompkins
Jona. Tompkins
Caleb Tompkins
Daniel Tait
George Taffey
Patr. F. Tighe
John Townsend
Henry I. Traver
John Thomas
Silas Titus
Alex. Tilford, jun.
William Titus
John Titus
David Tree
Samuel Titus
John Tomkins
Jacob Tucker
B. Tompkins
Cornelius Toby
Joshua Toby
Adhbel Thomas
John Tibbets
Simeon Tarpering
Daniel Taylor
John Tinkey
Conrade Tinkey
Joseph Tesman
Benjamin Thorby
Thomas Thorn
Gilbert Tompkins
Amos Underhill
Joseph Underhill
Joshua Underhill
Thomas Underhill
Anna Underhill
R. Underhill
John Underhill
Benj. Underhill
Bishop Underhill
Gilbert Underhill
John Underhill
Isaac Upton
Isaac Upton, jun.
Caleb Underhill
Abm. Underhill
Solomon Underhill
James Usher
S. Underhill
Nathl. Underhill
James Underhill
P. I. Vanpelt
G. Van Nostrand
I. A. Van Hook
A. Van Cleef
T. I. Vandyke
L. Van Nostrand
John Vanderpool
John Van Blascom
M. Van Giesom
Thomas Vaughan
Hester Va'an
James Varick
F. Vandeburgh
Robert Vantassel
J. Van Nostrand

A. Van Wyck
C. Van Wyck
John Van Vleck
D. Van Vaughton
Isaac Vidder
P. S. Van Renselaer
S. Van Renselaer
Elias Vanderlip
Samuel Vail
George Vance
Peter Vanboon
Matt. Van Vleck
John Van Vleck
D. Van Vechten
Isaac Vedeler
E. L. Vanznrwerp 30 cop.
Peter I. Vankiesk
Jacob Vanthielen
Wm. Valentine
Robert Vankeuren
Uriah Vaariper
Daniel Valentine
John Vanosdoll
John Van Duryee
Samuel Vail
Moses Vail
John Vail
John C. Voght
G. V. Valkenburgh
W. Van Renselaer
P. Van Renselaer
Solomon Vail
Jedediah Varney
Henry A. Vanulack
George D. Vail
Ezra Varney
Eben Whitney
Solomon Wheeler
Mary Woodward
Matthias Wall
James White
Silas B. Wells
Tunis A. Waldron
Elizabeth Wragg
A. Williams
James Walker
Charles Wheelock
Charles Wilcox
John Watson
Michael White
Amos White
Jonah Willets
Smith Wood
Henry Woolsey
R. Woolsey, jun.
B. I. Wooley
Cerick Westervelt
Wm. Woolley
John H. Warner
Cornelius Wilcox
Wm. I. Way
Benj. I. Way
Thomas Way
Bartow White
Abm. Witmore
Hugh Walsh
Benj. Whitaker
L. Whitmore
Robert Wingate
James Walker
Elias Willard
Dr. Woolruff
Elbert Willer
Stephen Warner
Elijah White
Thomas Watern
E. Willard & Co.
Eliza Willett
Hezekiah Williams
Wilson & Storm
J. Watts

Samuel Whallon
William Want
Luke Woodworth
James Walker
Robert Wingate
Peter Williams
E. White, jun.
J. Waltron
Edward Warrens
Joseph Warford
James Wood
Henry Wood
Asa Wall
David Webb
Francis Ward
John Watts
John Wardell
Daniel Westervelt
Francis Wilson
Charles Wright
Peter Wilson
Ebenezer White
Geo. Woodruff
John Ward
Joseph Whitney
John W. Wyman
Harman S. Wallark
John Westerfield
Henry Warts
Daniel D. Walters
J. & E. Wier
Joseph L. Wheeler
Dennis Ward
James Whitlock
Mary Woodress
Charles Walker
Thaddeus Whitlock
Benjamin Webb
George Woods
Aaron I. Westervelt
James Wiker
Charles Willits
Samuel Woodruff
Robert Watts
Thomas Wightman
P. V. Winkle
Fry Willis
Edmund Willis
Benjamin Wright
Jacob Willits
Richard Willits
Thomas Whitson
Gideon Wright
William Wright
Thomas Walker
John White
James Ward
Bartholomew Ward
Lydia Willis
Joseph Wilson
Cerah Wilson
Jonas Wood
John Willis
Jonathan Waring
Daniel Wood
Daniel Willett
...m Wright
John Wells
William Walker
W. H. Wilson
Samuel Williams
J. Wright
Benj. Wright, jun.
Henry Waters
Gilbert Williams
Richard Worth
William Worth
Noah Weed
Charles Williams
Stephen Willard
Cyrus Williams
Elijah Williams

John Wilkes
Reuben Ward
Jesse Wright
Nicholas Worell
Jacob Weekes
David Webb
Jacob Wilber
David Winslow
John J. Wolley
James Willets
Silas Wodell
Jesse Wakham
Abner White
Charles White
Nehemiah Wolley
Isaac White
Peregrine White
John H. Weaver
Amos Whitson
Jacob Willets
William Willets
Hugh Wabb
Moses Webb
Jotham Waring
James Watson
John Wright
John Wood
James Weeks
Caleb Weeks
John Young
Abraham Young
John Yates
Samuel You
Elisha Yale
James Youngs
Abigail Yelverton
Henry Youngs
James Young
John Young
Edward Young
William Young
A. C. Zabriskie

NEW-JERSEY.

John Adams
Elijah Ayres
Joshua Ayres
Samuel Ayres
Josiah Andrews
Samuel Atkinson
John Atkinson
Ralph Akerman
Marquis Alward
George Bacon
Levi Bond
Richard Bond
Benjamin Bacon
Thomas Bacon
David Bacon
Abel Bacon
Richard Barker
Uriah Bacon
Joel Bereman
Isaac Brown
Thomas Brown
Joseph Brown
Ephraim Bishop
Jeremiah Buck
John Buck
Thomas Burch
Daniel Burt
William Busby
John Brown, jr.
W. Bradway
Joseph Basset
Adna Bradway
John B. Bowman
Henry Brunce
Richard Barnard
Cyrus Barnard
Rich'd Barnard, jr.

Joseph Barnard
William Boswell
Thaddeus Bruin
Samuel F. Burdye
Isaac Beach
John Bantam
Samuel Ball
Mary Baldwin
Daniel Bodd
Jacob Bumstead
Samuel Baldwin
Ichabod Baldwin
Joseph Baldwin
John Bloomer
Isaac W. Crane
James Clark
Nathan Cooper
Reuben Cuff
Thomas Cock
Charles Collady
Robert Clendenen
John P. Cornell
William Clark
Ichabod Crane
William Crocker
Benj. Cleveland
John C. Crane
Mary Cocker
Job Copperthwaite
Nich's Cowohoven
Philip Carr
Harry Caldwell
John L. Cole
William Clark
Abm. T. Cadmus
Herman Cadmus
Peter I. Cadmus
John Cornitson
John Sheerman
David Clark
John Dare
Elnathan Davis
Jonathan Davis
Isaac Davis
Ebenezer Davis
Richard Davis
David Davis
Reuben Davis
Ephraim Dayton
James Dorsett
Priscilla Dears
Fred. Deetwieter
Samuel Dodd
Cyrus Dodd
T. S. Dodd
Moses Dodd
W. B. Ewing
Jacob Elwell
Jonathan Elmer
Timothy Elmer
Samuel Ellis
John Ellis, jun.
Lewis Evans
Mary Ellis
Joseph Erwin
William Ellison
Robert Easborn
Seely Fighiaro
Thomas French
John Furman
William Forman
Geo. M. Furman
Elizabeth Fraley
Benj. B. Frafee
David Gilman
John Gummere
Charles Gordon
Benj. Griscom
William Griscom
Peter H. Gorgas
John Green
William Grant

John R. Gould
Jonathan Holmes
John Holmes
Thomas Harris
Jeremiah Harris
Samuel Hains
Jonathan Hilyard
Jacob Hilyard
Isaac Harrison
Sam. W. Hartshorn
James Hinchman
Charles Hannah
Joseph Harris
John Hancock
Hezekiah P. Hart
Robinson Howel
M. M. Hardenbergh
James Houston
Esther Hayes
Sally Humniwell
William Hoyer
Alpheus Hews
Peter Hedenberg
John C. Hedenberg
James T. Harrison
Josiah Hornblower
Lemuel Jones
John L. Johnson
Agnes Jorden
Henry Johnson
Richard Jobs
Moses Jaques
Abel Jackson
Abm. Juralemon
P. Jackson
R. Kelley
Samuel Kirby
Jonathan Kerr
Aaron King
Reuben Ludlam
Joseph Ludlam
Ephraim Lummis
George Lanning
John Lanning, jun.
Pheneas Lord
Edmund Lafetra
James Lawrence
Peter Lintiman
James B. Low
Joseph Lyon
D. F. Lockwood
Richard Ludlow
Ephraim Mulford
David Mulford
John Miller
Isaac Mulford
Jacob Miller
Robert Magee
Enoch H. Moore
Jacob Merrot
Wm. T. Miller
James Morris
Joseph Miller
Christopher Mason
Robert M'Neely
George Mott
Mary Morrell
Alex. Montieth
Abijah Moore
John Morris, jun.
Elizab. M'Creckon
James M'Crenie
Jacob Marcell
Jon V. Mackett
Corn'. Mandeville
Peter Maverick
John Moore
Michael M. Null
William Nicholson
Mary Nace
James Nutman
Lewis Paullin

Stephen Paullin
Benajah Parvin
Caleb C. Pancoast
Isaac Pine
Aaron Pancoast
John Pesely
Alex. Provest
Caleb Pennock
James Pyle
Samuel Pennock
Stacy Potts
Thomas Peanier
Jacob Price
Samuel Pitt
John Poork
Nathaniel Rulon
William Rose
Enos Randolph
Samuel Reeves
Charles Reeves
Biddle Reeves
Jesse Redman
Abm. Rodgers
Richard Rird
Thos. H. Rogers
George Rohdee
Hugh P. Russ
Charles Ramsay
Charles Rogers
R. W. Shepherd
John Shepherd
Wm. Shepherd
Mary Shepherd
Ananias Statham
Richard Seely
David Shepherd
Wm. H. Sully
Harvy Shepherd
James Shepherd
Furman Shepherd
Abel Shepherd
Nathan Shepherd
Josiah Shepherd
Samuel M. Shute
Jacob Shull
Ebenezer Seely
Daniel P. Stratton
Michael Seving
Deborah Stewart
Gabriel Swain
Thomas Skin
Samuel Siuste
James Sretch, jun.
Jacob Sharp
Nehemiah Sullivan
Mary Shourds
Joseph Stewart
Peter Smiley
George Sherman
Jasper Smith
Eliza Shaw
Robert Shotwell
Daniel Shotwell
Nathan Seabury
Charles Shipman
Joseph Salter
Amos Salter
Gaius Smith
Mary G. Smith
Joseph Sigler
John Stimis
Daniel Seacord
Benjamin Tyler
Samuel Tyler
James Tomlinson
Abraham Tilton
George Tatum
Joah. Thompson, jr.
Jacob Thompson
Andrew Thompson
Thomas Tilton
Elizabeth Thomas

4 K

SUBSCRIBERS' NAMES

Benjamin Tayton	Wallace Boyd	Nathan Evans	Joseph Justice	William Munter
Benjamin Thorn	George Boxton	Thomas Edge	Edward Jones	Amos Mitchell
Nehem. Tichenor	John Burrows	Wm. Eberman	Halliday Jackson	John Meridith
H. Van Dorsdalen	Susanna Brinton	Joseph Ehenfried	Ann Johnson	Rudolph Morva
D. F. Van Liew	James Brinton	John Eberlien	James Johnson	Philip M'Elway
Isaac Vail	John Brumfield	Thomas Ewart	James Jackson	John M'Ilvaine
Jas. Vanderventer	Christian Breneman	John Ely 10 cop.	Margaret Jones	Giles Newton
Hannah Vanderbeek	Eleanor Barker	Mary Fougery	George Knox	James Nagbe
Hannah Vatorse	Thomas Brown	Hannah Ford	Andrew Kenedy	Isaac Nightingale
Sylves. Vanbeuren	William Barnett	Elizabeth Flanagan	Josiah S. Kay	Nathaniel Newlin
Simeon Van Houton	R. Burke 10 cop.	Elizabeth Farr	George Keates	John Noy
A. A. Van Houton	Thomas Baldwin	George Fitler	Margaretta Kerlin	David Nelson
Richard Wood	Jane Bavington	Joseph Fearon	Jesse Kersey	Sarah Osborne
Howel P. Watson	Mary C. Cryder	John Fisher	Nathaniel Kady	Jonathan Owen
Benjamin West	Solomon Cumming	Elizb. Flankinborn	Wm. Kirkwood	William Otley
Isaac Wheaton	Michael Crate	Arthur Forbis	William Kester	Hugh Orr
David Wood	Godfrey G. Cope	John Frailey	Israel Kenton	Jesse Owen
Ephraim Westcott	John Crockett	William Findley	Paul Knight	Richard Pryor
John Westcott	John Crates, jun.	Jonathan Furman	Betsy King	John Philips
Amos Westcott	Samuel Care	Miles Foster	Abm. Keyser	Henry Probasco
Samuel Westcott	John G. Capp	Richard French	William Laird	Benjamin Perkins
Grany. Woolman	George Climer	Elizabeth Gorden	John M. Leod	Alexander Purvis
Samuel Willis	Michael Casey	Sarah Graham	H. Lewis, jun.	Stephen Payran
Peter Welsh	John Craig	John H. Gartley	Joseph Lyndall	John Pemberton
Benj. Weatherby	Mary Cornell	Joseph Grubb	James F. Lee	Elisha Parker
Wm. Waddington	John Chapman	Conrad Gyrne	Samuel Lippincott	Sarah Price
Joseph Whitall	Jacob Carrigan	Peter Gardiner	Joseph Lea	Caleb Price
John F. Warner	John J. Cole	Wm. Gardiner	Jacob Lasher	Aaron Pursse
Sebastian Weender	Joseph Carter	Samuel Garrett	George C. Lenter	Mary Picard
George Weender	Benjamin Collins	Nathan Garrett	Samuel Levis	John Pugh
William Windle	John Cromwell	Thomas Garrett	Asher Lobb	David Pumeroy
John S. Wilson	Wm. Cummings	Joseph George	Samuel Levis, jun.	Dell Peanel
Matthew White	George Clark	Elisha Gatchel	Osborn Levis	Jonathan Pennell
Ambrose Williams	Jeremiah Clark	Wm. Gheen	Hester Lobb	John Powell
Philip Williams	Woodward Crosby	James Gamble	Samuel Long	Samuel Pugh
Alexander Wilson	Moses Coates	James Glasby	John Lightner	John Pim
Bethel Ward	Joseph Cottrell	Thomas Glasby	Samuel Lefever	Joseph Paxson
Benjamin Weiler	Wm. Chamberlain	Joseph Gest, jun.	Joel Lightner	Benjamin Paxson
Thomas Wills	John Chamberlain	Andrew Grivens	Isaac Leeds	Jonathan Paxson
Ezekiel Wade	John Carpenter	Wm. Glaspia	Hugh Lloyd	William Powers
Elisha Webb	Josh. Chamberlain	Joseph Gregg	John Milnor	Jacob Pennock
Timothy Willis	Samuel Carpenter	George Gregg	John Mitchell	Michael Pigeon
Isaac Yard	John Coohran	Joseph Guilkey	Mary M'Kinny	Robert Patton
	Isaac Conrad	Moses Gillingham	John M'Kinny	William Pyle
PENNSYLVA-	Calvin Cooper	Thomas Gilbert	Christian Miller	Jonathan Pyle
NIA.	Abraham Cornell	Y. Gillingham	Benjamin Mastin	Joshua Pusey
	Alex. Chandler	Hannah Gibbs	Ann M'Pherson	Joshua E. Pusey
John Alsop	William Chambers	Mary Gibbs	John M'Allister	Benjamin Packnil
Edwin A. Atlee	John Chipman	George J. Henry	John Morphey	George Quigley
Jane Allen	John Crosby	James Hunter	John M'Farland	Joel Ray
W. Adams	Joseph Dickinson	George C. Haas	John Milner, jun.	Wm. L. Read
Thomas Anderson	Wm. Dickinson	John Milee	Hugh S. Magee	John Renkirt
Nich. Armbruster	Chris. H. Denckla	Elizabeth Hilborn	Ruth Morris	Thomas Rose
Thomas Ashton	John Delavace	Elijah Hammond	James M'Clay	William Ruff
Wm. Anderson	Ann Drummond	John Hutchinson	Rebecca Mitchel	Elizabeth Ryal
Robert Arthurs	Richard Dougherty	John Hahn	Ferdinand Morayh	Joseph Richards
Thomas Agnew	Noah Davis	Martha Humphreys	William Moore	Mary Richards, jr.
John Allen	Nathan Dickinson	Jonathan Haycock	George Martin	Francis Renshaw
Jacob Bond	Thomas Downing	Jesse Hayes	Sarah Marshall	Cath. Richardet
Mary Barr	Richard Downing	Joseph Hibbaral	George Miller	John Reed
Wm. Beates	Joseph R. Downing	Joseph Hollowell	Jacob Malin	Thomas Roberts
Jacob Bable	Hunt Downing	Abraham Heston	Samuel Malin	Samuel Rhoads
Mary Barry	Samuel Downing	Isaac Hawlew	Samuel Moore	Israel Roberts
Aaron Boughman	Joseph Dunbar	Sarah E. Hannum	James Moxton	Joseph Richmond
Jacob Bennet	John M. Dill	Joseph Hunt	Charles Mowry	John Russel
G. Breitenhurt	B. Sure Drake	Joseph Harvuot	Samuel Moon	Robert Reed
Michael Boyle	Jacob M. Dill	William Hore	James M'Kin	Daniel Reigart
George Burden	Jacob Demuth	Thomas Henderson	Samuel F. Marsh	John Rose
Mary Ball	Francis Downing	Robert Hore	James M'Chesney	John Roth
Elisha Brown	Doctor Defresne	Aaron Howard	James M'Connaghy	Isaac Reed
Luther Bans	Amos Dixon	John J. Henry	James Manu	Richard Kue
Michael Baker	Samuel W. Doak	John Kantsch	Reuben Marsh	Gilbert Redman
Wm. Booth	Joseph Delany	Amos Harmer	Robert M'Chesney	William Rawlins
Frederick Boley	James Dyre	Israel Hoops	Robert M'Ilvaine	Jacob Rogers
Rebecca Brown	Caleb Dilworth	David Hillis	John M'Roy	Joseph Shoemaker
Thomas Boyle	Isaac Davis	Nathan Harper	George Mars	Amos Stackhouse
Matthew Brown	Thomas Evans	Abraham Harrison	Archibald M'Cordy	Richard Sermon
Sarah Boyle	Benjamin Esen	Robert Hollburn	Mary A. M'Donald	Stokely Sturgis
June Small	Joseph H. Erwin	Ebenezer Headly	Jesse Miller	Ann Sprogell
Mary S. Beavan	Thomas H. Elliott	Joseph Johnson	Jonathan Mifflin	Christian Sulger
Samuel Baldwin	William Evans	Ruth Jenkins	Francis Murray	John G. Simmons
John Baldwin	Jacob Edwards	Daniel James	Wm. Musgrove	John Smith

SUBSCRIBERS' NAMES

Daniel Stephen, Jr.
Jacob Smith
Abm. Shoemaker
Nathan Smith
William Stokes
Charles Shuster
Henry Snyder
Sophia Stretton
Leonard Snowden
William Salter
Wm. M. Stewart
Josiah Siddons
Edward Smith
Ezekiel Starrat
George Swayne
John Sharpless
Nathan Sharpless
Amos Staymaker
Isaac Smith
James Stewart
Jacob Souders
Wilson Smith
James Steel
Caleb Sharpless
Leonard Shallcross
John Shallcross
Th. Scattergood
Moses Stacy
John Starkton
Nathan A. Smith
Isaac Thomas
John Torr, jun.
David Thomas
John Tomlinson
James Thompson
Marg. Tittermary
Joseph Torr
Asher Tharp
John Thomas
Samuel Tremble
Abel Thomas
Eli Thomas
Jane Thompson
James Tygart
Jos. Thornsborough
Charles Tees
Samuel Temple
Jonathan Thomas
Joseph Thompson
Jesse Townsend
Alex. Urquhart
Geo. Vanderslice
Benj. Vandergrift
S. Witherill, jun.
James Wickham
Thomas Williams
John Willis
Thomas Whitear
Martha Williamson
John Wilson
Rebecca Wilson
Jacob Warren
Edward Wilson
Alexander Wilson
Mary Wilson
William Wester
William Watts
William Wallace
George Widdows
John Williams
Joseph Wain
Samuel West
Thomas Wallace
Roger Watkins
Joseph Williams
David Witmer
Ann Walter
William Wright
Samuel Wood
James Wright
Stephen Wilson
Clinton Walter

Joel Woolman
Jacob Warrell
Lewis Wernway
Thomas Warrell
Isaac Whitelock
Jesse Waterman
Abraham Warner
Seth Wells
Nicholas Waln
Elias Yarnall
Matthias Young
Jacob Zigler
Matthias Zahn

DELAWARE.

Benj. Brower
Solomon Beckley
Margaret W. Blake
Mary Bonsal
William Baldwin
William Clark
Saml Carnahan
John Crozier
Joseph Downing
William Foulk
Charles Hillyard
Evan Lewis
George Monro
Eliza. Montgomery
Richard Mowlan
Hannah Nichols
William Pool
Henry Rice
Margaret Rasin
James Smith
Samuel A. Smith
John Smith
James Stair
Joshua Vansant
Stephen Wilson
Esther Watter
Abijah Yates

MARYLAND.

Joseph Armstrong
John Armstrong
Michael Abbott
Martha Austin
Hugh Allen
I. & S. Addison
John Bants
L. Barry
Nancy Bouchill
Charles Brown
Benj. Berry
Thomas Bromlin
Alex. Buckanan
John Bonds
John Berry
Robert Benton
Nicholas Berton
Robert Bruice
Isaac Broughton
Eliza Bishop
Lewis Barker
Isaiah Balderston
S. Brown
John Burges
Joseph E. Bentley
John Connor
Nathaniel Cleever
Francis Clark
Samuel Cook
G. Comerly
Thomas Childs
Thomas Coulson
Martha Clark
Hannibal Chester
Samuel Chubb
Robert Craggs

Henry Cowshan
Henry Cook
Joseph Caldwell
Isabella Colaen
David Carson
Thomas Campbell
Samuel Cranford
James Clark
Patrick Coulson
John Cowman
William Canby
Leonard Dorsee
William Dunn
John Davidson
Richard Degroff
Philip Dever
Isaac Dear
John Davis
H. H. Dorsey
John B. Dixon
John W. Dutton
James M. Day.
Eliza. English
Sarah Ennis
James Emerson
N. W. Easton
Sarah Faber
Nicholas Ford
Susannah Foiks
Peter Fenby
Cath. Ferguson
Henry Freeman
Henry Fitch
David Grayham
James Grimes
John Gliddeman
Mary Gibbins
John Glinn
Henry Gracey
Ann Gurny
Bernard Gilpin
Hugh Hamilton
I. H. Hollingsworth
George Hussey
James Harrison
Edward Hall
I. H. W. Hawkins
Wm. B. Holmes
Daniel Horner
John Howser
James Hurs
Francis Horner
John Hory
Samuel Hopkins
Gerrard Hopkins
Samuel S. Hopkins
Andrew Jordan
I. I. Johnson
Walter Jinkins
Jacob Jones
Loyk Johnson
Solomon Johnson
John Kingston,
    To copies.
David Krouse
John Krebs
John Kelly
Samuel Kineard
James Lowrey
Joseph Leany
Barbary Lawton
Jacob Lafetra
John Mack
Architald M'Bread
John Merrikin
Alexander Marr
John M'Collochy
Christr. Meader
F. Morinernou
John M'Dormelly
Jacob Meyers
James M'Cormick

Levin Mills
Daniel M'Selton
Edward Morgan
Joshua Miles
James Mastin
Margaret M'Bull
Mary Magbill
Jesse Morgan
Lewis Miller
T. Mouldion
John M'Intire
William Morgan
Basil Nelson
John Nicholson
Michael Nary
Dennis Nowland
Benj. Nottu
James Norris
Nathan Norris
T. Norris, 2 copies
David Newton
James Oldham
Mary Ann Oldham
I. S. Ovacre
James Orr
Elizabeth Panou
Peter Poter
Nathaniel Phillips
Thomas Pattern
William Parks
Thomas Por
Thomas Ruse
Daniel T. Rankin
Alexander Russel
Jane Rigg
G. K. Kummel
Angus Ross
Anguilla Rose
John Randall
John Richardson
Wm. M. Rapp
George Rhodes
Wm. Robinson
Luke Reed
Conrad Roud
R. A. Shipley
John Sclatter
Adam Stove
Sarah Spencer
Amelia J. Smalley
G. Sharer
Ruth I. Staples
Susannah Sharer
Ann Stewart
John Snyder
John Seabel
James Smith
William Stilt
John Stewart
Matthew Saulsbey
Henry Shark
Wm. Shield
Fred. Sheffield
Daniel Stansbury
Mary Stanley
John Sykes
George Stout
Richard Snowden
Thomas Snowden
Philip Snowden
Agila Taylor
Jane Thompson
John E. Thornton
Henry Tumauns
Mary. I Thompson
Mary T. Thompson
Thomas Taylor
Elihu Toukard
John Valliant
John Whittemore
D. Whiteford
Henry Welley

Peter L. White
John Williams
John Woods
I. Winslandly
Josiah Willing
Joseph Williams
Michael Wall
John Waters
Joseph White
Eliza Winters
William Winters
William Wallice
Charles Waskey
Alexander Yearly
Samuel Yuell

DISTRICT OF COLUMBIA.

Thomas Adams
Jacob Bough
Stephen B. Blau
Enoch Busson
Aden B. Docket
Henry S. Earl
Ebenezer Eliason
Henry Ferris
Anna Fox
Martin Fisher
Thomas Gettens
James H. Hamilton
Nathaniel R. Heath
John Janny
William Jolliffe
Zenas Kinsey
Vincent King
John Little
Leonard Mackall
Wm. Markward
Bolitha Laws
Margaret Linnsdon
Rebecca Lawrence
William Lauphier
William Morgan
    2 copies.
Wm. M'Kinny
William Nevitt
Jerome Plummer
Thomas Patten
T. R. Richardson
George R. Riley
John Ross
Isaac Robbins
Edward Stabler
David Simmons
Samuel Swayne
M. Schofield
Thomas Shruce
Joseph Smith
Peter Saunders
H. Scott
Richard H. Till
John Thomas
Samuel Wheeler
Stephen Webster
John West
William Yates

VIRGINIA.

Joseph Bond
Nathaniel Hains
John Hains
Samuel Howel
Israel Janney
Jacob Janney
Samuel M'Pherson
Wm. M'Pherson
Asa Moore, 10 cops
Rebecca Neil
Samuel Swayne

SUBSCRIBERS' NAMES.

The following Names were received too late for insertion in their proper places.

NEW-YORK.

Ozias Ansley
Abm. R. Adriance
Theod. Adriance
William Aikens
Betsey Blossom
Abner Baker
Nathaniel Britton
James Butler
Nathaniel Butler
Samuel Bartin
Israel Bedell
Anthony Bird
Joseph Bailey
John Benjamin
Edward W. Blake
Vinant Bosline
James Bodine
John Campbell
Abm. Crocheron
Daniel Crocheron
Jacob Crocheron
Nathanel Colt
D. Chamberlain
F. Cheeeman
Matthias Dehart
John Dunn
Cor. Dissosway
Richard Dubois
I. R. Dissosway
David N. C. Davis
William Degrout
Walter Dongan
John Date
Jarvis Dusenberry
Mark Dissosway
Tunis Egbert
Isaac F. Griffith
George Faitoute
John Garretson
John Gore
James Guyon, jun.
Content Garrison
Jacob Gosline
Jacob Garretson
Mary Hiliker
Abm. P. Housman
John Hatfield

P. W. Haughwout
P. E. Haughwout
Rachel Henry
Thomas Hyatt
N. Hinchman
John Hewlett
Isaiah Jenings
Zacharias Kuyper
Daniel Laurens
Peter Low
Phebe Lott
David Lamberson
Deborah Mersereau
Mary Merrell
Daniel Merell
Lyon Merrell
John Morgan
William Micheau
Joshua Mersereau
Stephen Mersereau
John Morgan
Cha. M'Simonson
Cornelius Martins
Cath M'Millen
David Mersereau
John Martling
Benjamin Martino
Charity Moffic
Wm. Maxwell
J. S. Messenger
John Nickles
James Nation
Samuel Neilson
Israel Oakley
Daniel Owen
Abraham Parker
Abm. Prall, jun.
Benjamin Parker
John Phillips
Wm. Parremore
Isaac Platt
Peter Rushang
Matthew Ridgway
Nathaniel Robins
Abraham Rickrow
John Ray
George Ray
Ann Ryeras
Margaret Robertson

Ben. Rowland
Daniel Simonson
Barnt. Simonson
Reuben Simonson
William Seaman
Jane Seguine
James Seguine
John Storms
Ebenr. Shareman
Jonathan Stidefort
Thomas I. Storm
Abraham Sleight
Mary Sanderson
Adam Stauley
Benjamin Sneden
L. G. Stanbrough
Gilbert W. Sayres
Rem Snedeker
Abrm. Snedeker
John Skidmore
James Totten
Jacob Tyson
Oliver Taylor
John Taylor
Eleanor Talman
Henry Titus
John Vanpelt
Jacob Vreeland
Daniel Van Duzen
A. Van Duzen, jun.
John Vandebilt
J. Valentine
Stephen Wood
James Wood
Moses E. Woel
Jacob Winant
Peter Winant
Thomas Wright
Cornelius Woglam
Abner Wilcox
John Willsee
Samuel Weiling
Joshua Wright
C. Webster jun.

NEW-JERSEY.

Joseph Aitkinson
Grace Allen

George Arvis
John Butcher
Ann Bishop
Grace Bassett
Bethuel Berton
Isaac Cooper
Thomas Coles
Jonathan Colson
William Carpenter
Isaac Cade
Jacob Davis Jun.
Thomas Dickson
George Davis
Edmund Darnell
Gabriel Davis
William Eldridge
Edmund French
Sarah Garwood
Joseph Groff
Letitia Groff
Rachel Gibson
Richard Hunt
Amos Haines
Samuel Hancock
John Hall
John Hainet
Job Haines
Samuel Holmes
John Inskeep
Abel Jackson
Abrm. Jeralemon
P. Jackson
Joseph Kaighin
James Kaighin
S. B. Lippincot
Samuel Lippincot
Aaron Lippincot
Hope Lippincot
Abel Lippincot
Joshua Lippincot
Isaac Lippincot
Joseph Mickle
Isaac Mickle
Elizabeth W. Mil-
[ler
Thomas Mason
George Mickle
Joseph Matlack
John Matlack

Joseph Ogden
Hannah Pinim
Provost & Wash-
    ington
Abel Riclon
Pancoast Roberts
James Risby
Ben. Robinson
Enoch Roberts Jun.
William Rogers
Samuel Roberts
William Roberts
James Saunders
Isaiah Shinn
Uriah Shinn
Barzilla Scott
William Smith
James Simpson
Aguila Stokes
S. L. Saunders
John Stiles
John Tatum
Wallace Taylor
Hannah Thompson
Samuel Tonkin
Thomas Thorn
William Thorn
John L. Vanneman
Ezra Woodruff
John Woodward
Lewis Watson
William White
David Walker
Edmund Wetherly
John Wistar
Preston Worduat
Benjamin Wright
Joseph Wolf
Jacob Wilkins
John Morrell
Daniel Parvin
Charles Rufus
Henry Waddle
Henry Parshall
Edmund Trench
Thomas Keir
Joseph Haighton
James Haighton

CPSIA information can be obtained
at www.ICGtesting.com
Printed in the USA
BVHW070327120819
555626BV00004B/594/P

9 780371 018200